PRINCIPLES OF MICRO-ECONOMICS

SECOND EDITION

Principles of Micro-Economics

JOSEPH E. STIGLITZ

SECOND EDITION

STANFORD UNIVERSITY

W · W · NORTON & COMPANY · NEW YORK · LONDON

The text of this book is composed in Zapf Book
with the display set in Kabel
Composition by TSI Graphics
Manufacturing by Rand McNally
Book design by Antonina Krass
Cover painting: Laszlo Moholy-Nagy, *LIS*, 1922
Oil on canvas, 131 × 100 centimeters
Courtesy of the Kunsthaus, Zurich
Special thanks to Hattula Moholy-Nagy

Library of Congress Cataloging-in-Publication Data

Stiglitz, Joseph E.
    Principles of microeconomics / Joseph E. Stiglitz. — 2nd ed.
        p.   cm.
    Includes index.
    1. Microeconomics.   I. Title.
    HB172.S86   1996
    338.5 — dc20   95-22777

ISBN 0-393-96929-0 (pbk.)

W. W. Norton & Company, Inc., 500 Fifth Avenue, New York, N.Y. 10110
    http://web.wwnorton.com
W. W. Norton & Company Ltd., 10 Coptic Street, London WCIA IPU

2 3 4 5 6 7 8 9 0

To Jane,
my harshest critic and best friend,
from whom I have learned the strengths and limits of economics;

and to
Julia, Jed, Michael, and Siobhan
in the hope, and belief, that a better understanding of economics
will lead to a better world for them to inherit.

ABOUT THE AUTHOR:

Internationally recognized as one of the leading economists of his generation, Joseph Stiglitz has made important contributions to virtually all of the major subdisciplines of economics: macroeconomics, monetary economics, public and corporate finance, trade, development, and industrial organization. After teaching at Yale, Princeton, and Oxford, in 1988 he accepted a position at Stanford University, where he has taught a wide variety of courses reflecting his broad interests, including Economics 1, one of the most popular courses on campus. In 1995, President Clinton asked him to serve as chief economic adviser, appointing him Chairman of the Council of Economic Advisers and a member of the cabinet. In early 1997, Joseph Stiglitz will become the chief economist at the World Bank. Professor Stiglitz is the author and editor of hundreds of scholarly articles and books, including the best-selling undergraduate text *Economics of the Public Sector* (Norton) and, with Anthony Atkinson, *Lectures in Public Economics.* He is founding editor of the *Journal of Economic Perspectives,* established in 1987 to lower the barriers of specialization erected by other major economic journals, and a former vice president of the American Economic Association. Among his many prizes and awards, Professor Stiglitz has received the American Economic Association's John Bates Clark Award, given to the economist under forty who has made the most significant contributions to economics. Joe Stiglitz lives in Washington, D.C. with his wife and four children.

Contents in Brief

PART FOUR | POLICY ISSUES

Contents

CHAPTER **2** THINKING LIKE AN ECONOMIST • 27

CHAPTER **3** TRADE • 52

CHAPTER **4** DEMAND, SUPPLY, AND PRICE • 71

CHAPTER **5** USING DEMAND AND SUPPLY • 96

PART TWO

PERFECT MARKETS

CHAPTER **8** THE CONSUMPTION
DECISION • 171

CHAPTER **9** LABOR SUPPLY AND
SAVINGS • 199

CHAPTER **10**   A STUDENT'S GUIDE TO INVESTING • 226

CHAPTER **11**   THE FIRM'S COSTS • 250

CHAPTER **12**   PRODUCTION • 281

CHAPTER **13**   COMPETITIVE
EQUILIBRIUM • 309

PART THREE

IMPERFECT MARKETS

CHAPTER **14** MONOPOLIES AND IMPERFECT COMPETITION • 335

CHAPTER 15 OLIGOPOLIES • 363

CHAPTER 16 GOVERNMENT POLICIES TOWARD COMPETITION • 388

CHAPTER **19**

IMPERFECTIONS IN THE LABOR MARKET • 454

CHAPTER **20**

FINANCING, CONTROLLING, AND MANAGING THE FIRM • 475

PART FOUR

POLICY ISSUES

CHAPTER **23** PUBLIC DECISION
MAKING • 543

PREFACE

Introductory students should know the vitality of modern economics, and this book is intended to show it to them. When I set out to write the First Edition, I felt that none of the available texts provided an adequate understanding of the principles of *modern* economics—both the principles that are necessary to understanding how modern economists think about the world, and the principles that are required to understand current economic issues. Apparently, my feelings were shared by many, as indicated by the resounding success of the First Edition. Not only was the book widely adopted in colleges and universities throughout the world, it was also rapidly translated into many languages—from major editions in Spanish, German, Italian, Japanese, and Chinese, to small editions in countries such as Latvia. This Second Edition builds on the initiatives of its predecessor. With the benefit of a wealth of feedback from the market, I have made a painstaking effort to improve the book from cover to cover. I believe both students and their instructors will be pleased with the result.

This Second Edition is also informed by my recent professional activities. During the last two years I have enjoyed a direct role in U.S. policy making as Chairman of the President's Council of Economic Advisers and as a member of the cabinet. This experience reinforced my conviction that the traditional principles course is too far removed from our national policy concerns and the modern advances in economics that can illuminate them. Moreover, my service on the council afforded me the opportunity to discuss key economic problems with leaders throughout the world, both in the major industrialized countries, and in India, China, Russia, and elsewhere. It was thus with a unique perspective that I set to work on the revision during the last two years, carving out time on weekends and during countless hours before dawn.

Economics is the science of choice and writing a textbook involves many choices. As I began work on the Second Edition, I was convinced that the choices I had made in the First Edition—for instance, the attention to new topics such as technological change and finance, and the increased emphasis on international concerns—were moves in the right direction. However, I had become even more convinced that an understanding of these new topics had to be based on solid foundations in established fundamentals, such as the law of supply and demand, the theory of the firm, and traditional perspectives on unemployment, inflation, and economic growth. Thus, in the revision I simultaneously faced several challenges, not the least of which was to reinforce the exposition of the fundamentals at the same time as I strengthened the discussion of new topics.

As I began the revision, several of the dramatic changes that had loomed so large in the early 1990s seemed still to occupy center stage, but new issues and new perspectives had emerged. The Cold War has ended, with the political and economic system of Communism the clear loser. The economies of the former Soviet Union and Eastern Europe are making a slow and painful transition to market economies. The countries of East Asia have experienced unprecedented growth, in some cases at rates in excess of 10 percent, year after year; they have shown that development is indeed possible. Japan became an economic powerhouse, while Korea, Taiwan, and the other Asian "tigers" went from being poor, backward countries to major players in the international arena. Their growth was based on international trade, and trade throughout the world, including the United States, became increasingly important. Huge private capital flows helped finance the development of many countries as well as the huge deficits that the United States and other countries began to mount. When investors lost confidence in a country, as they did in Mexico in 1995, these same capital flows precipitated an economic crisis that quickly spread, and was only arrested through strong international cooperation.

The success of East Asia during the 1970s and 1980s stands out as an exception in a world economy facing disappointment; the countries of Africa saw their desperate economic conditions worsen. Beginning around 1973, growth in the industrialized countries, including the United States, slowed markedly. Europe, where unemployment rates in the 1960s had fallen to extremely low rates, saw them soar, often to double-digit levels, and stubbornly remain there; while in the United States, where growth had been benefiting all groups, but especially the poor, inequality increased, with those at the bottom actually seeing their living standards deteriorate.

Within the United States, the mid-1990s brought signs of a reversal of some of these trends. Unemployment and inflation rates fell to low levels that had not been seen for a quarter of a century. The poverty rate began to decline, and incomes of all groups, especially those at the bottom, began to rise. American manufacturing experienced rapid productivity growth, with matching success in the international arena—U.S. car production again became the largest in the world. But among many workers, anxiety remained high; while their real wages and incomes had begun to rise, they still had not recovered to their earlier peaks, and no one was sure these trends would continue. Overall productivity growth also remained below its previous levels. Though the soaring deficit was brought under control—it had been the largest experienced in the United States during peacetime, with the national debt quadrupling between 1981 and 1992—the long-run prospects appeared daunting; the aging of the baby boomers would put unprecedented strains on the Social Security and health care systems.

As the world has changed, expectations have changed as well. While there has been enormous improvement in the quality of air in cities like Pittsburgh and Gary, Indiana, and while Lake Erie has been rescued from becoming polluted to the point where life could not survive, our expectations about the environment have grown even faster; we have become increasingly aware of environmental costs. Longevity has increased, but our knowledge of how to prolong life has grown more rapidly, and rising medical costs have become a major political issue. The economic role of women has changed: not only have they taken a more active part in the labor force, there has been a revolution in expectations concerning the kinds of jobs women can hold.

And in virtually every one of the major issues facing the economy, there is a debate about the role of government. Government in the United States has grown enormously. Before World War II, government took less than one out of every five dollars; today it takes one out of three. Still, government in the United States is proportionately smaller than in most other industrialized countries. At one level, there is remarkable agreement about what the government should do: it has, for instance, a responsibility to help the economy remain at full employment with stable prices, to protect the environment, to support education, and to provide for the national defense. But how the government should fulfill its responsibilities in each of these areas is highly contentious. Issues concerning the responsibility, capability, and strategies of government in economics have come to the center of the political debate.

These are exciting issues and events, and they fill the front pages of our newspapers and the evening television news shows. Yet in the past, as a teacher of the introductory course in economics, I felt frustrated: none of the textbooks really conveyed this sense of excitement. Try as they might, none seemed to prepare students adequately for interpreting and understanding these important economic events.

As I thought about it more, one of the reasons for this became clear: the principles expounded in the classic textbook of Alfred Marshall of a hundred years ago, or that of Paul Samuelson, now almost fifty years old, were not the principles for today. The way we economists understand our discipline had changed to reflect the changing world, but the textbooks had not kept pace. Our professional discourse was built on a *modern* economics, but these new developments simply were not adequately reflected in any of the vast array of textbooks that were available to me as a teacher.

Indeed, changes in the economics discipline over the past half century have been as significant as the changes in world events. The basic competitive model of the economy was perfected in the 1950s. Since then, economists have gone beyond that model in several directions as they have come to better understand its limitations. Earlier researchers had paid lip service to the importance of incentives and to problems posed by limited information. However, it was only in the last two decades that real progress was made in understanding these issues. The 1996 Nobel Prize was awarded to two economists who pioneered our understanding of the role of information and incentives in the economy. Their work, and the work of others in this field, have found immediate applications. Both the collapse of the former Soviet bloc economies and the failure of the American S & L's can be viewed as consequences of the failure to provide appropriate incentives. A central question in the debate over growth and productivity has been, how can an economy provide stronger incentives for innovation? The debate over pollution and the environment centers around the relative merits of regulation and providing incentives not to pollute and to conserve resources.

The past fifty years have also seen a reexamination of the boundary between economics and business. Subjects like finance and management used to be relegated to business schools, where they were taught without reference to economic principles. Today we know that to understand how market economies actually work, we have to understand how firms finance and manage themselves. Tremendous insights can be gleaned through the application of basic economic principles, particularly those grounded in an understanding of incentives. Stories of corporate takeovers have been replaced on the front page by stories of bankruptcies as acquiring corporations have found themselves overextended. The 1990 Nobel Prize was awarded to three economists who had contributed most to the endeavor to integrate finance and economics. Yet the introductory textbooks had not yet built in the basic economics of finance and management.

We have also come to better appreciate the virtues of competition. We now understand, for instance, how the benefits of competition extend beyond price to competition for technological innovation. At the same time, we have come to see better why, in so many circumstances, competition appears limited. Again, as I looked over the available textbooks, none seemed to provide my students with a sense of this new understanding.

Samuelson's path-breaking textbook is credited with being the first to integrate successfully the (then) new insights of Keynesian economics with traditional microeconomics. Samuelson employed the concept of the neoclassical synthesis—the view that once the economy was restored to full employment, the old classical principles applied. In effect, there were two distinct regimes to the economy. In one, when the economy's resources were underemployed, macroeconomic principles applied; in the other, when the economy's resources were fully employed, microeconomic principles were relevant. That these were distinct and hardly related regimes was reflected in how texts were written and courses were taught; it made no difference whether micro was taught before macro, or vice versa. In the last few decades, economists came to question the split that had developed between microeconomics and macroeconomics. The profession as a whole came to believe that macroeconomic behavior had to be related to underlying microeconomic principles; there was one set of economic principles, not two. But this view simply was not reflected in any of the available texts.

This book differs from most other texts in several ways. Let me highlight some of the most prominent distinctions.

- Reflecting my recent involvement in policy making, throughout the text I have introduced examples to relate economic theory to recent policy discussions. In each chapter, there is a policy perspective box providing a vignette on one particular issue, such as the investment tax credit, health care policy, unfunded mandates in environmental regulation, and capital gains taxation. These policy discussions both enliven the course and enrich the student's command over the basic material.
- Economists are a contentious lot, yet on most issues differences between economists pale in comparison to differences between noneconomists. Indeed, there is a high degree of consensus among economists, and I have drawn attention to this throughout the book with 10 points of consensus in economics, among them scarcity, incentives, the benefits of trade, the role of prices, and competition.
- Rather than the traditional approach of stretching out the competitive model to fill the entire course, I teach it in a compact format in the first two parts of the book. This allows students to develop a complete picture of the basic model, before looking systematically at the role of imperfect markets. When I turn to the discussion of the latter in Parts Three and Four, a better foundation has been laid for an understanding of such issues as technological change (Chapter 17), information problems and other imperfections in the product and labor markets (Chapters 18 and 19), and decision making within the firm (Chapter 20)—all subjects which get short shrift in other texts.
- Finance is recognized as an important part of economics. Chapter 6 introduces the basic ideas of time and risk, Chapter 10 presents "A Student's Guide to Investing," and Chapter 20 discusses how firms raise the funds they need for investment and relates finance to the struggles for corporate control.
- Throughout, issues of incentives and the problems posed by incomplete information are given prominence. To take but two of many examples, Chapter 19 discusses the role that reputation plays in providing firms with incentives to maintain the quality of their products, and Chapter 20 discusses how firms try to motivate their managers and how managers try to motivate their workers—and the problems they encounter in doing so.
- As our understanding of the limitations of markets has increased, so has our understanding of the limitations of government, and the age-old questions of the appropriate balance between government and the private sector have to be reexamined. This book looks at a wide range of policy issues, including how government can respond to the inefficiencies that arise from limited competition (Chapter 16), and what the government should do to preserve the environment (Chapter 21) and to promote greater equality (Chapter 22). The related issues of how and why government makes the decisions it does are considered in Chapter 23 ("Public Decision Making").

I emphasize in this book that most economic tasks are beyond the scope of any one individual. This lesson certainly applies to the writing and revision of a textbook. In writing the First Edition, I benefited greatly from the reactions of my students in the introductory courses at Princeton and Stanford who class-tested early drafts. Their enthusiastic response to the manuscript provided much-needed boosts to motivate me at several critical stages. The reception of the First Edition showed that the venture was well worth the effort. Similarly, the revision has benefited from the experience of the thousands of students who have used the book and their teachers who offered invaluable feedback.

This edition, and the previous, have benefited from numerous reviewers. The book has been improved immeasurably by their advice—some of which, quite naturally, was conflicting. In particular, I would like to thank Robert T. Averitt, Smith College; Mohsen Bahmani-Oskooee, University of Wisconsin, Milwaukee; H. Scott Bierman, Carleton College; John Payne Bigelow, University of Missouri; Bruce R. Bolnick, Northeastern University; Adhip Chaudhuri, Georgetown University; Michael D. Curley, Kennesaw State College; John Devereux, University of Miami; K. K. Fung, Memphis State; Christopher Georges, Hamilton College; Ronald D. Gilbert, Texas Tech University; Robert E. Graf, Jr., United States Military Academy; Glenn W. Harrison, University of South Carolina; Marc Hayford, Loyola University; Yutaka Horiba, Tulane University; Charles Howe, University of Colorado; Sheng Cheng Hu, Purdue University; Glenn Hubbard, Columbia University; Allen C. Kelley, Duke University; Michael M. Knetter, Dartmouth College; Stefan Lutz, Purdue University; Mark J. Machina, University of California, San Diego; Burton G. Malkiel, Princeton University, Lawrence Martin, Michigan State University; Thomas Mayer, University of California, Davis; Craig J. McCann, University of South Carolina; Henry N. McCarl, University of Alabama, Birmingham; John McDermott, University of South Carolina; Marshall H. Medoff, University of California, Irvine; Peter Mieszkowski, Rice University; W. Douglas Morgan, University of California, Santa Barbara; John S. Murphy, Canisius College; William Nielson, Texas A&M University; Neil B. Niman, University of New Hampshire; David H. Papell, University of Houston; James E. Price, Syracuse University; Daniel M. G. Raff, Harvard Business School; Christina D. Romer, University of California, Berkeley; Richard Rosenberg, Pennsylvania State University; Christopher J. Ruhm, Boston University; Suzanne A. Scotchmer, University of California, Berkeley; Richard Selden, University of Virginia; Andrei Shleifer, Harvard University; John L. Solow, University of Iowa; George Spiva, University of Tennessee; Mark Sproul, University of California at Los Angeles; Frank P. Stafford, University of Michigan; Raghu Sundaram, University of Rochester; Hal R. Varian, University of Michigan; Franklin V. Walker, State University of New York at Albany; James M. Walker, Indiana University; Andrew Weiss, Boston University; Gilbert R. Yochum, Old Dominion University.

It is a pleasure also to acknowledge the help of a number of research assistants. Many of them went well beyond the assigned tasks of looking up, assembling, and graphing data to providing helpful criticism of the manuscript. These include Edwin Lai, now at Vanderbilt University; Chulsoo Kim, now at Rutgers University; Alexander Dyck, now at Harvard University; Patricia Nabti and Andres Rodriguez, now at University of Chicago; Marcie Smith; and Kevin

Woodruff. I am particularly indebted to John Williams, who supervised and coordinated the final stages of preparation of the manuscript for the First Edition, and who assisted me on the entire preparation of the second. But John did more than this: he has been a sounding board for new ideas, new organizational structures, and new expositions.

I have been indeed fortunate in both editions of enlisting the help of individuals who combined a deep understanding of economics with an editor's fine honed pen: Timothy Taylor in the first edition and Felicity Skidmore in the second. Both have remarkable editorial skills; both have long been committed to the notion that it is important that modern economic ideas be communicated widely and that they *can* be, in a way that is both enlightening and enjoyable. Timothy, John, and Felicity all gave their energy and creativity to the enterprise, and the book is immeasurably better as a result.

This is the second book I have published with Norton, a company that reflects many of the aspects of organizational design that I discuss in the text. This book would not be nearly the one it is without the care, attention, and most important, deep thought devoted to my work by so many there. A few deserve special mention. Donald Lamm, chairman of the board at Norton, managed not only to keep the incentives straight within his firm, but also found time to read early drafts of the First Edition at several critical stages and offered his usual insightful suggestions. I cannot sufficiently acknowledge my indebtedness to Drake McFeely, who served as my editor on the First Edition (and succeeded Don Lamm as president of Norton) and Ed Parsons, who served as my editor on the Second Edition. Both have been concerned about the ideas *and* their presentation, and both have been tough, but constructive, critics. The work of Kate Barry, the manuscript editor, was as energetic as it was cheerful. All four made my work harder, so that readers of this book would have an easier time. Several others at Norton also deserve mention: Rosanne Fox for her outstanding proofreading, Ashley Deeks and Claire Acher, for their work on the photographs, Antonina Krass for the splendid design of the book, and Roy Tedoff and Jane Carter for coordinating its production. Finally, Stephen King, Steve Hoge, and Linda Puckette have contributed their unique talents in the creation of innovative electronic ancillaries for the text.

I owe a special thanks to those who prepared the ancillary materials that accompany the text. Given the fact that this book represents a departure from the standard mold of the past, the tasks they faced were both more important and more difficult. Their enthusiasm, insight, and hard work have produced a set of truly superb ancillaries: Lawrence Martin of Michigan State University prepared the print Study Guide and oversaw its transformation into an electronic counterpart, Ward Hanson of Stanford has developed an on-line version of the Instructor's Manual, and Alan Harrison of McMaster University prepared the test bank for the Second Edition.

It is common practice at this point in the preface to thank one's spouse and children, who have had to sacrifice so much (presumably time that the author would otherwise have spent with them). My debt goes beyond these commonplaces. My wife and children have motivated me, partly by the thirst for economic understanding they have evidenced by their questions about the rapidly changing economic scene, and partly by their challenging spirit—easy explanations, making heavy use of standard economics jargon, would not satisfy them. Moreover, in their perspective, the only justification for diverting my attention away from them and from my principal job as a teacher and researcher was the production of a textbook that would succeed in communicating the basic ideas of modern economics more effectively than those already available. I hope that what I—together with all of those who have helped me so much—have produced will please them.

OUTLINE FOR A SHORT COURSE

This book is suitable for short courses offered under a quarter system or other abbreviated schedules. Below I offer a provisional outline for such a short course, omitting several chapters. Naturally, to a large extent, *which* topics get omitted is a matter of taste. The following is my selection for a short course using fifteen chapters.

Chapter Number	Chapter Title
1	The Automobile and Economics
2	Thinking Like an Economist
3	Trade
4	Demand, Supply, and Price
5	Using Demand and Supply
7	The Public Sector
8	The Consumption Decision
9	Labor Supply and Savings
11	The Firm's Costs
12	Production
14	Monopolies and Imperfect Competition
16	Government Policies Towards Competition
18	Imperfect Information in the Product Market
21	Externalities and the Environment
22	Taxes, Transfers, and Redistribution

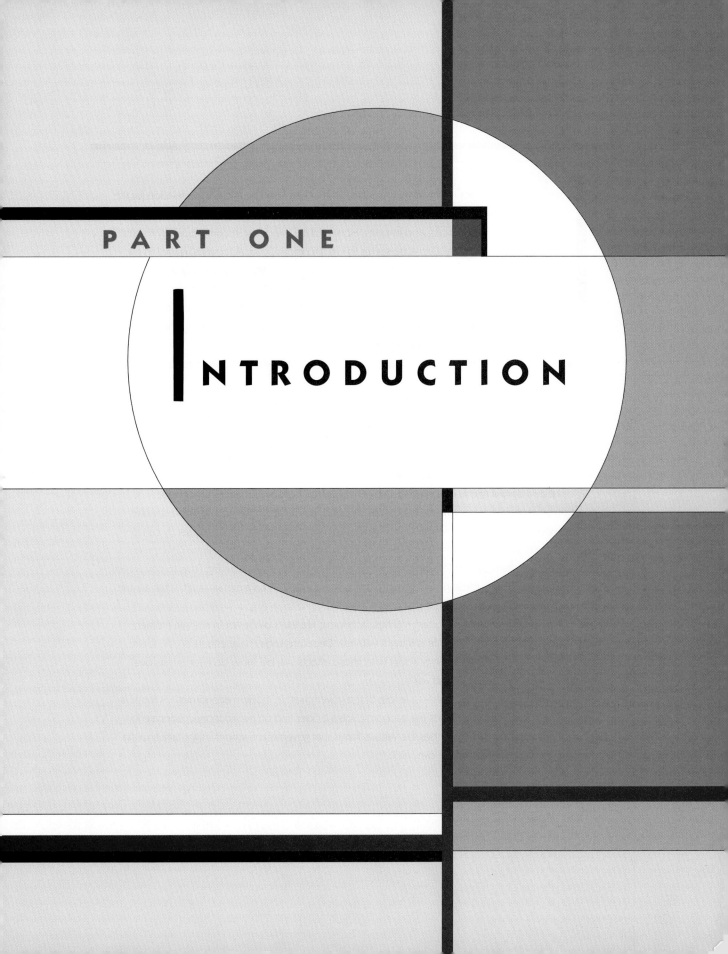

PART ONE

INTRODUCTION

These days economics is big news. If we pick up a newspaper or turn on the television for the prime-time news report, we are likely to be bombarded with statistics on unemployment rates, inflation rates, exports, and imports. How well are we doing in competition with other countries, such as Japan? Everyone seems to want to know. Political fortunes as well as the fortunes of countries, firms, and individuals depend on how well the economy does.

What is economics all about? That is the subject of Part One. Chapter 1 uses the story of the automobile industry to illustrate many of the fundamental issues with which economics is concerned. The chapter describes the four basic questions at the heart of economics, and how economists attempt to answer these questions.

Chapter 2 introduces the economists' basic model and explains why notions of property, profits, prices, and cost play such a central role in economists' thinking.

A fact of life in the modern world is that individuals and countries are interdependent. Even a wealthy country like the United States is dependent on foreign countries for vital imports. Chapter 3 discusses the gains that result from trade; why trade, for instance, allows greater specialization, and why greater specialization results in increased productivity. It also explains the patterns of trade—why each country imports and exports the particular goods it does.

Prices play a central role in enabling economies to function. Chapters 4 and 5 take up the question of what determines prices. Also, what causes prices to change over time? Why is water, without which we cannot live, normally so inexpensive, while diamonds, which we surely can do without, are very expensive? What happens to the prices of beer and cigarettes if the government imposes a tax on these goods? Sometimes the government passes laws requiring firms to pay wages of at least so much, or forbidding landlords to charge rents that exceed a certain level. What are the consequences of these government interventions?

Chapter 6 introduces two important realities: economic life takes place not in a single moment of time but over long periods, and life is fraught with risk. Decisions today have effects on the future, and there is usually much uncertainty about what those effects will be. How do economists deal with problems posed by time and risk?

Finally, Chapter 7 turns to the pervasive role of the government in modern economies. Its focus is on why the government undertakes the economic roles it does and on the economic rationale for government actions. It also describes the various forms that government actions might take and the changing roles of the government over time.

1

THE AUTOMOBILE AND ECONOMICS

Imagine the world 100 years ago: no cars, airplanes, computers (and computer games!), movies—to say nothing of atomic energy, lasers, and transistors. The list of inventions since then seems almost endless.

Of all the inventions that have shaped the world during the past century, perhaps none has had so profound an effect as the automobile. It has changed how and where people work, live, and play. But like any major innovation, it has been a mixed blessing: traffic jams on the one hand, access to wilderness on the other. And the new opportunities it created for some were accompanied by havoc for others. Some occupations—such as black-smiths—virtually disappeared. Others—such as carriage makers—had to transform themselves (into car body manufacturers) or go out of business. But the gains of the many who benefited from the new industry far out-weighed the losses of those who were hurt.

The story of the automobile is familiar. But looking at it from the per-spective of economics can teach us a great deal about the economic way of thinking.

KEY QUESTIONS

1. What *is* economics? What are the basic questions it addresses?

2. In economies such as that of the United States, what are the respective roles of government and the private, or "market," sector?

3. What are markets, and what are the principal markets that make up the economy?

4. Why is economics called a science?

5. Why, if economics is a science, do economists so often seem to disagree?

THE AUTOMOBILE: A BRIEF HISTORY

The idea of a motorized carriage occurred to many, in the United States and Europe, at roughly the same time. But ideas by themselves are not enough. Translating ideas into marketable products requires solving technical problems and persuading investors to finance the venture.

If you visit a museum of early cars, you will see that the technical problems were resolved in a variety of ways, by many people working independently. At the turn of the century, the area around Detroit was full of innovators developing cars—Ransom E. Olds, the Dodge brothers, and Henry Ford. The spirit must have been much like that of "Silicon Valley" (the area in California between San Francisco and San Jose) in the past quarter century, which has been at the center of computer technology development: a spirit of excitement, breakthroughs made, and new milestones reached. The various automobile innovators could draw upon a stock of ideas "floating in the air." They also had the help of specialized firms that had developed a variety of new technologies and skills: for example, new alloys that enabled lighter motors to be constructed and new techniques for machining that allowed for greater power, precision, and durability.

Henry Ford is generally given credit for having recognized the potential value of a vehicle that could be made and sold at a reasonable price. Before Ford, automobiles were luxuries, affordable only by the very rich. He saw the potential benefit from providing inexpensive transportation. After he introduced the Model T in 1909 at a "bargain" price of $900, he continued to cut the price—to $440 in 1914 and $360 in 1916. Sales skyrocketed from 58,000 in 1909 to 730,000 in 1916. Ford's prediction of a mass market for inexpensive cars had proved correct.

But success was neither sudden nor easy. To translate his idea into action

Ford had to put together a company to produce cars, figure out how to produce them cheaply, and raise the capital required to make all this possible.

Raising capital was particularly difficult, since the venture was extremely risky. Would Ford be successful in developing his automobile? Would someone else beat him to it? Would the price of a car be low enough for many people to buy it? If he was successful, would imitators copy his invention, robbing him of the mass market he needed to make money?

Ford formed a partnership to develop his first car. He was to supply the ideas and the work, while his partners supplied the funds. It took three partnerships before Ford produced a single car. The first two went bankrupt, with the financial partners in each case accusing Ford of spending all of his time developing ideas instead of acting on them.

But were the first two sets of partners treated unfairly? After all, they knew the risks. Ford could have entered each partnership in good faith and simply been unable to deliver.

But even in the third case, his partners were unhappy: They claimed he managed to garner for himself the lion's share of the profits. Ford may have argued that his ideas were far more important than the mere dollars that the financiers provided to carry them out.

Whatever the truth in Ford's case, the general problem of who contributes more in a partnership and who should get what share of any profits occurs often.

Ford's success was due as much to his ability to come up with innovative ways of providing incentives and organizing production as to his skill in solving technical problems. He demonstrated this ability with his original labor policies. He offered more than double the going wage and paid his workers the then princely sum of $5 a day. In exchange, Ford worked his employees hard; the moving assembly line he invented enabled him to set his workers a fast pace and push them to keep up. The amount produced per worker increased enormously. Still, it was clear that the high wages were ample compensation for the extra effort. Riots almost broke out as workers clamored for the jobs he offered. Ford had rediscovered an old truth: in some cases, higher wages for employees can repay the employer in higher productivity, through greater loyalty, harder work, and less absenteeism.

Ford's success in increasing productivity meant that he could sell his cars far more cheaply than his rivals could. The lower prices and the high level of sales that accompanied them made it possible for him to take full advantage of the mass production techniques he had developed. At one point, however, Ford's plans were almost thwarted when a lawyer-inventor named George Baldwin Selden claimed that Ford had infringed on his patent.

The U.S. government grants patents to enable inventors to reap the rewards of their innovative activity. These are generally for specific inventions, like a new type of braking system or transmission mechanism, not for general ideas. Ford's idea of an assembly line, for example, was not an invention that could be patented, and it was imitated by other car manufacturers. A patent gives the inventor the exclusive right to produce his invention for a limited time, thus helping to assure that inventors will be able to make some money from their successful inventions. Patents may lead to higher prices for these new products, since there is no competition from others making the same product. But the presumption is that the gains to society from the innovative activity more than compensate for the losses to consumers from the temporarily higher prices.

Selden had applied for, and been granted, a patent for a horseless, self-propelled carriage. He demanded that other car manufacturers pay him a royalty, which is a payment for the right to use a patented innovation. Ford challenged Selden's patent in court on the grounds that the concept of a "horseless, self-propelled carriage" was too vague to be patentable. Ford won. Providing cars to the masses at low prices made Ford millions of dollars and many millions of Americans better off, by enabling them to go where they wanted to go more easily, cheaply, and speedily.

CRISIS IN THE AMERICAN AUTOMOBILE INDUSTRY

Today people think of computers and gene-splicing, not automobiles, as the new technologies. The story of the automobile is no longer emblematic of the latest technological breakthroughs. The changing fortunes of the American automobile industry during the past two decades are similar to those of many other parts of U.S. industry.

There were more than a hundred U.S. automobile manufacturers in the fall of 1903, twenty-seven of which accounted for more than 70 percent of the total sales of the industry. By the early 1960s, however, only three companies were responsible for 88 percent of U.S. auto sales. Of the car manufacturers that existed at the beginning of the century, many had gone bankrupt or given up on the automobile business, and the remainder had been agglomerated into or taken over by the dominant firms.

The most serious problems faced by the auto industry in the 1960s involved air pollution and automobile safety. To reduce pollution, the government regulated the amount of exhaust fumes a car could produce, and design changes followed. On the safety front, automobile companies quickly responded to demands for increased safety by providing seat belts.

This relatively rosy picture changed dramatically in 1973. That year, the Organization of Petroleum Exporting Countries (OPEC)—mainly countries in the Middle East—combined forces to hold down the supply of oil, create a scarcity, and thus push up its price. OPEC actually cut off all oil exports for a few tense weeks late in 1973. Its power was a surprise to many, including the American automobile industry. American cars then tended to be bigger and heavier than those in Japan and Europe. This was easily explained: incomes in the United States were higher; Americans could afford larger cars and the gasoline they guzzled. Also, Japan and Europe imposed much heavier taxes on gasoline than did the United States, encouraging consumers in those countries to buy smaller, more fuel-efficient cars.

The U.S. auto industry, thus, was ill-prepared for the higher gas prices caused by OPEC's move. But other countries, especially Japan, stood ready to

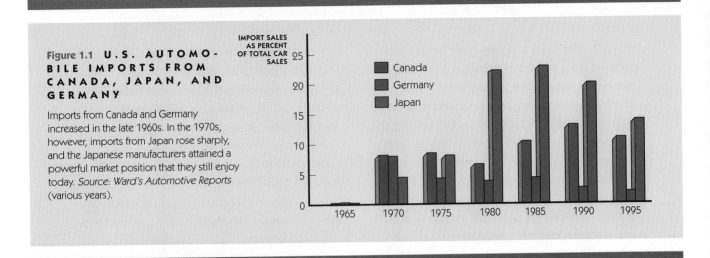

Figure 1.1 U.S. AUTOMOBILE IMPORTS FROM CANADA, JAPAN, AND GERMANY

Imports from Canada and Germany increased in the late 1960s. In the 1970s, however, imports from Japan rose sharply, and the Japanese manufacturers attained a powerful market position that they still enjoy today. *Source: Ward's Automotive Reports* (various years).

gain, with smaller, cheaper, and more fuel-efficient cars. Auto imports as a whole nearly doubled in the 1970s, from 15 percent of the total cars sold in the United States in 1970 to 27 percent by 1980, and they remained at a high level throughout the 1980s and into the 1990s. Figure 1.1 shows the dramatic increase in imports of new passenger cars from Canada, Germany, and especially Japan over the last thirty years.

It was clear that the Japanese firms were supplying what American consumers wanted, but the effect on the American automobile industry was devastating. Profits fell and workers were laid off.

CHRYSLER: GOVERNMENT TO THE RESCUE

In the late 1970s, one firm, Chrysler, was on the verge of bankruptcy. The company did not have and could not borrow the cash to pay off loans that were due, so it asked for help from the government. In the ensuing debate about whether the government should save Chrysler, advocates of a bailout (rescue from financial ruin) painted a picture of unemployed workers and empty, wasted factories.

Critics of the bailout pointed out that the workers, machines, and buildings of a bankrupt company do not disappear. Instead, they can be hired by or sold to new companies under new management. Redeployment of resources was appropriate, critics argued, because the impending bankruptcy demonstrated that Chrysler management had failed to manage its resources well.

In the end, the government guaranteed some new loans for Chrysler. If Chrysler failed to pay back its loans, the government would do so with tax money. Because of this guarantee, Chrysler was able to obtain loans from private investors and banks, and at a relatively low rate of interest. Its subsequent

POLICY PERSPECTIVE: WHEN IS A TRUCK A CAR?

In April 1994 U.S. trade negotiator Mickey Kantor headed up a team to negotiate with its counterparts from Japan. The United States has a huge trade imbalance with Japan, importing far more than it exports. Of the many factors causing this imbalance, the one that infuriates U.S. industry is "unfair trade practices" or subtle actions by the Japanese government to restrict American sales. Rice is a good example. The Japanese refused to import American rice until 1994. Automobile parts are another example. Regulations—justified on safety grounds—restricted sales of replacement parts produced by firms other than the car's manufacturer. Only Toyota could make replacement parts for Toyota cars. But since almost all cars sold in Japan are made in Japan, this effectively kept out non-Japanese parts producers.

Part of Kantor's mission was to reduce such un-

fair trade practices, and he used the mini-van as a weapon. The mini-van may seem to have nothing to do with rice, but in the context of those negotiations it did. Why? Because importers of vehicles into the United States must pay a tariff (tax)—a tax that is higher on cars than on trucks.

The mini-van is currently taxed as a truck. But, is it really a truck? The mini-van is commonly built on a truck frame, but it hauls people, not goods. With Japanese imports accounting for 7 percent of the U.S. mini-van market, U.S. producers would be delighted to reduce their Japanese competition by getting the mini-van reclassified as a car and taxed as such. The higher tariff, of course, would raise the price of Japanese mini-vans to U.S. consumers and reduce their attractiveness in the U.S. market. The unspoken threat of such a reclassification was not lost on the Japanese.

success is an often-told tale, with the president of Chrysler, Lee Iacocca, claiming a large share of the credit for himself.

It turns out that the government had strong incentives to step in and help Chrysler. Not only was there concern about losing one of the three major firms in the automobile industry, but the government stood to lose money through an insurance program for workers' pensions set up several years before. This program guaranteed that even if a company went bankrupt, workers would still receive their pensions. Had Chrysler gone bankrupt, the government might have had to pay Chrysler workers hundreds of millions of dollars in pensions.

The government even ended up making money in bailing out Chrysler. In return for guaranteeing the loans, the government insisted that, in effect, it be granted some share of ownership in the firm. With the company's subsequent success, these shares turned out to be quite valuable.

PROTECTION FROM FOREIGN COMPETITION

The problems at Chrysler also existed in reduced form at General Motors and Ford. But in the early 1980s, all three began to make a recovery from the hard times of the 1970s, for several reasons. Unions dramatically reduced their wage demands. Smaller and more fuel-efficient cars were developed. And the government again stepped in, this time to help protect the industry from foreign competition. Again the concern was layoffs: in 1980, unemployment in Michigan, a major auto-producing state, had reached 12.6 percent (as contrasted with the total U.S. unemployment rate of 7.1 percent). Rather than imposing a tariff (tax) on car imports, the American government negotiated with the Japanese government to restrain Japan's automobile exports. Although the export limits were called voluntary, they were actually negotiated under pressure. If the Japanese had not taken the "voluntary" step of limiting exports, Congress probably would have passed a law forcing them to do so.

The reduced supply of Japanese cars led not only to increased sales of American cars, but to higher prices, both for Japanese and American cars. The American industry was subsidized not by the taxpayers in general but by those who bought cars, through these higher prices. The Japanese car manufacturers had little to complain about, since they too benefited from the higher prices. Had Japanese manufacturers gotten together and agreed to reduce their sales and raise prices, the action would have been viewed as a violation of U.S. antitrust laws, which were designed to enforce competition. But here the American government itself was encouraging less competition!

The Japanese responded in still another way to these restrictions. They decided to circumvent the limitations on their exports by manufacturing cars here in the United States. As shown in Figure 1.2, in 1995 more than one out of three cars produced in the United States is produced by foreign-owned firms. These are referred to as **transplants.** Honda, Mazda, Nissan, and Toyota could all claim that at least some of their cars were made in America.

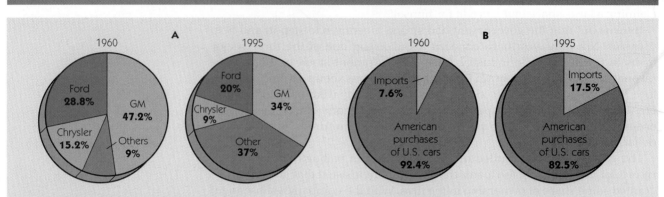

Figure 1.2 SHARES OF THE U.S. AUTOMOBILE MARKET

These pie charts show some of the changes in the U.S. auto market in recent decades. Panel A focuses on production, panel B on purchases. The charts in panel A show that production has remained concentrated. In 1960, the "other" firms were small American firms such as Studebaker and American Motors; in 1990, they were foreign-owned firms like Honda. The charts in panel B show the dramatic increase in imports. *Source: Ward's Automotive Reports* (various years).

THE REBIRTH OF THE AMERICAN AUTOMOBILE INDUSTRY

What would have happened had the automobile companies not been given the breather that the Japanese export restraints provided? We cannot tell. Perhaps they would have been forced to transform themselves more quickly. Perhaps one or more would have gone out of business. What we do know is that during the 1980s, the industry worked hard to compete effectively with its Japanese rivals. The different firms pursued different strategies.

General Motors, for instance, focused on automation, investing heavily in robots and other new equipment. Much of this turned out to be wasted. But GM did undertake a successful, major new venture—the Saturn project. In addition to innovations in product design and manufacturing, labor relations and marketing were improved. Worker participation in decision making was increased. And instead of the haggling that is typical of car purchases, Saturns were bought just like most other goods—at the prices on their stickers. The car generated so much customer loyalty that when the company invited owners to come to the factory in June 1994 to celebrate what was billed as its "homecoming," 44,000 people showed up.

THE HISTORY OF THE AUTOMOBILE IN STATISTICS

Figure 1.3 illustrates the history of U.S. car production. The ups and downs of the curve reflect the rise, fall, and recovery of the industry. Car production has

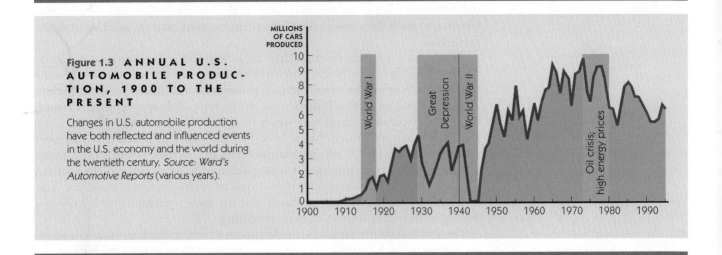

Figure 1.3 ANNUAL U.S. AUTOMOBILE PRODUCTION, 1900 TO THE PRESENT

Changes in U.S. automobile production have both reflected and influenced events in the U.S. economy and the world during the twentieth century. *Source: Ward's Automotive Reports* (various years).

been set against a backdrop of the major events affecting the economy as a whole. Different years are listed on the horizontal axis, while the number of cars built is provided on the vertical axis. Improvements in techniques of mass production led to the boom in sales early in this century. During the Great Depression of the 1930s, sales declined sharply, and civilian automobile production halted entirely during World War II. Production then rose during the boom of the 1950s and 1960s. In the 1970s, sharp increases in the price of gasoline helped trigger two worldwide recessions, reducing car sales. The U.S. economy recovered to a pattern of steady growth in the mid-1980s, halting, at least temporarily, the decline in automobile sales.

Heading into the economic downturn that began in 1990, the industry again showed its sensitivity to the health of the overall economy. Reduced confidence in the economy and lower incomes led consumers to put off purchasing cars. The reduced sales of cars, in turn, contributed to the slowdown of the economy. It was not until interest rates fell and the economy began to recover, in 1993, that automobile sales again began to recover; profits once again soared, reaching record levels.

WHAT IS ECONOMICS?

This narrative illustrates many facets of economics, but now a definition of our subject is in order. **Economics** studies how individuals, firms, governments, and other organizations within our society make **choices,** and how those choices determine the way the resources of society are used. **Scarcity** figures prominently in economics: choices matter because resources are scarce. Imagine an enormously wealthy individual who can have everything he wants. We might think that scarcity is not in his vocabulary—until we consider that time is a resource, and he must decide what expensive toy to devote his time to each day. Taking time into account, then, scarcity is a fact in everyone's life.

To produce a single product, like an automobile, thousands of decisions and choices have to be made. Since any economy is made up not only of automobiles but of millions of products, it is a marvel that the economy functions at all, let alone as well as it does most of the time. This marvel is particularly clear if you consider instances when things do not work so well: the Great Depression in the United States in the 1930s, when 25 percent of the work force could not find a job; the countries of the former Soviet Union today, where ordinary consumer goods like carrots or toilet paper are often simply unavailable; the less developed economies of many countries in Africa, Asia, and Latin America, where standards of living have remained stubbornly low, and in some places have even been declining.

The fact that choices must be made applies as well to the economy as a whole as it does to each individual. Somehow, decisions are made—by individuals, households, firms, and government—that together determine how the economy's limited resources, including its land, labor, machines, oil, and other natural resources, are used. Why is it that land used at one time for growing crops may, at another time, be used for an automobile plant? How was it that over the space of a couple of decades, resources were transferred from making horse carriages to making automobile bodies? that blacksmiths were replaced by auto mechanics? How do the decisions of millions of consumers, workers, investors, managers, and government officials all interact to determine the use of the scarce resources available to society? Economists reduce such matters to four basic questions concerning how economies function:

1. What is produced, and in what quantities? There have been important changes in consumption over the past fifty years. Spending for medical care, for example, was only 3.5 percent of total personal consumption in 1950. By 1995, more than one out of every seven dollars was spent on medical care. What can account for changes like these? The economy seems to spew out new products like videocassette recorders and new services like automated bank tellers. What causes this process of innovation? The overall level of production has also shifted from year to year, often accompanied by large changes in the levels of employment and unemployment. How can economists explain these changes?

In the United States, the question of what is produced, and in what quantities, is answered largely by the private interaction of firms and consumers, but government also plays a role. Prices are critical in determining what goods are produced. When the price of some good rises, firms are induced to produce more of that good, to increase their profits. Thus, a central question for economists is, why are some goods more expensive than others? And why have the prices of some goods increased or decreased?

2. How are these goods produced? There are often many ways of making something. Textiles can be made with hand looms. Modern machines enable fewer workers to produce more cloth. Very modern machines may be highly computerized, allowing one worker to monitor many more machines than was possible earlier. The better machines generally cost more, but they require less labor. Which technique will be used, the advanced technology or the labor-intensive one? Henry Ford introduced the assembly line. More recently, car manufacturers have begun using robots. What determines how rapidly technology changes?

In the U.S. economy, firms answer the question of how goods are produced, again with input from the government, which sets regulations and enacts laws that affect everything from the overall organization of firms to the ways they interact with their employees and customers.

3. For whom are these goods produced?   In the United States, individuals who have higher incomes can consume more goods. But that answer only pushes the question back one step: What determines the differences in income and wages? What is the role of luck? of education? of inheritance? of savings? of experience and hard work? These questions are difficult to answer. For now, suffice it to say that while incomes are primarily determined by the private interaction of firms and households in the United States, government also plays a strong role, with taxes as well as programs that redistribute income.

Figure 1.4 shows the relative pay in a variety of different occupations. To judge by income, each physician receives five times as much of the economy's output as a firefighter, and seven times as much as a butcher.

4. Who makes economic decisions, and by what process?   In a **centrally planned economy,** as the Soviet Union was, the government takes responsibility for virtually every aspect of economic activity. The government provides the answers to the first three questions. A central economic planning agency works through a bureaucracy to say what will be produced and by what method, and who shall consume it. At the other end of the spectrum are economies that rely primarily on the free interchange of producers and their customers

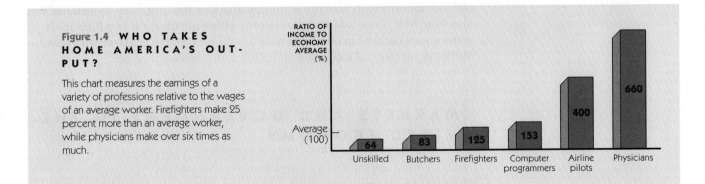

Figure 1.4 WHO TAKES HOME AMERICA'S OUTPUT?

This chart measures the earnings of a variety of professions relative to the wages of an average worker. Firefighters make 25 percent more than an average worker, while physicians make over six times as much.

RATIO OF INCOME TO ECONOMY AVERAGE (%)

Average (100)

Unskilled	Butchers	Firefighters	Computer programmers	Airline pilots	Physicians
64	83	125	153	400	660

BASIC QUESTIONS OF ECONOMICS

1. What is produced, and in what quantities?

2. How are these goods produced?

3. For whom are these goods produced?

4. Who makes economic decisions, and by what process?

to determine what, how, and for whom. The United States, which lies near this latter end, has a **mixed economy;** that is, a mix between public (governmental) and private decision making. Within limits, producers make what they want; they use whatever method of production seems appropriate to them; and the output is distributed to consumers according to their income.

When economists examine an economy, they want to know to what extent economic decisions are made by the government, and to what extent they are made by private individuals. In the United States, while individuals for the most part make their own decisions about what kind of car to purchase, the government has inserted itself in a number of ways: it has taken actions that affect the import of Japanese cars, that restrict the amount of pollutants a car can produce, and that promote fuel efficiency and automobile safety.

A related question is whether economic decisions are made by individuals for their own interests or for the interest of an employer such as a business firm or government agency. This is an important distinction.We can expect people acting on their own behalf to make decisions that benefit themselves. When they act on behalf of organizations, however, a conflict of interest may arise. Observers often refer to corporations and governments as if they were a single individual. Economists point out that organizations consist, by definition, of a multitude of individuals and that the interests of these individuals do not necessarily coincide with one another or, for that matter, with the interests of the organization itself. Organizations bring a number of distinctive problems to the analysis of choice.

As you can see by their concern with decision making, economists are concerned not only with *how* the economy answers the four basic questions, but also *how well.* They ask, is the economy efficient? Could it produce more of some goods without producing fewer of others? Could it make some individuals better off without making some other individuals worse off?

MARKETS AND GOVERNMENT IN THE MIXED ECONOMY

The primary reliance on private decision making in the United States reflects economists' beliefs that this reliance is appropriate and necessary for economic efficiency; however, economists also believe that certain interventions by government are desirable. Finding the appropriate balance between the public and the private sectors of the economy is a central issue of economic analysis.

MARKETS

The economic concept of markets is used to include any situation where exchange takes place, though this exchange may not necessarily resemble the traditional village markets. In department stores and shopping malls, customers rarely haggle over the price. When manufacturers purchase the materials they need for production, they exchange money for them, not other goods. Most goods, from cameras to clothes, are not sold directly from producers to consumers. They are sold from producers to distributors, from distributors to retailers, from retailers to consumers. All of these transactions are embraced by the concepts of **market** and **market economy.**

In market economies with competition, individuals make choices that reflect their own desires. And firms make choices that maximize their profits; to do so, they must produce the goods consumers want, and they must produce them at lower cost than other firms. As firms compete in the quest for profits, consumers benefit, both from the kinds of goods produced and the prices at which they are supplied. The market economy thus provides answers to the four basic economic questions—what is produced, how it is produced, for whom it is produced, and how these decisions are made. And on the whole, the answers the market gives ensure the efficiency of the economy.

But the answer the market provides to the question of for whom goods are produced is one that not everyone finds acceptable. Like bidders at an auction, what market participants are willing and able to pay depends on their income. Some groups of individuals—including those without skills that are valued by the market—may receive such a low income that they could not feed and educate their children without outside assistance. Government provides the assistance by taking steps to increase income equality. These steps, however, often blunt economic incentives. While welfare payments provide an important safety net for the poor, the taxation required to finance them may discourage work and savings. If the government takes one out of three or even two dollars that an individual earns, that individual may not be inclined to work so much. And if the government takes one out of two or three dollars a person earns from interest on savings, the person may decide to spend more and save less. Like the appropriate balance between the public and private sectors, the appropriate balance between concerns about equality (often referred to as **equity concerns**) and efficiency is a central issue of modern economics.

THE ROLE OF GOVERNMENT

The answers to the basic economic questions that the market provides on the whole ensure efficiency. But in certain areas the solutions appear inadequate to many. There may be too much pollution, too much inequality, and too little concern about education, health, and safety. When the market is not perceived to be working well, people often turn to government.

The government plays a major role in modern economies. We need to understand both what that role is and why government undertakes the activities that it does. The story of the automobile provides several instances. Early on, George Baldwin Selden was almost able to use government-created patent laws to change the course of the industry. In the late 1970s, government loan guarantees enabled Chrysler to survive. The automobile industry was helped by government restrictions on Japanese imports but probably hurt by government regulations concerning pollution. The strength of the auto unions, reflected in their success in raising wages to high levels, was partly a result of the rights that federal legislation had granted to them. Later on we will see more ways in which government policy has affected industry.

The U.S. government sets the legal structure under which private firms and individuals operate. It regulates businesses to ensure that they do not discriminate by race or sex, do not mislead customers, are careful about the safety of their employees, and do not pollute air and water. In some industries, the government operates like a private business: the government-owned Tennessee Valley Authority (TVA) is one of the nation's largest producers of electricity; most children attend government-owned public schools; and most mail is still delivered by the government-owned post office. In other cases, the government supplies goods and services that the private sector does not, such as providing for the national defense, building roads, and printing money. Government programs provide for the elderly through Social Security (which pays income to retired individuals) and Medicare (which funds medical needs of the aged). The government helps those who have suffered economic dislocation, through unemployment insurance for those temporarily unemployed and disability insurance for those who are no longer able to work. The government also provides a safety net of support for the poor, particularly children, through various welfare programs.

One can easily imagine a government controlling the economy more directly. In countries where decision-making authority is centralized and concentrated in the government, government bureaucrats might decide what and how much a factory should produce and set the level of wages that should be paid. Various European governments run steel companies, coal mines, and the telephone system. At least until recently, governments in countries like the former Soviet Union and China attempted to control practically all major decisions regarding resource allocation.

THE THREE MAJOR MARKETS

The market economy revolves around exchange between individuals (or households), who buy goods and services from firms, and firms, which take **inputs,** the various materials of production, and produce **outputs,** the goods and services that they sell. In thinking about a market economy, economists focus their attention on three broad categories of markets in which individu-

CLOSE-UP: A FAILED ALTERNATIVE TO THE MIXED ECONOMY

While the mixed economy now is the dominant form of economic organization, it is not the only possible way of answering the basic economic questions. Beginning in 1917, an experiment in almost complete government control was begun in what became the Soviet Union.

What was produced in such an economy, and in what quantities? Government planners set the targets, which workers and firms then struggled to fulfill.

How were these goods produced? Again, since government planners decided what supplies would be delivered to each factory, they effectively chose how production occurred.

For whom were these goods produced? The government made decisions about what each job was paid, which affected how much people could consume. In principle, individuals could choose what to buy at government-operated stores, at prices set by the government. But in practice, many goods were unavailable at these stores.

Who made economic decisions, and by what process? The government planners decided, basing the decisions on their view of national economic goals.

At one time, all this planning sounded very sensible, but as former Soviet premier Nikita Khrushchev once said, "Economics is a subject that does not greatly respect one's wishes." Many examples of Soviet economic woes could be cited, but two will suffice. In the shoe market, the Soviet Union was the largest national producer in the world. However, the average shoe was of such low quality that it fell apart in a few weeks, and inventories of unwanted shoes rotted in warehouses. In agriculture, the Soviet government had traditionally allowed small private plots. Although the government limited the time farmers could spend on these plots,

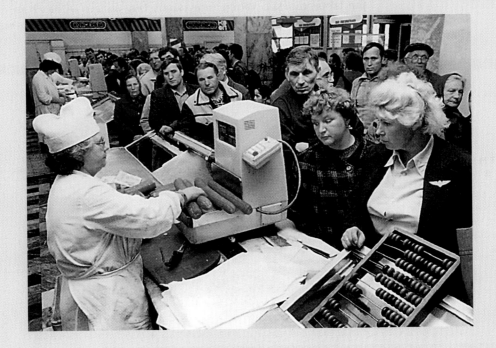

publicly run farming was so unproductive that the 3 percent of Soviet land that was privately run produced about 25 percent of the total farm output.

Today the standard of living in the former Soviet Union is not only below that in industrialized nations like the United States and those of Western Europe, but it is barely ahead of developing nations like Brazil and Mexico. Workers in the Soviet Union shared a grim one-liner: "We pretend to work and they pretend to pay us."

The collapse of the Soviet Union was, to a large extent, the result of the failure of its economic system. Much of this text is concerned with explaining why mixed economies work as well as they do.

als and firms interact. The markets in which firms sell their outputs to households are referred to collectively as the **product market.** Many firms also sell goods to other firms; the outputs of the first firm become the inputs of the second. These transactions too are said to occur in the product market.

On the input side, firms need (besides the materials that they buy in the product market) some combination of labor and machinery with which their goods can be produced. They purchase the services of workers in the **labor market.** They raise funds, with which to buy inputs, in the **capital market.** Traditionally, economists have also highlighted the importance of a third input, land, but in modern industrial economies, land is of secondary importance. For most purposes, it suffices to focus attention on the three major markets listed here, and this text will follow this pattern.

As Figure 1.5 shows, individuals participate in all three markets. When individuals buy goods or services, they act as **consumers** in the product market. When people act as **workers,** economists say they "sell their labor services" in the labor market. When individuals buy shares of stock in a firm or lend money to a business, economists note that they are participating in the capital market, and refer to them as **investors.**

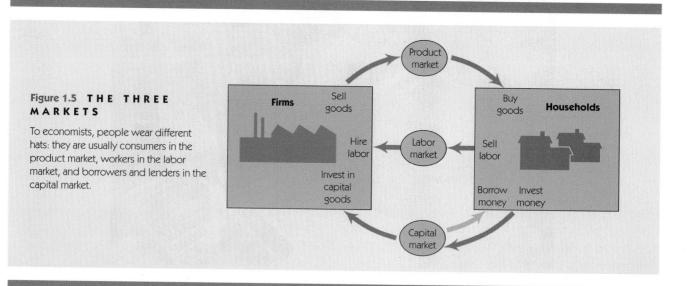

Figure 1.5 THE THREE MARKETS

To economists, people wear different hats: they are usually consumers in the product market, workers in the labor market, and borrowers and lenders in the capital market.

TWO CAVEATS

Terms in economics often are similar to terms in ordinary usage, but they can have special meanings. The terms **markets** and **capital** illustrate the problem.

Though the term "market" is used to conjure an image of a busy **marketplace,** there is no formal marketplace for most goods and services. There are buyers and sellers, and economists analyze the outcome *as if* there were a single marketplace in which all the transactions occurred.

Moreover, economists often talk about the "market for labor" as if all workers were identical. But workers obviously differ in countless ways. In some cases, these differences are important. We might then talk about the "market for skilled workers," or "the market for plumbers." But in other cases—such as when we are talking about the overall state of the economy and focusing on the unemployment rate (the fraction of workers who would like jobs but cannot get them)—these differences can be ignored.

When newspapers refer to the capital market, they mean the bond traders and stockbrokers and the companies they work for on Wall Street and other financial districts. When economists use the term capital market they have in mind a broader concept. It includes all the institutions concerned with raising funds (and, as we will see later, sharing and insuring risks), including banks and insurance companies.

The term "capital" is used in still another way—to refer to the machines and buildings used in production. To distinguish this particular usage, in this book we refer to machines and buildings as **capital goods.** Capital markets thus refers to the markets in which funds are raised, borrowed, and lent. **Capital goods markets** refers to the markets in which capital goods are bought and sold.

MICROECONOMICS AND MACROECONOMICS: THE TWO BRANCHES OF ECONOMICS

The detailed study of product, labor, and capital markets is called **microeconomics.** Microeconomics ("micro" is derived from the Greek word meaning "small") focuses on the behavior of the units—the firms, households, and individuals—that make up the economy. It is concerned with how the individual units make decisions and what affects those decisions. By contrast, **macroeconomics** ("macro" comes from the Greek word meaning "large") looks at the behavior of the economy as a whole, in particular the behavior of such aggregate measures as overall rates of unemployment, inflation, economic growth, and the balance of trade. The aggregate numbers do not tell us what any firm or household is doing. They tell us what is happening in total, or on average.

It is important to remember that these perspectives are simply two ways of looking at the same thing. Microeconomics is the bottom-up view of the economy; macroeconomics is the top-down view. The behavior of the economy as a whole is dependent on the behavior of the units that make it up.

The automobile industry is a story of both micro- and macroeconomics. It is a story of microeconomic interactions of individual companies, investors, and labor unions. It is also a story of global macroeconomic forces like oil shortages and economic fluctuations. When auto companies laid off workers in the late 1970s, their problems boosted the overall unemployment rate. The recession of the early 1990s brought heavy reductions in car sales. When the recovery occurred, auto sales grew rapidly.

THE SCIENCE OF ECONOMICS

Economics is a **social science.** It studies the social problem of choice from a scientific viewpoint, which means that it is built on a systematic exploration of the problem of choice. This systematic exploration involves both the formulation of theories and the examination of data.

A **theory** consists of a set of assumptions (or hypotheses) and conclusions derived from those assumptions. Theories are logical exercises: *if* the assumptions are correct, *then* the results follow. If all college graduates have a better chance of getting jobs and Ellen is a college graduate, then Ellen has a better chance of getting a job than a nongraduate. Economists make predictions with their theories. They might use a theory to predict what will happen if a tax is increased or if imports of foreign cars are limited. The predictions of a theory are of the form "If a tax is increased and if the market is competitive, then output will decrease and prices will increase."

In developing their theories, economists use models. To understand how economists use models, consider a modern car manufacturer trying to design a new automobile. It is extremely expensive to construct a new car. Rather than creating a separate, fully developed car for every engineer's or designer's conception of what she would like to see the new car be, the company uses models. The designers might use a plastic model to study the general shape of the vehicle and to assess reactions to the car's aesthetics. The engineers might use a computer model to study the air resistance, from which they can calculate fuel consumption and a separate model for judging the car's comfort.

Just as engineers construct different models to study particular features of a car, so too economists construct models of the economy—in words or equations—to depict particular features of the economy. An economic model might describe a general relationship ("When incomes rise, the number of cars purchased increases"), describe a quantitative relationship ("When incomes rise by 10 percent, the number of cars purchased rises, on average, by 12 percent"), or make a general prediction ("An increase in the tax on gasoline will decrease the demand for cars").

DISCOVERING AND INTERPRETING RELATIONSHIPS

A **variable** is any item that can be measured and that changes. Prices, wages, interest rates, quantities bought and sold, are all variables. What interests economists is the connection between variables. When economists see what appears to be a systematic relationship among variables, they ask, could it have arisen by chance, or is there indeed a relationship? This is the question of **correlation.**

Economists use statistical tests to measure and test correlations. Consider the problem of deciding whether a coin is biased. If you flip a coin 10 times and get 6 heads and 4 tails, is the coin a fair one? Or is it weighted to heads? Statistical tests will say that the result of 6 heads and 4 tails could easily happen by chance, so the evidence does not prove that the coin is weighted. This does not prove that it is *not* slightly weighted. The evidence is just not strong enough for either conclusion. But if you flip a coin 100 times and get 80 heads, statistical tests will tell you that the possibility of this happening by blind chance with a fair coin is extremely small. The evidence supports the assertion that the coin is weighted.

A similar logic can be used on correlations in economic data. People with more education tend to earn higher wages. Is the connection merely chance? Statistical tests show whether the evidence is too weak for a conclusion, or whether it supports the existence of a systematic relationship between education and wages.

CAUSATION VERSUS CORRELATION

Economists would like to accomplish more than just asserting that different variables are indeed correlated. They would like to conclude that changes in one variable *cause* the changes in the other variable. The distinction between correlation and **causation** is important. If one variable "causes" the other, then changing one variable necessarily will change the other. If the relationship is just a correlation, this may not be true.

Earlier, we saw that Japanese imports increased for more than a decade after 1973 and sales of U.S. cars decreased. The two variables were negatively correlated. But did that prove that increased Japanese sales caused the decreased American sales? If the decline in U.S. car production during this period was because American companies were producing large gas guzzlers that people no longer wanted, reducing Japanese car sales might not increase the sales of U.S.-made cars. In short, if there was a common cause to both changes—increased oil prices leading to increased sales of Japanese cars and decreased sales of U.S. cars—then these trends would be reversed only when American companies started to produce fuel-efficient cars.

In some cases, the *direction* of causation is not clear: did high Japanese sales cause low U.S. sales, or vice versa? For instance, it might have turned out, upon closer investigation, that the true explanation of decreased sales of U.S. cars was strikes that caused production shortages; when U.S. cars were not available, consumers turned to Japanese cars. To tell which explanation is valid—whether high Japanese sales cause low U.S. sales, whether low U.S. sales cause high Japanese sales, or whether both are caused by a third factor—requires closer examination of, for example, the circumstances in which the two variables moved in directions different from those normally observed.

EXPERIMENTS IN ECONOMICS

Many sciences use laboratory experiments to test alternative explanations, since experiments allow the scientist to change one factor at a time and see what happens. But the economy is not a chemistry lab. Instead, economics is like astronomy, in that both sciences must use the experiments that nature provides. Economists look for situations in which only one factor changes, and study the consequences of changing that factor. A change in the income tax system is an example of a natural experiment. But nature is usually not kind to economists; the world does not hold still. As the tax system changes, so do other features of the economy, and economists often have a difficult time deciding whether changes are the result of the new tax system or of some other economic change. Sometimes they can use what is called **econometrics,** the branch of statistics developed to analyze the particular measurement problems that arise in economics.

In a few cases, economists have engaged in social experiments. For example, they have given a selected group of individuals a different income tax schedule or welfare program from that faced by another, otherwise similar, group. In recent years, a major new branch of economics, called **experimental economics,** has analyzed certain aspects of economic behavior in a controlled, laboratory setting. One way of seeing how individuals respond to risk, for example, is to construct a risky situation in such a setting and force individuals to make decisions and act on them. By varying the nature of the risk and the rewards, one can learn about how individuals will respond to different risks in real life situations. Similarly, different kinds of auctions can be simulated in a controlled laboratory setting to see how buyers respond. Lessons learned from such auctions have already been used by government in designing some of the auctions it conducts. Both social and laboratory experiments have provided economists with valuable insights concerning economic behavior.

But even with all available tools, the problem of finding a variety of correlations between several different types of data and having to discern which connections are real and which are only apparent is a difficult one. Economists' interest in these questions is motivated by more than just curiosity. Often important policy questions depend on what one believes is really going on. Whether a country thinks it worthwhile to pour more resources into higher education may depend on whether it believes that the differences in wages observed between those with and without a college education are largely due to the skills and knowledge acquired during college, or whether they are mainly related to differences in ability between those who make it through college and those who do not.

The important lessons to remember here are (1) the fact of a correlation does not prove a causation; (2) the way to test different explanations of causation is to hold all of the factors constant except for one, and then allow that one to vary; (3) data do not always speak clearly, and sometimes do not allow any conclusions to be drawn.

WHY ECONOMISTS DISAGREE

Economists are frequently called upon to make judgments on matters of public policy. Should the government reduce the deficit? Should inflation be reduced? If so, how? In these public policy discussions, economists often disagree. They differ in their views of how the world works, in their *description* of the economy, in their predictions of the consequences of certain actions. And they differ in their values, in how they evaluate these consequences.

When they describe the economy, and construct models that predict either how the economy will change or the effects of different policies, they are engaged in what is called **positive economics.** When they evaluate alternative policies, weighing up the various benefits and costs, they are engaged in what is called **normative economics.** Positive economics is concerned with what "is," with describing how the economy functions. Normative economics deals with what "should be," with making judgments about the desirability of various courses of action. Normative economics makes use of positive economics. We cannot make judgments about whether a policy is desirable unless we have a clear picture of its consequences. Good normative economics also tries to be explicit about precisely what values or objectives it is incorporating. It tries to couch its statements in the form "If these are your objectives . . . , then this is the best possible policy."

Consider the normative and positive aspects of the proposal to restrict imports of Japanese cars. Positive economics would describe the consequences: the increased prices consumers have to pay; the increased sales of American cars; the increased employment and increased profits; the increased pollution and oil imports, because American cars on average are less fuel efficient than Japanese cars. In the end, the question is, *should there be restraints on imports of Japanese cars?* This is a normative question: Normative economics would weigh these various effects—the losses of the consumers, the gains to workers, the increased profits, the increased pollution, the increased oil imports—to reach an overall judgment. Normative economics develops systematic frameworks within which these complicated judgments can be conducted in a systematic way.

CLOSE-UP: ECONOMISTS AGREE!

Try the following six statements out on your class-mates or your family to see whether they, like the economists surveyed, disagree, agree with provisos, or agree:

	Percentage of economists who		
	Disagree	Agree with provisos	Agree
1. Tariffs and import quotas usually reduce general economic welfare.	6.5%	21.3%	71.3%
2. A ceiling on rents reduces the quantity and quality of housing available.	6.5%	16.6%	76.3%
3. The cause of the rise in gasoline prices that occurred in the wake of the Iraqi invasion of Kuwait is the monopoly power of large oil companies.	67.5%	20.3%	11.4%
4. The trade deficit is primarily a consequence of the inability of U.S. firms to compete.	51.5%	29.7%	18.1%
5. Cash payments increase the welfare of recipients to a greater degree than do transfers-in-kind of equal cash value.	15.1%	25.9%	58.0%

Among the general population, these are controversial questions. You will find many people who believe that restricting foreign imports is a good thing; that government regulation of rents has few ill effects; that the trade deficit is mainly caused by the inability of U.S. companies to compete; that government should avoid giving cash to poor people (because they are likely to waste it); and that oil companies are the cause of higher oil prices.

But when professional economists are surveyed, there is broad agreement that many of those popular answers are misguided. The percentages listed above are from a survey carried out by economists at Weber State University and Brigham Young University in 1990. Notice that healthy percentages of economists apparently believe that most import quotas are economically harmful; that government control of rents does lead to adverse consequences; that oil companies are not to blame for higher oil prices; that the trade deficit is not caused by the competitive problems of individual companies; that cash payments benefit the poor more than direct (in-kind) transfers of food, shelter, and medical care.

Sources: Richard M. Alston, J. R. Kearl, and Michael B. Vaughan, "Is There a Consensus Among Economists in the 1990s?" *American Economic Review* (May 1992).

DISAGREEMENTS WITHIN POSITIVE ECONOMICS

Even when they describe how the economy works, economists may differ for two main reasons. First, economists differ over what is the appropriate model of the economy. They may disagree about how well people and firms are able to perceive and calculate their self-interest, and whether their interactions take place in a competitive or a noncompetitive market. Different models will produce different results. Often the data do not allow us to say which of two competing models provides a better description of some market.

Second, even when they agree about the appropriate theoretical model, economists may disagree about quantitative magnitudes, which will cause their predictions to differ. They may agree, for instance, that reducing the tax on interest income will encourage individuals to save more, but they may produce different estimates about the amount of the savings increase. Again, many of these disagreements arise because of inadequate data. We may have considerable data concerning savings in the United States over the past century. But institutions and economic conditions today are markedly different from those of fifty or even ten years ago.

DISAGREEMENTS WITHIN NORMATIVE ECONOMICS

There are generally many consequences of any policy, some beneficial, some harmful. In comparing two policies, one may benefit some people more, another may benefit others. One policy is not unambiguously better than another. It depends on what you care more about. A cut in the tax on the profits from the sale of stocks might encourage savings, but at the same time, most of the benefits accrue to the very wealthy; hence, it increases inequality. A reduction in taxes to stimulate the economy may reduce unemployment, but it may also increase inflation. Even though two economists agree about the model, they may make different recommendations. In assessing the effect of a tax cut on unemployment and inflation, for instance, an economist who is worried more about unemployment may recommend in favor of the tax cut, while the other, concerned about inflation, may recommend against it. In this case, the source of the disagreement is a difference in values.

But while economists may often seem to differ greatly among themselves, in fact they agree more than they disagree: their disagreements get more attention than their agreements. Most importantly, when they do disagree, they seek to be clear about the source of their disagreement: 1) to what extent does it arise out of differences in models, 2) to what extent does it arise out of differences in estimates of quantitative relations, and 3) to what extent does it arise out of differences in values? Clarifying the sources of and reasons for disagreement can be a very productive way of learning more.

CONSENSUS ON THE IMPORTANCE OF SCARCITY

Most of what we have discussed in this chapter fits within the areas on which there is broad consensus among economists. This includes the observation that the U.S. economy is a mixed economy and that there are certain basic questions that all economic systems must address. We highlight the most important points of consensus throughout the book. Our first consensus point concerns scarcity. It is the most important point of consensus in this chapter.

1   Scarcity

There is no free lunch. Having more of one thing requires giving up something else. Scarcity is a basic fact of life.

REVIEW AND PRACTICE

SUMMARY

1. Economics is the study of how individuals, firms, and governments within our society make choices. Choices are unavoidable because desired goods, services, and resources are inevitably scarce.

2. There are four basic questions that economists ask about any economy. (1) What is produced, and in what quantities? (2) How are these goods produced? (3) For whom are these goods produced? (4) Who makes economic decisions, and by what process?

3. The United States has a mixed economy; there is a mix between public and private decision making. The economy relies primarily on the private interaction of individuals and firms to answer the four basic questions, but government plays a large role as well. A central question for any mixed economy is the balance between the public and private sectors.

4. The term "market" is used to describe any situation where exchange takes place. In America's market economy, individuals, firms, and government interact in product markets, labor markets, and capital markets.

5. Economists use models to study how the economy works and to make predictions about what will happen if something is changed. A model can be expressed in words or equations, and is designed to mirror the essential characteristics of the particular phenomena under study.

6. A correlation exists when two variables tend to change together in a predictable way. However, the simple existence of a correlation does not

prove that one factor causes the other to change. Additional outside factors may be influencing both.

7. Positive economics is the study of how the economy works. Disagreements within positive economics center on the appropriate model of the economy or market and the quantitative magnitudes characterizing the models. Normative economics deals with the desirability of various actions. Disagreements within normative economics center on differences in the values placed on the various costs and benefits of different actions.

KEY TERMS

centrally planned economy
mixed economy
market economy
product market

labor market
capital market
capital goods
microeconomics
macroeconomics

theory
correlation
causation
positive economics
normative economics

REVIEW QUESTIONS

1. Why are choices unavoidable?

2. How are the four basic economic questions answered in the U.S. economy?

3. What is a mixed economy? Describe some of the roles government might play, or not play, in a mixed economy.

4. Name the three main economic markets, and describe how an individual might participate in each one as a buyer and seller.

5. Give two examples of economic issues that are primarily microeconomic, and two examples that are primarily macroeconomic. What is the general difference between microeconomics and macroeconomics?

6. What is a model? Why do economists use models?

7. When causation exists, would you also expect a correlation to exist? When a correlation exists, would you also expect causation to exist? Explain.

8. "All disagreements between economists are purely subjective." Comment.

PROBLEMS

1. Characterize the following events as microeconomic, macroeconomic, or both.
    (a) Unemployment increases this month.

(b) A drug company invents and begins to market a new medicine.
(c) A bank loans money to a large company but turns down a small business.
(d) Interest rates decline for all borrowers.
(e) A union negotiates for higher pay and better health insurance.
(f) The price of oil increases.

2. Characterize the following events as part of the labor market, the capital market, or the product market.
(a) An investor tries to decide which company to invest in.
(b) With practice, the workers on an assembly line become more efficient.
(c) The opening up of the economies in Eastern Europe offers new markets for American products.
(d) A big company that is losing money decides to offer its workers a special set of incentives to retire early, hoping to reduce its costs.
(e) A consumer roams around a shopping mall, looking for birthday gifts.
(f) The federal government needs to borrow more money to finance its level of spending.

3. Discuss the incentive issues that might arise in each of the following situations. (Hint: Remember the history of the automobile industry at the start of this chapter.)
(a) You have some money to invest, and your financial adviser introduces you to a couple of software executives who want to start their own company. What should you worry about as you decide whether to invest?
(b) You are running a small company, and your workers promise that if you increase their pay, they will work harder.
(c) A large industry is going bankrupt and appeals for government assistance.

4. Name ways in which government intervention has helped the automobile industry in the last two decades, and ways in which it has injured the industry.

5. The back of a bag of cat litter claims, "Cats that use cat litter live three years longer than cats that don't." Do you think that cat litter actually causes an increased life expectancy of cats, or can you think of some other factors to explain this correlation? What evidence might you try to collect to test your explanation?

6. Life expectancy in Sweden is 78 years; life expectancy in India is 61 years. Does this prove that if an Indian moved to Sweden he would live longer? That is, does this prove that living in Sweden causes an increase in life expectancy, or can you think of some other factors to explain these facts? What evidence might you try to collect to test your explanation?

2

THINKING LIKE AN ECONOMIST

E veryone thinks about economics, at least some of the time. We think about money (we wish we had more of it) and about work (we wish we had less of it). But there is a distinctive way that economists approach economic issues, and one of the purposes of this course is to introduce you to that way of thinking. This chapter begins with a basic model of the economy. We follow this with a closer look at how the basic units that comprise the economy—individuals, firms, and governments—make choices in situations where they are faced with scarcity. In Chapters 3 through 5, we study ways in which these units interact with one another, and how those interactions "add up" to determine how society's resources are allocated.

1. What is the basic competitive model of the economy?

2. What are incentives, property rights, prices, and the profit motive, and what roles do these essential ingredients of a market economy play?

3. What alternatives for allocating resources are there to the market system, and why do economists tend not to favor these alternatives?

4. What are some of the basic techniques economists use in their study of how people make choices? What are the various concepts of costs that economists use?

THE BASIC COMPETITIVE MODEL

Though different economists employ different models of the economy they all use a basic set of assumptions as a point of departure. The economist's basic competitive model has three components: assumptions about how consumers behave, assumptions about how firms behave, and assumptions about the markets in which these consumers and firms interact. The model ignores government, because we need to see how an economy without a government might function before we can understand the role of government.

RATIONAL CONSUMERS AND PROFIT-MAXIMIZING FIRMS

Scarcity, which we encountered in Chapter 1, implies that individuals and firms must make choices. Underlying much of economic analysis is the basic assumption of **rational choice,** that people weigh the costs and benefits of each possibility. This assumption is based on the expectation that individuals and firms will act in a consistent manner, with a reasonably well-defined notion of what they like and what their objectives are, and with a reasonable understanding of how to attain those objectives.

In the case of an individual, the rationality assumption is taken to mean that he makes choices and decisions in pursuit of his own self-interest. Different people will, of course, have different goals and desires. Sally may want to drive a Porsche, own a yacht, and have a large house; to attain those objectives, she knows she needs to work long hours and sacrifice time with her family. Andrew is willing to accept a lower income to get longer vacations and more leisure throughout the year.

Economists make no judgments about whether Sally's preferences are "better" or "worse" than Andrew's. They do not even spend much time asking why different individuals have different views on these matters, or why tastes change over time. These are important questions, but they are more the province of psychology and sociology. What economists are concerned about are the consequences of these different preferences. What decisions can they expect Sally and Andrew, rationally pursuing their respective interests, to make?

In the case of firms, the rationality assumption is taken to mean that firms operate to maximize their profits.

COMPETITIVE MARKETS

To complete the model, economists make assumptions about the places where self-interested consumers and profit-maximizing firms meet: markets. Economists begin by focusing on the case where there are many buyers and sellers, all buying and selling the same thing. You might picture a crowded farmers' market to get a sense of the number of buyers and sellers—except that you have to picture everyone buying and selling just one good. Let's say we are in Florida, and the booths are all full of oranges.

Each of the farmers would like to raise his prices. That way, if he can still sell his oranges, his profits go up. Yet with a large number of sellers, each is forced to charge close to the same price, since if any farmer charged much more, he would lose business to the farmer next door. Profit-maximizing firms are in the same position. In an extreme case, if a firm charged any more than the going price, it would lose *all* its sales. Economists label this case **perfect competition.** In perfect competition, each firm is a **price taker,** which simply means that because it cannot influence the market price, it must accept that price. The firm takes the market price as given because it cannot raise its price without losing all sales, and at the market price it can sell as much as it wishes. Even if it sold ten times as much, this would have a negligible effect on the total quantity marketed or the price prevailing in the market. Markets for agricultural goods would be, in the absence of government intervention, perfectly competitive. There are so many wheat farmers, for instance, that each farmer believes he can grow and sell as much wheat as he wishes and have no effect on the price of wheat. (Later in the book, we will encounter markets with limited or no competition, like monopolies, where firms can raise prices without losing all their sales.)

On the other side of our farmers' market are rational individuals, each of whom would like to pay as little as possible for her oranges. Why can't she pay less than the going price? Because the seller sees another buyer in the crowd who will pay the going price. Thus, the consumers also take the market price as given, and focus their attention on other factors—their taste for oranges, primarily—in deciding how many to buy.

This model of consumers, firms, and markets—rational, self-interested consumers interacting with rational, profit-maximizing firms, in competitive markets where firms and consumers are both price takers—is the **basic competitive model.** The model has one very strong implication: if actual markets are well described by the competitive market, then the economy will be efficient: resources are not wasted, it is not possible to produce more of one good without producing less of another, and it is not even possible to make anyone better off without making someone else worse off. These results are obtained without government.

Virtually all economists recognize that actual economies are not *perfectly* described by the competitive model, but most still use it as a convenient benchmark—as we will throughout this book. We will also point out important differences between the predictions of the competitive model and observed outcomes, which will guide us to other models which provide a better description of particular markets and situations. Economists recognize too that, while the competitive market may not provide a *perfect* description of some markets, it may provide a good description—with its predictions matching actual outcomes well, though not perfectly. As we shall see, economists differ in their views about how many such markets there are, how good the "match" is, and how well alternative models do in rectifying the deficiencies of the competitive model in particular cases.

INGREDIENTS IN THE BASIC COMPETITIVE MODEL

1. Rational, self-interested consumers

2. Rational, profit-maximizing firms

3. Competitive markets with price-taking behavior

PRICES, PROPERTY RIGHTS, AND PROFITS: INCENTIVES AND INFORMATION

For market economies to work efficiently, firms and individuals must be informed and have incentives to act on available information. Indeed, incentives can be viewed as at the heart of economics. Without incentives, why would individuals go to work in the morning? Who would undertake the risks of bringing out new products? Who would put aside savings for a rainy day? There is an old expression about the importance of having someone "mind the store." But without incentives, why would anyone bother?

Market economies provide information and incentives through *prices, profits,* and *property rights.* Prices provide information about the relative scarcity of different goods. The **price system** ensures that goods go to those individuals and firms who are most willing and able to pay for them. Prices convey information to firms about how individuals value different goods.

The desire for profits motivates firms to respond to the information provided by prices. By producing what consumers want in the most efficient way, in ways that least use scarce resources, they increase their profits. Similarly, rational individuals' pursuit of self-interest induces them to respond to prices: they buy goods which are more expensive—in a sense relatively more scarce—only if they provide commensurately greater benefits.

For the profit motive to be effective, firms need to be able to keep at least some of their profits. Households, in turn, need to be able to keep at least some of what they earn or receive as a return on their investments. (The return on their investments is simply what they receive back in excess of what they invested. If they receive back less than they invested, the return is negative.) There must, in short, be **private property,** with its attendant **property rights.** Property rights include both the right of the owner to use the property as she sees fit and the right to sell it.

These two attributes of property rights give individuals the incentive to use property under their control efficiently. The owner of a piece of land tries to figure out the most profitable use of the land; for example, whether to build a store or a restaurant. If he makes a mistake and opens a restaurant when he should have opened a store, he bears the consequences: the loss in income. The profits he earns if he makes the right decisions—and the losses he bears if he makes the wrong ones—give him an incentive to think carefully about the decision and do the requisite research. The owner of a store tries to make sure that her customers get the kind of merchandise and the quality of service they want. She has an incentive to establish a good reputation, because if she does so, she will do more business and earn more profits.

The store owner will also want to maintain her property—which is not just the land anymore, but includes the store as well—because she will get more for it when the time comes to sell her business to someone else. Similarly, the owner of a house has an incentive to maintain *his* property, so that he can sell it for more when he wishes to move. Again, the profit motive combines with private property to provide incentives.

How the Profit Motive Drives the Market System

In market economies, incentives are supplied to individuals and firms by prices, profits, and property rights.

INCENTIVES VERSUS EQUALITY

While incentives are at the heart of market economies, they come with a cost: inequality. Any system of incentives must tie compensation with performance. Whether through differences in luck or ability, performance of different individuals will differ. In many cases, it will not be possible to identify why performance is high. The salesperson may claim that the reason his sales are high is superior skill and effort, while his colleague may argue that it is dumb luck.

If pay is tied to performance, there will inevitably be some inequality. And the more closely compensation is tied to performance the greater the inequality. The fact that the greater the incentives, the greater the resulting inequality is called the **incentive-equality trade-off.** If society provides greater incentives, total output is likely to be higher, but there will also probably be greater inequality.

One of the basic questions facing society in the choice of tax rates and welfare systems is how much would incentives be diminished by an increase in tax rates to finance a better welfare system and thus reduce inequality? What would be the results of those reduced incentives?

WHEN PROPERTY RIGHTS FAIL

Prices, profits, and property rights are the three essential ingredients of market economies. We can learn a lot about why they are so important by examining a few cases where property rights and prices are interfered with. Each example highlights a general point. Any time society fails to define the owner of its resources and does not allow the highest bidder to use them, inefficiencies result. Resources will be wasted or not used in the most productive way.

Ill-Defined Property Rights: The Grand Banks   Fish are a valuable resource. Not long ago, the area between Newfoundland and Maine, called the Grand Banks, was teeming with fish. Not surprisingly, it was also teeming with fishermen, who saw an easy livelihood scooping out the fish from the sea. Since there were no property rights, everyone tried to catch as many fish as he could. A self-interested fisherman would rationally reason that if he did not catch the fish, someone else would. The result was a tragedy: the Grand Banks was overfished, to the point where not only was it not teeming with fish, but commercial fishing became unprofitable. Today Canada and the United States have a treaty limiting the amount of fish that fishermen from each country can take from the Grand Banks, and gradually, over the years, the fish population has been restored.

Restricted Property Rights   In California the government allocates water rights among various groups. Water is scarce. Hence these rights to water are extremely valuable. But they come with a restriction. They are not transferable; they cannot be sold. Cattle ranchers currently have the right to about 10 percent of the state's water, slightly less than the fraction consumed by residences. Government charges ranchers as little as $50 per acre-foot for their water, in contrast to $256 per acre-foot charged to residences in San Francisco and much more in some towns. The value of water to thirsty urban consumers—what they would be willing to pay for the additional water—exceeds the profits from raising cattle. If the water rights could be sold, those in the cattle industry would have a strong incentive to sell their rights to the towns. If cattle owners could get out of the cattle business and sell their water rights to urban residents instead, everyone would be better off.[1] In this case, restrictions on property rights have led to inefficiencies.

Entitlements as Property Rights   Property rights do not always mean that you have full ownership or control. A **legal entitlement,** such as the right to occupy an apartment for life at a rent that is controlled, common in some large cities, is viewed by economists as a property right. Individuals do not own the apartment and thus cannot sell it, but they cannot be thrown out, either.

These partial and restricted property rights result in many inefficiencies. Because the individual in a rent-controlled apartment cannot (legally) sell the right to live in her apartment, as she gets older she may have limited incentives to maintain its condition, let alone improve it.

CONSENSUS ON INCENTIVES

Incentives, prices, profits, and property rights are central features of any economy, and highlight an important area of consensus among economists. This brings us to our second point of consensus:

2   Incentives

> *Providing appropriate incentives is a fundamental economic problem. In modern market economies, profits provide incentives for firms to produce the goods individuals want, and wages provide incentives for individuals to work. Property rights also provide people with important incentives, not only to invest and to save, but to put their assets to the best possible use.*

RATIONING

The price system is only one way of allocating resources, and a comparison with other systems will help to clarify the advantages of markets. When individuals get less of a good than they would like at the terms being offered, the good is said to be **rationed.** Different rationing schemes are different ways of deciding who gets society's scarce resources.

Rationing by Queues   Rather than supplying goods to those willing and able to pay the most for them, a society could give them instead to those most willing to wait in line. This system is called **rationing by queues,** after the British term for lines. Tickets are often allocated by queues, whether they are for

---

[1] The calculation of benefits and losses does not take into account the feelings of the cattle.

movies, sporting events, or rock concerts. A price is set, and it will not change no matter how many people line up to buy at that price. (The high price that scalpers can get for "hot" tickets is a good indication of how much more than the ticket price people would have been willing to pay.)

Rationing by queues is thought by many to be a more desirable way of supplying medical services than the price system. Why, it is argued, should the rich—who are most able to pay for medical services—be the ones to get better or more medical care? Using this reasoning, Britain provides free medical care to everyone on its soil. To see a doctor there, all you have to do is wait in line. Rationing medicine by queues turns the allocation problem around: since the value of time for low-wage workers is lower, they are more willing to wait, and therefore they get a disproportionate share of (government-supplied) medical services.

In general, rationing by queues is an inefficient way of distributing resources because the time spent in line is a wasted resource. There are usually ways of achieving the same goal within a price system that can make everyone better off. Returning to the medical example, if some individuals were allowed to pay for doctors' services instead of waiting in line, more doctors could be hired with the proceeds, and the lines for those unable or unwilling to pay could actually be reduced.

Rationing by Lotteries   **Lotteries** allocate goods by a random process, like picking a name from a hat. University dormitory rooms are usually assigned by lottery. So are seats in popular courses; when more students want to enroll in a section of a principles of economics course than the size of the section allows, there may be a lottery to determine who gets to enroll. The United States used to allocate certain mining rights and licenses to radio airwaves by lottery. Like queue systems, lotteries are thought to be fair because everyone has an equal chance. However, they are also inefficient, because the scarce resources do not go to the individual or firm who is willing and able to pay (and therefore values them) the most.

Rationing by Coupons   Most governments in wartime use **coupon rationing.** People are allowed so many gallons of gasoline, so many pounds of sugar, and so much flour each month. To get the good, you have to pay the market price *and* produce a coupon. The reason for coupon rationing is that without coupons prices might soar, inflicting a hardship on poorer members of society.

Coupon systems take two forms depending on whether coupons are tradable or not. Coupons that are not tradable give rise to the same inefficiency that occurs with most of the other nonprice systems—goods do not in general go to the individuals who are willing and able to pay the most. There is generally room for a trade that will make all parties better off. For instance, I might be willing to trade some of my flour ration for some of your sugar ration. But in a nontradable coupon system, the law prohibits such transactions. When coupons cannot be legally traded, there are strong incentives for the establishment of a **black market,** an illegal market in which the goods or the coupons for goods are traded.

OPPORTUNITY SETS

We have covered a lot of ground so far in this chapter. We have seen the economist's basic model, which relies on competitive markets. We have seen how prices, the profit motive, and private property supply the incentives that drive a market economy. And we have gotten our first glimpse at why economists believe that market systems, which supply goods to those who are willing and able to pay the most, provide the most efficient means of allocating what the economy produces. They are far better than the nonprice rationing schemes that have been employed. It is time now to return to the question of choice. Market systems leave to individuals and firms the question of what to consume. How are these decisions made?

For a rational individual or firm, the first step in the economic analysis of any choice is to identify what is possible—what economists call the **opportunity set,** which is simply the group of available options. If you want a sandwich and you have only roast beef and tuna fish in the refrigerator, then your opportunity set consists of a roast beef sandwich, a tuna fish sandwich, a strange sandwich combining roast beef and tuna fish, or no sandwich. A ham sandwich is out of the question. Defining the limitations facing an individual or firm is a critical step in economic analysis. One can spend time yearning after the ham sandwich, or anything else outside the opportunity set, but when it comes to making choices and facing decisions, only what is within the opportunity set is relevant.

BUDGET AND TIME CONSTRAINTS

Constraints limit choices and define the opportunity set. In most economic situations, the constraints that limit a person's choices—that is, those constraints that actually are relevant—are not sandwich fixings, but time and money. Opportunity sets whose constraints are imposed by money are referred to as **budget constraints;** opportunity sets whose constraints are prescribed by time are called **time constraints.** A billionaire may feel that his choices are limited not by money but by time; while for an unemployed worker, time hangs heavy—lack of money rather than time limits his choices.

The budget constraint defines a typical opportunity set. Consider the budget constraint of Alfred, who has decided to spend $100 on either cassette recordings or compact discs. A CD costs $10, a cassette $5. So Alfred can buy 10 CDs or 20 cassettes; or 9 CDs and 2 cassettes; or 8 CDs and 4 cassettes. The various possibilities are set forth in Table 2.1. And they are depicted graphically in Figure 2.1:[2] along the vertical axis, we measure the number of cassettes purchased, and along the horizontal axis, we measure the number of CDs. The line marked B_1B_2 is Alfred's budget constraint. The extreme cases,

Table 2.1 **ALFRED'S OPPORTUNITY SET**

Cassettes	CDs
0	10
2	9
4	8
6	7
8	6
10	5
12	4
14	3
16	2
18	1
20	0

[2] See the Chapter appendix for help in reading graphs.

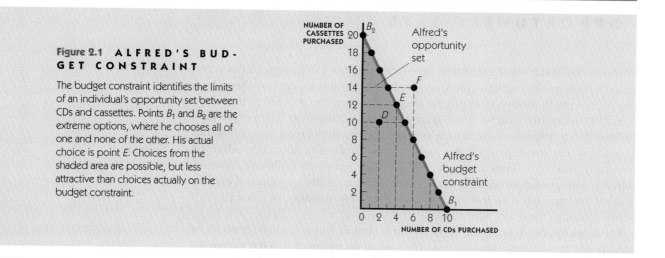

Figure 2.1 ALFRED'S BUD-GET CONSTRAINT

The budget constraint identifies the limits of an individual's opportunity set between CDs and cassettes. Points B_1 and B_2 are the extreme options, where he chooses all of one and none of the other. His actual choice is point E. Choices from the shaded area are possible, but less attractive than choices actually on the budget constraint.

where Alfred buys only CDs or cassettes, are represented by the points B_1 and B_2 in the figure. The dots between these two points, along the budget constraint, represent the other possible combinations. The cost of each combination of CDs and cassettes must add up to $100. The point actually chosen by Alfred is labeled E, where he purchases 4 CDs (for $40) and 12 cassettes (for $60).

Alfred's budget constraint is the line that defines the outer limits of his opportunity set. But the whole opportunity set is larger. It also includes all points below the budget constraint. This is the shaded area in the figure. The budget constraint shows the maximum number of cassettes Alfred can buy for each number of CDs purchased, and vice versa. Alfred is always happiest when he chooses a point on his budget constraint rather than below it. To see why, compare the points E and D. At point E, he has more of both goods than at point D. He would be even happier at point F, where he has still more cassettes and CDs, but that point, by definition, is unattainable.

Figure 2.2 depicts a time constraint. The most common time constraint simply says that the sum of what an individual spends her time on each day—including sleeping—must add up to 24 hours. The figure plots the hours spent watching television on the horizontal axis and the hours spent on all other activities on the vertical axis. People—no matter how rich or how poor—have only 24 hours a day to spend on different activities. The time constraint is quite like the budget constraint. A person cannot spend more than 24 hours or fewer than zero hours a day watching TV. The more time she spends watching television the less time she has available for all other activities. Point D (for dazed) has been added to the diagram at 5 hours a day—this is the amount of time the typical American chooses to spend watching TV.

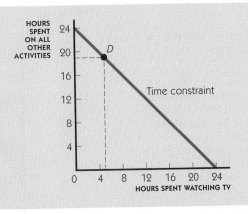

Figure 2.2 AN OPPORTUNITY SET FOR WATCHING TV AND OTHER ACTIVITIES

This opportunity set is limited by a time constraint, which shows the trade-off a person faces between spending time watching television and spending it on other activities. At 5 hours of TV time per day, point *D* represents a typical choice for an American.

THE PRODUCTION POSSIBILITIES CURVE

Business firms and whole societies face constraints. They too must make choices limited to opportunity sets. The amounts of goods a firm or society could produce, given a fixed amount of land, labor, and other inputs, are referred to as its **production possibilities.**

As one commonly discussed example, consider a simple description of a society in which all economic production is divided into two categories, military spending and civilian spending. Of course, each of these two kinds of spending has many different elements, but for the moment, let's discuss the choice between the two broad categories. For simplicity, Figure 2.3 refers to military spending as "guns" and civilian spending as "butter." The production of guns is given along the vertical axis, the production of butter along the horizontal. The possible combinations of military and civilian spending—of guns and butter—is the opportunity set. Table 2.2 sets out some of the possible combinations: 90 million guns and 40 million tons of butter, or 40 million guns and 90 million tons of butter. These possibilities are depicted in the figure. In the case of a choice involving production decisions, the boundary of the opportunity set—giving the maximum amount of guns that can be produced for each amount of butter and vice versa—is called the **production possibilities curve.**

The importance of the guns-butter trade-off can be seen dramatically by looking back at Figure 1.3, which shows that during World War II, car production plummeted almost to zero as the automobile factories were diverted to the production of tanks and other military vehicles.

When we compare the individual's opportunity set and that of society, reflected in its production possibilities curve, we notice one major difference. The individual's budget constraint is a straight line, while the production

Table 2.2 PRODUCTION POSSIBILITIES FOR THE ECONOMY

Guns (millions)	Butter (millions of tons)
100	0
90	40
70	70
40	90
0	100

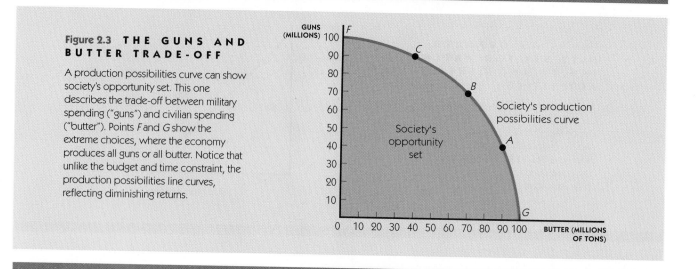

Figure 2.3 THE GUNS AND BUTTER TRADE-OFF

A production possibilities curve can show society's opportunity set. This one describes the trade-off between military spending ("guns") and civilian spending ("butter"). Points F and G show the extreme choices, where the economy produces all guns or all butter. Notice that unlike the budget and time constraint, the production possibilities line curves, reflecting diminishing returns.

possibilities curve bows outward. There is a good reason for this. An individual typically faces fixed **trade-offs:** if Alfred spends $10 more on CDs (that is, he buys one more CD), he has $10 less to spend on cassettes (he can buy two fewer cassettes).

On the other hand, the trade-offs faced by society are not fixed. If a society produces only a few guns, it will use those resources—the men and machines—that are best equipped for gun making. But as society tries to produce more and more guns, doing so becomes more difficult; it will increasingly depend on those resources that are less good at producing guns. It will be drawing these resources out of the production of other goods, in this case, butter. Thus, when the economy increases its production of guns from 40 million a year (point A) to 70 million (B), butter production falls by 20 million tons, from 90 million tons to 70 million tons. But if production of guns is increased further, to 90 million (C), an increase of only 20 million, butter production has to decrease by 30 million tons, to only 40 million tons. For each increase in the number of guns, the reduction in the number of tons of butter produced gets larger. That is why the production possibilities curve is curved.

In another example, assume that a firm owns land that can be used for growing wheat but not corn, and land that can grow corn but not wheat. In this case, the only way to increase wheat production is to move workers from the cornfields to the wheat fields. As more and more workers are put into the wheat fields, production of wheat goes up, but each successive worker increases production less. The first workers might pick the largest and most destructive weeds. Additional workers lead to better weeding, and better weeding leads to higher output. But the additional weeds rooted up are smaller and less destructive, so output is increased by a correspondingly smaller amount. This is an example of the general principle of **diminishing returns.**

Table 2.3 DIMINISHING RETURNS

Labor in cornfield (no. of workers)	Corn output (bushels)	Labor in wheat field (no. of workers)	Wheat output (bushels)
1,000	60,000	5,000	200,000
2,000	110,000	4,000	180,000
3,000	150,000	3,000	150,000
4,000	180,000	2,000	110,000
5,000	200,000	1,000	60,000

Adding successive units of any input such as fertilizer, labor, or machines to a fixed amount of other inputs—seeds or land—increases the output, or amount produced, but by less and less.

Table 2.3 shows the output of the corn and wheat fields as labor is increased in each field. Assume the firm has 6,000 workers to divide between wheat production and corn production. Thus, the second and fourth columns together give the firm's production possibilities, which are depicted in Figure 2.4.

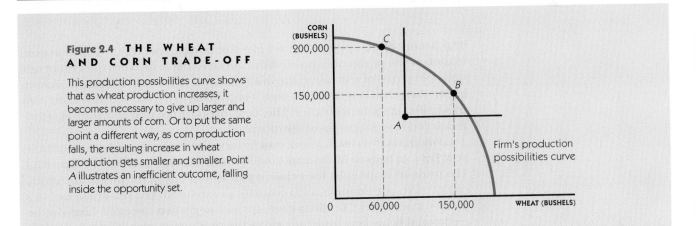

Figure 2.4 THE WHEAT AND CORN TRADE-OFF

This production possibilities curve shows that as wheat production increases, it becomes necessary to give up larger and larger amounts of corn. Or to put the same point a different way, as corn production falls, the resulting increase in wheat production gets smaller and smaller. Point A illustrates an inefficient outcome, falling inside the opportunity set.

INEFFICIENCIES: BEING OFF THE PRODUCTION POSSIBILITIES CURVE

There is no reason to assume that a firm or an economy will always be on its production possibilities curve. Any inefficiency in the economy will result in a point such as *A* in Figure 2.4, below the production possibilities curve. One of the major quests of economists is to look for instances in which the economy is inefficient in this way.

Whenever the economy is operating below the production possibilities curve, it is possible for us to have more of every good—more wheat and more corn, more guns and more butter. No matter what goods we like, we can have more of them. That is why we can unambiguously say that points below the production possibilities curve are undesirable. But this does not mean that every point on the production possibilities curve is better than any point below it. Compare points *A* and *C* in Figure 2.4. Corn production is higher at *C*, but wheat production is lower. If people do not like corn very much, the increased corn production may not adequately compensate them for the decreased wheat production.

There are many reasons why the economy may be below the production possibilities curve. If land better suited for the production of corn is mistakenly devoted to the production of wheat, the economy will operate below its production possibilities curve. If some of society's resources—its land, labor, and capital goods—are simply left idle, as happens when there is a depression, the economy operates below the production possibilities curve. The kinds of inefficiencies discussed earlier in the chapter with inadequately or improperly defined property rights also result in operating below the production possibilities curve.

COST

The beauty of an opportunity set like the budget constraint, the time constraint, or the production possibilities curve is that it specifies the cost of one option in terms of another. If the individual, the firm, or the society is operating on the constraint or curve, then it is possible to get more of one thing only by sacrificing some of another. The "cost" of one more unit of one good is how much you have to give up of the other.

Economists thus think about cost in terms of trade-offs within opportunity sets. Let's go back to Alfred choosing between CDs and cassettes in Figure 2.1. The trade-off is given by the **relative price,** the ratio of the prices of CDs and cassettes. In our example, a CD cost $10, a cassette $5. The relative price is $10 ÷ $5 = 2; for every CD Alfred gives up, he can get two cassettes. Likewise, societies and firms face trade-offs along the production possibilities curve, like the one shown in Figure 2.3. There, point *A* is the choice where 40 million guns and 90 million tons of butter are produced. The trade-off can be calculated by comparing points *A* and *B*. Society can have 30 million more guns by giving up 20 million tons of butter.

Trade-offs are necessary because resources are scarce. If you want something, you have to pay for it; you have to give up something. If you want to go to the library tomorrow night, you have to give up going to the movies. If a sawmill wants to make more two-by-four beams from its stock of wood, it will not be able to make as many one-by-four boards.

OPPORTUNITY COSTS

If someone were to ask you right now what it costs to go to a movie, you would probably answer, "Seven dollars," or whatever you paid the last time you went to the movies. But with the concept of trade-offs, you can see that a *full* answer is not that simple. To begin with, the cost is not the $7 but what that $7 could otherwise buy. Furthermore, your time is a scarce resource that must be figured into the calculation. Both the money and the time represent opportunities forgone in favor of going to the movie, or what economists refer to as the **opportunity cost** of the movie. To apply a resource to one use means that it cannot be put to any other use. Thus, we should consider the next-best, alternative use of any resource when we think about putting it to any particular use. This next-best use is the formal measurement of opportunity cost.

Some examples will help to clarify the idea of opportunity cost. Consider a student, Sarah, who enrolls in college. She thinks that the check for tuition and room and board represents the costs of her education. But the economist's mind immediately turns to the job she might have had if she had not enrolled in college. If Sarah could have earned $15,000 from September to June, this is the opportunity cost of her time, and this forgone income must be added to the college bills in calculating the total economic cost of the school year.

Now consider a business firm that has bought a building for its headquarters that is bigger than necessary. If the firm could receive $3 per month in rent for each square foot of space that is not needed, then this is the opportunity cost of leaving the space idle.

The analysis can be applied to the government as well. The federal government owns a vast amount of wilderness. In deciding whether it is worthwhile to convert some of that land into a national park, the government needs to take into account the opportunity cost of the land. The land might be used for growing timber or for grazing sheep. Whatever the value of the land in its next-best use, this is the economic cost of the national park. The fact that the government does not have to buy the land does not mean that the land should be treated as a free good.

Thus, in the economist's view, when rational firms and individuals make decisions—whether to undertake one investment project rather than another, whether to buy one product rather than another—they take into account *all* of the costs, the full opportunity costs, not just the direct expenditures.

Businesses often neglect one of the most important opportunity costs of all: the time of their top employees. The personnel agency Accountemps tried to measure some of that wasted time by surveying 200 executives from the 1,000 largest U.S. companies. The executives estimated that they spent an average of 15 minutes a day on hold on the telephone; an average of 32 minutes a day reading or writing unnecessary memos; and an average of 72 minutes a day at unnecessary meetings. Now multiply those numbers by 48 weeks (assuming that the executives take four weeks of vacation each year). The average executive would be spending 60 hours per year on telephone hold; 128 hours per year on unnecessary memos; and 288 hours a year in unnecessary meetings!

Of course, estimates like these are more for illustration than precision. Moreover, it may be impossible to tell in advance whether a meeting will be useful; the only way to have a productive meeting, after all, may be to risk having an unproductive one. But even taking the particular numbers with a grain of salt, it seems likely that many businesses schedule meetings believing that since they do not have to pay extra for people to attend, the cost of the meetings is zero. They ignore the opportunity cost, the fact that their highly paid managers could be doing something else with their time.

One semi-serious proposal is that businesses should measure and display the opportunity cost of their meetings with a scoreboard placed discreetly in the corner of their meeting rooms. As everyone entered the meeting room, she would enter her hourly salary, and the scoreboard would then start adding up the cost of everyone's time. For example, if there were twenty executives in a meeting who earned an average of $45 per hour, then the scoreboard would ring up $900 for every hour of meeting time. We could also include an opportunity cost of using the meeting room, of needing to return calls from other people who called during the meeting, and so on. Surely, as the scoreboard showed the opportunity cost of the regular afternoon meeting climbing into four figures, there would be strong incentive to finish quickly and let everyone return to her other tasks.

Source: "Executives on Hold 60 Hours a Year," *San Jose Mercury News,* July 10, 1990, p. 7A.

SUNK COSTS

Economic cost includes costs, as we have just seen, that noneconomists often exclude, but it also ignores costs that noneconomists include. If an expenditure has already been made and cannot be recovered no matter what choice is made, a rational person would ignore it. Such expenditures are called **sunk costs.**

To understand sunk costs, let's go back to the movies, assuming now that you have spent $7 to buy a movie ticket. You were skeptical about whether the movie was worth $7. Half an hour into the movie, your worst suspicions are realized: the movie is a disaster. Should you leave the movie theater? In making that decision, the $7 should be ignored. It is a sunk cost; your money is gone whether you stay or leave. The only relevant choice now is how to spend the next 90 minutes of your time: watch a terrible movie or go do something else.

Or assume you have just purchased a fancy laptop computer for $2,000. But the next week, the manufacturer announces a new computer with twice the power for $1,000; you can trade in your old computer for the new one by paying an additional $400. You are angry. You feel you have just paid $2,000 for a computer that is now almost worthless, and you have gotten hardly any use out of it. You decide not to buy the new computer for another year, until you have gotten at least some return for your investment. Again, an economist would say that you are not approaching the question rationally. The past decision is a sunk cost. The only question you should ask yourself is whether the extra power of the fancier computer is worth the additional $400. If it is, buy it. If not, don't.

MARGINAL COSTS

The third aspect of cost that economists emphasize is the extra costs of doing something, what economists call the **marginal costs.** These are weighed against the (additional) **marginal benefits** of doing it. The most difficult decisions we make are not whether to do something or not. They are whether to do a little more or a little less of something. Few of us waste much time deciding whether or not to work. We have to work; the decision is whether to work a few more or a few less hours. A country does not consider whether or not to have an army; it decides whether to have a larger or smaller army.

Jim has just obtained a job for which he needs a car. He must decide how much to spend on the car. By spending more, he can get a bigger and more luxurious car. But he has to decide whether it is worth a few hundred (or thousand) marginal dollars for a larger car or for extra items like fancy hubcaps, power windows, and so on.

Polly is considering flying to Colorado for a ski weekend. She has three days off from work. The air fare is $200, the hotel room costs $100 a night, and the ski ticket costs $35 a day. Food costs the same as at home. She is trying to decide whether to go for two or three days. The *marginal* cost of the third day is $135, the hotel cost plus the cost of the ski ticket. There are no additional transportation costs involved in staying the third day. She needs to compare the marginal cost with the additional enjoyment she will have from the third day.

People, consciously or not, think about the trade-offs at the margin in most of their decisions. Economists, however, bring them into the foreground. Like opportunity costs and sunk costs, marginal analysis is one of the critical concepts that enable economists to think systematically about the costs of alternative choices.

Investment tax credits have been a popular tool of policymakers. With a 10 percent investment tax credit, a firm that invests $100 million—say, in the construction of a new factory—gets a credit against its taxes of $10 million. The government is in effect paying 10 percent of the investment. In 1993, the Clinton administration proposed a new form of tax credit, one that would have rewarded businesses for increasing the amount they spent on new investment over what they had spent the previous year. This proposal differs from the usual investment tax credit, which rewards all new investment equally (including the vast amount that would have been invested anyway). The Clinton proposal, which Congress failed to pass, makes good economic sense. Since it focuses on the additional (marginal) dollar, which is the focus of a business's investment decision, it gets more bang for the tax buck.

Here is the logic. As we have seen, an investment tax credit that allows firms to reduce their tax bill by 10 percent of their investment expenditures effectively reduces the cost of investment by 10 percent. This is a strong incentive to invest. But it comes at a high cost, because most of the investment would have been undertaken anyway. If, for example, the economy would have undertaken $750 billion of investment, and the tax credit increases this to $810 billion, the cost of the $60 billion in increased investment is $81 billion in lost federal revenue.

The proposal that lost in the 1993 Congress, in contrast, was a net investment tax credit. The intent of this, as noted, is to reward only investment that would not have happened without the credit. How do we know what that is? We don't. But an acceptable if imperfect substitute is to provide the credit on investment increases over the previous year. In terms of the previous example, suppose that last year's investment was in fact $700 billion—an imperfect estimate of the $750 billion that would have occurred without the tax credit. Since it is only the marginal cost that is relevant to investment decision makers, a 10 percent net investment tax credit will increase investment to $810 billion, as before. But because the credit is only paid on $110 billion ($810 billion minus $700 billion), the Treasury loses only $11 billion ($110 billion × 10 percent)—$70 billion less than the revenues lost from the regular investment tax credit.

The 1993 Congress may have dropped the ball on the investment tax credit. But it did focus on policy at the margin when it renewed a provision that makes increases in research and development (R & D) expenditures eligible for a 20 percent tax credit.

BASIC STEPS OF RATIONAL CHOICE

Identify the opportunity sets.

Define the trade-offs.

Calculate the costs correctly, taking into account opportunity costs, sunk costs, and marginal costs.

USING ECONOMICS: USING MARGINAL ANALYSIS TO SET SAFETY STANDARDS

For the past two decades, the government has taken an active role in ensuring auto safety. It sets standards that all automobiles must meet. For instance, an automobile must be able to withstand a side collision of a particular velocity. One of the most difficult problems the government faces is deciding what those standards should be. It recently considered tightening standards for withstanding side collisions on trucks. The government calculated that the higher standards would result on average in 79 fewer deaths per year. It calculated that to meet the higher standards would increase the cost of an automobile by $81. (In addition, the heavier trucks would use more fuel.) In deciding whether to impose the higher standard, it used marginal analysis. It looked at the *additional* lives saved and at the *additional* costs.

REVIEW AND PRACTICE

SUMMARY

1. The basic competitive model consists of rational, self-interested individuals and profit-maximizing firms, interacting in competitive markets.

2. The profit motive and private property provide incentives for rational individuals and firms to work hard and efficiently. Ill-defined or restricted property rights can lead to inefficient behavior.

3. Society often faces choices between efficiency, which requires incentives that enable people or firms to receive different benefits depending on their performance, and equality, which entails people receiving more or less equal benefits.

4. The price system in a market economy is one way of allocating goods and services. Other methods include rationing by queue, by lottery, and by coupon.

5. An opportunity set illustrates what choices are possible. Budget constraints and time constraints define individuals' opportunity sets. Both show the trade-offs of how much of one thing a person must give up to get more of another.

6. A production possibilities curve defines a firm or society's opportunity set, representing the possible combinations of goods that the firm or society can produce. If a firm or society is producing below its production possibilities curve, it is said to be inefficient, since it could produce more of either good without producing less of the other.

7. The opportunity cost is the cost of using any resource. It is measured by looking at the next-best, alternative use to which that resource could be put.

8. A sunk cost is a past expenditure that cannot be recovered, no matter what choice is made in the present. Thus, rational decision makers ignore them.

9. Most economic decisions concentrate on choices at the margin, where the marginal (or extra) cost of a course of action is compared with its extra benefits.

KEY TERMS

perfect competition	budget constraints	opportunity cost
basic competitive model	time constraints	sunk costs
price system	production possibilities	marginal costs
rationing systems	trade-offs	marginal benefits
opportunity set	diminishing returns	

REVIEW QUESTIONS

1. What are the essential elements of the basic competitive model?

2. Consider a lake in a state park where everyone is allowed to fish as much as he wants. What outcome do you predict? Might this problem be averted if the lake were privately owned and fishing licenses were sold?

3. Why might government policy to make the distribution of income more equitable lead to less efficiency?

4. List advantages and disadvantages of rationing by queue, by lottery, and by coupon. If the government permitted a black market to develop, might some of the disadvantages of these systems be reduced?

5. What are some of the opportunity costs of going to college? What are some of the opportunity costs a state should consider when deciding whether to widen a highway?

6. Give two examples of a sunk cost, and explain why they should be irrelevant to current decisions.

7. How is marginal analysis relevant in the decision about which car or which house to purchase: After deciding the kind of car to purchase, how is marginal analysis relevant?

PROBLEMS

1. Imagine that many businesses are located beside a river, into which they discharge industrial waste. There is a city downstream, which uses the river as a water supply and for recreation. If property rights to the river are ill-defined, what problems may occur?

2. Suppose an underground reservoir of oil may reside under properties owned by several different individuals. As each well is drilled, it reduces the amount of oil that others can take out. Compare how quickly the oil is likely to be extracted in this situation with how quickly it would be extracted if one person owned the property rights to drill for the entire pool of oil.

3. In some states, hunting licenses are allocated by lottery; if you want a license, you send in your name to enter the lottery. If the purpose of the system is to ensure that those who want to hunt the most get a chance to do so, what are the flaws of this system? How would the situation improve if people who won licenses were allowed to sell them to others?

4. Imagine that during time of war, the government imposes coupon rationing. What are the advantages of allowing people to buy and sell their coupons? What are the disadvantages?

5. Kathy, a college student, has $20 a week to spend; she spends it either on junk food at $2.50 a snack, or on gasoline at $1 per gallon. Draw Kathy's opportunity set. What is the trade-off between junk food and gasoline? Now draw each new budget constraint she would face if
   (a) a kind relative started sending her an additional $10 per week;
   (b) the price of a junk food snack fell to $2;
   (c) the price of gasoline rose to $1.20 per gallon.
In each case, how does the trade-off between junk food and gasoline change?

6. Why is the opportunity cost of going to medical school likely to be greater than the opportunity cost of going to college? Why is the opportunity cost of

a woman with a college education having a child greater than the opportunity cost of a woman with just a high school education having a child?

7. Bob likes to divide his recreational time between going to movies and listening to compact discs. He has 20 hours a week available for recreation; a movie takes two hours, and a CD takes one hour to listen to. Draw his "time budget constraint." Bob also has a limited amount of income to spend on recreation. He has $60 a week to spend on recreational activities; a movie costs $5, and a CD costs $12. (He never likes to listen to the same CD twice.) Draw his budget constraint. What is his opportunity set?

APPENDIX: READING GRAPHS

Whether the old saying that a picture is worth a thousand words under- or overestimates the value of a picture, economists find graphs extremely useful.

For instance, look at Figure 2.5; it is a redrawn version of Figure 2.1, showing the budget constraint—the various combinations of CDs and cassettes he can purchase—of an individual, Alfred. More generally, a graph shows the relationship between two variables, here, the number of CDs and the number of cassettes that can be purchased. The budget constraint gives the maximum number of cassettes that can be purchased, given the number of CDs that have been bought.

In a graph, one variable (here, CDs) is put on the horizontal axis and the other variable on the vertical axis. We read a point such as E by looking down

Figure 2.5 READING A GRAPH: THE BUDGET CONSTRAINT

Graphs can be used to show the relationship between two variables. This one shows the relationship between the variable on the vertical axis (the number of cassettes Alfred can buy) and the variable on the horizontal axis (the number of CDs).

The slope of a curve like the budget constraint gives the change in the number of cassettes that can be purchased as Alfred buys one more CD. The slope of the budget constraint is negative.

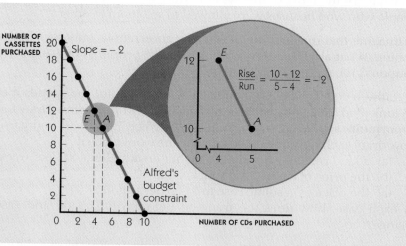

to the horizontal axis and seeing that it corresponds to 4 CDs, and by looking across to the vertical axis and seeing that it corresponds to 12 cassettes. Similarly, we read point *A* by looking down to the horizontal axis and seeing that it corresponds to 5 CDs, and by looking across to the vertical axis and seeing that it corresponds to 10 cassettes.

In the figure, each of the points from the table has been plotted, and then a curve has been drawn through those points. The "curve" turns out to be a straight line in this case, but we still use the more general term. The advantage of the curve over the individual points is that with it, we can read off from the graph points on the budget constraint that are not in the table.

Sometimes, of course, not every point on the graph is economically meaningful. You cannot buy half a cassette or half a CD. For the most part, we ignore these considerations when drawing our graphs; we simply pretend that any point on the budget constraint is actually possible.

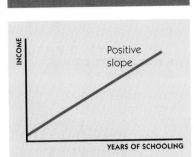

Figure 2.6 POSITIVELY SLOPED CURVE

Incomes increase with the number of years of schooling.

SLOPE

In any diagram, the amount by which the value along the vertical axis increases from a change in a unit along the horizontal axis is called the **slope,** just like the slope of a mountain. Slope is sometimes described as "rise over run," meaning that the slope of a line can be calculated by dividing the change on the vertical axis (the "rise") by the change on the horizontal axis (the "run").

Look at Figure 2.5. As we move from *E* to *A*, increasing the number of CDs by 1, the number of cassettes purchased falls from 12 to 10. For each additional CD bought, the feasible number of cassettes that can be purchased falls by 2. So the slope of the line is

$$\frac{\text{rise}}{\text{run}} = \frac{10 - 12}{5 - 4} = \frac{-2}{1} = -2.$$

When, as in Figure 2.5, the variable on the vertical axis falls when the variable on the horizontal axis increases, the curve, or line, is said to be **negatively sloped.** A budget constraint is always negatively sloped. But when we describe the slope of a budget constraint, we frequently omit the term "negative." We say the slope is 2, knowing that since we are describing the slope of a budget constraint, we should more formally say that the slope is negative 2. Alternatively, we sometimes say that the slope has an absolute value of 2.

Figure 2.6 shows the case of a curve that is **positively sloped.** The variable along the vertical axis, income, increases as schooling increases, giving the line its upward tilt from left to right.

In later discussions, we will encounter two special cases. A line that is very steep has a very large slope; that is, the increase in the vertical axis for every unit increase in the horizontal axis is very large. The extreme case is a perfectly vertical line, and we say then that the slope is infinite (Figure 2.7, panel A). At the other extreme is a flat, horizontal line; since there is no increase in the vertical axis no matter how large the change along the horizontal, we say that the slope of such a curve is zero (panel B).

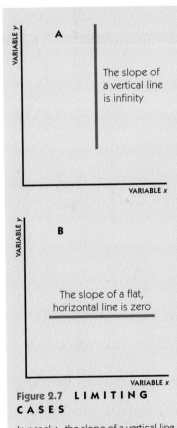

Figure 2.7 LIMITING CASES

In panel A, the slope of a vertical line is infinite. In panel B, the slope of a horizontal line is zero.

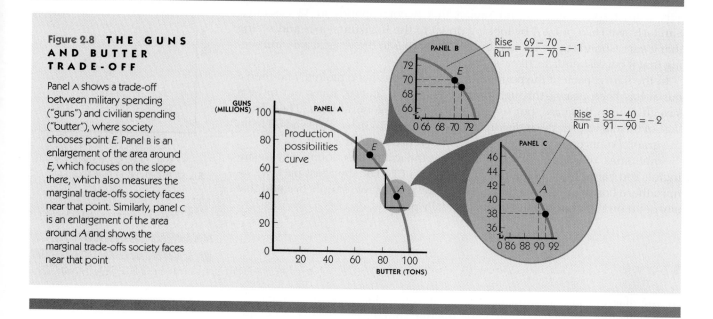

Figure 2.8 THE GUNS AND BUTTER TRADE-OFF

Panel A shows a trade-off between military spending ("guns") and civilian spending ("butter"), where society chooses point E. Panel B is an enlargement of the area around E, which focuses on the slope there, which also measures the marginal trade-offs society faces near that point. Similarly, panel c is an enlargement of the area around A and shows the marginal trade-offs society faces near that point

Figures 2.5 and 2.6 both show straight lines. Everywhere along the straight line, the slope is the same. This is not true in Figure 2.8, which repeats the production possibilities curve shown originally in Figure 2.3. Panel B of the figure blows up the area around point E. From the figure, you can see that if the output of butter increases by 1 ton, the output of guns decreases by 1 million guns. Thus, the slope is

$$\frac{\text{rise}}{\text{run}} = \frac{69 - 70}{71 - 70} = -1.$$

Now look at point A, where the economy is producing more butter. The area around A has been blown up in panel c. Here, we see that when we increase butter by 1 more unit, the reduction in guns is greater than before. The slope at A (again, millions of fewer guns produced per extra ton of butter) is

$$\frac{\text{rise}}{\text{run}} = \frac{38 - 40}{91 - 90} = -2.$$

With curves such as the production possibilities curve, the slope differs as we move along the curve.

INTERPRETING CURVES

Look at Figure 2.9. Which of the two curves has a larger slope? The one on the left appears to have a slope that has a larger absolute value. But look carefully at the axes. Notice that in panel A, the vertical axis is stretched relative to panel B. The same distance that represents 20 cassettes in panel B represents only 10

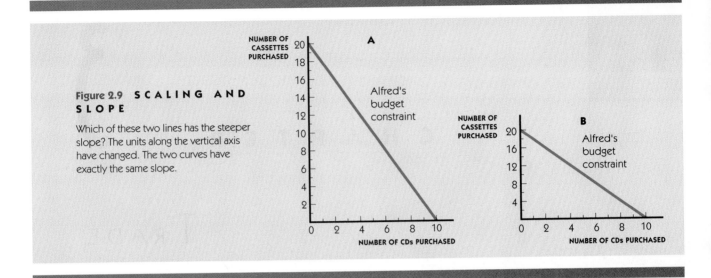

Figure 2.9 SCALING AND SLOPE

Which of these two lines has the steeper slope? The units along the vertical axis have changed. The two curves have exactly the same slope.

cassettes in panel A. In fact, both panels represent the same budget constraint. They have exactly the same slope.

This kind of cautionary tale is as important in looking at the graphs of data that were common in Chapter 1 as it is in looking at the relationships presented in this chapter that produce smooth curves. Compare, for instance, panels A and B of Figure 2.10. Which of the two curves exhibits more variability? Which looks more stable? Panel B appears to show that car production does not change much over time. But again, a closer look reveals that the axes have been stretched in panel A. The two curves are based on exactly the same data, and there is really no difference between them.

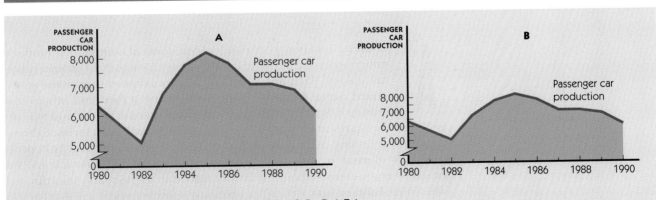

Figure 2.10 SCALING AND GRAPHS OF DATA

Which of these two curves shows greater variability in the output of cars over time? The two curves plot the same data. The vertical scale has again been changed. *Source: Ward's Automotive Reports* (1991).

CHAPTER 3

TRADE

 creature on another planet looking down at a developed modern economy on earth might compare human activity to an enormous ant colony. Each ant seemingly has an assigned task. Some stand guard. Some feed the young. Some harvest food and others distribute it. Some shuffle paper, scribble notes in books, and type on computer keyboards at computer consoles. Others work in factories, tightening screws, running machines, and so on. How is all of this activity coordinated? No dictator or superintelligent computer is giving instructions. Yet somehow an immense amount is accomplished in a reasonably coordinated way. Understanding how a complex economy operates—how it is that certain individuals do one task, others do another, how information is communicated and decisions made—is a central objective of economics.

This chapter discusses the problem of economic interdependence at two levels: individuals and firms within a country, and countries within the world economic community. Many of the same principles apply at both levels.

KEY QUESTIONS

1. Why is trade (exchange) mutually beneficial?

2. What are the similarities and differences between trade (exchange) between individuals within a country and trade between countries?

3. What determines what any particular country produces and sells on the international market? What is meant by

comparative advantage, and why does it play such an important role?

4. What are the gains from specialization?

5. How valid is the argument, so often heard in political circles, that trade should be restricted?

THE BENEFITS OF ECONOMIC INTERDEPENDENCE

We begin by considering the benefits of trade, specifically the exchange of those goods that are already available in the economy.

THE GAINS FROM TRADE

When individuals own different goods, have different desires, or both, there is an opportunity for trades that benefit all parties to the trade. Kids trading baseball cards learn the basic principles of exchange. One has two Ken Griffey, Jr. cards, the other has two Barry Bonds cards. A trade will benefit both of them. The same lesson applies to countries. Nigeria has more oil than it can use, but it does not produce enough food to feed its populace. The United States has more wheat than Americans can consume, but needs oil. Trade can benefit both countries.

Voluntary trade involves only winners. If the trade would make a loser of any party, that party would choose not to trade. Thus, a fundamental consequence of voluntary exchange is that it benefits everyone involved.

"FEELING JILTED" IN TRADE

In spite of the seemingly persuasive argument that individuals only voluntarily engage in trade if they think they will be better off as a result, people often walk away from a deal believing they have been hurt. It is important to understand that when economists say that a voluntary trade makes the two traders better off, they do not mean that it makes them both happy.

Imagine, for example, that Frank brings an antique rocking chair to a flea market to sell. He is willing to sell it for $100 but hopes to sell it for $200. Helen comes to the flea market planning to buy such a chair, hoping to spend only $100, but willing to pay as much as $200. They argue and negotiate, eventually settle on a price of $125, and make the deal. But when they go home, they both complain. Frank complains the price was too low, and Helen that it was too high.

From an economist's point of view, such complaints are self-contradictory. If Frank *really* thought $125 was too low, he would not have sold at that price. If Helen *really* thought $125 was too high, she would not have paid the price. Economists argue that people reveal their preferences not by what they say, but by what they do. If one voluntarily agrees to make a deal, one also agrees that the deal is, if not perfect, at least better than the alternative of not making it.

Two common objections are made to this line of reasoning. Both involve Frank or Helen "taking advantage" of the other. The implication is that if a buyer or a seller can take advantage, then the other party may be a loser rather than a winner.

The first objection is that either Frank or Helen may not really know what is being agreed to. Perhaps Helen recognizes the chair is an antique, but by neglecting to tell Frank, manages to buy it for only $125. Perhaps Frank knows the rockers fall off, but sells the chair without telling this to Helen, thus keeping the price high. In either case, lack of relevant information makes someone a loser after the trade.

The second objection concerns equitable division of the **gains from trade.** Since Helen would have been willing to pay as much as $200, anything she pays less than that is **surplus,** the term economists use for a gain from trade. Similarly, since Frank would have been willing to sell the chair for as little as $100, anything he receives more than that is also surplus. The total dollar value of the gain from trade is $100—the difference between the maximum price Helen was willing to pay and the minimum price at which Frank was willing to sell. At a price of $125, $25 of the gain went to Frank, $75 to Helen. The second objection is that such a split is not fair.

Economists do not have much patience with these objections. Like most people, they favor making as much information public as possible, and they think vendors and customers should be made to stand behind their promises. But economists also point out that second thoughts and "If only I had known" are not relevant. If Frank sells his antique at a flea market instead of having it valued by reputable antique dealers, he has made a voluntary decision to save his time and energy. If Helen buys an antique at a flea market instead of going to a reputable dealer, she knows she is taking a risk.

The logic of free exchange, however, does not say that everyone must express happiness with the result. It simply says that when people choose to make a deal, they prefer making it to not making it. And if they prefer the deal, they are by definition better off *in their own minds* at the time the transaction takes place.

The objections to trade nonetheless carry an important message: most exchanges that happen in the real world are considerably more complicated than the Frank-Helen chair trade. They involve problems of information, estimating risks, and expectations about the future. These complications will be discussed throughout the book. So without going into too much detail at the moment, let's just say that if you are worried that you do not have the proper information to make a trade, shop around, get a guarantee or expert opinion, or buy insurance. If you choose to plunge ahead without these precautions, don't pretend you didn't have other choices. Like those who buy a ticket in a lottery, you know you are taking a chance.

ECONOMIC RELATIONS AS EXCHANGES

Individuals in our economy are involved in masses of voluntary trades. They "trade" their labor services (time and skills) to their employer for dollars. They then trade dollars with a multitude of merchants for goods (like gasoline and groceries) and services (like plumbing and hair styling). The employer trades the goods it produces for dollars, and trades those dollars for labor services. Even your savings account can be viewed as a trade: you give the bank $100 today in exchange for the bank's promise to give you $105 at the end of the year (your original deposit plus 5 percent interest).

TRADE BETWEEN COUNTRIES

Why is it that people engage in this complex set of economic relations with others? The answer is that people are better off as a result of trading. Just as individuals *within* a country find it advantageous to trade with one another, so too do countries find trade advantageous. Just as it is impossible for any individual to be self-sufficient, it is impossible for a country to be self-reliant without sacrificing its standard of living. The United States has long been part of an international economic community. This participation has grown in recent decades increasing the interdependence between the United States and its trading partners. How has this affected the three main markets in the U.S. economy?

Interdependence in the Product Market   Foreign-produced goods are commonplace in U.S. markets. In the 1990s, for instance, more than a quarter of the cars sold in the United States were **imported** (imports are goods produced abroad but bought domestically), along with a third of apparel items, a third of the oil, and virtually all of the diamonds. Many of the minerals essential for the U.S. economy must also be imported from abroad. At the same time, U.S. farmers **export** almost two-fifths of the agricultural goods they produce (exports are goods produced domestically but sold abroad), including almost three-fourths of the wheat and one-third of the cotton.

Imports have grown in recent decades, not only in dollars, but also as a percentage of overall production. Exports have grown almost commensurately. Figure 3.1 shows how exports and imports have grown relative to the nation's total output: as a percentage of national output, both have more than doubled over the last twenty-five years. Smaller countries are typically even more

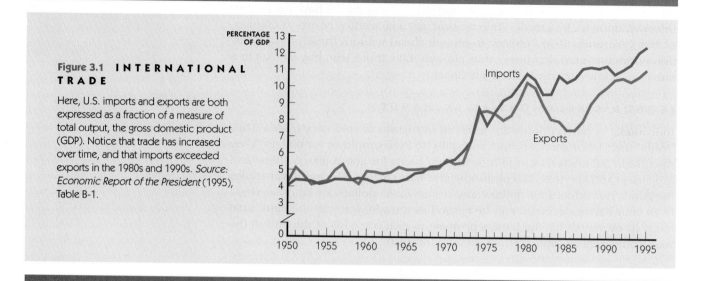

Figure 3.1 INTERNATIONAL TRADE

Here, U.S. imports and exports are both expressed as a fraction of a measure of total output, the gross domestic product (GDP). Notice that trade has increased over time, and that imports exceeded exports in the 1980s and 1990s. *Source: Economic Report of the President* (1995), Table B-1.

dependent on international trade than the United States. Britain and Canada import a quarter of their goods, France a fifth.

Earnings from abroad constitute a major source of income for some of our largest corporations; exports account for 45 percent of sales for Boeing, 20 percent for Hewlett-Packard, and 12 percent for Ford.

Interdependence in the Labor Market International interdependence extends beyond simply the shipping of goods between countries. More than 99 percent of U.S. citizens either immigrated here from abroad or are descended from people who did. Though the flow of immigrants, relative to the size of the population, has slowed since its peak at the turn of the century, it is still substantial, numbering in the millions every year. Today many rural American areas are dependent upon foreign-born doctors and nurses. Half of the engineers currently receiving doctorates at American universities are foreign-born. The harvests of many crops are highly dependent on migrant laborers from Mexico.

The nations of Europe have increasingly recognized the benefits that result from this international movement of workers. One of the important provisions of the treaty establishing the European Union, an agreement among most of the countries within Western Europe, allows for the free flow of workers within the member countries.

Interdependence in the Capital Market The United States has become a major borrower from abroad, but the country also invests heavily overseas. In 1995, for example, U.S. private investors owned approximately $2.5 trillion of assets (factories, businesses, buildings, loans, etc.) in foreign countries, while foreign investors owned $2.8 trillion of assets in the United States. American companies have sought out profitable opportunities abroad, where they can use their special skills and knowledge to earn high returns. They have established branches and built factories in Europe, Japan, Latin America, and elsewhere in the world.

Just as the nations of Western Europe have recognized the advantages that follow from the free flow of goods and labor among their countries, so too they have recognized the gains from the free flow of capital. Funds can be invested where they yield the highest returns. Knowledge and skills from one country can be combined with capital from another to produce goods that will be enjoyed by citizens of all countries. Though the process of liberalizing the flow of goods, labor, and capital among countries of the European Union has been going on for more than twenty years, 1992 marked the crucial date at which all remaining barriers were officially removed.

MULTILATERAL TRADE

Many of the examples to this point have emphasized two-way trade. Trade between two individuals or countries is called **bilateral trade.** But exchanges between two parties is often less advantageous than trade between several parties, called **multilateral trade.** Such trades are observed between sports teams. The New York Mets send a catcher to the St. Louis Cardinals, the Cardinals send a pitcher to the Los Angeles Dodgers, and the Dodgers send an outfielder to the Mets (see Figure 3.2A). No two of the teams was willing to make a two-way trade, but all can benefit from the three-way swap.

Countries function in a similar way. Japan has no domestic oil; it imports oil from Arabian countries. The Arabian countries want to sell their oil, but

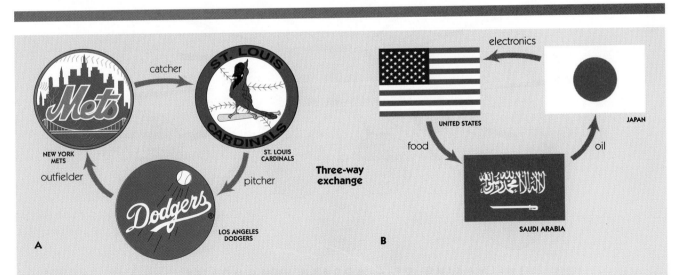

Figure 3.2 MULTILATERAL EXCHANGE

Panel A shows a multilateral, three-way trade between baseball teams. Notice that no two of the teams have the ingredients for a mutually beneficial exchange. Panel B illustrates a multilateral exchange in international trade.

they want wheat and food, not the cars and television sets that Japan can provide. The United States can provide the missing link by buying cars and televisions from Japan and selling food to the Arab nations. Again, this three-way trade, shown in Figure 3.2B, offers gains that two-way trade cannot. The scores of nations active in the world economy create patterns far more complex than these simplified examples.

Figure 3.3 illustrates the construction of a Ford Escort in Europe, and dramatizes the importance of multilateral and interconnected trade relations. The parts that go into an Escort come from all over the world. Similar diagrams could be constructed for many of the components in the diagram; the aluminum alloys may contain bauxite from Jamaica, the chrome plate may use chromium from South Africa, the copper for wiring may come from Chile.

Multilateral trade means that trade between any two participants may not balance. In Figure 3.2B, the Arab countries send oil to Japan but get no goods (only yen) in return. No one would say that the Arab countries have an unfair trade policy with Japan. Yet some congressional representatives, newspaper

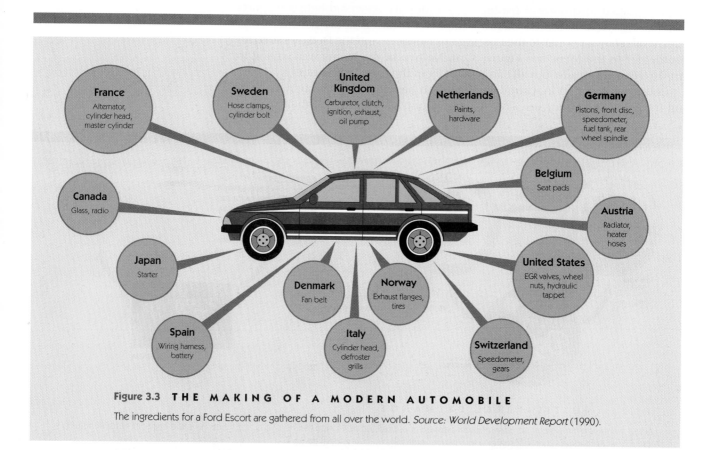

Figure 3.3 THE MAKING OF A MODERN AUTOMOBILE
The ingredients for a Ford Escort are gathered from all over the world. *Source: World Development Report* (1990).

columnists, and business executives complain that since the United States imports more from a particular country (often Japan) than it exports to that country, the trade balance is "unfair." A misguided popular cliché says that "trade is a two-way street." But trade in the world market involves hundreds of possible streets between nations. While there are legitimate reasons to be concerned with the overall U.S. trade deficit, there is no reason why U.S. exports and imports with any particular country should be balanced.

COMPARATIVE ADVANTAGE

We have so far focused on exchanges of existing goods. But clearly, most of what is exchanged must first be produced. Trade allows individuals and countries to concentrate on what they produce best.

Some countries are more efficient at producing almost all goods than are other countries. The possession of superior production skills is called having an **absolute advantage,** and these advanced countries are said to have an absolute advantage over the others. How can the countries with disadvantages successfully engage in trade? The answer lies in the principle of **comparative advantage,** which states that individuals and countries specialize in producing those goods in which they are *relatively*, not absolutely, more efficient.

To see what comparative advantage means, let's say that both the United States and Japan produce two goods, computers and wheat. The amount of labor needed to produce these goods is shown in Table 3.1. (These numbers are all hypothetical.) The United States is more efficient (spends fewer worker hours) at making both products. America can rightfully claim to have the most efficient computer industry in the world, and yet it imports computers from Japan. Why? The *relative* cost of making a computer (in terms of labor used) in Japan, relative to the cost of producing a ton of wheat, is low, compared with the United States. That is, in Japan, it takes 15 times as many hours (120/8) to produce a computer as a ton of wheat; in the United States, it takes 20 times as many hours (100/5) to produce a computer as a ton of wheat. While Japan has an absolute *dis*advantage in producing computers, it has a *comparative* advantage.

Table 3.1 **LABOR COST OF PRODUCING COMPUTERS AND WHEAT (worker hours)**

	United States	Japan
Labor required to make a computer	100	120
Labor required to make a ton of wheat	5	8

The principle of comparative advantage applies to individuals as well as countries. The president of a company might type faster than her secretary, but it still pays to have the secretary type her letters, because the president may have a comparative advantage at bringing in new clients, while the secretary has a comparative (though not absolute) advantage at typing.

PRODUCTION POSSIBILITIES SCHEDULES AND COMPARATIVE ADVANTAGE

The easiest way to understand the comparative advantage of different countries is to use the production possibilities schedule first introduced in Chapter 2. Figure 3.4 depicts parts of hypothetical production possibilities schedules for two countries, China and the United States, producing two commodities, textiles (garments) and airplanes. In both schedules, point E represents the current level of production. Let us look at what happens if each country changes its production by 100 airplanes.

China has a **comparative** advantage in producing textiles. If it reduces its airplane production by 100, its textile production can be increased by 10,000 garments. This trade-off between airplanes and garments is called the **marginal rate of transformation.** By contrast, if the United States reduces its airplane production by 100 airplanes, its textile production can be increased by only 1,000 garments. Conversely, if it increases its airplane production by 100, it will have to reduce its garment production by only 1,000 garments. We can now see why the world is better off if each country exploits its comparative advantage. If China moves from E to E' (decreasing airplane production by 100), 10,000 more garments can be produced. If the United States at the same time increases its airplane production by 100 from E to E'', it will produce only 1,000 fewer garments. In the new situation, the world production of airplanes is unchanged, but world production of garments has increased by 9,000. So long as the production trade-offs differ—that is, so long as the mar-

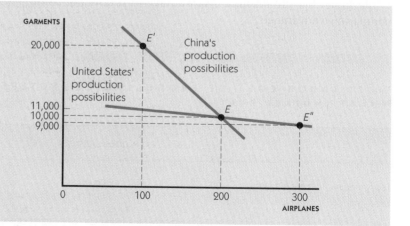

Figure 3.4 EXPLOITING COMPARATIVE ADVANTAGE

The production possibilities schedules for China and the United States, each manufacturing two commodities, textiles and airplanes, illustrate the trade-offs at different levels of production. Point E shows the current level of production for each country; E' and E'' illustrate production decisions that better exploit each country's comparative advantage.

Problem: Using the earlier example of Japan and the United States producing wheat and computers, calculate the trade-offs and the gains from specialization. Assume that both countries have 240,000 worker hours, initially divided equally between producing wheat and computers.

Solution: First, draw the production possibilities curves, as in the figure below. Since the costs (in worker hours) of producing each unit of each commodity are fixed, the production possibilities schedule is a straight line. If the United States used all its labor to produce computers, it would produce 2,400 computers; if it used all its labor to produce wheat, it would produce 48,000 tons of wheat. If Japan used all its labor to produce computers, it would produce 2,000 computers; if it used all its labor to produce wheat, it would produce 30,000 tons of wheat.

In both curves, use point A to mark the current point of production, at which labor is equally divided between computers and wheat.

Next, calculate the slope of the production possibilities curve, giving the trade-offs: in the United States, increasing wheat output by 1,000 tons leads to a reduction of computers by 50, while reducing wheat output by 1,000 tons in Japan leads to an increase in computers of 66⅔. Thus, each shift of wheat production by 1,000 tons from Japan to the United States increases world computer production by 16⅔.

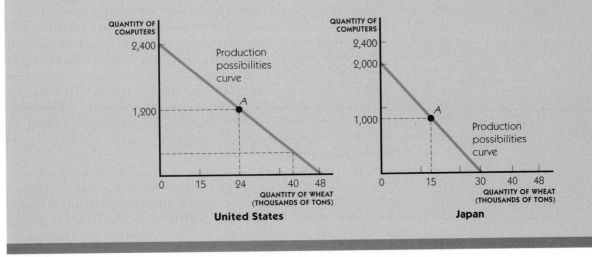

United States **Japan**

ginal rates of transformation differ—it pays for China to specialize increasingly in textiles, and the United States to specialize increasingly in airplanes. Notice that the analysis only requires knowledge about the production trade-offs. We do not need to know how much labor or capital is required in either country to produce either airplanes or garments.

Though it pays countries to increase production and export of goods in which they have a comparative advantage and to import goods in which they have a comparative disadvantage, this may not lead to complete specialization. Thus the United States continues to be a major producer of textiles, in spite of heavy imports from the Far East. This does not violate the principle of comparative advantage: not all textiles require the same skill and expertise in manufacturing. Thus, while China may have a comparative advantage in inexpensive textiles, the United States may have a comparative advantage in higher quality textiles. At the same time, the comparative advantage of other countries is so extreme in producing some goods that it does not pay for the United States to produce them at all: TVs, VCRs, and a host of other electronic gadgets, for example.

COMPARATIVE ADVANTAGE AND SPECIALIZATION

To see the benefits of specialization, consider the pencil. A tree, containing the right kind of wood, must be felled; it must be transported to a sawmill, and there cut into pieces that can be further processed into pencil casings. Then the graphite that runs through the pencil's center, the eraser at its tip, the metal that holds the two together must each be produced by specially trained people. The pencil is a simple tool. But to produce it by oneself would cost a fortune in money and an eternity in time.

Why Specialization Increases Productivity Specialization increases productivity, thus enhancing the benefits of trade, for three reasons. First, specializing avoids the time it takes a worker to switch from one production task to another. Second, by repeating the same task, the worker becomes more skilled at it. And third, specialization creates a fertile environment for invention.

Dividing jobs so that each worker can practice and perfect a particular skill (called the **division of labor**) may increase productivity hundreds or thousands of times. Almost anyone who practices simple activities—like sewing on a button, shooting a basketball, or adding a column of numbers—will be quite a lot better at them than someone who has not practiced. Similarly, a country that specializes in producing sports cars may develop a comparative advantage in sports cars. With its relatively large scale of production, it can divide tasks into separate assignments for different people; as each becomes better at his own tasks, productivity is increased.

At the same time, the division of labor often leads to invention. As someone learns a particular job extremely well, she might figure out ways of doing it better—including inventing a machine to do it. Specialization and invention reinforce each other. A slight initial advantage in some good leads to greater production of that good, thence to more invention, and thence to even greater production and further specialization.

Limits of Specialization The extent of division of labor, or specialization, is limited by the size of the market. There is greater scope for specialization in mass-produced manufactured goods like picture frames than in custom-made items like the artwork that gets framed. That is one reason why the costs of production of mass-produced goods have declined so much. Similarly, there is greater scope for specialization in a big city than a small town. That is why small stores specializing in a particular food or type of clothing thrive in cities but are rare in smaller towns.

The very nature of specialization limits its benefits. Repetitive jobs can lead to bored and unproductive workers. And single-track specialization inhibits the new insights and ideas that can come from engaging in a variety of work activities.

WHAT DETERMINES COMPARATIVE ADVANTAGE?

Earlier we learned that comparative advantage determines the pattern of trade. But what determines comparative advantage? In the modern world, this turns out to be a complex matter.

Natural Endowments   In first laying down the principle of comparative advantage in the early 1800s, the great British economist David Ricardo used the example of Portugal's trade with Britain. In Ricardo's example, Portugal had an absolute advantage in producing both wool and wine. But it had a comparative advantage in producing wine, and Britain had a comparative advantage in producing wool. In this and other early examples, economists tended to assume that a nation's comparative advantage was determined largely by its **natural endowments.** Countries with soil and climate that are *relatively* better for grapes than for pasture will produce wine; countries with soil and climate that are relatively better for pasture than for grapes will produce sheep (and hence wool).

In the modern economy, natural endowments still count: countries that have an abundance of low-skilled labor relative to other resources, such as China, have a comparative advantage in producing goods like textiles, which require a lot of handwork. But in today's technological age nations can also act to *acquire* a comparative advantage.

Acquired Endowments   Japan has little in the way of natural resources, yet it is a major player in international trade, in part because it has **acquired endowments.** Japan's case underscores the principle that by saving and accumulating capital and building large factories, a nation can acquire a comparative advantage in goods, like steel, that require large amounts of capital in their production. And by devoting resources to education, a nation can develop a comparative advantage in those goods that require a skilled labor force. Thus, the resources—human and physical—that a country has managed to acquire for itself can also give rise to comparative advantage.

Superior Knowledge   In the modern economy, comparative advantage may come simply from expertise in using resources productively. Switzerland has a comparative advantage in watches because, over the years, the people of the country have accumulated superior knowledge and expertise in watch making. Belgium has a comparative advantage in fine lace; its workers have developed the requisite skills. A quirk of fate might have led Belgium to acquire a comparative advantage in watches and Switzerland in lace.

Although patterns of specialization sometimes occur as an accident of history, in modern economies they are more likely to be a consequence of deliberate decisions. The United States' semiconductor industry is a case in point.

CLOSE-UP: THE COMPARATIVE ADVANTAGE OF THE UNITED STATES

What is the U.S. comparative advantage? Looking at the strengths of the United States in comparison with the rest of the world, one thinks of high technology. With over three-fourths of the world living in poor countries, without access even to the capital required for manufacturing, it would seem that these countries would have a *comparative* advantage in agriculture. Thus agriculture would be an area in which the United States had a comparative disadvantage. This intuitive answer is half right. The United States does export high technology products, like computing equipment, aircraft and aircraft engines, industrial organic chemicals, plastics and resins, and pharmaceuticals (drugs). In addition, the United States receives two billion dollars in payments from other countries using its patents.

But the United States is also a major exporter of agricultural goods, dominating world exports of wheat, corn, and cereals. It also exports rice, dairy products, and a host of other agricultural commodities.* For some commodities, this is a consequence of governmental intervention overruling the workings of the market: the costs of production of dairy products exceeds what is received on the international market, with the taxpayer making up the difference through subsidies to exports. In

most cases, however, the United States has a true comparative advantage: American farmers substitute sophisticated knowledge of farming, using skilled labor, advanced seeds, fertilizers, pesticides, and equipment instead of unskilled labor.

*The seemingly paradoxical observation that the United States was exporting less-capital-intensive goods, and importing more-capital-intensive goods, was first noted by Nobel Prize-winning economist Wassily Leontief, in a famous paper written in 1953. It is referred to as the Leontief paradox in his honor.

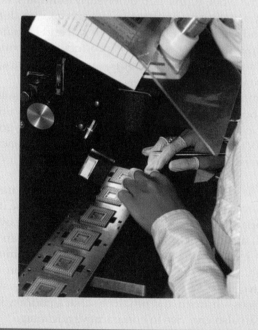

This industry manufactures the tiny silicon brains that control computers. Semiconductors were invented by an American, Robert Noyce, and in the 1970s, the United States had a powerful comparative advantage in manufacturing semiconductors; but Japan managed to become a close competitor in the 1980s. The rise of the U.S. semiconductor industry was built in part on decisions by the federal government to fund the necessary research (primarily so the semiconductors could be used in guided missiles and other weapons). The rise of the Japanese industry was similarly based on decisions by that government to support its semiconductor industry.

Stories like that of the semiconductor industry have led some economists to argue that government should encourage certain industries, in order for them to gain a technological advantage, for instance, through the support of research relevant to that industry.

Specialization   Earlier we saw how comparative advantage leads to specialization. Specialization may also lead to comparative advantage. The Swiss make fine watches, and have a comparative advantage in that market based on years of unique experience. Such superior knowledge, however, does not explain why Britain, Germany, and the United States, which are at roughly the same level of technological expertise in building cars, all trade cars with one another. How can each country have a comparative advantage in making cars? The answer lies in specialization.

Both Britain and Germany may be better off if Britain specializes in producing sports cars and Germany in producing luxury cars, or conversely, because specialization increases productivity. Countries enhance, or simply develop, a comparative advantage by specializing just as individuals do. As a result, similar countries enjoy the advantages of specialization even when they specialize in different variations of basically similar products.

THE FOUR BASES OF COMPARATIVE ADVANTAGE

Natural endowments, which consist of geographical determinants such as land, natural resources, and climate

Acquired endowments, which are the physical capital and human skills a nation has developed

Superior knowledge, including technological advantages, which may be acquired either as an accident of history or through deliberate policies

Specialization, which may create comparative advantages between countries that are similar in all other respects

THE PERCEIVED COSTS OF INTERNATIONAL INTERDEPENDENCE

If the argument that voluntary trade must be mutually beneficial is so compelling, why has there been, from time to time, such strong antitrade sentiment in the United States and many other countries? This antitrade feeling is often labeled **protectionism,** because it calls for "protecting" the economy from the effects of trade. Those who favor protectionism raise a number of concerns. Some of the objections to international trade parallel the objections to trade among individuals noted earlier. Was the trade a fair deal? Was the seller in a stronger bargaining position? Such concerns, for individuals and countries, revolve around how the *surplus* associated with the gains from trade is divided. Weak countries may feel that they are being taken advantage of by stronger countries. Their weaker bargaining position may mean that the stronger countries get *more* of the gains from trade. But this does not contradict the basic premise: both parties gain from voluntary exchange. All countries—weak as well as strong—are better off as a result of voluntary exchange.

But an important difference exists between trade among individuals and trade among countries. Some individuals within a country benefit from trade and some lose. Since the trade as a whole is beneficial to the country, the gains to the winners exceed the losses to the losers. Thus, in principle, those who benefit within the country could more than compensate those who lose. In practice, however, those who lose remain losers and obviously oppose trade, using the argument that trade results in lost jobs and reduced wages. These concerns have become particularly acute as unskilled workers face competition with low-wage unskilled workers in Asia and Latin America: how can they compete, without lowering their wages?

These concerns played a prominent role in the debate in 1993 over ratification of the North American Free Trade Agreement (NAFTA), which would allow Mexican goods into the United States with no duties at all. Advocates of NAFTA pointed out that (1) more jobs would be created by the new export opportunities than would be lost through competition from Mexican firms; and (2) the jobs created paid higher wages, reflecting the benefits from specialization in areas where the United States had a comparative advantage.

Opponents of NAFTA, in particular, and trade, in general, are not swayed by these arguments, but instead stress the costs to workers and communities as particular industries shrink in response to foreign imports. The textile worker in North Carolina who loses his job as a result of imports of inexpensive clothing from China cannot instantly convert himself into a computer programmer in California or an aircraft engineer working for Boeing. But the fact is that jobs are being destroyed and created all the time, irrespective of trade. And over the long run, the economic incentive of the new jobs at Boeing may induce someone in the Midwest to leave his semi-skilled job and get the training that makes him eligible for one of the skilled jobs at Boeing. The vacancy created may be filled by someone who moves in from Kentucky, leaving a vacancy there for the laid-off textile worker in North Carolina.

Because of the practical complications and the very real costs of retraining and relocation, there is increasing recognition that government may need to play a role in facilitating job movements. To the extent that such assistance increases the number of winners from trade, it should reduce opposition to trade.

The North American Free Trade Agreement (NAFTA)—which will eliminate all trade barriers between the United States, Canada, and Mexico within fifteen years—will result in the largest free trade zone in the world, embracing 380 million people and a gross national product of $8 trillion. NAFTA was so vehemently opposed, however, that it was in grave danger of being defeated in the U.S. Congress. Two opponents in particular —labor unions and environmental groups—commanded enough votes in Congress that the potential gains from free trade were in danger of being lost—until a set of side agreements allayed their concerns.

Both groups feared the effects of competition from Mexico, in spite of evidence—consistent with the law of comparative advantage—that freer trade would increase national income, perhaps substantially. Labor unions were against NAFTA because they feared competition from Mexico's low-wage economy. Environmentalists were against NAFTA because they feared that competition with

Mexico (and its low environmental standards) would force the United States to lower its environmental standards to remain competitive.

For the Clinton administration, it was clear that quoting the law of comparative advantage was not going to be effective in disarming these critics. The administration pushed to have the three countries sign side agreements ensuring that each country abided by its own labor and environmental laws, changing enough votes to secure passage. A particularly important safeguard was the establishment of a joint U.S.-Mexico air-quality board to help alleviate the severe environmental problems along the Mexican-American border. With this and other safeguards in place, NAFTA promises to improve labor and environmental standards south of the border.

While NAFTA is thought primarily as reducing barriers in the product market, it has important effects on labor and capital markets. Ross Perot, in his attacks on NAFTA, conjured up a strong image of jobs and investment flowing south of the border, in

what he dramatically described as a "giant sucking sound." Fortunately, his premonitions have not been realized. In the long run, access to the American market will make investments in Mexico far more attractive; but the funds for investing will be attracted from throughout the global capital market. And increased access to Mexico will make investments in many industries in the United States more attractive. Higher wages in Mexico will reduce the immigration pressure on the United States. Finally, concerns about job loss are greatly exaggerated. It is not only that exports to Mexico will, in the long run, create more American jobs than will be lost through competition from Mexican imports; most of those jobs would have been lost anyway, to competition from Mexico or Asia or other Latin American countries. Though Mexico pays lower wages, its workers on average are less productive. It is precisely because American workers are more productive that American firms can pay higher wages.

Overall, America and Mexico both benefit from NAFTA, as each takes advantage of its comparative advantage, and living standards in both countries increase as a result.

While the perceived costs of economic interdependence cannot be ignored—especially when they become the subject of heated political debate—the fact that the country as a whole benefits from freer trade is one of the central tenets in which there is a consensus among the vast majority of economists. Trade is the subject of our third consensus point.

3 Trade

There are gains from voluntary exchanges. Whether between individuals or across national borders, all can gain from voluntary exchange. Trade allows parties to specialize in activities in which they have a comparative advantage.

REVIEW AND PRACTICE

SUMMARY

1. The benefits of economic interdependence apply to individuals and firms within a country as well as to countries within the world. No individual and no country is self-sufficient.

2. Both individuals and countries gain from voluntary trade. There may be cases when there are only limited possibilities for bilateral trade (exchange between two parties), but the gains from multilateral trade (exchange between several parties) may be great.

3. The principle of comparative advantage asserts that countries should export the goods in which their production costs are *relatively* low.

4. Specialization tends to increase productivity for three reasons: specializing avoids the time it takes a worker to switch from one production task

to another; workers who repeat a task become more skilled at it; specialization creates a fertile environment for invention.

5. A country's comparative advantage can arise from natural endowments, acquired endowments, superior knowledge, or specialization.

6. There is a basic difference between trade among individuals and trade among countries: with trade among countries, some individuals within the country may actually be worse off. Though in principle, those who gain could more than compensate those who lose, such compensations are seldom provided. Though free trade enhances national income, fears about job loss and wage reductions among low-skilled workers have led to demands for protection. Government assistance to facilitate the required adjustments may be desirable.

KEY TERMS

gains from trade
surplus
imports
exports
bilateral trade
multilateral trade

absolute advantage
comparative
  advantage
marginal rate of
  transformation
division of labor

natural endowments
acquired
  endowments
protectionism

REVIEW QUESTIONS

1. Why are all voluntary trades mutually beneficial?

2. Describe a situation (hypothetical, if need be) where bilateral trade does not work, but multilateral trade is possible.

3. What are some of the similarities of trade between individuals and trade between countries? What is a key way in which they differ?

4. Does a country with an absolute advantage in a product necessarily have a comparative advantage in that product? Can a country with an absolute disadvantage in a product have a comparative advantage in that product? Explain.

5. Why does specialization tend to increase productivity?

6. "A country's comparative advantage is dictated by its natural endowments." Discuss.

7. "If trade with a foreign country injures anyone in this country, the government should react by passing protectionist laws to limit or stop that particular trade." Comment.

PROBLEMS

1. Four players on a Little League baseball team discover that they have each been collecting baseball cards, and they agree to get together and trade. Is it possible for everyone to benefit from this agreement? Does the fact that one player starts off with many more cards than any of the others affect your answer?

2. Leaders in many less developed countries of Latin America and Africa have often argued that because they are so much poorer than the wealthy nations of the world, trade with the more developed economies of North America and Europe will injure them. They maintain that they must first become self-sufficient before than can benefit from trade. How might an economist respond to these claims?

3. If the United States changes its immigration quotas to allow many more unskilled workers into the country, who is likely to gain? Who is likely to lose? Consider the impact on consumers, on businesses that hire low-skilled labor, and on low-skilled labor in both the United States and the workers' countries of origin.

4. David Ricardo illustrated the principle of comparative advantage in terms of the trade between England and Portugal in wine (port) and wool. Suppose that in England it takes 120 laborers to produce a certain quantity of wine, while in Portugal it takes only 80 laborers to produce that same quantity. Similarly, in England it takes 100 laborers to produce a certain quantity of wool, while in Portugal it takes only 90. Draw the opportunity set for each country, assuming that each has 72,000 laborers. Assume that each country commits half its labor to each product in the absence of trade, and designate that point on your graph. Now describe a new production plan, with trade, that can benefit both countries.

5. Relate the comparative advantage of two countries to differences in the slope of their production possibilities schedules. In what sense might a small, poor country trading with a much larger, rich country be at a disadvantage? How might the differences affect how the gains from trade are divided?

6. In 1981, the U.S. government prodded Japanese automakers to limit the number of cars they would export to the United States. Who benefited from this protectionism in the United States and in Japan? Who was injured in the United States and in Japan? Consider companies that produce cars (and their workers) and consumers who buy cars.

7. For many years, an international agreement called the Multifiber Agreement has limited the amount of textiles that the developed economies of North America and Europe can buy from poor countries in Latin America and Asia. Textiles can be produced by relatively unskilled labor with a reasonably small amount of capital. Who benefits from the protectionism of the Multifiber Agreement, and who suffers?

4

DEMAND, SUPPLY, AND PRICE

C hoice in the face of scarcity, as we have seen, is the fundamental concern of economics. The **price** of a good or service is what must be given in exchange for the good. When the forces of supply and demand operate freely, price measures scarcity. As such, prices convey critical economic information. When the price of a resource used by a firm is high, the company has a greater incentive to economize on its use. When the price of a good that the firm produces is high, the company has a greater incentive to produce more of that good, and its customers have an incentive to economize on its use. In these ways and others, prices provide our economy with incentives to use scarce resources efficiently. This chapter describes how prices are determined in competitive market economies.

THE ROLE OF PRICES

Prices are the way participants in the economy communicate with one another. Assume a drought hits the country, reducing drastically the supply of corn. Households will need to reduce their consumption of corn or there will not be enough to go around. But how will they know this? Suppose newspapers across the country ran an article informing people they would have to eat less corn because of a drought. What incentive would they have to pay attention to it? How would each family know how much it ought to reduce its consumption? As an alternative to the newspaper, consider the effect of an increase in the price of corn. The higher price conveys all the relevant information. It tells families corn is scarce at the same time as it provides incentives for them to consume less of it. Consumers do not need to know anything about why corn is scarce, nor do they need to be told by how much they should reduce their consumption of corn.

Price changes and differences present interesting problems and puzzles. In the early 1980s, while the price of an average house in Los Angeles went up by 41 percent, the price of a house in Milwaukee, Wisconsin, increased by only 4 percent. Why? During the same period, the price of computers fell dramatically, while the price of bread rose, but at a much slower rate than the price of housing in Los Angeles. Why? The "price" of labor is just the wage or salary that is paid. Why does a physician earn three times as much as a college professor, though the college professor may have performed better in the college courses they took together? Why did average wage rates fall in the United States between 1973 and 1983? Why is the price of water, without which we cannot live, very low in most cases, but the price of diamonds, which we can surely live without, very high? The simple answer to all these questions is that in market economies like the United States, price is determined by supply and demand. Changes in prices are determined by changes in supply and demand.

Understanding the causes of changes in prices and being able to predict their occurrence is not just a matter of academic interest. One of the events that precipitated the French Revolution was the rise in the price of bread, for which the people blamed the government. Large price changes have also given rise to recent political turmoil in several countries, including Morocco, the Dominican Republic, Russia, and Poland.

Noneconomists see much more in prices than the impersonal forces of supply and demand. It was the landlord who raised the rent on the apartment; it was the oil company or the owner of the gas station who raised the price of gasoline. These people and companies *chose* to raise their prices, says the noneconomist, in moral indignation. True, replies the economist, but there must be some factor that made these people and companies believe that a higher price was not a good idea yesterday, but is today. And economists point out that at a different time, these same impersonal forces can force the same landlords and oil companies to cut their prices. Economists see prices, then, as symptoms of underlying causes, and focus on the forces of demand and supply behind price changes.

DEMAND

Economists use the concept of **demand** to describe the quantity of a good or service that a household or firm chooses to buy at a given price. It is important to understand that economists are concerned not just with what people desire, but with what they choose to buy given the spending limits imposed by their budget constraint and given the prices of various goods. In analyzing demand, the first question they ask is how the quantity of a good purchased by an individual changes as the price changes, keeping everything else constant.

THE INDIVIDUAL DEMAND CURVE

Think about what happens as the price of candy bars changes. At a price of $5.00, you might never buy one. At $3.00, you might buy one as a special treat. At $1.25, you might buy a few, and if the price declined to $.50, you might buy a lot. The table in Figure 4.1 summarizes the weekly demand of one individual, Roger, for candy bars at these different prices. We can see that the lower the price, the larger the quantity demanded. We can also draw a graph that shows the quantity Roger demands at each price. The quantity demanded is measured along the horizontal axis, and the price is measured along the vertical axis. The graph in Figure 4.1 plots the points.

A smooth curve can be drawn to connect the points. This curve is called the **demand curve.** The demand curve gives the quantity demanded at each price. Thus, if we want to know how many candy bars a week Roger will demand at a price of $1.00, we simply look along the vertical axis at the price

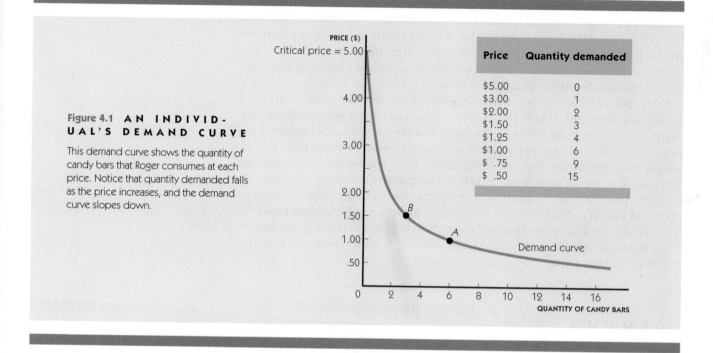

Figure 4.1 AN INDIVIDUAL'S DEMAND CURVE

This demand curve shows the quantity of candy bars that Roger consumes at each price. Notice that quantity demanded falls as the price increases, and the demand curve slopes down.

Price	Quantity demanded
$5.00	0
$3.00	1
$2.00	2
$1.50	3
$1.25	4
$1.00	6
$ .75	9
$ .50	15

$1.00, find the corresponding point A along the demand curve, and then read down to the horizontal axis. At a price of $1.00, Roger buys 6 candy bars each week. Alternatively, if we want to know at what price he will buy just 3 candy bars, we look along the horizontal axis at the quantity 3, find the corresponding point B along the demand curve, and then read across to the vertical axis. Roger will buy 3 candy bars at a price of $1.50.

As the price of candy bars increases the quantity demanded decreases. This can be seen from the numbers in the table in Figure 4.1, and in the shape of the demand curve, which slopes downward from left to right. This relationship is typical of demand curves and makes common sense: the cheaper a good is (the lower down we look on the vertical axis), the more of it a person will buy (the farther right on the horizontal axis); the more expensive, the less a person will buy.

DEMAND CURVE

The demand curve gives the quantity of the good demanded at each price.

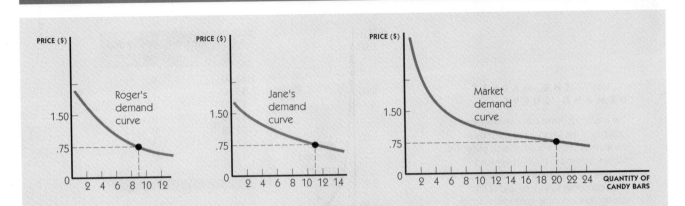

Figure 4.2 DERIVING THE MARKET DEMAND CURVE

The market demand curve is constructed by adding up, at each price, the total of the quantities consumed by each individual. The curve here shows what market demand would be if there were only two consumers. Actual market demand, as depicted in Figure 4.3, is much larger because there are many consumers.

THE MARKET DEMAND CURVE

Suppose there was a simple economy made up of two people, Roger and Jane. Figure 4.2 illustrates how to add up the demand curves of these two individuals to obtain a demand curve for the market as a whole. We "add" the demand curves horizontally by taking, at each price, the quantities demanded by Roger and by Jane and adding the two together. Thus, in the figure, at the price of $.75, Roger demands 9 candy bars and Jane demands 11, so that the total market demand is 20 candy bars. The same principles apply no matter how many people there are in the economy. The **market demand curve** gives the total quantity of the good that will be demanded at each price. The table in Figure 4.3 summarizes the information for our example of candy bars; it gives the total quantity of candy bars demanded by everybody in the economy at various prices. If we had a table like the one in Figure 4.1 for each person in the economy, we would construct Figure 4.3 by adding up, at each price, the total quantity of candy bars purchased. Figure 4.3 tells us, for instance, that at a price of $3.00 per candy bar, the total market demand for candy bars is 1 million candy bars, and that lowering the price to $2.00 increases market demand to 3 million candy bars.

Figure 4.3 also depicts the same information in a graph. As with Figure 4.1, price lies along the vertical axis, but now the horizontal axis measures the quantity demanded by everyone in the economy. Joining the points in the figure together, we get the **market demand curve.** If we want to know what the total demand for candy bars will be when the price is $1.50 per candy bar, we

Figure 4.3 THE MARKET DEMAND CURVE

The market demand curve shows the quantity of the good demanded by all consumers in the market at each price. The market demand curve is downward sloping, for two reasons: at a higher price, each consumer buys less, and at high enough prices, some consumers decide not to buy at all—they exit the market.

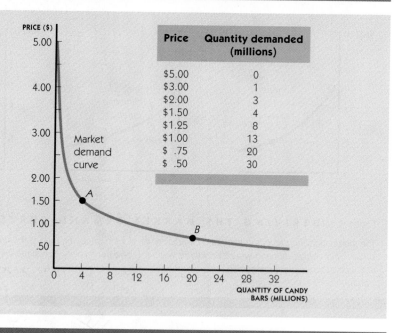

Price	Quantity demanded (millions)
$5.00	0
$3.00	1
$2.00	3
$1.50	4
$1.25	8
$1.00	13
$ .75	20
$ .50	30

look on the vertical axis at the price $1.50, find the corresponding point *A* along the demand curve, and read down to the horizontal axis; at that price, total demand is 4 million candy bars. If we want to know what the price of candy bars will be when the demand equals 20 million, we find 20 million along the horizontal axis, look up to find the corresponding point *B* along the market demand curve, and read across to the vertical axis; the price at which 20 million candy bars are demanded is $.75.

Notice that just as when the price of candy bars increases, the individual's demand decreases, so too when the price of candy bars increases, market demand decreases. Thus, the market demand curve also slopes downward from left to right. This general rule holds both because each individual's demand curve is downward sloping and because as the price is increased, some individuals will decide to stop buying altogether. In Figure 4.1, for example, Roger **exits the market**—consumes a quantity of zero—at the price of $5.00, at which his demand curve hits the vertical axis. At successively higher prices more and more individuals exit the market.

SHIFTS IN DEMAND CURVES

When the price of a good increases, the demand for that good decreases—when everything else is held constant. But in the real world, everything is not held constant. Any changes other than the price of the good in question shift

POLICY PERSPECTIVE: GOOD NEWS IS BAD NEWS

In the second half of 1993, oil prices fell dramatically, by nearly 25 percent. For consumers, this was good news, but for the Clinton administration, it presented a problem. In August 1992, the United States had signed the Framework Convention on Climate Change, known as the Rio convention, committing the country by the year 2000 to reduce its emissions of greenhouse gases to the level they had been in 1990. (Greenhouse gases, such as carbon dioxide, contribute to global warming.) Since the economy in 2000 would be substantially larger than in 1990, there would have to be corresponding increases in energy efficiency

to meet this goal. In September 1993, the United States had outlined an ambitious "National Action Plan" for fulfilling the country's commitments. But the plan was predicated on oil prices remaining the same. Falling oil prices would increase demand. Demand curves of the kind discussed in this chapter enabled analysts to calculate the increased energy consumption—and greenhouse gas emissions—that could be expected. These calculations indicated that there would be a substantial shortfall in meeting U.S. commitments, unless further steps were taken.

the (whole) demand curve—that is, change the amount that will be demanded at each price. How the demand curve for candy has shifted as Americans have become more weight conscious provides a good example. Figure 4.4 shows hypothetical demand curves for candy bars in 1960 and in 1995. We can see from the figure, for instance, that the demand for candy bars at a price of $.75 has decreased from 20 million candy bars (point E_{1960}, the original equilibrium) to 10 million (point E_{1995}), as people have reduced their "taste" for candy.

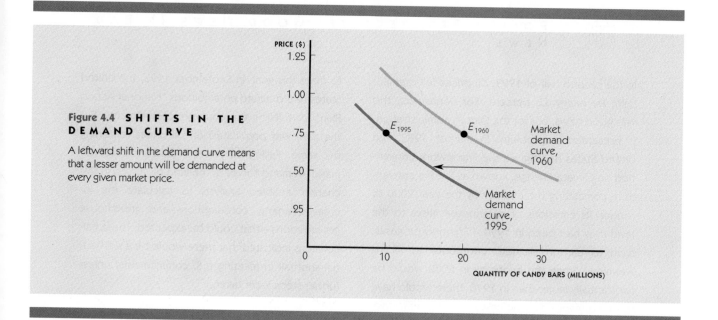

Figure 4.4 SHIFTS IN THE DEMAND CURVE

A leftward shift in the demand curve means that a lesser amount will be demanded at every given market price.

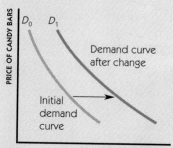

Figure 4.5 A RIGHT-WARD SHIFT IN THE DEMAND CURVE

If, at each price, there is an increase in the quantity demanded, then the demand curve will have shifted to the right, as depicted. An increase in income, an increase in the price of a substitute, or a decrease in the price of a complement can cause a rightward shift in the demand curve.

SOURCES OF SHIFTS IN DEMAND CURVES

Two of the factors that shift the demand curve—changes in income and in the price of other goods—are specifically economic factors. As an individual's income increases, she normally purchases more of any good. Thus, rising incomes shift the demand curve to the right, as illustrated in Figure 4.5. At each price, she consumes more of the good.

Changes in the price of other goods, particularly closely related goods, will also shift the demand curve for a good. For example, when the price of margarine increases, some individuals will substitute butter. Two goods are **substitutes** if an increase in the price of one *increases* the demand for the other. Butter and margarine are thus substitutes. When people choose between butter and margarine, one important factor is the relative price, that is, the ratio of the price of butter to the price of margarine. An increase in the price of butter and a decrease in the price of margarine both increase the relative price of butter. Thus, both induce individuals to substitute margarine for butter.

Candy bars and granola bars can also be considered substitutes, as the two goods satisfy a similar need. Thus, an increase in the price of granola bars makes candy bars relatively more attractive, and hence leads to a rightward shift in the demand curve for candy bars. (At each price, the demand for candy is greater.)

Sometimes, however, an increase in a price of other goods has just the opposite effect. Consider an individual who takes sugar in her coffee. In deciding on how much coffee to demand, she is concerned with the price of a cup of coffee *with* sugar. If sugar becomes more expensive, she will demand less

CLOSE-UP: GASOLINE PRICES AND DEMAND FOR SMALL CARS

When demands for several products are intertwined, conditions affecting the price of one will affect the demand for the other. When gasoline prices in the United States increased in the 1970s, for example, the change affected the demand for small cars.

Actually, the price of gasoline soared twice in the 1970s: once when the Organization of Petroleum Exporting Countries (OPEC) shut off the flow of oil to the United States in 1973, and again when the Shah of Iran was driven from power in 1979, leading to a disruption in oil supplies. The price of gasoline at the pump rose from $.27 a gallon in 1973 to $1.40 a gallon by 1981. How could Americans conserve on gasoline? The distance from home to office was not going to shrink, and people had to commute to their jobs. One solution found by American drivers was that when the time came to replace their old cars, they purchased smaller cars that offered more miles to the gallon.

Analysts classify car sales according to car size. Just after the first rise in gas prices, about 2.5 million large cars, 2.8 million compacts, and 2.3 million subcompacts were bought per year. By 1985, the proportions had shifted drastically. About 1.5 million large cars were sold that year, a significant decline from the mid-1970s. The number of subcompacts sold was relatively unchanged at 2.2 million, but the number of compacts sold soared to 3.7 million.

The demand curve for any good (like cars) assumes that the price of complementary goods (like gasoline) is fixed. The rise in gasoline prices caused the demand curve for small cars to shift out to the right and the demand curve for large cars to shift back to the left.

The reason is easy to see. Imagine that you drive 15,000 miles per year. A large car gets 15 miles to the gallon, meaning that you would need to buy 1,000 gallons of gasoline per year, while a small car gets 30 miles to the gallon, meaning that you would only have to buy 500 gallons of gas per year. When the price of gasoline was at its 1981 peak of $1.40 per gallon, this higher mileage translated into a savings of $700 per year.

Sources: Gasoline prices taken from various issues of *Survey of Current Business;* auto sales figures from Linda Williams and Patricia Hu of Oak Ridge National Laboratory; *Light Duty Vehicle Summary: Model Year 1976 to the First Half of Model Year 1989.*

coffee. For this person, sugar and coffee are **complements;** an increase in the price of one *decreases* the demand for the other. A price increase of sugar shifts the demand curve of coffee to the left: at each price, the demand for coffee is less. Similarly a *decrease* in the price of sugar shifts the demand curve for coffee to the right.

Noneconomic factors can also shift market demand curves. The major ones are changes in tastes and in composition of the population. The candy example shown earlier was a change in taste. Other taste changes over the past decade in the United States include a shift from hard liquor to wine and from fatty meats to low-cholesterol foods. Each of these taste changes has shifted the whole demand curve of the goods in question.

Population changes that shift demand curves are often related to age. Young families with babies purchase disposable diapers. The demand for new houses and apartments is closely related to the number of new households, which in turn depends on the number of individuals of marriageable age. The U.S. population has been growing older, on average, both because life expectancies are increasing and because birthrates fell somewhat after the baby boom that followed World War II. So there has been a shift in demand away from diapers and new houses. Economists working for particular firms and industries spend considerable energy ascertaining population effects, called **demographic effects,** on the demand for the goods their firms sell.

Sometimes demand curves shift as the result of new information. The shifts in demand for alcohol and meat—and even more so for cigarettes—are related to improved consumer information about health risks.

Changes in the availability of credit also can shift demand curves—for goods like cars and houses that people typically buy with the help of loans. When banks, for example, reduce the money available for consumer loans, the demand curves for cars and houses shift.

SOURCES OF SHIFTS IN MARKET DEMAND CURVES

A change in income

A change in the price of a substitute

A change in the price of a complement

A change in the composition of the population

A change in tastes

A change in information

A change in the availability of credit

A change in expectations

Finally, what people think will happen in the future can shift demand curves. If people think they may become unemployed, they will reduce their spending. In this case, economists say that their demand curve depends on expectations.

SHIFTS IN A DEMAND CURVE VERSUS MOVEMENTS ALONG A DEMAND CURVE

The distinction between changes that result from a *shift* in the demand curve and changes that result from a *movement along* the demand curve is crucial to understanding economics. A movement along a demand curve is simply the change in the quantity demanded as the price changes. Figure 4.6A illustrates a movement along the demand curve from point A to point B; *given a demand curve,* at lower prices, more is consumed. Figure 4.6B illustrates a shift in the demand curve to the right; *at a given price,* more is consumed. Quantity again increases from Q_0 to Q_1, but now the price stays the same.

In practice, both effects are often present. Thus, in panel C of Figure 4.6, the movement from point A to point C—where the quantity demanded has been

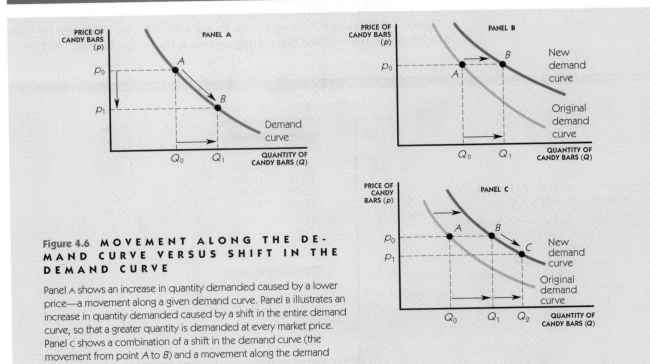

Figure 4.6 MOVEMENT ALONG THE DE-MAND CURVE VERSUS SHIFT IN THE DEMAND CURVE

Panel A shows an increase in quantity demanded caused by a lower price—a movement along a given demand curve. Panel B illustrates an increase in quantity demanded caused by a shift in the entire demand curve, so that a greater quantity is demanded at every market price. Panel C shows a combination of a shift in the demand curve (the movement from point A to B) and a movement along the demand curve (the movement from B to C).

increased from Q_0 to Q_2—consists of two parts: a change in quantity demanded resulting from a shift in the demand curve (the increase in quantity from Q_0 to Q_1), and a movement along the demand curve due to a change in the price (the increase in quantity from Q_1 to Q_2).

SUPPLY

Economists use the concept of **supply** to describe the quantity of a good or service that a household or firm would like to sell at a particular price. Supply in economics refers to such seemingly disparate choices as the number of candy bars a firm wants to sell and the number of hours a worker is willing to work. As with demand, the first question economists ask is how does the quantity supplied change when price changes, keeping everything else the same?

Figure 4.7 shows the number of candy bars that the Melt-in-the-Mouth Chocolate Company would like to sell, or supply to the market, at each price. As the price rises, so does the quantity supplied. Below $1.00, the firm finds it unprofitable to produce. At $2.00, it would like to sell 85,000 candy bars. At $5.00, it would like to sell 100,000.

Figure 4.7 also depicts these points in a graph. The curve drawn by connecting the points is called the **supply curve.** It shows the quantity that Melt-

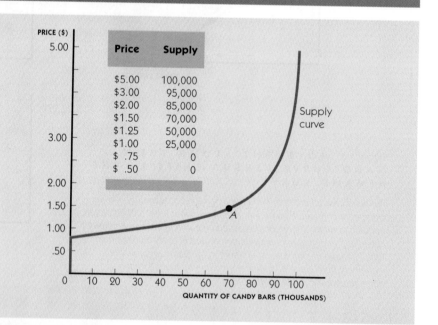

Figure 4.7 ONE FIRM'S SUPPLY CURVE

The supply curve shows the quantity of a good a firm is willing to produce at each price. Normally a firm is willing to produce more as the price increases, which is why the supply curve slopes upward.

Price	Supply
$5.00	100,000
$3.00	95,000
$2.00	85,000
$1.50	70,000
$1.25	50,000
$1.00	25,000
$ .75	0
$ .50	0

in-the-Mouth will supply at each price, holding all other factors constant. As with the demand curve, we put the price on the vertical axis and the quantity supplied on the horizontal axis. Thus, we can read point A on the curve as indicating that at a price of $1.50 the firm would like to supply 70,000 candy bars.

In direct contrast to the demand curve, the typical supply curve slopes upward from left to right; at higher prices, firms will supply more.[1] This is because higher prices yield suppliers higher profits—giving them an incentive to produce more.

SUPPLY CURVE

The supply curve gives the quantity of the good supplied at each price.

MARKET SUPPLY

The **market supply** of a good is simply the total quantity that all the firms in the economy are willing to supply at a given price. Similarly, the market supply of labor is simply the total quantity of labor that all the households in the economy are willing to supply at a given wage. Figure 4.8 tells us, for instance, that at a price of $2.00, firms will supply 70 million candy bars, while at a price of $.50, they will supply only 5 million.

Figure 4.8 also shows the same information graphically. The curve joining the points in the figure is the **market supply curve.** The market supply curve gives the total quantity of a good that firms are willing to produce at each price. Thus, we read point A on the market supply curve as showing that at a price of $.75, the firms in the economy would like to sell 20 million candy bars.

As the price of candy bars increases, the quantity supplied increases, other things equal. The market supply curve slopes upward from left to right for two reasons: at higher prices, each firm in the market is willing to produce more; and at higher prices, more firms are willing to enter the market to produce the good.

The market supply curve is calculated from the supply curves of the different firms in the same way that the market demand curve is calculated from the demand curves of the different households: at each price, we add horizontally the quantities that each of the firms is willing to produce.

[1] Chapter 9 will describe some unusual situations where supply curves may not be upward sloping.

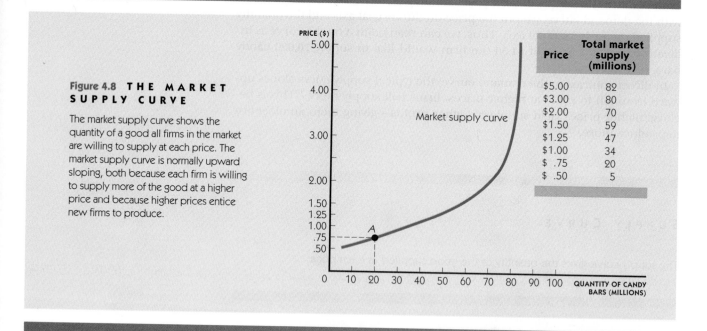

Figure 4.8 THE MARKET SUPPLY CURVE

The market supply curve shows the quantity of a good all firms in the market are willing to supply at each price. The market supply curve is normally upward sloping, both because each firm is willing to supply more of the good at a higher price and because higher prices entice new firms to produce.

Price	Total market supply (millions)
$5.00	82
$3.00	80
$2.00	70
$1.50	59
$1.25	47
$1.00	34
$ .75	20
$ .50	5

Figure 4.9 shows how this is done in a market with only two producers. At a price of $1.25, Melt-in-the-Mouth Chocolate produces 50,000 candy bars, while the Chocolates of Choice Company produces 40,000. So the market supply is 90,000 bars. The same principle applies to markets with many firms.

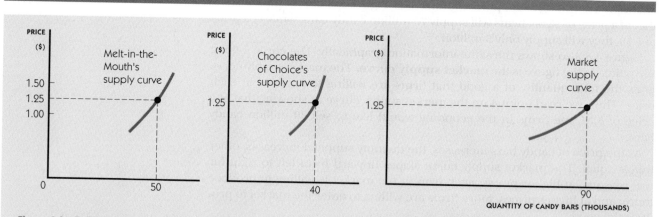

Figure 4.9 DERIVING THE MARKET SUPPLY CURVE

The market supply curve is constructed by adding up the quantity that each of the firms in the economy is willing to supply at each price. The figure here shows what market supply would be if there were only two producers. Actual market supply, as depicted in Figure 4.8, is much larger because there are many producers.

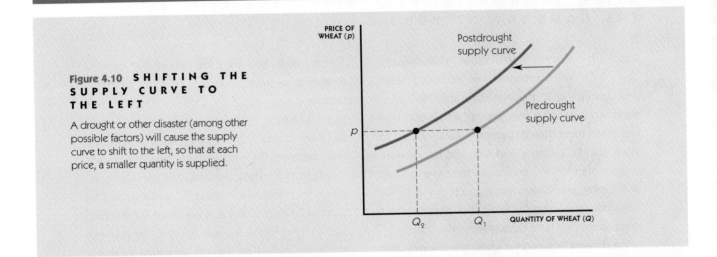

Figure 4.10 SHIFTING THE SUPPLY CURVE TO THE LEFT

A drought or other disaster (among other possible factors) will cause the supply curve to shift to the left, so that at each price, a smaller quantity is supplied.

SHIFTS IN SUPPLY CURVES

Just as demand curves can shift, supply curves too can shift, so that the quantity supplied at each price increases or decreases. Suppose a drought hits the breadbasket states of mid-America. Figure 4.10 illustrates the situation. The supply curve for wheat shifts to the left, which means that at each price of wheat, the quantity firms are willing to supply is smaller.

SOURCES OF SHIFTS IN SUPPLY CURVES

There are several sources of shifts in market supply curves, just as in the case of the market demand curves already discussed. One is changing prices of the inputs used to produce a good. Figure 4.11 shows that as corn becomes less expensive, the supply curve for cornflakes shifts to the right. Producing cornflakes costs less, so at every price, firms are willing to supply a greater quantity. That is why the quantity supplied along the curve S_1 is greater than the quantity supplied, at the same price, along the curve S_0.

Another source of shifts is changes in technology. The technological improvements in the computer industry over the past two decades have led to a rightward shift in the market supply curve. Yet another source of shifts is nature. The supply curve for agricultural goods may shift to the right or left depending on weather conditions, insect infestations, or animal diseases.

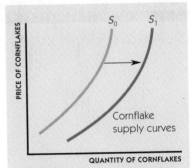

Figure 4.11 SHIFTING THE SUPPLY CURVE TO THE RIGHT

An improvement in technology or a reduction in input prices (among other possible factors) will cause the supply curve to shift to the right, so that at each price, a larger quantity is supplied.

For the midwestern United States, 1988 brought one of the worst droughts ever recorded. Corn production was 35 percent lower than had been expected before the drought; soybean production was down more than 20 percent, wheat was down more than 10 percent, and oats and barley were down more than 40 percent. As these events were developing, economists attempted to predict their consequences, using the basic laws of supply and demand that we have developed in this chapter.

The drought reduced the amount of any crop that would be supplied at any given price. The drought can be viewed as shifting the supply curve to the left. Predictably, with a given demand curve, the large shift of the supply curve resulted in much higher prices for these farm products: corn prices rose by 80 percent by the end of the summer, soybeans by almost 70 percent, and wheat by 50 percent.

Economists also used the supply and demand models to predict the effects on other products. Grain is a major input into cattle production. With cattle production less profitable, many farmers slaughtered their cattle sooner than they had originally planned. As a result, meat production rose slightly in 1988. The increased short-run supply resulted in a decrease in meat prices (adjusted for inflation). Grain is also a major input for the production of chicken. The supply curves for chickens and eggs shifted to the left, resulting in higher prices for these commodities. The higher prices of these agricultural goods resulted in a shift to the right of the demand curve for other foods which were substitutes. Thus, prices for foods, such as vegetables and fruits, whose supply was not affected by the midwestern drought, still increased—by 5 percent in July 1988 alone.

Reduction in the availability of credit may curtail firms' ability to borrow to obtain inputs needed for production, and this too will induce a leftward shift in the supply curve. Finally, changed expectations can also lead to a shift in the supply curve. If firms believe that a new technology for making cars will become available in two years' time, this belief will discourage investment today and will lead to a temporary leftward shift in the supply curve.

SOURCES OF SHIFTS IN MARKET SUPPLY CURVES

A change in the prices of inputs
A change in technology
A change in the natural environment
A change in the availability of credit
A change in expectations

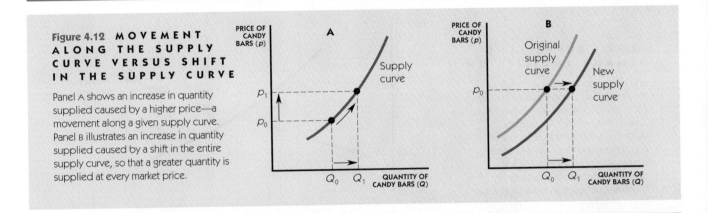

Figure 4.12 MOVEMENT ALONG THE SUPPLY CURVE VERSUS SHIFT IN THE SUPPLY CURVE

Panel A shows an increase in quantity supplied caused by a higher price—a movement along a given supply curve. Panel B illustrates an increase in quantity supplied caused by a shift in the entire supply curve, so that a greater quantity is supplied at every market price.

SHIFTS IN A SUPPLY CURVE VERSUS MOVEMENTS ALONG A SUPPLY CURVE

Distinguishing between a movement *along* a curve and a *shift* in the curve itself is just as important for supply curves as it is for demand curves. In Figure 4.12A, the price of candy bars has gone up, with a corresponding increase in quantity supplied. Thus, there has been a movement along the supply curve.

By contrast, in Figure 4.12B, the supply curve has shifted to the right, perhaps because a new production technique has made it cheaper to produce candy bars. Now, even though the price does not change, the quantity supplied increases. The quantity supplied in the market can increase either because the price of the good has increased, so that for a *given supply curve*, the quantity produced is higher; or because the supply curve has shifted, so that at a *given price*, the quantity supplied has increased.

LAW OF SUPPLY AND DEMAND

This chapter began with the assertion that supply and demand work together to determine the market price in competitive markets. Figure 4.13 puts a market supply curve and a market demand curve on the same graph to show how this happens. The price actually paid and received in the market will be determined by the intersection of the two curves. This point is labeled E_0, for equilibrium, and the corresponding price ($.75) and quantity (20 million) are called, respectively, the **equilibrium price** and the **equilibrium quantity.**

Since the term **equilibrium** will recur throughout the book, it is important to understand the concept clearly. Equilibrium describes a situation where

Figure 4.13 SUPPLY AND DEMAND EQUILIBRIUM

Equilibrium occurs at the intersection of the demand and supply curves, at point E_0. At any price above E_0, the quantity supplied will exceed the quantity demanded, the market will be out of equilibrium, and there will be excess supply. At any price below E_0, the quantity demanded will exceed the quantity supplied, the market will be out of equilibrium, and there will be excess demand.

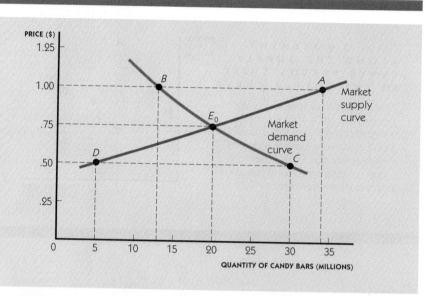

there are no forces (reasons) for change. No one has an incentive to change the result—the price or quantity consumed or produced in the case of supply and demand.

Physicists also speak of equilibrium in describing a weight hanging from a spring. Two forces are working on the weight. Gravity is pulling it down; the spring is pulling it up. When the weight is at rest, it is in equilibrium, with the two forces just offsetting each other. If one pulls the weight down a little bit, the force of the spring will be greater than the force of gravity, and the weight will spring up. In the absence of any further intrusions, the weight will bob back and forth and eventually reach its equilibrium position.

An economic equilibrium is established in the same way. At the equilibrium price, consumers get precisely the quantity of the good they are willing to buy at that price, and producers sell precisely the quantity they are willing to sell at that price. Neither producers nor consumers have any incentive to change.

But consider the price of $1.00 in Figure 4.13. There is no equilibrium quantity here. First find $1.00 on the vertical axis. Now look across to find point A on the supply curve, and read down to the horizontal axis; point A tells you that at a price of $1.00, firms want to supply 34 million candy bars. Now look at point B on the demand curve. Point B shows that at a price of $1.00, consumers only want to buy 13 million candy bars. Like the weight bobbing on a spring however, this market will work its way back to equilibrium, in the following way. At a price of $1.00, there is **excess supply.** As producers discover that they cannot sell as much as they would like at this price, some of them will lower their prices slightly, hoping to take business from other producers. When one producer lowers prices, his competitors will have to respond, for fear that they will end up unable to sell their goods. As prices come

Every economic model, including the model of how supply and demand determine the equilibrium price and quantity in a market, is constructed of three kinds of relationships: identities, behavioral relationships, and equilibrium relationships. Recognizing these component parts will help in understanding not only how economists think but also the source of their disagreements.

The market demand is equal to the sum of individual demands. This is an identity. An identity is a statement that is true simply because of the definition of the terms. In other words, market demand is *defined* to be the sum of the demands of all individuals. Similarly, it is an identity that market supply is equal to the sum of the supplies of all firms; the terms are defined in that way.

The demand curve represents a relationship between the price and the quantity demanded. Normally, as prices rise, the quantity of a good demanded decreases. This is a description of how individuals behave, and is called a behavioral relationship. The supply curve for each firm is also a behavioral relationship.

Economists may disagree over behavioral relationships. They may agree about the direction of the relationship but disagree about the strength of the connection. For any given product, does a change in price lead to a large change in the quantity demanded or a small one? But they may even disagree over the direction of the effect. As later chapters will discuss, in some special cases a higher price may actually lead to a *lower* quantity supplied.

Finally, an equilibrium relationship exists when there are no forces for change. In the supply and demand model, the equilibrium occurs when the quantity demanded is equal to the quantity supplied. An equilibrium relationship is not the same as an identity. It is possible for the economy to be out of equilibrium, at least for a time. Of course, being out of equilibrium implies that there are forces for change pushing toward equilibrium. But an identity must always hold true at all times, as a matter of definition.

Economists usually agree about what an equilibrium would look like, but they often differ on whether the forces pushing the markets toward equilibrium are strong or weak, and thus on whether the economy is typically close to equilibrium or may stray rather far from it.

down, consumers will also buy more, and so on until the market reaches the equilibrium price and quantity.

Similarly, assume that the price is lower than $.75, say $.50. At the lower price, there is **excess demand:** individuals want to buy 30 million candy bars (point *C*), while firms only want to produce 5 million (point *D*). Consumers unable to purchase all they want will offer to pay a bit more; other consumers, afraid of having to do without, will match these higher bids or raise them. As prices start to increase, suppliers will also have a greater incentive to produce more. Again the market will tend toward the equilibrium point.

To repeat for emphasis: at equilibrium, no purchaser and no supplier has an incentive to change the price or quantity. In competitive market economies actual prices tend to be the equilibrium prices, at which demand equals supply.

This is called the **law of supply and demand.** Note: this law does not mean that at every moment of time the price is precisely at the intersection of the demand and supply curves. As with the example of the weight and the spring, the market may bounce around a little bit when it is in the process of adjusting. What the law of supply and demand does say is that when a market is out of equilibrium, there are predictable forces for change.

USING DEMAND AND SUPPLY CURVES

The concepts of demand and supply curves—and market equilibrium as the intersection of demand and supply curves—constitute the economist's basic model of demand and supply. This model has proven to be extremely useful. It helps explain why the price of some commodity is high, and that of some other commodity is low. It also helps *predict* the consequences of certain changes. Its predictions can then be tested against what actually happens. One of the reasons that the model is so useful is that it gives reasonably accurate predictions.

Figure 4.14 repeats the demand and supply curve for candy bars. Assume, now, however, that sugar becomes more expensive. As a result, at each price, the amount of candy firms are willing to supply is reduced. The supply curve shifts to the left, as in panel A. There will be a new equilibrium, at a higher price and a lower quantity of candy consumed.

Alternatively, assume that Americans become more health conscious, and as a result, at each price fewer candy bars are consumed: the demand curve shifts to the left, as shown in panel B. Again, there will be a new equilibrium, at a lower price and a lower quantity of candy consumed.

This illustrates how changes in observed prices can be related either to shifts in the demand curve or shifts in the supply curve. When the war in

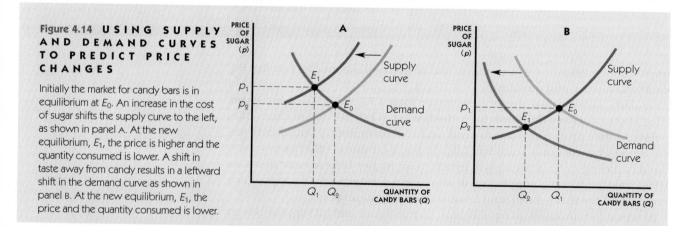

Figure 4.14 USING SUPPLY AND DEMAND CURVES TO PREDICT PRICE CHANGES

Initially the market for candy bars is in equilibrium at E_0. An increase in the cost of sugar shifts the supply curve to the left, as shown in panel A. At the new equilibrium, E_1, the price is higher and the quantity consumed is lower. A shift in taste away from candy results in a leftward shift in the demand curve as shown in panel B. At the new equilibrium, E_1, the price and the quantity consumed is lower.

Kuwait interrupted the supply of oil from the Middle East in 1990, that was a shift in the supply curve. The model predicted the result: an increase in the price of oil. This increase was the natural process of the law of supply and demand.

CONSENSUS ON THE DETERMINATION OF PRICES

The law of supply and demand plays such a prominent role in economics that there is a joke about teaching a parrot to be an economist simply by teaching it to say "supply and demand." That prices are determined by the law of supply and demand is one of the most long-standing and widely accepted ideas of economists. It forms our fourth point of consensus.

4 Prices

In competitive markets, prices are determined by the law of supply and demand. Shifts in the demand and supply curves lead to changes in the equilibrium price. Similar principles apply to the labor and capital markets. The price for labor is the wage, and the price for capital is the interest rate.

PRICE, VALUE, AND COST

Price, to an economist, is what is given in exchange for a good or service. Price, in this sense, is determined by the forces of supply and demand. Adam Smith, often thought of as the founder of modern economics, called our notion of price "value in exchange," and contrasted it to the notion of "value in use":

> The things which have the greatest value in use have frequently little or no value in exchange; and, on the contrary, those which have the greatest value in exchange have frequently little or no value in use. Nothing is more useful than water, but it will purchase scarce any thing; scarce any thing can be had in exchange for it. A diamond, on the contrary, has scarce any value in use; but a very great quantity of other goods may frequently be had in exchange for it.[2]

The law of supply and demand can help to explain the diamond-water paradox, and many similar examples where "value in use" is very different from "value in exchange." Figure 4.15 presents a demand and a supply curve for water. Individuals are willing to pay a high price for the water they need to live, as illustrated by point *A*, on the demand curve. But above some quantity, *B*, people will pay almost nothing more for additional water. In most of the

---

[2]*The Wealth of Nations* (1776), Book I, Chapter IV.

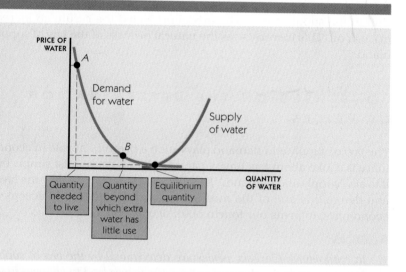

Figure 4.15 SUPPLY AND DEMAND FOR WATER

Point A shows that people are willing to pay a relatively high price for the first few units of water. But to the right of B, people have plenty of water already and are not willing to pay much for an additional amount. The price of water will be determined at the point where the supply curve crosses the demand curve. In most cases, the resulting price is extremely low.

inhabited parts of the world, water is readily available, so it gets supplied in plentiful quantities at low prices. Thus, the supply curve of water intersects the demand curve to the right of *B*, as in the figure; hence the low equilibrium price. Of course, in the desert, the water supply may be very limited and the price, as a result, very high.

To an economist, the statements that the price of diamonds is high and the price of water is low are statements about supply and demand conditions. They say nothing about whether diamonds are "more important" or "better" than water. In Adam Smith's terms, they are not statements about value in use.

Price is related to the *marginal* value of an object, that is, the value of an additional unit of the object. Water has a low price not because the *total* value of water is low—it is obviously high, since we could not live without it—but because the marginal value, what we would be willing to pay to be able to drink one more glass of water a year, is low.

Just as economists take care to distinguish the words "price" and "value," they also distinguish the *price* of an object (what it sells for) from its *cost* (the expense of making the object). This is another crucial distinction in economics. The costs of producing a good affect the price at which firms are willing to supply that good. An increase in the costs of production will normally cause prices to rise. And in the competitive model, *in equilibrium*, the price of an object will normally equal its (marginal) cost of production (including the amount needed to pay a firm's owner to stay in business rather than seek some other form of employment). But there are important cases—as we shall see in later chapters—where price does not equal cost.

In thinking about the relationship of price and cost, it is interesting to consider the case of a good in fixed supply, such as land. Normally, land is something that cannot be produced, so its cost of production can be considered infinite (though there are situations where land can be produced, as when Chicago filled in part of Lake Michigan to expand its lake shore). Yet there is still an equilibrium price of land—where the demand for land is equal to its (fixed) supply.

REVIEW AND PRACTICE

SUMMARY

1. An individual's demand curve gives the quantity demanded of a good at each possible price. It normally slopes down, which means that the person demands a greater quantity of the good at lower prices and a lesser quantity at higher prices.

2. The market demand curve gives the total quantity of a good demanded by all individuals in an economy at each price. As the price rises, demand falls, both because each person demands less of the good and because some people exit the market.

3. A firm's supply curve gives the amount of a good the firm is willing to supply at each price. It is normally upward sloping, which means that firms supply a greater quantity of the good at higher prices and a lesser quantity at lower prices.

4. The market supply curve gives the total quantity of a good that all firms in the economy are willing to produce at each price. As the price rises, supply rises, both because each firm supplies more of the good and because some additional firms enter the market.

5. The law of supply and demand says that in competitive markets, the equilibrium price is that price at which quantity demanded equals quantity supplied. It is represented on a graph by the intersection of the demand and supply curves.

6. A demand curve *only* shows the relationship between quantity demanded and price. Changes in tastes, in demographic factors, in income, in the prices of other goods, in information, in the availability of credit, or in expectations are reflected in a shift of the entire demand curve.

7. A supply curve *only* shows the relationship between quantity supplied and price. Changes in factors such as technology, the prices of inputs, the natural environment, expectations, or the availability of credit are reflected in a shift of the entire supply curve.

8. It is important to distinguish movements along a demand curve from shifts in the demand curve, and movements along a supply curve from shifts in the supply curve.

KEY TERMS

demand curve
substitutes
complements

demographic effects
supply curve
equilibrium price

excess supply
excess demand

REVIEW QUESTIONS

1. Why does an individual's demand curve normally slope down? Why does a market demand curve normally slope down?

2. Why does a firm's supply curve normally slope up? Why does a market supply curve normally slope up?

3. What is the significance of the point where supply and demand curves intersect?

4. Explain why, if the price of a good is above the equilibrium price, the forces of supply and demand will tend to push the price toward equilibrium. Explain why, if the price of the good is below the equilibrium price, the market will tend to adjust toward equilibrium.

5. Name some factors that could shift the demand curve out to the right.

6. Name some factors that could shift the supply curve in to the left.

PROBLEMS

1. Imagine a company lunchroom that sells pizza by the slice. Using the following data, plot the points and graph the demand and supply curves. What is the equilibrium price and quantity? Find a price at which excess demand would exist and a price at which excess supply would exist, and plot them on your diagram.

Price per slice	Demand (number of slices)	Supply (number of slices)
$1	420	0
$2	210	100
$3	140	140
$4	105	160
$5	84	170

2. Suppose a severe drought hit the sugarcane crop. Predict how this would affect the equilibrium price and quantity in the market for sugar and the market for honey. Draw supply and demand diagrams to illustrate your answers.

3. Imagine that a new invention allows each mine worker to mine twice as much coal. Predict how this will affect the equilibrium price and quantity in the market for coal and the market for heating oil. Draw supply and demand diagrams to illustrate your answer.

4. Americans' tastes have shifted away from beef and toward chicken. Predict how this change affects the equilibrium price and quantity in the market for beef, the market for chicken, and the market for roadside hamburger stands. Draw supply and demand diagrams to illustrate your answer.

5. During the 1970s, the postwar baby boomers reached working age, and it became more acceptable for married women with children to work. Predict how this increase in the number of workers is likely to affect the equilibrium wage and quantity of employment. Draw supply and demand curves to illustrate your answer.

5

USING DEMAND AND SUPPLY

T he concepts of demand and supply are among the most useful in economics. The demand and supply framework explains why doctors are paid more than lawyers, or why the income of unskilled workers has increased less than that of skilled workers. It can also be used to predict what the demand for condominiums or disposable diapers will be fifteen years from now, or what will happen if the government increases the tax on cigarettes. Not only can we predict that prices will change, we can predict by how much they will change.

This chapter has two purposes. The first is to develop some of the concepts required to make these kinds of predictions, and to illustrate how the demand and supply framework can be used in a variety of contexts.

The second is to look at what happens when people interfere with the workings of competitive markets. Rents may seem too high for poor people to afford adequate housing. The price of corn may seem unfairly low, not adequate to compensate farmers for their work. Political pressure constantly develops for government to intervene on behalf of the group that has been disadvantaged by the market—whether it be poor people, farmers, or oil companies (which ask for government help when the price of oil falls). The second part of this chapter traces the consequences of political interventions into the workings of some markets.

KEY QUESTIONS

1. What is meant by the concept of elasticity? Why does it play such an important role in predicting market outcomes?

2. What happens when market outcomes are interfered with, as when the government imposes price floors and ceilings? Why do such interferences give rise to shortages and surpluses?

SENSITIVITY TO PRICE CHANGES: THE PRICE ELASTICITY OF DEMAND

If tomorrow supermarkets across the country were to cut the price of bread or milk by 5 percent, the quantity demanded of these items would not change much. If stores offered the same reduction on premium ice cream, however, demand would increase substantially. Why do price changes sometimes have small effects and at other times large ones? The answer lies in the shape of the demand and supply curves.

The demand for ice cream is more sensitive to price changes than is the demand for milk, and this is reflected in the shape of the demand curves as illustrated in Figure 5.1. The demand curve for ice cream (panel A) is much flatter than the one for milk (panel B). When the demand curve is somewhat flat, a change in price, say from $2.00 a gallon to $2.10, has a large effect on the quantity consumed. In panel A, the demand for ice cream decreases from 100 million pints at a price of $2.00 a pint to 90 million pints at a price of $2.10 per pint.

By contrast, when the demand curve is steep, it means that a change in price has little effect on quantity. In panel B, the demand for milk decreases from 100 million gallons at $2.00 per gallon to 99 million gallons at $2.10 per gallon. But saying that the demand curve is steep or flat just pushes the question back a step: why are some demand curves steeper than others?

The answer is that though substitutes exist for almost every good or service, substitution will be more difficult for some goods and services than for others. When substitution is difficult, when the price of a good increases the quantity demanded will not decrease by much, and when the price falls the quantity demanded will not increase much. The typical consumer does not substitute milk for beer—or for anything else—even if milk becomes a good deal cheaper.

When substitution is easy, on the other hand, a fall in price may lead to a large increase in quantity demanded. For instance, there are many good substitutes for ice cream, including sherbets and frozen yogurts. The price decrease for ice cream means that these close substitutes have become relatively more expensive, and the demand for ice cream would thus increase significantly.

For many purposes, economists need to be precise about how steep or how flat the demand curve is. For precision they use the concept of the **price elasticity of demand** (for short, the price elasticity or the elasticity of demand). The price elasticity of demand is defined as the percentage change in the quantity demanded divided by the percentage change in price. In mathematical terms,

$$\text{elasticity of demand} = \frac{\text{percentage change in quantity demanded}}{\text{percentage change in price}}.$$

If the quantity demanded changes 8 percent in response to a 2 percent change in price, then the elasticity of demand is 4.

(Price elasticities of demand are really *negative* numbers; that is, when the price increases, quantities demanded are reduced. But the convention is to simply refer to the elasticity as a number with the understanding that it is negative.)

It is easiest to calculate the elasticity of demand when there is just a 1 percent change in price. Then the elasticity of demand is just the percent change in the quantity demanded. In the telescoped portion of Figure 5.1A, we see that increasing the price of ice cream from $2.00 a pint to $2.02—a 1 percent

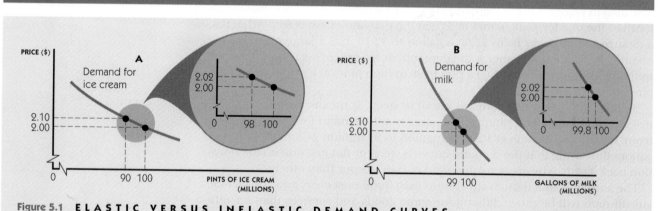

Figure 5.1 ELASTIC VERSUS INELASTIC DEMAND CURVES

Panel A shows a hypothetical demand curve for ice cream. Note that quantity demanded changes rapidly with fairly small price changes, indicating that demand for ice cream is elastic. The telescoped portion of the demand curve shows that a 1 percent rise in price leads to a 2 percent fall in quantity demanded. Panel B shows a hypothetical demand curve for milk. Note that quantity demanded changes very little, regardless of changes in price, meaning that demand for milk is inelastic. The telescoped portion of the demand curve shows that a 1 percent rise in price leads to a .2 percent fall in quantity demanded.

increase in price—reduces the demand from 100 million pints to 98 million, a 2 percent decline. So the price elasticity of demand for ice cream is 2.

By contrast, assume that the price of milk increases from $2.00 a gallon to $2.02 (again a 1 percent increase in price), as shown in the telescoped portion of Figure 5.1B. This reduces demand from 100 million gallons per year to 99.8 million. Demand has gone down by .2 percent, so the price elasticity of demand is therefore .2. Larger values for price elasticity indicate that demand is more sensitive to changes in price. Smaller values indicate that demand is less sensitive to price changes.

PRICE ELASTICITY AND REVENUES

The revenue received by a firm in selling a good is price times quantity. We write this in a simple equation. Letting R denote revenues, p price, and Q quantity:

$$R = pQ$$

This means that when price goes up by 1 percent, whether revenues go up or down depends on the magnitude of the decrease in quantity. If quantity decreases by more than 1 percent, then total revenues decrease; by less than 1 percent, they increase.

We can express this result in terms of the concept of price elasticity. When the elasticity of demand is greater than unity, the change in quantity more than offsets the change in prices, we say that the demand for that good is **relatively elastic,** or *sensitive* to price changes, and revenues decrease as price increases and increase as price decreases.

In the case where the price elasticity is **unity,** or 1, the decrease in the quantity demanded just offsets the increase in the price, so price increases have no effect on revenues. If the price elasticity is less than unity, then when the price of a good increases by 1 percent, the quantity demanded is reduced by less than 1 percent. Since there is not much reduction in demand, elasticities in this range, between 0 and 1, mean that price increases will increase revenues. And price decreases will decrease revenues. We say the demand for that good is **relatively inelastic,** or *insensitive* to price changes.

Business firms must pay attention to the price elasticity of demand for their products. Suppose a cement producer, the only one in town, is considering a 1 percent increase in price. The firm hires an economist to estimate the elasticity of demand, so that the firm will know what will happen to sales when it raises its price. The economist tells the firm that its demand elasticity is 2. This means that if the price of cement rises by 1 percent, the quantity sold will decline by 2 percent.

The firm's executives will not be pleased by the findings. To see why, assume that initially the price of cement was $1,000 per ton, and 100,000 tons were sold. To calculate revenues, you multiply the price times the quantity sold. So initially revenues were $1,000 × 100,000 = $100 million. With a 1 percent increase, the price will be $1,010. If the elasticity of demand is 2, then a

Table 5.1 SOME PRICE ELASTICITIES IN THE U.S. ECONOMY

Industry	Elasticity
Elastic demands	
Purchased meals	2.27
Metals	1.52
Furniture, timber	1.25
Motor vehicles	1.14
Transportation	1.03
Inelastic demands	
Gas, electricity, water	.92
Oil	.91
Chemicals	.89
Beverages	.78
Tobacco	.61
Food	.58
Housing services	.55
Clothing	.49
Books, magazines, newspapers	.34
Meat	.2

Sources: Ahson Mansur and John Whalley, "Numerical Specification of Applied General Equilibrium Models: Estimation, Calibration, and Data," in Scarf and Shoven, eds., *Applied General Equilibrium Analysis* (New York: Cambridge University Press, 1984), p. 109; Hendrik S. Houthakker and Lester D. Taylor, *Consumer Demand in the United States: Analysis and Projections* (Cambridge: Harvard University Press, 1970).

1 percent price increase results in a 2 percent decrease in the quantity sold. With a 2 percent quantity decrease, sales are now 98,000 tons. Revenues are down to $98.98 million ($1,010 × 98,000), a fall of just slightly over 1 percent. Because of the high elasticity, this cement firm's price *increase* leads to a *decrease* in revenues.

The price elasticity of demand works the same way for price decreases. Suppose the cement producer decided to decrease the price of cement 1 percent, to $990. With an elasticity of demand of 2, sales would then increase 2 percent, to 102,000 tons. Thus, revenues would *increase* to $100,980,000 ($990 × 102,000), that is, by a bit less than 1 percent.

EXTREME CASES

There are two extreme cases that deserve attention. One is that of a flat demand curve, a curve that is perfectly horizontal. We say that such a demand curve is perfectly elastic, or has **infinite elasticity,** since even a slight increase in the price results in demand dropping to zero. The other case is that of a steep demand curve, a curve that is perfectly vertical. We say that such a demand curve is perfectly inelastic, or has **zero elasticity,** since no matter what the change in price, demand remains the same.

PRICE ELASTICITIES IN THE U.S. ECONOMY

The elasticity of demand for most foods is low (an increase in price will not affect demand much). The elasticity of demand for most luxuries, such as perfume, ski trips, and Mercedes cars, is high (an increase in price will lead to much less demand). Table 5.1 gives the elasticities of demand for some important goods. For example, the price elasticity of food and of tobacco is about .6, in contrast to the price elasticity for motor vehicles, which is 1.14. The table also shows the price elasticities for broad groups of goods. It may be easy to substitute purchased meals for home-cooked food, but it is difficult to do without food. Thus, the price elasticity of purchased meals is 2.27, while the price elasticity of all food is much lower, at .58. More generally, goods for which it is easy to find substitutes will have high price elasticities; goods for which substitutes cannot easily be found will have low price elasticities.

ELASTICITY AND SLOPE

The elasticity of a curve is not the same as its slope. The best way to see the distinction is to look at the **linear** demand curve. The linear demand curve is a straight line, depicted in Figure 5.2. With a linear demand curve, the quantity demanded is related to the price by the equation

$$Q = a - bp.$$

If $a = 120$, and $b = 2$, at a price of 10, $Q = 100$; at a price of 11, $Q = 98$; at a price of 12, $Q = 96$, and so forth.

The demand curve also gives the price at which a particular quantity of the good will be demanded. Thus, we can rewrite the equation to read

$$p = \frac{a}{b} - \frac{Q}{b},$$

so that (with $a = 120$, $b = 2$ as before), at $Q = 100$, $p = 10$; at $Q = 99$, $p = 10.5$; at $Q = 98$, $p = 11$.

Slope gives the change along the vertical axis per unit change along the horizontal axis. Recall that when we draw the demand curve, we put price on the vertical axis and output on the horizontal axis.

$$\text{slope} = \frac{\text{change in price}}{\text{change in quantity}} = \frac{\Delta p}{\Delta Q}.$$

where the symbol Δ—the Greek letter delta—signifies a change. Thus, ΔQ means the change in quantity and Δp means the change in price. Equivalently, slope is the change in price for a unit change in quantity. In our example, as we

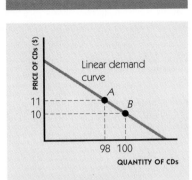

Figure 5.2 LINEAR DEMAND CURVE

The linear demand curve is a straight line; it is represented algebraically by the equation $Q = a - bp$. The slope of the demand curve is a constant. However, the elasticity varies with output. At low outputs (high prices) it is very high. At high outputs (low prices) it is very low.

PRICE ELASTICITY OF DEMAND

Elasticity	Description	Effect on Quantity Demanded of 1% Increase in Price	Effect on Revenues of 1% Increase in Price
Zero	Perfectly inelastic (vertical demand curve)	Zero	Increased by 1%
Between 0 and 1	Inelastic	Reduced by less than 1%	Increased by less than 1%
1	Unitary elasticity	Reduced by 1%	Unchanged
Greater than 1	Elastic	Reduced by more than 1%	Reduced; the greater the elasticity, the more revenue is reduced
Infinite	Perfectly elastic (horizontal demand curve)	Reduced to zero	Reduced to zero

change quantity by 1, price changes by ½. More generally, the slope of the linear demand equation above is ⅙.[1]

The elasticity, as we know, is given by

$$\text{elasticity} = \frac{\text{percentage change in quantity}}{\text{percentage change in price}}.$$

The percentage change in quantity is

$$\text{percentage change in quantity} = \frac{\text{change in quantity}}{\text{quantity}} = \frac{\Delta Q}{Q}.$$

Similarly,

$$\text{percentage change in price} = \frac{\text{change in price}}{\text{price}} = \frac{\Delta p}{p}.$$

We can now rewrite the expression for elasticity as

$$\text{elasticity} = \frac{\Delta Q/Q}{\Delta p/p} = \frac{\Delta Q}{\Delta p} \times \frac{p}{Q}$$

$$= b \times \frac{p}{Q}$$

$$= \frac{1}{\text{slope}} \times \frac{p}{Q}.$$

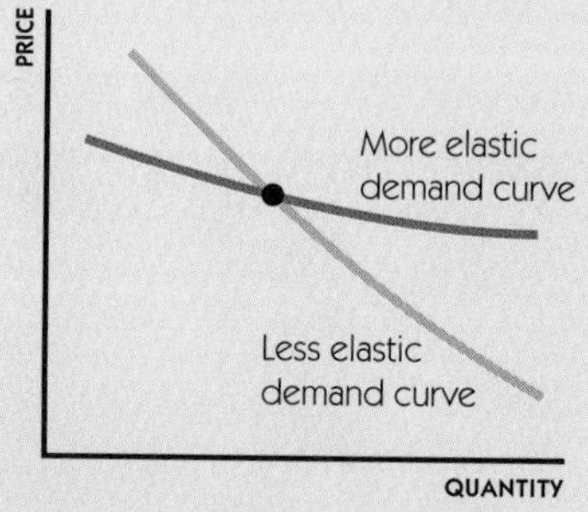

Everywhere along a linear demand curve, the slope is the same; but the elasticity is very high at low levels of output and very low at high levels of output.

The formula for elasticity has one other important implication, illustrated in Figure 5.3. Of two demand curves going through the same point, the flatter demand curve has the higher elasticity at the point of intersection. At the point where they intersect, p and Q (and therefore p/Q) are the same. Only the slopes differ. The one with the smaller slope has the greater elasticity.

Figure 5.3 COMPARING ELASTICITIES

If two demand curves intersect, at the point of intersection, the flatter demand curve has the greater price elasticity.

[1]To see this, observe that at $Q + 1$, the price is

$$\frac{a}{b} - \frac{Q+1}{b}.$$

The change in price is

$$\frac{a}{b} - \frac{Q}{b} - \left(\frac{a}{b} - \frac{Q+1}{b}\right) = \frac{a}{b} - \frac{Q}{b} - \frac{a}{b} + \frac{Q+1}{b} = \frac{1}{b}.$$

SMALL VERSUS LARGE PRICE CHANGES

Often, economists are interested in what would happen if there is a large price change. For instance, if a 50 percent tax is imposed on cigarettes, what will happen to demand?

When price changes are small or moderate, we can *extrapolate*. That is, often we have information about the effect of a small price change. We then extrapolate, assuming that a slightly larger price change will have proportionately larger effects. For example, if a 1 percent change in price results in a 2 percent change in quantity, then a 3 percent change in price will probably result in an approximately 6 percent change in quantity.

With large price changes, however, such extrapolation becomes riskier. The reason is that *price elasticity is typically different at different points along the demand curve.*

THE DETERMINANTS OF THE ELASTICITY OF DEMAND

In our earlier discussion, we noted one of the important determinants of the elasticity of demand: the availability of substitutes. There are two important determinants of the degree of substitutability: the relative price of the good consumed and the length of time it takes to make an adjustment.

When the price of a commodity is low, and the consumption is high, a variety of substitutes exist. Figure 5.4 illustrates the case for aluminum. When the price of aluminum is low, it is used as a food wrap (aluminum foil), as con-

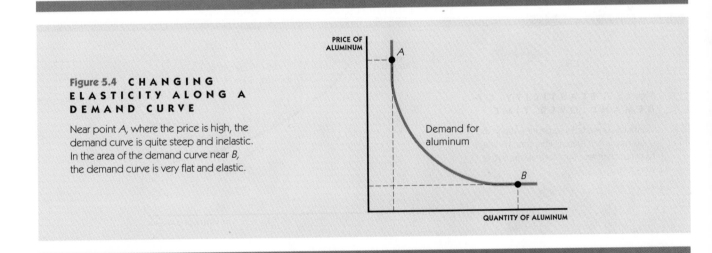

Figure 5.4 CHANGING ELASTICITY ALONG A DEMAND CURVE

Near point *A*, where the price is high, the demand curve is quite steep and inelastic. In the area of the demand curve near *B*, the demand curve is very flat and elastic.

tainers for canned goods, and in airplane frames because it is lightweight. As the price increases, customers seek out substitutes. At first, substitutes are easy to find, and the demand for the product is greatly reduced. For example, plastic wrap can be used instead of aluminum foil. As the price rises still further, tin is used instead of aluminum for cans. At very high prices, say near point *A*, aluminum is used only where its lightweight properties are essential, such as in airplane frames. At this point, it may take a *huge* price increase before some other material becomes an economical substitute.

A second important determinant of the elasticity of demand is time. Because it is always easier to find substitutes and to make other adjustments when you have a longer time to make them, the elasticity of demand is normally larger in the *long run*—in the period in which all adjustments can be made—than it is in the *short run*, when at least some adjustments cannot be made. Figure 5.5 illustrates the difference in shape between short-run and long-run demand curves for gasoline.

The sharp increase in oil prices in the 1970s provides an outstanding example. The short-run price elasticity of gasoline was .2 (a 1 percent increase in price led to only a .2 percent decrease in quantity demanded), while the long-run elasticity was .7 or more; the short-run elasticity of fuel oil was .2, and the long-run elasticity was 1.2. In the short run, consumers were stuck with their old gas-guzzling cars, their drafty houses, and their old fuel-wasting habits. In the long run, however, consumers bought smaller cars, became used to houses with slightly lower temperatures, installed better insulation in their homes, and turned to alternative energy sources. The long-run demand curve was therefore much more elastic (flat) than the short-run curve. Indeed, the long-run elasticity turned out to be much larger than anticipated.

How long is the long run? There is no simple answer. It will vary from product to product. In some cases, adjustments can occur rapidly; in other cases, they are very gradual. As old gas guzzlers wore out, they were replaced with

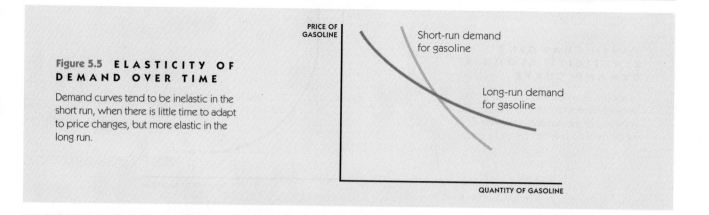

Figure 5.5 ELASTICITY OF DEMAND OVER TIME

Demand curves tend to be inelastic in the short run, when there is little time to adapt to price changes, but more elastic in the long run.

PRICE OF GASOLINE

Short-run demand for gasoline

Long-run demand for gasoline

QUANTITY OF GASOLINE

fuel-efficient compact cars. As furnaces wore out, they were replaced with more efficient ones. New homes are now constructed with more insulation, so that gradually, over time, the fraction of houses that are well insulated is increasing.

THE PRICE ELASTICITY OF SUPPLY

Supply curves normally slope upward. As with demand curves, they are steep in some cases and flat in others. The degree of steepness reflects sensitivity to price changes. A steep supply curve, like the one for oil in Figure 5.6A, means that a large change in price generates only a small change in the quantity firms want to supply. A flatter curve, like the one for chicken in Figure 5.6B, means that a small change in price generates a large change in supply. Economists have developed a precise way of representing the sensitivity of supply to prices in a way that parallels the one already introduced for demand. The **price elasticity of supply** is defined as the percentage change in quantity supplied divided by the percentage change in price (or the percentage change in quantity supplied corresponding to a price change of 1 percent).

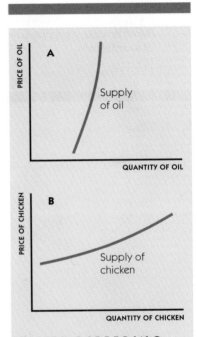

Figure 5.6 DIFFERING ELASTICITIES OF SUPPLY

Panel A shows a supply curve for oil. It is inelastic: quantity supplied increases only a small amount with a rise in price. Panel B shows a supply curve for chicken. It is elastic: quantity supplied increases substantially with a rise in price.

$$\text{Elasticity of supply} = \frac{\text{percentage change in quantity supplied}}{\text{percentage change in price}}.$$

The elasticity of supply of oil is low—an increase in the price of oil will not have a significant effect on the total supply. The elasticity of supply of chicken is high, as President Nixon found out when he imposed price controls in August 1971. When the price of chicken was forced lower than the market equilibrium price, less than 10 percent lower, farmers found it was simply unprofitable to produce chickens and sell them at that price; there was a large decrease in the quantity supplied, and the result was huge shortages.

As is the case with demand, if a 1 percent increase in price results in more than a 1 percent increase in supply, we say the supply curve is elastic. If a 1 percent increase in price results in less than a 1 percent increase in supply, the supply curve is inelastic. In the extreme case of a vertical supply curve—where the amount supplied does not depend at all on price—the curve is said to be perfectly inelastic, or to have *zero* elasticity; and in the extreme case of a horizontal supply curve, the curve is said to be perfectly elastic, or to have *infinite* elasticity.

Just as the demand elasticity differs at different points of the demand curve, so too does the supply curve. Figure 5.7 shows a typical supply curve in manufacturing. An example might be ball bearings. At very low prices, plants are just covering their operating costs. Some plants shut down. In this situation, a small increase in price elicits a large increase in supply. The supply curve is relatively flat (elastic). But eventually, all machines are being worked, and factories are

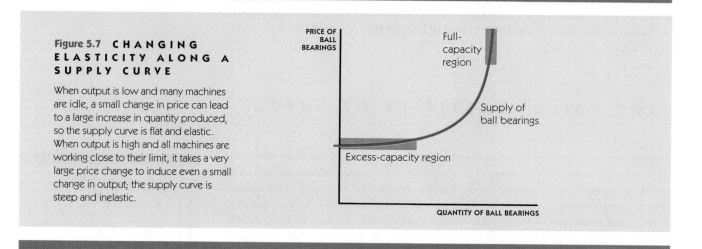

Figure 5.7 CHANGING ELASTICITY ALONG A SUPPLY CURVE

When output is low and many machines are idle, a small change in price can lead to a large increase in quantity produced, so the supply curve is flat and elastic. When output is high and all machines are working close to their limit, it takes a very large price change to induce even a small change in output; the supply curve is steep and inelastic.

also working all three shifts. In this situation, it may be hard to increase supply further, so that the supply curve becomes close to vertical (inelastic). That is, however much the price increases, the supply will not change very much.

PRICE ELASTICITY OF SUPPLY

Elasticity	Description	Effect on Quantity Supplied of 1% Increase in Price
Zero	Perfectly inelastic (vertical suppply curve)	Zero
Between 0 and 1	Inelastic	Increased by less than 1%
1	Unitary elasticity	Increased by 1%
Greater than 1	Elastic	Increased by more than 1%
Infinite	Perfectly elastic (horizontal supply curve)	Infinite increase

SHORT RUN VERSUS LONG RUN

Economists distinguish between the responsiveness of supply to price in the short run and in the long run, just as they do with demand. The long-run supply elasticity is greater than the short-run. We define the short-run supply curve as the supply response *given the current stock of machines and buildings.* The long-run supply curve assumes that firms can adjust the stock of machines and buildings.

Farm crops are a typical example of a good whose supply in the short run is not very sensitive to changes in price; that is, the supply curve is steep (inelastic). After farmers have done their spring planting, they are committed to a certain level of production. If the price of their crop goes up, they cannot go back and plant more. If the price falls, they are stuck with the crop they have. In this case, the supply curve is relatively close to vertical, as illustrated by the steeper curve in Figure 5.8.

The long-run supply curve for many crops, in contrast, is very flat (elastic). A relatively small change in price can lead to a large change in the quantity supplied. A small increase in the price of soybeans relative to the price of corn may induce many farmers to shift their planting from corn and other crops to soybeans, generating a large increase in the quantity of soybeans. This is illustrated in Figure 5.8 by the flatter curve.

Earlier, we noted the response of consumers to the marked increase in the price of oil in the 1970s. The long-run demand elasticity was much higher than the short-run. So too for supply. The higher prices drove firms, both in the United States and abroad in places like Canada, Mexico, and the North Sea off the coast of Great Britain, to explore for more oil. Though the alternative supplies could not be increased much in the short run (the short-run supply curve was inelastic, or steep), in the long run new supplies were found. Thus, the long-run supply elasticity was much higher (the supply curve was flatter) than the short-run supply elasticity.

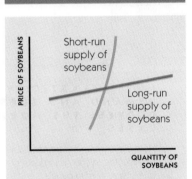

Figure 5.8 ELASTICITY OF SUPPLY OVER TIME

Supply curves may be inelastic in the short run and very elastic in the long run, as in the case of agricultural crops like soybeans.

USING DEMAND AND SUPPLY ELASTICITIES

When the demand curve for a good such as wine shifts to the right—when, for instance, wine becomes more popular, so that at each price the demand is greater—there is an increase in both the equilibrium price of wine and the quantity demanded, or consumed. Similarly, when the supply curve for a good such as corn shifts to the left—because, for instance, of a drought that hurt the year's crop, so that at each price farmers supply less—there is an increase in the equilibrium price of corn and a decrease in quantity. Knowing that the shifts in the demand or supply curve will lead to an adjustment in both price *and* quantity is helpful, but it is even more useful to know whether most of the impact of a change will be on price or on quantity. For this, we have to consider the price elasticity of both the demand and supply curves.

Figure 5.9 illustrates the typical range of outcomes. If the supply curve is highly elastic (approaching the horizontal, as in panel A), shifts in the demand curve will be reflected more in changes in quantity than in price. If the supply curve is *relatively* inelastic (approaching the vertical, as in panel B), shifts in the demand curve will be reflected more in changes in price than in quantity.

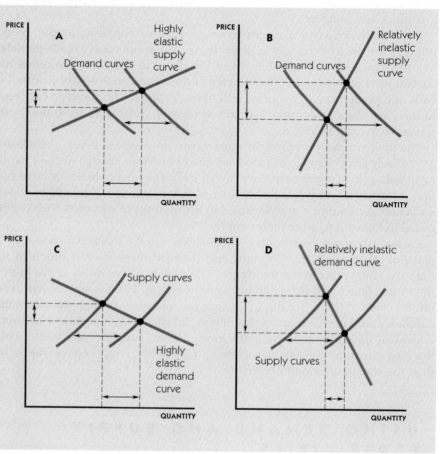

Figure 5.9 ELASTICITY OF DEMAND AND SUPPLY CURVES: THE NORMAL CASES

Normally, shifts in the demand curve will be reflected in changes in both price and quantity, as seen in panels A and B. When the supply curve is highly elastic, shifts in the demand curve will result mainly in changes in quantities; if it is relatively inelastic, shifts in the demand curve will result mainly in price changes. Likewise, shifts in the supply curve will be reflected in changes in both price and quantity, as seen in panels C and D. If the demand curve is highly elastic, shifts in the supply curve will result mainly in changes in quantities; if it is relatively inelastic, shifts in the supply curve will result mainly in price changes.

If the demand curve is highly elastic (approaching the horizontal as in panel C), shifts in the supply curve will be reflected more in changes in quantity than in price. Finally, if the demand curve is *relatively* inelastic (approaching the vertical as in panel D), shifts in the supply curve will be reflected more in changes in price than in quantity.

The extreme cases can be easily seen by extending the graphs in Figure 5.9. If one tilts the supply curve in panel A to be completely flat (perfectly elastic), a shift in the demand curve will have no effect on price. If one tilts the supply curve in panel B to be vertical (perfectly inelastic), a shift in the demand curve will have no effect on quantity.

LONG-RUN VERSUS SHORT-RUN ADJUSTMENTS

Because demand and supply curves are likely to be less elastic (more vertical) in the short run than in the long run, shifts in the demand and supply curves are more likely to be reflected in price changes in the short run, but in quantity changes in the long run. In fact, price increases in the short run provide the signals to firms to increase their production. Therefore, short-run price increases can be thought of as responsible for the output increases that occur in the long run.

TAX POLICY AND THE LAW OF SUPPLY AND DEMAND

For many questions of public policy, understanding the law of supply and demand is vital. One of the important ways economists use this law is in projecting the effect of taxes. Assume that the tax on a pack of cigarettes is increased by 10 cents, that the tax is imposed on cigarette manufacturers, and that all the companies try to pass on the cost increase to consumers, by raising the price of a pack by 10 cents. At the higher price, fewer cigarettes will be consumed, with the decrease in demand depending on the price elasticity of demand. With lower demand, firms must reduce their price if demand is to equal supply; by how much depends on the price elasticity of supply. The new equilibrium is depicted in Figure 5.10A.

For firms to produce the same amount as before, they must receive 10 cents more per pack (which they pass on to the government). Thus, the supply curve is shifted up by 10 cents. Since the demand for cigarettes is relatively inelastic, this shift will result in a large increase in price and a relatively small decrease in quantity demanded.

When a tax on producers results in consumers paying a higher price, economists say the tax is "passed on" or "shifted" to consumers. The fact that the consumer bears the tax (even though it is collected from the producers) does not mean that the producers are "powerful" or have conspired together. It simply reflects the system of supply and demand. Note, however, that the price did not rise the full 10 cents. Producers receive slightly lower after-tax prices and therefore bear a small fraction of the tax burden.

A tax imposed on a good for which the demand is very elastic leads to a different result. Assume, for instance, that the government decides to tax cheddar cheese (but no other cheeses). Since many cheeses are almost like cheddar, the demand curve for cheddar cheese is very elastic. In this case, as Figure 5.10B makes clear, most of the tax is absorbed by the producer, who receives (net of tax) a lower price. Production of cheddar cheese is reduced drastically as a consequence.

SHORTAGES AND SURPLUSES

The law of supply and demand works so well in a developed modern economy, most of the time, that everyone can take it for granted. If you are willing to pay the "market price"—the prevailing price of the good, determined by the

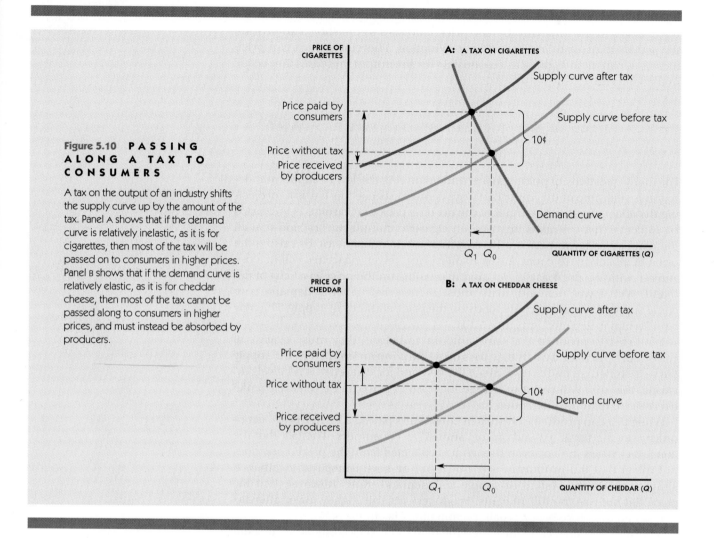

Figure 5.10 PASSING ALONG A TAX TO CONSUMERS

A tax on the output of an industry shifts the supply curve up by the amount of the tax. Panel A shows that if the demand curve is relatively inelastic, as it is for cigarettes, then most of the tax will be passed on to consumers in higher prices. Panel B shows that if the demand curve is relatively elastic, as it is for cheddar cheese, then most of the tax cannot be passed along to consumers in higher prices, and must instead be absorbed by producers.

intersection of demand and supply—you can obtain almost any good or service. Similarly, if a seller of a good or service is willing to charge no more than the market price, he can always sell what he wants to.

When the price is set so that demand equals supply—so that any individual can get as much as she wants at that price, and any supplier can sell the amount he wants at that price—economists say that the **market clears.** But when the market does not clear, there are shortages or surpluses. To an economist, a **shortage** means that people would like to buy something, but they simply cannot find it for sale at the going price. A **surplus** means that sellers would like to sell their product, but they cannot sell as much of it as they would like at the going price. These cases where the market does not seem to be working are often the most forceful reminders of the importance of the

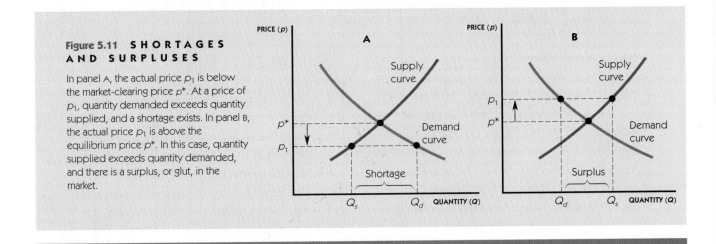

Figure 5.11 SHORTAGES AND SURPLUSES

In panel A, the actual price p_1 is below the market-clearing price p^*. At a price of p_1, quantity demanded exceeds quantity supplied, and a shortage exists. In panel B, the actual price p_1 is above the equilibrium price p^*. In this case, quantity supplied exceeds quantity demanded, and there is a surplus, or glut, in the market.

law of supply and demand. The problem is that the "going price" is not the market equilibrium price.

Shortages and surpluses can be seen in the standard supply and demand diagram shown in Figure 5.11. In both panels A and B, the market equilibrium price is p^*. In panel A, the going price, p_1, is below p^*. At this price, demand exceeds supply; you can see this by reading down to the horizontal axis. Demand is Q_d; supply is Q_s. The gap between the two points is the "shortage." With the shortage, consumers scramble to get the limited supply available at the going price.

In panel B, the going price, p_1, is above p^*. At this price, demand is less than supply. Again we denote the demand by Q_d and the supply by Q_s. There is a surplus in the market of $Q_s - Q_d$. Now sellers are scrambling to find buyers.

At various times and for various goods, markets have not cleared. There have been shortages of apartments in New York; farm surpluses have plagued both Western Europe and the United States; in 1973, there was a shortage of gasoline, with cars lined up in long lines outside of gasoline stations. Unemployment is a type of surplus, when people who want to work find that they cannot sell their labor services at the going wage.

In some markets, like the stock market, the adjustment of prices to shifts in the demand and supply curves tends to be very rapid. In other cases, such as in the housing market, the adjustments tend to be sluggish. When price adjustments are sluggish, shortages or surpluses may appear as prices adjust. Houses tend not to sell quickly, for instance, during periods of decreased demand, which translate only slowly into lower housing prices.

When the market is not adjusting quickly toward equilibrium, economists say that prices are **sticky.** Even in these cases, the analysis of market equilibrium is useful. It indicates the direction of the changes—if the equilibrium price exceeds the current price, prices will tend to rise. Moreover, the rate at

No government likes to increase taxes. It doesn't sit well with voters. In 1990, as pressures to reduce the mounting federal deficit increased, and the scope for expenditure reduction seemed to be exhausted, there was an attempt to find the least painful way of increasing taxes. A 10 percent luxury tax was imposed on such big ticket items as pleasure boats, private airplanes, high-priced cars, jewelry, and furs. Such luxury taxes are often popular because no one *has* to pay them: rich people pay them only because they *choose* to buy these goods. All taxes are painful to someone, but a tax that weighs only on rich people who are buying frivolous luxuries is one of the more socially painless ways to raise money.

But the success of these taxes depends on the elasticity of demand. If the demand is highly elastic, slight increases in the price resulting from the tax will drive demand down, so little revenue would be raised.

As it turned out, the demand for these luxury goods was reasonably elastic. Sales of pleasure boats fell by nearly 90 percent in south Florida in early 1991, as prospective buyers bought boats in the Bahamas to avoid paying the tax. Sales of high-priced cars like Mercedes and Lexus also fell substantially. The situation of sellers of luxury goods was made even worse by the recession in 1991, which reduced the income of many prospective buyers, thus shifting the demand curve for luxuries back to the left as well.

This unexpected high elasticity of demand carried two bits of bad news for the economy. First, rather than falling on the wealthy as had been hoped, the burden of the new luxury tax actually ended up falling on the workers and retailers who manufacture and sell these luxury items. Second, the luxury tax raised far less money than had been expected. The Congressional Budget Office had forecast that the tax would raise about $1.5 billion over five years. But in 1991, it raised only about $30 million. Once the costs of setting up and enforcing the new tax were considered, it probably lost money for the government in its first year. Not surprisingly, the tax was repealed in 1993.

Sources: Bernard Baumohl, "Tempest in a Yacht Basin," *Time,* July 1, 1991, p. 52; Nick Ravo, "Big Boats Take It on the Chin," *New York Times,* April 14, 1991, sec. III, p. 9.

which prices fall or rise is often related to the gap, at the going price, between the quantity demanded and the quantity supplied.

INTERFERING WITH THE LAW OF SUPPLY AND DEMAND

The law of supply and demand, which governs how prices are set, can produce results that some individuals or groups do not like. For example, a reduced supply of oil may lead to a higher equilibrium price for oil. The higher price is not a malfunction of the law of supply and demand, but this is little comfort to those who use gasoline to power their cars and oil to heat their homes. Low demand for unskilled labor may lead to very low wages for unskilled workers. An increase in the demand for apartments in New York City leads, in the short run (with an inelastic supply), to an increase in rents—to the delight of landlords, but the dismay of renters.

In each of these cases, pressure from those who did not like the outcome of market processes has led government to act. The price of oil and natural gas was, at one time, regulated; minimum wage laws set a minimum limit on what employers can pay, even if the workers are willing to work for less; and rent control laws limit what landlords can charge. The concerns behind these interferences with the market are understandable, but the agitation for government action is based on two errors.

First, someone (or some group) was assigned blame for the change: the oil price rises were blamed on the oil companies, low wages on the employer, and rent increases on the landlord. As already explained, economists emphasize the role of anonymous market forces in determining these prices. After all, if landlords or oil companies are basically the same people today as they were last week, there must be some reason that they started charging different prices this week. Sometimes the price increase is the result of producers colluding to raise prices. This was the case in 1973, when the oil-exporting countries got together to raise the price of oil. The more common situation, however, is illustrated by the increase in the price of oil in August 1990, after Iraq's invasion of Kuwait. There was no collusion this time. The higher price simply reflected the anticipated reduction in the supply of oil. People rushed to buy, increasing short-term demand and pushing up the equilibrium price.

The second error was to forget that as powerful as governments may be, they can no more repeal the law of supply and demand than they can repeal the law of gravity. When they interfere with its working, the forces of supply and demand will not be balanced. There will either be excess supply or excess demand. Shortages and surpluses create problems of their own, often worse than the original problem the government was supposed to resolve.

Two straightforward examples of government overruling the law of supply and demand are **price ceilings,** which impose a maximum price that can be charged for a product, and **price floors,** which impose a minimum price. Rent control laws are price ceilings, and minimum wage laws and agricultural

CLOSE-UP: RENT CONTROL IN NEW YORK CITY

New York City adopted rent control on a "temporary" basis during World War II. Half a century later, it is still in effect. Journalist William Tucker has been collecting stories of well-to-do New Yorkers who benefit from this situation. The minority leader in the state senate, for example, pays $1,800 a month for a *ten-room* apartment overlooking Central Park. A newcomer pays $1,500 for a one-bedroom apartment in midtown Manhattan. A housing court judge who hears rent-control cases pays $93 a month for a two-bedroom apartment in a building where studio apartments (with no separate bedroom) rent for $1,200.

Of course, people who have been able to pay far below market value for decades tend to favor rent control. But since rent control is effectively a price ceiling, economists, looking to the law of supply and demand, would expect it to lead to problems and indeed it has.

For example, despite a serious shortage of housing in New York City, over 300,000 rental units have simply been abandoned. Almost no new rental housing is being built. Only about 2 percent of the apartments in New York are vacant at any time, as opposed to vacancy rates averaging 6 percent in East Coast cities, like Baltimore, that do not have rent control. When many people are struggling to obtain one of the few available apartments, poor people tend to lose out.

Even with rent control, the *average* rent in New York City is little different from some other large cities, like Chicago. But in Chicago, a newcomer can find an apartment at something close to the average rent. In New York, newcomers often have to make special payments to secure an apartment, and then pay extraordinarily high rents that help to subsidize those who have been living there for a long time.

Attempting to provide moderate and low-cost housing is a worthy public goal. But the example of New York and other rent-controlled cities shows that even when the goal is worthy, the law of supply and demand does not simply fade away.

Sources: William Tucker, "We All Pay for Others' Great Apartment Deals," *Newsday,* May 24, 1986; Tucker, "Moscow on the Hudson," *The American Spectator* (July 1986), pp. 19–21; Tucker, "Where Do the Homeless Come From?" *National Review,* September 25, 1987, pp. 32–43.

price supports are price floors. A closer look at each will help highlight the perils of interfering with the law of supply and demand.

PRICE CEILINGS: THE CASE OF RENT CONTROL

Price ceilings—setting a maximum charge—are always tempting to governments because they seem an easy way to assure that everyone will be able to afford a particular product. Thus, in the last couple of decades in the United States, price ceilings have been set for a wide range of goods, from chickens to oil to interest rates. In each case the result has been to create shortages at the controlled price. People want to buy more of a good than producers want to sell, because producers have no incentive to produce more of the good. Those who can buy at the cheaper price benefit; producers and those unable to buy suffer.

The effect of **rent control** laws—setting the maximum rent that a landlord can charge for a one-bedroom apartment, for example—is illustrated by Figure 5.12. In panel A, R^* is the market equilibrium rental rate, at which the demand for housing equals the supply. However, the local government is concerned that at R^*, many poor people cannot afford housing in the city, so it imposes a law that says that rents may be no higher than R_1. At R_1, there is an excess demand for apartments. While the motives behind the government

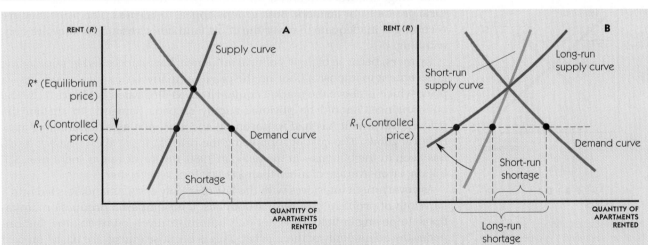

Figure 5.12 A PRICE CEILING: RENT CONTROL

Rent control laws limit the rents apartment owners may charge. If rents are held down to R_1, below the market-clearing level R^*, as in panel A, there will be excess demand for apartments. Panel B shows the long-run response. The supply of rental housing is more elastic in the long run, since landlords can refuse to build new apartment buildings, or they can sell existing apartments as condominiums. The price ceiling eventually leads to the quantity supplied being even farther below the quantity demanded.

action may well have been praiseworthy, the government has created an artificial scarcity.

The problems caused by rent control are likely to be worse in the long run than in the short run, because long-run supply curves are more elastic than short-run supply curves. In the short run, the quantity of apartments does not change much. But in the long run, the quantity of apartments can decline for several reasons, as landlords try to minimize the losses from rent control. Apartments may be abandoned as they deteriorate; they can be converted to condominiums and sold instead of rented; and apartment owners may not wish to construct new ones if they cannot charge enough in rent to cover their costs.

Figure 5.12B illustrates how the housing shortages under rent control will increase over time. Rent control results in all *existing* renters being better off, at least as long as the landlord stays in the business. But the quantity of available rental housing will decrease, so that many would-be residents will be unable to find rental housing in the market. Since renters tend to be poorer than those who can buy a home, a shortage of rental housing will tend to hurt the poor most.

PRICE FLOORS: THE CASE OF AGRICULTURAL SUPPORTS

Just as consumers try to get government to limit the prices they pay, sellers would like the government to put a floor on the prices they receive: a minimum wage for workers and a minimum price on wheat and other agricultural products for farmers. Both groups appeal to fairness. The price they are receiving is inadequate to cover the effort (and other resources) they are contributing.

Farmers, because of their political influence, have succeeded in persuading government to impose a floor on the prices of many agricultural products—a price which is above the market equilibrium, as illustrated in Figure 5.13. The consequences should be obvious: supply exceeds demand. To sustain the price, government has had to purchase and stockpile huge amounts of agricultural goods. The cost of supporting the price at these above market levels has been in the billions—at the peak, in 1986, the government spent over $25 billion, or an average of more than $11,000 for every farmer.

As government interferes with the law of supply and demand, it is led into a labyrinth of problems. To reduce supplies, it has imposed production limitations. Imposing limitations is not only administratively cumbersome, but impedes the adaptability of the market. This is because quotas are based on past production, but some areas should be expanding, and others contracting, in response to changed circumstances. The quota system does not allow this to happen easily. Worse still, wheat farmers have to keep producing wheat, lest they lose their quota. But this means that they cannot rotate their crops—and this is bad for the soil and the environment. To avoid the build up of surpluses, Congress has enacted a program to subsidize exports. But these subsidies have angered other countries, which view it as unfair competition. Our

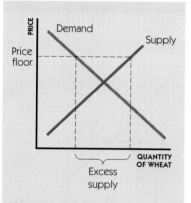

Figure 5.13 PRICE FLOORS

If the government imposes a price floor on, say, wheat—at a price in excess of the market equilibrium—there will be excess supply. Either the government will have to purchase the excess, putting it into storage or discarding it in some way, or it will have to limit production.

subsidies of wheat exports to Mexico have hurt our economic relations with Argentina. Even Mexico has viewed them with alarm, as they have interfered with Mexico's attempts to reform its agricultural sector.

Government is aware of these problems, but the political pressures to maintain high prices kept the price support program in place for a long time. The agricultural bill passed in 1996 is intended to lead to a phase-out for most major crops.

ALTERNATIVE SOLUTIONS

Large changes in prices cause distress. It is natural to try to find scapegoats and to look to the government for a solution. Such situations call for compassion, and the economists' caution can seem coldhearted. But the fact remains

USING ECONOMICS: CALCULATING RESPONSES TO OIL PRICE CHANGES

As oil prices have fluctuated during the past decade, government analysts have repeatedly had to calculate the implications of those changes for oil consumption. If the United States consumes more oil, it will need to import more, and that in turn affects the balance of payments.

Assume prices of oil are expected to rise by 10 percent over the next two years. What will this do to the consumption of oil in the United States, if the elasticity of demand is .7? An elasticity of demand of .7 means that a 1 percent increase in price reduces demand by .7 percent. So a 10 percent increase in price will reduce demand by 7 percent. If the initial level of demand is 100 million barrels, demand will fall to 93 million.

What happens to total expenditures? If the initial price was $20 a barrel, total expenditures initially were $2 billion. Now, with a price of $22 a barrel (a 10 percent increase from $20), they have gone up to $22 × 93 million = $2.04 billion.

What happens to imports? The United States imports oil from abroad, and because the price of each barrel it imports has increased, it is worse off. But this is partly offset by the decreased use of oil. Assume the United States produces 50 million barrels, and that production remains unchanged. Initially, it imported 50 million, but now, it imports only 43 million. U.S. expenditures on imports actually fall: before the expenditures were 50 million × $20 = $1 billion; now they are 43 million barrels × $22 per barrel = $946 million.

In the long run, the elasticity of demand is greater, so the reduction in consumption is larger. If the long-run elasticity is 1, then consumption falls to 90 million barrels, and expenditures remain unchanged. Imports fall to 40 million barrels, with a value of $880 million.

that in competitive markets, price changes are simply the impersonal workings of the law of supply and demand; without price changes, there will be shortages and surpluses. The examples of government attempts to interfere with the workings of supply and demand provide an important cautionary tale: one ignores the workings of the law of supply and demand only at one's peril. This does not mean, however, that the government should simply ignore the distress caused by large price and wage changes. It only means that government must take care in addressing the problems; price controls, including price ceilings and floors, are unlikely to be effective instruments.

Later chapters will discuss ways in which the government can address dissatisfaction with the consequences of the law of supply and demand—by making use of the power of the market rather than trying to fight against it. For example, if the government is concerned with low wages paid to unskilled workers, it can try to increase the demand for these workers. A shift to the right in the demand curve will increase the wages these workers receive. The government can do this either by subsidizing firms that hire unskilled workers or by providing more training to these workers and thus increasing their productivity.

If the government wants to increase the supply of housing to the poor, it can provide housing subsidies for the poor, which will elicit a greater supply. If government wants to conserve on the use of gasoline, it can impose a tax on gasoline. Noneconomists often object that these sorts of economic incentives have other distasteful consequences, and sometimes they do. But government policies that take account of the law of supply and demand will tend to be more effective, with fewer unfortunate side effects, than policies that ignore the predictable economic consequences that follow from disregarding the law of supply and demand.

REVIEW AND PRACTICE

SUMMARY

1. The price elasticity of demand describes how sensitive the quantity demanded of a good is to changes in the price of the good. When demand is inelastic, an increase in the price has little effect on quantity demanded and the demand curve is steep; when demand is elastic, an increase in the price has a large effect on quantity demanded and the curve is flat. Demand for necessities is usually quite inelastic; demand for luxuries is elastic.

2. The price elasticity of supply describes how sensitive the quantity supplied of a good is to changes in the price of the good. If price changes do not induce much change in supply, the supply curve is very steep and is said to be inelastic. If the supply curve is very flat, indicating that price changes cause large changes in supply, supply is said to be elastic.

3. The extent to which a shift in the supply curve is reflected in price or quantity depends on the shape of the demand curve. The more elastic the demand, the more a given shift in the supply curve will be reflected in changes in equilibrium quantities and the less it will be reflected in changes in equilibrium prices. The more inelastic the demand, the more a given shift in the supply curve will be reflected in changes in equilibrium prices and the less it will be reflected in changes in equilibrium quantities.

4. Likewise, the extent to which a shift in the demand curve is reflected in price or quantity depends on the shape of the supply curve.

5. Demand and supply curves are likely to be more elastic in the long run than in the short run. Therefore a shift in the demand or supply curve is likely to have a larger price effect in the short run and a larger quantity effect in the long run.

6. Elasticities can be used to predict to what extent consumer prices rise when a tax is imposed on a good. If the demand curve for a good is very inelastic, consumers in effect have to pay the tax. If the demand curve is very elastic, the quantities produced and the price received by producers are likely to decline considerably.

7. Government regulations may prevent a market from moving toward its equilibrium price, leading to shortages or surpluses. Price ceilings lead to excess demand. Price floors lead to excess supply.

KEY TERMS

price elasticity of
  demand
infinite elasticity
zero elasticity

price elasticity of
  supply
market clearing
sticky prices

price ceilings
price floors

REVIEW QUESTIONS

1. What is meant by the elasticity of demand and the elasticity of supply? Why do economists find these concepts useful?

2. Is the slope of a perfectly elastic demand or supply curve horizontal or vertical? Is the slope of a perfectly inelastic demand or supply curve horizontal or vertical? Explain.

3. If the elasticity of demand is unity, what happens to total revenue as the price increases? What if the demand for a product is very inelastic? What if it is very elastic?

4. Under what condition will a shift in the demand curve result mainly in a change in quantity? in price?

5. Under what condition will a shift in the supply curve result mainly in a change in price? in quantity?

6. Why do the elasticities of demand and supply tend to change from the short run to the long run?

7. Under what circumstances will a tax on a product be passed along to consumers?

8. Why do price ceilings tend to lead to shortages? Why do price floors tend to lead to surpluses?

PROBLEMS

1. Suppose the price elasticity of demand for gasoline is .2 in the short run and .7 in the long run. If the price of gasoline rises 28 percent, what effect on quantity demanded will this have in the short run? in the long run?

2. Imagine that the short-run price elasticity of supply for a farmer's corn is .3, while the long-run price elasticity is 2. If prices for corn fall 30 percent, what are the short-run and long-run changes in quantity supplied? What are the short- and long-run changes in quantity supplied if prices rise by 15 percent? What happens to the farmer's revenues in each of these situations?

3. Assume that the demand curve for hard liquor is highly inelastic and the supply curve for hard liquor is highly elastic. If the tastes of the drinking public shift away from hard liquor, will the effect be larger on price or on quantity? If the federal government decides to impose a tax on manufacturers of hard liquor, will the effects be larger on price or on quantity? What is the effect of an advertising program that succeeds in discouraging people from drinking? Draw diagrams to illustrate each of your answers.

4. Imagine that wages (the price of labor) are sticky in the labor market, that is, wages do not change in the short run, and that a supply of new workers enters that market. Will the market be in equilibrium in the short run? Why or why not? If not, explain the relationship you would expect to see between the quantity demanded and supplied, and draw a diagram to illustrate. Explain how sticky wages in the labor market affect unemployment.

5. For each of the following markets, explain whether you would expect prices in that market to be relatively sticky or not:
   (a) the stock market;
   (b) the market for autoworkers;
   (c) the housing market;
   (d) the market for cut flowers;
   (e) the market for pizza-delivery people.

6. Suppose a government wishes to assure that its citizens can afford adequate housing. Consider three ways of pursuing that goal. One method is

to pass a law requiring that all rents be cut by one-quarter. A second method offers a subsidy to all builders of homes. A third provides a subsidy directly to renters equal to one-quarter of the rent they pay. Predict what effect each of these proposals would have on the price and quantity of rental housing in the short run and the long run.

CHAPTER 6

TIME AND RISK

 hen Bill Clinton ran for the presidency in 1992, a central part of his platform was that the country was not investing enough in its future. The *choices* we make today affect living standards in the future. Much of economics is thus *future oriented.* The basic principles of markets and making choices—the law of supply and demand—apply here as well. But there are some distinctive aspects of future-oriented choices that contrast with the static nature of the conventional supply and demand equilibrium analysis. The first part of this chapter focuses on those aspects. We show how prices in the present, for instance, are linked to expectations of prices in the future.

While the Republicans and Democrats differ on many issues, they are united on the importance of encouraging entrepreneurship. A large percentage of new jobs are created in new and small businesses. But starting new businesses is risky—one of the many risks that permeate the economy. How do individuals and firms respond to risks? And how does uncertainty affect markets? The function of insurance is to protect against risk. Homeowners typically buy fire insurance, for instance. But many risks cannot be protected against so easily. A firm planning to bring out a new product, for example, cannot buy insurance to protect against the risk that it will fail in the marketplace. How well market economies handle the problems created by risk has much to do with their successes. The second part of this chapter investigates insurance and other markets that protect against risk.

KEY QUESTIONS

1. How do we compare a dollar received next year or in five years' time with a dollar received today?

2. What determines the demand for an asset like gold, which is purchased mainly with the intent of selling it at some later date? What determines shifts in the demand curve for assets?

3. How do individuals, firms, and markets respond to risk?

4. What are some of the central problems facing insurance firms? Why are there many risks for which insurance is not available?

5. Why is entrepreneurship so important?

INTEREST

When you put money into a bank account you are involved in a future-oriented transaction. You have loaned your money to the bank, and the bank has promised to pay you back. But banks offer more than security; they offer you a *return* on your savings. This return is called **interest.** If you put $1,000 in the bank at the beginning of the year, and the interest rate is 10 percent per year, you will receive $1,100 at the end of the year. The $100 is the payment of interest, while the $1,000 is the repayment of the **principal,** the original amount lent to the bank.

To an economist, the interest rate is a price. Normally, we express prices in terms of dollars. If the price of an orange is $1.00, that means we must give up $1.00 to get one orange. Economists talk about the relative price of two goods as the amount of one good you have to give up to get one more unit of the other. The relative price is the ratio of the two "dollar" prices.

For example, if the price of an apple is $.50 and the price of an orange is $1.00, then the relative price (that is, the ratio of the prices) is 2. If we wish to consume one more orange, we have to give up two apples. Thus, the relative price describes a trade-off. Similarly, if the interest rate is 10 percent, by giving up $1.00 worth of consumption today, a saver can have $1.10 worth of consumption next year. Thus, the rate of interest tells us how much future consumption we can get by giving up $1.00 worth of current consumption. It tells us the relative price between the present and the future.

THE TIME VALUE OF MONEY

Interest rates are normally positive. If you have $1.00 today, you can put it into the bank and, if the interest rate is 5 percent, receive $1.05 at the end of next year. In short, $1.00 becomes, in this example, $1.05 next year.

A dollar today is worth more than a dollar in the future. Economists call this the **time value of money.** The concept of **present discounted value** tells us precisely how to measure the time value of money. The present discounted value of $100 a year from now is what you would pay today for $100 a year from now. Suppose the interest rate is 10 percent. If you put $90.91 in the bank today, at the end of the year you will receive $9.09 interest, which together with the original amount will total $100. Thus, $90.91 is the present discounted value of $100 a year from now, if the interest rate is 10 percent.

There is a simple formula for calculating the present discounted value of any amount to be received a year from now: just divide the amount by 1 plus the annual rate of interest. The annual rate of interest is often denoted by r.

To check this formula, consider the present discounted value of $100. According to the formula, it is $100 / (1 + r)$. In other words, take the present discounted value, $100 / (1 + r)$, and put it in the bank. At the end of the year you will have

$$\frac{\$100}{1+r} \times (1+r) = \$100,$$

confirming our conclusion that $100 / (1 + r)$ today is the same as $100 one year from now.

PRESENT DISCOUNTED VALUE

Present discounted value of $1.00 next year $= \dfrac{\$1.00}{1 + \text{interest rate}}$.

Equivalently, denoting the interest rate by r, the right-hand side of the equation

becomes $\dfrac{\$1.00}{1 + r}$.

If the interest rate increases, the present discounted value of $100 a year from now will decrease. If the interest rate should rise to 20 percent, for example, the present discounted value of $100 a year from now becomes $83.33 (100/1.2).

The concept of present discounted value is important because so many decisions in economics are oriented to the future. Whether the decision is made by a person buying a house or saving money for retirement, or by a company building a factory or making an investment, the decision maker must be able to value money that will be received one, two, five, or ten years in the future.

THE MARKET FOR LOANABLE FUNDS

The previous section explained how the interest rate is a price, similar to the price of any other good, like apples and oranges. The price of borrowing a dollar (what you have to pay back in a year) is the dollar plus the annual rate of interest. In calculating the present discounted values, firms or individuals take the interest rate as given. But obviously the interest rate changes over time. How is the interest rate determined? Like other prices, the interest rate is determined by the law of supply and demand.

At any given time, there are some people and companies who would like to borrow, so they can spend more than they currently have. Rachel has her first job and knows she needs a car for transportation; George needs kitchen equipment, tables, and chairs to open his sandwich shop. Others would like to save, or spend less than they currently have. John is putting aside money for his children's college education and for his retirement; Bill is putting aside money to make a down payment on a house.

Exchanges that occur over time are called **intertemporal trades.** The gains from trade discussed in Chapter 3 apply equally well here. When one individual lends money to another, both gain. John and Bill can lend money to Rachel and George. John and Bill will get paid interest in the future, to compensate them for letting Rachel and George use their funds now. Rachel and George are willing to pay the interest because to them, having the funds today is worth more to them than waiting. The borrower may be a business firm like the one owned by George, who believes that with these funds he will be able to make an investment that will yield a return far higher than the interest rate he is charged today. Or the borrower may be an individual facing some emergency, such as a medical crisis, that requires funds today. The borrower may simply be a free spirit, wishing to consume as much as he can (as much as lenders are willing to give him), and letting the future take care of itself.

How is the supply of funds to be equated with the demand? As the interest rate rises, some borrowers will be discouraged from borrowing. Rachel may decide to ride her bicycle to work and postpone buying a new car until she can save up the money herself (or until interest rates come down). At the same time, as the interest rate rises, some savers may be induced to save more. Their incentives for savings have increased. John realizes that every extra dollar he saves today will produce more money in the future, so he may put more aside.[1] Figure 6.1 shows the supply and demand curves for loanable funds. Here the interest rate is the "price," and the amount of money loaned and borrowed is the quantity. At r^*, the demand for funds equals the supply of funds.

We can now explain why the equilibrium interest rate is positive. If it were zero or negative, prospective borrowers would demand more funds than prospective savers would be willing to supply. Indeed, negative interest rates would mean that people could borrow to consume today and pay back less in the future, and that savers would receive less in the future than the amount they saved. Only at a positive interest rate can the demand for loans be equated to the supply.

In our economy, borrowers and lenders do not usually meet face to face. Instead, banks and other financial institutions serve as intermediaries, collecting savings from those who want to save and disbursing money to those who want to borrow. These intermediaries help make the market for loans work smoothly. For their services, the intermediaries charge fees, which can be measured as the difference between the interest rate they pay savers and the interest rate they charge borrowers.

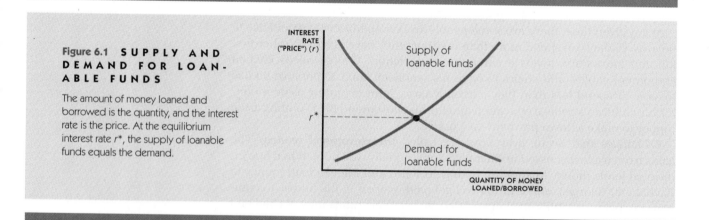

Figure 6.1 SUPPLY AND DEMAND FOR LOANABLE FUNDS

The amount of money loaned and borrowed is the quantity, and the interest rate is the price. At the equilibrium interest rate r^*, the supply of loanable funds equals the demand.

[1]In Chapter 9, we will see that there is some controversy about whether higher interest rates always induce people to save more.

INFLATION AND THE REAL RATE OF INTEREST

The interest rate, we have seen, is a price. It tells how many dollars next period we can get if we give up one dollar today. But except for misers like Scrooge who store money for its own sake, dollars are of value only because of the goods that can be bought with them. Because of inflation—the increase in prices over time—dollars in the future buy fewer goods than dollars today. In deciding both whether to borrow and whether to lend, individuals want to know how much *consumption* they get tomorrow if they give up a dollar's worth of consumption today. The answer is given by the **real rate of interest.** This is distinguished from the **nominal rate of interest,** the rate one sees posted at one's bank and in the newspaper, which simply describes the number of dollars one gets next year in exchange for a dollar today. There is a simple relationship between the real interest rate and the nominal interest rate: the real interest rate equals the nominal interest rate minus the rate of inflation (the annual rate of change of prices on average). If the nominal interest rate is 10 percent and the rate of inflation is 6 percent, then the real interest rate is 4 percent. By lending out (or saving) a dollar today, you can increase the amount of goods that you get in one year's time by 4 percent.

Consider an individual who decides to deposit $1,000 in a savings account. At the end of the year, at a 10 percent interest rate, she will have $1,100. But prices meanwhile have risen by 6 percent. A good that cost $1,000 in the beginning of the year now costs $1,060. In terms of "purchasing power," she has only $40 extra to spend ($1,100 − $1,060)—4 percent more than she had at the beginning of the year. This is her real return. In an inflationary economy, a borrower is in a similar situation. He knows that if he borrows money, the dollars he gives back to repay the loan will be worth less than the dollars he receives today. Thus, what is relevant for individuals to know when deciding either how much to lend (save) or how much to borrow is the *real* interest rate, which takes account of inflation. It is the real interest rate that should appear on the vertical axis of Figure 6.1.

REAL INTEREST RATE

Real interest rate = nominal interest rate − rate of inflation

THE MARKET FOR ASSETS

Gardeners today would have been shocked at the price of tulip bulbs in early seventeenth-century Holland, where one bulb sold for the equivalent of $16,000 in today's dollars. The golden age of tulips did not last long, however, and in 1637, prices of bulbs fell by over 90 percent. Dramatic price swings are not only curiosities of history. Between 1973 and 1980, the price of gold rose from $98 to $613, or by 525 percent; then from 1980 to 1985, it fell to $318. Between 1977 and 1980, the price of farmland in Iowa increased by 40 percent, only to fall by over 60 percent from 1980 to 1987. On October 19, 1987, prices in the U.S. stock market fell by one-half *trillion* dollars, almost 25 percent. Even a major war would be unlikely to destroy a quarter of the U.S. capital stock in a single day. But there was no war or other external event to explain the 1987 drop.

How can the demand and supply model of Chapters 4 and 5 explain these huge price swings? Supply curves for these goods certainly could not have shifted so dramatically. Nor could changes in tastes, incomes, or other goods have caused such fantastic shifts in demand. The solution to this puzzle does lie in shifts of the demand curve, but not directly for the reasons we saw in Chapter 4.

The first step in the solution is to recognize that the goods in the examples above are unlike ice cream cones, newspapers, or any other goods that are valued by the consumer mainly for their present use. Gold, land, stock, and even tulips in seventeenth-century Holland are all examples of **assets.** Assets are long-lived and thus can be bought at one date and sold at another. For this reason, the price individuals are willing to pay for them today depends not only on today's conditions—the immediate return or benefits—but also on some expectation of what tomorrow's conditions will be; in particular, on what the assets can be sold for in the future.

The concept of present discounted value tells us how to measure and compare returns anticipated in the future. Changes in present discounted value shift demand curves, as shown in Figure 6.2, because the amount that someone is willing to pay today depends on the present discounted value of what she believes she can get for it in the future.

Present discounted values can change for two reasons. First, they can change because the interest rate changes. An increase in the interest rate reduces the present discounted value of the dollars you expect to receive in the future. This is one reason why increases in the interest rate are often accompanied by drops in the price of shares on the stock market, and vice versa. Smart investors thus try to forecast interest rates accurately. Second, present discounted values can change because of a change in the expected price of an asset at the time one expects to sell it. Again, this will lead to a shift in the demand curve. Such **expectations** can be quite volatile, which explains a great deal of the volatility in asset prices.

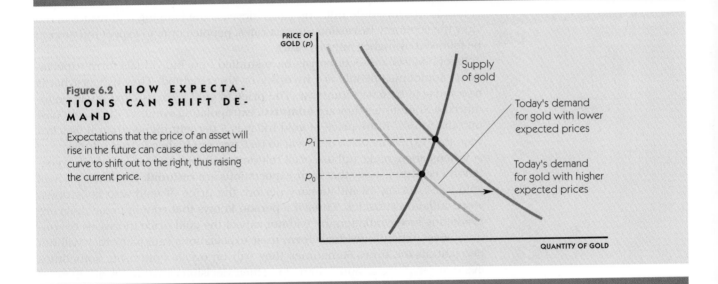

Figure 6.2 HOW EXPECTA-TIONS CAN SHIFT DE-MAND

Expectations that the price of an asset will rise in the future can cause the demand curve to shift out to the right, thus raising the current price.

To see how expectations concerning future events affect *current* prices, consider a hypothetical example. People suddenly realize that new smog-control devices will, ten years from now, make certain parts of Los Angeles much more attractive places to live than they are today. As a result, future-oriented individuals will think that ten years from now the price of land in those areas will be much higher, say $1 million an acre. But, they also think, nine years from now it will already be recognized that in one short year an acre will be worth $1 million. Hence, nine years from now investors will be willing to pay almost $1 million for the land—even if, at that date (nine years from now), the smog has not yet been eliminated. But then, these same individuals think, eight years from now investors will realize that in one short year the price will rise to almost $1 million and will pay close to that amount. Working backward like this makes it apparent that if people are confident land is going to be much more valuable in ten years, its price rises today.

Thus, while changes in tastes or technology or incomes or the prices of other goods *today* could not account for some of the sharp changes in asset values described at the start of this section, changes in expectations concerning any of these variables in the future will have an effect *today* on the demand. Markets for assets are linked together over time. An event that is expected to happen in ten or fifteen or even fifty years can have a direct bearing on today's market.

FORMING EXPECTATIONS

Changes in expectations about future returns or interest rates, then, can be reflected in large changes in asset prices today. How do individuals and firms form expectations? Partly by looking at past experience. If a company has steadily grown more valuable, investors may come to expect that pattern to continue. If every time inflation rates increase the banking authorities act to slow the economy by raising interest rates, people come to expect inflation to be followed by higher interest rates.

Psychologists and economists have studied how individuals form expectations. Sometimes people are **myopic,** or short-sighted. They expect what is true today to be true tomorrow. The price of gold today is what it will be tomorrow. Sometimes they are **adaptive,** extrapolating events of the recent past into the future. If the price of gold today is 5 percent higher than it was last year, they expect its price next year to be 5 percent higher than it is today.

When people make full use of all relevant available data to form their expectations, economists say that their expectations are **rational.** While the price of gold rises during an inflationary period, the price of gold also goes down when inflation subsides. Thus, if a person knows that economic analysts are predicting lower inflation, he will not expect the gold price increases to continue. Even when individuals form their expectations rationally, they will not be right all the time. Sometimes they will be overly optimistic, sometimes overly pessimistic (although in making their decisions, they are aware of these possibilities). But the assumption of rational expectations is that on average they will be right.

The 1970s were a period when adaptive expectations reigned. Many investors came to expect prices of assets such as land and housing to continue to rise rapidly. The more you invested, the more money you made. The idea that the price of a house or of land might fall seemed beyond belief—even though history is full of episodes (most recently during the 1930s) when such prices fell dramatically. The weak real estate markets of the 1980s in many regions reminded investors of the importance of incorporating historical data in forming expectations.

But in this, as in all types of fortune-telling, history never repeats itself exactly. Since the situation today is never precisely like past experience, it is never completely clear which facts will be the relevant ones. Even the best-informed experts are likely to disagree. When it comes to predicting the future, everyone's crystal ball is cloudy.

THE MARKET FOR RISK

Most of us do not like the risk that accompanies most future-oriented economic activity. We might spend a few dollars on some lottery tickets or playing the slot machines at Las Vegas or Atlantic City, but for the most part, we try to avoid or minimize serious risks. Psychologists who have studied this "risk-avoidance behavior," focus on the anxiety to which uncertainty gives rise. Economists refer to risk-avoidance behavior by saying that individuals are **risk averse.**

RESPONDING TO RISK

Even though most individuals are risk averse, our economy needs to encourage risk taking. New ventures are risky, but they are the engine of economic growth. Our economy has developed a number of ways by which risks are transferred, transformed, and shared. The institutions and arrangements by which this is done are known collectively as the **market for risk.**

AVOIDING AND MITIGATING RISKS

The simplest way to respond to risk is to avoid it: don't gamble. But if everyone avoided all risks, economic activity would come to a standstill. No investments would be made. Firms wouldn't even hire workers: there is always the chance that an employee won't work out.

So risks cannot be avoided. But there is much individuals and firms can do to reduce the degree of risk and soften its impact. Firms invest in fire detection and suppression equipment to reduce the damage from a fire. Thorough research—obtaining as complete information as possible—before undertaking an investment project reduces the risk.

MAINTAINING OPTIONS

A second way to respond to risk is to keep one's options open. Many uncertainties get resolved over time. At the beginning of the week, Tim doesn't know whether it will rain on Saturday. By Friday, the weather forecasters will have provided him with much better information—a better estimate of the probability of rain. By Saturday morning, he will have a still better estimate. Tim would like to go to the football game Saturday afternoon, provided it does not rain. If it rains, he would rather go to the movies. But by Friday all the football tickets will be sold out. He has to make his decision earlier. He may decide to buy the ticket on Monday, knowing that there is a chance that he will not use it (if it rains). Buying the ticket on Monday maintains his options. Failing to buy the ticket forecloses the option of going to the football game. On Saturday morning it does rain. Tim recognizes that the expenditure on the football ticket is a sunk cost. Even though he spent the money, he prefers spending an extra $5 and going to the movies, than getting cold and drenched at the football game. It was worth spending the money to keep his options open.

Businesses often spend considerable amounts to maintain options. They may enter a market, for example, knowing they will lose money for the next year or two. But they hope to learn a lot from the experience, and they know that if they fail to enter the market, it will be much harder (costlier) to enter later. It is worth losing money for a while to keep their options open.

DIVERSIFYING

A third response to risk is: don't put all of your eggs in the same basket. Firms, for instance, may enter several lines of business to reduce risk. Farmers may grow several different crops. If things go badly in one area, there is a good chance they will go better in some other area.

TRANSFERRING AND SHARING RISKS

A fourth response to risk is to transfer or share it. If I have no homeowner's insurance and my house burns down, I would suffer a financial calamity. But if some rich person agrees to pay me $100 if my house burns down, his $100 loss would not have a major effect on his finances. He will be willing to accept the small risk, for a fee a bit above the average payment he expects to make in the event of my house burning down. Thus, if there is a 1 percent chance that my house will burn down, the "expected" payment of someone who agrees to pay me $100 if that happens is

$$\text{expected payment} = \text{probability of loss} \times \text{payment in event of loss}$$
$$= .01 \times \$100 = \$1.$$

The *risk premium* is the *extra* payment an individual or firm must receive to be willing to bear risks. If he were willing to accept the risk in return for a payment of $1.10, then the $.10 is the risk premium. I would be more than willing to pay him $1.10 to absorb the risk. Ideally, I would like to find 1,000 such people to insure my $100,000 house; for then, I would have completely transferred the risk of a fire to them.

Insurance Firms   Insurance firms are the institutions in our economy that specialize in absorbing risks. The earliest insurance firms—collectively known as Lloyd's of London—did nothing more than pull together a group of investors willing to absorb large risks, such as those associated with shipwrecks. Today, insurance firms absorb risk directly.

LIMITS ON INSURANCE AS PROTECTION AGAINST RISK

Even though insurance companies specialize in absorbing risks, individuals and firms cannot buy insurance to protect themselves against all types of risk. A business, for example, cannot buy insurance that protects it against the risk that the demand for its product will fall, or the risk that a competitor will develop a better product that will drive the company into bankruptcy. Economists have identified two inherent problems that limit the use of insurance as a mechanism for handling risk: adverse selection and moral hazard. Although the following discussion focuses on these problems in the context of insurance, they apply more generally to methods of sharing risk, including stocks and bonds.

Adverse Selection   The probability that an individual will have an accident depends on characteristics of that individual's life and behavior that an insurance firm cannot perfectly observe. If the accident probabilities of different individuals could be accurately estimated, then in a competitive insurance market, premiums would accurately reflect those accident probabilities. For example, "hot dog" skiers would pay higher medical insurance rates than people with safer pastimes, reflecting the higher average medical expenses.

What do you do as a policymaker to combat the practice of "cream skimming" in the health insurance industry? This is the practice of providing insurance to those who are in good health and have a low health-risk profile (inexpensive to insure) and refusing insurance to those who are already sick or who are at known high risk for future health problems (expensive to insure). This type of adverse selection in the health insurance industry adds to the problem of the medically uninsured in the United States today.

Among proposed reforms are (1) making it illegal for firms to refuse insurance to those with "pre-existing conditions," that is, medical conditions that existed prior to the purchase of insurance, and (2) requiring community rating, a risk-rating scheme that requires the insurance industry to charge the same premium, regardless of medical condition, age, or sex.

Such reforms may help, but they are unlikely to solve the problem because insurance companies can still select the favorable risks. They can, for example, locate their offices on the fifth floor of a building with no elevator and make prospective customers apply in person. They can also design their insurance packages to appeal to the young and healthy—by providing especially generous "sports medicine" benefits, for example, or giving free memberships to health clubs.

One way to prevent cream skimming would be to tax or subsidize insurance firms depending on the health risks of their particular client pool. These tax/subsidy arrangements are called "risk adjustments" and remove the cost advantage of selecting the best risks. Another way is to standardize benefits, thus preventing the use of special benefit packages to attract lower risk groups. These and similar proposals to regulate the insurance market have problems of their own, however. Most are imperfect, and some would require extensive and expensive bureaucracies to develop, administer, and enforce.

But insurance firms do not know everything about each individual's risks. Insurance rates can only be based on observable factors; auto insurance rates, for example, depend on the record of past accidents, age of driver, and type of vehicle. The same rate is charged to all people with identical observable traits. When an insurance company perceives that the premiums it is charging for a particular group of individuals is too low for the risks of the group, it raises the premiums. This is when the problem of adverse selection can appear.

The **adverse selection** problem arises when insurance companies try to raise their premiums and the best risks stop buying insurance. The best risks may either decide to self-insure (not buy insurance from any company) or switch to another company. The worst risks—those who know that they really need insurance because they are unhealthy, for example, and so will not self-insure, or those who cannot get insurance elsewhere—stick with the firm. As the best risks leave, the *average* riskiness of the insured risks worsens. It may deteriorate so much that average profits actually fall—the increased average riskiness more than offsets the increased premiums.

Though the term adverse selection was coined to capture this *adverse* effect on the mix of those buying insurance as premiums increase, it has come to refer to the whole array of actions which can affect the mix of those buying insurance.

For many kinds of insurance, such as fire insurance, adverse selection problems may not be too bad. The critical information (determining the likelihood of a fire) can easily enough be observed—for instance, by building inspectors. But for many of the kinds of risks against which individuals would like to buy insurance, adverse selection effects are important. With health or automobile insurance, for instance, an insurance firm is likely to find it difficult to determine any particular individual's risk. Even worse, consider the problem of measuring the risk that a firm's new product will fail to meet expectations. It would be nearly impossible for an insurance company to decide precisely what the prospects for the product are. The business firm itself is certainly more likely to be better informed than the insurance company about the markets in which it is trying to sell the product. Not surprisingly, then, because of their disadvantage in obtaining crucial information, insurance firms do not supply insurance against such business risks.

Moral Hazard   A second problem faced by insurance companies is an incentive problem: insurance affects people's incentives to avoid whatever contingencies they are insured against. A person who has no fire insurance on a house, for example, may choose to limit the risk of fire by buying smoke alarms and home fire extinguishers and being especially cautious. But if that same person had fire insurance, he might not be so careful. Indeed, if the insurance would pay more than the house's market value, he might even be tempted to burn his own house down to collect the insurance.

This general feature of insurance, that it reduces the individual's incentives to avoid the insured-against accident, is called **moral hazard.** Of course, from an economist's point of view, what is at issue is not a question of morality, but only a question of incentives. If a person bears only a portion, or none, of the consequences of his actions—as he does when he has purchased insurance—his incentives are altered.

In the late 1960s, after urban riots plagued many major cities in the United States, inner-city property values plunged. Insurance coverage adjusted, but slowly. In the meantime many buildings were insured at amounts that considerably exceeded their reduced market value. Was it purely coincidental that the value of fire losses nationwide increased 55 percent between 1966 and 1970?

Moral hazard concerns may not be important for many kinds of insurance; an individual who buys a large life insurance policy and thus knows that her children will be well cared for in the event of her demise is hardly likely to take much bigger risks with her life. (There was, however, a grisly case in California some years ago in which a person cut off one foot with an axe to try to collect on disability insurance.) But for many kinds of risks against which a firm's managers would *like* to buy insurance, moral hazard concerns are important. For example, if a company could buy insurance to guarantee a minimum level of profit, managers would have less incentive to exert effort. When moral hazard problems are strong, insurance firms will offer limited—or even no—insurance.

THE RISK-INCENTIVE TRADE-OFF

We have seen that insurance reduces incentives. The greater the insurance coverage, the more incentives are reduced. If my house is insured for only 50 percent of any loss, I have a strong incentive to make sure that there is no fire. If it is insured for 100 percent of any loss, I have little incentive to expend any resources to avoid a fire.

There is thus a risk-incentive trade-off. The more the individual divests himself of risk, the weaker his incentives to avoid "bad results" and to foster "good results." This principle applies in many contexts other than simple insurance markets. A store manager whose salary is guaranteed faces little risk, but also has little incentive. If his pay depends on the store's sales, he has stronger incentives, but faces greater risk. In spite of his best efforts, sales may be low—perhaps because of an economic downturn, perhaps because buyers have simply turned away from his products; in either case, his income will be low.

In many cases, the market reaches a compromise: partial insurance, providing the purchaser of insurance with some incentives, but making her also bear some risk. With medical insurance, for example, it is common for an insurance company to pay only some percentage (like 80 percent) of expenses (this is called coinsurance). In this case, an individual will have a financial motivation to be cautious in the use of medical care, but still be largely protected.

Similarly, a firm that borrows money for a project is generally required to invest some of its own funds in the project, or to supply the lender with collateral; that is, provide the lender with an asset that the firm forfeits if it fails to repay the loan. Lenders know that with more of their own money at stake, borrowers will have better incentives to use the funds wisely.

CLOSE-UP: AUTO INSURANCE AND ADVERSE SELECTION IN NEW JERSEY

The charge for private passenger automobile insurance in the United States skyrocketed during the mid- and late 1980s. The general price level rose by 3.5 percent per year during that time. Auto insurance prices rose by 9 percent per year. Perhaps no state had worse auto insurance problems than New Jersey.

New Jersey was a likely candidate for several reasons. It has the highest population per square mile of any state in the country crowding the highways. Nine of the nation's top twenty-five cities for car theft are in New Jersey. New Jersey was one of only two states with no upper limit on the medical costs that could be claimed from any accident. It cost $1,000 a year on average to insure a car in New Jersey at the start of the 1990s, more than double the national average.

But New Jersey contributed to its own woes. In 1983, the state set up a Joint Underwriting Authority (JUA), which was intended to offer auto insurance to those too risky for private companies to insure. JUA rates were supposed to be comparable to those in private companies, which is a bit difficult to figure, since the private insurance companies did not want to insure these risky drivers at all. In practice, anyone could be insured by the JUA at rates not much different from the average for low-risk drivers.

This law, though well-meant, set up what should have been anticipated patterns of adverse selection. Private insurance companies directed their worst risks to the JUA, insuring only the lower risks themselves. By the end of the 1980s, half of New Jersey's drivers were enrolled in the JUA, which had accumulated a deficit of $3 billion that was growing by $1 billion a year. Extra taxes were needed to cover the lost money, creating a political furor in the Garden State.

As is so often the case, the insurance industry got blamed for the mess. The government started regulating insurance premiums and compelling the insurance firms to insure high-risk cars. These constraints had the predictable effects. Insurance companies sued the state, and several, like Allstate, left the state altogether rather than sell insurance at a loss. Insurance spreads and shares risk, but it cannot provide something for nothing.

Sources: Insurance Information Institute, *1990 Property/Casualty Insurance Facts;* "Insurers Under Siege: Lawmakers, Consumers, and Corporate Customers Are Fighting Mad," *Business Week,* August 21, 1989, pp. 72–79; Joseph J. Sullivan, "Compromise on Insurance Isn't Working in New Jersey," *New York Times,* January 15, 1989, p. D6; Jay Romano, "Why Auto Insurance Costs So Much," *New York Times,* October 22, 1989, sec. XII, p. 1; Romano, "New Law on Auto Insurance Draws Fire," *New York Times,* March 18, 1990, sec. XII, p. 1.

ENTREPRENEURSHIP

Innovation gives life to a capitalist economy. It also demonstrates the vital roles played by time and risk. Consider for a moment the many new products and new processes of production that have so enriched (or at least altered) everyone's life in the last century: fast food, transistors, computers, airplanes, cars, televisions—the list is endless. Each of these innovations required more than just an idea. It needed people willing to follow the advice of David Lloyd George, once prime minister of Great Britain, who said: "Don't be afraid to take a big step if one is indicated. You can't cross a chasm in two small jumps."

Innovations require people and businesses to take risks. Innovators need capital too, since those who have innovative ideas, like Henry Ford, often do not have the capital to carry them out. They must turn to others to supply them with resources, generally in exchange for part of any eventual return. After all, someone who lends to an innovator bears a risk, and he must receive compensation to be willing to undertake these risks.

In forming judgments about whether to pursue a possible innovation, innovators and investors form expectations about the future. But because they are dealing with new ideas, products, and processes, the expectations of reasonable men and women may differ. When the returns are in and the project has proved to be a success or a failure, it is often difficult to ascertain the reasons why, even with the wisdom of hindsight. Thus, those whose jobs require them to make decisions—the lending officers of banks, the managers of pension funds and other financial institutions, the leaders of corporations—face a difficult task. But lack of any simple formula does not mean that there are not better and worse ways of making these decisions. Forming expectations and evaluating risks are like playing football in a fog; you cannot always tell what is going on, but skilled players with good foresight still have an advantage.

Thus, **entrepreneurs**—the individuals responsible for creating new businesses, bringing new products to market, developing new processes of production—face all the problems we have discussed. All business decision making involves risk taking. But entrepreneurs who take responsibility for managing a new business generally face more risk than established companies. Businesses often require additional financing for new projects, but new enterprises almost always require extensive outside financing. The problem of selection, of determining which of a set of potential investment projects and entrepreneurs ought to receive funds, is particularly acute, since because these projects are new, they have yet to establish a reputation. Lenders may be reluctant, for instance, to provide funds for fear of default.

Since entrepreneurs cannot buy insurance to cover most of the risks they face, they must also be willing to bear the risks themselves. Entrepreneurs need a return to compensate them for their efforts and the risks they undertake. Similarly, those who provide these new enterprises with capital must receive a return greater than they might receive elsewhere, to compensate them for the additional risks they have to bear. There has been ongoing concern about the effect of a variety of public policies, especially tax policy, on these returns. Does the current tax system discourage entrepreneurship? Can policies be designed to encourage it? These questions will be addressed later in the book.

AN OVERVIEW OF FINANCIAL MARKETS

Our economic system is often referred to as capitalism, reflecting the importance that capital markets—or more generally, financial markets—play in our economy. The central role of these markets constitutes another major area of consensus among economists. Here is our fifth consensus point:

5 Financial Markets

Financial markets are a central part of modern economies. They are essential for raising capital for new enterprises, expanding on-going businesses, and sharing risks.

REVIEW AND PRACTICE

SUMMARY

1. Much of economics is future oriented, which means that households and firms must form expectations about the future and cope with problems of risk and uncertainty.

2. The interest rate is a price. It equates the supply of funds by savers and the demand by borrowers. Savers receive interest for deferring consumption, and borrowers pay interest so that they can consume or invest now and pay later.

3. The fact that the market interest rate is positive means that a dollar received today is worth more than a dollar received in the future. This is the time value of money. The present discounted value of a dollar in the future is the value in dollars today of receiving a dollar in the future, given the prevailing rate of interest.

4. The real interest rate, which measures a person's actual increase in buying power when she saves money, is equal to the nominal interest rate (the amount paid in dollars) minus the inflation rate.

5. What investors are willing to pay today for an asset depends largely on what they believe they can sell it for in the future. Changes in expectations can thus shift the demand curve for an asset and change current prices.

6. Most people are risk averse. They respond to risks by trying to avoid them and mitigate their impacts; by keeping options open; by diversifying; and by transferring risks to and sharing risks with others.

7. Among the most important institutions for absorbing risks are insurance firms. Insurance firms face two problems. One is that people who buy insurance tend to be those most at risk, and charging higher prices for insurance will discourage those less at risk from buying insurance at all. This effect is called adverse selection. The second problem is that insurance reduces the incentives individuals have to avoid whatever they are insured against. This is called moral hazard.

8. Entrepreneurial innovation plays a central role in modern economies.

KEY TERMS

interest	nominal rate of	rational expectations
principal	interest	risk averse
present discounted	assets	adverse selection
value	expectations	moral hazard
intertemporal trades	myopic expectations	entrepreneurs
real rate of interest	adaptive expectations	

REVIEW QUESTIONS

1. Who is on the demand side and who is on the supply side in the market for loanable funds? What is the price in that market?

2. Would you prefer to receive $100 one year from now, or five years from now? Why? Does your answer change if the rate of inflation is zero?

3. What is the relationship between the nominal interest rate and the real interest rate?

4. True or false: "Demand curves depend on what people want now, not on their expectations about the future." Explain your answer.

5. What is meant by risk aversion? What are some consequences of the fact that most people are risk averse?

6. Why do people pay insurance premiums if they hope and expect that nothing bad is going to happen to them?

7. What is moral hazard? What is adverse selection? How do they affect insurance markets?

8. Why is there a trade-off between risk and incentives? Give an example of this trade-off.

PROBLEMS

1. Occasionally, firms issue bonds that promise to pay a fixed amount, say, in one year, but pay no interest in the interim. What is the market value today of a bond that promises to pay $1,000 next year, if the interest rate is 5 percent? 10 percent? 20 percent?

2. A machine costs $1 million and produces output of $1.1 million (net of other costs) next year, at which point it will be worn out and useless. At what rate of interest is the present discounted value of the return ($1.1 million) equal to the cost of the machine? If the current interest rate in the economy is higher than the rate for the present discounted value of the return, would you buy the machine? Why or why not?

3. Many states have passed laws that put a ceiling on the rate of interest that can be charged; these laws are called usury laws. Using a supply and demand diagram, show the effect of interest rate ceilings on the quantity (supply) of lending. Who is better off as a result of usury laws? Who is worse off?

4. Suppose the workers at a particular company have been complaining that their medical insurance does not cover enough items. To help build loyalty among the staff, the company agrees to cover more items. However, it finds that the number of sick days taken and its expenses for health care both rise sharply. Why might this happen? What is the name for it?

5. You hire someone to paint your house. Since it is a large job, you agree to pay him by the hour. What moral hazard problem must you consider? Explain the trade-off between risk and incentives in this situation.

6. (This problem depends on the chapter appendix below.) Imagine that $1,000 is deposited in an account for five years; the account pays 10 percent interest per year, compounded annually. At the end of the first year, the account is credited with $100 interest, and then starts earning interest on the interest, and similarly at the end of each successive year. How much money will be in the account after five years? What if the rate of interest is 12 percent? What if the annual rate of interest is 12 percent, but the interest is compounded monthly?

7. (This problem depends on the chapter appendix below.) Suppose you want to buy a car three years from now, and you know that the price of a car at that time will be $10,000. If the interest rate is 7 percent per year, how much would you have to set aside today to have the money ready when you need it? If the interest rate is 5 percent, how much would you have to set aside today?

APPENDIX: CALCULATING PRESENT DISCOUNTED VALUE

In the text, we described how to calculate the present discounted value (PDV) of a dollar received a year from now. The present discounted value of a dollar received two years from now can be calculated in a similar way. But how much *today* is equivalent to, say, $100 two years from now? If I were given $PDV today, and I put it in the bank, at the end of the year, I would have PDV(1 + r)$. If I left it in the bank for another year, in the second year I would earn interest on the total amount in the bank at the end of the first year, $r \times$ PDV$(1 + r)$. Therefore, at the end of the two-year period I would have:

$$\text{PDV}(1 + r) + [r \times \text{PDV }(1 + r)]$$
$$= \text{PDV}(1 + r)(1 + r)$$
$$= \text{PDV}(1 + r)^2.$$

Thus, the $PDV of $100 in two years is $100 / $(1 + r)^2$. If I put $100 / $(1 + r)^2$ in the bank today, I would have $100 / $(1 + r)^2 \times (1 + r)^2 = $100 in two years. In performing these calculations, we have taken account of the interest on the interest. This is called **compound interest.**

(By contrast, **simple interest** does not take into account the interest you earn on interest you have previously earned.) If the rate of interest is 10 percent and is compounded annually, $100 today is worth $110 a year from now and $121 (*not* $120) in two years' time. Thus, the present discounted value today of $121 two years from now is $100. Table 6.1 shows how to calculate the present discounted value of $100 received next year, two years from now, and three years from now.

Table 6.1   **PRESENT DISCOUNTED VALUE OF $100**

Year received	Present discounted value
Next year	$\frac{1}{1+r} \times 100 = \frac{100}{1+r}$
Two years from now	$\frac{1}{1+r} \times \frac{100}{1+r} = \frac{100}{(1+r)^2}$
Three years from now	$\frac{1}{1+r} \times \frac{100}{(1+r)^2} = \frac{100}{(1+r)^3}$

We can now see how to calculate the value of an investment project that will yield a return over several years. We look at what the returns will be each year, adjust them to their present discounted values, and then add these values up. Table 6.2 shows how this is done for a project that yields $10,000 next year and $15,000 the year after, and that you plan to sell in the third year for $50,000. The second column of the table shows the return in each year. The third column shows the discount factor—what we multiply the return by to obtain the present discounted value of that year's return. The calculations assume an interest rate of 10 percent. The fourth column multiplies the return by the discount factor to obtain the present discounted value of that year's return. In the bottom row of the table, the present discounted values of each year's return have been added up to obtain the total present discounted value of the project. Notice that it is much smaller than the number we obtain simply by adding up the returns, which is the "undiscounted" yield of the project.

Table 6.2 CALCULATING PRESENT DISCOUNTED VALUE OF A THREE-YEAR PROJECT

Year	Return	Discount factor ($r = 0.10$)	Present discounted value ($r = 0.10$)
1	$10,000	$\frac{1}{1.10}$	$ 9,091
2	$15,000	$\frac{1}{(1.10)^2} = \frac{1}{1.21}$	$12,397
3	$50,000	$\frac{1}{(1.10)^3} = \frac{1}{1.331}$	$37,566
Total	$75,000	—	$59,054

THE PUBLIC SECTOR

Most Americans have a great deal of faith in our economic system, with its primary reliance on private markets. Yet despite this basic faith, the United States has a public, or governmental, sector that reaches out into all spheres of economic activity. How do economists explain the role of government in the economy?

In earlier chapters, we have seen how the profit system provides firms with the incentive to produce the goods consumers want. Prices give firms the incentive to economize on scarce resources. Prices also coordinate economic activity and signal changes in economic conditions. Private property provides incentives for individuals to invest in and to maintain buildings, machines, land, cars, and other possessions. Chapter 3 demonstrated the incentives individuals and countries have to engage in mutually advantageous trades and

1. What distinguishes the private from the public sector?

2. What explains the economic roles the government has undertaken?

3. What are externalities and public goods, and why do they imply that markets may not work well?

4. What are the various ways the government can affect the economy and attempt to achieve its economic objectives?

5. How has the role of government changed in recent decades? And how does the role of government in the United States compare with its role in other industrial countries?

6. What are some of the current controversies concerning the roles of government? Why do failures of the market system not necessarily imply that government action is desirable?

to specialize in areas of comparative advantage. Chapters 4 and 5 showed how, in free markets, prices are determined by the interaction of demand and supply.

We have thus seen how the private market answers the four basic questions set out in Chapter 1: *What is produced and in what quantities* is determined by the interaction of demand and supply, reflecting both the goods consumers want and what it costs firms to produce those goods. *How it is produced* is determined by competition among firms, which must produce the goods in the least expensive way possible in order to stay in business. *For whom it is produced* is determined by the incomes of individuals in the economy. Those with high incomes get more of the economy's goods and services, and those with low incomes get less. These incomes, in turn, are established by the demand and supply for labor, which determines what workers are paid, and the demand and supply for capital, which determines the return people get on their savings. *Who makes the decisions?* Everyone. Which goods are produced depends on millions of decisions made in households and firms throughout the economy. Moreover, firms, competing against one another, have incentives to choose as managers those most able to make the hard decisions—whether to enter some new market or develop some new product—that every firm must face if it is to survive.

If this private-market system works so well, what role do economists see for the government? Economists recognize that the government must set and enforce the basic laws of society, and provide a framework within which firms can compete fairly against one another. Beyond this, however, economists' understanding of the market's ability to answer the basic economic questions leads them to look hard at any additional function the government serves: why are private markets not serving that function? This chapter will explore the roles the government has undertaken, and how and why it carries out those roles.

THE CHANGING ROLES OF GOVERNMENT

The appropriate balance between the public and private sectors is a subject of constant debate, with different countries giving different answers to this question. In Switzerland, the public sector is small and government economic activities are severely limited. In the Soviet Union before its collapse and China before its reforms, the government tried to control or **nationalize** virtually all aspects of economic activity, though the difficulty of doing this created increasing pressures for change. Between these extremes lies a wide spectrum: free market economies like Hong Kong, where businesses do not face many of the regulations facing businesses in the United States and Western Europe; welfare state economies like Sweden, where the government takes major responsibilities for health care, child care, and a host of other social services, but where there is also a large private sector; and a number of European economies, like Great Britain, where the government until recently dominated major industries like steel, coal, railroads, airlines, and public utilities. The United States is nearer the free market end of this spectrum than most countries with industrialized, developed economies.

Government has almost always been responsible for certain activities that the vast majority of citizens believe are fundamentally public functions—the justice system, police protection, and national defense, for example. But government's role in other areas has changed over time, usually in response to perceived failures of the market economy. In the late nineteenth century, the U.S. government began regulating railroads and breaking up huge monopolies such as Standard Oil, in response to concerns that they were ruthlessly using their market power to control the economy and exploit consumers. In the 1930s, the economic havoc inflicted by the Great Depression—one out of four Americans was out of work, banks failed and the stock market crashed, plummeting agricultural prices forced farmers to default on their loans and lose their farms—led government into a whole new set of responsibilities known collectively as the New Deal.

In 1946, with the Full Employment Act, the U.S. government extended its role to include responsibility for maintaining the economy at full employment. This commitment contributed in part to a period of unprecedented prosperity. But the fruits of that prosperity were distributed very unequally. Many Americans were born into squalor and poverty. Their educational prospects were dim, as were their chances of getting good jobs. In the 1960s, the government responded by again increasing its responsibility, this time in the form of President Johnson's Great Society programs, including the War on Poverty.

The 1970s saw a change in direction: government regulations were seen as excessively burdensome, interfering with rather than helping the economy. There was, in fact, a worldwide movement toward **deregulation**—eliminating, for instance, the regulations that controlled airline and trucking prices—

and **privatization**—relying on the private sector to provide services that were formerly provided by the government. In the late 1980s, a new set of concerns emerged having to do with the competitiveness of the American economy. Americans were saving less than were citizens of other industrialized powers. The rapid increases in productivity that had marked the 1950s and early 1960s slowed. There were new calls for government activity to spur the economy. Government increased its support for research and development (R & D) aimed at commercial rather than defense objectives, which had been the primary focus of public R & D funding in previous periods.

THE PICTURE IN STATISTICS

Changes in the size and role of government can be seen clearly in government statistics measuring the share of the total output of the economy (gross domestic product or GDP) devoted to government expenditures. In 1900, government spending accounted for 8 percent of GDP. By 1950, this share had grown to 21 percent, and by 1980—the year before Ronald Reagan took office—to 32 percent. Today it stands at 34 percent.

Figure 7.1 shows where federal dollars go. In 1950, just over half went to defense, and about an eighth each to Social Security/welfare and to interest pay-

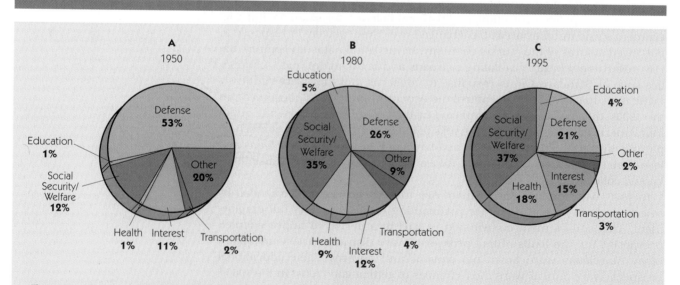

Figure 7.1 THE CHANGING PATTERN OF FEDERAL EXPENDITURES

Since 1950, there has been a steady increase in the share of federal funds allotted to health, Social Security, and welfare coupled with a marked decrease in the share allotted to defense. The share going for interest on the debt rose between 1980 and 1995 as a result of soaring deficits during the 1980s and early 1990s. *Sources: Statistical Abstract of the United States (1995), Table 520, Mid-Session Review of the 1997 Budget, July 16, 1996.*

POLICY PERSPECTIVE: THE "PEACE DIVIDEND"—NOW YOU SEE IT, NOW YOU DON'T

A dramatic event ushered in the decade of the 1990s—the end of the Cold War. With it came the promise of what came to be known as the "peace dividend." The arms race would be replaced with international cooperation, and the resources that had formerly been dedicated to the arms buildup could be spent on domestic needs for a change. But discussions of how to spend the peace dividend have turned into a consensus that there is no dividend to spend. Advocates of U.S. military strength argued that new weapons were required to face the new challenges of the post-Cold War world. The

United States had to be able to fight in two regions simultaneously. While the need for nuclear deterrence was undoubtedly reduced, the need for conventional forces was possibly increased.

So far, in spite of the widespread consensus of the importance of unmet social needs, investments in education and research, and deficit reduction, the views of advocates of continued defense spending have prevailed. In real terms defense is projected to decline only slightly over the next ten years. Somehow, the peace dividend disappeared before anyone saw it.

The Berlin Wall, after it fell in November 1989.

ments on the national debt, leaving the remaining quarter to finance all other government programs. Since then, the share of federal spending going to defense has fallen dramatically: in 1995 only one in five federal dollars went to defense. The shares going for Social Security/welfare and health programs, on the other hand, have steadily increased, to the point where today they account for half of the total. In 1950, interest payments were relatively high as a result of the huge debt accumulated to fight World War II. But the deficit increases of the Reagan and Bush years caused interest payments on the national debt to rise to record levels, currently 15 percent of all federal expenditures. After defense, Social Security/welfare, health, and interest payments, only 9 percent of the budget is left to spend on everything else, including running the government itself!

STATE AND LOCAL GOVERNMENT

Most of the services that people look for from government—police protection, schools, roads, fire, libraries, parks—are provided largely by states and localities, which account for 40 percent of public sector spending in the United States. In many areas state and local responsibility is growing. For a few services, such as education, federal funding has increased. For instance, today, while states and localities remain *responsible* for elementary and secondary education, the federal government provides about 6 percent of the funds.

WHAT DISTINGUISHES THE PRIVATE AND PUBLIC SECTORS?

In a democracy, two important features distinguish private from public institutions. First, the people responsible for running public institutions are elected or appointed by someone who is elected. The legitimacy of the person holding the position is derived directly or indirectly from the electoral process. Second, any government has certain rights of compulsion. For instance, the U.S. government has the right to force its citizens to pay taxes; if they fail to do so, it can confiscate their property and even imprison them. The government has the right to force its young people to serve in the armed forces at wages below those that would induce them to volunteer. The government also has the right of **eminent domain,** which is the right to seize private property for public use, provided it compensates the owner fairly.

Its ability to use compulsion means that the government can do things private institutions cannot do. Once a decision has been made to build a public road, for instance, a local government can make sure that everyone in town helps to pay for it. Sometimes governments create rules to bind their own hands, so that they cannot do *anything* they wish. For instance, the government has established elaborate hiring procedures for itself that private firms generally do not find worthwhile. The owner of a private firm can decide whom she wants to hire; if she hires someone incompetent, she and her firm suffer. If the manager of a public enterprise hires someone incompetent, however, the public pays. The government's strict hiring procedures help avoid bad hiring, but they may also result in rigidities that make it difficult for government enterprises to compete against private firms for the most talented individuals.

These and other constraints imposed on the public sector—as well as the absence of the profit motive which provides the private sector with strong in-

The increase in central (federal) government expenditures during the twentieth century has been dramatic, but expenditures in the United States are still among the smallest of any of the major industrial countries in proportion to the size of the economy. In the Netherlands and the United Kingdom, government expenditures are approximately half of GDP as compared to about one-quarter for the United States. Of the major developed countries, only Japan and Australia spend under one-third of GDP on the public sector. As a significant portion of U.S. federal expenditures goes to defense (about 4 percent of GDP), the relative size of nondefense expenditures is particularly low viewed from this international perspective.

In the United States federal spending on nondefense public sector programs amounts to about 19 percent of GDP. In the Netherlands and the United Kingdom this figure is 50 and 39 percent respectively. The key difference is that Social Security and welfare programs are much larger in those countries relative to the United States.

These foreign comparisons prove different things to different people. Advocates of more government spending argue that the United States is out of step. Opponents of more government spending argue that all of these countries would do better to reduce public expenditures.

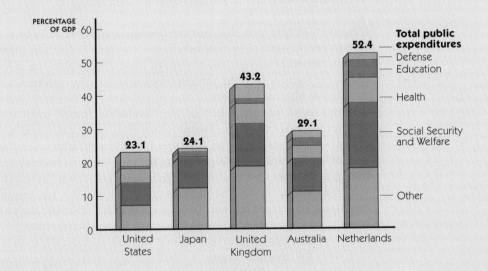

Source: Government Finance Statistics Yearbook (1995).

centives to be efficient, reduce costs, and produce what consumers want—put the public sector at a general disadvantage relative to the private sector in markets that work well. Economists, concerned with the most efficient solutions to economic problems ask: When do markets work well? When do they fail? And, when they fail, when might government improve matters?

ADAM SMITH'S "INVISIBLE HAND" AND THE CENTRAL ROLE OF MARKETS

The modern economic faith in private markets can be traced back to Adam Smith's 1776 masterpiece *The Wealth of Nations*. Smith argued that workers and producers, interested only in helping themselves and their families, were the basis of the success of the economy. The public interest would best be promoted by individuals pursuing their own self-interest. As Smith put it:

> Man has almost constant occasion for the help of his brethren, and it is in vain for him to expect it from their benevolence only. He will be more likely to prevail if he can interest their self-love in his favor, and show them that it is for their own advantage to do for him what he requires of them. . . . It is not from the benevolence of the butcher, the brewer, or the baker, that we expect our dinner, but from their regard to their own interest. We . . . never talk to them of our own necessities but of their advantages.[1]

Smith's insight was that individuals work hardest to help the overall economic production of society when their efforts help themselves. He argued that an "obvious and simple system of liberty" provided the greatest opportunities for people to help themselves and thus, by extension, to create the greatest wealth for a society.

Smith used the metaphor of the **"invisible hand"** to describe how self-interest led to social good: "He intends only his own gain, and he is in this as in many other cases led by an invisible hand to promote an end which was no part of his intention . . . By pursuing his own interest he frequently promotes that of the society more effectually than when he really intends to promote it."

Economics has progressed since Adam Smith, but his fundamental argument still has great appeal. Greater liberty for individuals in country after country has indeed led to huge increases in production that have benefited if not everyone, almost everyone. Nevertheless, it is not difficult to find discontent with the market. There is concern that markets produce too much of some things, like air and water pollution, and too little of other things, such as support for the arts or child care facilities. Generally, concern with market outcomes can be placed into three broad categories: those that are based on ignorance of the laws of economics, those having to do with redistribution of income, and those having to do with genuine failures of private markets.

[1]Book 1, Chapter 2.

CLOSE-UP: ADAM SMITH—FOUNDER OF MODERN ECONOMICS

Adam Smith, the founder of modern economics, was a professor of moral philosophy at the University of Glasgow, in the latter part of the eighteenth century. His great masterpiece, *The Wealth of Nations,* was published in 1776, the year the United States signed the Declaration of Independence. The American Revolution coincided with two other revolutions. The industrial revolution marked the transformation of the economy both from agriculture to industry and from rural to urban life. A revolution in ideas and ideology began to question the earlier view in which social institutions had been accepted as a matter of course, as part of a God-given order. Intellectuals began to inquire into the functions of social institutions (schools, churches, government) and to consider changes that could make society better off. This thinking is strongly reflected in the Federalist papers that form the background of the U.S. Constitution, and in the French Revolution at the turn of the nineteenth century.

No precise date or place marks the beginning of either the industrial or the ideological revolution. Glasgow was at the center of both, and this was perhaps no accident: both revolutions fed upon each other. The key idea in Adam Smith's economics was that individuals, in pursuing their self-interest, could more assuredly attain the common interest than if it were pursued by government (at that time, a monarch). This view contrasted with the earlier *mercantilist* view, which held that government should actively pursue the commercial interests of the country, particularly by promoting exports. Because of his emphasis on markets, Adam Smith is often held up as a champion of very limited government. A closer look at his *Wealth of Nations* shows a far more balanced view. Though he did not use the modern "market failures" vocabulary, he recognized many limitations of markets, and he saw government as performing an important role, such as supporting education. He also recognized the tendencies for firms to try to reduce or suppress competition, as well as the adverse consequences of lack of competition.

Adam Smith

GOVERNMENT AND IGNORANCE OF ECONOMICS

"Wouldn't the world be a better place if we still lived in the Garden of Eden?" epitomizes complaints about markets that ignore the laws of economics. Things have a price because they are scarce. If the price of oil is high, it is because oil is scarce and the high price reflects that scarcity. In Chapter 4, we saw that economists regard such situations not as market failures but as the hard facts of economic life. Much as everyone would like to live in a world where all individuals could have almost everything they wanted at a price they could afford, this is simply unrealistic. Those calling on government to "solve" the problem of scarcity by passing laws about prices simply shift the problem. They reduce prices for some and cause shortages for everyone else.

GOVERNMENT AND REDISTRIBUTION

A second category of complaints against the market represents a dissatisfaction with the distribution of income. Market economies may be productive and efficient at producing wealth, but they may also cause some people to get very rich and others to starve. Someone who has a rare and valuable skill will, by the laws of supply and demand, receive a high income. Someone else who has few skills, and common ones at that, will find his wage low—perhaps even too low for survival. The economy may have a very unequal distribution of income.

Most economists see an important role for the government in income redistribution, taking income from those who have more and giving it to those who have less. In their view, society need not accept whatever distribution of income results from the workings of private markets. Federal income and estate taxes on the rich and welfare programs for the poor are part of the government's role in redistribution.

Concern for greater economic equality is a generally accepted role for government, but there is still much disagreement about the benefits and costs of programs aimed at reducing inequality. And even if government reaches agreement on the degree to which income inequality should be reduced, economists will disagree as to what is the best method because income redistribution affects incentives.

Questions of redistribution are often posed as, How should the economy's pie be divided? What size slice should each person get? By looking at the pie in panel A of Figure 7.2, you can see that the poorest 20 percent of the population

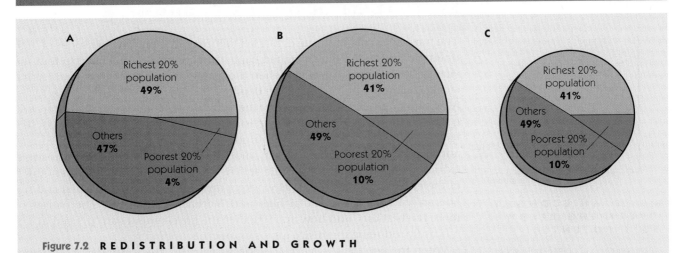

Figure 7.2 REDISTRIBUTION AND GROWTH

Panel A shows that the poor receive only a small share of the economy's output. Plans for redistribution often assume the situation in panel B, where the poor simply receive a larger share. But if the redistribution is poorly managed or too great, it may substantially reduce the size of the overall pie, as in panel C, making all groups worse off. *Source: 1994 Current Population Reports, Bureau of the Census (June 1996).*

get a relatively small slice—that is, 20 percent receive only 4 percent of the economy's income—while the richest 20 percent of the population get a relatively large slice, 49 percent of the economy's income. Often redistribution is viewed as simply cutting the pie differently, giving the poor somewhat larger slices and the rich somewhat smaller, as in panel B. But if the process of redistributing income weakens economic incentives and makes the economy less productive, the size of the whole pie will shrink, as illustrated in panel C. There the poor get a larger share of a smaller pie. The rich are much worse off now—they get a smaller share of a smaller pie. If the size of the pie has shrunk enough, even the poor may be worse off. By designing government redistribution programs appropriately, it may be possible to limit the size of these effects on productivity.

GOVERNMENT AND MARKET FAILURES

The final category of discontent with private markets represents cases where the market does indeed fail in its role of producing economic efficiency. Economists refer to these problems as **market failures,** and have studied them closely. When there is a market failure, government may be able to correct the market failure and enhance the economy's efficiency.

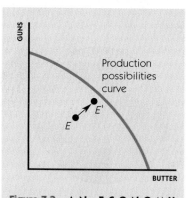

Figure 7.3 AN ECONOMY OPERATING BELOW FULL POTENTIAL

The economy is at point *E*, below the edge of its production possibilities curve. The government seeks to have it operate closer to the curve, at point *E'*, for instance.

STABILIZATION OF THE ECONOMY

The most dramatic example of market failures is the periodic episodes of high unemployment that have plagued capitalist economies. It is hard to tout the virtues of an efficient market when a quarter of the labor force and capital stock sits idle, as it did during the depth of the Great Depression of the 1930s. Although many economists believe there are forces that eventually restore the economy to full employment, the costs of waiting for the economy to correct itself—in terms of both forgone output and human misery—are enormous, and virtually all governments today take it as their responsibility to *try* to avoid extreme fluctuations in economic activity—both the downturns (when much of the economy's resources, its workers and machines, remain idle) and the booms (which may result in high and increasing inflation). The causes of these fluctuations, and how and whether the government can succeed in significantly reducing them, are topics in macroeconomics.

When the economy's scarce resources are idle, the economy is operating below its production possibilities curve, as shown in Figure 7.3. As usual, the curve has been simplified to two goods, guns and butter, which represent the general output levels in the public and private sectors. The government attempts to move the economy from point *E* to a point closer to the production possibilities curve, *E'*.

Even when the economy is at full employment, resources will not be efficiently allocated (1) if competition is limited, (2) if there are externalities, (3) if public goods are involved, (4) if markets are missing, and (5) if information is limited.

LACK OF COMPETITION

Competition is essential for a market to function efficiently. Competition is what forces firms to look for more efficient ways of producing goods and to meet the desires of consumers more effectively. Without competition, prices will be higher and production lower than with competition. But life for the firms themselves is easier without competition, and profits are higher. Thus, firms try to reduce the extent of competition. Governments have passed numerous laws, called antitrust and fair competition laws, attempting to enhance competition in the market economy.

EXTERNALITIES

But even when there is competition, the market may supply too much of some goods and too little of others. One of the reasons for this is the presence of **externalities.** Externalities are present whenever an individual or firm can take an action that directly affects others but for which it neither pays nor is paid compensation. It therefore does not bear all the consequences of its action. (The effect of the action is "external" to the individual or firm.) Externalities

Economists have attempted to calculate the externalities associated with driving and smoking. When individuals drive, they ignore the costs of accidents and congestion they impose on other drivers and the air pollution they cause. Estimates of the total annual value of these external costs range into the billions of dollars. Gasoline taxes discourage driving, and thus are one way of offsetting "overconsumption." Say the appropriate gasoline tax is 20 cents a gallon. Assume the pretax price of gasoline is $1 and the supply of gasoline is perfectly elastic. The tax raises the price of gasoline by approximately 20 percent. If the gasoline price elasticity of the demand for driving is 0.5, this should decrease driving by about 10 percent.

Smoking also causes externalities. Some studies argue that second-hand smoke has adverse health effects. And typically, individuals pay only a fraction of their total health bills. There is strong evidence that smoking leads to lung and heart diseases, increasing health care expenditures. Offsetting this effect is the fact that smoking has one external "benefit": it causes people to die younger, reducing Social Security and other retirement benefits. While the negative externalities outweigh the positive, a relatively small tax, of approximately 20 cents per pack, was at one time thought to be appropriate. Such a tax, with a price elasticity of 0.3 and with a before-tax price of $2.00, would reduce consumption by 3 percent ($10\% \times 0.3$). This calculation, however, ignored one important effect: smoking has adverse effects on pregnancy, indicated, for instance, by increased low birth weights. The costs of these adverse effects are believed to be very large.

are pervasive. A hiker who litters, a driver whose car emits pollution, a child who leaves a mess behind after he finishes playing, a person who smokes a cigarette in a crowded room—all create externalities. In each case, the actor is not the only one who must suffer the consequences of his action; others suffer them too. Externalities can be thought of as instances when the price system works imperfectly. The hiker is not "charged" for the litter she creates, nor does the car owner pay for the pollution his car makes.

The examples so far are negative externalities. A common example of a negative externality is a factory that emits air pollution. The factory benefits from emitting the pollution, since by doing so, the company can make its product more cheaply than if it put in pollution-control devices. Society as a whole bears the negative external costs of pollution. If the factory had to pay for its pollution, it would find ways to produce less of it. And indeed, government environmental regulations are often aimed at just that goal.

Externalities can also be positive. A common example of a positive externality is a new invention. When someone makes a new discovery that leads to greater economic productivity, other people (or companies) benefit. The inventor receives, through the prices he charges, only a fraction of the total gains to society from the invention. Other firms will copy it and learn from it. Inventions like the laser and the transistor have benefited consumers, both by providing new products and allowing other products to be made less expensively. While the individual researcher bears the costs of making a discovery, society receives positive external benefits. If everyone who benefited from an invention had to pay money to the inventor, there would be far higher incentives for research and development. And indeed, patents and other government laws aimed at protecting intellectual property enable the investors to get a larger return than they otherwise would.

When externalities are present, the market's allocation of goods will be inefficient. When the production of a good such as steel entails a negative externality—like smoke and its effect on the air—the market level of production is too high. This is because the producer fails to take into account the "social costs" in deciding how much to produce. To put it another way, the price of steel determined in competitive markets by the law of supply and demand only reflects *private costs*, the costs actually faced by firms. If firms do not have to pay *all* of the costs (including the costs of pollution), equilibrium prices will be lower and output higher than they would be if firms took social costs into account.

The government can offset this effect in several ways. For instance, it might impose a tax. Panel A of Figure 7.4 shows the demand and supply curves for steel, and depicts the market equilibrium at the intersection of the two curves, Q_0. If the government imposes a tax on the production of steel, the supply curve will shift to the left—the quantity produced at each price will be lower—and the equilibrium level of production will be less, Q_1.

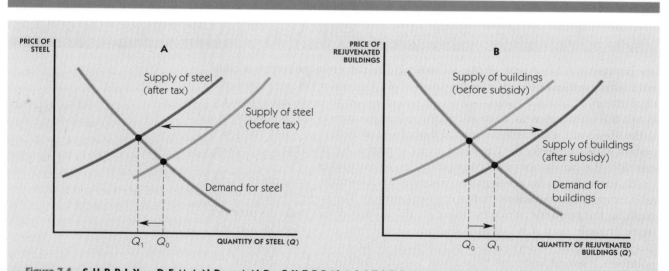

Figure 7.4 SUPPLY, DEMAND, AND EXTERNALITIES

The steel industry produces a negative externality of pollution. In panel A, a tax on steel production shifts the supply curve to the left, reducing both steel production and pollution. In panel B, a subsidy for rejuvenated buildings, which create the positive externality of neighborhood beautification, shifts the supply curve to the right, causing more buildings and neighborhoods to be renovated.

When the production of a good involves positive externalities, the market level of production is too low, and the government can try to enlarge the supply. The rejuvenation of an apartment building in a decaying part of a city provides an example of a positive externality; it will probably enhance the value of buildings around it. Panel B of Figure 7.4 shows the demand and supply curve for rejuvenated buildings. A government subsidy to rejuvenation shifts the supply curve to the right, increasing the number of rejuvenated buildings from Q_0 to Q_1.

PUBLIC GOODS

A particular category of goods, called **public goods,** is an extreme case of positive externalities. The consumption (or enjoyment) of a public good by one individual does not subtract from that of other individuals (consumption is accordingly said to be **nonrivalrous**). Public goods also have the property of **nonexcludability**—that is, it costs a great deal to exclude any individual from enjoying the benefits of a public good. The standard example of a public good is defense. Once the United States is protected from attack, it costs nothing extra to protect each new baby from foreign invasion. Furthermore, it would be virtually impossible to exclude a newborn from the benefits of this protection.

Public parks along the sides of a highway are another example. Anyone driving along the highway enjoys the view. The fact that one person is enjoying the view does not exclude others from enjoying it; and it would in fact be expensive to stop anyone who is driving along the highway from benefiting from the view. A lighthouse to guide ships around dangerous shoals or rocks is still another example of a public good. No additional costs are incurred as an additional ship navigates near the lighthouse, and it would be difficult to shut off the light in the lighthouse at just the right time to prevent a ship passing by from taking advantage of the lighthouse.

A **pure public good** is one where the marginal costs of providing it to an additional person are strictly zero and where it is impossible to exclude people from receiving the good. Many public goods that government provides are not *pure* public goods in this sense. The cost of an additional person using an uncrowded interstate highway is very, very small, but not zero, and it is possible, though relatively expensive, to exclude people from (or charge people for) using the highway.

Figure 7.5 compares examples of publicly provided goods against the strict definition of a pure public good. It shows the ease of exclusion along the horizontal axis and the (marginal) cost of an additional individual using the good along the vertical axis. The lower left-hand corner represents a pure public good. Of the major public expenditures, only national defense is close to a pure public good. Completely uncongested highways, to the extent they exist, are another example. The upper right-hand corner represents a pure private good (health services or education), where the cost of exclusion is low and the marginal cost of an additional individual using the good is high.

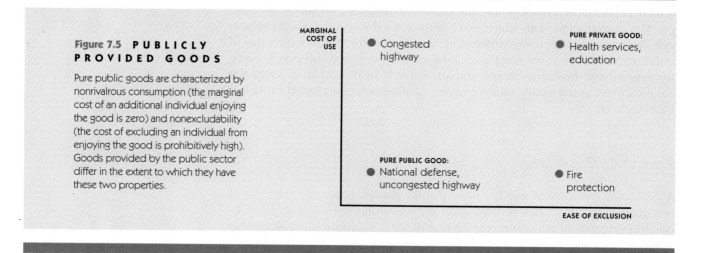

Figure 7.5 PUBLICLY PROVIDED GOODS

Pure public goods are characterized by nonrivalrous consumption (the marginal cost of an additional individual enjoying the good is zero) and nonexcludability (the cost of excluding an individual from enjoying the good is prohibitively high). Goods provided by the public sector differ in the extent to which they have these two properties.

Many goods are not pure public goods but have one or the other property to some degree. Fire protection is like a private good in that exclusion is relatively easy—individuals who refuse to contribute to the fire department could simply not be helped in the event of a fire. But fire protection is like a public good in that the marginal cost of covering an additional person is low. Most of the time, firefighters are not engaged in fighting fires but are waiting for calls. Protecting an additional individual has little extra cost. Only in that rare event when two fires break out simultaneously will there be a significant cost to extending fire protection to an additional person.

Sometimes the marginal cost of using a good to which access is easy (a good that possesses the property of nonexcludability) will be high. When an uncongested highway turns congested, the costs of using it rise dramatically, not in terms of wear and tear on the road but in terms of the time lost by drivers using the road. It is costly to exclude by charging for road use—as a practical matter, this can only be done on toll roads, and, ironically, the tollbooths often contribute to the congestion.

Many of the goods that are publicly provided, such as education and health services, have high costs associated with providing the service to additional individuals. For most of these goods, exclusion is also relatively easy. In fact, many of these goods and services are provided privately in some countries, or provided both publicly and privately. Though they are publicly provided in this country, they are not *pure* public goods, in the technical sense in which the term is defined.

Private markets undersupply public goods. If a single shipowner used the port near which a lighthouse is constructed, he could weigh the costs and benefits of the lighthouse. But if there were one large shipowner and many smaller owners, it would not pay any one of the small owners to build the lighthouse; and the large shipowner, in deciding whether to construct the lighthouse, would only take into account the benefits he would receive, not the benefits to the small shipowners. If the costs of construction exceeded the benefits that he alone would receive, he would not build the lighthouse. But if the benefits accruing to *all* the shipowners, large and small, were taken into account, those benefits might exceed the costs; it would then be desirable to build the lighthouse.

One can imagine a voluntary association of shipowners getting together to construct a lighthouse in this situation. But what happens if some small shipowner refuses to contribute, thinking that even if he does not contribute, the lighthouse will be built anyway? This is the **free-rider** aspect of public goods; because it is difficult to preclude anyone from using them, those who benefit from the goods have an incentive to avoid paying for them. Every shipowner has an incentive to "free ride" on the efforts of others. When too many decide to do this, the lighthouse will not be built.

Governments bring an important advantage to bear on the problem of public goods. They have the power to coerce citizens to pay for them. There might be *some* level of purchase of public goods—lighthouses, highway parks, even police or fire services—in the absence of government intervention. But society would be better off if the level of production were increased, and citizens were forced to pay for the increased level of public services through taxes.

MISSING MARKETS

Market economies only work well when there are, in fact, markets or good substitutes for markets. Before government provided unemployment insurance, disability insurance, and Social Security, individuals could not purchase these forms of insurance in the market.[2] In many areas, flood insurance, crop insurance, or even theft insurance is not available. Seventy-five years ago, before government became involved, many households could not obtain mortgages to buy a home. These are all examples of important **missing markets.** In later chapters, we will consider the reasons for these missing markets. For now, we simply note that the absence of these markets has served as an impetus for government programs to fill the gaps.

INFORMATION AND KNOWLEDGE

The efficiency with which it handles information is one of the great strengths of the market economy. Producers do not have to know what each consumer likes; and consumers do not have to know the details of production of any of the products which they consume. Prices convey information about scarcity. Working through the law of supply and demand, prices convey information from consumers to producers about how consumers value different goods, and from producers to consumers about the resources required (at the margin) to produce different goods.

---

[2]Even in those limited instances when insurance was available, the price was much higher than could be simply justified by the risks.

ECONOMIC ROLES FOR THE GOVERNMENT

Redistributing income
Correcting market failures

MAJOR MARKET FAILURES

Episodes of high unemployment
Lack of competition
Externalities
Public goods
Missing markets
Information and knowledge (including innovation)

But some kinds of information, like information about the weather, are public goods: the marginal cost of an additional individual benefiting from the information is negligible, and the cost of excluding individuals from this information may be considerable. This kind of information can also be important for efficient functioning of the economy, but markets do not produce efficient amounts of it. Thus, weather information is supplied by the U.S. Meteorological Service, an agency of the U.S. government.

Earlier, we saw how innovations typically give rise to externalities. Research can be thought of as the process of acquiring information, and innovation as the process of translating ideas, information, into new products. Later, we will discuss the array of government actions and programs that are trying to ensure not only that the level of resources allocated to knowledge acquisition is appropriate, but that it is directed in the right way.

BEYOND MARKET FAILURES

Markets, when they work well and do not suffer from one of the market failures described above, ensure that the economy is efficient—that resources are not wasted and that the economy operates on its production possibilities curve.

But efficiency is not everything. Even when a market is efficient, it may result in a distribution of income in which some individuals have hardly enough to live on, while others live in opulence.

Government actions are, of course, not limited to issues of economics. Governments try, for instance, to discourage robbery, rape, and murder. By and large, however, so long as an individual's action does not directly affect another, individuals are left to do what they please. I may think it strange that someone prefers vanilla to chocolate ice cream, or cherry to blueberry pie, but why should I impose my preferences? The principle that individuals are the best judges of what is in their own interests and that their preferences should be respected is called the **principle of consumer sovereignty.** There are, however, instances when government violates this principle: by smoking marijuana, an individual may cause no one else harm, yet governments in most states have made smoking marijuana illegal. Often, other rationales (such as externalities) for such actions are put forward; yet the underlying basis for government action remains inconsistent with the principle of consumer sovereignty. For instance, from 1920 to 1933, it was illegal to produce or sell alcoholic beverages in the United States. One of the reasons for this prohibition was the ill effects of drinking on others (such as alcohol-related accidents); but the view that drinking was *morally* wrong was what provided the fervor to the prohibition movement.

Government intervenes not only to discourage or prohibit certain actions, but to encourage or force others. It requires parents to send their children to school, for instance. Goods the government encourages because it believes there is some "public interest" in their consumption that is not an externality (although it goes beyond the private interests of those consuming the goods) are called **merit goods.**

GOVERNMENT'S OPTIONS

Once society has decided that government should do something, there is a second question: how can government accomplish society's ends most efficiently? The government has four choices. It can do something directly, it can provide incentives for the private sector to do something, it can mandate the private sector to do something, or it can take some combination of these.

TAKING DIRECT ACTION

One option is for government simply to take charge itself. If it believes there is a market failure in the provision of medical care, for instance, it can nationalize the medical sector, as Britain did after World War II. If the government believes there is a market failure in the airline or railroad industry, it can nationalize the industry, or the part of the industry with which it is discontent, and run the industry itself. If it believes there is a market failure in the provision of housing for the poor, it can build government housing projects.

Direct action does not require government to produce the good itself. It can also purchase the good from the private sector. Health care in the United States is an example. Although the government pays for much of the medical care of the poor and the elderly (through Medicaid and Medicare, respectively), it pays private doctors and hospitals to provide the actual care. Veteran's Hospitals, on the other hand, are run by the government.

PROVIDING INCENTIVES TO THE PRIVATE SECTOR

The government can also choose to operate at a distance, providing incentives to alter the workings of private markets in desirable ways. It can provide such incentives directly through subsidies, as it does for agriculture, or indirectly through the tax system, as is more commonly done in the United States. The government has used energy tax credits to encourage energy conservation. It has also used an investment tax credit, which gives firms a tax break for investing in new machines, to encourage investment. And special provisions of the tax code encourage employers to provide health insurance and pensions for their employees.

Subsidies and taxes put the government in the position of manipulating the price system to achieve its ends. If the government is worried about the supply of adequate housing for the poor, for example, it can provide builders with direct payments, or it can grant tax reductions for those who invest in slum areas. Both shift the supply curve of low cost housing to the right. If the government wants to encourage oil conservation, it can impose a tax on oil or gasoline, which will encourage conservation by raising the price of oil. It can also tax cars that are not energy efficient, raising their price.

MANDATING ACTION IN THE PRIVATE SECTOR

Concern about the effectiveness of incentives in achieving the desired result or about their cost (in tax forgiveness or outright payments) may lead government to mandate the desired action. A mandate is simply a requirement backed up by the threat of legal punishment. The government may mandate, for instance, that private firms provide health insurance to their employees.

GOVERNMENT'S OPTIONS

Taking direct action
   Production of a good or service
   Purchase of a good or service
Providing incentives to the private sector
   Direct subsidies
   Tax subsidies
Mandating private sector action

The government may mandate that automobile manufacturers produce fuel-efficient cars, specifying particular standards for miles per gallon of gas. Real estate developers who want to get a permit for a large housing project may be required to provide a certain number of units for low-income individuals, or to help improve a local road or build a loca l school. In all these cases, the government requirement does not show up as a cost on the government's budget. Mandates do have costs, however. These costs are borne indirectly by workers, firms, and consumers, and can be very high.

COMBINING OPTIONS

The government often combines two or more courses of action in its attempts to achieve some objective. Consider, for instance, the concern over medical care. The U.S. government pays for medical care for the aged and the poor; it provides actual medical care for veterans in hospitals it operates; it provides incentives for employers to offer health insurance by giving these expenditures favorable tax treatment; and there have been proposals to mandate firms to provide a minimum level of health insurance for employees. Different countries have chosen different mixes of these policies. In several countries, such as the United Kingdom, the government actually runs the entire health service; in other countries, government supplies health insurance to everyone and pays for that insurance with taxpayers' dollars.

GOVERNMENT FAILURES

Whenever there is a market failure, there is a *potential* role for government. Government needs to consider each of the alternatives discussed in the previous section, and assess the likelihood that one or the other alternative will succeed. Such an assessment may conclude that it is better not to intervene after all. Recent decades have provided numerous examples of government programs that have either not succeeded to the extent their sponsors had hoped, or have failed altogether. Urban renewal programs, meant to revive the inner cities and to provide housing for the poor, wound up destroying more low-income housing than they created. Welfare programs, intended to provide a safety net for the poor, are thought by some to have helped perpetuate the cycle of poverty. Out of the failures and limited successes of government programs has emerged a better understanding of the causes of government failure.

IMPERFECT INFORMATION

Imperfect information poses a problem in the public as well as the private sector. The government would like to make sure, for instance, that public welfare assistance goes only to those who really need it. But it is costly to sort out the truly deserving from those who are not. Spending more on screening applicants lets fewer of the undeserving through the application process. But spending more on administration leaves less to spend on benefits. As always, there are trade-offs.

INCENTIVES AND THE EFFICIENCY OF GOVERNMENT

Problems of incentives can be worse in the public than in the private sector. Homeowners, for example, have an incentive to maintain their property, not only because an attractive house is more enjoyable to live in, but also because when they sell, an attractive house will yield a higher price. Owners of a private apartment building, similarly, have incentives to maintain the building. And tenants in private apartments have an incentive not to abuse the property (they can be evicted or fail to have their lease renewed). Tenants in public housing have no such incentives. From their perspective, the quality of their apartment building is like a public good; each individual has too little incentive to maintain public amenities. Managers of public housing have no incentives comparable to private landlords, and they typically have limited discretion in evicting tenants or even in refusing to renew leases. The problem of incentives is made worse in the public sector because public officials work under a set of civil service rules about salary levels and job tenure that can make it difficult to hire first-rate workers or to reward workers for efficient performance. The rules make it difficult to pay good public officials a salary comparable to what similarly qualified and hardworking people receive in the private sector, or to offer them opportunities for rapid promotion. It is even more difficult to fire or demote incompetent and lazy workers.

Incentives in the public sector can actually lead to decisions that are not in the national interest in a broad sense. Legislators' concern about votes leads to "pork barrel" legislation, whose primary value is to create jobs or improve amenities in a legislator's home district. Presumably, most pork barrel projects would not be undertaken if those who lived in the district had to pay for it themselves, but the projects sound good if the rest of the country is footing the bill. It is widely believed, for instance, that a large number of unneeded military bases have been kept open because of congressional pressure.

Moreover, elected officials need funds to run their campaigns, and this makes them particularly attentive to those who can assist with campaign finances. The influence of the farm lobby in obtaining support, far out of proportion to the number of voters whose livelihood depends on agriculture, is frequently attributed to this sort of "special interest" lobbying. Unions and many other groups have formed Political Action Committees (PACs) to provide funds to congressional representatives who are sympathetic to their views. Naturally, lobbyists for these special interest groups claim they are not buying politicians but simply providing them with information needed to make an informed judgment—and then supporting those who have seen the truth. Some economists, including Nobel Prize winners James Buchanan and George Stigler, go so far as to see the problems of the public sector as perhaps the inevitable consequence of the political process.

WASTE IN GOVERNMENT

Whether for these or other reasons, many Americans view government as *necessarily* less efficient than private firms. These views have been supported by stories of government spending $1,000 for toilet seats and $200 for hammers, as well as some statistical studies which show systematic higher costs, associated with public housing (by as much as 20 percent) as opposed to private firms. While there are numerous instances of government inefficiency, the evidence casts doubt on the view that the public sector is inevitably less efficient than the private sector. When, for instance, government enterprises are subjected to competition—as in the case of the Canadian National Railroad (a government enterprise), which competes vigorously against the Canadian Pacific Railroad—the discipline of competition forces them to be equally efficient. The administrative costs of many private insurance companies—amounting to up to 30 percent or more of the premiums—are considerably higher than the administrative expenses of public social insurance, such as Social Security. France's state-run electricity company is reputedly as efficient as any private firm.

There are also theoretical reasons to question the conclusion that public enterprises are doomed to be less efficient. This is because *some* of the problems generating inefficiencies in the public sector plague the private sector also. Just as public sector employees typically do not receive any incentive pay (that is, pay is not linked to performance, so there are few *direct* returns to performing better), neither do most employees in the private sector. And large (with more than 500 employees) corporations—which still produce one-half of the economy's output—face bureaucratic problems no less than does government.

A consensus is thus emerging among economists that although the government is *often* less efficient than private firms performing similar tasks, it is not necessarily so. Major efforts are currently underway to increase government efficiency.

UNFORESEEN RESPONSES TO A PROGRAM

The success or failure of programs in the public sector depends not only on public officials, but also on how the private sector responds. Predicting those private responses is difficult, and many government programs have faced problems because of this difficulty. For example, providing almost free medical care to the aged, through Medicare, greatly increased the demand for medical services by the aged, leading to increases in costs well beyond those originally projected. In 1990, the government required that drug companies provide drugs to the government at the lowest price sold on the market. The government had observed that drug companies sold drugs to some customers at prices below those at which they were selling drugs to government under the Medicare program, and calculated that it could save billions of dollars by taking advantage of these discounts. But the drug companies cancelled

In 1993, President Clinton charged Vice President Al Gore with heading up a task force to identify systematically ways in which the government was doing its business inefficiently and recommend changes that would make it more efficient. This was the mandate to "reinvent government." The task force identified serious problems with procurement, how the government goes about buying goods from the private sector. For instance, when the government wants to buy a plain, ordinary T-shirt it takes more than thirty pages of fine print to describe the item in question. No wonder that a government-bought T-shirt costs more than its civilian counterpart, even if it is bought from the same dealer!

The government got itself into this mess with the best of motives. It puts up to competitive bidding most of what it purchases to ensure that it gets what it wants at the lowest price. But to get what it wants, the government must be precise in its specifications. Without such specifications for T-shirts, for example, a bidder might skimp on quality (cloth) or workmanship (stitching). Skimping might save only a dime a shirt. But if the government is in the market for a million shirts, the company that skimps stand to make an additional $100,000 in profits.

But drawing up specifications in such detail is almost certain to result in a T-shirt that is different from the standard T-shirts manufactured by the popular manufacturers—requiring a separate run, which raises the cost. Moreover, since most manufacturers simply do not find the inconvenience of filling a government contract worthwhile, the number of bidders is limited—raising the price still higher. Thus, rather than reducing prices, the competitive bidding process results in government actually paying higher prices.

The procurement reform proposed by the Gore task force to solve this general problem is simple.

It allows government to purchase off-the-shelf items through standard commercial channels, as long as the off-the-shelf prices are lower than the government can obtain through competitive bidding. Procurement reform may save the government several billion dollars a year. Other aspects of reinventing government entail efforts to get government to follow the best practices of America's most efficient companies—including a proposal to convert the nation's air traffic control system into a government-owned corporation.

Competition is enough to force the private sector constantly to "reinvent" itself, to look for better and more efficient ways of doing what it does. But it is political pressures—including the pressure of the huge government deficit—that provide the incentive to reinvent government.

all discounts, recognizing that it did not pay to discount at all if they had to give the government a discount every time they gave someone else a discount. As a result, instead of saving the government money, the legislation wound up costing other users of drugs more money!

Often a problem arises not from the overall design of a government program, but from a particular regulation. The Aid to Families with Dependent Children program (AFDC) used to have an eligibility requirement that there not be a man in the household (some states still have this requirement). The program may thus have contributed to the breakup of families. At other times, a problem occurs as an almost inevitable result of the program. Providing better Social Security benefits has enabled many elderly to live on their own, rather than being dependent on their children. These elderly, whose only or major source of income is Social Security, may (apart from the benefits of independence) be actually worse off than they were when they were living with their children. The true beneficiaries of increased Social Security may be not the elderly but their children, who have been relieved of a burden they otherwise would have assumed.

SOURCES OF PUBLIC FAILURES

Imperfect information

Problems of incentives, particularly for those charged with administering government programs, sometimes leading to waste

Failure to assess the full consequences of government programs, including responses of the private sector

AN APPRAISAL OF THE ROLE OF GOVERNMENT

The appropriate role of government is one of the most highly contested political issues. Consider the case of government's role in income redistribution. There are disagreements in assessing the trade-offs, such as the magnitude of the negative incentive effects arising from taxes upon the well-off to finance programs for the poor. And even if there were agreement about the magnitude of the incentive effects, there may be disagreements about whether the costs—in terms of reduced efficiency and reduced welfare of those who are hurt by higher taxes—are worth the gains—in terms of the benefits to the poor who are helped. Also, there are disagreements about basic values, such as whether the higher income of the well-off is their "just reward" for greater effort. Nonetheless, while there is disagreement about what role the government ought to play in the economy, there is general consensus among economists over the important role the government currently does play. This is our sixth consensus point:

6 The Role of Government

Government plays an important role in modern economies: it redresses market failures, redistributes income, and provides social insurance against risks such as unemployment, health care costs, disability, and retirement. Although the design and scope of government activity are often debated, there is broad agreement about the importance of the role of government in the economy.

REVIEW AND PRACTICE

SUMMARY

1. Government plays a pervasive role in the economy of almost every industrialized country. U.S. government expenditures are approximately one-third of national output—a much larger proportion than forty years ago, but a smaller proportion than in most countries of Western Europe. The major reason for the increase has been increased expenditures on Social Security/welfare, health programs, and interest payments.

2. In a democracy, the public sector differs from the private in two main ways. Its legitimacy and authority are derived from the electoral process; it also has certain powers of compulsion, such as requiring households and firms to pay taxes and obey laws.

3. By and large, private markets allocate resources efficiently. But in a number of areas they do not, as is the case with externalities and public

goods. Moreover, the economy sometimes fails to use the available resources fully; there may be idle industrial capacity and unemployed workers. Even when the economy is efficient, there may be dissatisfaction with the distribution of income.

4. Individuals and firms produce too much of a good with a negative externality, such as air or water pollution, since they do not bear all the costs. They produce too little of a good with a positive externality, such as a new invention, since they cannot receive all the benefits.

5. Public goods are goods that it costs little or nothing for an additional individual to enjoy, but that it costs a great deal to exclude any individual from enjoying. National defense and lighthouses are two examples. Free markets underproduce public goods.

6. Government has a variety of instruments it can use when markets are not functioning efficiently. It can take direct action, provide incentives to the private sector, or mandate action by the private sector.

7. While market failures provide a potential rationale for government action, government action may not provide an effective remedy. There are systematic reasons for "government failure" just as there are for "market failure."

8. The proper balance between the public and private sectors is a major concern of economics.

KEY TERMS

nationalization	market failures	missing markets
deregulation	externalities	principle of
privatization	public goods	consumer
"invisible hand"	free-rider problem	sovereignty

REVIEW QUESTIONS

1. Name some of the ways government touches the lives of all citizens, both in and out of the economic sphere.

2. "Since democratic governments are elected by the consent of a majority of the people, they have no need for compulsion." Comment.

3. How can individual selfishness end up promoting social welfare?

4. Name areas in which market failure can occur.

5. Why do goods with negative externalities tend to be overproduced? Why do goods with positive externalities tend to be underproduced? Give an example for each.

6. What two characteristics define a public good? Give an example.

7. What three broad types of instruments does government have to try to achieve its goals?

8. Does the presence of a market failure necessarily mean that government action is desirable? If not, why not?

PROBLEMS

1. In each of the following areas, specify how the government is involved, either as a direct producer, a regulator, a purchaser of final goods and services distributed directly to individuals or used within government, or in some other role:
  (a) education
  (b) mail delivery
  (c) housing
  (d) air travel
  (e) national defense.
In each of these cases, can you think of ways that part of the public role could be provided by the private sector?

2. Can you explain why even a benevolent and well-meaning government may sometimes have to use the power of eminent domain? (Hint: Consider the incentives of one person who knows that her property is the last obstacle to building a highway.)

3. Explain why government redistribution programs involve a trade-off between risk and incentives for *both* rich and poor.

4. Each of the situations below involves an externality. Tell whether it is a positive or negative externality, or both, and explain why free markets will overproduce or underproduce the good in question:
  (a) a business performing research and development projects
  (b) a business that discharges waste into a nearby river
  (c) a concert given in the middle of a large city park
  (d) an individual who smokes cigarettes in a meeting held in a small, unventilated room.

5. When some activity causes a negative externality like pollution, would it be a good idea to ban the activity altogether? Why or why not? (Hint: Consider marginal costs and benefits.)

6. Highways are often referred to as public goods. That designation is basically fair, but not perfect. What are the costs of "exclusion"? Can you describe a case where the marginal cost of an additional driver on a highway might be relatively high? How might society deal with this problem?

PART TWO

PERFECT MARKETS

art Two explores in depth the basic microeconomic assumptions of rational, well-informed consumers interacting with profit-maximizing firms in competitive markets. This set of assumptions, as we learned in Chapter 2, constitutes the economist's basic model. Here, we study the implications of this model and examine the powerful insights it affords. It turns out that while this basic model is a good starting point, consumers are often not as well-informed, and markets are often not as competitive, as the model assumes them to be. Part Three expands on and enriches the basic model in ways that make it more realistic.

The economy consists of three groups of participants—individuals or households, firms, and government—interacting in three markets, the labor, capital, and product markets. Part Two follows those divisions, with one important exception: the discussion of government is postponed to Part Three. The object in Part Two is to understand how a purely private market economy might operate. Chapters 8–10 discuss how individuals and households make their choices of what goods to consume, how much to save, how to invest their savings, and how much labor to supply. Chapters 11 and 12 analyze how firms make their decisions concerning how much to produce and how to produce it.

Finally, Chapter 13 brings households and firms together in the three markets. Households supply labor, and firms demand labor. The interaction of this supply and demand for labor determines wages. Similarly, households supply capital and firms demand capital to build factories and buy new machines. Their interaction in the capital market determines the interest rate and the equilibrium level of savings and investment in the economy. Households take their income, both what they earn as workers and the return on their savings, and use it to buy goods. They demand goods. With the workers they have hired, machines they have purchased, and factories they have built, firms produce goods. Firms' supply of goods and households' demand for goods interact in the product market, and this interaction determines the prices of the myriad of goods we consume.

CHAPTER 8

THE CONSUMPTION DECISION

M ore than 100 million U.S. households taken together make an astounding number of spending choices every day. These decisions contribute to the overall demand for cars and bicycles, clothes and housing, and masses of other products available on the market. The members of each household also make decisions that affect how much income they will have to spend, like whether to work overtime or whether both partners in a marriage should work. They decide how much of their income to save. And they decide where to put the nest eggs they do save.

These four sets of decisions—about spending, working, saving, and investing—represent the basic economic choices facing the household. This chapter focuses on spending decisions and how these decisions are affected by taxes and other government policies. Chapter 9 discusses working and saving decisions. Chapter 10 deals with household decisions concerning how to invest savings.

These microeconomic decisions have macroeconomic consequences as well. Household decisions about whether to buy a car that is imported from Japan or one that is American-made will affect the U.S. trade deficit. Choices about how much one should work will affect overall levels of unemployment and production. Household decisions about savings and investment will affect the future growth of the economy.

1. Where does the demand curve come from? Why is it normally downward sloping?

2. How does an increase in income shift the demand

curve? How do changes in the prices of other goods shift the curve?

THE BASIC PROBLEM OF CONSUMER CHOICE

The first basic problem facing a consumer is easy to state, though hard to resolve: what should he do with whatever (after tax) income he has to spend. He must allocate (that is, divide) his available income among alternative goods. Should he buy CDs, go to the movies, eat candy bars, or purchase sweaters? In the absence of scarcity the answer would be easy: have it all!

Chapter 2 provided the basic framework for economic decision making. The consumer defines his opportunity set, what is *possible* given the constraints he faces, and then chooses the most preferred point within this set. This chapter begins by reviewing how we define the opportunity set, and then asks how it changes—and how what the individual chooses changes—when incomes and prices change.

THE BUDGET CONSTRAINT

The individual's opportunity set is defined by the budget constraint. If, after taxes, a person's weekly paycheck comes to $300 and he has no other income, this is his budget constraint. Total expenditures on food, clothing, rent, entertainment, travel, and all other categories cannot exceed $300 per week. (For now we ignore the possibilities that individuals may borrow money, or save money, or change their budget constraints by working longer or shorter hours.)

The line *BC* in Figure 8.1A shows a simplified individual budget constraint. A student, Fran, has a total of $300 each semester to spend on "fun" items. Figure 8.1 assumes that there are two goods, candy bars and compact discs. The simplified assumption of only two goods is an abstraction that highlights the main points of the analysis.

Let's say that a candy bar costs $1, while a compact disc costs $15. If Fran spent all her income on candy bars, she could purchase 300 candy bars (point *B* on the budget constraint). If she spent all her income on CDs, she could buy

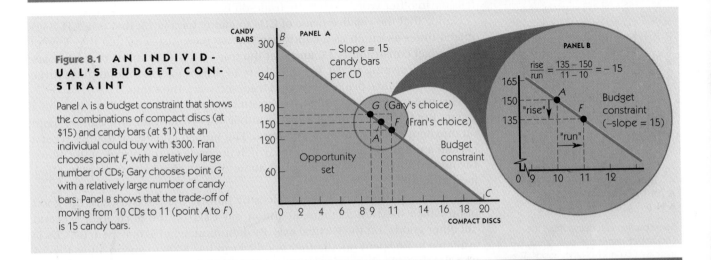

Figure 8.1 AN INDIVID-UAL'S BUDGET CONSTRAINT

Panel A is a budget constraint that shows the combinations of compact discs (at $15) and candy bars (at $1) that an individual could buy with $300. Fran chooses point F, with a relatively large number of CDs; Gary chooses point G, with a relatively large number of candy bars. Panel B shows that the trade-off of moving from 10 CDs to 11 (point A to F) is 15 candy bars.

20 CDs (point C on the budget constraint). Fran can also choose any of the intermediate choices on line BC. For example, she could buy 10 CDs (for $150) and 150 candy bars (for $150), or 15 CDs ($225) and 75 candy bars ($75). Each combination of purchases along the budget constraint totals $300.

As we learned in Chapter 2, a budget constraint diagram has two important features. First, although any point in the shaded area of Figure 8.1A is feasible, only the points on the line BC are really relevant. This is because Fran is not consuming her entire budget if she is inside her budget constraint. Second, by looking along the budget constraint, we can see the trade-offs she faces—how many candy bars she has to give up to get 1 more CD, and vice versa. Look at points F and A. This part of the budget constraint is blown up in panel B. At point A, Fran has 10 CDs; at F, she has 11. At F, she has 135 candy bars; at A, 150. To get 1 more CD, she has to give up 15 candy bars.

These are her trade-offs, and they are determined by the relative prices of the two goods. If one good costs twice as much as another, to get 1 more unit of the costly good, we have to give up 2 units of the cheaper good. If, as here, one good costs fifteen times as much as another, to get 1 more unit of the costly good, we have to give up 15 units of the less costly good.

The **slope** of the budget constraint also tells us what the trade-off is. The slope of a line measures how steep it is. As we move 1 unit along the horizontal axis (from 10 to 11 CDs), the slope measures the size of the change along the vertical axis. The slope is the rise (the movement up or down on the vertical axis) divided by the run (the corresponding horizontal movement). The slope of this budget constraint is thus 15.[1] It tells us how much of one good, at

---

[1]We ignore the negative sign. See the appendix to Chapter 2 for a more detailed explanation of the slope of a line.

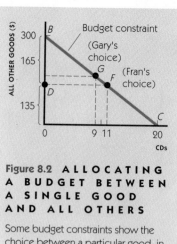

Figure 8.2 ALLOCATING A BUDGET BETWEEN A SINGLE GOOD AND ALL OTHERS

Some budget constraints show the choice between a particular good, in this case CDs, and all other goods. The other goods that might be purchased are collectively measured in money terms, as shown on the vertical axis.

a given price, we need to give up if we want 1 more unit of the other good; it tells us, in other words, what the trade-off is.

Notice that the relative price of CDs to candy bars is 15; that is, a CD costs fifteen times as much as a candy bar. But we have just seen that the slope of the budget constraint is 15, and that the trade-off (the number of candy bars Fran has to give up to get 1 more CD) is 15. It is no accident that these three numbers—relative price, slope, and trade-off—are the same.

This two-product example was chosen because it is easy to illustrate with a graph. But this logic can cover any number of products. Income can be spent on one item or a combination of items. The budget constraint defines what a certain amount of income can buy, which depends on the prices of the items. Giving up some of one item would allow the purchase of more of another item or items.

Economists represent these choices by putting the purchases of the good upon which they are focusing attention, say CDs, on the horizontal axis and "all other goods" on the vertical axis. By definition, what is not spent on CDs is available to be spent on all other goods. Fran has $300 to spend altogether. A more realistic budget constraint for her is shown in Figure 8.2. The intersection of the budget constraint with the vertical axis, point *B*—where purchases of CDs are zero—is $300. If Fran spends nothing on CDs, she has $300 to spend on other goods. The budget constraint intersects the horizontal axis at 20 CDs (point *C*); if she spends all her income on CDs and CDs cost $15 each, she can buy 20. If Fran chooses a point such as *F*, she will buy 11 CDs, costing $165, and she will have $135 to spend on other goods ($300–$165). The distance 0*D* on the vertical axis measures what she spends on other goods; the distance *BD* measures what she spends on CDs.

CHOOSING A POINT ON THE BUDGET CONSTRAINT: INDIVIDUAL PREFERENCES

The budget constraint and a recognition of possible trade-offs is the starting point for the study of consumer behavior. The process of identifying the budget constraints and the trade-offs is the same for *any* two people. If a person walks into a store (that only accepts cash) with $300, any economist can tell you his budget constraint and the trade-offs he faces by looking at the money in his pocket and the prices on the shelves. What choice will he make? Economists narrow their predictions to points on his budget constraint; any individual will choose *some* point along the budget constraint. But the point actually chosen depends on the individual's preferences: Fran, who likes to listen to music, might choose point *F* in Figure 8.1, while Gary, who loves candy, might choose *G*.

Few people will choose either of the extreme points on the budget constraint, *B* or *C* in Figure 8.1, where only one of the goods is consumed. The reason for this is that the more you have of a good—say, the more CDs you have relative to another good such as candy—the less valuable is an additional unit of that good relative to additional units of another good. At points near *C*, it seems safe to assume that to most individuals, an extra CD does not look as attractive as some candy bars. Certainly, at *B*, most people would be so full of candy bars that an extra CD would look preferable.

Where the individual's choice lies depends on how she values the two goods. Chapter 2 emphasized the idea that in making decisions, people look at the *margin;* they look at the extra costs and benefits. In this case, the choice at each point along the budget constraint is between 1 more CD and 15 more candy bars. If Gary and Fran choose different points along the budget constraint, it is because they value the marginal benefits (how much better off they feel with an *extra* CD) and the marginal costs (how much it hurts to give up 15 candy bars) differently. Gary chooses point *G* in Figure 8.1 because that is the point where, for him, the marginal benefit of an extra CD is just offset by what he has to give up to get the extra CD, which is 15 candy bars. When Fran, who loves listening to music, considers point *G*, she realizes that for her, at that point, CDs are more important and candy bars less important than they are for Gary. So she trades along the line until she has enough CDs and few enough candy bars that, for her, the marginal benefits of an extra CD and the marginal costs of 15 fewer candy bars are equal. This point, as we have supposed, is *F.*

The same reasoning holds for a budget constraint like the one shown in Figure 8.2. Here, Gary and Fran are choosing between CDs and all other goods, measured in dollar terms. Now in deciding to buy an extra CD, each one compares the marginal benefit of an extra CD with the marginal cost, what has to be given up in other goods. With CDs priced at $15, choosing to buy a CD means giving up $15 of other goods. For Gary, the marginal benefit of an extra CD equals the cost, $15, when he has only 9 CDs and can therefore spend $165 on other goods. For Fran, who has more of a taste for CDs, the marginal benefit of an extra CD does not equal this marginal cost until she reaches 11 CDs, with $135 to spend elsewhere. Thus, the price is a quantitative measure of the marginal benefit.

WHAT HAPPENS TO CONSUMPTION WHEN INCOME CHANGES?

When an individual's income increases, he has more to spend on consumption. Normally, he will buy a little more of many goods, although his consumption of some goods will increase more than that of others, and different individuals will spend their extra income in different ways. Jim may spend much of his extra income going out to eat in restaurants more often, while Bill may spend much of his extra income buying a more expensive car.

The **income elasticity of demand** (which parallels the *price* elasticity of demand presented in Chapter 5) measures how much the consumption of a particular good increases with income:

$$\text{income elasticity of demand} = \frac{\text{percentage change in consumption}}{\text{percentage change in income}}.$$

The income elasticity of demand, in other words, is the percentage change in consumption that would result from a one percent increase in income. If the income elasticity of demand of a certain good is greater than one, a 1 percent increase in an individual's income results in a more than 1 percent increase in expenditures on that good. That is, the amount he spends on that good increases more than proportionately with income. By definition, if the income elasticity of demand is less than one, then a 1 percent increase in income results in a less than 1 percent increase in expenditures. In this case, the share of income a consumer spends on that good decreases with a rise in income.

As people's incomes increase, the types of goods they choose to buy also change. In particular, they have more money to spend on goods other than those required just to survive. For instance, while they may spend some of the extra income to buy better-quality food and other necessities, more money goes toward movies, more expensive automobiles, vacations, and other luxuries. Accordingly, poor individuals spend a larger percentage of their income on food and housing and a smaller percentage of their income on perfume. In other words, the income elasticity of necessities is less than one, and the income elasticity of luxuries is greater than one.

The consumption of some goods actually decreases as income increases and increases as income decreases. These goods are called **inferior** goods. They are in sharp contrast to **normal** goods, the consumption of which increases with income. In other words, goods for which the income elasticity is *negative* are, by definition, inferior, while all other goods are called normal. For instance, if Fran, who has been riding the bus to work, gets a large raise, she may find that she can afford a car. After buying the car, she will spend less on bus tokens. Thus, in this particular sense, bus rides represent an inferior good.

Figure 8.3 shows how typical families at different income levels spend their income. In the figure, we see that *on average*, the poorest 20 percent of the population spend more than 100 percent of their before-tax income on housing—more than 100 percent is only possible because of government subsidies. This contrasts with the richest 20 percent, who spend only a fifth of their income on housing. Similarly, the poorest 20 percent spend nearly half their before-tax income on food, while the richest 20 percent spend less than a tenth.

Table 8.1 provides the income elasticities of some consumer goods. Chapters 4 and 5 pointed out that consumers and firms could make greater adjustments the longer the time they had to make changes. Thus, long-run price elasticities are normally larger—often much larger—than short-run price elasticities. The same is true for responses to changes in income. Long-run income elasticities are larger—often much larger—than short-run income elasticities. The data provided in the table are long-run elasticities. An example of the difference between long-run and short-run elasticity is provided by gasoline and oil; their long-run elasticity is 1.36; their short-run elasticity is only .55.

Note that the income elasticity of water is .59. It may seem surprising that water has any elasticity at all—don't poor people have to drink water just as much as rich people do to survive? The fact that there is a systematic relation-

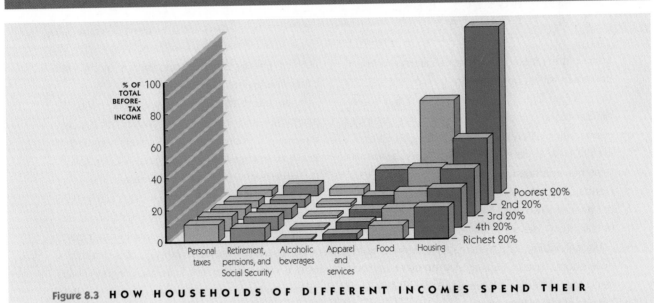

Figure 8.3 HOW HOUSEHOLDS OF DIFFERENT INCOMES SPEND THEIR MONEY

The poor spend far higher proportions of their income on basic necessities like food and housing than do the rich. *Note:* Before-tax income does not include borrowing or benefits received from government programs, which explains expenditures greater than 100 percent. *Source: Consumer Expenditure Survey Data,* 1984–87, Bulletin 2333.

Table 8.1 SOME INCOME ELASTICITIES OF DEMAND

Elastic (long-run)		Inelastic (long-run)	
Motion pictures	3.41	Car repairs	.90
Drugs and medicines	3.04	Tobacco products	.86
Owner-occupied housing	2.45	China, glassware, and utensils	.77
Nondurable toys	2.01	Shoe repairs	.72
Electricity	1.94	Alcoholic beverages	.62
Restaurant meals	1.61	Water	.59
Local buses and trains	1.38	Furniture	.53
Gasoline and oil	1.36	Clothing	.51
Car insurance	1.26		
Physicians' services	1.15		
Car purchases	1.07		

Source: H. S. Houthakker and Lester D. Taylor, *Consumer Demand in the United States* (Cambridge, Mass.: Harvard University Press, 1970).

Some of the differences in choices along a budget constraint reflect nothing more than differences in tastes—Fran likes CDs more than Gary. But some differences in choices are systematic, for instance representing differences in circumstances. Eleanor lives in New England and spends more on oil to heat her apartment than does Jim, who lives in Florida; Amy, who lives in Montana, 200 miles from the nearest town, buys more gas and spends more on cars than does someone from New York City.

Understanding such systematic determinants in how people spend their money helps us understand the markedly different responses in different regions of the country to government proposals to tax different goods. A case in point arose in 1993, after the Clinton administration took office with a pledge to reduce the huge federal deficit. Many policy analysts, both inside and outside government, favored a tax on energy. Most energy sources are relatively cheap in the United States compared to many other industrialized countries. Low energy prices lead Americans to consume high quantities of energy, thus increasing urban congestion, air pollution, and greenhouse gas emissions. A tax on energy would provide incentives to conserve energy—making such a tax an environmentally sound way of raising revenue and cutting the deficit.

The administration proposed a BTU tax—named after the British Thermal Unit, a standard measure of energy. The intent was to levy the tax on the basis of energy used, treating all energy sources alike. The tax proposal generated immediate opposition from heavy energy users. Americans living in the Northeast, who needed to heat their homes for much of the year, claimed that the tax would hit them unfairly. The aluminum industry, a heavy user of energy, strongly opposed it along with other energy-intensive industries.

In an effort to make the tax more politically palatable—and increase the chance of passage through the Congress—policymakers whittled it down to a single-form-of-energy tax—on gasoline. The proposal turned into an increase in the gasoline tax from 14.1 cents to 20.6 cents per gallon. Americans in the West, who drive much longer distances in a typical day than people in other parts of the country, were up in arms. Politics dictated a reduction in the proposed gas tax. Congress finally passed, and the President signed, a mere 4.3 cents per gallon increase in the tax on gasoline, which raises about $24 billion from 1993 to 1998, or less than $5 billion a year more in federal revenue than before the gas tax increase. This tax rate is too low to have a major effect on driving, let alone on energy use as a whole, and the extra revenues will have a similarly small effect on the federal deficit.

ship between income and water consumption simply emphasizes the point that, with effort, you can economize on almost any resource. At lower income levels, you may wash your car less often, water your lawn less often, and so on.

Information like that contained in Figure 8.3 is of great practical importance. For example, it helps determine how a tax will affect different groups. Anybody who consumes alcohol will be hurt by a tax on alcohol. But if the poor spend a larger fraction of their income on alcohol, as the figure suggests, they will bear a disproportionately large share of the tax.

A CLOSER LOOK AT THE DEMAND CURVE

In Chapter 4, we saw the principal characteristic of the demand curve: when prices rise, the quantity of a good demanded normally falls. Here, we take a closer look at why. This will help us understand why some goods respond more strongly to price changes, that is, have a greater price elasticity.

Let us return to our earlier example of Fran buying CDs in Figure 8.2. If the price of CDs rises from $15 to $20, Fran will face a new budget constraint. If she didn't buy any CDs, she would still have $300 to spend on other goods; but if she decided to spend all of her income on CDs, she could only buy 15 rather than 20. Her budget constraint is now the blue line in Figure 8.4.

The increase in the price of CDs has one obvious and important effect: Fran cannot continue to buy the same number of CDs and the same amount of other goods as she did before. Earlier, Fran bought 11 CDs. If she bought the same number of CDs, it would cost her $55 more, and she would have $55 less to spend on other goods. No matter what she does, Fran is worse off as a result of the price increase. It is *as if* she had less income to spend. When she has less income to spend, she reduces her expenditure on each good, including CDs. This part of the response to the higher price is called the **income effect.** An increase in income of about $55, or 18 percent ($55 out of $300), would offset the price increase.[2] Assume the income elasticity is approximately 1; that is, with income reduced by 18 percent, she would reduce purchases of CDs by 18 percent, which is about 2 CDs. This part of the reduction of the demand of CDs, from 11 to 9, is the income effect.

The magnitude of the income effect depends on two factors: how important the commodity is to the individual—that is, how large a fraction of the individual's income is spent on the good—and how large the income elasticity is. Since, in most cases, individuals spend a relatively small fraction of their income on any particular good, the income effect is relatively small. But in the case of housing, for example, on which individuals spend between a quarter

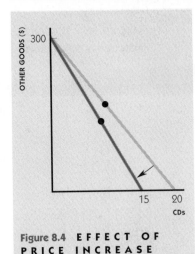

Figure 8.4 EFFECT OF PRICE INCREASE

An increase in the price of CDs moves the budget constraint down as shown. Fran must cut back on the consumption of some goods. Here, we show her cutting back both on the consumption of CDs and other goods.

---

[2]Actually, it would slightly overcompensate. With the $55 increase, Fran could buy exactly the same bundle of goods as before, but as we shall shortly see, she will *choose* to reallocate her spending. The reallocation will make her better off.

In recent years, the government has contemplated a variety of "sin" taxes—taxes on smoking and drinking—as well as environmental taxes—taxes on gasoline—as a way of raising revenue. To calculate the revenue raised from any tax, the government must estimate the elasticity of demand. If the elasticity of demand is high, then a tax which raises the price will reduce quantity consumed, and hence the revenue raised will be greatly reduced. Even if the elasticity is not high, if huge taxes are imposed—such as has been proposed for cigarettes—the reduction in consumption may be large.

For instance, the price elasticity of demand for cigarettes is estimated to be 0.3. In 1994, the tax stood at 24 cents, or 12 percent of the price. There have been proposals to raise the tax to 69 cents, 99 cents, or $2.00, raising the price (assuming that the tax is passed on to consumers) by 22.5, 37.5, or 88 percent. If the trend towards less smoking and other sources of price increases is ignored, the tax would thus reduce consumption by 6.8, 11.3, or 26.4 percent, and the estimated revenues would be far less than if there were no demand response. For instance, if the tax were quadrupled to 99 cents, rather than quadrupling tax revenue (as would be the case if demand remained unchanged), revenue would be increased only by a factor of 2.5.

and a third of their income on average, the income effect of an increase in the price of housing is significant.

Let us go back to Fran and the CDs. At the higher price, giving up one CD gets her more of other goods—more candy bars, more movies, more tapes, more sweaters. The relative price of CDs, or the trade-off between CDs and other goods has changed. At the higher price, she *substitutes* goods that are less expensive for the more expensive CDs. Not surprisingly, this effect is called the **substitution effect.** The magnitude of the substitution effect depends on how easily Fran can substitute other goods. If Fran still owns her tape player, and if the price of tapes remains unchanged, then the substitution effect might be large. She may drop the number of CDs she purchases to 2. But if Fran has no tape player, if the only entertainment she likes is listening to music, and if she dislikes all the music played by the local radio stations, then the substitution effect may be small. She may drop the number of CDs she purchases only to 8.

DERIVING DEMAND CURVES

We can now see both how to derive the demand curve and why it has the shape it does. At each price, we draw the budget constraint and identify the point along the budget constraint that is chosen. As the price of CDs increases, Fran will choose points along the successive budget constraints with fewer CDs purchased: higher prices mean she is less well off, and therefore, through the income effect, decrease her purchases of all goods. The higher price *relative to other goods* means she will substitute other goods for CDs.

THE IMPORTANCE OF DISTINGUISHING BETWEEN INCOME AND SUBSTITUTION EFFECTS

Distinguishing between the income and substitution effects of a change in price is important for two reasons.

Understanding Responses to Price Changes   First, the distinction improves our understanding of consumption responses to price changes. Thinking about the substitution effect helps us understand why some demand curves have a low price elasticity and others a high price elasticity. It also helps us understand why the price elasticity may well differ at different points along the demand curve. Recall from Chapter 5 that when an individual is consuming lots of some good, substitutes for the good are easy to find, and a small increase in price leads to a large reduction in the quantity demanded; but as consumption gets lower, it becomes increasingly difficult to find good substitutes.

Or consider the effect of an increase in the price of one good on the demand for *other* goods. There is always an income effect; the income effect, by itself, would lead to a reduced consumption of all commodities. But the substitution effect leads to *increased* consumption of substitute commodities. Thus, an increase in the price of Coke will lead to increased demand for Pepsi at each price; the demand curve for Pepsi shifts to the right, because the substitution effect outweighs the slight income effect.

Understanding Inefficiencies Associated with Taxes   A second reason to focus on income and substitution effects is to identify some of the inefficiencies associated with taxation. The purpose of a tax is to raise revenue so that the government can purchase goods; it represents a transfer of purchasing power from the household to the government. If the government is to obtain more resources, individuals have to consume less. Thus, any tax must have an income effect.

But beyond that, taxes often distort economic activity. The distortion caused by taxation is associated with the substitution effect. Take the window tax imposed in medieval England. It was intended to raise revenue. It led, instead, to the construction of windowless houses—a major distortion of the tax. Most of the distortions associated with modern taxes are somewhat more subtle. Take a tax on airline tickets or on telephone calls. Reducing consumption of things that are against society's interest can be a legitimate goal of taxation. But the government does not think flying or making telephone calls is a bad thing. The tax is levied to raise revenues. But it results in fewer air flights and telephone calls anyway—an unintentional consequence. Any tax leads to *some* reduction in consumption, through the income effect. But most taxes also

USING ECONOMICS: INCOME AND SUBSTITUTION EFFECTS

After the huge increase in oil prices in the late 1970s, President Carter wanted to conserve energy by discouraging the use of oil. One plan entailed the government raising the price of gasoline by imposing a tax, but then refunding the tax to consumers by reducing their income taxes. Some commentators ridiculed this idea. What's the point of collecting a tax and then refunding it? The answer is simple: the substitution effect.

Imagine that before this plan, Lucy has an income of $20,000. She spends $500 a year (2.5 percent of her income) on gasoline; at a price of $1.00 a gallon, she can buy 500 gallons of gasoline. Assume first that the tax on a gallon of gasoline is raised by $.20, increasing the price Lucy pays to $1.20 a gallon. If the price elasticity of demand for gasoline is .5, then this price increase will lead to a fall in quantity demanded of 10 percent

(20 percent × .5 = 10 percent). Now Lucy is buying 450 gallons (90 percent of 500) at a price of $1.20 a gallon—and spending a total of $540. Government revenue is $.20 × 450 = $90. Assume that the government refunds Lucy the $90. (The refund depends not on the actual amount of the gasoline tax paid by Lucy but on the average amount paid by all taxpayers. In this example, Lucy is an average person, so her refund is just equal to the gasoline tax she paid.) Is the government undoing the effect of the higher gasoline prices by giving consumers income? Not entirely. If Lucy continues to spend about 2.5 percent of her additional income on gasoline, her expenditure on gasoline goes up by just over $2 (2.5 percent × $90 refund). Her consumption of gasoline is still lower than it would have been without the tax combined with the rebate.

change relative prices; so they have a substitution effect. It is the substitution effect that gives rise to the distortion. If the substitution effect is small, the distortion is small; if the substitution effect is large, the distortion is large.

UTILITY AND THE DESCRIPTION OF PREFERENCES

We have seen that people choose a point along their budget constraint by weighing the benefits of consuming more of one good against the costs— what they have to forgo of other goods. Economists refer to the benefits of consumption as the **utility** that individuals get from the combination of goods they consume. Presumably a person can tell you whether or not he prefers a certain combination of goods to another. Economists say that the preferred bundle of goods gives that individual a higher level of utility than the other bundle of goods he could have chosen. Similarly, economists say that the individual will choose the bundle of goods—within the budget constraint—that maximizes his utility.

In the nineteenth century, social scientists, including the British philosopher Jeremy Bentham, hoped that science would someday develop a machine that could actually measure utility. A scientist could simply hook up some electrodes to an individual's head and read off how "happy" she was. Most modern economists believe that there is no *unique* way to measure utility, but that there are useful ways of measuring changes in how well-off a person is.

For our purposes, a simple way to measure utility will suffice: we ask how much an individual would be willing to pay to be in one situation rather than another. For example, if Joe likes chocolate ice cream more than vanilla, it stands to reason that he would be willing to pay more for a scoop of chocolate ice cream than for a scoop of vanilla. Or if Diane would rather live in California than in New Jersey, it stands to reason that she would be willing to pay more for the West Coast location.

Notice that how much a person is willing to pay is different from how much he *has* to pay. Just because Joe is willing to pay more for chocolate ice cream than for vanilla does not mean he will have to pay more. What he has to pay depends on market prices; what he is willing to pay reflects his preferences. Willingness to pay is a useful measure of utility, which is often helpful for purposes such as thinking about how an individual allocates his income along his budget constraint. But the hopes of nineteenth-century economists, that we could find some way of measuring utility that would allow us to compare how much utility Fran got from a bundle of goods with how much utility Gary obtained, are now viewed as pipe dreams.

Using willingness to pay as our measure of utility, we can construct a diagram like Figure 8.5A, which shows the level of utility Mary receives from sweatshirts as the number of sweatshirts she buys increases. This information is also given in Table 8.2. Here we assume that Mary is willing to pay $200 for 5 sweatshirts, $228 for 6 sweatshirts, $254 for 7 sweatshirts, and so on. Thus, 5 sweatshirts give her a utility of 200, 6 a utility of 228, and 7 sweatshirts a utility of 254. Mary's willingness to pay increases with the number of sweatshirts, reflecting the fact that additional sweatshirts give her additional utility. The extra utility of an additional sweatshirt, measured here by the additional amount she is willing to pay, is the **marginal utility.** The numbers in the third column of Table 8.2 give the marginal (or extra) utility she received from her last sweatshirt. When Mary owns 5 sweatshirts, an additional sweatshirt yields her an additional or marginal utility of 28 (228 − 200); when she owns 6 sweatshirts, an additional one gives her a marginal utility of only 26 (254 − 228). Panel B traces the marginal utilities of each of these increments.[3]

As an individual's bundle of goods includes more and more of a good, each successive increment increases her utility less. This is the law of **diminishing**

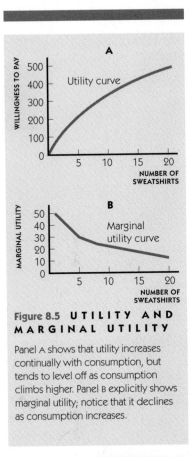

Figure 8.5 UTILITY AND MARGINAL UTILITY

Panel A shows that utility increases continually with consumption, but tends to level off as consumption climbs higher. Panel B explicitly shows marginal utility; notice that it declines as consumption increases.

---

[3]Since marginal utility is the extra utility from an extra unit of consumption, it is measured by the slope of the utility curve in panel A.

Table 8.2 UTILITY AND MARGINAL UTILITY

Number of sweatshirts	Mary's willingness to pay (utility)	Marginal utility	Number of pizzas	Mary's willingness to pay (utility)	Marginal utility
0	0	50	0	0	18
1	50	45	1	18	16
2	95	40	2	34	15
3	135	35	3	49	14
4	170	30	4	63	13
5	200	28	5	76	12
6	228	26	6	88	11
7	254	24	7	99	10
8	278	23	8	109	9
9	301	22	9	118	8
10	323	21	10	126	7
11	344	20	11	133	6
12	364	19	12	139	5
13	383	18	13	144	4
14	401	17	14	148	
15	418	16			
16	434	15			
17	449	14			
18	463	13			
19	476	12			
20	488				

marginal utility. The first sweatshirt is very desirable, and additional ones are attractive as well. But each sweatshirt does not increase utility by as much as the one before, and at some point, Mary may get almost no additional pleasure from adding to her sweatshirt wardrobe.

When Mary has a given budget and must choose between two goods that cost the same, say sweatshirts and pizza, each of which costs $15, she will make her choice so that the marginal utility of each good is the same. Table 8.2 shows Mary's willingness to pay (utility) for both sweatshirts and pizza. Look at what happens if Mary buys 20 sweatshirts with her $300 and no pizza. The marginal utility of the last sweatshirt is 12, and that of the first pizza is 18. If she switches $15 from sweatshirts to pizza, she loses a utility of 12 from the decreased sweatshirts, but gains 18 from her first pizza. It obviously pays for her to switch.

Now look at the situation when she has decreased her purchases of sweat-shirts to 17 and increased purchases of pizza to 3. The marginal utility of the last sweatshirt is 15, and that of the last pizza is also 15. At this point, she will not want to switch anymore. If she buys another sweatshirt, she gains 14, but the *last* pizza, her 3rd, which she will have to give up, has a marginal utility of 15; she loses more than she gains. If she buys another pizza, she gains 14, but the last sweatshirt (her 17th) gave her 15; again, she loses in net. We can thus see that with her budget, she is best off when the marginal utility of the two goods is the same.

The same general principle applies when the prices of two goods differ. Assume that a sweatshirt costs twice as much as a pizza. So long as the marginal utility of sweatshirts is more than twice that of pizzas, it still pays for Mary to switch to sweatshirts. To get one more sweatshirt, she has to give up two pizzas, and we reason, as before, that she will adjust her consumption until she gets to the point where the marginal utilities of the two goods, *per dollar spent,* are equal. This is a general rule: in choosing between two goods, a consumer will adjust her choices to the point where the marginal utilities are proportional to the prices. Thus, the last unit purchased of a good that costs twice as much as another must generate twice the marginal utility as the last unit purchased of the other good; the last unit purchased of a good that costs three times as much must generate three times the marginal utility as the last unit purchased of the other good; and so on.

We can write this result simply as

$$\frac{MU_x}{p_x} = \frac{MU_y}{p_y}$$

where Mu_x is the marginal utility of good x, MU_y is the marginal utility of good y, p_x is the price of good x, and p_y is the price of good y. The ratio of the marginal utility to price should be the same for all goods.

In the example we have just analyzed, we assumed Mary's willingness to pay for sweatshirts—her measure of utility—does not depend on how many pizzas, or other goods, she has. This is seldom the case. The utility, and hence marginal utility, of sweatshirts will depend on the number of pizzas, books, and other goods she has. Thus, even when the price of sweatshirts remains the same, if the price of other goods changes, she will change her consumption of those other goods *and* sweatshirts. The same thing will happen if Mary's income changes.

CONSUMER SURPLUS

Assume you go into a store to buy a can of soda. The store charges you 50 cents. You would have been willing to pay $1.00. The difference between what you paid and what you would have been willing to pay is called **consumer surplus.**

We can calculate the consumer surplus Mary gets from buying pizza from her demand curve. To see how we do this, use the marginal utility analysis of the previous section. We saw that at 11 pizzas, Mary is willing to pay $6 for one more; at 12, she is willing to pay $5.

Mary buys pizza up to the point where the price is equal to the marginal utility of the last pizza she chooses to buy. Of course, she pays the same price for each of the pizzas she purchases. Suppose pizzas cost $5 and Mary buys 13. The 13th pizza gives her a marginal utility of 5 and costs $5. Mary is getting a bargain: she would have been willing to pay more for the earlier pizzas. For her first pizza, she would have been willing to pay $18, for the second $16, and so forth. She would have been willing to pay a total of $144 ($18 + $16 + $15 + $14 + $13 + $12 + $11 + $10 + $9 + $8 + $7 + $6 + $5) for the 13 pizzas. The difference between what she *has* to pay for 13 pizzas—$5 × 13, or $65—and what she would have been willing to pay, $144, is her consumer surplus. In this case, her consumer surplus is $79.

There is always some consumer surplus, so long as a consumer has to pay only a fixed price for all the items she purchases. The fact that demand curves are downward sloping means that the previous units the consumer purchases are more valuable than the marginal units. She would have been willing to pay more for these earlier units than for the last unit, but she does not have to.

In Figure 8.6, the total amount Mary would have been willing to pay for 13 pizzas is the total area under the demand curve between the vertical axis and 13, the combination of the lightly and heavily shaded areas. This area is the sum of the willingness to pay for the 1st, 2nd, 3rd, and so on, up to 13 pizzas. The amount Mary actually has to pay is the heavily shaded area—the price, $5, times the quantity, 13 pizzas. Her consumer surplus is the *difference*, the lightly shaded area above the price line and below the demand curve, over the range of the quantity purchased.

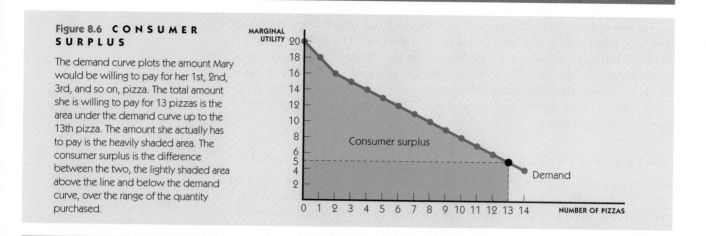

Figure 8.6 CONSUMER SURPLUS

The demand curve plots the amount Mary would be willing to pay for her 1st, 2nd, 3rd, and so on, pizza. The total amount she is willing to pay for 13 pizzas is the area under the demand curve up to the 13th pizza. The amount she actually has to pay is the heavily shaded area. The consumer surplus is the difference between the two, the lightly shaded area above the line and below the demand curve, over the range of the quantity purchased.

LOOKING BEYOND THE BASIC MODEL: HOW WELL DO THE UNDERLYING ASSUMPTIONS MATCH REALITY?

In the market economy, "For whom are goods produced?" has a simple answer: goods are produced for consumers. A theory of consumer choice is, therefore, critical to understanding market economies. The model of budget constraints and individual preferences sketched in this chapter is the economist's basic model of consumer choice. It is a powerful one whose insights carry well beyond this course. Still, the model has been criticized. Four criticisms are summarized here. The first has no economic merit. The other three are somewhat relevant. The first criticism is that the model does not reflect the thought processes consumers really go through. This line of criticism is like criticizing the physicist's model of motion, which predicts with great precision how billiard balls will interact, simply because most pool players do not go through the equations before taking a shot. The appropriate question is whether the economic model of consumer choice can reliably be used to make predictions. By and large it can. Many businesses, for example, have found the model useful for predicting the demand for their products. And economists have used the model with remarkable success to predict consumer behavior in a variety of circumstances.

The second criticism questions the model's assumption that individuals know what they like, which is to say that they have well-defined preferences. This criticism has some merit. Having well-defined preferences means that if you gave someone a choice between two bundles of goods—one consisting of two apples, three oranges, and one pear and the other consisting of three apples, two oranges, and four pears—he could tell you quickly which he preferred. Furthermore, well-defined preferences imply that if you asked him tomorrow and the day after, he would give you the same answer. But in many cases, if you asked someone which of two things he preferred, he would say, "I don't know. Let me try them out." And what he likes may change from day to day. His preferences may, moreover, be affected by what others like. How else can we account for the frequent fads in foods and fashions as well as other aspects of our lives?

The third criticism has to do with the model's assumption that individuals know the prices of each good in the market. People often do not know prices. They know that there are bargains to be found, but they know it is costly to search for them. While we can talk meaningfully about the price of a bushel of wheat, what do we mean by the "price" of a couch, or a house? If we are lucky and stumble onto a deal, we might find a leather couch for $1,000. If unlucky, even after searching all day, we may not find one for under $1,500. When we

CLOSE-UP: INTERNATIONAL PRICE AND INCOME ELASTICITIES FOR FOOD

For many in the poorer nations, getting enough food to live on is a daily struggle. But for residents of wealthy nations, food is easy to come by. These differences in circumstances are reflected in differences in income and price elasticities. The left-hand column of the table below lists selected countries from the poorest to richest, with their per capita income given as a percentage of per capita income in the United States in the second column. The third column gives an income elasticity for food in that country, while the fourth column lists a price elasticity for food.

Notice that the income elasticity of demand for food declines as income rises. This makes intuitive sense: as poor people receive more income, they will tend to spend a larger proportion of their additional money on food than wealthier people will. In India, a 10 percent increase in income will lead to a 7.6 percent increase in the quantity of food demanded. Looking at the fourth column, we see that for the richer countries such as the United States and Canada, a 10 percent increase in the price of food leads only to a 1 percent reduction in the quantity of food purchased.

More of the expenditures on food in the richer countries are luxuries—restaurants, lobsters, steaks. One might have thought that this would imply that the price elasticity in richer countries would be larger than in poorer countries. But there is another effect that dominates. In poorer

Country	Per capita income (as % of U.S.)	Income elasticity of food	Price elasticity of food
India	5.2%	.76	−.32
Nigeria	6.7%	.74	−.33
Indonesia	7.2%	.72	−.34
Bolivia	14.4%	.68	−.35
Philippines	16.8%	.67	−.35
Korea	20.4%	.64	−.35
Poland	34.6%	.55	−.33
Brazil	36.8%	.54	−.33
Israel	45.6%	.49	−.31
Spain	55.9%	.43	−.36
Japan	61.6%	.39	−.35
Italy	69.7%	.34	−.30
United Kingdom	71.7%	.33	−.22
France	81.1%	.27	−.19
Germany	85.0%	.25	−.17
Canada	99.2%	.15	−.10
United States	100.0%	.14	−.10

Source: Ching-Fun Cling and James Peale, Jr., "Income and Price Elasticities," in Henri Thell, ed., *Advances in Econometrics Supplement* (Greenwich, CT: JAI Press, 1989). Data are from 1980.

countries, people spend a much larger fraction of their income on food. When the price of food goes up, they almost have to reduce food consumption. This is not the case in the wealthier countries. Because expenditures on food represent a larger fraction of total expenditures in poor countries, the income effect of a rise in the price of food there is larger.

get the bargain leather couch home, if we are lucky, we will find it is even better than we thought. If unlucky, the couch will fall apart.

The final criticism points out that sometimes prices and preferences interact in a more complicated way than this chapter has depicted. People's attitudes toward a good can depend on its price. More expensive goods may have snob appeal. And when the quality of certain goods cannot easily be checked, individuals may judge quality by price. Because, on average, better (more durable) things are more costly, a cheap item is assumed to be of poor quality and an expensive item of good quality. In either case, demand curves will look quite different from those described in this chapter. Lowering the price for a good may actually lower the demand.

The fact that the basic economic model needs to be extended or modified for some goods in some instances does not deny its usefulness in the vast majority of situations where it provides just the information that businesses and governments need for making important decisions. Even in those instances where the model does not work so well, it provides a basic framework that allows us to enhance our understanding of the behavior of households. By asking which of the assumptions underlying the model seems inappropriate in that particular situation, we are guided in our search for a better model of consumption.

REVIEW AND PRACTICE

SUMMARY

1. The amount of one good a person must give up to purchase another good is determined by the relative prices of the two goods, and is illustrated by the slope of the budget constraint.

2. As a good becomes more expensive relative to other goods, an individual will substitute other goods for the higher-priced good. This is the substitution effect.

3. As the price of a good rises, a person's buying power is reduced. The response to this lower "real" income is the income effect. Consumption of a normal good rises as income rises. Thus, normally, when price rises both the substitution and income effects lead to decreased consumption of that good.

4. When substitution is easy, demand curves tend to be elastic, or flat. If substitution is difficult, demand curves tend to be inelastic, or steep.

5. Economists sometimes describe the benefits of consumption by referring to the utility that people get from a combination of goods. The extra utility of consuming one more unit of a good is referred to as the marginal utility of that good.

KEY TERMS

slope	normal good	marginal utility
income elasticity of demand	income effect	diminishing marginal utility
inferior good	substitution effect	consumer surplus
	utility	

REVIEW QUESTIONS

1. How is the slope of the budget constraint related to the relative prices of the goods on the horizontal and vertical axes?

2. How can the budget constraint appear the same even for individuals whose tastes and preferences differ dramatically?

3. Is the income elasticity of demand positive or negative for a normal good?

4. If the price of a normal good increases, how will the income effect cause the quantity demanded of that good to change?

5. What is the substitution effect? Why do the substitution and income effects normally reinforce each other? Is this true for an inferior good?

6. Does a greater availability of substitutes make a demand curve more or less elastic? Explain.

7. Why does marginal utility tend to diminish?

8. What is meant by consumer surplus?

PROBLEMS

1. A student has an entertainment budget of $120 per term, and spends it on either concert tickets at $10 apiece or movie tickets at $6 apiece. Suppose movie tickets decrease in price, first falling to $4, then $3, then $2. Graph the four budget constraints, with movies on the horizontal axis. If the student's demand for movies, D, is represented by the function $D = 60 - 10p$, where p is the price, graph both the demand curve for movies and the point she will choose on the budget line corresponding to each price.

2. Choose two normal goods and draw a budget constraint illustrating the trade-off between them. Show how the budget line shifts if income increases. Arbitrarily choose a point on the first budget line as the point a particular consumer will select. Now find two points on the new budget line such that the new preferred choice of the consumer must fall between these points.

3. DINKs are households with "double income, no kids," and such households are invading your neighborhood. You decide to take advantage of this influx by starting a gourmet take-out food store. You know that the price elasticity of demand for your food from DINKs is .5 and the income elasticity of demand is 1.5. From the standpoint of the quantity that you sell, which of the following changes would concern you the most?

   (a) The number of DINKs in your neighborhood falls by 10 percent.
   (b) The average income of DINKs falls by 5 percent.

4. Compare one relatively poor person, with an income of $10,000 per year, with a relatively wealthy person who has an income of $60,000 per year. Imagine that the poor person drinks 15 bottles of wine per year at an average price of $10 per bottle, while the wealthy person drinks 50 bottles of wine per year at an average price of $20 per bottle. If a tax of $1 per bottle is imposed on wine, who pays the greater amount? Who pays the greater amount as a percentage of income? If a tax equal to 10 percent of the value of the wine is imposed, who pays the greater amount? Who pays the greater amount as a percentage of income?

   The data in Table 8.1 show an income elasticity of .62 for alcoholic beverages. Consider two people with incomes of $20,000 and $40,000. If all alcohol is taxed at the same rate, by what percentage more will the tax paid by the $40,000 earner be greater than that paid by the $20,000 earner? Why might some people think this unfair?

5. Consider two ways of encouraging local governments to build or expand public parks. One proposal is for the federal government to provide grants for public parks. A second proposal is for the government to agree to pay 25 percent of any expenditures for building or expansion. If the same amount of money would be spent on each program, which do you predict would be most effective in encouraging local parks? Explain your answer, using the ideas of income and substitution effects.

APPENDIX: INDIFFERENCE CURVES AND THE CONSUMPTION DECISION[4]

This chapter explained the consumption decision in terms of the budget constraint facing the individual and the individual's choice of her most preferred

[4]This appendix may be skipped without loss of understanding of later chapters.

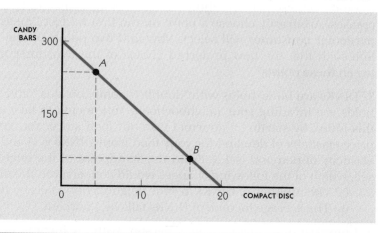

Figure 8.7 BUDGET CON-STRAINT

The budget constraint defines the opportunity set. Fran can choose any point on or below the budget constraint. if she has strong preferences for CDs, she might choose B; if she has strong preferences for candy bars, she might choose point A.

point on the budget constraint. Effects of changes in prices on the quantity demanded were analyzed in terms of income and substitution effects.

To facilitate a more rigorous analysis of choices and the consequences of changes in prices, economists have developed an extremely useful tool called **indifference curves.** Indifference curves give the combinations of goods among which an individual is indifferent or which yield the same level of utility. This appendix shows how indifference curves can be used to derive the demand curve and to separate more precisely changes in consumption into income and substitution effects.

USING INDIFFERENCE CURVES TO ILLUSTRATE CONSUMER CHOICES

In this chapter solutions to consumer choice problems were characterized as having two stages: first, identify the opportunity set, and second, find the most preferred point in the opportunity set. For consumers with a given income to spend on goods, the budget constraint defines her opportunity set. Figure 8.7 repeats the budget constraint for Fran, who must divide her income between candy bars and CDs. In the chapter, we simply said that Fran chose the most preferred point along the budget constraint. If she likes CDs a lot, she might choose point B; if she has a stronger preference for candy, she might choose point A.

The concept of the indifference curve can help us see which of these points she chooses.

The indifference curve shows the various combinations of goods that make a person equally happy. For example, in Figure 8.8, the indifference curve I_0 gives all those combinations of candy bars and compact discs that Fran finds just as attractive as 150 candy bars and 10 CDs (point A on the curve). At B, for instance, she has 12 CDs but only 130 candy bars—not so much candy, but in

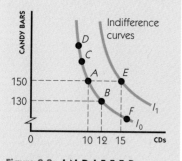

Figure 8.8 INDIFFER-ENCE CURVES

An indifference curve traces combinations of goods among which anindividual is indifferent. Each reflects Fran's taste for CDs and for candy bars. She is just as well off (has an identical amount of utility) at all points on the indifference curve I_0: A, B, C, D, or F.

her mind the extra CDs make up for the loss. The fact that B and A are on the same indifference curve means that Fran is indifferent. That is, if you asked her whether she preferred A to B or B to A, she would answer that she couldn't care less.

Indifference curves simply reflect preferences between pairs of goods. Unlike demand curves, they have nothing to do with budget constraints or prices. The different combinations of goods along the indifference curve cost different amounts of money. The indifference curves are drawn by asking an individual which he prefers: 10 candy bars and 2 CDs or 15 candy bars and 1 CD? or 11 candy bars and 2 CDs or 15 candy bars and 1 CD? or 12 candy bars and 2 CDs or 15 candy bars and 1 CD? When he answers, "I am indifferent between the two," the two points that represent those choices are on the same indifference curve.

Moving along the curve in one direction, Fran is willing to accept more CDs in exchange for fewer candy bars; moving in the other direction, she is willing to accept more candy bars in exchange for fewer CDs. Any point on the same indifference curve, by definition, makes her just as happy as any other— whether it is point A or C or an extreme point like D, where she has many candy bars and very few CDs, or F, where she has relatively few candy bars but more CDs.

However, if Fran were to receive the same number of candy bars but more CDs than at A—say 150 candy bars and 15 CDs (point E)—she would be better off on the principle that "more is better." The new indifference curve I_1 illustrates all those combinations of candy bars and CDs that make her just as well off as the combination of 150 candy bars and 15 CDs.

Figure 8.8 shows two indifference curves for Fran. Because more is better, Fran (or any individual) will prefer a choice on an indifference curve that is higher than another. On the higher indifference curve, she can have more of both items. By definition, we can draw an indifference curve for *any* point in the space of an indifference curve diagram. Also by definition, indifference curves cannot cross, as Figure 8.9 makes clear. Assume that the indifference curves I_0 and I_1 cross at point A. That would mean that Fran is indifferent between A and all points on I_0, and between A and all points on I_1. In particular, she would be indifferent between A and B, between A and C, and accordingly between B and C. But B is clearly preferred to C; therefore, indifference curves cannot cross.

INDIFFERENCE CURVES AND MARGINAL RATES OF SUBSTITUTION

The slope of the indifference curve measures the number of candy bars that the individual is willing to give up to get another compact disc. The technical term for the slope of an indifference curve is the **marginal rate of substitution.** The marginal rate of substitution tells us how much of one good an individual is *willing* to give up in return for one more unit of another. This concept is quite distinct from the amount a consumer *must* give up, which is determined by the budget constraint and relative prices.

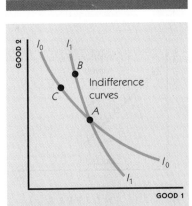

Figure 8.9 WHY INDIFFERENCE CURVES CANNOT CROSS

If two indifference curves crossed, a logical contradiction would occur. If curves crossed at point A, then Fran would be indifferent between A and B, between A and C, and therefore between B and C. But since B involves higher consumption of both goods than C, B is clearly preferred to C.

If Fran's marginal rate of substitution of candy bars for CDs is 15 to 1, this means that if she is given 1 more CD, she is willing to give up 15 candy bars. If she only had to give up 12 candy bars, she would be happier. If she had to give up 20, she would say, "That's too much—having one more CD isn't worth giving up twenty candy bars." Of course, Gary could have quite different attitudes toward CDs and candy bars. His marginal rate of substitution might be 25 to 1. He would be willing to give up 25 candy bars to get 1 more CD.

The marginal rate of substitution rises and falls according to how much of an item an individual already has. For example, consider point F back in Figure 8.8, where Fran has a lot of CDs and few candy bars. In this case, Fran already has bought all her favorite CDs; the marginal CD she buys now will be something she likes, but not something she is wild over. In other words, because she already has a large number of CDs, having an additional one is less important. She would rather have some candy bars instead. Her marginal rate of substitution of candy bars for CDs at F is very low; for the sake of illustration, let's say that she would be willing to give up the marginal CD for only 10 candy bars. Her marginal rate of substitution is 10 to 1 (candy bars per CD).

The opposite situation prevails when Fran has lots of candy bars and few CDs. Since she is eating several candy bars almost every day, the chance to have more is just not worth much to her. But since she has few CDs, she does not yet own all of her favorites. The marginal value of another candy bar is relatively low, while the marginal value of another CD is relatively high. Accordingly, in this situation, Fran might insist on getting 30 extra candy bars before she gives up 1 CD. Her marginal rate of substitution is 30 to 1 (candy bars per CD).

As we move along an indifference curve, we increase the amount of one good (like CDs) that an individual has. In Fran's case, she requires less and less of the other good (candy bars) to compensate her for each one-unit decrease in the quantity of the first good (CDs). This principle is known as the **diminishing marginal rate of substitution.** As a result of the principle of diminishing marginal rate of substitution, the slope of the indifference curve becomes flatter as we move from left to right along the curve.

USING INDIFFERENCE CURVES TO ILLUSTRATE CHOICES

By definition, an individual does not care where he sits on any *given* indifference curve. But he would prefer to be on the highest indifference curve possible. What pins him down is his budget constraint. As Figure 8.10 illustrates, the highest indifference curve that a person can attain is the one that just touches the budget constraint—that is, the indifference curve that is *tangent* to the budget constraint. The point of tangency (labeled E) is the point the individual will choose. Consider any other point on the budget constraint, say A. The indifference curve through A is below the curve through E; the individual is better off at E than at A. But consider an indifference curve above I_0, for instance I_1. Since every point on I_1 lies above the budget constraint, there is no point on I_1 that the individual can purchase given his income.

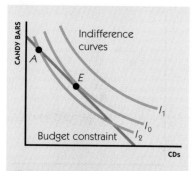

Figure 8.10 INDIFFERENCE CURVES AND THE BUDGET CONSTRAINT

The highest feasible indifference curve that can be reached is the one just tangent to the budget constraint, or indifference curve I_0 here. This individual's budget constraint does not permit her to reach I_1, nor would she want to choose point A, which would put her on I_2, since along I_2 she is worse off.

When a curve is tangent to a line, the curve and line have the same slope at the point of tangency. Thus, the slope of the indifference curve equals the slope of the budget constraint at the point of tangency. The slope of the indifference curve is the marginal rate of substitution; the slope of the budget constraint is the relative price. This two-dimensional diagram therefore illustrates a basic principle of consumer choice: *individuals choose the point where the marginal rate of substitution equals the relative price.*

This principle makes sense. If the relative price of CDs and candy bars is 15 (CDs cost $15 and candy bars cost $1) and Fran's marginal rate of substitution is 20, Fran is willing to give up 20 candy bars to get 1 more CD, but only *has* to give up 15; it clearly pays her to buy more CDs and fewer candy bars. If her marginal rate of substitution is 10, she is willing to give up 1 CD for just 10 candy bars; but if she gives up 1 CD, she can get 15 candy bars. She will be better off buying more candy bars and fewer CDs. Thus, if the marginal rate of substitution exceeds the relative price, Fran is better off if she buys more CDs; if it is less, she is better off if she buys fewer CDs. When the marginal rate of substitution *equals* the relative price, it does not pay for her to either increase or decrease her purchases.

INCOME ELASTICITY

Budget constraints and indifference curves show why, while goods normally have a positive income elasticity, some goods may have a negative income elasticity. As incomes increase, the budget constraint shifts out to the right in a parallel line, say from BC in Figure 8.11 to B_1C_1 to B_2C_2. The choices—the points of tangency with the indifference curves—are represented by the points E_0, E_1, and E_2. In panel A, we see the normal case, where as the budget constraint shifts out, more of both candy bars and CDs are consumed. But panel B illustrates the case of inferior goods. Potatoes are on the horizontal

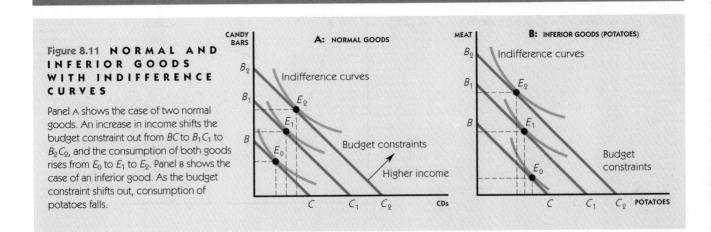

Figure 8.11 NORMAL AND INFERIOR GOODS WITH INDIFFERENCE CURVES

Panel A shows the case of two normal goods. An increase in income shifts the budget constraint out from BC to B_1C_1 to B_2C_2, and the consumption of both goods rises from E_0 to E_1 to E_2. Panel B shows the case of an inferior good. As the budget constraint shifts out, consumption of potatoes falls.

axis, and meat is on the vertical. As incomes rise, the points of tangency (E_1 and E_2) move to the left; potato consumption actually falls.

USING INDIFFERENCE CURVES TO DERIVE DEMAND CURVES

Indifference curves and budget constraints can be used to derive the demand curve, to show what happens when prices increase. The analysis consists of two steps.

First, we identify what happens to the budget constraint as, say, the price of CDs increases. In the budget constraint drawn in Figure 8.12A, we find CDs on the horizontal axis and all other goods on the vertical axis. If Fran buys no CDs, she has $300 to spend on all other goods. At a CD price of $15, she can

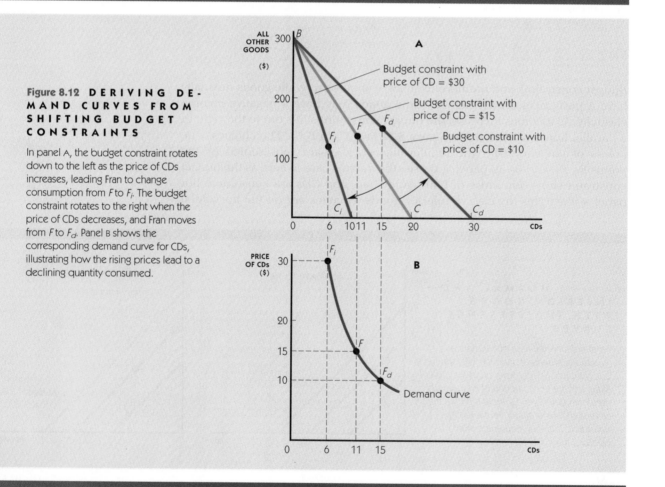

Figure 8.12 DERIVING DE-MAND CURVES FROM SHIFTING BUDGET CONSTRAINTS

In panel A, the budget constraint rotates down to the left as the price of CDs increases, leading Fran to change consumption from F to F_i. The budget constraint rotates to the right when the price of CDs decreases, and Fran moves from F to F_d. Panel B shows the corresponding demand curve for CDs, illustrating how the rising prices lead to a declining quantity consumed.

buy up to 20 CDs. As the price of CDs increases, the budget constraint rotates. If she buys no CDs, the amount of other goods she can purchase is unchanged, at $300. But if she buys only CDs, the number of CDs she can purchase decreases in proportion to the increase in price. If the price rises to $30, she can buy half the number of CDs.

For each budget constraint, we find the point of tangency between the indifference curve and the budget constraint, the points labeled F_i, F, and F_d. This shows the point chosen along each budget constraint. Looking at the horizontal axis, we see, at each price, the quantity of CDs purchased. Panel B then plots these quantities for each price. At the price of $15, Fran chooses 11 CDs, at a price of $30, only 6.

SUBSTITUTION AND INCOME EFFECTS

Indifference curves also permit a precise definition of the substitution and income effects. Figure 8.13 plots some of Jeremy's indifference curves between CDs and candy bars. Jeremy's original budget constraint is line BC and his indifference curve is I_0; the point of tangency, the point he chooses, is point E_0. Suppose the price of candy increases. Now he can buy fewer candy bars, but the number of CDs he can buy, were he to spend all of his income on CDs,

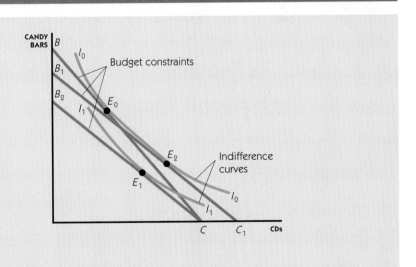

Figure 8.13 SUBSTITUTION AND INCOME EFFECTS WITH INDIFFERENCE CURVES

As the price of candy bars increases, the budget constraint rotates down. The change of Jeremy's choice from E_0 to E_1 can be broken down into an income and a substitution effect. The line B_1C_1 shows the substitution effect, the change in the budget constraint that would occur if relative prices shifted but the level of utility remained the same. (Notice that Jeremy stays on the same indifference curve in this scenario.) The substitution effect alone causes a shift from E_0 to E_2. The shift in the budget constraint from B_1C_1 to B_2C shows the income effect, the change that results from changing the amount of income but leaving relative prices unchanged. The income effect alone causes a shift from E_2 to E_1.

is unchanged. Thus, his budget constraint becomes flatter; it is now line B_2C. While Jeremy originally chose point E_0 on the indifference curve I_0, now he chooses E_1 on the *lower* indifference curve I_1.

The price change has moved Jeremy's choice from E_0 to E_1 for two reasons: the substitution effect and the income effect. To see how this has happened, let's isolate the two effects. First, we focus on the substitution effect by asking what would happen to Jeremy's consumption if we changed relative prices, but did not change how well off he was. To keep him just as well off as before the price change, we must keep him on the same indifference curve, I_0. Thus, the substitution effect is a movement along an indifference curve. As the price of candy rises, Jeremy, moving down the indifference curve, buys more CDs and fewer candy bars. The movement from E_0 to E_2 is the substitution effect. The budget constraint B_1C_1 represents the *new* prices, but it does not account for the income effect, by definition, since Jeremy is on the same indifference curve that he was on before.

To keep Jeremy on the same indifference curve when we increase the price of candy requires giving Jeremy more income. The line B_1C_1 is the budget constraint with the *new* prices that would leave Jeremy on the same indifference curve. Because prices are the same, the budget constraint B_1C_1 is parallel to B_2C. We now need to take away the income that left Jeremy on the same indifference curve. We keep prices the same (at the new levels), and we take away income until we arrive at the new budget constraint B_2C, and the corresponding new equilibrium E_1. The movement from E_2 to E_1 is called the income effect, since only income is changed. We have thus broken down the movement from the old equilibrium, E_0, to the new one, E_1, into the movement from E_0 to E_2, the substitution effect, and the movement from E_2 to E_1, the income effect.

LABOR SUPPLY AND SAVINGS

T he first of the four basic decisions of the household—how individuals choose to spend their money—was discussed in Chapter 8. How much money people have to spend depends, in turn, on two other basic decisions: how much they choose to work (and earn) and how much they save (or spend from savings). This chapter focuses on these two decisions. We will see that consumer theory can be applied directly to analyzing the work and saving decisions. We will also see how the supply curve for labor and the supply curve for savings can be derived, and why they have the shapes they do. Chapter 10 then focuses on the fourth basic decision: how individuals invest what they save.

KEY QUESTIONS

1. How can the basic tools introduced in Chapter 8 to analyze consumers' expenditure decisions be applied to such important aspects of life as work, education, and savings?

2. What determines the number of hours an individual works, or whether she chooses to work or not? How

do income and substitution effects help us to understand why labor supply may not be very responsive to changes in wages, or savings to changes in interest rates?

3. Why do economists think of education as an investment, and refer to the result as human capital?

THE LABOR SUPPLY DECISION

Patterns of labor supply have changed greatly in the past three decades. The average work week for a production worker has declined by one-eighth since 1950. At the same time, the fraction of women in the labor force has increased enormously. As a result, the typical married household now devotes more hours to work outside the home than it did in 1900. The number of hours worked in different jobs and industries also varies. As Figure 9.1 shows, miners work 45 hours per week on average, for instance, while those in the retail sector work fewer than 30 hours.

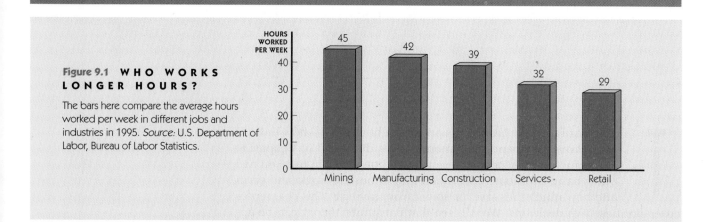

Figure 9.1 WHO WORKS LONGER HOURS?

The bars here compare the average hours worked per week in different jobs and industries in 1995. *Source:* U.S. Department of Labor, Bureau of Labor Statistics.

THE CHOICE BETWEEN LEISURE AND CONSUMPTION

Economists use the basic model of choice to help understand these patterns of labor supply. The decision about how much labor to supply is a choice between consumption, or income, and leisure. (Leisure to an economist means all the time an individual could potentially work for pay that he actually spends not working. The time parents spend caring for their children, for example, is leisure in this special sense.) By giving up leisure, a person receives additional income, and therefore increases his consumption. By working less and giving up some consumption, a person obtains more leisure. An increase in income does not necessarily translate *immediately* into consumption; the individual has to decide whether to spend his extra income now or in the future. We tackle this later in the chapter. Here we assume that the person spends all his income.

Even though the typical job seems to represent a fixed time requirement, there are a variety of ways in which people can influence how much labor they will supply. Many workers may not have discretion as to whether they will work full time, but they have some choice in whether or not they will work overtime. In addition, many individuals moonlight; they take up second jobs that provide them with additional income. Most of these jobs—like driving a taxi—provide considerable discretion in the number of hours worked. Hence, even when people have no choice about how much they work at their primary job, they still have choices. Further, the fact that jobs differ in their normal work week means that a worker has some flexibility in choosing a job that allows her to work the amount of hours she wishes. Finally, economists believe that the social conventions concerning the "standard" work week—the 40-hour week that has become the 35-hour week—respond over time to the attitudes (preferences) of workers.

We now apply the analysis of Chapter 8 to an individual's choice between work and leisure. Figure 9.2 shows the budget constraint of Steve, who earns an hourly wage of $5. Accordingly, for each hour less of leisure Steve enjoys—for each extra hour he works—he earns $5 more; that is, his consumption increases by $5. Underlying this budget constraint is his time constraint. He has only so many hours a day, say 16, to spend either working or at leisure. For each extra hour he works, he has 1 less hour of leisure. If he works 1 hour, his income is $5, if he works 2 hours, his income is $10, and so forth. If he works 16 hours—he has no leisure—his income is $5 × 16 = $80. The budget constraint trade-off is $5 per hour.

Steve will choose a point on the budget constraint according to his own preferences, just as he chose between two goods in Chapter 8. He must choose the appropriate trade-off between consumption and leisure. Let's suppose that he chooses point E_0. At E_0, he has 10 hours of leisure, which means that he works 6 hours out of a total available time of 16 hours, and makes $30.

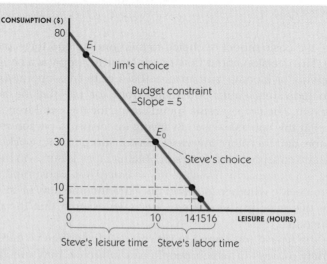

Figure 9.2 A BUDGET CONSTRAINT BE-TWEEN LEISURE AND INCOME

Individuals are willing to trade leisure for an increase in income, and thus in consumption. The budget constraint shows Steve choosing E_0, with 10 hours of daily leisure, 6 hours of work, and $30 in daily wages.

In deciding which of the points along the budget constraint to choose, Steve balances out the marginal benefits of what he can buy with an additional hour's wages with the marginal costs—the value of the hour's worth of leisure that he will have to forgo. Steve and his brother Jim assess the marginal benefits and marginal costs differently: Steve chooses point E_0, while his brother chooses point E_1. Jim values the material things in life more and leisure less.

For Steve, at E_0, the marginal benefit of the extra concert tickets or other goods he can buy with the money he earns from working an extra hour just offsets the marginal cost of that hour, the extra leisure he has to give up. At points to the left of E_0, Steve has less leisure (so the marginal value of leisure is greater) and he has more goods (so the marginal value of the extra goods he can get is lower). The marginal benefit of working more exceeds the marginal costs, and so he works more—he moves toward E_0. Converse arguments apply to Steve's thinking about points to the right of E_0.

We can use the same kind of reasoning to see why the workaholic Jim chooses a point to the left of E_0. At E_0, Jim values goods more and leisure less; the marginal benefit of working more exceeds the marginal cost. At E_1, the marginal benefit of working an extra hour (the extra consumption) just offsets the marginal cost.

This framework can be used to analyze the effect of changes in income and wages on the work–leisure decision in the same way that we discussed the effects of changes in income and prices on purchases of goods and services. For instance, an increase in nonwage income normally leads individuals to consume more of all "goods," including leisure: at fixed wages, as nonwage incomes rise, labor supply decreases.

Changes in wages have both an income effect and a substitution effect. An increase in wages makes individuals better off. When individuals are better off they work less. This is the income effect. But an increase in wages also changes the trade-offs. By giving up one more hour of leisure, the individual can get more goods. Because of this, individuals are willing to work more. This is the substitution effect.

In the case of the typical good, we saw that the income and substitution effects reinforced each other. A higher price meant individuals were worse off, and this lead to reduced consumption of the good; and a higher price meant that individuals substituted away from the good whose price had increased. *With labor supply, income and substitution effects work in opposite directions, so the net affect of an increase in wages is ambiguous.*

We derive the labor supply curve in the same way we derived the demand curve for a good in Chapter 8. Figure 9.3 shows two possible outcomes.

Figure 9.3A shows the normal case of an upward-sloping labor supply curve, where the substitution effect dominates. Panel B illustrates the case of a backward-bending labor supply curve. At high wages, the income effect of further increases in wages outweighs the substitution effect, so that labor supply decreases. Doctors, dentists, and other high-income professionals who work only a four-day week may be evidence of a labor supply curve that is backward bending at high-income levels.

If income and substitution effects just outweigh each other, then labor supply will be relatively unaffected by wage changes. The evidence is that, at least for men, the labor supply elasticity—the percentage increase in hours worked as a result of a 1 percent increase in real wages—is positive but small. That is

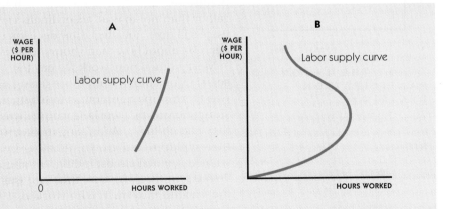

Figure 9.3 THE LABOR SUPPLY CURVE

Panel A shows the case where the substitution effect exceeds the income effect by just a bit, so increases in wages lead to only a small change in labor supply, and the labor supply curve is almost vertical. In panel B, the substitution effect dominates the income effect at low wages, so that the labor supply curve is upward sloping; and the income effect dominates the substitution effect at high wages, so that the labor supply is downward sloping over that range. Thus, the labor supply curve bends backward.

why in spite of the huge increase in wages over the past fifty years, average hours worked, for men, has not changed much.

WAGE CHANGES AND LABOR SUPPLY

As wages rise, individuals become better off. This income effect induces them to work less. Offsetting this is the substitution effect—the greater return to working provides an incentive to work longer hours. Either effect may dominate. Thus, the quantity of labor supplied may increase or decrease with wage increases.

LABOR FORCE PARTICIPATION

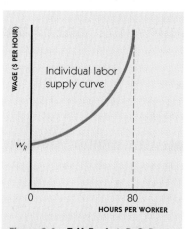

Figure 9.4 THE LABOR PARTICIPATION DECISION

The reservation wage W_R is the minimum wage at which an individual supplies labor.

The decision about how much labor to supply can be divided into two parts: whether to work and, if so, how much to work. The decision about *whether* to work is called the **labor force participation decision.** Figure 9.4 shows the labor supply curve for an individual, that is, how many hours he is willing to supply at each wage. The minimum wage at which the individual is willing to work, W_R, is called the **reservation wage.** Below the reservation wage, the individual does not participate in the labor force.

For men, the question of whether to work has traditionally had an obvious answer. Unless they were very wealthy, they have had to work to support themselves (and their families). The wage at which they would decide to work rather than not to was, accordingly, very low. For most men, a change in the wage still does not affect their decision of whether to work. It affects only their decision about how many hours to work, and even this effect is small.

Most women now work for pay too. Women, however, have faced different social expectations from those facing men. Only a few decades ago, not only was there some question as to whether women should work, the social presumption was that working women would drop out of the labor market when they had children. And many mothers did not reenter the market even after their children had grown. Whether by social convention or by choice, most women seemed almost indifferent about whether they worked for pay. Small changes in the wage rate thus had the potential of causing large changes in the fraction of women who worked. The labor supply curve for women appeared to be very elastic (flat). Some economists have estimated a female labor supply elasticity as large as .9; that is, a 1 percent increase in wages leads to a .9 percent increase in labor supply.

Today the traditional presumptions about the role of women have changed. Most women without small children participate in the labor market, and

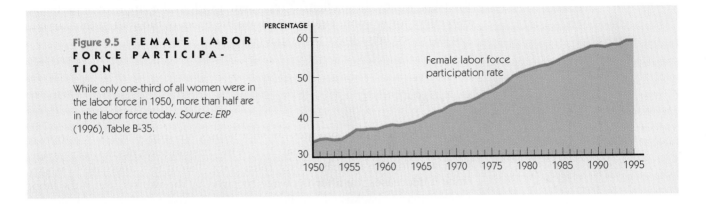

Figure 9.5 FEMALE LABOR FORCE PARTICIPATION

While only one-third of all women were in the labor force in 1950, more than half are in the labor force today. *Source: ERP (1996), Table B-35.*

many with children leave only for relatively short periods of time. It is important to note here that the labor force, as economists define it, includes not only those who have jobs but also those who are looking for jobs. In 1890, only 17 percent of all women were in the labor force; the figure now stands at 57 percent. Figure 9.5 shows the dramatic increase in female labor force participation during the past 40 years.

This change can be viewed partly as a *shift* in the labor supply curve and partly as a *movement* along it. Figure 9.6 shows how the number of women participating in the labor force increases with the wage rate. Such a curve is called the labor force participation curve. If all women supplied a fixed number of hours (say, 35 hours per week), then the labor force participation curve and the female labor supply curve would look the same.

Job opportunities for women have increased enormously in the past thirty years, and relative wages have risen. Thus, the return to working has increased and the opportunity cost of being out of the labor force has gone up. Even in the absence of social change, these factors would be expected to lead to increased labor force participation by women. The increased participation of women as a result of higher wages is a *movement* along the labor force participation curve. This change is seen in Figure 9.6 as the increase in labor force participation from L_0 to L_1.

But two other changes have contributed to the trend as well. Beginning around 1973, (real) wages stopped growing at the rate they had been during the period following World War II. Individuals and families had come to expect regular increases in their income. When these increases stopped, they felt the loss. This development encouraged many married women to take part-time or full-time jobs as a way of keeping the family income increasing, and in some cases, to prevent it from decreasing.

There has also been a change in attitudes, both on the part of women and on the part of employers. Enrollments of women in professional schools increased dramatically, reflecting changed attitudes among the women themselves. And outright discrimination against women was barred by federal law

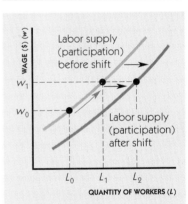

Figure 9.6 EXPLAINING CHANGES IN LABOR FORCE PARTICIPATION

The increased labor force participation of women results in part from a movement along the supply curve resulting from higher wages (the movement from L_0 to L_1), and in part from a shift of the supply curve itself (the movement from L_1 to L_2).

in 1963. Reduced discrimination made it more attractive for women to enter the labor force. These changes represent a *shift* in the labor force participation curve for women. Figure 9.6 shows the effect of the shift in the curve in the increased labor force participation from L_1 to L_2.

TAX POLICY AND LABOR SUPPLY

The effect of a change in wages on labor supply has important policy implications. For example, we often hear that an increase in taxes discourages people from working. An increase in tax rates is equivalent to a decrease in wages, since it decreases the after-tax wage received by the worker. But if the labor supply curve is backward bending, then a tax increase and its accompanying reduction in the after-tax wage can actually increase the labor supply.

Differences in views about the relative magnitudes of the income and substitution effects on labor supply have played an important role in recent debates over tax policy. When asked how they would respond to a tax increase, workers do not answer in terms of income and substitution effects. They say things like "I have to work longer hours to maintain my standard of living" or "I work less, because it doesn't pay to work so hard." But economists interpret these different responses in the analytical framework of income and substitution effects. In particular, economists are interested in what happens *on average*, and what happens to particular groups of people within the economy.

For men, the consensus is that the labor supply elasticity is relatively low, so that changing taxes has little effect on either labor force participation or hours worked. But some economists believe that men's labor supply elasticity is quite large, and that the 50 percent tax rate on high incomes that prevailed until 1986 had a strong adverse effect on labor supply. Indeed, some "Supply Siders" (named for their emphasis on incentives that affect supply) predicted that high-income groups would supply so much more labor in response to a tax reduction that government revenue would actually increase (even with lower tax *rates*). The evidence by and large indicates that the labor supply response elasticity for men is actually low. Hours worked increased little if at all as a result of the tax cuts of the 1980s, and overall tax revenues dropped. But tax revenues from *upper* income groups did increase. It is not clear that the rich worked more as a result of the reduced tax rates, however. Two other explanations are at least as plausible. First, the lower tax rates meant that the value of avoiding taxes through tax shelters fell, and investors moved their money back into taxable activities. Second, and more important, wage inequality continued to increase over the period. The rich became richer, not because they worked more hours but because they earned more per hour worked.

In contrast to the small labor supply response of men to tax rate changes, the labor supply response of women is large. Higher wages bring many more women into the labor force and higher taxes send many more women out of it. A look at the U.S. income tax makes it easy to see why taxes can have such a large effect on female labor force participation. For a family of four, no tax is

POLICY PERSPECTIVE: THE AMBIGUOUS EFFECTS OF THE EARNED INCOME CREDIT

In 1993, Congress greatly expanded the earned income credit (EIC). With the EIC, low-income workers actually get a check from the government, rather than pay taxes. The intent of the EIC is to *make* work pay. Even a minimum wage worker with a family earns enough, with EIC, to bring him (almost) out of poverty. The government pays a subsidy of approximately 30 percent. Thus, a worker receiving $8,000 with two children would receive an additional $2,400. But above $11,000, the benefit is "phased out," that is, the size of the check received from the government becomes smaller. A family of four with a salary of $25,300 receives no benefit at all.

For low-wage workers, the EIC encourages labor force participation (the decision to look for a job rather than stay home). It succeeds in making work pay, at least pay more than before. But for workers in the phase-out range, the EIC discourages working long hours. The extra return for working an extra hour is greatly reduced. There is thus a strong substitution effect—the same effect that would have occurred if workers faced a 17.7 percent tax rate. After adjusting for the EIC phase-out, the *net* increase in income of a $5.00 per hour worker is only $4.12 for each hour worked. In addition, the worker may have to pay federal income tax of 15 percent, making the net income after adjustment for the EIC and income tax only $3.37 per hour—a marginal tax rate of 33 percent!

imposed on the first $16,000 of earned income. But if the household's primary breadwinner earns more than this, every dollar the spouse earns is taxed. In fact, if the primary breadwinner earns more than about $54,000, the household faces a federal income tax rate of 28 percent for every dollar the spouse earns (not to speak of the Social Security and state income taxes).

The situation is aggravated further because families in which both adults work have additional costs, like child care or the higher food bills from eating out or buying frozen dinners. Between the higher tax rate and the fact that much of the extra income may go to cover the extra expenses, the financial incentive for many secondary earners to work is low. Thus, changes in the after-tax wage rate can have large effects on the number of secondary earners who decide to work. A sobering fact of American life is that the spouse looking for the household's second job is usually the wife.

Before 1986, the tax laws recognized this problem, and did not tax the wages of the second worker in a family as heavily. But this tax provision created inequities as well. Consider a single-earner family where the father is working two jobs, one full-time and one part-time, for a total of 60 hours a week. Compare that with a two-earner family where the two wage earners' combined hours equal 60 hours a week. Why should the two-earner family deserve a lower tax rate than the man working overtime? Arguments like this one led to the 1986 repeal of the tax provision that benefited the second wage earner in a family.

THE RETIREMENT DECISION

Retirement is another important aspect of the labor force participation decision. In 1900, a 40-year-old American man could expect to live until age 68. At the same time, 68 percent of men over age 65 were in the labor force. Thus, the typical worker stayed on the job until he died, or until he was too sick to work. Today a 40-year-old man can expect to live to be 76, but only 16 percent of men over 65 are working or looking for work. In addition, only 67 percent of men between the ages of 55 and 64 are in the labor force. Retirement before 65 has become the expectation, and the number of middle-aged retirees is expected to continue to grow.

These retirement decisions too can be understood in terms of a basic economic model. Increased lifetime wealth has led individuals to choose more leisure over their lifetime. The fact that when people are better off they wish to enjoy more leisure is, as we saw earlier, the income effect. The decision to retire earlier can be thought of as a decision to enjoy more leisure. Indeed, it makes sense for people to choose more leisure in their later years, when their productivity has reached its peak and their wages are not going to increase much further.

At the same time, wages today are much higher than they were fifty years ago. This means that it is more costly for people to retire early—the amount of consumption (income) they have to give up is larger. This is the substitution effect. Evidently, for many people, the income effect dominates the substitution effect.

HUMAN CAPITAL AND EDUCATION

The nation's output depends not only on the number of hours people work but also on how productive those hours are. One of the important determinants of workers' productivity—and therefore wages—is education.

By staying in school longer, which usually means delaying entry into the labor force, people can increase their expected annual income. In addition, working *harder* in school and giving up leisure may result in better grades and skills, which in turn will result in higher wages in the future. Thus, students face a trade-off between leisure today and consumption, or income, in the future.

Spending a year in college has its obvious costs—tuition, room, and board. But there are also opportunity costs, such as the income that would have been received from a job. These opportunity costs are costs of going to school just as much as are any direct tuition payments. Economists say that the investment in education produces **human capital,** making an analogy to the **physical capital** investments that businesses make in plant and equipment. Human capital is developed by formal schooling, on-the-job learning, and many other investments of time and money that parents make in their children.

Table 9.1 **YEARS OF SCHOOLING BY AGE**

Age group (in 1993)	% with less than high school degree	% with a high school degree but no bachelor's degree	% with at least a bachelor's degree
25–44	12.3	62.5	25.2
45–64	19.8	57.8	22.4
65 and older	39.7	48.3	12.0

The United States invests an enormous amount in human capital. In fact, human capital is more significant than physical capital. As much as two-thirds to three-fourths of all capital is human capital. This investment is financed both publicly and privately. Local, state, and federal governments spend about one-quarter of a trillion dollars a year on education. Government expenditures on primary and secondary education are the largest category of expenditure at the local and state levels, accounting for more than 20 percent of total expenditures.

The enormous increase in education in the past fifty years is illustrated in Table 9.1. Among those 65 and older, nearly 40 percent do not have a high school degree; of those 25–44 only one in eight have not received a high school degree. Similarly the percentage with at least a bachelor's degree is twice as high for those 25–44 in relation to those 65 and older.

EDUCATION AND ECONOMIC TRADE-OFFS

The production possibilities curve introduced in Chapter 2 can illustrate how decisions concerning investments in human capital are made. To accomplish this, we divide an individual's life into two periods: "youth" and "later working years." Figure 9.7 depicts the relationship between consumption in youth and in later life. As the individual gives up consumption in his youth, staying in school longer increases his expected future consumption because he can expect his income to go up. The curve has been drawn to show diminishing returns: spending more on education today (reducing consumption) raises future income, but each additional investment in education provides a smaller and smaller return.

Point A represents the case where Everett is a full-time student through four years of college, with little income until graduation (his youth) but with a high income in later life. Point B represents the consequences of dropping out of school after high school. When he does this, Everett has a higher income in his youth but a lower income in later life. Other possible points between A and B represent cases where Everett drops out of college after one or two years.

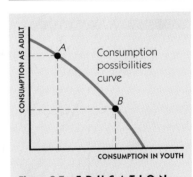

Figure 9.7 EDUCATION AND THE TRADE-OFF BETWEEN CURRENT AND FUTURE CONSUMPTION

Point A represents a choice of a reduced consumption and better education in the present, with a higher consumption in the future. Point B represents the choice of higher consumption and less education now, with a lower level of consumption in the future.

THE WIDENING WAGE GAP

Those who have a college education are paid more on average than those who fail to complete high school. The average wage of workers with at least four years of college is two-thirds greater than that of workers whose formal education ended with a high school diploma. Because unskilled workers generally cannot perform the same jobs as skilled workers, it is useful to think about the wages of the two groups as determined in separate labor markets, as illustrated in Figure 9.8. Panel A shows the demand and supply curves of unskilled workers, panel B those of skilled workers. The equilibrium wage for skilled workers is higher than that for unskilled workers.

What happens if a change in technology shifts the demand curve for skilled labor to the right, to DS_1, and the demand curve for unskilled labor to the left, to DU_1? The wages of unskilled workers will decrease from wu_0 to wu_1, and those of skilled workers will increase from ws_0 to ws_1. In the long run, this increased wage gap induces more people to acquire skills, so the supply of unskilled workers shifts to the left, and that of skilled workers shifts to the right. As a result, the wage of unskilled workers rises from wu_1 to wu_2, and that of skilled workers falls from ws_1 to ws_2. These long-run supply responses thus dampen the short-run movements in wages.

Over the past two decades, the ratio of wages of college graduates to high school graduates, and the ratio of wages of high school graduates to nongrad-

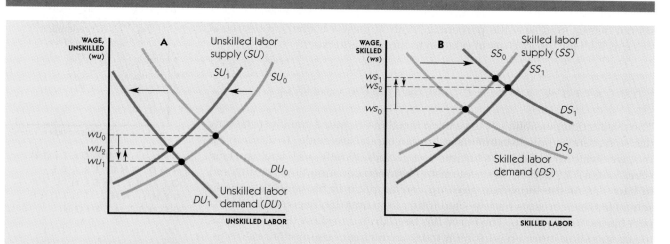

Figure 9.8 **THE MARKET FOR SKILLED AND UNSKILLED LABOR**

In panel A, new advanced technology shifts the demand curve for unskilled labor to the left, and reduces wages from wu_0 to wu_1. In panel B, the new technology shifts the demand curve for skilled labor out to the right, and thus raises wages from ws_0 to ws_1. Over time, this increased difference in wages may lead more individuals to obtain skills, shifting the supply curve for unskilled labor back to the left, raising wages for unskilled labor somewhat from wu_1 to wu_2, and shifting the supply curve for skilled labor to the right, reducing wages for skilled labor from ws_1 to ws_2.

Savings and labor supply are two of the key household decisions that can be analyzed using our basic model of consumer choice. But there are other important household decisions that can be analyzed using this model. Among the more important of these decisions is the number of children, a decision which affects the labor supply of the economy in the long run. Imagine the scene. A romantic, candlelit dinner, and two newlyweds discussing their future. They know about family planning and want to make a rational decision about the size of their future family. As their shared anticipation of the joys of parenthood increases, they push back their plates and bring out their calculators. Naturally, they have both taken economics.

As they consider all the costs of children—including the opportunity cost of wages lost from time the mother could otherwise spend working outside the home—they realize that the wife's expected earning power is an important part of their calculations. They structure their thinking about family size by weighing the marginal costs and marginal benefits of having children. From this per-spective they see the decision to have children as the demand for children, and higher earning power for the mother as increasing the "price" of a child, causing a downward movement along the demand curve.

In case you have any doubt, this is *not* how the typical family makes decisions about children, at least explicitly. But economists have noted that this model does explain the facts. Women with higher real wages have smaller families, on average. And birthrates in high-wage countries are lower than birthrates in countries with reduced earnings opportunities. This association has been confirmed repeatedly across time and across countries.

uates has increased enormously. Indeed, the real wages (that is, wages adjusted for changes in the cost of living) of unskilled workers has fallen dramatically (by as much as 30 percent). Though there have been shifts in both demand and supply curves, the primary explanation of these shifts is a change in the relative demand for skilled labor, probably attributable largely to changes in technology.

While we can be fairly confident of the predicted shifts in long-run labor supply, how fast they will occur is less clear. At the same time that these supply shifts occur, there may be further shifts in the demand curves, exacerbating wage differences. The question is how long will it take for the wage gap to be reduced to the levels that prevailed in the 1960s? In the meantime, many worry about the social consequences of steadily increasing wage (and income) inequality.

BUDGET CONSTRAINTS AND SAVINGS

The assumption that individuals spend their money in a rational manner, thinking through the alternatives clearly, holds for the savings as well as the spending and working decisions. In making their savings decisions, individuals are making a decision about *when* to spend, or consume. If they consume less today—if, that is, they save more today—they can consume more tomorrow.

We use the budget constraint to analyze this choice. Instead of showing the choice between two goods, the budget constraint now shows, as in Figure 9.9, the choice between spending in two time periods. This is similar to our discussion of human capital investment decisions. The only difference is that instead of "youth" and "later working years," the two time periods here are "working years" and "retirement years." Consider the case of Joan. She faces the lifetime budget constraint depicted in the figure. The first period is represented on the horizontal axis, the second on the vertical. Her wages during her working life (the first period) are w. Thus, at one extreme, she could consume all of w the first period (point C) and have nothing for her retirement. At the other extreme, she could consume nothing in the first period, save all of her income, and consume her savings with accumulated interest in the second (point B). If we use r to denote the rate of interest, her consumption in the second period is $w(1 + r)$. In between these extremes lies a straight line that defines the rest of her choices. She can choose any combination of first- and

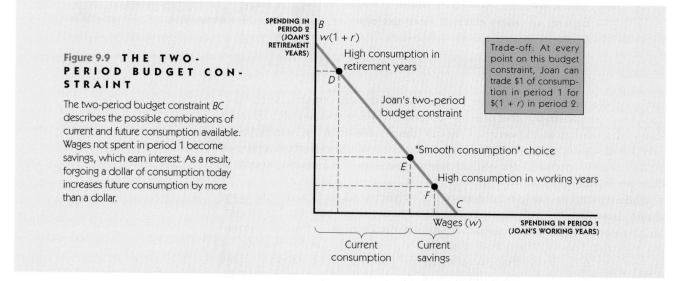

Figure 9.9 THE TWO-PERIOD BUDGET CONSTRAINT

The two-period budget constraint *BC* describes the possible combinations of current and future consumption available. Wages not spent in period 1 become savings, which earn interest. As a result, forgoing a dollar of consumption today increases future consumption by more than a dollar.

second-period consumption on this line. This is Joan's two-period budget constraint.

By postponing consumption—that is, by saving—Joan can increase the total amount of goods that she can obtain because she is paid interest on her savings. The cost, however, is that she must wait to enjoy the goods. But what is the relative price, the trade-off between future and current consumption? To put it another way, how much extra future consumption can she get if she gives up one unit of current consumption?

If Joan decides not to consume one more dollar today, she can take that dollar, put it in the bank, and get back at the end of the year that dollar plus interest. If the interest rate is 10 percent, for every dollar of consumption that Joan gives up today, she can get $1.10 of consumption next year. The relative price (of consumption today relative to consumption tomorrow) is thus 1 plus the interest rate. Because Joan must give up more than $1.00 of consumption in the second period to get an additional $1.00 worth of consumption today, current consumption is more expensive than future consumption. As was emphasized in Chapter 6, what Joan cares about in evaluating the trade-offs between consumption during her working years versus consumption in retirement is the *real* rate of interest, taking into account inflation.

In this example, where Joan's life is divided into a working period and a retirement period, what is relevant is the average length of time between the time that money is earned and saved, and the time that the savings are used in retirement. For an average person, this is perhaps 35 years. In making her calculations, Joan will take into account the fact that if she leaves her money in the bank, it will earn compound interest, meaning that interest will be paid on interest already earned, not just on the amount of principal saved.

In recent years, the real rate of interest has been around 4 percent a year. If interest were not compounded, earning 4 percent a year for 35 years would simply provide an overall return of 35×4 percent = 140 percent. If Joan puts $1.00 in the bank today, in 35 years, with no compounding of interest, she will get back $2.40 in real terms. However, if interest is compounded annually, for each dollar deposited the calculation is $(1 + .04)^{35}$.[1] So the total interest paid will be 294.6 percent. If she puts $1.00 in the bank today, in 35 years she will get back—in real terms—$3.94 (that is, her original dollar *plus* the interest). Compound interest makes a big difference.

Thus, the slope of Joan's budget constraint is 3.94—for every dollar of consumption she gives up during her working years, she gets $3.94 of additional consumption in retirement.

Joan chooses among the points on this budget constraint according to her personal preferences. Consider, for example, point *D*, where Joan is consuming very little during her working life. Since she is spending very little in the present, any additional consumption now will have a high marginal value. She will be relatively eager to substitute present consumption for future consumption. At the other extreme, if she is consuming a great deal in the pre-

---

[1] At the end of the first year, Joan has 1.04. In the second year, she earns 4 percent interest on this, so she has 1.04 *plus* $.04 \times \$1.04$, or $(1.04)^2$. In the third year, she earns 4 percent on this cumulated amount, or $.04 \times (1.04)^2$. Her total account is thus $(1.04)^2 + .04 \times (1.04)^2 = (1.04)^3$.

sent, say at point *F*, additional consumption today will have a relatively low marginal value, while future consumption will have a high marginal value. Hence, she will be relatively eager to save more for the future. She chooses a point in between, *E*, where consumption in the two periods is not too different. She has **smoothed** her consumption; that is, consumption in each of the two different periods is about the same. This kind of savings, motivated to smooth consumption over one's lifetime and to provide for retirement, is called **life-cycle** savings. In Figure 9.9, the difference between the first period income, *w*, and what she consumes is her savings.

SAVINGS AND THE INTEREST RATE

What happens to Joan's savings if the interest rate increases? Her new budget constraint is shown in Figure 9.10 as *B'C*. If she does no saving, the interest rate has no effect on her consumption. She simply consumes her income during her working years, with nothing left over for retirement. But for all other choices, she gets more consumption during her retirement years.

The increased interest rate has both an income and a substitution effect. Because Joan is a saver, higher interest rates make her better off. Because she is better off, she consumes more today, that is, she reduces savings. This is the income effect. But her return to savings—to postponing consumption—is increased. For each dollar of consumption she postpones, she gets more consumption when she retires. This induces her to consume less—to save more.

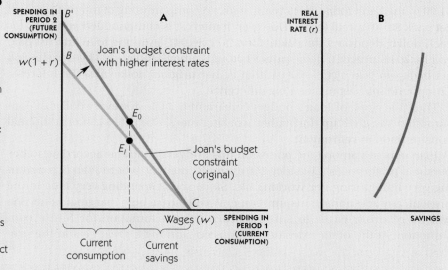

Figure 9.10 SAVINGS AND THE INTEREST RATE

An increase in interest rates rotates the budget constraint out from *BC* to *B'C* (panel A). The fact that the individual is better off means that there is an income effect, leading to greater consumption in the present (and the future). Higher current consumption implies lower savings. However, the higher interest rate makes future consumption cheaper; the substitution effect, associated with the changed slope, leads to greater savings now (panel B). The savings function in panel B gives the level of savings at each level of the real interest rate. The curve depicted has the typical shape: increases in the real interest rate lead to slight increases in savings; the substitution effect slightly outweighs the income effect.

This is the substitution effect. Thus, the substitution and income effects work in opposite directions, and the *net* effect is ambiguous. Either may dominate. A higher interest rate may lead to more or less savings. In the case shown, current consumption—and hence savings—is unchanged.

What happens on *average* is a difficult empirical question. Most estimates indicate that the substitution effect outweighs the income effect, so that an increase in real interest rates has a slightly positive effect on the rate of savings.

Panel B of Figure 9.10 shows the savings function, which gives the level of savings for each level of the real interest rate. It is derived by finding the choices between consumption today and in the future for different real interest rates, represented by rotating the budget constraint. The curve depicted has the typical shape. Increases in the real interest rate lead to slight increases in savings; the substitution effect slightly outweighs the income effect. But the savings curve could be vertical; the income effect just outweighs the substitution effect. Or it can even be backward bending; the income effect slightly outweighs the substitution effect.

The magnitude of the response of savings to interest rates is an important question. Government policies aimed at increasing the interest rate individuals receive, such as exempting certain forms of savings from taxation, are based on the belief that an increase in the interest rate on savings will significantly increase total (aggregate) savings in the economy. Since wealthy people save more, reducing taxes on interest—which increases the effective interest rate to the saver—obviously benefits them more, and increases the degree of income inequality.

THE SAVINGS DECISION

The savings decision is a decision of *when* to consume: today or tomorrow.

The slope of the budget constraint between consumption today and consumption tomorrow is determined by the rate of interest.

A principal motive of savings is to smooth consumption, so that consumption during working years and consumption during retirement years is about the same.

OTHER FACTORS AFFECTING SAVINGS

We have now seen how individuals' decisions about savings can be looked at using the techniques of consumer choice analysis presented in Chapter 8. For savings, the two basic determinants are income and interest rates. As incomes rise, individuals want to consume more in their retirement, and hence must

The interest elasticity of savings is a key parameter in evaluating policies aimed at promoting savings through reducing the tax on the return to savings. Assume that the interest elasticity of savings is .1, so that a 1 percent increase in the after-tax return to savings leads to a 0.1 percent increase in savings. Then if household savings is $150 billion, and if the average saver faces a 28 percent tax rate, eliminating the tax on the return to capital (interest) would increase household saving by 2.8 percent x $150 billion = $4.2 billion. Meanwhile, if the average return (before tax) on capital is 10 percent, and the aggregate capital owned by households is $2 trillion, then the revenue lost by the government is 28 percent x $2 trillion = $56 billion. The increased federal deficit more than offsets the increased household savings, and eliminating the tax on interest has failed to achieve its purpose of increasing total U.S. savings.

save more. As interest rates change, the income and substitution effects work in different directions, so the net effect is ambiguous.

The savings decision in the United States also involves an even more important determinant: Social Security. How much individuals need to save for their retirement depends on how large a check they get from the Social Security Administration when they retire. A generous Social Security system reduces the need to save for retirement. If this is the case, why have private pension programs grown at the same time that Social Security payments have become more generous? Two explanations are commonly put forward. First, as individuals' life spans have increased well beyond the normal retirement age, the need for retirement income has increased faster than has the generosity of Social Security. Second, with higher incomes, as we saw earlier in the chapter, individuals decide to enjoy more leisure, one form of which is earlier retirement. With earlier retirement, the need for retirement income increases.

AGGREGATE SAVINGS

The sum of the savings of all individuals in society is **aggregate savings.** At any time, some individuals are saving and others are spending their savings (or, as economists say, **dissaving**). Aggregate savings is the two activities taken together. The **aggregate savings rate** is aggregate savings divided by aggregate income. **Demographic** factors, in particular the rate of growth of the population, are important determinants of the aggregate savings rate. Retirees typically dissave. That is, they withdraw from savings accounts and cash in stocks and bonds if they have any (to supplement their main income sources, Social Security and interest on investments). There is considerable concern about the low aggregate savings rate in the United States (discussed further below). Our aging population is one reason for this. A more slowly growing population, like that of the United States, has a larger proportion of elderly and, on

CLOSE-UP: WHY IS THE U.S. SAVINGS RATE SO LOW?

When Taiwan proposed becoming a major investor in McDonnell-Douglas in 1992, many observers got a jolt. Only a short while ago, Taiwan had been one of the poorer countries; now it was buying a major share of one of the world's premier aerospace firms. How come?

At one level the answer is easy. Households in Taiwan (and Japan, and many of the United States' major competitors) save a much larger proportion of their incomes than their U.S. counterparts. But the question still remains. Why? Several reasons are given by economists. First, U.S. Social Security benefits are relatively generous, reducing the need to save for retirement. Second, it has become much easier to borrow for all kinds of pur-

poses. In other words the capital market in this country has improved in its capacity to serve individual borrowers. Third, Americans have a greater taste than many for consumption now rather than later. If more people spend more, aggregate savings goes down. Fourth, the need to save for a rainy day has been reduced in this country with better medical insurance, unemployment insurance, and so on. Finally, the household wealth tied up in housing and corporate stocks in the United States rose dramatically through the 1980s—each by about $800 billion. As people saw their wealth embodied in real estate and stocks rise, they spent more of their income and saved less.

that account, a lower aggregate savings rate than faster-growing populations with higher birth rates.

The basic model provides great insight into the determinants of savings. But several motives for saving fall outside the basic model and have important implications for understanding the determinants of savings.

First, people typically want to leave something to their descendants. This is the **bequest savings motive.** Lawrence Summers, Deputy Secretary of the Treasury, and Laurence Kotlikoff, Boston University, argue that the sum of

One of the most popular policy programs designed to increase households' savings has been **individual retirement accounts** (IRAs). In its original form the tax law allowed people to deduct from their taxable income money invested in an IRA (up to an annual limit of say $2,000). **In** addition, the interest earned on this money is not taxed until it is withdrawn during retirement. Why are they popular? Because individuals rich enough to have savings can simply transfer money from a taxed account into their tax-free IRA account—they get a tax benefit without doing any additional saving. This may sound cynical but economic theory supports this reasoning. For anyone who is already saving more than the $2,000 per year allowed, there is no *marginal* incentive. The return from saving an additional dollar is unchanged. There is no substitution effect, and it is the substitution effect that drives additional savings. More generally, evidence indicates that interest elasticities of savings are low. In this case, even if there were no limit on the amount that could be deposited, savings would not be stimulated much. Moreover, poorer Americans are least likely to take advantage of IRAs, making the tax break for these accounts a benefit for the middle class and the wealthy.

Whether this is good or bad, of course, depends on the value one places on equity.

Despite the theoretical arguments suggesting that the IRAs would do little to stimulate savings, they are turning out to be more effective in increasing savings than expected. One reason is that banks advertise aggressively to recruit the IRA accounts. Advertisers "sell" savings, just as they sell cars and cigarettes.

More recently, a more tax-equitable IRA has been proposed. This would allow for tax deductibility for contributions to an IRA account that exceeded a target, say 10 percent of income. Richer individuals would thus have a higher target.

savings of the small group of very wealthy people exceeds that of the entire rest of the population, and the main reason for saving by the wealthy is the bequest motive. Another motive for savings is the **precautionary** motive. This "saving for a rainy day" protects against emergencies for which one has no insurance coverage. Precautionary savings is particularly important for owners of small businesses and farmers whose incomes can vary enormously from year to year. Still another (related) motive is to save for a particular purpose. **Target savings** is directed toward needs for which it may be hard to borrow sufficient funds, such as a down payment on a house or a college education for one's children.

REVIEW AND PRACTICE

SUMMARY

1. The decision about how to allocate time between work and leisure can be analyzed using the basic ideas of budget constraints and preferences. Individuals face a trade-off along a budget constraint between leisure and income. The amount of income a person can obtain by giving up leisure is determined by the wage rate.

2. In labor markets, the substitution and income effects of a change in wages work in opposite directions. An increase in wages makes people better off, and they wish to enjoy more leisure now as well as more consumption; this is the income effect. But an increase in wages raises the opportunity cost of leisure, and encourages more work; this is the substitution effect. The overall effect of a rise in wages will depend on whether the substitution or income effect is actually larger.

3. An upward-sloping labor supply curve represents a case where the substitution effect of higher wages outweighs the income effect. A relatively vertical labor supply curve represents a case where the substitution and income effects of higher wages are nearly equal. A backward-bending labor supply curve represents a case where the substitution effect dominates at low wages (labor supply increases as the wage increases), but the income effect dominates at high wages (labor supply decreases as the wage increases).

4. The basic model of choice between leisure and income also can be used to analyze decisions concerning labor force participation, including when to enter the labor force and when to retire.

5. Human capital adds to economic productivity just as physical capital does. It is developed by education, on-the-job learning, and investments of time and money that parents make in their children.

6. In making a decision to save, people face a trade-off between current and future consumption. The amount of extra consumption an individual can obtain in the future by reducing present consumption is determined by the real rate of interest.

7. An increase in the real rate of interest makes individuals who save better off. The resulting income effect leads to an increase in current consumption (*and* future consumption) and a decrease in savings. An increase in the real rate of interest also makes it more attractive to save; this is the substitution effect, and it leads to a decrease in current consumption. The net effect is thus ambiguous, though in practice it appears that an increase in the real interest rate has a slightly positive effect on savings.

KEY TERMS

labor force partici- pation decision reservation wage human capital	life-cycle savings aggregate savings bequest savings motive	precautionary savings motive target savings motive

REVIEW QUESTIONS

1. How do people make choices about the amount of time to work, given their personal tastes and real wages in the market?

2. How will the income effect of a fall in wages affect hours worked? How will the substitution effect of a fall in wages affect hours worked? What does the labor supply curve look like if the income effect dominates the substitution effect? If the substitution effect dominates the income effect?

3. Describe how students invest time and money to acquire human capital.

4. How does a choice to consume in the present determine the amount of consumption in the future?

5. What is the price of future consumption in terms of present consumption?

6. For savers, how will the income effect of a higher interest rate affect current savings? How will the substitution effect of a higher interest rate affect current savings?

7. What are some of the other factors, besides incomes and interest rates, that affect savings?

PROBLEMS

1. Imagine that a wealthy relative dies and leaves you an inheritance in a trust fund that will provide you with $20,000 per year for the rest of your life. Draw a diagram to illustrate this shift in your budget constraint between leisure and consumption. After considering the ideas of income and substitution effects, decide whether this inheritance will cause you to work more or less.

2. Most individuals do not take a second job (moonlight), even if they could get one, for instance as a taxi driver. This is in spite of the fact that their "basic job" may require them to work only 37 hours a week. Most moonlighting jobs pay less per hour than the basic job. Draw a typical worker's budget constraint. Discuss the consequences of the kink in the budget constraint.

3. Under current economic conditions, let's say that an unskilled worker will be able to get a job at a wage of $5 per hour. Now assume the government decides to assure that all people with a weekly income of less than $150 will be given a check to bring them up to the $150 level. Draw one such worker's original budget constraint and the constraint with the welfare program. Will this welfare program be likely to cause a recipient who originally worked 30 hours to work less? How about a recipient who worked less than 30 hours? More than 30 hours? Explain how the government might reduce these negative effects by offering a wage subsidy that would increase the hourly wage to $6 per hour for each of the first 20 hours worked, and draw a revised budget constraint to illustrate.

4. This chapter analyzed the savings decision of an individual who worked for one period, and was retired the next, and received no social security payment in his retirement.
   (a) Show how the budget constraint changes if the individual receives a fixed social security payment in retirement. Discuss what this does to savings.
   (b) Show how the budget constraint changes if the individual is taxed the first period of his life and receives a fixed social security payment in retirement. Discuss what this does to savings.

5. This chapter focused on how interest rates affect savers. If an individual is a net debtor (that is, he owes money), what is the income effect of an increase in interest rates. Will an increase in the interest rates that he has to pay induce him to borrow more or less?

6. In the context of the life-cycle model of savings, explain whether you would expect each of the following situations to increase or decrease household savings.
   (a) More people retire before age 65.
   (b) There is an increase in life expectancy.
   (c) The government passes a law requiring private businesses to provide more lucrative pensions.

7. Explain how each of the following changes might affect people's saving.
   (a) Inheritance taxes are increased.
   (b) A government program allows college students to obtain student loans more easily.
   (c) The government promises to assist anyone injured by natural disasters like hurricanes, tornadoes, and earthquakes.
   (d) More couples decide against having children.
   (e) The economy does far worse than anyone was expecting in a given year.

8. Economists are fairly certain that a rise in the price of most goods will cause people to consume less of those goods, but they are not sure whether a rise in interest rates will cause people to save more. Use the ideas of substitution and income effects to explain why economists are confident of the conclusion in the first case, but not in the second.

9. There is a negative correlation between a woman's real wage and her family size. Two possible explanations have been put forward. One is that women with higher real wages *choose* to have smaller families. Explain why this might be so. The second is that larger family sizes might cause women to receive lower wages, for instance, because they have to accept jobs where they can be absent when their children are sick. What evidence might help you choose between these two explanations?

APPENDIX: INDIFFERENCE CURVES AND THE LABOR SUPPLY AND SAVINGS DECISIONS[2]

This appendix investigates the labor supply and savings decisions using the indifference curve approach applied in the appendix to Chapter 8 to the consumption decision. Let's first look at the choice between leisure and consumption.

Figure 9.11 shows Tom's budget constraint between leisure and consumption. The slope of the budget constraint is the wage. The figure also shows two indifference curves; each gives the combinations of leisure and consumption among which Tom is indifferent. As usual, since people prefer more of both consumption and leisure if that is possible, Tom will move to the highest indifference curve he can attain. This will be the one that is just tangent to the budget constraint.

The slope of the indifference curve is the marginal rate of substitution between leisure and consumption. It measures the amount of extra consumption Tom requires to compensate him for forgoing one additional hour of leisure. At the point of tangency between the indifference curve and the budget constraint, point E, both have the same slope. That is, the marginal rate of substitution equals the wage at this point.

As in the appendix to Chapter 8, we can easily see why Tom chooses this point. Assume his marginal rate of substitution is $15 (dollars per hour), while his wage is $20 (dollars per hour). If he works an hour more—gives up an hour's worth of leisure—his consumption goes up by $20. But to compensate him for the forgone leisure, he only requires $15. Since he gets more than he requires by working, he clearly prefers to work more.

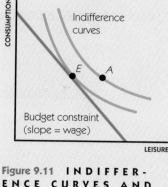

Figure 9.11 INDIFFERENCE CURVES AND LEISURE-INCOME CHOICES

An individual will choose the combination of leisure and income at E. Point A would be more desirable, but it is not feasible. Other points on the budget line or inside it are feasible, but they lie on lower indifference curves and are therefore not as desirable.

DECIDING WHETHER TO WORK

Figure 9.12 shows how to use indifference curves to analyze how people decide whether to work or not. Consider a low-wage individual facing a welfare system in which there is a fixed level of benefits if one's income is below a

---

[2]You will need to have read the appendix to Chapter 8 in order to follow this appendix.

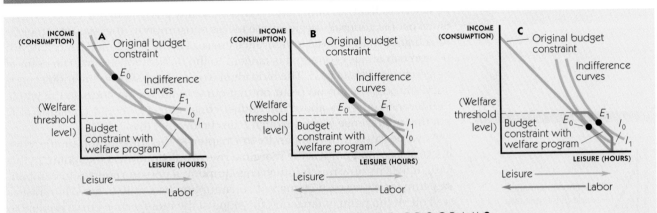

Figure 9.12 INDIFFERENCE CURVES AND WELFARE PROGRAMS

Panel A shows the case of an individual who chooses to work whether or not the welfare program exists. In panel B, before a welfare program is introduced, the individual is earning more than the welfare threshold. With the availability of welfare, she relies on welfare benefits to work less and move to a higher indifference curve. Panel C shows the case of someone who is earning less than the welfare threshold, but would choose to work still less if the welfare program existed.

threshold level. Benefits are cut off once income exceeds a certain level. The indifference curve I_0 is tangent to the budget constraint without welfare, and the point of tangency is E_0. The curve I_1 is the highest indifference curve consistent with the person receiving welfare.

The three possible cases are illustrated in panels A, B, and C. In panel A, the indifference curve through point E_0, I_0, is higher than the curve I_1. The individual chooses to work at E_0, and is unaffected by the welfare program. In panels B and C, the person works sufficiently little to be eligible for welfare; that is, I_1 is higher than I_0, and so he chooses point E_1. In panel B, the individual realizes that if he works more, he will lose his welfare benefits. He earns just (little) enough to be eligible for welfare. In panel C, the welfare system has only an income effect. If the welfare benefits are large enough, the individual may choose not to work at all (at E_1 there is zero labor).

DECIDING HOW MUCH TO SAVE

The decision of how much to save is a decision about how much of lifetime income to consume now and how much to consume in the future. This trade-off is summarized in the two-period budget constraint introduced in the chapter, with present consumption measured along the horizontal axis and future consumption along the vertical axis. The slope of the budget constraint is $1 + r$, where r is the rate of interest, the extra consumption we get in the future from forgoing a unit of consumption today.

Figure 9.13 shows three indifference curves. The indifference curve through point A gives all the combinations of consumption today and con-

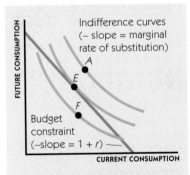

Figure 9.13 INDIFFERENCE CURVES AND SAVINGS BEHAVIOR

An individual will choose the combination of present and future consumption at E. Point A would be more desirable, but it is not feasible. Point F is feasible, but it lies on a lower indifference curve and is therefore less desirable.

sumption in the future among which the individual is indifferent (she would be just as well off, no better and no worse, at any point along the curve as at A). Since people generally prefer more to less consumption, they would rather be on a higher than a lower indifference curve. The highest indifference curve a person can attain is one that is tangent to the budget constraint. The point of tangency we denote by E. The individual would clearly prefer the indifference curve through A, but no point on that curve is attainable because the whole indifference curve is above the budget constraint. She could consume at F, but the indifference curve through F lies below that through E.

As we learned in the appendix to Chapter 8, the slope of the indifference curve at a certain point is the marginal rate of substitution at that point. In this case, it tells us how much future consumption a person requires to compensate him for a decrease in current consumption by 1 unit, to leave him just as well off. At the point of tangency, the slope of the indifference curve is equal to the slope of the budget constraint. The marginal rate of substitution at that point, E, equals $1 + r$. If the individual forgoes a unit of consumption, he gets $1 + r$ more units of consumption in the future, and this is exactly the amount he requires to compensate him for giving up current consumption. On the other hand, if the marginal rate of substitution is less than $1 + r$, it pays the individual to save more. To see why, assume $1 + r = 1.5$, while the person's marginal rate of substitution is 1.2. By reducing his consumption by a unit, he gets 1.5 more units in the future, but he would have been content getting only 1.2 units. He is better off saving more.

CHANGING THE INTEREST RATE

With indifference curves and budget constraints, we can see the effect of an increase in the interest rate. Figure 9.14 shows the case of an individual, Maggie, who works while she is young and saves for her retirement. The vertical axis gives consumption during retirement years, the horizontal axis consumption during working years. An increase in the rate of interest rotates the budget constraint, moving it from BC to B_2C. It is useful to break the change down into two steps. In the first, we ask what would have happened if the interest rate had changed but Maggie remained on the same indifference curve. This is represented by the movement of the budget constraint from BC to B_1C_1. As a result of the increased interest rate, Maggie consumes less today— she saves more. This is the substitution effect, and it is seen in the movement from E_0 to E_2 in the figure.

In the second step we note that, since Maggie is a saver, the increased interest rate makes her better off. To leave Maggie on the same indifference curve after the increase in the interest rate, we needed to reduce her income. Her true budget constraint, after the interest rate increase, is B_2C, parallel to B_1C_1. The two budget constraints have the same slope because the after-tax interest rates are the same. The movement from B_1C_1 to B_2C is the second step. It induces Maggie to increase her consumption from E_2 to E_1. At higher incomes and the same relative prices (interest rates), people consume more every pe-

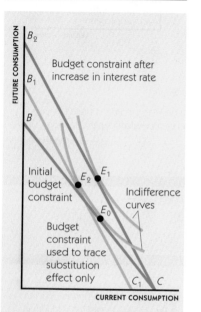

Figure 9.14 INCOME AND SUBSTITUTION EFFECTS OF A HIGHER INTEREST RATE

An increase in the interest rate rotates the budget constraint, moving it from BC to B_2C. The substitution effect describes what happens when relative prices are changed but Maggie remains on the same indifference curve; there is a shift in the budget line from BC to B_1C_1, and an increase in savings from E_0 to E_2. The income effect is the result of an outward shift of the budget line, keeping relative prices the same; the income effect is described by the shift from B_1C_1 to B_2C, and the increase in present consumption from E_2 to E_1.

riod, which implies that they save less. The movement from E_2 to E_1 is the income effect.

Thus, the substitution effect leads her to save more, the income effect to save less, and the net effect is ambiguous. In this case, there is a slight increase in savings.

A STUDENT'S GUIDE TO INVESTING

E very decision to save is accompanied by a decision about what to do with the savings. They might go under a mattress, but usually savings are invested—in bank accounts, the stock or bond market, the real estate market, and other financial opportunities. Individually and collectively, these opportunities can be thought of as enticements to defer consumption—to save. Broadly speaking, an **investment** is the purchase of an asset in the expectation of receiving a return. For the economy as a whole, real investment must be distinguished from financial investment. Real investment includes the purchase of new factories and new machines. Financial investment includes bank accounts, stocks, bonds, and so on. The two markets are linked: the financial investments people make provide firms with the funds they need to undertake real investments.

This chapter is about financial investment. It first takes up the major alternatives available to savers and discusses the characteristics of the different alternatives that are important to investors. From these characteristics, we can establish a simple theory to explain how asset prices are determined. The chapter closes with strategies for intelligent investing.

KEY QUESTIONS

1. What are the principal alternatives available in which to invest savings?

2. What are the important characteristics of each?

3. Why do some assets yield a higher return than others?

4. What is meant by an efficient market? Is it possible to "beat the market"?

5. What are some of the basic ingredients in an intelligent investment strategy?

INVESTMENT ALTERNATIVES

Every saver faces a myriad of possibilities when it comes to investing her savings. The choices she makes depend on the amount of money she has to invest, her motivations to save, her willingness to bear risk, and her age and health. Of the seemingly endless array of places to put one's money, five are most important: bank deposits, including certificates of deposit (CDs); housing; bonds; stocks; and mutual funds. In making choices among them, investors focus on four characteristics: return, risk, liquidity, and tax liability.

BANK DEPOSITS

As a student, your major savings are likely to be earnings from a summer job that will be spent during the next school year. If so, the decision of where to invest is generally uncomplicated. A **bank savings account** (or a similar account) offers three advantages: it pays you interest, it allows easy access to your money, and it offers security, because even if the bank itself goes broke the federal government, through the Federal Deposit Insurance Corporation, insures bank deposits of up to $100,000.

After leaving school, investment decisions become more difficult. You may want to put away some savings to make a down payment on a house. (With the average house selling for $120,000, a 20 percent down payment would be $24,000.) As savings increase, the value of a few extra percentage points of interest also increases. A **certificate of deposit (CD)**, in which you deposit money in a bank for a preset length of time, is as safe as an ordinary bank account and yields a slightly higher return. The drawback of a CD is that if you withdraw the money before the preset time has expired, you pay a penalty. The ease with which an investment can be turned into cash is called its **li-quidity.** Perfectly liquid investments can be converted into cash speedily and without any loss in value. CDs are less liquid than standard savings accounts.

HOUSING

Two-thirds of American households invest by owning their own homes. This investment is far riskier than putting money into a bank or a certificate of deposit. Home prices usually increase over time, but not always. In 1986, the price of housing in Houston declined by 11 percent, and in 1990, the price of housing in the Northeast and in the West declined by 6.8 percent and 3.5 percent, respectively. In addition, when prices do rise, the rate of increase is uncertain. Prices may be almost level for a number of years, and then shoot up by 20 percent in a single year. Note that while the bank may provide most of the funds for the purchase of a house, the owner bears the risk, since she is responsible for paying back the loan regardless of the market price of the house.

Housing as an investment has two other attributes—one attractive and one unattractive. On the positive side, real estate taxes, property taxes, and the interest on the mortgage are tax deductible, and the capital gains usually escape taxation altogether. On the negative side, housing is usually fairly illiquid. Houses differ one from another, and it often takes considerable time to find someone who really likes your house; if you try to sell your house quickly, on average you will receive less than you would if you had two or three months in which to sell it. Moreover, the costs of selling a house are substantial, often more than 5 percent of the value of the house—in any case more than the costs of selling stocks and bonds.

BONDS

Bonds are a way for corporations and government to borrow. The borrower—whether it is a company, a state, a school district, or the U.S. government—promises to pay the lender (the purchaser of the bond, or investor) a fixed amount in a specified number of years. In addition, the borrower agrees to pay the lender each year a fixed return on the amount borrowed. Thus, if the interest rate on a ten-year bond is 10 percent, a $10,000 bond will pay the lender $1,000 every year, and $10,000 at the end of ten years. The period remaining until a loan or bond is to be paid in full is called its **maturity.** Bonds that mature within a few years are called **short-term bonds;** those that mature in more than 10 years are called **long-term bonds.** A long-term government bond may have a maturity of 20 or even 30 years.

Bonds may seem relatively safe, because the investor knows what amounts will be paid. But consider a corporate bond that promises to pay $10,000 in 10 years and pays $1,000 every year until then. Imagine that an investor buys the bond, collects interest for a couple of years, and then realizes that he needs cash and wants to sell the bond. There is no guarantee that he will get $10,000 for it. He may get more and he may get less. If the market interest rate has fallen to 5 percent since the original bond was issued, a new $10,000 bond now would pay only $500 a year. Clearly, the original bond, which pays $1,000 a year, is worth considerably more. Thus, a decline in the interest rate leads to a rise in the value of bonds; and by the same logic, a rise in the interest rate leads to a decline in the value of bonds. This uncertainty about market value is what makes long-term bonds risky.[1]

Even if the investor holds the bond to maturity, that is, until the date at which it pays the promised $10,000, there is still a risk, since he cannot know for sure what $10,000 will purchase 10 years from now. If the general level of prices increases at a rate of 7 percent over these 10 years, the real value of the $10,000 will be just one-half what it would have been had prices remained stable during that decade.[2]

Because of the higher risk caused by these uncertainties, long-term bonds must compensate investors by paying higher returns, on average, than comparable short-term bonds. And because every corporation has at least a slight chance of going bankrupt, corporate bonds must compensate investors for the higher risk by paying higher returns than government bonds. The higher returns more than compensate for the additional bankruptcy risk, however, according to economic research. That is, if an investor purchases a very large number of good-quality corporate bonds, the likelihood that more than one or two will default is very small, and the overall return will be considerably higher than the return from purchasing government bonds of the same maturity (the same number of years until they come due).

Some corporate bonds are riskier than others—that is, there is a higher probability of default. These bonds must pay extremely high returns to induce investors to take a chance on them. When Chrysler looked on the verge of bankruptcy in 1980, Chrysler bonds were yielding returns of 23 percent. Obviously, the more a firm is in debt, the more likely it is to be unable to meet its commitments, and the riskier are its bonds. Especially risky bonds are called **junk bonds;** the yields on such bonds are much higher than those from a financially solid firm, but the investor must take into account the high probability of default.

SHARES OF STOCK

You might also choose to invest in shares of corporate stock. When a person buys shares in a firm, she literally owns a fraction (a share) of the total firm. Thus, if the firm issues 1 million shares, an individual who owns 100 shares

---

[1]The market price of the bond will equal the present discounted value of what it pays. For instance, a 3-year bond that pays $10 per year each of 2 years and $110 at the end of the 3rd year has a value of

$$\frac{10}{1+r} + \frac{10}{(1+r)^2} + \frac{110}{(1+r)^3},$$

where r is the market rate of interest. We can see that as r goes up, the value of the bond goes down, and vice versa.

[2]If prices rise at 7 percent a year, with compounding, the price level in 10 years is $(1.07)^{10}$ times the level it is today; $(1.07)^{10}$ is approximately equal to 2; prices have doubled.

owns .01 percent of the firm. Investors choose stocks as investments for two reasons.

First, firms pay some fraction of their earnings—its receipts after paying workers, suppliers of materials, and all interest due on bank and other loans—directly to shareholders. These payments are called **dividends.** On average, firms distribute one-third of earnings as dividends; the remainder, called **retained earnings,** is kept for investment in the company. The amount of a dividend, unlike the return on a bond, depends on a firm's earnings and on what proportion of those earnings it chooses to distribute to shareholders.

In addition to receiving dividends, those who invest in stocks hope to make money by choosing stocks that will appreciate in value, and then sell them at the higher price. The increase in the realized price of a share (or any other asset) is called a **capital gain.** (If the asset is sold at a price below that at which it was purchased, the investor realizes a **capital loss.**)

Shares of stock are risky for a number of reasons. First, the earnings of firms vary greatly. Even if firms do not vary their dividends, differences in profits will lead to differences in retained earnings, and these will be reflected in the value of the shares. In addition, the stock price of a company depends on the beliefs of investors as to, for instance, the prospects of the economy, the industry, and that particular firm. Loss of faith in any one could lead to a drop in the stock price. Thus, an individual who had to sell all his shares because of some medical emergency might find they had declined significantly in value. Even if the investor believes the shares will eventually return to a higher value, he may be unable to wait.

Shares of stock are riskier than bonds. This is because, when a firm goes bankrupt and must pay off its investors, the law requires bondholders to be paid off as fully as possible before shareholders receive any money at all. As a result, a bondholder in a bankrupt company is likely to be paid some share of her original investment, while a shareholder may receive nothing. Over the long run, shares of stock have yielded very high returns. While corporate bonds yielded on average an annual real rate of return of 2 percent in the period from 1926 to 1994, shares of stock yielded a real return of nearly 7 percent in the same period.

MUTUAL FUNDS

A **mutual fund** gathers funds from many different investors into a single large pool of funds, with which it can then purchase a large number of assets. A *money market* mutual fund invests its funds in CDs and comparably safe assets.

The advantage of a money market mutual fund is that you get higher rates of interest than on bank accounts and still enjoy liquidity. The fund managers know that most individuals will leave their money in the account, and some will be adding money to the account as others pull money out. They are thus able to put a large proportion of the fund in certificates of deposit and still not have to pay the penalties for early withdrawal. In this way, money market mutual funds give investors the easy access to their funds associated with banks, while providing them the higher returns associated with CDs.

Money market mutual funds may also invest their customers' money in short-term government bonds, called **Treasury bills, or T-bills.** Treasury bills are available only in large denominations ($10,000 or more). They promise to repay a certain amount (their face value, say, $10,000) in a relatively short period, less than 90 or 180 days, and investors buy them at less than their face value. The difference between the amount paid and the face value becomes the return to the purchaser.

With most money market mutual funds, you can even write a limited number of checks a month against your account. The major disadvantage of mutual funds is that they are not guaranteed by the federal government, as bank accounts are. However, some money market funds invest only in government securities or government-insured securities, making them virtually as safe as bank accounts.

Other mutual funds invest in stocks and bonds. Typically, they buy stock or bonds in dozens, sometimes hundreds, of different companies. Investors recognize the advantage of **diversification**—of not putting all their eggs in the same basket. If you put all your savings into a single stock and that firm has a bad year, you'll suffer a large loss. If you own stock in two companies, losses in one company may offset gains in the other. Mutual funds, in effect, allow much broader diversification. Of course, if the whole stock market does badly, a stock mutual fund will suffer too. When stocks go down, bonds often go up, so some mutual funds invest in both stocks and bonds. Others invest in risky ventures which, if successful, promise high returns; these are sometimes referred to as "growth" funds. There are many other specially designed mutual funds, and together they are enormously popular. For most investors, the first foray into the bond or stock market is through the purchase of a mutual fund.

DESIRABLE ATTRIBUTES OF INVESTMENTS

Table 10.1 sets forth the various investment opportunities we have described, with a list of their most important attributes. We now take a closer look at these attributes. As investors survey the broad range of opportunities available to them, they balance their personal needs against what the different investment options have to offer them. The ideal investment would have a high rate of return, be low risk, and be tax-exempt. But finding such an asset is as likely as finding the fountain of eternal youth. You can only expect to get more of one desirable property—say, higher returns—at the expense of another desirable property, such as safety. To understand what is entailed in these trade-offs, we need to take a closer look at each of the principal attributes.

Table 10.1 **ALTERNATIVE INVESTMENTS AND HOW THEY FARE**

Investment	Expected returns	Risk	Tax advantages	Liquidity
Bank savings accounts	Low	Low	None	High
CDs (certificates of deposit)	Slightly higher than savings	Low	None	Slightly less than savings accounts
Houses	High returns from mid-1970s to mid-1980s; in many areas, negative returns in late 1980s, early 1990s	Used to be thought safe; viewed to be somewhat riskier now	Many special tax advantages	Relatively illiquid; may take long time to find "good buyer"
Federal government long-term bonds	Normally slightly higher than T-bills	Uncertain market value next period; uncertain purchasing power in long run	Exempt from state income tax	Small charge for selling before maturity
Corporate bonds	Higher return than federal bonds	Risks of long-term federal bonds plus risk of default	None	Slightly less liquid than federal bonds (depends on corporation issuing bond)
Stocks	High	High	Capital gains receive slight tax preference	Those listed on major stock exchange are highly liquid; others may be highly illiquid
Mutual funds	Reflect assets in which funds are invested	Reflect assets in which funds are invested; reduced risk from diversification	Reflect assets in which funds are invested	Highly liquid
T-bills	About same as CDs	Low	Exempt from state income tax	Small charge for selling before maturity

EXPECTED RETURNS

First on the list of desirable properties are high returns. As we have noted, returns have two components: the interest (on a bond), dividend payments (on a stock), or rent (on real estate), and the capital gain. Thus, if you buy some stock for $1,000, receive $150 in dividends during the year, and at the end of the year sell the stock for $1,200, your total return is $150 + $200 = $350. If you sell the stock for $900, your total return is $150 − $100 = $50. If you sell it for $800, your total return is a *negative* $50.

In estimating the total return to an asset, the wise investor combines the asset's ongoing return (interest payments on a bank account or bond, dividends, rent, and so on) with its potential capital gain. But two problems still remain in comparing the returns to different assets. First, the returns may occur in different years. An asset that costs $1,000 and yields a $300 return next year is far preferable to one that costs the same amount and yields $300 in ten years. Dollars received at later dates are worth less than dollars today, as was demonstrated in Chapter 6. To make adjustments for the difference in timing, we need to compare the present discounted value of the returns.

The second problem is that, even if each of two assets will yield all of its returns next year, neither will have a guaranteed return. To make the right comparison in this case, we apply the concept of **expected returns.** The expected return to an asset is a statistical summing up—a single number that combines the various possible returns per dollar invested with the chances that each of these returns will actually be paid. Average returns *expected* in the future are the relevant focus here. Past returns should only be considered to the extent they give us a clue about expected future performance.

For simplicity, suppose that one of the two assets is a stock costing $100 that has a long tradition of paying $4 each year in dividends. The dividend thus supplies a 4 percent return; but some estimate is needed of its potential capital gain. Figure 10.1 plots the probabilities of different expected returns for this stock, and gives three possible outcomes for when the stock is sold a year from now. One possibility is that the stock will fetch only $97. The stock will nevertheless produce a 1 percent return ($97 + $4 = $101). Suppose, further, that experts give this outcome a 1 in 4 chance of occurring (a 25 percent probability). A second possibility is that the stock's price will be $104 and thus produce an 8 percent return ($104 + $4 = $108). This possibility is given a 2 in 4 chance of occurring (a 50 percent probability). The third possibility is that the stock will sell for $111, producing a return of 15 percent ($111 + $4 = $115). Like the first possibility, this is given a 1 in 4 chance of occurring (a 25 percent probability). (The sum of the probabilities, by definition, must add up to 1.)

The next step in calculating the expected return is to multiply each of the possible outcomes by the chance, or probability, that it will occur, as illustrated in Table 10.2. The sum of these products, 8 percent, is the expected

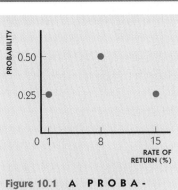

Figure 10.1 A PROBA-BILITY DISTRIBU-TION OF POSSIBLE RATES OF RETURN

There are three possible levels of return for this asset: a 1 in 4 chance of a 1 percent return, a 2 in 4 chance of an 8 percent return, and a 1 in 4 chance of a 15 percent return. The expected return is calculated by multiplying the possible returns times their probability of happening, and adding the results.

Table 10.2 CALCULATING EXPECTED RETURNS

Outcome (return)	Probability	Outcome x probability
1 percent	25 percent	0.25 percent
8 percent	50 percent	4 percent
15 percent	25 percent	3.75 percent
		Sum = 8 percent

return. We would then go through the same series of calculations with the other investment opportunity. If all other important characteristics of the two opportunities were the same, we would presumably choose the one with the higher expected return.

Different individuals will differ in their judgments concerning the likelihood of various returns. To some extent, people's views are based on historical experience. When economists say that the average return to stocks is higher than the return to bonds, they mean that historically, on average, over the past century, the returns to stocks have been higher. This does not necessarily mean that the return to stocks next year will be higher than the return to bonds, or that the return to particular stocks will be higher than the return to particular bonds. An individual who believes that a major economic downturn is likely may believe that the expected return to stocks next year will be lower than the return to bonds, and will weight his expected return calculation accordingly.

An important first lesson in investment theory is: *If there were no differences between assets other than the ways in which they produce returns (interest, dividends, etc.), then the expected returns to all assets would be the same.* Why? Because investors seeing the return to an asset that yielded more than this average would bid more for the asset. If the 8 percent return given in the stock example above looked high relative to other options, investors desirous of that return would bid the stock price up above $100. As the price rose, the expected return would decline. The upward pressure would continue until the expected return declined to match the level of all other investments.

In fact, the expected returns per dollar invested for different assets differ markedly from one another. This is because a number of other important attributes affect an asset's return. These include the risk that it will not pay the expected return; its treatment under tax law; and its liquidity, or the ease with which it can be sold. An asset that is less risky or more liquid or receives favorable tax treatment will have higher demand. The higher demand will lead to higher prices and thus to lower returns. Therefore, the before-tax expected return will be lower on assets that are safer, more liquid, or tax-favored. Economists say that such desirable assets sell at a **premium,** while assets that are riskier or more illiquid sell at a **discount.** Still, market forces assure that assets of comparable risk, liquidity, and tax treatment must yield the same expected returns.

We can see the effect of changes in risk, taxes, or liquidity in Figure 10.2. A reduction in the riskiness of an asset, a reduction in the taxes that are imposed on it, or an increase in its liquidity shifts the demand curve for the asset to the right. In the short run, the supply of an asset is inelastic. Even in the longer run, supply is likely not to be perfectly elastic. Accordingly, as illustrated in the figure, the price of the assets goes up, from p_0 to p_1. Accompanying the increase in price is a reduction in the return per dollar invested.

The next three sections explore these three additional attributes of investments—risk, tax considerations, and liquidity—and how they create premiums and discounts.

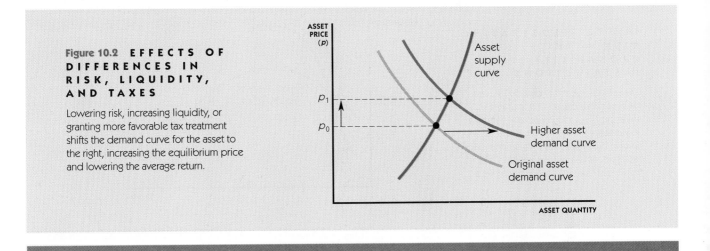

Figure 10.2 EFFECTS OF DIFFERENCES IN RISK, LIQUIDITY, AND TAXES

Lowering risk, increasing liquidity, or granting more favorable tax treatment shifts the demand curve for the asset to the right, increasing the equilibrium price and lowering the average return.

RISK

It has been said that financial markets are the places where risk is bought and sold. A full appreciation of this insight is beyond our scope here; but it does underline the important risks associated with most assets. The investor may receive a high or a low return. She may even get back less than she put in—a loss. Often this uncertainty concerns what the asset will be worth next week, next month, or next year. The price of a stock may go up or down. Long-term bonds are risky; even though the interest they pay is known, their market value may fluctuate. Moreover, because there is uncertainty about future inflation, there is uncertainty about the *real* return paid by a bond, even though the nominal return is fixed.

A prime consideration for any investor, therefore, is the riskiness of any investment alternative. Bank accounts, in this regard, are safe. Since government deposit insurance came into play in the 1930s after the great stock market crash, no one in the United States has lost her money in an insured bank account. But investments in housing, stocks, bonds, and most other investments all involve risk. The return may be substantially lower than what you expected, or you may lose some or all of your money.

Some assets are riskier than others; that is, they may have a greater chance of very low returns and a greater chance of very high returns. Figure 10.3 provides a slightly more complex version of Figure 10.1. This time, instead of describing only three possible payoffs, the diagram depicts all possible payoffs for each of two stocks. The two stocks represented here have the same average return, but the stock whose return is described by curve *A* is riskier than the stock whose return is described by curve *B*. There is a greater chance of both very low and very high returns.

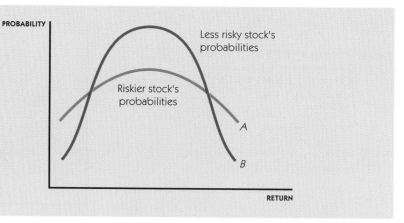

Figure 10.3 ILLUSTRATING RISK WITH PROBABILITY DISTRIBUTIONS

These two probability distributions are both symmetrical, around the same midpoint; thus, they both have the same expected return. However, the stock shown by curve *A* has a higher chance of very high or very low returns, and thus is riskier than the stock shown by curve *B*.

TAX CONSIDERATIONS

The government is a silent partner in almost all investments. It is not the kind of partner you would ordinarily choose—it takes a fraction of the profits, but leaves you with almost all the losses. Still, investors must take into account the fact that a substantial fraction of the returns to a successful investment will go to the government as taxes. Since different assets are treated differently in the tax code, tax considerations are obviously important in choosing a portfolio. After all, individuals care about after-tax returns, not before-tax returns. Investments that face relatively low tax rates are said to be **tax-favored.**

State and municipal bonds illustrate this point. These bonds yield a lower return than do corporate bonds of comparable risk and liquidity. So why do people buy them? The answer is that the interest on bonds issued by states and municipalities is generally exempt from federal tax. The higher your income, the more valuable this tax exemption is, because your tax savings are greater the higher your tax *rate*. The higher demand for these tax-exempt bonds from high-income investors drives up their price, which drives down the return received on the bonds. We can expect the return to decline to the point where the after-tax return for high-income individuals is at most only slightly higher than for an ordinary taxable bond of comparable risk.

Consider two bonds, identical in all respects except their tax treatment. Both promise to pay $110 next year, $10 of which is interest. The price of the taxable bond is $100. The equilibrium price for a municipal bond is greater than $100. This means that its average return, before tax, is less than 10 percent—less than the return on the taxable bond. If most investors have to pay 30 percent of any interest income in taxes, then the after-tax return is $7, not

On the single day of October 19, 1987, stock prices fell by 22.6 percent on the New York Stock Exchange. It was the largest one-day crash in the history of the stock market.

Stock market crashes are difficult for economists to explain. Who can explain the exact path of a stampede or the precise direction of an avalanche? The Presidential Task Force on Market Mechanisms was appointed soon after the 1987 crash to give it a try. Headed by Nicholas Brady, later appointed secretary of the Treasury, the task force did offer some insight.

In an efficient stock market, one in which most information was widely distributed and new information was what caused prices to move, a stock market crash would make sense *if* it was preceded by some extremely bad news. However, while the weeks before October 19 held their share of bad news, there was no news bad enough—like an earthquake or a plague—to cause this sort of collapse. In fact, the economy continued to grow after the crash for almost another three years.

If the cause of the crash was not fundamental economic factors, the task force reasoned, it must have been related to the mechanisms through which stocks are traded. In theory, at least, it is conceivable that the existing mechanisms for trading stocks somehow pushed stock prices too high—higher than the underlying value of the company could justify—and then pushed them too low during the crash. Economists have been working for some time on how price movements might become exaggerated in this way.

One possible explanation is that a number of stock traders have a tendency to buy whatever stocks are going up and to sell whatever stocks are going down. In a rising stock market, these traders would bid stock prices still higher; in a falling market, they would push prices still lower.

This explanation may sound plausible, but a number of economists are not happy with it. It presumes, for example, that a high stock price leads to more purchasers for that stock, which violates the basic notion that demand curves slope down. And wouldn't these investors learn from the stock market crash that the market cannot be pushed higher forever? Perhaps most troubling, the worst days of the stock market since the Great Depression seem to be concentrated in the second half of the 1980s. Is there some factor in the modern stock market that is making crashes more likely?

Some observers proposed to stop a future crash by shutting down the market whenever it declined substantially. Critics of this plan pointed out that stocks are traded worldwide, and the U.S. government has no power to shut down private trading. If shutting down the market leads to further panic, it could even prove counterproductive. Despite these doubters, in the aftermath of the 1987 crash, the New York Stock Exchange announced a rule that if stock prices move in a single day more than 50 points on the Dow Jones industrial average, trading will be interrupted.

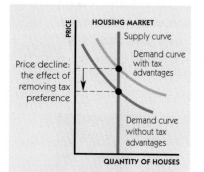

Figure 10.4 EFFECT OF REMOVING TAX PREFERENCES FOR HOUSING

Removing tax preferences for housing will shift the demand curve for housing down, and this will, in the short run (with an inelastic housing supply), cause marked decreases in the price of housing.

$10. They will be willing to buy the tax-exempt bond so long as its yield is at least 7 percent. Below that level, they will buy the taxable bond instead. Thus, the equilibrium price of the tax-exempt bond is $110 ÷ 1.07 = $102.80. That is, the tax-exempt bond yields the same return at a price of approximately $103 as the taxable bond does at $100.

Investing in housing, particularly a house to live in, is another tax-favored form of investment enjoyed by most Americans. You can deduct the interest payments on your mortgage and real estate taxes when you calculate your income for tax purposes. In addition, the capital gain from owning the house is not taxed until the house is sold. Even then, if you use the money to buy another house or if you are above age fifty-five, the capital gain (up to $155,000) from selling your house is not taxed at all. If the tax advantages of home ownership were ever withdrawn, we could expect housing prices to decline precipitously in the short run (in which supply is inelastic), as illustrated in Figure 10.4. It is not likely that tax preferences for housing will be suddenly removed, however, because most voters own houses, and politicians are loathe to anger such a large number of their constituents.

LIQUIDITY

The fourth important attribute to consider is liquidity. An asset is liquid if the costs of selling it are very low. A bank account is completely liquid (except when the bank goes bankrupt), because you can turn it into cash at virtually no charge by writing a check. Corporate stock in a major company is fairly liquid, because the costs of selling at a well-defined market price are relatively small.

In the basic competitive model, all assets are assumed to be perfectly liquid. There is a well-defined price at which anything can be bought and sold; any household or firm can buy or sell as much as it wants at that price; and the transaction is virtually without cost. But these assumptions are not always met. There are often significant costs of selling or buying an asset. The costs of selling a house, for instance, can be 5 percent or more of the value of the house. At times, even municipal bonds have been fairly illiquid. The prices at which such bonds could be bought and sold have been known to differ by more than 20 percent.

Taxes not only reduce after-tax returns, but they also affect investment strategies in a variety of ways. This is particularly true of the capital gains tax.

The stock market was very successful in 1995. Though stockholders became much wealthier, they only had to pay taxes on these gains if they sold their stocks. As long as investors hold on to their investments, they can postpone the capital gains tax. This reduces the pain—or in more technical terms, the present discounted value—of the tax. Indeed, if a person holds the stock until death, the tax is completely avoided.[*] This can be looked at another way. If John acquired a stock for $100 that is now worth $1,100, if he sells it, he must pay a capital gains tax on the $1,000 gain; assuming he is in the 28 percent tax bracket, he will be left with $820 to reinvest. Suppose John puts the $820 in a new investment that yields a 10 percent before-tax return, but he needs the cash in one year to pay for his daughter's college education. He will end up with $879.[**] If he had left his money in the old stock—which he expected to grow by only 8 percent, far slower than the alternative investment—at the end of next year he would have $883.[†] The effect of the capital gains tax is to make holding the old stock more attractive for John, even though it returns less. This is called the *locked-in effect*.

Now suppose that instead of cashing in to pay for his daughter's education, John died, leaving his shares to his daughter. In this case, the locked-in effect would be even greater. If John switched to the higher return asset, his daughter could have sold the shares for a net proceed of $902—the capital gain on the new stock goes untaxed. But if he had left it in the old stock, she would have $1,188.

Temporarily lowering the capital gains tax induces people to sell shares in which they have unrealized capital gains. It is like a sale. And like a sale, so many people may sell their shares, and "realize" their gains that tax revenues may rise. Of course, though revenues are increased while the sale is on, they may be reduced later. A permanent lowering of the capital gains tax rate has a much smaller effect. There is considerable controversy over whether revenues will be increased in the short run, and even more controversy over whether they will be increased in the long run. When the Democrats controlled Congress, they calculated that a capital gains tax reduction would reduce revenues even in the short run; but when the Republicans took control of Congress in 1994, they calculated that it would increase revenues, at least in the short run.

As Congress focused on balancing the budget by the year 2002, attention was focused on the impact of tax policy in that year—and the fact that in the official calculations, a tax decrease raised revenue in that time horizon made a capital gains tax reduction seem particularly attractive. Although eliminating the loophole that allows capital gains accumulated over a lifetime to be completely avoided at death would be the most effective way of reducing the locked-in effect and, it is estimated, raise a considerable amount of revenue, proposals to do so received scant attention in the political debate.

[*] This loophole is called "step-up-in basis." The person inheriting the stock gets to treat it *as if* he had purchased it at the date of inheritance. His benefactor's capital gain is completely ignored.

[**] The $820 will generate a capital gain of $82, but he will have to pay $23 in taxes.

[†] The $1,100 will be worth $1,188. He will pay a capital gains tax of $.28 \times \$1,088$, or approximately $305.

EFFICIENT MARKET THEORY

The demand for any asset depends on all four of the attributes just discussed—average return, risk, tax treatment, and liquidity. In a well-functioning market, there are no bargains to be had; you get what you pay for. If some asset yields a higher average return than most other investments, it is because that asset has a higher risk, is less liquid, or receives less favorable tax treatment.

That there are no bargains does not mean the investor's life is easy. He still must decide what he wants, just as he does when he goes into a grocery store. Figure 10.5 shows the kind of choices he faces. For simplicity, we ignore liquidity and tax considerations and focus only on average returns and risk. Panel A shows the opportunity set in the way that is usual for this case. Because "risk" is bad, to get less risk we have to give up some average returns. That is why the trade-off has a positive slope. Panel B shows the more familiar version of an opportunity set, by putting a measure of "safety" on the horizontal axis. Greater safety can only be obtained at the expense of a lower average return. Reading from either panel, we can see that assets with greater risk (lower safety) have a higher average return. Point A represents a government T-bill—no risk but low return. Point B might represent a stock or mix of stocks of average riskiness, point C one of high risk. A very risk-averse person might choose A, a less risk-averse person B, a still less risk-averse person C.

The theory that prices perfectly reflect the characteristics of assets—there are no bargains—is called the **efficient market theory.** Since much of the work on efficient market theory has been done on publicly traded stocks, our discussion centers on them. The lessons, however, can be applied to all asset prices.

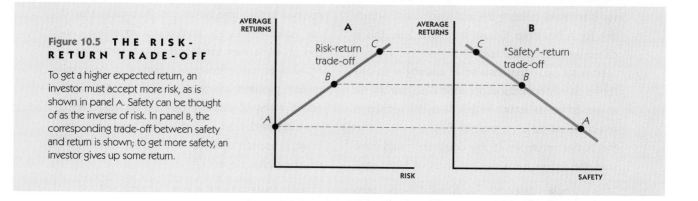

Figure 10.5 THE RISK-RETURN TRADE-OFF

To get a higher expected return, an investor must accept more risk, as is shown in panel A. Safety can be thought of as the inverse of risk. In panel B, the corresponding trade-off between safety and return is shown; to get more safety, an investor gives up some return.

The general presumption of the efficient markets theory is that high returns can only be obtained as a result of bearing high risks. Occasionally there are opportunities for making high returns at little or no risk—but competitive markets ensure that these opportunities quickly disappear. The most famous of these opportunities are called *arbitrage*. Arbitrage opportunities arise when the same item is being bought and sold at different prices. Thus, if gold can be bought or sold in New York at $350 an ounce, and in Zurich at $351 an ounce, it would pay someone to buy it in New York and sell it in Zurich, assuming that it is essentially costless to transfer gold from New York to Zurich. Arbitrage means that, at most, small price differences can survive long in the market. As investors buy gold in New York, the price there will be driven up; and as investors sell gold in Zurich, the price there will be driven down. The process stops when the prices are essentially the same.

Sometimes arbitrage takes on much more subtle forms. A closed-end mutual fund is a company that has bought stocks in a large number of other com-panies. Those are its only assets. The value of the company should be equal to the value of the shares it owns. Occasionally, closed-end funds have sold at a significant discount from the value of their shares. To see how arbitrage would work to eliminate this discount—at least shortly before the fund has announced that it will terminate, that is, sell its shares and send its owners a check for their value—notice that an investor could buy shares in the company and, at the same time agree to sell shares in the *underlying* stocks in a com-mensurate amount. For simplicity, assume the mu-tual fund owns only GM shares, and that there are a million shares in the mutual fund, and the fund owns 1 million GM shares. Buying a share in the mutual fund is *equivalent* to buying a share in GM. Assume a GM share sells for $30, and a share in the mutual fund sells for $25. An investor could buy a share in the mutual fund for $25 and agree to sell a share in GM, receiving $30, for a guaranteed profit of $5.

Good investors look for arbitrage opportunities, as elusive as they are.

EFFICIENCY AND THE STOCK MARKET

Most people do not think they can wander over to the racetrack and make a fortune. They are not so skeptical about the stock market. They believe that even if they themselves cannot sit down with the *Wall Street Journal* and pick out all the best stocks, someone who studies the stock market for a living could do so. But economists startled the investment community in the early 1960s by pointing out that choosing successful stocks is no easier—and no harder—than choosing the fastest horses.

The efficient market theory explains this discrepancy in views. When econ-omists refer to an efficient market, they are referring to one in which relevant information is widely known and quickly distributed to all participants. To oversimplify a bit, they envision a stock market where all investors have access to *Barron's* and *Fortune* magazines and many other sources of good information about business, and where government requires businesses to disclose certain information to the public. Thus, each stock's expected return, its risk, its tax treatment, and so on will be fully known by all investors. Because participants have all the information, asset prices will reflect it.

It turns out, however, that this broad dissemination of information is not only unrealistic but unnecessary. Economists have shown that efficient markets do not require that *all* participants have information. If enough participants have information, then prices will move as if the whole market had the information. All it takes is a few people knowledgeable enough to recognize a bargain, and prices will quickly be bid up or down to levels that reflect complete information. And if prices reflect complete information, even uninformed buyers, purchasing at current prices, will reap the benefit; while they cannot beat the market, neither do they have to worry about being "cheated" by an overpriced security.

You cannot "beat" an efficient market any more than you can beat the track. You can only get lucky in it. All the research done by the many big brokerage houses and individual investors adds up to a market that is in some respects like a casino. This is the irony of the view, held by most economists, that the stock market is an efficient one. If you are trying to make money in an efficient stock market, it is not enough to choose companies that you expect to be successful in the future. If you expect a company to be successful and everyone else also expects it to be successful, based on the available information, then the price of shares in that company will already be quite high. The only way to make abnormally high profits on stock purchases is to pick companies that will surprise the market by doing better than is generally expected.

The one exception is not really an exception because it involves trading with knowledge that other stock market participants do not have. **Inside traders** are individuals who buy and sell shares of companies for which they work. Studies show that their inside knowledge does in fact enable them to obtain above average returns. Federal law requires inside traders to disclose when they buy and sell shares in their own company. People who may not have the inside knowledge but imitate the stock market behavior of the insiders also do slightly above average. The law also restricts the ability of insiders to share their information with outsiders and profit from their extra knowledge, and exacts penalties for violations. Ivan Boesky made untold millions trading on insider information in the 1980s and paid large fines and even served time in jail.

Because prices in an efficient market already reflect all available information, any price changes are a response to *unanticipated* news. If it was already known that something good was going to occur, for instance some new computer model better than all previous computers was going to be unveiled, the price of the firm's stock would reflect this (it would be high) before the computer actually hit the market. You might not know precisely how much better than its competitors the new computer was, and hence you could not predict precisely by how much future earnings were likely to rise. You would make an estimate. The market will reflect the average of these estimates. When the new computer is introduced, there is some chance that it will be better than this average, in which case the price will rise further. But there is also a chance that it will not be quite as good as this average estimate, in which case the price will fall, even though the computer is in fact better than anything else on the market. In this case, the "surprise" is that the computer is not as good as the market anticipated.

Since tomorrow's news is, by definition, unanticipated, no one can predict whether it will cause the stock price to rise or fall. In an efficient stock market, prices will move unpredictably, depending on unexpected news. When a stock has an equal chance of rising or falling in value relative to the market as a whole, economists say that its price moves like a **random walk.** Figure 10.6 shows a computer-generated random walk, giving an idea of how unpredictable such a path is.

Random walk conjures up the image of a drunk who rambles down the street with generally unstable—and unpredictable—movements.

So too with the stock market. Although there is an upward drift in the level of all stock prices, whether any particular stock will do better or worse than that average is unpredictable. If the stock market is indeed a random walk, it is virtually impossible for investors to beat the market. You can do just as well by throwing darts at the newspaper financial page as you can by carefully studying the prospects of each firm. The only way to do better than the market, on average, is to take greater risks; but taking greater risks means that there is a larger chance of doing worse than the market too.

The randomness of the market has one important consequence: *some* individuals are going to be successful. This is bad news for people who want to believe that their insights, rather than luck, are what has enabled them to beat the market.

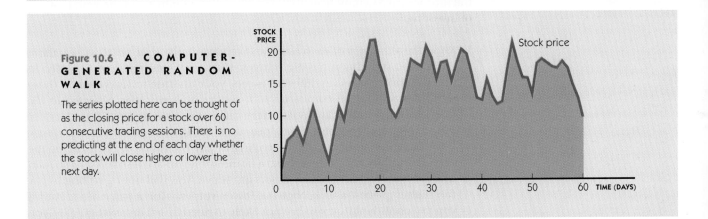

Figure 10.6 A COMPUTER-GENERATED RANDOM WALK

The series plotted here can be thought of as the closing price for a stock over 60 consecutive trading sessions. There is no predicting at the end of each day whether the stock will close higher or lower the next day.

EFFICIENT MARKETS OR RANDOM NOISE?

While most economists agree that there is little evidence individuals can, even by spending considerable money on information, consistently beat the market, there is controversy about how to interpret this finding. Some see it as evidence of the efficiency of the market, as we have seen. But some economists view it as evidence of nothing more than the market's randomness. Those who hold this view point out that there often seem to be large changes in stock market prices without any "news" of sufficient magnitude to account for these changes. For example, there are usually ten or fifteen days in the year when the stock market changes by more than 2 percent—a very large change for a single day—without any obvious news-related explanation.

The famous economist John Maynard Keynes compared predictions of the stock market to predictions of the winner of a beauty contest, where what one had to decide was not who was the greatest beauty, but who the other judges would think was the most beautiful. If investors suddenly "lose confidence" in a particular stock or in the whole stock market, or if they believe that others are losing confidence, share prices may fall dramatically.

STRATEGIES FOR INTELLIGENT INVESTING

So far, we have investigated major investment alternatives available to those who save, some of the important attributes of each, and the ways in which their prices reflect these attributes. If you are lucky enough (have enough money) to be considering some of these alternatives, keep in mind the following four simple rules. These rules will not tell you how to make a million by the time you are twenty-five, but they will enable you to avoid the worst pitfalls of investing.

1. *Know the attributes of each asset, and relate them to your personal situation.* Each asset has characteristic returns, risk, tax treatment, and liquidity. In making choices among different assets, your attitude toward each of these attributes should be *compared with the average attitudes reflected in the marketplace.* Most individuals prefer safer, tax-favored, more liquid assets. That is why those assets sell at a premium (and produce a correspondingly lower average return). Are you willing to pay the amount required by the market for the extra safety or extra liquidity? If you are less risk averse than average, you will find riskier assets attractive. You will not be willing to pay the higher price—and accept the lower return—for a safer asset. And if you are confident that you are not likely to need to sell an asset quickly, you will not be willing to pay the premium that more liquid assets require. If you are putting aside money for tuition next year, on the other hand, you probably will want to choose a relatively liquid asset.

2. *Give your financial portfolio a broad base.* In choosing among financial assets, you need to look not only at each asset separately, but at all of your assets together. A person's entire collection of assets is called her **portfolio.** (The portfolio also includes liabilities—what she owes—but they take us beyond the scope of this chapter.) This rule is seen most clearly in the case of risk. One of the ways you reduce risk is by diversifying your investment portfolio. With a well-diversified portfolio, it is extremely unlikely that something will go wrong with all the assets simultaneously. An investor with a diversified portfolio must still worry about events like recessions or changes in the interest rate, which will tend to make all stocks go up or down. But events that affect primarily one firm will have a small impact on the overall portfolio.

Many mutual funds claim more than just diversification: they claim that their research and insight into markets enable them to pick winners. Our discussion of efficient markets casts doubt on these claims. Many mutual funds do no research, claim no insights, and do nothing more than provide portfolio diversification. These are called **indexed funds.** There are several measures of the average price of stocks in the market. For instance, the Standard & Poor's (S&P) 500 index is the average price of 500 stocks chosen to be representative of the market as a whole. Other indices track prices of various categories of stocks, such as transportation, utilities, or high technology. Indexed funds link their portfolio to these stock market indexes. Thus, there are a number of index funds that buy exactly the same mix of stocks that constitute the S&P 500 index. Naturally, these indexed funds do about as well as—no better and no worse than—the S&P 500 index, after accounting for a small charge for managing the fund.

Because the index funds have low expenses, particularly in comparison with funds that are trying to outguess the market, they yield higher average returns to their investors than other funds with comparable risk.

3. *Look at* all *of the risks you face, not just those in your financial portfolio.* Many people may be far less diversified than they believe. For example, consider someone who works for the one big company in town. She owns a house, has a good job, has stock in the company, money in the bank, and a pension plan. But if that single company goes broke, she will lose her job, the value of her stock will fall, the price of her house is likely to decline as the local economy suffers, and even the pension plan may not pay as much as expected.

4. *Think twice before you think you can beat the market!* Efficient market theory delivers an important message to the personal investor. If an investment adviser tells you of an opportunity that beats the others on all counts, don't believe him. The bond that will produce a higher than average return carries with it more risk. The bank account that has a higher interest rate has less liquidity. The dream house at an unbelievable price probably has a leaky roof. The tax-favored bond will have a lower return—and so on. Efficient market theory, as we have seen, says that information about these characteristics is built into the price of assets, and hence built in to the returns. Basically, investors can adjust the return to their portfolio only by adjusting the risk they face. Burton Malkiel, author of the best-selling book

CLOSE-UP: JUST HOW SMART IS THE "SMART MONEY"?

The financial press pays attention to keeping track of the winners and losers in the investment world. Major newspapers, including the *Wall Street Journal,* regularly publish lists of the best- and worst-performing mutual funds for classes of investments. Now, everybody wants to put their investment money with the "smart money." But do the top experts really do that much better than average? One way to find out is to look at the return you would get if you followed the "dumb" strategy of buying and holding all the stocks on the S&P 500 list of the 500 largest U.S. companies. Since 1976, a mutual fund company has offered a fund that does exactly that—the Vanguard Index Trust 500 portfolio, which today has over $8 billion in assets. One advantage of such an "index fund" is that the amount the mutual fund spends on market research and buying and selling stocks is extremely low. The return to the investor of the Vanguard 500 over the last 10 years was 14.8 percent. This is a standard by which the "smart money" can be evaluated. One of the biggest success stories has been the Fidelity Magellan fund managed by mutual fund guru Peter Lynch until his recent retirement. This fund beat the Vanguard 500 fund by about 3.8 percent per year. But is the Magellan fund the exception or the rule?

As we know, riskier investments require an added return, or risk premium. So, to compare apples to apples, we look at investment portfolios with riskiness similar to that of the S&P 500 list. The 10-year returns to investors from 52 actively managed mutual funds are shown in the figure. Their average return was only 13.9 percent per year, nearly one percentage point per year below that of the Vanguard 500 fund. The smart money was not so smart after all! In fact, less than 30 percent of the funds "beat the market." Economists see this as further support for the efficient market theory. Whether one fund does better than another is a matter of luck (and holding down costs).

Source: Morningstar (1994).

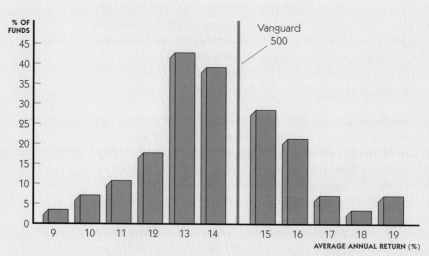

A Random Walk Down Wall Street, applies this theory to personal investing. "Every investor must decide the trade-off he or she is willing to make between eating well and sleeping well. The decision is up to you. High investment rewards can be achieved only at the cost of substantial risk-taking."[3]

REVIEW AND PRACTICE

SUMMARY

1. Investment options for individuals include putting savings in a bank account of some kind or using them to buy real estate, bonds, shares of stock, or mutual funds.

2. Returns on investment can be received in four ways: interest, dividends, rent, and capital gains.

3. Assets can differ in four important ways: in their average returns, their riskiness, their treatment under tax law, and their liquidity.

4. The expected return of an asset is calculated by multiplying each of the possible outcomes times the probability of its occurring, and adding the results.

5. By holding assets that are widely diversified, individuals can avoid many of the risks associated with specific assets, but not the risks associated with the market as a whole.

6. The efficient market theory holds that all available information is fully reflected in the price of an asset. Accordingly, changes in price reflect only unanticipated events and, therefore, are random and unpredictable.

7. There are four rules for intelligent investors: (1) evaluate the characteristics of each asset and relate them to your personal situation; (2) give your financial portfolio a broad base; (3) look at all the risks you face, not just those in your financial portfolio; (4) think twice before believing you can beat the market.

KEY TERMS

investment	capital gain	efficient market
certificate of deposit	mutual fund	theory
(CD)	Treasury bills	random walk
liquidity	(T-bills)	portfolio
dividends	expected returns	

[3]6th ed. (New York: Norton, 1995).

REVIEW QUESTIONS

1. Suppose an investor is considering two assets with identical expected rates of return. What three characteristics of the assets might help differentiate the choice between them?

2. List the principal alternative forms of investment that are available. What are the returns on each called? Rate them in terms of the characteristics described in question 1.

3. True or false: "Two assets must have equal expected returns." If we modify the statement to read "Two assets that are equally risky must have equal expected returns," is the statement true? Explain your answer.

4. If you found out that several company presidents were buying or selling stock in their own companies, would you want to copy their behavior? Why or why not?

5. What is the efficient market theory? What implications does it have for whether you can beat the market? Does it imply that all stocks must yield the same expected return?

6. Why do economists expect the market to be efficient?

7. What alternative interpretations are given to the observation that individuals cannot, even by spending considerable money on information, consistently beat the market?

8. List and explain the four rules for intelligent investing.

9. True or false: "A single mutual fund may be a more diversified investment than a portfolio of a dozen stocks." Explain.

PROBLEMS

1. Imagine a lottery where 1 million tickets are sold at $1 apiece, and the winning ticket receives a prize of $700,000. What is the expected return to buying a ticket in this lottery? Will a risk-averse person buy a ticket in this lottery?

2. Would you expect the rate of return on bonds to change with their length of maturity? Why or why not?

3. Why might a risk-averse investor put some money in junk bonds?

4. Would you predict that
    (a) the before-tax return on housing would be higher or lower than the before-tax return on other assets?
    (b) investors would be willing to pay more or less for a stock with a high return when the economy is booming and a low return when the economy is in a slump than they would pay for a stock with just the opposite pattern of returns?

(c) an investment with low liquidity would sell at a premium or a discount compared with a similar investment with higher liquidity?

5. Each of two investments has a 1 in 10 chance of paying a return of −10 percent; a 1 in 5 chance of paying 2 percent; a 1 in 3 chance of paying 6 percent; a 1 in 5 chance of paying 10 percent; and a 1 in 6 chance of paying 12 percent. Draw this probability distribution, and calculate the expected return for these two investments. If investment A is a house and investment B is a share of corporate stock, how might liquidity or tax considerations help you decide which of these investments you prefer?

6. Imagine a short-term corporate $1,000 bond that promises to pay 8 percent interest over three years. This bond will pay $80 at the end of the first year and the second year, and $1,080 at the end of the third year. After one year, however, the market interest rate has increased to 12 percent. What will the bond be worth to an investor who is not too concerned about risk at that time? If the firm appears likely to go bankrupt, how will the expected return on this bond change?

7. Golfer Lee Trevino once said: "After losing two fortunes, I've learned. Now, when someone comes to me with a deal that's going to make me a million dollars, I say, 'Tell it to your mother.' Why would a stranger want to make me a million?" Explain how Trevino's perspective fits the efficient market theory.

11

THE FIRM'S COSTS

The previous three chapters focused on the decisions of house-holds and individuals. In this chapter, the focus shifts to the deci-sions of firms. Firms make decisions concerning what and how much to produce, and how to produce it, with the aim of maxi-mizing their profits.

The basic competitive model is, once again, our starting point. Many firms, all making the same product, compete with one another to sell that product to well-informed customers, who instantaneously recognize and act upon any price differences. Because customers are well informed about prices, all firms in a competitive market must accept the price set for their product by the forces of supply and demand in the market as a whole. Any firm trying to sell above that price will lose all its customers. Firms in competitive markets are, therefore, **price takers.** The classic example of competitive markets are agricultural markets—thousands of farmers, say, producing milk. A dairy farmer does not waste time wondering what price to set for the milk he has to sell. He knows he will get the "going price."

A firm does, however, have some control over its costs. The firm's total costs are affected by, among other things, its level of production, and its choice of inputs (how to produce what it produces). Chapter 12 shows how a firm uses this relationship to choose the level of production that maximizes its profits. This chapter focuses on how firms minimize their costs, and how costs are affected by the level of production.

Even though we talk in terms of "production" and "goods," it is important to bear in mind that only one-third of the U.S. economy consists of industries that produce goods in the conventional sense—manufacturing, mining, construction, and agriculture. The other two-thirds of the economy produces primarily services—industries like transportation, education, health care, wholesale and retail trade, and finance. The principles laid out here, however, apply equally to these other sectors.

PROFITS, COSTS, AND FACTORS OF PRODUCTION

A business that continually incurs losses over time will cease to exist because it will not have enough money to pay its bills. Businesses are under constant pressure to make money. The motivation of making as much money as possible—maximizing profits—provides a useful starting point for discussing the behavior of firms in competitive markets.

The definition of **profits** is simple:

profits = revenues − costs.

The **revenue** a business receives from selling its products are calculated as the quantity it sells of the product multiplied by the price of the product. A firm's **costs** are defined as the total expense of producing the good.

What the firm uses to produce the goods are called inputs or **factors of production**: labor, materials, and capital goods. The firm's total costs are simply the sum of the costs of these inputs. Labor costs are what the company pays for the workers it hires and the managers it employs to supervise the workers. The costs of materials include raw materials and intermediate goods. Intermediate goods are whatever supplies the company purchases from other firms—such as seeds, fertilizer, and gasoline for a farm; iron ore, coal, coke, limestone, and electric power for a steel company. The cost of capital goods include the cost of machinery and structures such as buildings and factories.

All firms work to keep their costs as low as possible. For given prices and levels of output, a firm maximizes its profits by finding the least costly way of producing its output. Thus, profit-maximizing firms are also cost-minimizing firms. Within limits, firms can vary the mix of labor, materials, and capital goods they use; and they will do so until they find the lowest cost method of producing a given quality and quantity of product. The simplest way of understanding how firms find the lowest cost point is to look at a firm with only two factors of production, one fixed, one variable. Not surprisingly, inputs which vary with the level of production are said to be variable.

PRODUCTION WITH ONE VARIABLE INPUT

A wheat farmer with a fixed amount of land who uses only labor to produce his crop is our example. The more labor he applies to the farm (his own time, plus the time of workers that he hires), the greater the output. Labor is the single variable factor (input).

The relationship between the quantity of inputs used in production and the level of output is called the **production function.** Figure 11.1 shows the farmer's production function; the data supporting the figure are set forth in Table 11.1. The increase in output corresponding to a unit increase in any factor of production, labor in this case, is the **marginal product** of that factor. For example, when the number of hours worked per year rises from 8,000 to 9,000, output increases by 10,000 bushels, from 155,000 to 165,000. The marginal product of an extra 1,000 hours of labor is, accordingly, 10,000 bushels. The marginal product is given in the last column of the table. Diagrammatically, it is given by the slope of the production function. The slope of a curve

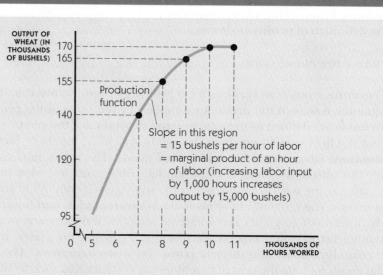

Figure 11.1 PRODUCTION FUNCTION WITH DIMINISHING RETURNS TO AN INPUT

As the amount of the input (labor) increases, so does the output (wheat). But there are diminishing returns to labor; each increase in labor results in successively smaller increases in wheat output. Since the slope of the curve is the marginal product of labor, on the graph, this means the slope flattens out as the amount of labor increases.

Table 11.1 **LEVEL OF OUTPUT WITH DIFFERENT AMOUNTS OF LABOR**

Number of hours worked	Amount of wheat produced (bushels)	Marginal product (additional bushels produced by 1,000 additional hours of labor)
5,000	95,000	25,000
6,000	120,000	20,000
7,000	140,000	15,000
8,000	155,000	10,000
9,000	165,000	5,000
10,000	170,000	0
11,000	170,000	

is the change along the vertical axis (the increase in output) from a unit increase along the horizontal axis (the increase in labor input).

DIMINISHING RETURNS

In the case of the wheat farmer, as more labor is added to a fixed amount of land, the marginal product of labor diminishes. This is another application of the concept of **diminishing returns,** which we originally encountered in Chapter 2. In the case of a firm's production function, diminishing returns implies that each additional unit of labor generates a smaller increase in output than the last. Increasing the number of hours worked from 7,000 to 8,000 raises output by 15,000 bushels, but increasing the hours worked from 8,000 to 9,000 raises output by only 10,000 bushels. Diminishing returns sets in with a vengeance at higher levels of input; moving from 10,000 to 11,000 hours worked adds nothing. Diagrammatically, diminishing returns are represented by the slope flattening out as the amount of labor increases. It is clear that, with diminishing returns, increases in output lead to less than proportionate increases in input; doubling the input results in output that is less than twice as large.

DIMINISHING RETURNS

As more and more of one input is added, *while other inputs remain unchanged,* the marginal product of the added input diminishes.

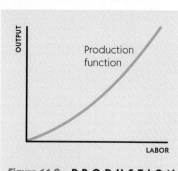

Figure 11.2 PRODUCTION FUNCTION WITH IN-CREASING RETURNS TO AN INPUT

As the amount of labor increases, so does output. But the returns to labor are increasing in this case; successive increases in labor result in successively larger increases in output. On the graph, this means the slope becomes steeper as the amount of labor increases.

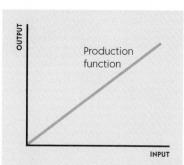

Figure 11.3 PRODUCTION FUNCTION WITH CONSTANT RETURNS TO AN INPUT

The marginal product of labor is constant, neither increasing nor diminishing as the firm expands production. On the graph, this means that the slope does not change.

INCREASING RETURNS

Although a production function with diminishing returns is an important case, other cases do occur. Figure 11.2 shows a production function where increasing an input (here, labor) raises output more than proportionately. A firm with this kind of production function has **increasing returns.** In the single-input case depicted, it is clear that the marginal product of the input increases with the amount produced; that is, when the firm is producing a lot, adding one more worker increases output by more than it does when the firm is producing little.

Imagine a business that picks up garbage. If this business counts only one out of every five houses as customers, it will have a certain cost of production. But if the company can expand to picking up the garbage from two out of every five houses, while it will need more workers, the workers will be able to drive a shorter distance and pick up more garbage faster. Thus, a doubling of output can result from a less than doubling of labor. Many examples of increasing returns, like garbage collection, involve providing service to more people in a given area. Telephone companies and electric utilities are two other familiar instances.

CONSTANT RETURNS

In between the cases of diminishing and increasing returns lies the case of **constant returns,** shown in Figure 11.3. Each additional unit of input increases output by the same amount, and the relationship between input and output is a straight line.

FIXED VERSUS VARIABLE INPUTS

Firms typically require a certain level of input just to be in business. Before it can open its doors, for instance, a firm may need land (or space) and some machines. It will have to hire someone to run the personnel office and someone to supervise the workers. These are called **fixed inputs,** because they do not depend on the level of output. The quantities of **variable inputs,** in contrast, rise and fall with the level of production. For instance, the firm can work its space and machines for one shift a day, or it can run them for all twenty-four hours. It simply hires more workers and uses more materials. These workers and materials are variable inputs.

Figure 11.4 shows a production function with fixed and variable inputs. At L_0, the fixed inputs are in place. At first, when the firm increases inputs beyond L_0, output increases more than proportionately. Output at L_2 is more than twice output at L_1, even though L_2 is twice L_1. This is due to the effect of the fixed input. As the variable input is increased, the increase in output generated by each successive unit of input decreases due to diminishing returns. Beyond L_3, the effect of diminishing returns outweighs that of fixed inputs and output rises *less* than proportionately with inputs.

The ratio of output to input at any point on the production function is called the **average productivity.** At point A, for example, the average productivity is the distance up the vertical axis from the origin (Q_3) divided by the dis-

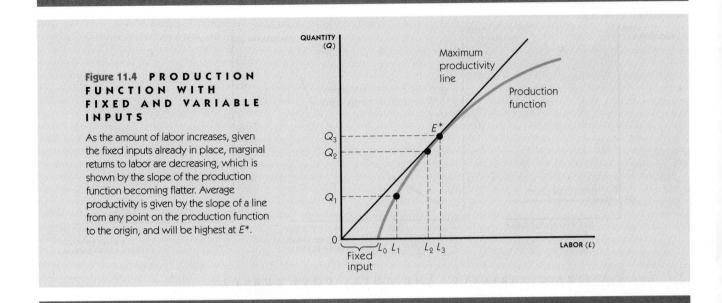

Figure 11.4 PRODUCTION FUNCTION WITH FIXED AND VARIABLE INPUTS

As the amount of labor increases, given the fixed inputs already in place, marginal returns to labor are decreasing, which is shown by the slope of the production function becoming flatter. Average productivity is given by the slope of a line from any point on the production function to the origin, and will be highest at E^*.

tance along the horizontal axis (L_3). This is the slope of the line from the origin to E^*. The steepest line from the origin to the production function touches the production function at E^*. This is the level of production at which output per unit of input is maximized. Notice that average productivity—the slope of the line from the origin to the production function—increases as output increases to point E^*, and falls thereafter. Marginal productivity—the slope of the production function itself—continuously decreases as employment increases beyond L_0.

COST CURVES

The production function is important to the firm because the inputs it depicts determine the costs of production. The case of the production function with fixed inputs described in Figure 11.4 is the most common production function in the economy, and a look at the kinds of costs it generates will give us an overview of the major categories of cost upon which economists concentrate.

FIXED AND VARIABLE COSTS

The costs associated with inputs that do not vary with the level of production are called **fixed costs.** Whether the firm produces nothing or produces at maximum capacity, it antes up the same fixed cost. Figure 11.5 shows how costs depend on output. Panel A depicts fixed costs as a horizontal line—by definition, they do not depend on the level of output. As an example, consider a would-be wheat farmer who has the opportunity to buy a farm and its equipment for $25,000. His fixed costs are $25,000.

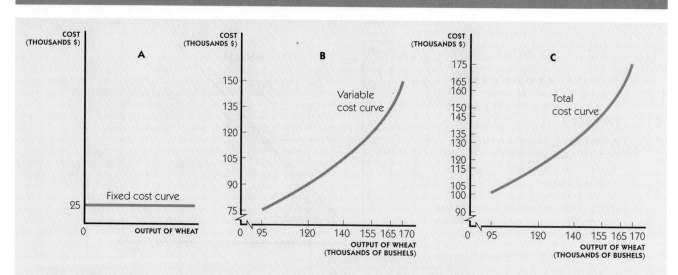

Figure 11.5 FIXED, VARIABLE, AND TOTAL COST CURVES

Panel A shows a firm's fixed cost; by definition, fixed costs do not depend on the level of output. Panel B shows a firm's variable costs, which rise with the level of production. The increasing slope of the curve indicates that it costs more and more to produce at the margin, which is a sign of diminishing returns. Panel C shows a total cost curve. It has the same slope as the variable cost curve, but is higher by the amount of the fixed costs.

Variable costs correspond to variable inputs. These costs rise or fall with the level of production. Any cost that the firm can change during the time period under study is a variable cost. To the extent that such items as labor costs or costs of materials can go up or down as output does, these are variable costs. If we give our farmer only one variable input, labor, then his variable costs would be, say, $15 per hour for each worker. The variable costs corresponding to levels of output listed in Table 11.1 are shown in Table 11.2 and plotted in Figure 11.5B. As output increases, so do variable costs, so the curve slopes upward.

TOTAL COSTS

Table 11.2 also includes a column labeled "Total cost." **Total costs** are defined as the sum of variable and fixed costs, so this column differs from the variable costs column by $25,000, the amount of the firm's fixed cost. The total cost curve, summarizing these points, is shown in Figure 11.5C.

MARGINAL COST AND MARGINAL PRODUCT

As with the economic decisions we have discussed earlier in this book, the most important cost for the firm's decision makers is the **marginal cost.** This is the extra cost corresponding to each additional unit produced. In the case

Table 11.2 **COST OF PRODUCING WHEAT**

Output (bushels)	Labor required (hours)	Total variable cost (at a wage of $15 per hour)	Total cost ($)	Marginal cost ($ per bushel)	Average cost ($ per bushel)	Average variable cost ($ per bushel)
95,000	5,000	75,000	100,000	—	1.05	.79
120,000	6,000	90,000	115,000	.60	.96	.75
140,000	7,000	105,000	130,000	.75	.93	.75
155,000	8,000	120,000	145,000	1.00	.94	.77
165,000	9,000	135,000	160,000	1.50	.97	.82
170,000	10,000	150,000	175,000	3.00	1.03	.88

of the wheat farmer's costs (Table 11.2), as he increases labor input from 7,000 hours to 8,000 hours, output increases by 15,000 bushels. Thus, to produce 1,000 extra bushels requires 1,000/15 = 66⅔ extra hours. The cost of producing an extra 1,000 bushels is 66⅔ hours × wage per hour. If the wage is $15 per hour, the marginal cost of 1,000 bushels is $1,000.

More generally, if *MPL* is the marginal product of labor (15 bushels per hour), and *w* is the (hourly) wage ($15 per hour), the marginal cost of producing an extra unit of output is just *w/MPL* ($1 per bushel).

The marginal cost curve depicted in Figure 11.6 is upward sloping, reflect-

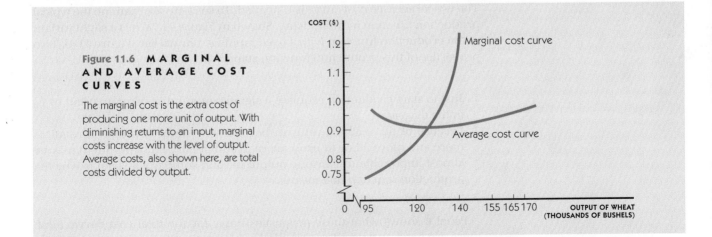

Figure 11.6 MARGINAL AND AVERAGE COST CURVES

The marginal cost is the extra cost of producing one more unit of output. With diminishing returns to an input, marginal costs increase with the level of output. Average costs, also shown here, are total costs divided by output.

ing the fact that as more is produced, it becomes harder and harder to increase output further—an example of the familiar principle of diminishing marginal returns.

RELATIONSHIP BETWEEN MARGINAL AND TOTAL COST CURVES

There is a simple relationship between the marginal cost curve and the total cost curve. The marginal cost is just the slope of the total cost—the change in total costs (movement along the vertical axis, in Figure 11.5C) resulting from a unit change in output (movement along the horizontal axis).

AVERAGE COST

The final set of costs that concern the business firm are its **average costs.** These are simply total costs divided by output. The average cost curve gives average costs corresponding to different levels of output. Figure 11.6 also shows the average cost curve corresponding to the total cost curve depicted in Figure 11.5C. To find the average cost for any level of output, we draw a line from the origin to the point on the total cost curve for that level of output. The slope of that line is

$$\frac{\text{total costs}}{\text{output}} = \text{average costs.}$$

AVERAGE VARIABLE COSTS

The concept of **average variable costs** will be useful in the next chapter when we discuss the production decision. These are total variable costs divided by output.

THE U-SHAPED AVERAGE COST CURVE

The typical average cost curve is U-shaped. To see why, we examine the typical production function in more detail. Shown in Figure 11.7A, it is a slight variant of the production function with a fixed input we saw earlier (Figure 11.4). Two properties of this production function stand out:

1. Just to start production requires a significant input of labor, marked by L_0 in the diagram.
2. Because of diminishing returns, beyond some level of output it requires more and more labor to produce each additional unit of output. It may be almost impossible to increase output beyond some point. That is why the production function flattens out.

Panel B shows what these properties imply for the total cost curve. First, there are fixed costs, c_0. Second, diminishing returns mean that not only do total costs rise as output increases, but the total cost curve becomes steeper

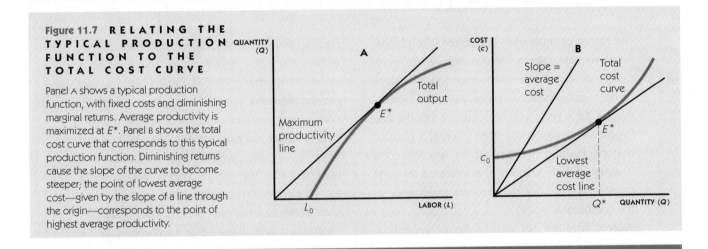

Figure 11.7 RELATING THE TYPICAL PRODUCTION FUNCTION TO THE TOTAL COST CURVE

Panel A shows a typical production function, with fixed costs and diminishing marginal returns. Average productivity is maximized at E^*. Panel B shows the total cost curve that corresponds to this typical production function. Diminishing returns cause the slope of the curve to become steeper; the point of lowest average cost—given by the slope of a line through the origin—corresponds to the point of highest average productivity.

and steeper. Third, average costs, total costs divided by output, are minimized at the output level Q^*. This is shown in Figure 11.8. Average cost is the sum of the average fixed cost—the fixed cost divided by output—and average variable cost. As output increases, average fixed cost declines. Average variable cost, on the other hand, increases with output as the law of diminishing returns sets in with strength. At low levels of output, the first effect dominates, so average costs declines. But once a high enough level of output is achieved, the second effect dominates, so average cost increases with output, as shown in Figure 11.8.

Even if the average cost curve is U-shaped, the output at which average costs are minimized may be very great, so high that there is not enough demand to justify producing that much. Thus, when economists refer to declining average costs, they mean that those costs are declining over the level of output that is likely to prevail in the market.

Relationship between Average and Marginal Cost Curves   The relationship between average costs and marginal costs is reflected in Figure 11.8. The marginal cost curve intersects the average cost at the bottom of the U—the *minimum* average cost. To understand why the marginal cost curve will *always* intersect the average cost curve at its lowest point, consider the relationship between average and marginal costs. As long as the marginal cost is below the average cost, producing an additional unit will pull down the average. Thus, everywhere that the marginal cost is below average cost, the average cost curve is declining. If marginal cost is above average cost, then producing an additional unit will raise the average. So everywhere that the marginal cost is above average cost, the average cost curve must be rising. The point between where the U-shaped average cost curve is falling and where it is rising is the minimum point.

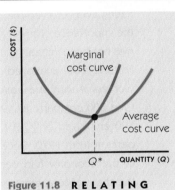

Figure 11.8 RELATING THE MARGINAL COST CURVE TO THE AVERAGE COST CURVE

The average cost curve is usually U-shaped. it initially declines as the fixed costs are spread over a larger amount of output, and then rises as diminishing returns to the variable input become increasingly important. With a U-shaped average cost curve, the marginal cost curve will cross the average cost curve at its minimum.

CLOSE-UP: HOW IMPORTANT IS THE FORTUNE 500?

The model of small and very competitive companies may seem like an abstraction. When many people think of the American economy, they think of huge companies like Exxon, IBM, and General Motors. Each year, *Fortune* magazine lists the 500 largest companies in the United States; it is a sort of honor roll of corporate America, where success is equated with size. But the existence of large companies does not disprove the importance of the competitive model.

Large firms are not immune from competition, either from other large firms or from upstarts. For the last few decades, the importance of the Fortune 500 has been declining relative to growth in the rest of the economy. Competitive pressure is eating away at even the largest companies, while the importance of small- and middle-sized companies has been increasing. In 1970, for example, the Fortune 500 employed a total of 14.6 million workers. About one worker in five was with a Fortune 500 company. By 1990, though, the Fortune 500 employed only 12.4 million, a decline of 15 percent from 1970. Since employment in the rest of the economy had been growing in that time, the share of total employment in the Fortune 500 fell. Only about one person in ten worked for one of the biggest 500 companies.

Sales figures tell a similar story. Between 1970 and 1990 sales reported by the Fortune 500 increased by 59 percent in real terms. However, the economy as a whole grew by 72 percent over that time, so the Fortune 500 was lagging well behind.

The reduced role of the biggest American corporations has given rise to considerable debate. Some argue that a globally connected economy increases the importance of bigness. Big companies can invest in larger projects, distribute and sell all over the globe, and compete with huge companies from other countries. Others respond that the rise of smaller, often new companies promotes competition and innovation and thus serves consumers better. For example, the David and Goliath story of Apple, whose first computer was launched from the garage of its founders, versus longtime computer giant IBM in the market for personal computers has fascinated industry observers. Confronted with a myriad of competitors in the personal computer market—including Compaq, Dell, Toshiba, and many others—IBM has not been able to dominate. Its share of the world market in personal computers has fallen to only 8 percent.

Sources: Fortune 500 numbers taken from April issues of *Fortune;* U.S. figures are from *Economic Report of the President* (1991).

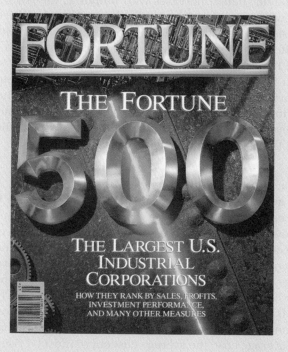

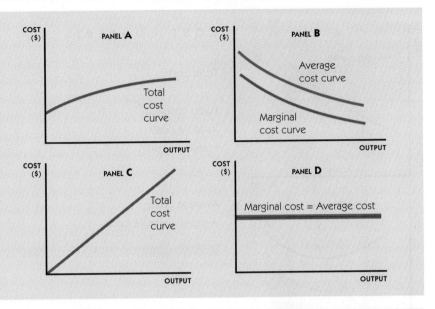

Figure 11.9 COST CURVES WITH INCREASING OR CONSTANT RETURNS

Panels A and B show total, marginal, and average cost curves with increasing returns. Average costs decline as production increases. Panel C shows a total cost curve with constant returns; since returns to the variable factor are constant and fixed costs are zero, the total cost curve begins at the origin and its slope does not change. Panel D shows marginal and average costs with constant returns; marginal cost does not change, and so the average cost does not change either.

ALTERNATIVE SHAPES OF COST CURVES

Earlier, we saw that production functions may exhibit increasing or constant returns. If there are increasing returns, output increases more than proportionately with the input and total costs increase more slowly than output, as seen in panel A of Figure 11.9. In this case average costs decline, as illustrated in panel B. Marginal costs are also declining, corresponding to a situation where the marginal product of labor increases as output decreases.

If there are constant returns, doubling inputs doubles output, which will cost twice as much. In this case, total costs are simply proportional to output (panel C), and average and marginal costs are constant and equal (panel D).

CHANGING FACTOR PRICES AND COST CURVES

The cost curves shown thus far are based on the fixed prices of each of the inputs firms purchase. An increase in the price of a variable factor, such as the wage, or the price of some raw material, shifts the total, average, and marginal cost curves upward, as illustrated in Figure 11.10. An increase in the price of a fixed factor shifts only the total and average cost curves upward.

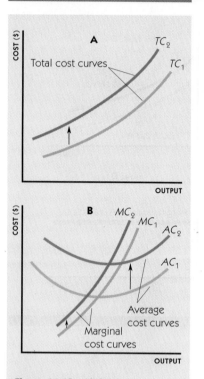

Figure 11.10 HOW CHANGING INPUT PRICES AFFECT COST CURVES

An increase in the price of a variable factor shifts the total, average, and marginal cost curves upward.

COST CONCEPTS

Total costs:	Total costs of producing output = fixed costs + variable costs
Fixed costs:	Costs that do not depend on output
Variable costs:	Costs that depend on output
Marginal costs:	Extra cost of producing an extra unit = total cost of $(Q + 1)$ units minus total cost of Q units of output
Average costs:	Total costs divided by output
Average variable costs:	Total variable costs divided by output

PRODUCTION WITH MANY FACTORS

The basic principles of the case with only two factors—one fixed, one variable—apply also to firms producing many products with many different inputs. The only fundamental difference is that with many factors it becomes possible to produce the same output in several different ways. Cost minimization, therefore, involves weighing the costs of different mixes of inputs. (The analysis is somewhat more complicated, and is in the appendix to this chapter.)

COST MINIMIZATION

There are usually several ways a good can be produced, using different quantities of various inputs. Table 11.3 illustrates two alternative ways of making car frames, one a highly automated process requiring little labor and the other a less automated process that uses more assembly-line workers. The table shows the daily wage and capital costs for each process. Each method produces the same quantity of output (say, 10,000 car frames per day). In this simple example, we assume all workers are identical (of equal skill) and hence get paid the same wage, and that all machines cost the same. As we can see from the table, the less automated process clearly costs more at the given costs of labor ($20 per worker per hour) and machines (rental costs equal $1,000 per day).

Although this table provides only two stark alternatives, it should be clear that in some cases the alternative possibilities for production will form a con-

Table 11.3 **COSTS OF PRODUCTION**

Inputs	More automated process	Less automated process
Labor	50 man hours @ $20 = $1,000	500 man hours @ $20 = $10,000
Machines	5 machines @ $1,000 = $5,000	2 machines @ $1,000 = $ 2,000
Total	$6,000	$12,000

tinuum, where the input of one increases a bit, the input of another falls a bit, and output remains the same. In other words, the firm can smoothly substitute one input for another. For instance, in producing cars, different machines vary slightly in the degree of automation. Machines requiring less and less labor to run them cost more. When firms make their decisions about investment, they thus have a wide range of intermediate choices between the two described in the table.

THE PRINCIPLE OF SUBSTITUTION

One of the most important consequences of the principle of cost minimization in the case of multiple factors of production is that when the price of one input (say, oil) increases relative to that of other factors of production, the change in relative prices causes firms to substitute cheaper inputs for the more costly factor. This is an illustration of the general **principle of substitution** we encountered in Chapter 4.

THE PRINCIPLE OF SUBSTITUTION

An increase in the price of an input will lead the firm to substitute other inputs in its

place.

In some cases, substitution is quick and easy; in other cases, it may take time and be difficult. When the price of oil increased fourfold in 1973 and doubled again in 1979, firms found many ways to economize on the use of oil. For instance, companies switched from oil to gas (and in the case of electric power companies, often to coal) as a source of energy. More energy-efficient cars and trucks were constructed, often using lighter materials like aluminum and plastics. These substitutions took time, but they did eventually occur.

The principle of substitution should serve as a warning to those who think they can raise prices without bearing any consequences. Argentina has almost a world monopoly on linseed oil. At one time, linseed oil was universally used for making high-quality paints. Since there was no competition, Argentina decided that it would raise the price of linseed oil and assumed everyone would have to pay it. But as the price increased, paint manufacturers learned to substitute other natural oils that could do almost as well.

Raising the price of labor (wages) provides another example. Unions in the auto and steel industries successfully demanded higher wages for their members during the boom periods of the 1960s and 1970s, and firms paid the higher wages. But at the same time, the firms redoubled their efforts to mechanize their production and to become less dependent on their labor force. Over time, these efforts were successful and led to a decline in employment in those industries.

DIAGRAMMATIC ANALYSIS

We can see the principle of substitution at work using our average cost diagrams. The car manufacturer described earlier has two alternative ways of producing cars, each with its own average cost curve. Both are shown in Figure 11.11. The general principle of cost minimization requires that the firm use the method of production with the lowest average costs at the planned level of production. In the figure, at high levels of production (above Q_1), the more mechanized process with average cost curve AC_2 dominates the less mechanized process with average cost curve AC_1. A smaller-scale producer, however, uses the less mechanized process. Assume now the cost of labor increases. This shifts up the cost curves for both ways of producing, but obviously, the less mechanized process—which is more dependent on labor—has its cost curve shifted up more. As a result, the critical output at

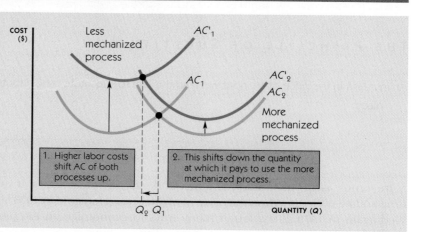

Figure 11.11 MINIMIZING COSTS AS INPUT PRICES CHANGE

With two production processes, as the price of an input increases—in this case, labor—both average cost curves shift up. However, AC_1 relies more heavily on labor, so it shifts up more. This means that firms will switch to the more mechanized technology of AC_2 at a lower level of output (Q_2 instead of Q_1), and there will tend to be a shift away from the more expensive input, labor, and toward the relatively cheaper capital.

1. Higher labor costs shift AC of both processes up.

2. This shifts down the quantity at which it pays to use the more mechanized process.

In the two hundred years since the beginning of the industrial revolution, there has been an enormous increase in the amount of carbon dioxide (CO_2) in the atmosphere; and concentrations are expected to increase rapidly over coming decades. There is an increasing consensus that the increased concentration of this and related gases (called greenhouse gases) will lead to global warming, with potentially significant impacts on the environment. Reflecting this consensus, the nation's of the world signed an agreement in Rio de Janeiro in 1992 to work towards limiting their growth. Slowing down the rate of increase of these greenhouse gases will entail using less energy, and substituting away from sources of energy that produce large amounts of greenhouse gases—like coal—towards sources of energy that produce less—like natural gas—or none at all, like hydroelectric power. A carbon tax, levied on various fuels in proportion to how much they contribute to greenhouse gases, has been suggested as one way of encouraging firms to substitute away from coal and toward fuels that are environmentally more sound.

which it pays to use the more mechanized production process is lowered, from Q_1 to Q_2. Thus, as the price of labor is increased, more firms switch to a more mechanized process—capital goods (machines) are substituted for labor.

An increase in the price of any input shifts the cost function up. The amount by which the cost function shifts up depends on several factors, including how much of the input was being used in the first place and how easy it is to substitute other inputs. If the production process uses a great deal of the input, then the cost will shift up a lot. If there is a large increase in the price of an input, and the firm cannot easily substitute other inputs, then the cost curve will shift up more than it would if substitution of other inputs were easy.

SHORT-RUN AND LONG-RUN COST CURVES

Up to this point, we have referred to the distinction between inputs that are fixed (their cost does not vary with quantity produced) and inputs that are variable (their cost does depend on quantity produced). We have sidestepped the fact that inputs, and costs, may be fixed for some period of time, but if the time period is long enough, they can vary with production. Take the inputs of labor and machines, for example. In the short run, the supply of machines may be fixed. Output is then increased only by increasing labor. In the longer run, both machines and workers can be adjusted. The short-run cost curve, then, is the cost of production with a *given* stock of machines. The long-run cost curve is the cost of production when all factors are adjusted.[1]

SHORT-RUN COST CURVES

If we think of the number of machines as being fixed in the short run, and labor as the principal input that can be varied, our earlier analysis of production with a single variable factor provides a good description of short-run cost curves. Thus, short-run *average* cost curves are normally U-shaped.

The short-run *marginal* cost curve in Figure 11.12 presents a pattern often seen in manufacturing. Marginal costs are approximately constant over a wide range. As long as their newest machines are not being fully used, firms find that increasing production by 10 percent requires increasing the number of production workers by 10 percent and the inputs of other materials (raw materials, intermediate goods) by 10 percent. Idle machines are simply put to work. Eventually, however, the cost of producing extra units goes up. Workers have to work more hours (and often they get paid more—time and a half or double time—for these extra hours). Overworked machines break down more frequently. Older, poorer machines have to be put to use. At some level of output, it may be impossible, without extraordinary costs, to push a factory to a higher level of production in the short run.

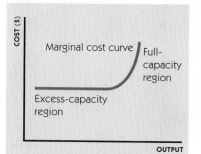

Figure 11.12 SHORT-RUN MARGINAL COSTS

When there is excess capacity, the marginal cost of producing an extra unit may not increase much, and so the marginal cost curve is flat. But when capacity is approached, marginal costs may rise rapidly.

[1]The distinction between short-run and long-run costs corresponds to the distinction between short-run and long-run supply curves introduced in Chapter 4. Chapter 12 will make clear the relationship. It is an exaggeration to think that only capital goods are fixed in the short run while all of labor is variable. In some cases, capital goods may easily be varied; a firm can, for instance, rent cars. And in some cases, as when a company has long-term contracts with its workers, it may be very difficult to vary labor in the short run.

We have thus identified two key properties of the short-run marginal cost curve. (1) When there is unused or excess capacity, the marginal cost of producing each extra unit does not increase much; the marginal cost curve is relatively flat. (2) But eventually the marginal cost curve becomes steeply upward sloping. (Remember, we are focusing here on the short run, so we assume the number of machines is fixed; there is a particular capacity for which the plant was designed.)

Before we turn to the long run, it is useful to rethink the meaning of fixed costs. So far, we have used the term to mean costs that do not depend on the level of output. This in fact blurs the distinction between two related concepts. Even if a firm could instantaneously adjust all factors of production, some overhead costs would still be required for the company to exist at all. From now on, **overhead costs** will be defined as costs that a firm must bear simply to operate, whether or not they can be varied in the short run. For a firm to be in business at all, for example, it probably needs telephone service. **Fixed costs** will be defined as costs that are fixed in the short run, whether or not they represent overhead costs. For example, if a firm signs a contract to rent a warehouse at $5,000 a month for ten years, its warehouse rental costs are fixed in the short run.

LONG-RUN COST CURVES

Even if the short-run average cost curves for a given manufacturing facility are U-shaped, the long-run average cost curve may not have the same shape. As production grows, it will pay at some point to build a second plant, and then a third, a fourth, and so on. Panel A of Figure 11.13 shows the total costs of producing different levels of output, assuming that the firm builds one plant. This curve is marked TC_1. It also shows the total costs of producing different levels of output assuming the firm builds two plants (TC_2) and three plants (TC_3). How many plants will the company build? Clearly, the firm wishes to minimize the (total) costs of producing at any level of output. Thus, the *relevant* total cost curve is the lower boundary of the three curves, which is heavily shaded. Between 0 and Q_1, the firm produces using one plant; between Q_1 and Q_2, it uses two plants; and for outputs larger than Q_2, it uses three plants.

We can see the same results in panel B, using average cost curves. Obviously, if the firm minimizes the total costs of producing any particular output, it minimizes the average cost of producing that output. The figure shows the average cost curves corresponding to the firm's producing with one, two, and three plants. The company chooses the number of plants that minimizes its average costs, given the level of output it plans to produce. Thus, if the firm plans to produce less than Q_1, it builds only one plant; AC_1 is less than AC_2 for all outputs less than Q_1. If the firm plans to produce between Q_1 and Q_2, it builds two plants, because AC_2 is, in this interval, less than either AC_1 or AC_3. Similarly, for outputs greater than Q_2, the firm builds three plants.

In this case, the long-run average cost curve is the shaded bumpy curve in

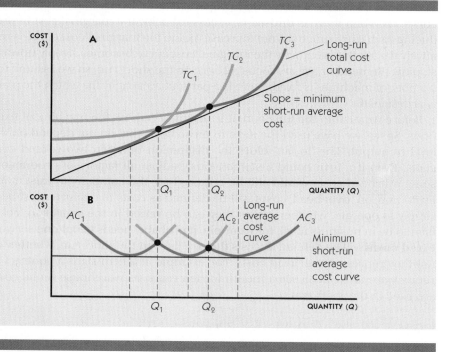

Figure 11.13 SHORT-RUN AND LONG-RUN COST CURVES

Panel A shows a series of short-run total cost curves, TC_1, TC_2, and TC_3, each representing a different level of fixed capital input. In the long run, a cost-minimizing firm can choose any of these, so the long-run total cost curve will be the lowest cost of producing any level of output, as shown by the heavily shaded lower boundary of the curves. Panel B shows a series of short-run average cost curves, AC_1, AC_2, and AC_3, each representing a different level of fixed capital input. in the long run, a cost-minimizing firm can choose any of these, so the long-run average cost curve will be the shaded lower boundary of the curves.

Figure 11.13B. For large outputs, the bumps look very small. In drawing long-run average cost curves, therefore, we typically ignore the bumps and draw smooth curves.

We now need to ask whether long-run average cost curves are normally flat or slope upward or downward. To answer this question, remember how we analyzed the shape of the short-run average cost curve, or the average cost curve with a single variable input. We first described the production function, relating the level of input to the level of output. If output increases less than proportionately with the input because there are diminishing returns, the average cost curve is rising. If output increases more than proportionately with the input, there are increasing returns, and the average cost curve is falling.

Exactly the same kind of analysis applies when there are many inputs. We ask, what happens when all of the inputs increase together? If, when all of the inputs increase together and in proportion, output increases just in proportion, there are **constant returns to scale;** if output increases less than proportionately, there are **diminishing returns to scale;** and if output increases more than proportionately, there are **increasing returns to scale,** or **economies of scale.**

Many economists argue that constant returns to scale are most prevalent in manufacturing; a firm can increase its production simply by replicating its plants. Then the long-run average and marginal costs equal minimum short-run average costs. The average and marginal cost curves for such a case are depicted in Figure 11.14, where there are many, many plants, and the long-run average cost curve is flat. (The small "bumps" are caused by the fact that output may not be a simple multiple of the output at which a plant attains its

Figure 11.14 THE SHAPE OF THE LONG-RUN AVERAGE COST CURVE

If there are many possibilities for varying the scale of the firm, such as by adding new machines and thus many short-run average cost curves, the long-run average cost curve defined by their joint boundary can be thought of as very flat, or smooth. In this case, the long-run average cost curve is drawn as horizontal. The firm can increase output simply by replicating identical plants, and there are constant returns to scale.

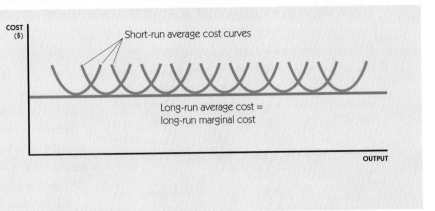

minimum average costs; but, as the figure shows, these bumps become relatively insignificant if output is very large.)

There are, however, also costs to running a firm—the overhead costs. The firm must bear these costs whether it operates 1, 2, or 100 plants. These overhead costs include not only the costs of the corporate headquarters, but also the basic costs of designing the original plant. Thus, we commonly think of the long-run average cost curve as slightly downward sloping, as in Figure 11.15A.

But sometimes small is beautiful, and big is bad. In these cases there are diminishing returns to scale. As the firm tries to grow, adding additional plants, it faces increasing managerial problems; it may have to add layer upon layer of management, and each of these layers increases its cost. When the firm is very small, the owner can watch all his workers. When the firm has grown to 10 employees, the owner can no longer supervise his workers effectively; a new supervisor may be needed every time his firm hires 10 more workers. By the time the firm has grown to 100 workers, he has 10 supervisors. Now the owner spends most of his time looking after the supervisors, not the workers directly.

Eventually, the owner finds it difficult to keep tabs on the supervisors, so it becomes necessary to hire a manager for them. Notice that in this pattern, the number of supervisors and managers is a growing proportion of the workers in the firm. An organization with 10 workers requires only 1 supervisor; with 100 workers, it requires 10 supervisors and a manager; with 1,000 workers, 100 supervisors, 10 managers, and 1 supermanager. Besides the raw numbers of administrative people, decisions now must pass through a number of layers of bureaucracy, and communication will often be slower.

Eventually, average costs may start to increase, as illustrated in Figure 11.15 B. Whether any particular industry is best described by Figure 11.14, 11.15A, or 11.15B depends on the importance of overhead costs and the extent to which managerial problems grow with size.

Increasing returns to scale are also possible in some industries, even for

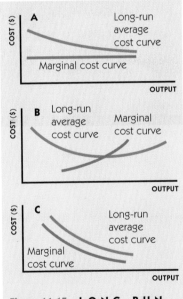

Figure 11.15 LONG-RUN AVERAGE COSTS

Panel A shows that with overhead costs, long-run average costs may be declining, but they flatten out as output increases. In panel B, with managerial costs increasing with the scale of the firm, eventually average and marginal costs may start to rise. Panel C shows that if there are increasing returns to scale, long-run costs may be continuously falling.

very large outputs. As the firm produces a higher output, it can take advantage of larger and more efficient machines, which it would not pay a small firm to purchase. If there are increasing returns to scale, then the long-run average cost curve and the marginal cost curve will be downward sloping, as in Figure 11.15c.

LOOKING BEYOND THE BASIC MODEL: COST CURVES AND THE COMPETITIVENESS OF MARKETS

The degree of competition in an industry depends to a considerable degree on the structure of costs in that industry. This leads us to several insights that take us beyond the basic model. Consider the case of one company that is producing all the market wants in an industry with declining average costs. If any new company wishes to enter this market and produce less than the incumbent firm, its average costs will be higher than that of the incumbent company. So long as the original firm produces more than the entrant, its costs will be lower, so it can undercut the newcomer—and in fact charge a price so low that the new firm suffers a loss while the incumbent firm still makes a profit. Indeed, if the original merchant charges a price just equal to his average costs (or threatens to do so if an entrant tries to crash into his market), there is no way that a rival can profitably enter.

If, in contrast, the incumbent firm is the only firm producing for the entire market but is on the upward-sloping portion of an average cost curve, a new company might aim at producing less with a lower average cost. Now, at least one new company will be able to undersell the original firm, and competitive forces will have some power.

The magnitude of the output at which average costs are minimized depends largely on the size of overhead costs, relative to total costs. In industries in which overhead costs are low, there will normally be many firms, since average costs will reach their minimum value at a relatively low level of output. Since the average cost curve may begin to rise quite rapidly beyond a relatively small output, small firms have the power to undersell larger firms, and there will be many firms in the market. Businesses with low overhead costs include real estate and travel agencies. In these industries, the typical firm is small, and there are thousands of them.

In industries in which overhead costs are high, however, the minimum average costs will be attained at a very high output, so there will be relatively few firms. Low-cost producers in these industries tend to be large firms, and relatively few fill the market demand. Makers of automobiles and household appliances are examples. In some industries, overhead average costs are declining throughout the output levels demanded in the market. In these cases, at least within any locality, there will be only one firm. Examples include electricity and other utility companies and cement plants. A main cost for most utilities is the cost of the wires (for electricity and telephone) or pipes (for water and sewage).

Expenditures to develop a new product are like high overhead costs in their effect on entry into a market. Firms can, of course, choose to spend more or less on research or on developing new products, but these costs do not increase with the firm's level of output. It is not surprising, then, that in many of the sectors of the economy in which research and development expenditures are important, there are relatively few firms. For example, the chemical industry is dominated by a small number of large firms.

ECONOMIES OF SCOPE

Most firms produce more than one good. Deciding which goods to produce and in what quantities, and how to produce them (the first and second basic economic questions), are central problems facing firm managers. The problems would be fairly straightforward, were it not for some important interrelations among the products. The production of one product may affect the costs of producing another.

In some cases, products are produced naturally together; we say they are **joint products.** Thus, a sheep farm naturally produces wool, lamb meat, and mutton. If more lambs are slaughtered for meat, there will be less wool and less mutton.

If it is less expensive to produce a set of goods together than separately, economists say that there are **economies of scope.** The concept of economies of scope helps us understand why certain sets of activities are often undertaken by the same firms. Issues of economies of scope have also played an important role in discussions of regulation over the past two decades. At the time of the breakup of AT&T, which previously had dominated both local and long-distance telephone service as well as research in telecommunications, some economists argued against the breakup on the grounds that there were important economies of scope among these activities.

REVIEW AND PRACTICE

SUMMARY

1. A firm's production function specifies the level of output resulting from any combination of inputs. The increase in output corresponding to a unit increase in any input is the marginal product of that input.

2. Short-run marginal cost curves are generally upward sloping, because diminishing returns to a factor of production imply that it will take ever increasing amounts of the input to produce a marginal unit of output.

3. The typical short-run average cost curve is U-shaped. With U-shaped average cost curves, the marginal and average cost curves will intersect at the minimum point of the average cost curve.

4. When a number of different inputs can be varied, and the price of one input increases, the change in relative prices of inputs will encourage a firm to substitute relatively less expensive inputs; this is an application of the principle of substitution.

5. Economists often distinguish between short-run and long-run cost curves. In the short run, a firm is generally assumed not to be able to change its capital stock. In the long run, it can. Even if short-run average cost curves are U-shaped, long-run average cost curves can take on a variety of shapes. They can, for instance, be flat, continuously declining, or declining and then increasing.

6. Economies of scope exist when it is less expensive to produce two products together than it would be to produce each one separately.

KEY TERMS

profits
revenues
production function
marginal product
fixed inputs
variable inputs
average productivity

fixed costs
overhead costs
variable costs
total costs
marginal cost
average costs
average variable
    costs

constant, diminish-
    ing, or increasing
    returns to scale
    (economies of
    scale)
economies of scope

REVIEW QUESTIONS

1. What is a production function? When there is a single (variable) input, why does output normally increase less than in proportion to input? What are the alternative shapes that the relationship between input and output takes? What is the relationship between these shapes and the shape of the cost function?

2. What is meant by these various concepts of cost: total, average, average variable, marginal, and fixed? What are the relationships between these costs? What are short-run and long-run costs? What is the relationship between them?

3. Why are short-run average cost curves frequently U-shaped? With U-shaped average cost curves, what is the relationship between average and marginal costs? If the average cost curve is U-shaped, what does the total cost curve look like?

4. What happens to average, marginal, and total costs when the price of an input rises?

5. If a firm has a number of variable inputs and the price of one of them rises, will the firm use more or less of this input? Why?

6. What are diminishing, constant, and increasing returns to scale? When might you expect each to occur? What is the relationship between these properties of the production function and the shape of the long-run average and total cost curves?

7. What are economies of scope, and how do they affect what a firm chooses to produce?

PROBLEMS

1. Tom and Dick, who own the Tom, Dick, and Hairy Barbershop, need to decide how many barbers to hire. The production function for their barbershop looks like this:

Number of barbers	Haircuts provided per day	Marginal product
0	0	
1	12	
2	36	
3	60	
4	72	
5	80	
6	84	

Calculate the marginal product of hiring additional barbers, and fill in the last column of the table. Over what range is the marginal product of labor increasing? constant? diminishing? Graph the production function. By looking at the graph, you should be able to tell at what point the average productivity of labor is highest. Calculate average productivity at each point to illustrate your answer.

2. The overhead costs of the Tom, Dick, and Hairy Barbershop are $160 per day, and the cost of paying a barber for a day is $80. With this information, and the information in problem #1, make up a table with column headings in this order: Output, Labor required, Total variable cost, Total cost, Marginal cost, Average variable cost, and Average cost. If the price of a haircut is $10 and the shop sells 80 per day, what is the daily profit?

3. Using the information in problems #1 and #2, draw the total cost curve for the Tom, Dick, and Hairy Barbershop on one graph. On a second graph, draw the marginal cost curve, the average cost curve, and the average variable cost curve. Do these curves have the shape you would expect? Do the minimum and average cost curves intersect at the point you expect?

4. Suppose a firm has the choice of two methods of producing: one method entails a fixed cost of $10 and a marginal cost of $2; the other entails a fixed cost of $20 and a marginal cost of $1. Draw the total and average cost curves for both methods. At what levels of output will the firm use the low fixed-cost technology? At what levels of output will it use the high fixed-cost technology?

5. A firm produces cars using labor and capital. Assume that average labor productivity—total output divided by the number of workers—has increased in the last few months. Does that mean that workers are working harder? Or that the firm has become more efficient? Explain.

APPENDIX: COST MINIMIZATION WITH MANY INPUTS

This appendix shows how the basic principles of cost minimization can be applied to a firm's choice of the mix of inputs to use in production. To do this, we make use of a set of concepts and tools similar to those presented in the appendix to Chapter 8, in the analysis of how households make decisions about what mix of goods to purchase.

ISOQUANTS

The alternative ways of producing a particular quantity of output can be graphically represented by **isoquants.** The first part of the term comes from the Greek word *iso*, meaning "same," while "quant" is just shorthand for quantity. Thus, isoquants illustrate the different combinations of inputs that produce the same quantity.

Consider this simple extension of the example of Table 11.3 on page 263. A firm can buy three different kinds of machines, each of which produces car frames. One is a highly mechanized machine that requires very little labor. Another is much less automated and requires considerably more labor. In between is another technique. These represent three different ways of producing the same quantity.

Assume the firm wishes to produce 10,000 car frames a day. It could do this by using highly mechanized machines, moderately mechanized machines, or nonmechanized machines. The total capital and labor requirements for each of these possibilities are represented in Figure 11.16. The horizontal axis shows the capital requirements, while the vertical axis shows the labor requirements. The labor and capital associated with the highly mechanized production process is shown by point *A*, the moderately mechanized by point *B*, and the low mechanized by point *C*.

If the firm wishes, it can produce half of its output on the highly mechanized machines and half on the moderately mechanized machines. If it chooses this option, its capital requirements will be halfway between the capital that would be required if it used only *A* or only *B*, and its labor requirements will also be halfway between. This halfway-between choice is illustrated by point *X*. By similar logic, the firm can achieve any combination of capital and labor requirements on the straight line joining *A* and *B* by changing the proportion of highly mechanized and moderately mechanized machines. And by changing the proportion of moderately mechanized and low-mechanized machines, it can achieve any combination of capital and labor requirements on the straight line joining *B* and *C*. The curve *ABC* is the isoquant. It gives all those combinations of capital and labor that can produce 10,000 automobile frames per day. All of these input combinations give the same output.

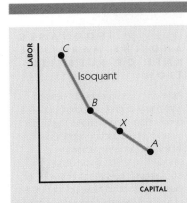

Figure 11.16 THREE ALTERNATIVE METHODS OF PRODUCING A CERTAIN AMOUNT

Point *A* represents the inputs for a highly mechanized way of producing a certain number of car frames; point *C* represents a technique of production that uses a much less expensive machine, but more labor; point *B* represents a technique that is in between. By using different techniques in different proportions, the firm can use a combination of labor and capital on the line joining *A* and *B*, such as point *X*. The curve *ABC* is an isoquant.

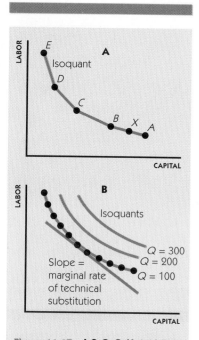

Figure 11.17 ISOQUANTS AND THE MARGINAL RATE OF SUBSTITUTION

Panel A shows an isoquant defined with many alternative techniques of production. Panel B shows that as the number of production techniques increases, isoquants appear as a smooth curve. The slope of the isoquant tells how much of one input must be added to make up for the loss of a unit of the other input; this is the marginal rate of technical substitution.

Consider now what happens if many techniques are available instead of only three. The isoquant consists of points designating each of the techniques, and the short line segments connecting these points that represent combinations of two techniques, as shown in Figure 11.17A. When many, many production techniques are available, the isoquant looks much like a smooth curve, and economists often draw it that way, as in panel B.

Many different isoquants can be drawn, each representing one particular level of output, as in panel B. Higher isoquants represent higher levels of production; lower isoquants represent lower levels.[2] There is also a simple relationship between the production functions discussed above and isoquants. The production function gives the output corresponding to each level of inputs. The isoquant tells what are the levels of inputs that can yield a given level of output.

MARGINAL RATE OF TECHNICAL SUBSTITUTION

The idea of marginal rate of substitution was introduced in the appendix to Chapter 8 to describe how individuals are willing to trade off less of one good for more of another. The concept is also useful in analyzing what technology firms will choose. In the case of firms, the marginal rate of substitution is defined not by individual preferences but by actual physical facts. If a firm reduces one input by a unit and then raises another input enough so that the final output remains the same, the amount of extra input required is called the **marginal rate of technical substitution.**

An example should help to clarify this idea. If a firm can reduce the amount of capital it uses by 1 machine, hire 2 more workers, and produce the same quantity, then it is possible for 2 workers to replace 1 machine. In this case, the marginal rate of technical substitution between workers and machines is 2/1. The marginal rate of technical substitution is just the slope of the isoquant, as Figure 11.17B shows diagrammatically: the slope simply tells how much of an increase in labor is needed to offset a one-unit decrease in capital to produce the same amount of output.[3]

Notice that the marginal rate of technical substitution and the slope of the isoquant change with the quantities of labor and capital involved. With fewer and fewer machines, it becomes increasingly difficult to substitute workers for machines. The marginal rate of technical substitution rises, and the slope of the isoquant becomes steeper and steeper. At the other end of the isoquant, with more and more machines, it becomes easier and easier to replace one of

[2] Readers who have read the Chapter 8 appendix on indifference curves should recognize the similarities between isoquants and indifference curves: while indifference curves give those combinations of goods that yield the individual the same level of utility, the isoquant gives those combinations of goods (inputs) that yield the firm the same level of output.

[3] Again, readers who earlier studied indifference curves will recall that the slope of the indifference curve is also called the marginal rate of substitution; it tells us how much extra of one good is required when consumption of another good is reduced by one unit, if we wish to leave the individual at the same level of welfare—on his indifference curve.

them. The marginal rate of technical substitution diminishes as the number of machines increases, and the slope of the isoquant becomes flatter. There is a **diminishing marginal rate of technical substitution** in production, just as there was a diminishing marginal rate of substitution in consumption.

The marginal rate of technical substitution can be calculated from the marginal products of labor and capital. If adding 1 more worker increases the output of automobile frames by 1, the marginal product of an extra worker in this industrial process is 1 (car frame). Let us also imagine that adding 1 machine leads to an increase in car output of, say, 2 a day. So in this industrial process, the marginal product of a machine is 2. In this example, adding 2 workers and reducing machine input by 1 leaves output unchanged. Thus, the marginal rate of technical substitution is 2/1. In general, the marginal rate of technical substitution is equal to the ratio of the marginal products.

The principle of diminishing returns explains why the marginal rate of technical substitution diminishes as a firm adds more and more machines. As it adds more machines, the marginal product of an additional machine diminishes. As the number of workers is reduced, the marginal product of an additional worker is increased. As workers are becoming more productive at the margin and machines are becoming less productive at the margin, it becomes increasingly easier to replace machines with additional workers.

Notice that calculating the marginal rate of substitution does not tell the firm whether it *should* substitute workers for machines, or machines for workers. The number itself only provides factual information about what the trade-off would be, based on the technology available to the firm. To decide which combination of inputs should be chosen, the firm must also know the market prices of the various inputs.

COST MINIMIZATION

Minimizing costs requires marginal decision making. Firms know the technology they are currently using and can consider changing it by trading off some inputs against others. To decide whether such a trade-off will reduce costs, they calculate the marginal rate of technical substitution and simply compare the market price of the input they are reducing with the price of the input they are increasing. If a firm can replace 1 machine with 2 workers and maintain the same output, and if a worker costs $12,000 a year and a machine costs $25,000 a year to rent, then by reducing machines by 1 and hiring 2 workers, the firm can reduce total costs. On the other hand, if a worker costs $13,000, it would pay to use 2 fewer workers (for a saving of $26,000) and rent 1 machine (for a cost of $25,000).

The only time that it would not pay the firm either to increase labor and reduce the number of machines or to decrease labor and increase the number of machines is when the marginal rate of technical substitution is equal to the relative price of the two factors. The reason for this is similar to the reason why individuals set their personal marginal rates of substitution equal to the ratio of market prices. The difference is that the individual's marginal rate of substitution is determined by individual preferences, while the firm's marginal rate of technical substitution is determined by technology.

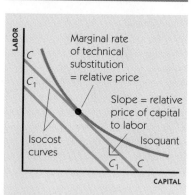

Figure 11.18 COST MINI-MIZATION

Cost-minimizing firms will wish to produce as much output as they can given a particular level of expenditure, so they will choose the highest isoquant they can reach with a given isocost curve, which will be the isoquant tangent to the isocost curve.

ISOCOST CURVES

The **isocost** curve gives those combinations of inputs that cost the same amount. The isocost curve is analogous to an individual's budget constraint, which gives those combinations of goods that cost the same amount. If a firm faces fixed prices for its inputs, the isocost curve is a straight line, whose slope indicates the relative prices; that is, if each worker costs, say, $50 per day, then if the firm reduces the labor used by one, it could spend $50 per day on renting more machines. If renting a machine for a day costs $100, then the firm can rent one more machine with the amount it would save by reducing the input of labor by two. There are, of course, many isocost lines, one for each level of expenditure. Lower isocost lines represent lower expenditures on inputs. Costs along line C_1C_1 in Figure 11.18 are lower than costs along CC. The different isocost lines are parallel to one another, just as different household budget constraints representing different income levels are parallel.

Notice that all firms facing the same prices for inputs will have the same isocost lines. Similarly, different individuals with the same income face the same budget constraint, even when their preferences differ. However, the isoquant curves that describe each firm are based on the product the firm is making and the technology and knowledge available to the firm. Thus, isoquant curves will differ from firm to firm.

Isoquant curves and isocost lines can illuminate the behavior of a cost-minimizing firm. For example, any efficient profit-maximizing firm will wish to maximize the output it obtains from any given expenditure. Or to rephrase the same point, the firm must reach the highest possible isoquant, given a particular level of expenditure on inputs, represented by a particular isocost line. The highest possible isoquant will touch the isocost line at a single point; the two curves will be tangent.

The problem of cost minimization can be described in a different way. Consider a firm that has a desired level of output and wishes to minimize its cost. The firm chooses an isoquant, and then tries to find the point on the isoquant that is on the lowest possible isocost line. Again, the cost-minimizing firm will choose the point of tangency between the isocost line and the isoquant.

At the point of tangency, the slopes of the two curves are the same. The slope of the isoquant is the marginal rate of substitution. The slope of the isocost line is the relative price. Thus, *the marginal rate of technical substitution must equal the relative price.*

APPLYING THE DIAGRAMMATIC ANALYSIS

The isoquant/isocost diagram can be used to show how a change in relative prices affects the optimal mix of inputs. A change in relative prices changes the isocost line. In Figure 11.19, an increase in the wage makes the isocost curves flatter. CC is the original isocost curve that minimizes the costs of producing output Q_0 (that is, CC is tangent to the isoquant Q_0). C_1C_1 is the isocost line with the new higher wages that is tangent to the original isoquant. Obviously, to produce the same level of output will cost more if wages are in-

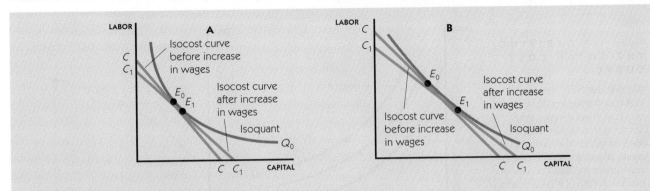

Figure 11.19 CHANGING FACTOR PRICES

This firm has chosen the level of production associated with the isoquant shown, and the cost-minimizing combination of labor and capital for producing that amount is originally at E_0. But as wages rise, relative prices shift, and the cost-minimizing method of producing the given amount becomes E_1. In panel A, an increase in wages leads to little substitution. But in panel B, an increase in wages leads to a much larger amount of substitution.

creased. The figure also shows what this change in relative prices in the form of higher wages does to the cost-minimizing combination of inputs: as one would expect, the firm substitutes away from labor toward capital (from point E_0 to E_1).

Of course, the magnitude of the substitution will differ from industry to industry, depending on an industry's isoquant. In addition, substitution is likely to be much greater in the long run than in the short run, as machines wear out, firms try to find out how to conserve on the more expensive inputs, and so on. The figure represents these different possibilities for substitution. In panel A, the possibilities for substitution are very limited. The isoquant is very "curved." This figure illustrates a case where it is very difficult to substitute (at least in the short run) machines for labor (illustrated, perhaps, by the use of blast furnaces in producing steel). In panel B, substitution is very easy; the isoquant is very flat. This illustrates an opposite case; it is relatively easy for a firm to substitute machines for labor, say, by using robots.

DERIVING COST CURVES

The cost curves in this chapter represent the minimum cost of producing each level of output, at a particular level of input prices. Figure 11.20A shows the cost-minimizing way of producing three different levels of output, Q_1, Q_2, and Q_3. Panel B then plots the actual level of costs associated with each of these levels of output. That is, the isocost curves tangent to the isoquants in panel A show the minimum level of costs associated with each output. Tracing out the costs associated with each level of output provides the total cost curve.

Figure 11.20 DERIVING THE TOTAL COST CURVE

The total cost curve describes how total cost changes at different levels of output. Panel A shows three isoquants representing different levels of output, and three isocost curves tangent to those isoquants, representing the least-cost way of producing each of these amounts. Panel B plots the actual level of costs for each of these levels of output, producing the familiar total cost curve.

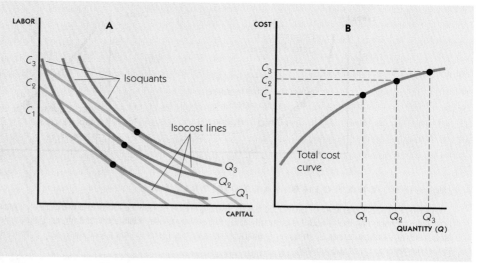

And once we have the total cost curve, we know how to derive the marginal cost curve (the slope of the total cost curve) and the average cost curve (the slope of a line from the origin to the total cost curve).

12

PRODUCTION

hapter 11 defined profits as the difference between revenues and costs. We learned the basic tools for assessing the costs of production. In this chapter, we learn how to calculate the benefits from production, and examine how firms weigh costs against these benefits. This balancing process dictates the profit-maximizing firm's production decision.

This chapter rounds out the discussion of markets because, in making their production decisions, firms provide the final ingredients for a complete model of the economy. With all the ingredients in hand—the basic economic decisions of individuals and households to maximize satisfaction, and the basic economic decisions of firms seeking to maximize profits—we will be able to construct a complete model of the economy in Chapter 13.

KEY QUESTIONS

1. What determines the level of output a firm will supply at any given price? How do we derive, in other words, the firm's supply curve?

2. What determines whether or when a firm will enter or exit a market?

3. How do the answers to these questions enable us to analyze the market supply curve, why it is upward sloping and why it may be more elastic than the supply curve of any single firm?

4. How do we reconcile economists' view that competition drives profits to zero with accountants' reports showing that most of the time most firms earn positive profits?

5. What determines a firm's demand for inputs, such as labor or capital? Why is a firm's demand curve for labor downward sloping?

REVENUE

Consider the hypothetical example of the High Strung Violin Company, manufacturers of world-class violins. The company hires labor; it buys wood, utilities, and other materials; and it rents a building and machines. Its violins sell for $40,000 each. Last year the company sold 7 of them, for a gross revenue of $280,000. Table 12.1 gives a snapshot of the firm's financial health, its profit-and-loss statement for last year.

We see that High Strung's revenues were $280,000, and its costs were

Table 12.1 **PROFIT-AND-LOSS STATEMENT FOR THE HIGH STRUNG VIOLIN COMPANY**

Gross revenue		$280,000
Costs		$180,000
Wages (including fringe benefits)	$150,000	
Purchases of wood and other materials	$ 20,000	
Utilities	$ 1,000	
Rent of building	$ 5,000	
Rent of machinery	$ 2,000	
Miscellaneous expenses	$ 2,000	
Profits		$100,000

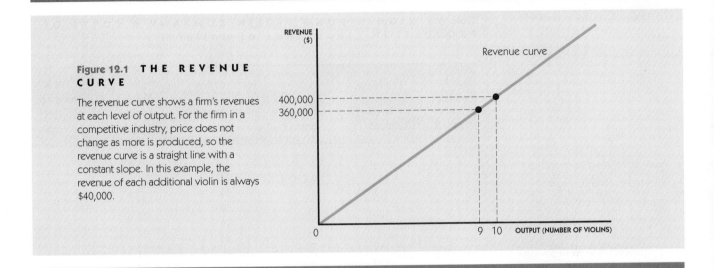

Figure 12.1 THE REVENUE CURVE

The revenue curve shows a firm's revenues at each level of output. For the firm in a competitive industry, price does not change as more is produced, so the revenue curve is a straight line with a constant slope. In this example, the revenue of each additional violin is always $40,000.

$180,000, so its profits were $100,000. If its costs had been $400,000 instead of $180,000, its profits would have been −$120,000. The firm would have made a negative profit, in other words, a loss.

The relationship between revenue and output is shown by the **revenue curve** in Figure 12.1. The horizontal axis measures the firm's output, while the vertical axis measures the revenues. When the price of a violin is $40,000 and the firm sells 9 violins, its revenue is $360,000; when it sells 10, revenue rises to $400,000.

The extra revenue that a firm receives from selling an extra unit is called its **marginal revenue.** Thus, $40,000 is the extra (or marginal) revenue from selling the tenth violin. It is no accident that the marginal revenue equals the price of the violin. A fundamental feature of competitive markets is that firms receive the same market price for each unit they sell, regardless of the number of units they sell. Thus, the extra revenue that firms in competitive markets receive from selling one more unit—the marginal revenue—is the same as the market price of the unit.

COSTS

High Strung's costs increase as it expands its level of output. Total costs are given in column 1 of Table 12.2 and depicted diagrammatically in Figure 12.2A. Panel B shows the corresponding average and marginal costs. High Strung's average cost curve exhibits the typical U-shape that we associate with manufacturing firms.

Even before it builds its first violin, the company must spend $90,000. Space must be rented. Some employees will have to be hired. Equipment must be

Table 12.2 HIGH STRUNG VIOLIN COMPANY'S COSTS OF PRODUCTION (thousands of dollars)

Output	(1) Total cost	(2) Average cost	(3) Marginal cost	(4) Total variable cost	(5) Average variable cost
0	90				
1	100	100	10	10	10
2	110	55	10	20	10
3	120	40	10	30	10
4	130	32.5	10	40	10
5	140	28	10	50	10
6	150	25	10	60	10
7	175	25	25	85	12.1
8	215	26.9	40	125	15.6
9	270	30	55	180	20
10	400	40	130	210	21

purchased. No matter how many or how few violins High Strung produces, its fixed costs will remain $90,000.

The *extra* cost of producing an additional violin, the marginal cost, is shown in column 3. Marginal cost is always associated with the additional cost of producing a *particular* unit of output. The marginal cost of increasing production from 1 to 2 violins, for example, is $10,000. Each additional violin costs $10,000 more until production reaches 6 violins. The extra (or marginal) cost of producing the seventh violin is $25,000. The marginal cost of producing the eighth violin is $40,000.

The High Strung Violin Company's average costs initially decline as its production increases, since the fixed costs can be divided among more units of production. But after 7 violins, average costs begin to increase, as the effect of the increasing average variable costs dominates the effect of the fixed costs.

BASIC CONDITIONS OF COMPETITIVE SUPPLY

In choosing how much to produce, a profit-maximizing firm will focus its decision at the margin. Having incurred the fixed cost of getting into this market, the decision is generally not the stark one of whether or not to produce, but

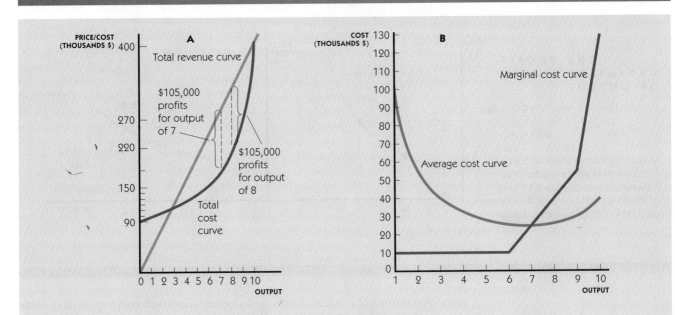

Figure 12.2 RELATING REVENUES AND COSTS

The firm's revenue and total cost curves can be diagrammed on the same graph, as in panel A. When total revenue exceeds total costs, the firm is making profits at that level of output. Profits, the difference between revenues and costs, are measured by the distance between the two curves; in this case, the highest level of profit is being made at a production level of 7 or 8. When total costs exceed total revenue, the firm is making losses at that level of output. When the two lines cross, the firm is making zero profits. The marginal and average cost curves for this company have their expected shape in panel B. Marginal costs are constant until a production level of 6, and then they begin to increase. The average cost curve is U-shaped.

whether to produce one more unit of a good or one less. For a firm in a competitive market, the answer to this problem is relatively simple: the company simply compares the marginal revenue it will receive by producing an extra unit—which is just the price of the good—with the extra cost of producing that unit, the marginal cost. As long as the marginal revenue exceeds the marginal cost, the firm will make additional profit by producing more. If marginal revenue is less than marginal cost, then producing an extra unit will cut profits, and the firm will reduce production. In short, the firm will produce to the point where the marginal cost equals marginal revenue, which in a competitive market is equal to price.

The profit-maximizing level of output, where price equals marginal cost, can be seen in panel A of Figure 12.3, which shows the marginal cost curve for a firm facing increasing marginal costs. The firm produces up to the point where price (which equals marginal revenue) equals marginal cost. If it produces more than that, the extra cost will be greater than the extra revenue received. The figure shows how much output the firm will produce at each price. At the price p_1, it will produce the output Q_1. At the price p_2, it will pro-

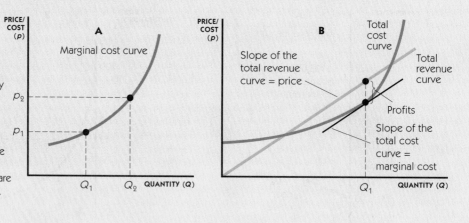

Figure 12.3 THE PROFIT-MAXIMIZING LEVEL OF OUTPUT

A competitive firm maximizes profits by setting output at the point where price equals marginal cost. In panel A, at the price of p_1, this quantity is Q_1. Panel B shows total revenue and total costs. Profits are maximized when the distance between the two curves is maximized, which is the point where the two lines are parallel (and thus have the same slope).

duce the output Q_2. With an upward-sloping marginal cost curve, it is clear that the firm will produce more as price increases.

The marginal cost curve is upward sloping, just as the supply curves in Chapter 4 were upward sloping. This too is no accident: a firm's marginal cost curve is actually the same as its supply curve. The marginal cost curve shows the additional cost of producing one more unit at different levels of output. A competitive firm chooses to produce at the level of output where the cost of producing an additional unit (that is, the marginal cost) is equal to the market price. We can thus read from the marginal cost curve what the firm's supply will be at any price: it will be the quantity of output at which marginal cost equals that price.

Figure 12.2A shows total revenues as well as total costs of the High Strung Violin Company. We can see that profits—the gap between revenues and costs—are maximized at an output of either 7 or 8. If the price were just slightly lower than $40,000, profits would be maximized at 7, and if the price were just slightly higher than $40,000, profits would be maximized at 8.

The profit-maximizing level of output can also be seen in panel B of Figure 12.3, which shows the total revenue and total cost curves. Profits are the dif-

EQUILIBRIUM OUTPUT FOR COMPETITIVE FIRMS

In competitive markets, firms produce at the level where price equals marginal cost.

ference between revenues and costs. In panel B, profits are the distance between the total revenue curve and the total cost curves. The profit-maximizing firm will choose the output where that distance is greatest. This occurs at Q_1. Below Q_1, price (the slope of the revenue curve) exceeds marginal costs (the slope of the total cost curve) so profits increase as output increases; above Q_1, price is less than marginal cost, so profits decrease as output increases.

ENTRY, EXIT, AND MARKET SUPPLY

We are now in a position to tackle the market supply curve. To do so, we need to know a little more about each firm's decision to produce. First let's consider a firm that is currently not producing. Under what circumstances should it incur the fixed costs of entering the industry? This is a relatively easy problem: the company simply looks at the average cost curve and the price. *If price exceeds minimum average costs, it pays the firm to enter.* This is because if it enters, it can sell the goods for more than the cost of producing them, thus making a profit.

Figure 12.4A shows the U-shaped average cost curve. Minimum average cost is c_{min}. If the price is less than c_{min}, then there is no level of output at which the firm could produce and make a profit. If the price is above c_{min}, then the firm will produce at the level of output at which price (p) equals marginal cost, Q^*. At Q^*, marginal cost exceeds average costs. (This is always true

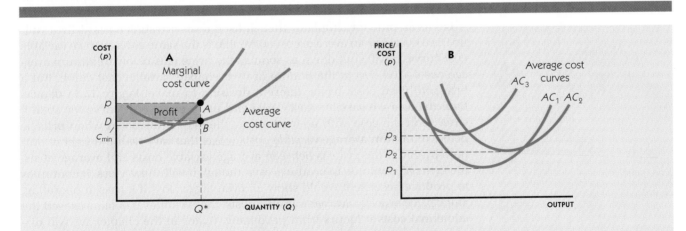

Figure 12.4 **COST CURVES, PROFITS, AND ENTRY**

Panel A shows that if price is above the minimum of the average cost curve, profits will exist. Profits are measured by the area formed by the shaded rectangle, the profit per unit (price minus average cost, corresponding to the distance AB) times the output, Q^*. Panel B shows average cost curves for three different firms. At price p_1, only one firm will enter the market. As price rises to p_2 and then to p_3, first the firm whose cost curve is AC_2 and then the firm whose cost curve is AC_3 will enter the market.

at output levels greater than that at which average costs are minimum.) Profit per unit is the difference between price and average costs. Total profits are the product of profit per unit and the level of output (the shaded area in the figure).

Different companies may have different average cost curves. Some will have better management. Some will have a better location. Accordingly, firms will differ in their minimum average cost. As prices rise, additional firms will find it attractive to enter the market. Figure 12.4B shows the U-shaped average cost curves for three different firms. Firm 1's minimum average cost is AC_1, firm 2's minimum average cost is AC_2, and firm 3's minimum average cost is AC_3. Thus, firm 1 enters at the price p_1, firm 2 at the price p_2, and firm 3 at the price p_3.

SUNK COSTS AND EXIT

The converse of the decision of a firm to enter the market is the decision of a firm already producing to exit the market. **Sunk costs** are costs that are not recoverable, even if a firm goes out of business. The High Strung Violin Company, for example, may have had an extensive television advertising campaign. The cost of this campaign is a sunk cost. There is no way this expenditure can be recouped even if production ceases. If there were no sunk costs the decision to enter and the decision to exit would be mirror images of each other. Firms would exit the market when their average costs rose above the price. But if some costs remain even if a firm exits the market, the question facing that firm is whether it is better off continuing to produce or exiting.

Let us assume for simplicity that all fixed costs are sunk costs. A firm with no fixed costs has an average cost curve that is the same as its average variable cost curve. It will shut down as soon as the price falls below minimum average costs—the cost at the bottom of its U-shaped variable cost curve. But a firm *with* fixed costs has a different decision to make. Figure 12.5A depicts both the average variable cost curve and the average cost curve for such a case. As in the case with no sunk costs, the firm shuts down when price is below minimum average *variable* costs (costs that vary with the level of output), p_1. But if the price is *between* average variable costs and average costs, the firm will continue to produce, even though it will show a loss. It continues to produce because it would show an even bigger loss if it ceased operating. Since price exceeds average variable costs, the revenues it obtains exceed the additional costs it incurs from producing. (Later in the chapter we will discuss the case when fixed costs are not necessarily sunk costs.)

Different firms in an industry will have different average variable costs, and so will find it desirable to exit the market at different prices. Figure 12.5B shows the average variable cost curves for three different firms. Their cost curves differ; some may, for instance, have newer equipment than others. As the price falls, the firm with the highest minimum average variable costs finds it is no longer able to make money at the going price, and decides not to operate. Thus, firm 3 (represented by the curve AVC_3) shuts down as soon as the

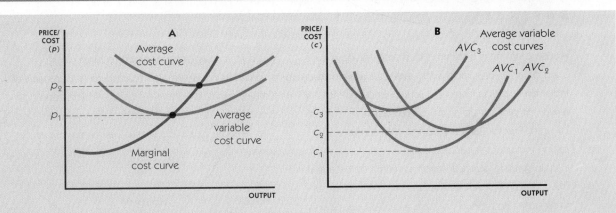

Figure 12.5 AVERAGE VARIABLE COSTS AND THE DECISION TO PRODUCE

Panel A shows a firm's average variable cost curves. In the short run, firms will produce as long as price exceeds average variable costs. Thus, for prices between p_1 and p_2, the firm will continue to produce, even though it is recording a loss (price is less than average cost). Panel B shows that firms with different average variable cost curves will decide to shut down at different price levels. As price falls below c_3, the minimum average variable cost for firm 3, firm 3 shuts down; as price falls still lower, below c_2, firm 2 shuts down. Finally, when price falls below c_1, firm 1 shuts down.

price falls below c_3, firm 2 shuts down as soon as the price falls below c_2, and firm 1 shuts down as soon as the price falls below c_1.

THE FIRM'S SUPPLY CURVE

We can now draw the firm's supply curve. As Figure 12.6A shows, for a firm contemplating entering the market, supply is zero up to a critical price, equal to the minimum average cost. Thus, for prices below $c_{min} = p$, the firm produces zero output. For prices greater than $c_{min} = p$, the firm produces up to the point where price equals marginal cost, so the firm's supply curve coincides with the marginal cost curve. For a firm that has incurred sunk costs of entering the market (panel B), the supply curve coincides with the marginal cost curve so long as price exceeds the minimum value of average *variable* costs; when price is below the minimum value of average variable costs, the firm exits, so supply is again zero.

THE MARKET SUPPLY CURVE

With this information about the cost curves of individual firms, we can derive the overall market supply curve. Back in Chapter 4, the market supply curve was defined as the sum of the amounts that each firm was willing to supply at

USING ECONOMICS: ENTERING THE PAINTING BUSINESS

House painting is a summer business, for days that are hot and long, and with available low-skilled labor on vacation from high school and college. As a way of picking up some cash, Michael decided to start Presto Painters during the summer after taking introductory economics.

Just getting started involves some substantial fixed costs. Michael ran the business out of his parents' home so he had no costs for office space. His fixed costs ended up looking like this:

Fixed costs	
Used van	$5,000
Paint and supplies	$2,000
Flyers and signs	$1,200
Business cards and estimate sheets	$ 500
Phone line and answering machine	$ 300
Total	$9,000

Michael went to work drumming up business. He took calls from potential customers and knocked on doors, made estimates of what he thought it would cost to paint someone's home, and then offered them a price. Of course, he was in direct competition with many other painters and had to meet the competition's price to get a job.

Michael found that the going rate for labor was $10 per hour. In the real world, labor is not the only variable input required for house painting. There are also costs from buying additional paint and brushes, but for the sake of simplicity, let's assume that he started off the summer with all the paint he needed. Thus, his variable costs were re-lated to the labor he needed to hire.

Variable costs are also related to the amount of time it takes to paint a house, which varies depending on the quality of the labor you can find. The variable costs for Presto Painters were as follows:

Houses painted	Hours of labor hired	Payroll cost
5	100	$ 1,000
10	300	$ 3,000
15	600	$ 6,000
20	1,000	$10,000
25	1,500	$15,000
30	2,100	$21,000

Given this information, Michael could calculate cost curves for Presto Painters (see next page).

Based on his marginal and average cost curves, Michael figured that if market conditions allowed him to charge $1,000 or more for a typical house, then he could make a profit by painting at least 25 houses. Roughly speaking, that is how his summer worked out; painting 25 houses for $1,000 apiece. Thus, he earned $1,000 in profits.

Or so he thought. Nowhere in this list of costs did Michael consider the opportunity cost of his time. He was not getting paid $10 an hour for painting houses; he was out there stirring up business, hiring and organizing workers, taking calls from customers, dealing with complaints.

Imagine that Michael had an alternate job possibility waiting on tables. He could earn $6 per hour (including tips) and work 40-hour weeks during a

12-week summer vacation. Thus, he could have earned $2,880 during the summer with little stress or risk. If this opportunity cost is added to the fixed costs of running the business, then his apparent profit turns into a loss. Since Presto Painters did not cover Michael's opportunity cost *and* compensate him for the risk and aggravation of running his own business, he would have been financially better off sticking to the business of filling people's stomachs rather than painting their houses.

Number of homes	Total cost	Average cost	Marginal cost (per house)
0	$ 9,000		$ 200
5	$10,000	$2,000	$ 400
10	$12,000	$1,200	$ 600
15	$15,000	$1,000	$ 800
20	$19,000	$ 950	$1,000
25	$24,000	$ 960	$1,200
30	$30,000	$1,000	

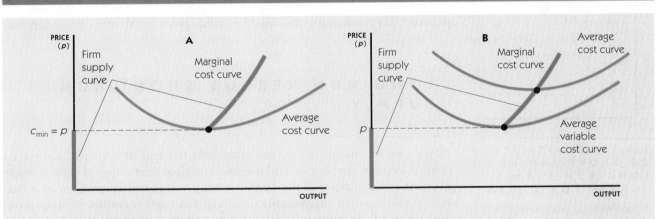

Figure 12.6 THE SUPPLY CURVE FOR A FIRM

Panel A shows that for a firm contemplating entering the market, supply is zero up to a critical price, equal to the firm's minimum average cost, after which the firm's supply curve coincides with the marginal cost curve. Panel B shows a firm that has already entered the market, incurring positive sunk costs; this firm will produce as long as price exceeds the minimum of the average variable cost curve.

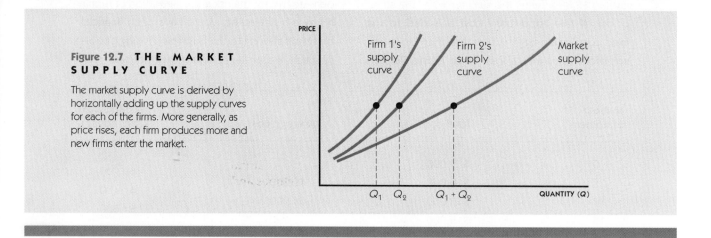

Figure 12.7 THE MARKET SUPPLY CURVE

The market supply curve is derived by horizontally adding up the supply curves for each of the firms. More generally, as price rises, each firm produces more and new firms enter the market.

any given price. Figure 12.7 provides a graphical description of the supply curve for a market with two firms. More generally, if the price rises, the firms already in the market (firms 1 and 2) will find it profitable to increase their output and new firms (with higher average variable cost curves) will find it profitable to enter the market. Because higher prices induce more firms to enter a competitive market, the market supply response to an increase in price is greater than if the number of firms were fixed. In the same way, as price falls, there are two market responses. The firms that still find it profitable to produce at the lower price will produce less, and the higher cost firms will exit the market. In this way, the competitive market ensures that whatever the product, it is produced at the lowest possible price by the most efficient firms.

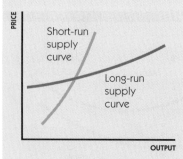

Figure 12.8 ELASTICITY OF SHORT-RUN AND LONG-RUN SUPPLY CURVES FOR A FIRM

Because there is a greater chance for a firm to adjust to changes in price in the long run, the price elasticity of the supply curve is greater in the long run than in the short run.

LONG-RUN VERSUS SHORT-RUN SUPPLY

As we saw in Chapter 11, in the short run the typical firm will have a U-shaped average cost curve, and a rising marginal cost curve at output levels above the lowest point of the U. But its long-run marginal cost curve is flatter. This is because adjustments to changes in market conditions take time, and some adjustments take longer than others. In the short run, you can add workers, work more shifts, run the machines harder (or reduce the rate at which these things are done), but you are probably stuck with your existing plant and equipment. In the long run, you can acquire more buildings and more machines (or sell them). Thus, the long-run supply curve for a firm is more elastic (flatter) than the short-run supply curve, as shown in Figure 12.8.

The same thing is true, only more so, for the industry—again because the number of firms is not fixed. Even if each firm can operate only one plant, the industry's output can be increased by 5 percent by increasing the number of firms by 5 percent. The extra costs of increasing output by 5 percent are approximately the same as the average costs. Accordingly, the long-run market supply curve is approximately horizontal. Under these conditions, even if the demand curve for the product shifts drastically, the market will supply much more of the product at pretty much the same price, as additional plants are constructed and additional firms enter the market.

Thus, the market supply curve is much more elastic in the long run than in the short run. Indeed, in the *very* short run, a firm may find it impossible to hire more skilled labor or to increase its capacity. Its supply curve, and the market supply curve, would be nearly vertical. In the short run machines and the number of firms are fixed, but labor and other inputs can be varied. Figure 12.9A shows the short-run supply curve. Contrast the short-run market supply curve with the long-run market supply curve. The short-run curve slopes up much more sharply. A shift in the demand curve has a larger effect on price and a smaller effect on quantity than it does in the long run. In the long run, the market supply curve may be horizontal. In this case, shifts in the demand curve have an effect *only* on quantity, as in panel B. Price remains at the level of minimum average costs; competition leads to entry to the point where there are zero profits.

Again, it is worth asking, "How long is the long run?" That depends on the industry. It takes an electric power company years to change its capacity. For most other firms, buildings and equipment can be added, if not within months, certainly within a year or two. Recent improvements in technology, like computer-aided design and manufacturing, have made it possible for many companies to change what they are producing more rapidly, and thus have reduced the length of the long run and made supply curves more elastic than in the past.

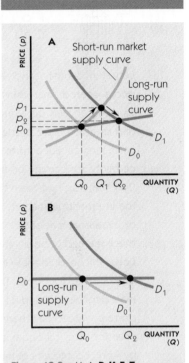

Figure 12.9 MARKET EQUILIBRIUM IN THE SHORT RUN AND LONG RUN

In panel A, the market equilibrium is originally at a price p_0 and an output Q_0. In the short run, a shift in the demand curve from D_0 to D_1 raises the price to p_1 and quantity to Q_1. In the long run, the supply elasticity is greater, so the increase in price is smaller—price is only p_2—and quantity is greater, Q_2. If supply is perfectly elastic in the long run, as shown in panel B, shifts in demand will only change the quantity produced in the long run, not the market price.

ADJUSTMENTS IN THE SHORT RUN AND THE LONG RUN

In the very short run, firms may be unable to adjust production at all; only the price changes.

In the short run, firms may be able to hire more labor and adjust other variable inputs.

In the long run, firms may be able to buy more machines, and firms may decide to enter or to exit.

The times required for these adjustments may vary from industry to industry.

Between January and April of 1996, gasoline prices soared, increasing by nearly 20 percent. One reason was the unusually cold winter, which had diverted more crude oil into the production of heating oil. But a more important factor was uncertainty concerning oil from Iraq. After the 1991 Gulf War, Iraq had been barred from selling oil on the international market. In early 1996, in the face of increasing evidence of food shortages in Iraq, there seemed to be significant progress in negotiations which would allow Iraq to sell $2 billion of oil in exchange for food. This additional oil would have depressed world oil prices, and American importers were clearly nervous about holding large inventories of oil under these circumstances. But by April, no agreement had been reached.

One proposed response to ease the burden on consumers was to reduce the gasoline tax temporarily by 4.3 cents a gallon,. Most economists believed that in the short run, the reduction would have little effect. They believed that the short-run supply curve for gasoline was very inelastic; American refineries were working to capacity. In this view, the price was high because of the limited supply. Any lowering of the prices consumers paid would result in demand exceeding supply in the short run. In this view, all the benefits of the reduced tax would accrue to the oil companies, in the form of higher profits.

Eventually, of course, more gasoline could and would be imported from abroad. In this case, the long-run supply curve—taking into account the response of imports—would come into play within a month or two.

LOOKING BEYOND THE BASIC MODEL: SUNK COSTS, ENTRY, AND COMPETITION

The degree of competition envisioned in the basic competitive model requires a large number of firms, vying with one another to sell a product. Competition among these firms drives the market price down to a level where there are no profits (as economists define them) in the market. (Recall that opportunity costs of the owners of the business and the cost of capital are included in the costs.)

Even without a large number of firms in the market, the predictions of the basic competitive model may still hold. Here is where the distinction between overhead (or *fixed*) and *sunk* costs becomes important. Overhead costs are costs that are incurred regardless of the scale of production of the firm. A company's headquarters is an overhead cost in this sense. But if a company ceases to operate, it can resell the building and might well recover its cost. The cost of the building in this case, though fixed, is not sunk. Now take the case of a company that not only bought a building but spent a lot of money commissioning a logo, which it then mounted conspicuously on its building. If this firm went out of business it could recover the cost of its building but *not* its logo. Who wants the secondhand logo of a bankrupt company? Advertising expenditures are typically sunk costs. Expenditures on assets that can readily be put to other uses—buildings and cars—are, for the most part, not sunk.

The theory of **contestable markets** predicts that even in a market with only one firm, that firm will make zero profits, just as in a market with many firms, *if* sunk costs are low. The threat that other firms will enter is sufficient to deter the single firm from raising its price beyond average cost. This result holds even in the presence of high fixed or overhead costs, so long as those costs consist of buildings, cars, airplanes, and other assets that can be easily sold. A firm entering the industry has little to lose, since it can always reverse its decision and recover its investment.

But when the assets include major ones with no alternative use—such as a nuclear power plant—then these costs become sunk costs, and the threat of competition diminishes. The firm that would otherwise have entered the market might now worry that if it enters, competition will get fierce. And the firm would be right to worry, as high sunk costs will make all firms reluctant to exit. If competition is fierce enough, the price might even drop below average costs, and still the firm's rivals may not leave. With prices below average costs, the new firm will not be able to get a return on its investment. Until it enters the market, the firm has an advantage: it has not taken on the sunk costs. Given the scenario just described, it may very well avert its gaze from the lure of high profits, knowing they are like a mirage. The profits will disappear if the new firm tries to grab them by entering the market, but will remain for the limited number of firms already in the market if they can keep the would-be newcomer out. Thus, markets with high sunk costs may be able to sustain high profits without much fear of entry—a clear departure from the basic competitive model.

CLOSE-UP: PAN AM'S EXIT

Pan American World Airways passed away on December 4, 1991. The company had been flying since 1927, and for many decades had been the dominant global airline. In fact, some said that the Pan Am logo may have been the most widely recognized corporate logo in the world at one time.

The death came as no surprise. Pan Am had lost money in every year except one between 1980 and 1991—losses that totaled nearly $2 billion. It had officially declared bankruptcy in January 1991. But what life support system delayed the exit of Pan Am from commercial aviation? How can our economic model account for a company that makes losses for a decade and even continues to operate after it has officially declared bankruptcy?

The model of entry and exit based on cost curves gives a useful explanation of why Pan Am would not exit after a single year of losses. As long as a firm can charge a price above average variable costs, it makes economic sense to stay in business, even if the price is below average total costs and the firm is making losses.

In fact, Pan Am seems to have continued to operate even when price was less than average variable cost. It hoped that market conditions would improve, and it wanted to keep alive its option. But it paid a high price for doing so.

To stay in business while making losses, though, a company must have assets to sell. In its many profitable years, Pan Am had built up many such assets, and in the 1980s it proceeded to sell them off. The company sold the Pan Am Building to Metropolitan Life Insurance for $400 million; its Intercontinental Hotels subsidiary for $500 million; its Pacific operations and later its London routes to United Airlines; and a considerable amount of Tokyo real estate. By the end of 1991, Pan Am was proposing to sell off most of its other routes to Delta and become a small airline based in Miami, serving mainly Latin American destinations. In other words, although Pan Am continued to fly during the 1980s while losing money, it was slowly exiting during most of that time.

In fact, economists sometimes disagree over whether a market economy forces exit to happen quickly enough. As the case of Pan Am demonstrates, exit can be a drawn-out process. This surely benefits some workers who could avoid switching jobs for a longer time. But shareholders in Pan Am would have been better off if the company had been sold off in the early 1980s before it had a chance to lose more money.

Sources: Brett Pulley, "Pan Am Ceases Operations, Race Opens to Get Its Valuable Latin American Routes," *Wall Street Journal,* December 5, 1991, p. A7; Agis Salpukas, "Its Cash Depleted, Pan Am Shuts," *New York Times,* December 5, 1991, p. D1; Severin Borenstein, "The Evolution of U.S. Airline Competition," *Journal of Economic Perspectives* (Spring 1992).

ACCOUNTING PROFITS AND ECONOMIC PROFITS

We have learned in previous chapters that firms maximize profits, but now it appears that with competition, profits are driven to zero. To most individuals, this seems like a contradiction: if profits were truly zero, why would firms ever produce? How do we reconcile the conclusion that competition drives profits to zero with the fact that, throughout the economy, firms regularly report making profits?

The answer is that accountants and economists think about profits differently in two important respects. The first is that economists take opportunity costs into account. The second has to do with the economic concept of rent. Both deserve a closer look.

OPPORTUNITY COSTS

To begin to see how opportunity costs affect the economist's view of profits, consider a small firm in which the owner has invested $100,000. Assume the owner receives a small salary, and devotes sixty hours a week to running the enterprise. An economist would argue that the owner ought to calculate his opportunity costs related to his investment of time and money into the business. The opportunity cost of his time is the best wage available to him if he worked sixty hours a week at an alternate job. The opportunity cost of his capital is the return that the $100,000 invested in this enterprise would produce in another investment. These are the true costs of the owner's time and capital investment. To calculate profits of the firm as the economist sees them, these opportunity costs have to be subtracted out.

One can easily imagine a business whose accountant reports a profit equal to 3 percent of the capital investment. An economist would note that if the investment capital had been put in a bank account, it would have earned at least 5 percent. Thus, the economist would say the business is making a loss. Failure to take into account opportunity costs means that reported profits often overstate true economic profits.

Taking opportunity costs into account is not always a simple matter; it is not always easy to determine the alternative uses of a firm's resources. Managerial time spent in expanding the firm in one direction, for example, might have been spent in controlling costs or expanding the firm in another direction. Land that is used for a golf course for the firm's employees might have been used for some other purpose, which could have saved more than enough money to buy golf club memberships for all who want them. In making decisions about resources like these, firms must constantly ask what price the resources might fetch in other uses.

Sometimes market data can provide appropriate prices for calculating opportunity costs. For example, the opportunity cost of giving huge offices to top executives can be gauged by the money those offices would bring if they were rented to some other company. But often the calculation is more difficult: how can, for example, a company measure the opportunity cost of the vice-president who cannot be fired and will not retire for five years?

What about the costs associated with an expenditure already made, say on a building that is no longer really needed by the firm? The relevant opportunity cost of this building is not the original purchase or lease price, but instead the value of the building in alternate uses, such as the rent that could be earned if the building were rented to other firms.

The fundamental point is that you cannot use past expenditures to calculate opportunity costs. Consider an automaker that has purchased a parcel of land for $1 million an acre. It turns out, however, that the company made a mistake and the land is worth only $100,000 an acre. The firm now must choose between two different plants for producing new cars, one of which uses much more land than the other. In figuring opportunity costs, should the land be valued at the purchase price of $1 million an acre, or what the land could be sold for—$100,000 an acre? The answer can make a difference between whether or not the firm chooses to conserve on land. From an economics viewpoint, the answer to this valuation problem should be obvious: the firm should evaluate costs according to the *current* opportunity costs. The fact that the company made a mistake in purchasing the land should be irrelevant for the current decision.

Individuals and firms frequently do compound their economic errors, however, by continuing to focus on past expenditures. Business executives who were originally responsible for making a bad decision may be particularly reluctant to let bygones be bygones. Publicly announcing that the correct market price of land is $100,000 an acre, for example, would be equivalent to announcing that a major mistake had been made. Acknowledging such a mistake could jeopardize a business executive's future with the firm.

ECONOMIC RENT

A second difference between an economist's and an accountant's definition of profit concerns **economic rent.** Economic rent is the difference between the price that is actually paid and the price that would have to be paid in order for the good or service to be produced.

Although economic rent has far broader applications than its historic use to refer to payments made by farmers to their landlords for the use of their land, the example of rent for land use is still instructive. The critical characteristic of land in this regard is that its supply is inelastic. Higher payments for land (higher rents) will not elicit a greater supply. Even if landlords received virtually nothing for their land, the same land would be available. Many other factors of production have the same inelastic character. Even if you doubled his salary, Greg Maddux would not "produce" more pitches for the Atlanta Braves. The extra payments for this kind of rare talent fall into the economist's definition of rent. Anyone who is in the position to receive economic rents is fortunate indeed, because these "rents" are unrelated to effort. They are payments determined entirely by demand.

Firms earn economic rent to the extent that they are more efficient than other firms. We saw earlier that a firm is willing to produce at a price equal to its minimum average cost. Some firms might be more efficient than others, so their average cost curves are lower. Consider a market in which all firms except one have the same average cost curve, and the market price corresponds to the minimum average cost of these firms. The remaining firm is super-efficient, so its average costs are far below those of the other firms. The company would have been willing to produce at a lower price, at its minimum average cost. What it receives in excess of what is required to induce it to enter the market are rents—returns on the firm's superior capabilities.

Thus, when economists say that competition drives profits to zero, they are focusing on the facts that in competitive equilibrium, price equals marginal cost for every firm producing. A company will not increase profits by expanding production, and it will not pay for firms outside the industry to enter. We say that competition drives profits to zero at the margin.

In some cases, supplies of inputs are inelastic in the short run but elastic in the long run. An example is payment for the use of a building. In the short run, the supply of buildings does not depend on the return, and hence payments for the use of a building are rents, in the economist's sense. But in the long run, the supply of buildings does depend on the return—investors will not construct new buildings unless they receive a return equal to what they could obtain elsewhere. So the "rent" received by the building's owner is not really a rent, in the sense in which economists use the term.[1]

ACCOUNTANTS' VERSUS ECONOMISTS' PROFITS

Accounting profits: revenues minus expenditures

Economic profits: revenues minus rents minus economic costs (including opportunity costs of labor and capital)

FACTOR DEMAND

In the process of deciding how much of each good to supply and what is the lowest-cost method of producing those goods, firms also decide how much of various inputs they will use. This is called **factor demand.** It is sometimes

[1]Economists sometimes use the term "quasi-rents" to describe payments for the use of buildings or other factors that are inelastically supplied in the short run, but elastically supplied in the long run.

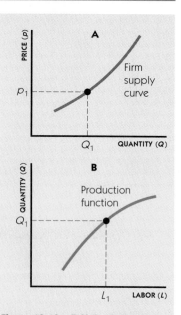

Figure 12.10 THE DE-MAND FOR LABOR

The demand for labor can be calculated from the firm's supply curve and the production function. Panel A shows how the firm, given a market price p_1, chooses a level of output Q_1 from its supply curve. Panel B shows that to produce the output Q_1 requires L_1 units of labor. L_1 is the demand for labor.

called a derived demand, because it flows from other decisions the profit-maximizing firm makes. In Chapter 11, the analysis of cost was broken up into two cases, one in which there was a single variable input, or factor of production, and one in which there were several factors. We proceed along similar lines here. Labor is used as our main example of an input. The same principles apply to any factor of production.

When there is only a single factor of production, say labor, then the decision about how much to produce is the same as the decision about how much labor to hire. As soon as we know the price of the good, we can calculate the supply (output) from the marginal cost curve; and as soon as we know the output the firm plans to produce, we know the labor required, simply by looking at the production function, which gives the output for any level of input of labor, or, equivalently, the labor required for any level of output. Thus, in Figure 12.10 at the price p_1, the output is Q_1 (panel A), and the labor required to produce that output (factor demand) is L_1 (panel B).

There is another way of deriving the demand for a factor. If a firm hires one more worker, for example, the extra cost is the wage, w. The extra benefit of the worker is the price of the good times the extra output. The extra output corresponding to the extra worker is the marginal product of labor. (Marginal products can be calculated for any other factor of production as well.) The price of the good thus produced times the marginal product of labor is referred to as the **value of the marginal product of labor.** The firm hires labor up to the point where the value of its marginal product (the marginal benefit) equals its price, in this case, the wage.

Using p for the price of the good, MPL for the marginal product of labor, and w for the wage of the worker, we can write this equilibrium condition as

$$\text{value of marginal product of labor} = p \times MPL = w = \text{wage}.$$

From this equilibrium condition we can derive the demand curve for labor. Figure 12.11 plots the value of the marginal product of labor for each level of

Figure 12.11 THE DEMAND CURVE FOR LABOR

The value of the marginal product of labor declines with the level of employment. Since labor is hired up to the point where the wage equals the value of the marginal product, at wage w_1, employment is L_1, and at wage w_2, employment is L_2. The demand curve for labor thus traces out the values of the marginal product of labor at different levels of employment.

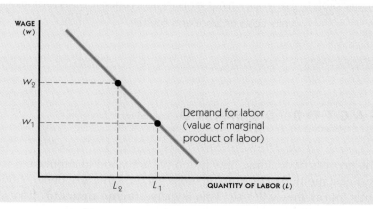

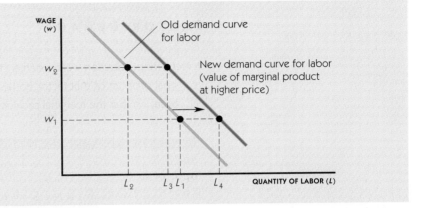

Figure 12.12 EFFECT OF PRICE CHANGE ON THE DEMAND CURVE FOR LABOR

An increase in the price received by a firm shifts the value of the marginal product of labor curve up, so that at each wage, the demand for labor is increased. At wage w_1, employment rises from L_1 to L_4; at wage w_2, employment rises from L_2 to L_3.

labor. Since the marginal product of labor decreases as labor increases, the value of the marginal product of labor decreases. When the wage is w_1, the value of the marginal product of labor equals the wage with a level of labor at L_1. This is the demand for labor at a wage w_1. When the wage is w_2, the value of the marginal product of labor equals the wage with a level of labor at L_2. This is the demand for labor at a wage w_2. Thus, the curve giving the value of the marginal product of labor at each level of employment *is* the demand curve for labor.

It is easy to use this diagram to see the effect of an increase in the price of the good the firm produces. In Figure 12.12, the higher price increases the value of the marginal product of labor at each level of employment, and it immediately follows that at each wage, the demand for labor increases; the demand curve for labor shifts to the right.

Thus, the demand for labor depends on both the wage and the price the firm receives for the goods it sells. In fact, the demand for labor depends only on the ratio of the two, as we will now see.

If we divide both sides of the equation giving the equilibrium condition by the price, we obtain the condition

$MPL = w/p.$

The wage divided by the price of the good being produced is defined as the **real product wage.** It measures what firms pay workers in terms of the goods the worker produces rather than in dollar terms. Thus, the firm hires workers up to the point where the real product wage equals the marginal product of labor.

This principle is illustrated in Figure 12.13, which shows the marginal product of labor. Because of diminishing returns, the marginal product diminishes as labor (and output) increases. As the real product wage increases, the demand for labor decreases.

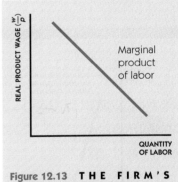

Figure 12.13 THE FIRM'S DEMAND CURVE FOR LABOR AND THE REAL PRODUCT WAGE

Firms hire labor up to the point where the real product wage equals the marginal product of labor. As the real product wage increases, the demand for labor decreases.

FACTOR DEMAND

A factor of production will be demanded up to the point where the value of the marginal product of that factor equals the price. In the case of labor, this is the same as saying that the marginal product of labor equals the real product wage.

FROM THE FIRM'S FACTOR DEMAND TO THE MARKET'S FACTOR DEMAND

Once we have derived the firm's demand curve for labor, we can derive the total market demand for labor. At a given set of prices, we simply add up the demand for labor by each firm at any particular wage rate. The total is the market demand at that wage rate. Since each firm reduces the amount of labor that it demands as the wage increases, the market demand curve is downward sloping. Figure 12.14 shows how we add up diagrammatically the demand curves for labor for two firms, the High Strung Violin Company and Max's Fine Tunes Violin Company. At a wage of w_1, High Strung demands 30

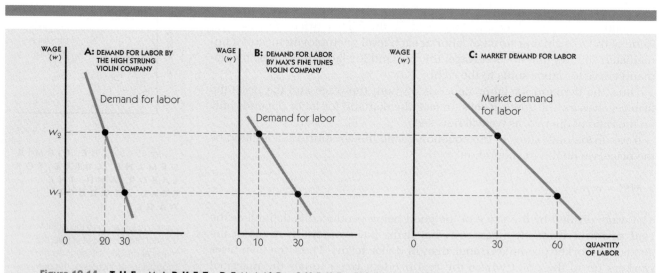

Figure 12.14 THE MARKET DEMAND CURVE FOR LABOR

The market demand curve for labor at each wage is obtained by horizontally adding up the demand curves for labor of each individual firm. As the wage rises, at a fixed price of output, less labor is demanded.

On the farm, basic inputs like durable equipment, real estate, and energy can be used to produce a variety of different outputs. However, as the price of an input rises, it may be harder to conserve on its use for some products than for others.

The elasticity relationships between three farm inputs and three outputs are shown in the table here. The first three rows of the table show how much the output of livestock, milk, and grains will change as the price of the three inputs changes. These figures allow an analyst to predict which products' supply would be affected most severely by changes in the price of various inputs. A 10 percent change in the price of durable equipment would have by far the smallest impact on the supply of grain, while a 10 percent change in the price of real estate would have the smallest effect on the supply of livestock.

Another result of a change in input prices will be that less of the input itself is demanded, because less of it will be used for every unit of output, and output will be lower; this is where the second three rows come in. The first column in the row for durable equipment shows that demand for durable equipment will fall 12.71 percent if the price of that equipment rises by 10 percent.

The third effect of a change in input prices will be on how much other inputs are demanded. In this example, raising the price of any input will lead to less of other inputs being used as well. This may seem surprising. As the price of one input increases, shouldn't a sensible farmer substitute other inputs? Such substitution is surely likely to occur. But the overall decrease in the amount produced will mean that fewer of all inputs are needed, even if the proportion of the inputs that are used shifts. If the price of energy increases by 10 percent, for example, the quantity of energy demanded will fall by 9.41 percent, the quantity of durable equipment demanded will fall by 3.21 percent, and the quantity of real estate by 2.06 percent. Since the amount of energy demanded will decline by the greatest amount, the production process will now be using relatively less energy than before. But since overall supply of all products will fall, fewer of all inputs will be needed.

Source: U. F. Ball, *American Journal of Agricultural Economics* (November 1988), p. 823. Data are from 1978 and 1979, and all elasticities are short-run.

| | Elasticity with respect to the price of | | |
	Durable equipment	Real estate	Energy
Livestock	−.534	−.275	−.286
Fluid milk	−.556	−.319	−.409
Grains	−.192	−.425	−.166
Durable equipment	−1.271	−.192	−.321
Real estate	−.237	−.584	−.206
Energy	−.647	−.336	−.941

workers and Max's Fine Tunes demands 30 workers, for a total demand of 60 workers. At a wage of w_2, High Strung demands 20 workers and Max's demands 10 workers, for a total demand of 30 workers.

FACTOR DEMANDS WITH TWO OR MORE FACTORS

It is now time to relax our assumption that firms require only one factor of production. With more than one factor, when the price of any input falls, the demand for that input will increase for two reasons. First, the firm (and the industry as a whole) substitutes the cheaper input for other inputs, so that for each unit of output produced, more of the cheaper input is employed. Second, the lower price of the input lowers the marginal cost of production at each level of output, and this leads to an increase in the level of production. Since

total demand for an input = demand for input per unit output × output,

and since both factor demand per unit of output and output have been increased, total demand for the input has increased.

When we draw the demand curve for labor, which shows the quantity of labor demanded at each wage, in the background we are keeping the price of output and the price of other inputs fixed. When any of these prices changes, the demand curve for labor shifts. For instance, as we have seen, if the price of output increases, the value of the marginal product of labor increases and the demand curve shifts to the right.

THE THEORY OF THE COMPETITIVE FIRM

We have now completed our description of the theory of the competitive firm. The firm takes the prices it receives for the goods it sells as given, and it takes the prices it pays for the inputs it uses, including the wages it pays workers and the costs of capital goods, as given. The firm chooses its outputs and inputs in order to maximize its profits.

We have seen where the supply curves for output and the demand curves for labor and capital that were used in Part One came from, and why they have the shape they do. As prices increase, output increases; firms produce more, and more firms produce. Thus, supply curves are upward sloping.

As wages increase, with the price of other inputs fixed, firms' marginal cost curve shifts up. This causes them to produce less at each price of their output. The higher *relative* price of labor induces firms to substitute other inputs for labor; they use less labor to produce each unit of output. Therefore, the demand curve for labor (and other inputs) is downward sloping.

In the next chapter, we will use these results, together with the analysis of the household's behavior in Chapters 8–10, to form a model of the entire economy.

REVIEW AND PRACTICE

SUMMARY

1. A revenue curve shows the relationship between a firm's total output and its revenue. For a competitive firm, the marginal revenue it receives from selling an additional unit of output is the price of that unit.

2. A firm in a competitive market will choose the level of output where the market price—the marginal revenue it receives from producing an extra unit—equals the marginal cost.

3. A firm will enter a market if the market price for a good exceeds its minimum average costs, since it can make a profit by selling the good for more than it costs to produce the good.

4. If the market price is below minimum average costs and a firm has no sunk costs, the firm will exit the market immediately. If the market price is below minimum average costs and a firm has sunk costs, it will continue to produce in the short run as long as the market price exceeds its minimum average variable costs.

5. For a firm contemplating entering a market, its supply is zero up to the point where price equals minimum average costs. Above that price, the supply curve is the same as the marginal cost curve.

6. The market supply curve is constructed by adding up the supply curves of all firms in an industry. As prices rise, more firms are willing to produce, and each firm is willing to produce more, so that the market supply curve is normally upward sloping.

7. The economist's and the accountant's concepts of profits differ in how they treat opportunity costs and economic rents.

8. A firm's demand for factors of production is derived from its decision about how much to produce. Inputs will be demanded up to the point where the value of the marginal product of the input equals its price.

9. The demand curve for factors of production is downward sloping for two reasons. Output is reduced as the price of the factor increases, and at each level of output, the firm substitutes away from the factor whose price has increased.

KEY TERMS

sunk costs	contestable markets	real product wage
revenue curve	economic rents	
marginal revenue	factor demand	

REVIEW QUESTIONS

1. In a competitive market, what rule determines the profit-maximizing level of output? What is the relationship between a firm's supply curve and its marginal cost curve?

2. What determines firms' decisions to enter a market? to exit a market? Explain the role of the average variable cost curve in determining whether firms will exit the market.

3. What is the relationship between the way accountants use the concept of profits and the way economists use that term?

4. How do firms decide how much of an input to demand? Why is the demand curve for inputs (like labor) downward sloping?

PROBLEMS

†1. The market price for painting a house in Centerville is $10,000. The Total Cover-up House-Painting Company has fixed costs of $4,000 for ladders, brushes, and so on, and the company's variable costs for house painting follow this pattern:

Output (houses painted)	2	3	4	5	6	7	8	9	10
Variable cost (in thousands of dollars)	26	32	36	42	50	60	72	86	102

Calculate the company's total costs, and graph the revenue curve and the total cost curve. Do the curves have the shape you expect? Over what range of production is the company making profits?

2. Calculate and graph the marginal cost, the average costs, and the average variable costs for the Total Cover-up House-Painting Company. Given the market price, at what level of output will this firm maximize profits? What profit (or loss) is it making at that level? At what price will the firm no longer make a profit? Assume its fixed costs are sunk; there is no market for used ladders, brushes, etc. At what price will the company shut down?

3. Draw a U-shaped average cost curve. On your diagram, designate at what price levels you would expect entry and at what price levels you would expect exit if all the fixed costs are sunk. What if only half the fixed costs are sunk? Explain your reasoning.

4. José is a skilled electrician at a local company, a job that pays $50,000 per year, but he is considering quitting to start his own business. He talks it over with an accountant, who helps him to draw up the following chart with their best predictions about costs and revenues.

Predicted annual costs		Predicted annual revenues
Basic wage	$20,000	$75,000
Rent of space	$12,000	
Rent of equipment	$18,000	
Utilities	$ 2,000	
Miscellaneous	$ 5,000	

The basic wage does seem a bit low, the accountant admits, but she tells José to remember that as owner of the business, José will get to keep any profits as well. From an economist's point of view, is the accountant's list of costs complete? From an economist's point of view, what are José's expected profits?

APPENDIX: ALTERNATIVE WAYS OF CALCULATING THE DEMAND FOR LABOR

We have now seen three different ways for determining the demand for labor. One uses the condition for equilibrium output, that price equals marginal cost—to determine the equilibrium level of output and then determine the required labor. The second is derived directly from the profit-maximizing condition for the demand for labor: the value of the marginal product of labor is set equal to the wage. The third is to set the real product wage equal to the marginal product of labor. This appendix shows how these conditions are, in fact, alternative ways of writing the same condition.

With a single factor of production, labor, the extra cost of producing an extra unit of output is just the extra labor required times the wage. The extra labor required is $1/MPL$, 1 divided by the marginal product of labor. If 1 extra worker produces 2 violins a year, it takes ½ of a worker to produce an extra violin. Hence, the competitive equilibrium condition, price equals marginal cost, can be rewritten as

$$p = w/MPL.$$

If we multiply both sides of this equation by MPL, we obtain

$$p \times MPL = w,$$

the familiar condition that the value of the marginal product ($p \times MPL$)

equals the wage. And if we now divide both sides of the equation by p, we obtain

$$MPL = w/p,$$

the condition that the marginal product of labor equals the real product wage. All of these conditions are in fact three ways of writing the same equation.

Two important consequences follow from these conditions. First, note that the demand for labor depends only on the real product wage, that is, the wage divided by the price of the good produced. If wages and prices both double, then the demand for labor and the supply of output are unaffected. Second, an increase in the wage, keeping prices fixed, reduces the demand for labor. This effect can be seen in several different ways. The real product wage has increased. Therefore, for the condition "the marginal product of labor equals the real product wage" to be satisfied, the marginal product of labor must increase. But the principle of diminishing returns says that to increase the marginal product of labor, the input of labor must be reduced.

Alternatively, an increase in the wage can be seen as increasing the marginal cost of hiring an additional unit of labor, while with a fixed output price, the marginal benefit remains the same. Thus, at the old level of employment, the marginal benefit of the last worker hired is less than the marginal cost, and it pays firms to lower their level of production. At a high enough wage, the average variable costs of production may exceed the price, and the firm will shut down.

COMPETITIVE EQUILIBRIUM

N ow that we have considered each aspect of the basic competitive model separately—the consumption decision, the work and savings decision, the investment decision, and the production decision—it is time to put the pieces together. In doing so, we will come to understand how markets answer the basic economic questions posed in Chapter 1: what is to be produced and in what quantities, how these goods are to be produced, for whom they are to be produced, and, most fundamental, how these resource allocation decisions are to be made.

This chapter also provides a first glance at the interconnectedness of a modern economy. In the giant web of transactions that is the U.S. economy, pressure on any one part will affect all the rest. In 1982, for example, the sharp fall in the price of oil reduced oil-drilling activity in the United States. This led to lower economic activity in oil-drilling states, most notably Texas, which resulted in lower real estate prices. Many real estate developers were unable to pay off the money they had borrowed to build new homes, and defaulted. Since most of these loans had been made through savings and loan associations (S & Ls), many S & Ls went bankrupt. The cost of rescuing the Texas S & Ls was so great that it threatened the nation's entire S & L system, requiring a federal bailout. Thus, a shiver in one part of the economy sent a chill through many other sectors.

Finally, this chapter explains why economists believe that, by and large, the market answers the fundamental economic questions efficiently.

KEY QUESTIONS

1. What is meant by the competitive equilibrium of the economy? Why is it that in competitive equilibrium, a disturbance to one part of the economy may have reverberations in others?

2. What implications does the interconnectedness of the economy have for policy issues such as the corporate income tax?

3. What is the circular flow diagram, and how does it show the many links between the different parts of the economy?

4. Why do so many economists believe that, by and large, reliance on private markets is desirable? How do competitive markets result in economic efficiency?

5. If markets result in distributions of income that society views as unacceptable, should the market be abandoned, or can the government intervene in a more limited way to combine efficient outcomes with acceptable distributions?

GENERAL EQUILIBRIUM ANALYSIS

In Chapter 4 where we introduced the idea of a market equilibrium, we focused on one market at a time. The price of a good was determined when the demand for that good equaled its supply. The wage rate was determined when the demand for labor equaled its supply. The interest rate was determined when the demand for savings equaled its supply. This kind of analysis is called **partial equilibrium analysis.** In analyzing what is going on in one market, we ignore what is going on in other markets.

Interdependencies in the economy make partial equilibrium analysis overly simple because demand and supply in one market depend on prices determined in other markets. For instance, the demand for skis depends on the price of ski tickets, ski boots, and possibly even airline tickets. Thus, the equilibrium price of skis will depend on the price of ski tickets, ski boots, and airline tickets. But by the same token, the demand for ski tickets and ski boots will depend on the price of skis. Accordingly, the equilibrium price of ski tickets and ski boots will depend on the price of skis. **General equilibrium analysis** broadens the perspective, taking into account the interactions and interdependencies within the various parts of the economy.

EXAMPLE: THE CORPORATE INCOME TAX

Ascertaining the effect of the corporate income tax—the tax the federal government imposes on the net income of corporations—provides an example of why general equilibrium analysis is often essential. A partial equilibrium

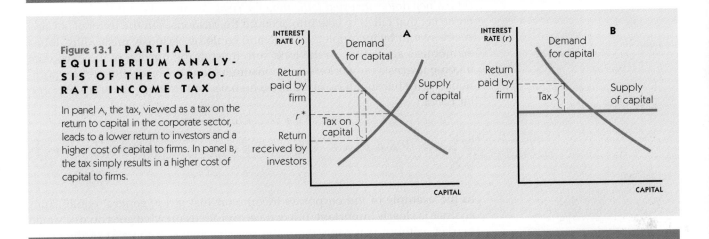

Figure 13.1 PARTIAL EQUILIBRIUM ANALYSIS OF THE CORPORATE INCOME TAX

In panel A, the tax, viewed as a tax on the return to capital in the corporate sector, leads to a lower return to investors and a higher cost of capital to firms. In panel B, the tax simply results in a higher cost of capital to firms.

analysis of this tax is provided in Figure 13.1, where we have drawn the demand and supply curves for capital in the corporate sector. The corporate income tax is shown as a tax on capital because much of a corporation's income is, in fact, a return on the capital invested in it. As can be seen, this tax drives a wedge between the price of capital paid by the firm and the return received by investors.

Who bears the burden of the tax? The partial equilibrium analysis shown in panel A of Figure 13.1 makes it clear that investors bear only a part of the burden. Their after-tax return is lowered, but not by the full amount of the tax. Panel B of the figure, indeed, shows a case in which investors bear none of the burden, when the supply of capital is horizontal (infinitely elastic).

If investors do not bear the burden of the tax, who does? Because the interest rate which firms pay increases, firms' costs have gone up, and this will be reflected in higher equilibrium prices. Thus, consumers bear some of the costs. If sales decrease as a result, the demand for labor may decrease, and thus wages may fall, in which case workers will bear some of the burden. But other factors need to be taken into account as well. The higher cost of capital may induce firms to substitute labor for machines, in which case the demand for labor may actually increase. At higher prices to consumers, however, the return to working is reduced. In this case, workers might supply less labor.

Account must also be taken of the interactions between capital in the corporate and unincorporated sectors of the economy. Because over 80 percent of nonfarm business takes place in the corporate sector, activities in that sector have major ramifications on the rest of the economy. If investors find it less attractive to invest in the corporate sector, they will shift their savings from the corporate to the unincorporated sector. As capital flows into the unincorporated sector, the return to capital in that sector will be reduced to the point that it equals the rate of return in the corporate sector. A full general equilibrium analysis needs to take all these factors into account.

General equilibrium analysis focuses on the fact that, in equilibrium, the re-

turns to all investments throughout the economy must provide the same rate of return per dollar invested (adjusting for risk). An analysis of the corporate income tax that failed to take into account the responses in the unincorporated sector would be incomplete at best, and could be seriously misleading. (Most economists agree that, in the long run, most of the burden of the corporate income tax rests on workers and consumers, and relatively little on corporations, their shareholders, or others who have lent money—contrary to popular belief.)

WHEN PARTIAL EQUILIBRIUM ANALYSIS WILL DO

In the example of the corporate income tax just given, general equilibrium analysis is clearly important. But can we ever focus on what goes on in a single market, without worrying about the reverberations in the rest of the economy? Are there circumstances in which partial equilibrium analysis will provide a fairly accurate answer to the effect of, say, a change in a tax? Fortunately, the answer is yes.

Partial equilibrium analysis is adequate, for example, when the reverberations from the initial imposition of a tax are so dispersed that they can be ignored without distorting the analysis. Such is the case when individuals shift their demand away from the taxed good toward many, many other goods. Each of the prices of those goods changes only a very little. And the total demand for factors of production (like capital and labor) changes only negligibly, so that the prices of different factors are virtually unchanged. Moreover, the slight changes in the prices of different goods and inputs have only a slight effect on the demand and supply curve of the industry upon which the analysis is focusing. In these circumstances, partial equilibrium analysis will provide a good approximation to what will actually happen.

EXAMPLE: A TAX ON CIGARETTES

The effect of a tax on cigarettes is an example where partial equilibrium analysis works well. Back in 1951, the federal tax on a pack of cigarettes was worth 42 percent of the total price paid by a consumer. Since the tax has not been adjusted for inflation, while the price of cigarettes (and everything else) has increased, by the late 1980s, the tax had dropped to only about 15 percent of the market price of a pack. A case could be made for increasing the tax, particularly since even doubling the tax—still well within the 42 percent figure—on each pack of cigarettes would raise nearly $3 billion a year. What predictions can be made about the consequences of increasing the tax?

A tax paid by firms can be thought of as increasing the costs of production. Figure 13.2 shows the tax as shifting the supply curve of cigarettes up by the amount of the tax. Demand is reduced from Q_0 to Q_1. Since expenditures on cigarettes are a small proportion of anyone's income, a 15 percent increase in their price will have a small effect on overall consumption patterns. While the

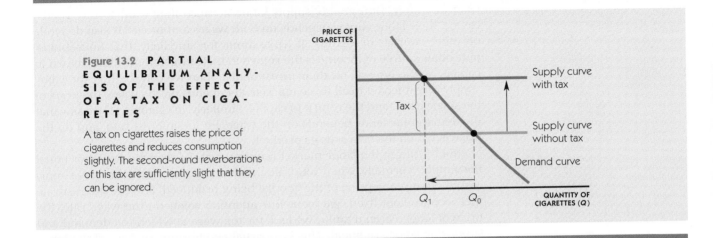

Figure 13.2 PARTIAL EQUILIBRIUM ANALYSIS OF THE EFFECT OF A TAX ON CIGARETTES

A tax on cigarettes raises the price of cigarettes and reduces consumption slightly. The second-round reverberations of this tax are sufficiently slight that they can be ignored.

reduced quantity demanded of cigarettes (and the indirect changed demand for other goods) will have a slight effect on the total demand for labor, this effect is so small that it will have no noticeable effect on the wage rate. Similarly, the tax will have virtually no effect on the return to capital.

Under these circumstances, where more distant general equilibrium effects are likely to be so faint as to be indiscernible, a partial equilibrium analysis of a tax on cigarettes is appropriate.

THE BASIC COMPETITIVE EQUILIBRIUM MODEL

General equilibrium analysis requires a model of the entire economy. To analyze the effects of imposing a tax or the immigration of labor or any other change, one "solves" for the full equilibrium before and after the change, and looks at how each of the variables—wages, prices, interest rates, outputs, employment, and so forth—has changed.

To see how this is done, we focus on a simplified version of the full competitive equilibrium model.

In this simplified model, we assume all workers have identical skills. Ignoring differences in skill level enables us to talk about the labor market as if all workers received the same wage. Similarly, we ignore all aspects of risk in our analysis of the capital market. This allows us to use a single interest rate. Finally, we assume that all firms produce the same good; in other words, the product market consists of only one good. We now have an economy made up of three markets—the labor market, the capital market, and the product market—and can use general equilibrium analysis to trace through how they depend on one another.

In Chapter 9, we saw how households determine the amount of labor they wish to supply. Households supply labor because they want to buy goods. Hence, their labor supply depends on both wages and prices. It also depends on other sources of income. If we assume, for simplicity, that households' only other source of income is the return to their investments (their return to capital, or the interest on their investments), then we can see that the labor supply is connected to all three markets. It depends on the wage, the price of the single good, and the return to capital. Similarly, in Chapter 11, we saw that the demand for labor depends on the wage, on the interest rate, and on the price at which the firm sells its product.

Equilibrium in the labor market requires that the demand for labor equal the supply. Normally, when we draw the demand curve for labor, we simply assume that p, the price of the good(s) being produced, and the interest rate (here, r) are kept fixed. We focus our attention solely on the wage rate, the price of labor. *Given p and r,* we look for the wage at which the demand and supply for labor are equal. This is a partial equilibrium analysis of the labor market.

The labor market is only one of the three markets, even in our highly simplified economy. There is also the market for capital to consider. In Chapter 9, we saw how households determine their savings, which in turn determine the available supply of capital. The supply of capital is affected, in general, by the return it yields (the interest rate, r) plus the income individuals have from other sources, in particular from wages. Since the amount individuals are willing to save may depend on how well off they feel, and how well off they feel depends on the wage rate relative to prices, we can think of the supply of capital too as depending on wages, interest rates, and prices. In Chapter 11, we learned how to derive firms' demand for capital. This too will depend on the interest rate they must pay, the price at which goods can be sold, and the cost of other inputs.

Equilibrium in the capital market occurs at the point where the demand and supply for capital are equal. Again, partial equilibrium analysis of the capital market focuses on the return to capital, r, at which the demand and supply of capital are equal, but both the demand and the supply depend on the wage and the price of goods as well.

Finally, there is the market for goods. Chapters 8 and 9 showed how to derive households' demand for goods. We can think of the household as first deciding on how much to spend (Chapter 9), and then deciding how to allocate what it spends over different goods (Chapter 8). Of course, with a single consumption good, the latter problem no longer exists. In our simplified model, then, we can think of the demand for goods at any price as being determined by household income, which in turn depends on the wage and the interest rate.

Similarly, in Chapter 12, we analyzed how firms determine how much to produce: they set price equal to marginal cost, where marginal cost depends on wages and the interest rate. Equilibrium in the goods market requires that the demand for goods equal the supply of goods. Again, while in the simple partial equilibrium analysis we focus on how the demand and supply of goods depend on price, p, we know that the demand and supply of goods also depend on both the wage rate and the return to capital.

EQUILIBRIUM IN THE BASIC COMPETITIVE MODEL

The labor market clearing condition: The demand for labor must equal the supply.
The capital market clearing condition: The demand for capital must equal the supply.
The goods market clearing condition: The demand for goods must equal the supply.

The labor market is said to be in equilibrium when the demand for labor equals the supply. The product market is in equilibrium when the demand for goods equals the supply. The capital market is in equilibrium when the demand for capital equals the supply. The economy as a whole is in equilibrium only when all markets clear simultaneously (demand equals supply in all markets). The general equilibrium for our simple economy occurs at a common wage rate, w, price, p, and interest rate, r, at which all three markets are all in equilibrium.

In the basic equilibrium model, there is only a single good, but it is easy to extend the analysis to the more realistic case where there are many goods. The same web of interconnections exists between different goods and between different goods and different inputs. Recall from Chapter 4 that the demand curve depicts the quantity of a good—for instance, beer—demanded at each price; the supply curve shows the quantity of a good that firms supply at each price. But the demand curve for beer depends on the prices of other goods and the income levels of different consumers; similarly, the supply curve for beer depends on the prices of inputs, including the wage rate, the interest rate, and the price of hops and other ingredients. Those prices, in turn, depend on supply and demand in their respective markets. The general equilibrium of the economy requires finding the prices for each good and for each input such that the demand for each good equals the supply, and the demand for each input equals the supply.

THE CIRCULAR FLOW OF FUNDS

General equilibrium analysis is not the only way to think about the interrelations of the various parts of the economy. Another way is to consider the flow of funds through the economy. Households buy goods and services from firms. Households supply labor and capital to firms. The income individuals receive, whether in the form of wages or the return on their savings, is spent to buy the goods that firms produce. All these transactions constitute what is called the **circular flow.**

Figure 13.3 A SIMPLE CIR-CULAR FLOW DIA-GRAM

In this simple circular flow diagram, only labor and product markets and only the household and firm sectors are represented. It can be analyzed from any starting point. For example, funds flow from households to firms in the form of purchases of goods and services. Funds flow from firms to households in the form of payments for the labor of workers and profits paid to owners.

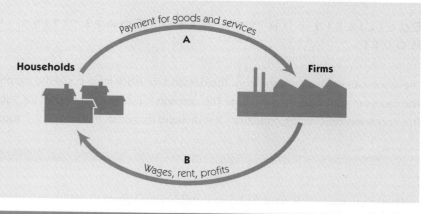

The circular flow for a simplified economy—in which there are only households and firms, households do not save, and firms do not invest—is shown in Figure 13.3. This circular flow diagram serves two purposes. First, it keeps track of how funds flow through the economy. We can see this by starting at point A and following the circular flow around to the right. The top arrow shows that households pay money to firms to buy goods for their consumption. The lower arrow (point B) shows that firms use the money to pay household members in the form of wages (for labor), rent (to the owners of land), and profit (to the owners of firms). The second purpose of the circular flow diagram is to focus on certain balance conditions in the economy that must always be satisfied. In the case of the simple flow in Figure 13.3, there is one balance condition. The income of households (the flow of funds from firms, lower arrow) must equal the expenditures of households (the flow of funds to firms, upper arrow).

Figure 13.4 expands the circular flow in three ways. First, savings and capital are included. Thus, the funds that flow from the firm to the household now include a return on capital (interest on loans and bonds, dividends on stocks). The funds that flow from the household to the firm now include savings, which go to purchase machines and buildings. And firms now retain some of their earnings to finance investment.

Second, the circular flow now includes funds flowing into and out of the government. Thus, some households receive transfer payments from the government (benefits like Social Security and welfare payments). Some sell their labor services to the government rather than private firms. Some receive interest on loans to the government (U.S. government bonds). And there is now an important additional outflow from households: income that goes to the government in the form of taxes. Similarly, firms have additional sources of inflow in the sales of goods and services they make to the government and in government subsidies to firms, and an additional outflow in the taxes they must pay to the government.

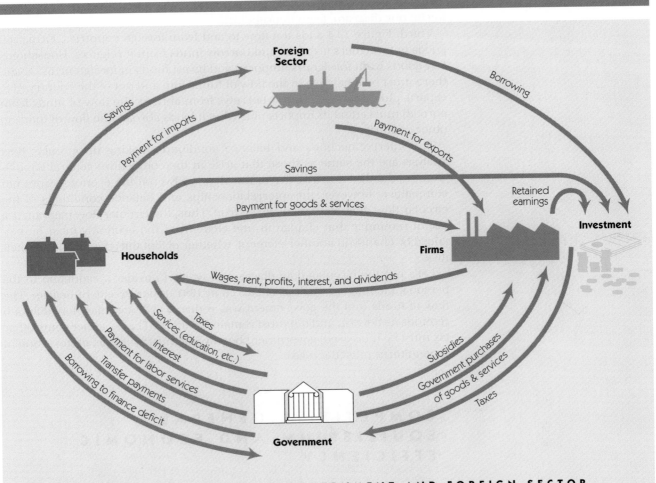

Figure 13.4 CIRCULAR FLOW WITH GOVERNMENT AND FOREIGN SECTOR ADDED

This expanded circular flow diagram shows the labor, capital, and product markets along with households, firms, government, and foreign countries; it too can be analyzed from any starting point. The flow of funds into each sector must balance the flow of funds out of each sector.

Just as the flow of funds into and out of households and firms must balance, the flow of funds into the government must balance the flow of funds out.[1] When there is a deficit—that is, when the government spends more than it collects in taxes, as has been the case in recent years—funds go into the gov-

---

[1]We ignore here the possibility that the government can simply pay for what it obtains by printing money. In the United States, the government always finances any shortfall in revenue by borrowing.

ernment as borrowings. The government finances the difference by borrowing (in our diagram, from households).

Third, Figure 13.4 adds the flow to and from foreign countries. Firms sell goods to foreigners (exports) and borrow funds from foreigners. Households buy goods from foreigners (imports) and invest funds in foreign firms. Again, there must be a balance in the flow of funds into and out of the country. U.S. exports plus what the country borrows from abroad (the flow of funds from abroad) must equal its imports plus what it lends abroad (the flow of funds to other countries).[2]

The interconnections and balance conditions making up circular flow analysis are the same as those that arise in the competitive general equilibrium model discussed earlier in the chapter. Even if the economy were not competitive, however, the interrelationships and balance conditions of the circular flow diagram would still be true. Thus, the circular flow diagram is a useful reminder that change in one element of the economy *must* be balanced by change in another element, whether or not the economy is competitive.

Let's put the circular flow diagram to work. Consider a reduction in the personal income tax, such as occurred in 1981 under President Reagan. The flow of funds into the government was reduced. The circular flow diagram reminds us flows in and out must remain balanced. That is, either some other tax must be increased, government borrowing must increase, or government expenditures must decrease.

COMPETITIVE GENERAL EQUILIBRIUM AND ECONOMIC EFFICIENCY

The first part of this chapter introduced the basic model of competitive general equilibrium. Competitive general equilibrium entails prices, wages, and returns to capital such that all markets—for goods, labor, capital (and other factors of production)—clear. A change in economic conditions, such as the imposition of a tax, a migration of labor, or a sudden decline in the quantity supplied of a good at each price, results in a new equilibrium to the economy. We have seen how the effects of such changes can be traced out.

Economists are interested, however, not only in describing the market equilibrium, but in evaluating it. Do competitive markets do a "good" job in allocating resources? Chapter 7 introduced the idea of Adam Smith's "invisible hand," which said that market economies are efficient. One of the most important achievements of modern economic theory has been to establish in what sense and under what conditions the market is efficient.

---

[2]This condition can be put another way. The difference between U.S. imports and exports must equal the net flow of funds from abroad (the difference between what the country borrows from abroad and what it lends).

CLOSE-UP: THE MINIMUM WAGE AND GENERAL EQUILIBRIUM

When the first minimum wage law was adopted by passage of the Fair Labor Standards Act of 1938, it had general equilibrium effects that altered the character of the country.

When enacted, the minimum wage law required that wages be no lower than 32.5 cents per hour. Because wages were much lower in the South than in the North, many more workers were affected there. For example, 44 percent of Southern textile workers were paid below the minimum wage, but only 6 percent of Northern textile workers were. African-Americans in the South were particularly affected. Many lost their jobs and migrated North. The economy of the South, no longer able to pay low wages, adapted by seeking out investment, which over the years has helped make states like Texas and Florida among the fastest-growing in the country.

Gavin Wright, professor of economics at Stanford University described the situation this way: "The overall effect of this history on black Americans is complex, mixed, and ironic. Displacement and suffering were severe. Yet in abolishing the low-wage South, the federal government also destroyed the nation's most powerful bastion of racism and white supremacy. The civil rights movement of the 1960s was able to use the South's hunger for capital inflows as an effective weapon in forcing desegregation. Similarly, migration to the North allowed dramatic increases in incomes and educational opportunities for many blacks; yet the same migration channeled other blacks into the high-unemployment ghettos which if anything have worsened with the passage of time."

A partial equilibrium analysis of the effects of enacting a minimum wage would only look at how the law affected labor markets. But for society as a whole, the effects of enacting such a law were far more momentous, touching on issues like racial desegregation and the growth of urban ghettos.

Source: Gavin Wright, "The Economic Revolution in the American South," *Journal of Economic Perspectives* (Summer 1987) 1:161–78.

PARETO EFFICIENCY

To economists, the concept of efficiency is related to concern with the well-being of those in the economy. When no one can be made better off without making someone else worse off the allocation of resources is called **Pareto efficient,** after the great Italian economist and sociologist Vilfredo Pareto (1848–1923). Typically when economists refer to efficiency, Pareto efficiency is what they mean. Saying that a market is efficient is a compliment. In the same way that an efficient machine uses its inputs as productively as possible, an efficient market leaves no way of increasing output with the same level of inputs. The only way one person can be made better off is by taking resources away from another, thereby making the second person worse off.

It is easy to see how an allocation of resources might not be Pareto efficient. Assume the government is given the job of distributing chocolate and vanilla ice cream and pays no attention to people's preferences. Assume, moreover, that some individuals love chocolate and hate vanilla, while others love vanilla and hate chocolate. Some chocolate lovers will get vanilla ice cream, and some vanilla lovers will get chocolate ice cream. Clearly, this is Pareto inefficient. Allowing people to trade resources, in this case, ice cream, makes both groups better off.

There is a popular and misguided view that *all* economic changes represent nothing more than redistributions. Gains to one only subtract from another. Rent control is one example. In this view, the only effect of rent control is redistribution—landlords receive less, and are worse off, by the same amount that their tenants' rents are reduced (and the tenants are better off). In some countries, unions have expressed similar views, and see wage increases as having no further consequences than redistributing income to workers from those who own or who manage firms. This view is mistaken, because in each of these instances, there are consequences beyond the redistribution. Rent control that keeps rents below the level that clears the rental housing market results in inefficiencies. For those concerned about renters who cannot afford the going rate, there are better approaches that make the renters as well as the landlords better off than under rent control. Thus, with rent control, the economy is not Pareto efficient.

CONDITIONS FOR THE PARETO EFFICIENCY OF THE MARKET ECONOMY

For the economy to be Pareto efficient, it must meet the conditions of exchange efficiency, production efficiency, and product-mix efficiency. Considering each of these conditions separately shows us why the basic competitive model attains Pareto efficiency. (Recall the basic ingredients of that model: rational, perfectly informed households interacting with rational, profit-maximizing firms in competitive markets, and in an environment in which the market failures discussed in Chapter 7 do not occur.)

EXCHANGE EFFICIENCY

Exchange efficiency requires that whatever the economy produces must be distributed among individuals in an efficient way. If I like chocolate ice cream and you like vanilla ice cream, exchange efficiency requires that I get the chocolate and you get the vanilla.

When there is exchange efficiency, there is no scope for further trade among individuals. Chapter 3 discussed the advantages of free exchange among individuals and nations. Any prohibition or restriction on trade results in exchange inefficiency. For instance, in war times, governments often ration scarce goods, like sugar. People are given coupons that allow them to buy, say, a pound of sugar a month. If sugar carries a price of $1 a pound, having $1 is not enough; you must also have the coupon. There is often considerable controversy about whether people should be allowed to sell their coupons, or trade their sugar coupons for, say, a butter coupon. If the government prohibits the sale or trading of coupons, then the economy will not be exchange efficient—it will not be Pareto efficient.

The price system ensures that exchange efficiency is attained. In deciding how much of a good to buy, people balance the marginal benefit they receive by buying an extra unit with the cost of that extra unit, its price. Hence, price can be thought of as a rough measure of the *marginal* benefit an individual receives from a good—that is, the benefit a person receives from one more unit of the good. For those who like chocolate ice cream a great deal and vanilla ice cream very little, this will entail consuming many more chocolate ice cream cones than vanilla. And conversely for the vanilla lover. Notice that no single individual or agency needs to know who is a chocolate and who is a vanilla lover for the goods to get to the right person. Not even the ice cream stores have to know individual preferences. Each consumer, by his own action, ensures that exchange efficiency is attained.

Notice too that if different individuals face *different* prices, then the economy will not, in general, be exchange efficient. This is because the difference in price opens up an opportunity for exchange. For example, Jim would love to fly to Hawaii but feels it is not worth it at the full fare offered. At the same time, Madeleine, whose mother is an airline executive and only has to pay half fares, is not keen on going to Hawaii but cannot pass up the good deal. Both can be made better off if they are allowed to make an exchange.

PRODUCTION EFFICIENCY

For an economy to be Pareto efficient, it must also be **production efficient.** That is, it must not be possible to produce more of some goods without producing less of other goods. In other words, Pareto efficiency requires that the economy operate along the production possibilities curve first introduced in Chapter 2.

Figure 13.5 shows the production possibilities curve for a simple economy that produces only two goods, apples and oranges. If the economy is at point *I*, inside the production possibilities curve, it cannot be Pareto efficient. Society could produce more of both apples and oranges, and by distributing them to

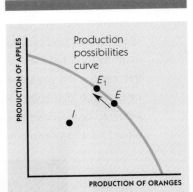

Figure 13.5 THE PRO-DUCTION POSSIBIL-ITIES CURVE

The production possibilities curve shows the maximum level of output of one good given the level of output of other goods. Production efficiency requires that the economy be on its production possibilities curve. Along the curve, the only way to increase production of one good (here, apples) is to decrease the production of other goods (oranges).

CLOSE-UP: PARETO IMPROVEMENT IN THE SKIES

Airlines want their planes to fly as full as possible. They also know that a certain percentage of people who purchased a ticket for any given flight are not going to show up. This gives the airlines an incentive to "overbook" flights. They sell more tickets than there are seats in the reasonable expectation that there will be room to take everyone who actually shows up. But sometimes everyone does show up, and a decision must be made about who will be bumped from the flight. Several methods of making this choice are possible.

In the 1960s, the airlines simply bumped whoever showed up last, and gave those people tickets for a later flight. Bumped passengers had no recourse. This sort of policy causes high blood pressure.

To avoid imposing these costs on frustrated passengers, a second policy might be for the government to forbid airlines to overbook flights. But in this case, some planes will be forced to fly with empty seats that some people would have been willing to buy. Airlines would lose revenues, prices would have to rise to offset the lost revenue, and travelers who could have flown in the empty seat but could not get reservations under the no-overbooking rule would all be losers.

There is an alternative solution which is a Pareto improvement both over the practice of bumping and over rules forbidding overbooking. Today airlines offer a free ticket on a future flight or other bonus as compensation to anyone willing to wait. People willing to accept such a deal are clearly better off in their own estimation. The airlines benefit because they are allowed to continue their practice of overbooking and thus keeping their flights as full as possible. In fact, since the person who receives a free ticket will often occupy a seat that would have been vacant anyway, the marginal cost of offering the free ticket for the airline is very close to zero. This is a real-world Pareto improvement. Everyone involved is at least no worse off and many are better off.

Source: Julian L. Simon, "An Almost Practical Solution to Airline Overbooking," *Journal of Transport Economics and Policy* (May 1968), pp. 201–2.

different individuals, it could make people better off. Prices signal to firms the scarcity of each of the inputs they use. When all firms face the same prices of labor, capital goods, and other inputs, they will take the appropriate actions to economize on each of these inputs, ensuring that the economy operates along its production possibilities curve.

PRODUCT-MIX EFFICIENCY

The third condition for Pareto efficiency is **product-mix efficiency.** That is, the mix of goods produced by the economy must reflect the preferences of those in the economy. The economy must produce along the production possibilities curve at a point that reflects the preferences of consumers. The price system again ensures that this condition will be satisfied. Both firms and households look at the trade-offs. Firms look at how many extra oranges they can produce if they reduce their production of apples. The result is given by the slope of the production possibilities curve, and is called **the marginal rate of transformation.** Firms compare this trade-off with the relative benefits of producing the two goods—given by the relative prices. Similarly, households look at the relative costs of apples and oranges—again given by the relative prices—and ask, given those trade-offs, whether they would like to consume more apples and fewer oranges or vice versa.

Changes in preferences are reflected quickly—through the operation of demand and supply curves—in changes in prices. These changes are then translated into changes in production by firms. Assume that the economy is initially producing at a point along the production possibilities curve, E in Figure 13.5. Consumers decide that they like apples more and oranges less. The increased demand for apples will result in the price of apples increasing, and this will lead to an increased output of apples; at the same time, the decreased demand for oranges will result in the price of oranges falling, and this in turn will lead to a decreased output of oranges. The economy will move from E to a point such as E_1, where there are more apples and fewer oranges produced; the mix of goods produced in the economy will have changed to reflect the changed preferences of consumers.

THREE CONDITIONS FOR PARETO EFFICIENCY

1. Exchange efficiency: Goods must be distributed among individuals in a way that means there are no gains from further trade.

2. Production efficiency: The economy must be on its production possibilities curve.

3. Product-mix efficiency: The economy must produce a mix of goods reflecting the preferences of consumers.

Many states require small children in cars to ride in specially designed safety seats. So why shouldn't small children traveling by plane be required to ride in safety seats as well? Congressional hearings were held on this subject in the summer of 1990. Everyone agreed that in at least a few cases, such seats would save a child's life in an airplane crash. Nevertheless, after considering the potential consequences and side effects of such a rule, the Federal Aviation Administration (FAA) argued against it.

On the benefit side, the FAA estimated that mandatory safety seats would save the life of one child in one airline crash every 10 years. But parents would have to pay as much as $185 to buy the safety seats themselves, in addition to paying for a regular airplane seat for the child. Now, children under two years old are allowed to sit in their parents' laps, avoiding the expense of an airline ticket. With those extra costs, the FAA estimated that 20 percent of the families who now fly with small children would either stay home or drive. The additional driving would lead to 9 additional highway deaths, 52 serious injuries, and 2,300 minor injuries over the same ten-year period, according to FAA estimates.

Even those who feel that saving an additional child's life has a value that cannot be reduced to a price tag, however high, must look beyond the market being regulated. Looking beyond airlines makes it clear that reducing airline deaths by requiring child safety seats for infants and toddlers is almost certain to cause even greater loss of life.

COMPETITIVE MARKETS AND PARETO EFFICIENCY

We now know that when economists say that market economies are efficient, or that the price system results in economic efficiency, they mean that the economy is Pareto efficient: no one can be made better off without making someone else worse off. We have also learned why competitive markets ensure that all three of the basic conditions for Pareto efficiency are attained: exchange efficiency, production efficiency, and product-mix efficiency.

The argument that competitive markets ensure Pareto efficiency can be put somewhat loosely in another way: a rearrangement of resources can only benefit people who voluntarily agree to it. But in competitive equilibrium, people have already agreed to all the exchanges they are willing to make; no one wishes to produce more or less or to demand more or less, given the prices he faces.

Pareto efficiency does *not* say that there are no ways to make one or many individuals better off. Obviously, resources could be taken from some and given to others, and the recipients would be better off. We have seen how, for instance, government interventions with the market, such as rent control, do benefit some individuals—those who are lucky enough to get the rent-controlled apartments. But in the process, someone is made worse off.

COMPETITIVE MARKETS AND INCOME DISTRIBUTION

Efficiency is better than inefficiency, but it is not everything. In the competitive equilibrium, some individuals might be very rich, while others live in dire poverty. One person might have skills that are highly valued, while another does not. Competition may result in an efficient economy with a very unequal distribution of resources.

The law of supply and demand in a competitive economy determines how the available income will be divided up. It determines how much workers get paid for their labor and the return to owners of capital on their investments. By determining wages and the return to capital, the market thus determines the distribution of income.

Knowing how the distribution of income is determined is important, because it tells us how the nation's economic pie is divided: it provides the answer to the question: "For whom are goods produced?" While competitive markets produce economic *efficiency*—no one can be made better off without making someone else worse off—competitive markets may also produce distributions of income that seem, at least to some, morally repugnant. An economy where some individuals live in mansions while others barely eke out a living may be efficient, but that still hardly makes the situation desirable. Left to themselves, competitive markets may provide an answer to the question "For whom are goods produced?" that seems unacceptable.

This unacceptable response does not mean that the competitive market mechanism should be abandoned, at least not under the conditions assumed in our basic model, with perfectly informed, rational consumers and firms interacting in perfectly competitive markets. Even if society as a whole wishes to redistribute income, it should not dispense with competitive markets. Instead, all that is needed is to redistribute the wealth that people possess, and then leave the rest to the workings of a competitive market. With appropriate redistributions of wealth, the economy can achieve any desired distribution of income.

As a practical matter, perhaps the most important impact of government on the distribution of "wealth" is through education—in providing everyone a certain amount of human capital. By providing all individuals, regardless of the wealth of their parents, with a free basic education, government reduces the degree of inequality that otherwise would exist. Still, as we shall see in Chapter 23, the magnitude of inequality in the United States remains high— larger than in most other developed countries.

Frequently government interferences with the market are justified on the grounds that they increase equality. These government policies are often based on the widely held but mistaken (as we have already seen) view that all redistributions are just that, some individuals get more, others get less, but there are no further repercussions. We now know that changing relative prices to achieve redistribution—such as rent control—will have effects in addition to redistributing income. Such changes interfere with the economy's efficiency. One consequence of lower rents for apartments, for example, is that the return on capital invested in rental housing will fall, and the economy will as a result invest too little in rental housing. Because of this underinvestment, the economy is not efficient.

Thus, interventions in the economy justified on the grounds that they increase equality need to be treated with caution. To attain an efficient allocation of resources with the desired distribution of income, *if* the assumptions of the competitive model are satisfied by the economy, the *sole* role of the government is to redistribute initial wealth. Not only can one rely on the market mechanism thereafter, but interfering with the market may actually result in the economy not being Pareto efficient.

Both of the results just presented—that competitive markets are Pareto efficient, and that every Pareto-efficient allocation, regardless of the desired distribution of income, can be obtained through the market mechanism—are **theorems.** That is, they are logical propositions that follow from basic definitions and assumptions, such as what is meant by a competitive economy and what is meant by Pareto efficiency. These theorems are based on other assumptions as well, such as the absence of externalities. When their assumptions are not satisfied, market economies may not be Pareto efficient, and more extensive government interventions may be required to obtain Pareto-efficient allocations. Later chapters will explore these circumstance in greater detail.

LOOKING BEYOND THE BASIC MODEL: MARKET FAILURES AND THE ROLE OF GOVERNMENT

This chapter has brought together the pieces of the basic competitive model. It has shown how the competitive equilibrium in an ideal economy is achieved. To the extent that conditions in the real world match the assumptions of the basic competitive model, there will be economic efficiency.

Government will have little role in the economy beyond establishing a legal framework within which to enforce market transactions.

One group of economists, referred to as **free-market economists** for their strong faith in unfettered markets as the path to economic efficiency, believe that the competitive model provides a good description of most markets most of the time. These economists, who include Nobel laureates Milton Friedman of Stanford University's Hoover Institution and the late George Stigler of the University of Chicago, believe that there is a very limited role for government in economic affairs. In their view, government intervention should be restricted mainly to changing unacceptable distributions of income, and even in this area government should operate with restraint.

Another group of economists, called **imperfect-market economists,** see significant discrepancies between the basic competitive model and the conditions they observe when they study actual consumers, firms, and markets. Such discrepancies lead them to question whether private markets, left to operate on their own, will produce economically efficient outcomes.

Imperfect-market economists would not, however, discard the model. For them, it is an important baseline for investigation. For example, many economists who specialize in the study of the economy's industrial structure, such as Joseph Bain of the University of California at Berkeley or F. M. Scherer of Harvard, argue that competition is limited, and explain why this is so. If the cigarette market is not competitive, the competitive model will yield incorrect predictions concerning, for instance, the consequences of an increase in the tax on cigarettes.

Other economists, such as Nobel laureate Kenneth J. Arrow of Stanford University, contend that firms do not have perfect information about the quality of their workers and investors do not have perfect information about the returns to different investment opportunities. This imperfect information, they argue, results in capital and labor markets functioning in ways quite different from that described by the basic competitive model.

Still other economists, such as MIT's Nobel laureate Robert Solow, argue that the model is generally appropriate, but there are important instances where markets cannot be relied upon without government intervention. They are concerned about pollution of the environment and about unemployment. Further, economists such as Paul Romer of the University of California at Berkeley and Paul David of Stanford University worry that firms on their own will invest too little in research, and as a result, economic growth will be hampered. These economists believe that these are instances where one or more of the assumptions of the basic competitive model are violated and that there is, therefore, scope for government intervention to increase economic efficiency.

What are the consequences when the underlying assumptions are not valid? Which of the assumptions are most suspect? What evidence do we have with which we can assess either the validity of the model's underlying assumptions or its implications? The next part of this book is devoted to these questions, and to the role of government that emerges from the answers.

A warning is in order before we embark on our study of market imperfections. That markets do not work perfectly—suggesting a possible role for government—does not necessarily mean that government intervention will improve matters.

Two Views of the Basic Competitive Model

Free-market view: The competitive model provides a good description of the economy, and government intervention is not required.

Imperfect-market view: In many markets, the competitive model does not provide a good description—for instance, because competition is limited and information is imperfect. There are important market failures, evidenced by unemployment and environmental pollution, requiring at least selective government intervention.

Free-market and imperfect-market economists continue to debate the extent to which the basic competitive model provides a good description of the economy. However, these disagreements should not mask the large, and growing areas of consensus about the efficiency of competitive markets, which we highlight with our seventh consensus point:

7 The Efficiency of Competitive Markets

At the center of the modern economy are competitive markets. Through the profit motive and the price system, competitive markets lead to economic efficiency. However, there are important exceptions, where markets fail to produce efficient outcomes. For instance, markets may not be competitive, and markets produce too much of goods with negative externalities (like pollution), and too little of goods with positive externalities (like basic research).

REVIEW AND PRACTICE

SUMMARY

1. When an economic change affects many markets at once, general equilibrium analysis is used to study the interactions among various parts of the economy. But when the secondary repercussions of a change are small, partial equilibrium analysis, focusing on only one or a few markets, is sufficient.

2. General equilibrium in the basic competitive model occurs when wages, interest rates, and prices are such that demand is equal to supply in all labor, capital, and product markets. All markets clear.

3. Circular flow of funds diagrams show capital, labor, and product market interrelationships between households, firms, government, and the foreign sector. The flow of funds in and out of each sector must balance.

4. Under the conditions of the basic competitive model, the economy's resource allocation is Pareto efficient; that is, no one can be made better off without making someone else worse off.

5. The distribution of income that emerges from competitive markets may possibly be very unequal. However, under the conditions of the basic competitive model, a redistribution of wealth can move the economy to a more equal allocation that is also Pareto efficient. No further government intervention is required.

6. Some economists hold that the basic competitive model provides an essentially accurate view of most of the economy; markets ensure economic efficiency, and there is only a limited role for government. Others maintain that many markets are quite imperfect, the basic competitive model provides no more than a starting point for analysis, and government intervention is required to deal with some of society's problems.

KEY TERMS

partial equilibrium
analysis
general equilibrium
analysis

circular flow
Pareto-efficient
allocations
exchange efficiency

production
efficiency
product-mix
efficiency

REVIEW QUESTIONS

1. What is the difference between partial and general equilibrium analysis? When is each one especially appropriate?

2. List the principal flows into and out of firms, households, government, and the foreign sector.

3. How does the economy in general equilibrium answer the four basic economic questions: What is produced, and in what quantities? How are these goods produced? For whom are they produced? Who decides how resources are allocated?

4. What is meant by Pareto efficiency? What is required for the economy to be Pareto efficient? If the conditions of the basic competitive model are satisfied, is the economy Pareto efficient?

5. If the distribution of income in the economy is quite unequal, is it necessary to impose price controls or otherwise change prices in the competitive marketplace to make it more equal?

PROBLEMS

1. Decide whether partial equilibrium analysis would suffice in each of these cases, or whether it would be wise to undertake a general equilibrium analysis:

(a) a tax on alcohol;
(b) an increase in the Social Security tax;
(c) a drought that affects farm production in the Midwestern states;
(d) a rise in the price of crude oil;
(e) a major airline going out of business.

Explain your answers.

2. Use the extended circular flow diagram, with the foreign sector included, to trace out the possible consequences of the following:

(a) a law requiring that businesses raise the wages of their employees;
(b) a decision by consumers to import more and save less;
(c) an increase in government expenditure financed by a corporate income tax;
(d) an increase in government expenditure without an accompanying increase in taxes.

3. Explain how each of the following might interfere with exchange efficiency:

(a) airlines that limit the number of seats they sell at a discount price;
(b) doctors who charge poor patients less than rich patients;
(c) firms that give volume discounts.

In each case, what additional trades might be possible?

4. Assume that in the steel industry, given current production levels and technology, 1 machine costing $10,000 can replace 1 worker. Given current production levels and technology in the automobile industry, 1 machine costing $10,000 can replace 2 workers. Is this economy Pareto efficient; that is, is it on its production possibilities curve? If not, explain how total output of both goods can be increased by shifting machines and labor between industries.

5. Consider three ways of helping poor people to buy food, clothing, and shelter. The first way is to pass laws setting price ceilings to keep these basic goods affordable. The second is to have the government distribute coupons that give poor people a discount when they buy these necessities. The third is for the government to distribute income to poor people. Which program is more likely to have a Pareto-efficient outcome? Describe why the other programs are not likely to be Pareto efficient.

APPENDIX: PARETO EFFICIENCY AND COMPETITIVE MARKETS

The concept of the marginal rate of substitution, introduced in the appendices to Chapters 8 and 9, can be used to see more clearly why competitive markets are Pareto efficient.

EXCHANGE EFFICIENCY

Exchange efficiency can be achieved only when all individuals have the same marginal rate of substitution, the amount of one good a person is willing to give up to get one unit of another. In competitive markets, individuals choose a mix of goods for which the marginal rate of substitution is equal to relative prices. Since all individuals face the same relative prices, they all have identical marginal rates of substitution, ensuring the exchange efficiency of the economy.

To see why exchange efficiency requires that all people have the same marginal rate of substitution, let's look at a simple example of Crusoe and Friday and their island economy. Assume that Crusoe's marginal rate of substitution between apples and oranges is 2; that is, he is willing to give up 2 apples for 1 extra orange. Friday's marginal rate of substitution between apples and oranges is 1; he is willing to give up 1 apple for 1 orange. Since their marginal rates of substitution are not equal, we can make one of them better off without making the other worse off (or we can make both of them better off). The allocation is not Pareto efficient.

To see how this is done, suppose we take 1 orange away from Friday and give it to Crusoe. Crusoe would then be willing to give up 2 apples, and be just as well off as before. If he gave up only 1½ apples to Friday, Friday would also be better off. Friday would have given up 1 orange in return for 1½ apples; he would have been willing to make the trade if he had received just 1 apple in return.

It is easy to see that Crusoe and Friday will continue to trade until their marginal rates of substitution are equal. As Friday gives up oranges for apples, his marginal rate of substitution increases; he insists on getting more and more apples for each orange he gives up. Similarly, as Crusoe gives up apples and gets more oranges, his marginal rate of substitution decreases; he is willing to give up fewer apples for each extra orange he gets. Eventually, the two will have identical marginal rates of substitution, at which point further trade will stop. Thus, the basic condition for exchange efficiency is that the marginal rates of substitution of all individuals must be the same.

PRODUCTION EFFICIENCY

The condition of production efficiency—when the economy is on its production possibilities curve—is very similar to the condition of exchange efficiency. An economy can only be productively efficient if the marginal rate of technical substitution between any two inputs in any two firms is the same. The marginal rate of technical substitution is the amount that one input can be reduced if another input is increased by one unit, while output remains constant (see appendix to Chapter 11).

Profit-maximizing firms in a competitive economy choose a mix of inputs such that the marginal rate of technical substitution of different inputs is equal to the relative prices of those inputs. If all firms face the same relative prices of inputs, their marginal rates of technical substitution will all be the same, and production efficiency will result.

For example, consider a case involving the steel and auto industries. Assume that in steel, the marginal rate of technical substitution between capital expenditures and labor is $2,000; that is, if a company uses one more worker, it can save $2,000 on equipment (or equivalently, two $1,000 machines substitute for one worker). In the auto industry, the marginal rate of technical substitution is $1,000; one $1,000 machine substitutes for one worker. The marginal rates of technical substitution between inputs are not equal, which means that the economy is not productively efficient.

Consider a worker moving from the auto to the steel industry. If the steel industry keeps its output at the same level, the additional worker in that industry frees up two machines. One of those machines can be transferred to the auto industry, and production in that industry would stay at the same level. (We are assuming that in the auto industry one $1,000 machine substitutes for one worker.) But one machine is left over. It can be used in the steel industry, the auto industry, or both to increase production.

As we increase the number of workers in the steel industry, the marginal productivity of labor in that industry will diminish, while as we reduce workers in the automobile industry, the marginal productivity of labor in that industry will increase; conversely for machines. As a result, the marginal rates of technical substitution will shift in the two industries, so that they are closer. Spurred on by the profit motive of the individual companies in competitive markets, labor and capital will tend to move between companies until marginal rates of technical substitution are equated, and production efficiency is reached. Thus, production efficiency, which means that the economy is on its production possibilities curve, requires that the marginal rate of technical substitution between any two inputs be the same in all uses.

PRODUCT-MIX EFFICIENCY

This third condition of Pareto efficiency requires that the economy operate at the point along the production possibilities curve that reflects consumers' preferences. Look at a particular point on the production possibilities curve in Figure 13.5, say point E. The **marginal rate of transformation** tells us how many extra units of one good the economy can get if it gives up one unit of another good—how many extra cases of beer the economy can produce if it reduces production of potato chips by a ton, or how many extra cars the economy can get if it gives up one tank. The slope of the production possibilities curve is equal to the marginal rate of transformation. The slope tells us how much of one good, measured along the vertical axis, can be increased if the economy gives up one unit of the good along the horizontal axis.

Product-mix efficiency requires that consumers' marginal rate of substitution equal the marginal rate of transformation. To see why this is so, and how competitive economies ensure product-mix efficiency, consider an economy producing two fruits, apples and oranges. Assume that the marginal rate of substitution between apples and oranges is 2—that is, individuals are willing to give up 2 apples for an additional orange; while the marginal rate of transformation is 1—they only have to give up 1 apple to get an additional orange. Clearly, it pays firms to increase orange production and reduce apple production.

The competitive price system ensures that the economy satisfies the condition for product-mix efficiency. We know that consumers set the marginal rate of substitution equal to the relative price. In a similar way, profit-maximizing firms have an incentive to produce more of some goods and less of others according to the prices they can sell them for, until their marginal rate of transformation is equal to the relative price. If consumers and producers both face the same relative prices, the marginal rate of substitution will equal the marginal rate of transformation. Thus, product-mix efficiency comes about when both consumers and firms face the same prices.

To see more clearly why competitive firms will set the marginal rate of transformation equal to relative prices, consider a firm that produces both apples and oranges. If the company reallocates labor from apples to oranges, apple production is reduced and orange production is increased. Assume apple production goes down by 2 cases and orange production goes up by 1 case. The marginal rate of transformation is 2. If a case of apples sells for $4 and a case of oranges sells for $10, the firm loses $8 on apple sales but gains $10 on orange sales. It is clearly profitable for the firm to make the switch. The firm will continue to switch resources from apples to oranges until the marginal rate of transformation equals the relative price. The same result will occur even if oranges and apples are produced by different firms.[3]

Thus, the basic condition for product-mix efficiency, that the marginal rate of substitution must equal the marginal rate of transformation, will be satisfied in competitive economies because firms set the marginal rate of transformation equal to relative prices, and consumers set their marginal rate of substitution equal to relative prices.

---

[3]The concept of product-mix efficiency can be illustrated by superimposing a family of indifference curves (Chapter 8, appendix) in the same diagram with the production possibilities curve. Assume, for simplicity, that all individuals are the same. The highest level of welfare that one representative individual can attain is represented by the tangency of her indifference curve with the production possibilities curve. The slopes of two curves that are tangent to each other are equal at the point of tangency. The slope of the indifference curve is the consumer's marginal rate of substitution; the slope of the production possibilities curve is the marginal rate of transformation. Thus, the tangency—and Pareto efficiency—requires that the marginal rate of substitution equal the marginal rate of transformation.

PART THREE

IMPERFECT
MARKETS

n Part Two, the basic model of perfectly competitive markets was developed. If the real world matched up to its assumptions, then markets could be given free rein. They would supply efficient outcomes. If an outcome seemed inequitable, society would simply redistribute initial wealth and let markets take care of the rest.

In the two centuries since Adam Smith enunciated the view that markets ensure economic efficiency, economists have investigated the model with great care. Nothing they have discovered has shaken their belief that markets are, by and large, the most efficient way to coordinate an economy. However, they have found significant departures between modern economies and the competitive model. Still, its insights are powerful, and most economists use the basic competitive model as the starting point for building a richer, more complete model. In Part Three, and later in Part Four, we will explore many of the ways in which the real world deviates from the competitive model. We can enumerate the basic differences here.

1. Most markets are not as competitive as those envisioned by the basic model. For evidence, one need look only as far as the nearest brand name. When we think of beer, we think of Budweiser, Miller, and Coors (among domestic beers). Automobiles bring to mind Chevrolets, Fords, Chryslers, and Toyotas. The examples go on forever; in fact, it is hard to think of a consumer product without attaching a brand name to it. The basic competitive model focuses on products like wheat or pig iron, for which the products produced by different firms are essentially identical, and are perfect substitutes for one another. In that model, there is no room for brand names. In the basic competitive model, if a firm raises its price slightly above that of its rivals, it loses all of its customers, as they switch; in the real world, a firm that raises its price slightly above that of its rivals loses some, but far from all, of its customers. A Budweiser enthusiast would probably pay 10 cents more for a six-pack of Bud than for one of Coors. In the basic competitive model, when firms contemplate how much to produce, they take the market price as given, and do not need to consider how their rivals will react. In the real world, many firms spend enormous energies trying to anticipate the actions and reactions of rivals. In Chapters 14–16, we will take up failures of competition in product markets and government responses to them. In Chapter 19, we will also encounter restricted competition in the labor market.

2. The basic model simply ignores technological change. It tells us about the striving for efficiency that occurs as consumers and firms meet in competitive markets, but it assumes that all firms operate with a given technology. Competition in the basic model is over price, yet in the real world, a primary focus of competition is the development of new and better products and the improvements in production, transportation, and marketing that allow products to be brought to customers at lower costs and thus at a lower price. This competition takes place not between the multitude of small producers envisaged in the basic competitive model, but often between the industrial giants like Du Pont and Dow Chemical, and between the industrial giants and upstarts, like IBM and the slew of small computer firms that eventually

took away a major share of the computer market. Chapter 17 will enrich the model to help us understand better this more general view of competition, and to enable us to see how technological change can be encouraged.

3. The individuals and firms envisioned in the basic model have easy and inexpensive access to the information they need in order to operate in any market they enter. Buyers know that they are buying, whether it is stocks or bonds, a house, a car, or a refrigerator. Firms know perfectly the productivity of each worker they hire, and when a worker goes to work for a firm, he knows precisely what is expected of him in return for his promised pay.

Imperfections of information and competition arise in all markets—in product, labor, and capital markets—and in each they take on different forms. Consider, for instance, the product market (Chapter 18). Consumers cannot ascertain all the characteristics of a product before they buy it; they rely in part on the seller's reputation. They may worry that if the price is too low, the product is likely to be shoddy; they use price in part to *judge* quality—a quite different role from that upon which Part Two focused, with important consequences.

Or consider the labor market, discussed in Chapter 19: in the basic model, the employer knows precisely what he wants the worker to do, and he knows whether the worker has done what he is supposed to do. The employer pays the worker if and only if he does what he was contracted for. Issues of incentives, of motivating workers, simply never arise. In practice, designing compensation schemes— often based on performance—to motivate workers is a central concern of management.

Or consider the capital market: a central issue facing firms is how best to meet their capital requirements, whether by borrowing or issuing new equity. A somewhat surprising implication of the basic competitive model is that how the firm raises its capital makes no difference. Chapter 20 explains how factors not taken into account in that basic model help us understand why it does make a difference, and how firms actually make these crucial decisions.

There are other important questions which the basic model does not address—because in that model the answer is either trivial or unimportant. For instance, *who* makes economic decisions makes no difference, when the outcome of that decision-making process would be the same whoever sat in the managers' chair. It would make no difference whether one firm took over another because the profit-maximizing decisions—what and how much should be produced and how it should be produced— would be the same in either case. But the decision about who manages a firm *is* an important decision; the takeover of one firm by another *can* have important consequences. Chapter 20 discusses some of the key issues concerning controlling and managing firms.

While beyond the scope of Part Three, the following points are noted here to complete our comparison of the competitive model and the real world.

4. The competitive model assumes that the costs of bringing a good to market accrue fully and completely to the seller, and that the benefits of consuming a good go fully and completely to the buyer.

In Chapter 7, however, we encountered the possibility of externalities, which are extra costs or benefits that do not figure in the market calculation. There may be positive externalities (such as national defense) and negative externalities (such as pollution). We will return to negative externalities in Part Four.

5. The basic model answers the question "What goods will be produced, and in what quantities?" by assuming that all desired goods that *can* be brought to market *will* be brought to market. Trees that bloom in gold coins and tablets that guarantee an eternal youth are out of the question. But if customers want to buy green hair coloring, cancer-causing tobacco products, or life insurance policies overladen with extras, then producers can be expected to supply such goods. However, there are many cases where markets have not provided goods or services that could be provided at a cost consumers would be willing to pay. Some of the most obvious examples are in insurance markets, where government has intervened with such programs as unemployment insurance, Social Security, and medical insurance for the aged. We first considered this problem of missing markets in Chapter 7, and will return to it in Part Four.

6. In the basic model, all markets clear—supply meets demand at the market price. Decades of evidence, however, suggest that labor markets often do not clear. The result is involuntary unemployment, sometimes on a massive scale. During the Great Depression, for instance, one out of four workers was out of a job. While beyond our scope in Part Three, the recurrence of involuntary unemployment in the economy is an important deviation from the competitive model of Part Two.

7. Even if markets are efficient, the way they allocate resources may appear to be socially unacceptable. We addressed this issue in Chapter 7, in the discussion of how government may redistribute income when the distribution produced by the market is deemed socially unacceptable. We will return to this subject in Part Four.

In the competitive model, there is little role for government, because markets ensure economic efficiency. The foregoing discussion highlights several reasons why there may be dissatisfaction with markets—why they may not in fact ensure efficiency or why, even if markets were efficient, the outcomes may not be acceptable. In each of these instances, government may be called upon. In each of the ensuing chapters, we will not only explore the limitations of the markets, but also describe and assess the roles government has undertaken to address those limitations.

THE BASIC MODEL VERSUS THE REAL WORLD

The Basic Model	The Real World
1. All markets are competitive.	1. Most markets are *not* characterized by the degree of competition envisioned in the basic model.
2. Technological know-how is fixed and cannot change.	2. Technological change is a central part of competition in modern industrial economies.
3. Firms, consumers, and any other market participants have easy access to information that is relevant to the markets in which they participate.	3. Good information may be impossible to come by, and in most cases is costly to obtain. In many markets, buyers of products know less than the sellers.
4. Sellers bear the full and complete costs of bringing goods to market, and buyers reap the full benefit.	4. Externalities mean that market transactions may not accurately account for costs and benefits and the private market provides an inadequate supply of public goods.
5. All desired markets exist.	5. Some markets may not exist, even though goods or services in that market might be provided at a cost consumers would be willing to pay.
6. There is no involuntary unemployment.	6. There is involuntary unemployment.
7. Competitive markets provide an efficient allocation of resources.	7. Efficiency is not enough. The income distribution generated by the market may be socially unacceptable.
8. There is little role for government.	8. Government plays an important role in the economy. Among its roles are correcting market failure, providing social insurance, and redistributing income.

CHAPTER 14

MONOPOLIES AND IMPERFECT COMPETITION

In the competitive model discussed in Part Two, markets have so many buyers and sellers that no individual household or firm believes its actions will affect the market equilibrium price. The buyer or seller takes the price as given, and then decides how much to buy or sell. At the "market" price, the seller can sell as much as she wants. But any effort to outfox the market has dramatic consequences. If, for instance, she raises her price above that of her competitors, her sales will be zero.

Not all markets are very competitive, however. For years, AT&T was the only long distance telephone carrier. Kodak controlled the market for film, and Alcoa the market for aluminum. Some firms so dominated a product that their brand name became synonymous with the product, as with Kleenex and Jell-O.

In some industries, such as soft drinks (Coca-Cola, Pepsi, Canada Dry), a handful of firms dominate a market, producing similar but not identical products. When one such firm raises its price a little—say, by 2 or 3 percent—it loses some customers but far from all. If it lowers its price by 2 or 3 percent, it gains additional customers, but not the entire market. As a result, these companies do not simply "take" the price as dictated to them by the market. They "make" the price. They are the **price makers.** Markets in which competition is limited are the subject of this chapter and the next.

1. If there is only one firm in a market—a monopoly—how does it set its price and output? In what sense is the monopoly price too high?

2. Why do firms with no competition or imperfect competition face downward-sloping demand curves?

3. What are the barriers to entry that limit the number of firms in a market?

4. What does equilibrium look like in a market with imperfect competition, where barriers to entry are small enough that profits are driven to zero, yet in which there are few enough firms that each faces a downward-sloping curve?

MARKET STRUCTURES

One way to simplify an economy is to break it up into its constituent markets. One market in the United States is the passenger car market, with Ford, General Motors, Chrysler, and various foreign firms the suppliers.

When economists look at markets, they look first at the **market structure,** that is, at how that market is organized. The market structure that forms the basis of the competitive model of Part Two is called perfect competition. For example, there are so many wheat farmers (producers) that no individual wheat farmer can realistically hope to move the price of wheat from that produced by the law of supply and demand.

Frequently, however, competition is not "perfect." Rather, it is limited. Economists group markets in which competition is limited into three broad structures. In the most extreme, there is no competition. A single firm supplies the entire market. This is called **monopoly.** Your local electric company probably has a monopoly in supplying electricity in your area. Since one would expect the profits of a monopolist to attract entry into that market, for a firm to maintain its monopoly position, there must be some barrier to entry. Below, we learn what these barriers are.

In the second structure, several firms supply the market, so there is *some* competition. This is called **oligopoly.** The automobile industry is an example, with three main producers in the United States. The defining characteristic of oligopolies is that the small number of firms forces each to be concerned with how its rivals will react to any action it undertakes. If General Motors offers low-interest-rate financing, for instance, the other companies may feel compelled to match the offer; and before making any such offer, GM will have to take this into account. By contrast, a monopolist has no rivals and thus considers only whether special offers help or hurt itself. And a firm facing perfect competition can sell as much as it wants at the market price without having to resort to any special offers.

In the third market structure, there are more firms than in an oligopoly, but not enough for perfect competition. This is called **monopolistic competition.** An example is the market for moderately priced clothing as represented by J. C. Penney, Sears, Kmart, and other such chains of stores. Each chain has its own make of clothing, which no other chain sells. But the clothing in each chain is similar enough to that supplied by other chains that there is considerable competition. Even so, the clothing supplied by the different chains is different enough to make competition limited, so that the chain is not a price taker. The degree of competition under monopolistic competition is greater than that of oligopoly. This is because monopolistic competition involves a sufficiently large number of firms that each firm can ignore the reactions of any rival. If one company lowers its price, it may garner for itself a large number of customers. But the number of customers it takes away from any single rival is so small that none of the rivals is motivated to retaliate.

With both oligopolies and monopolistic competition, there is some competition, but it is more limited than under perfect competition. These in-between market structures are referred to as **imperfect competition.**

ALTERNATIVE MARKET STRUCTURES

Perfect competition: Many, many firms; each believes that nothing it does will have any effect on the market price.

Monopoly: One firm.

Imperfect competition: Several firms, each aware that its sales depend on the price it charges and possibly other actions it takes, such as advertising. There are two special cases:

Oligopoly: Sufficiently few firms that each worries about how rivals will respond to any action it undertakes.

Monopolistic competition: Sufficiently many firms that each believes that its rivals will not change the price they charge should it lower its own price.

This chapter focuses on monopoly and monopolistic competition. Oligopolies are left for Chapter 15. We begin with an analysis of how a monopolist sets its price and quantity, and how monopoly outcomes compare with competitive outcomes. We then switch to imperfect competition, a more common structure, and analyze the principal determinants of competition within any market. We follow this with an analysis of the barriers to entry that enable imperfectly competitive firms to sustain higher than normal profits for long periods of time. The final section looks at the case where barriers to entry are weak enough that profits are driven to zero, but competition is still sufficiently limited that each firm can change its prices without losing all its customers.

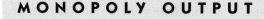

MONOPOLY OUTPUT

Economists' concerns about monopolies and other forms of restricted competition stem mainly from the observation that the output, or supply, of firms within these market structures is less than that of firms faced with perfect competition. To address these concerns, we consider a monopolist that charges the same price to all its customers and show how it determines its level of output.

A monopolist and a competitive firm are similar in some ways. Both try to maximize profits. In determining output, they compare the extra (or marginal) revenue they would receive from producing an extra unit of output with the extra (or marginal) cost of producing that extra unit. If marginal revenue exceeds marginal cost, it pays to expand output. Conversely if marginal revenue is less than marginal cost, it pays to reduce output. Thus, the basic principle for output determination for both a competitive firm and a monopolist is the same. Each produces at the output level at which marginal revenue equals marginal cost.

The essential difference between a monopolist and a competitive firm is that a competitive firm takes the price set by market forces. When such a firm increases production by one unit, its marginal revenue is just the price. For instance, the marginal revenue a wheat farmer receives from producing one more bushel of wheat is the price of a bushel of wheat. But the only way a monopolist can sell more is to lower the price it charges, so marginal revenue is *not* equal to the present market price.

The difference can be put another way. The demand curve facing a competitive firm is perfectly horizontal, as illustrated in Figure 14.1A. The price, p^*, is the "market price." The firm can sell as much as it wants at that price, and nothing at any higher price. In an industry such as wheat farming, if there are one million wheat farmers, each farmer on average accounts for one-millionth of the market. If a single average farmer even doubled his production, the total production would increase by one-millionth—a truly negligible amount that could be absorbed by the market with no perceptible change in price.

The demand curve facing a monopolist, in contrast, is downward sloping, as illustrated in Figure 14.1B. By definition, the monopolist controls the entire industry, so that a doubling of *its* output is a doubling of industry output, which will have a significant effect on price. If Alcoa, in the days when it had a monopoly on aluminum, had increased its production by 1 percent, the total supply of aluminum would have increased by 1 percent. Market prices would have fallen observably in response to a change in supply of even that magnitude.

The marginal revenue a monopolist receives from producing one more unit can be broken into two separate components. First, the firm receives revenue from selling the additional output. This additional revenue is just the market price. But to sell more, the firm must reduce its price. Unless it does

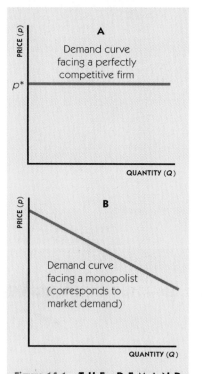

Figure 14.1 THE DEMAND CURVE FACING A PERFECTLY COMPETITIVE FIRM AND A MONOPOLIST

A price-taking, perfectly competitive firm can sell any quantity it wishes at the market price, but cannot raise the price at all without losing all its business. It faces the horizontal demand curve shown in panel A. A monopolist provides all the output in a market, so an increased amount can only be sold at a reduced price. Panel B shows the downward-sloping demand curve—the market demand curve—faced by a monopolist.

so, it cannot sell the extra output. Marginal revenue is the price it receives from the sale of the one additional unit *minus* the loss in revenues from the price reduction on all other units. Thus, for a monopolist, the marginal revenue for producing one extra unit is always less than the price received for that extra unit. (Only at the "first" unit produced are marginal revenue and price the same.)

This can be represented by a simple equation:

marginal revenue = net increase in revenue from selling one more unit

$$= \text{price} + \Delta p \times Q$$

where Δp represents the change in price and Q represents the initial quantity sold. For a competitive firm, $\Delta p = 0$, so marginal revenue equals price. For a monopolist, Δp is negative, so marginal revenue is less than the price.

Figure 14.2A shows the output decision of a competitive firm. Marginal revenue is just equal to the market price, $p*$. Panel B shows the output decision of a monopolist. Marginal revenue is always less than price. Note that with a monopoly, since marginal revenue is less than price and marginal revenue equals marginal cost, marginal cost is less than price. The price is what individuals are willing to pay for an extra unit of the product; it measures the marginal benefit to the consumer of an extra unit. Thus, the marginal benefit of

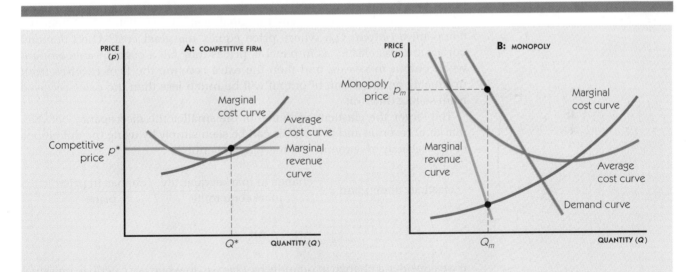

Figure 14.2 MARGINAL REVENUE EQUALS MARGINAL COST

A perfectly competitive firm gains or loses exactly the market price ($p*$) when it changes the quantity produced by one unit. To maximize profits, the firm produces the quantity where marginal cost equals marginal revenue, which in the competitive case also equals price. Panel B shows the downward-sloping marginal revenue curve for a monopolist. A monopolist also chooses the level of quantity where marginal cost equals marginal revenue. In the monopolistic case, however, marginal revenue is lower than price.

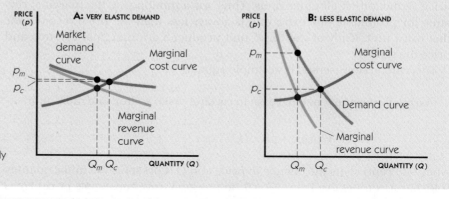

Figure 14.3 MONOPOLY AND THE ELASTICITY OF DEMAND

In panel A, a monopoly faces a very elastic market demand, so prices do not fall much as output increases, and monopoly price is not much more than the competitive price. In panel B, a monopoly faces a less elastic market demand, so price falls quite a lot as output increases, and price is substantially above the competitive price.

an extra unit exceeds the marginal cost. This is the fundamental reason that monopolies reduce economic efficiency.[1]

The extent to which output is curtailed depends on the magnitude of the difference between marginal revenue and price. This in turn depends on the shape of the demand curve. When demand curves are very elastic (relatively flat), prices do not fall much when output increases. As shown in Figure 14.3A, marginal revenue is not much less than price. The firm produces at Q_m, where marginal revenue equals marginal cost. Q_m is slightly less than the competitive output, Q_c, where price equals marginal cost. When demand curves are less elastic, as in panel B, prices may fall a considerable amount when output increases, and then the extra revenue the firm receives from producing an extra unit of output will be much less than the price received from selling that unit.

The larger the elasticity of demand, the smaller the discrepancy between marginal revenue and price. This can be seen simply by using the definitions of the elasticity of demand and marginal revenue:

$$\text{elasticity of demand} = -\frac{\text{change in market quantity}}{\text{market quantity}} \bigg/ \frac{\text{change in price}}{\text{price}}$$

$$= -\frac{\Delta Q}{Q} \bigg/ \frac{\Delta p}{p}.$$

If we consider a change in quantity by 1 (as we do when we calculate marginal revenue), so that $\Delta Q = 1$,

$$\text{elasticity of demand} = -\frac{1}{Q} \bigg/ \frac{\Delta p}{p} = -\frac{p}{\Delta p \times Q}, \text{ and}$$

[1]Chapter 16 will describe more precisely how the magnitudes of the losses associated with monopoly can be quantified.

marginal revenue = price + change in price × quantity sold

$$= p + (\Delta p \times Q)$$

$$= p \left(1 + \frac{\Delta p \times Q}{p} \right)$$

$$= p \, (1 - 1/\text{elasticity of demand}).$$

Hence, if the elasticity of demand is 2, marginal revenue is ½ of price. If the elasticity of demand is 10, marginal revenue is 9/10 of price.

THE FIRM'S SUPPLY DECISION

All firms maximize profits at the point where marginal revenue (the revenue from selling an extra unit of the product) equals marginal cost.

For a competitive firm, marginal revenue equals price.

For a monopoly, marginal revenue is less than price.

AN EXAMPLE: THE ABC-MENT COMPANY

Table 14.1 gives the demand curve facing the ABC-ment Company, which has a monopoly on the production of cement in its area. There is a particular price at which it can sell each level of output. As it lowers its price, it can sell

Table 14.1 DEMAND CURVE FACING ABC-MENT COMPANY

Cubic yards (thousands)	Price	Total revenues	Marginal revenues	Total costs	Marginal costs
1	$10,000	$10,000	$8,000	$15,000	$2,000
2	$ 9,000	$18,000	$6,000	$17,000	$3,000
3	$ 8,000	$24,000	$4,000	$20,000	$4,000
4	$ 7,000	$28,000	$2,000	$24,000	$5,000
5	$ 6,000	$30,000	0	$29,000	$6,000
6	$ 5,000	$30,000		$35,000	

more cement. Local builders will, for instance, use more cement and less wood and other materials in constructing a house.

For simplicity, we assume cement is sold in units of 1,000 cubic yards. At a price of $10,000 per unit (of 1,000 cubic yards), the firm sells 1 unit, at a price of $9,000, it sells 2 units, and at a price of $8,000, 3 units. The third column of the table shows the total revenues at each of these levels of production. The total revenues are just price times quantity. The marginal revenue from producing an extra unit (of 1,000 cubic yards) is just the difference between, say, the revenues received at 3 units and 2 units or 2 units and 1 unit. Notice that in each case, the marginal revenue is less than the price.

Figure 14.4 shows the demand and marginal revenues curves, using data from Table 14.1. At each level of output, the marginal revenue curve lies below the demand curve. As can be seen from the table, not only does price decrease as output increases, but so does marginal revenue.

The output at which marginal revenues equal marginal costs—the output chosen by the profit-maximizing monopolist—is denoted by Q_m. In our example, $Q_m = 4,000$ cubic yards. When the number of cubic yards increases from 3,000 to 4,000, the marginal revenue is $4,000, and so is the marginal cost. At this level of output, the price, p_m, is $7,000 (per 1,000 cubic yards), which is considerably in excess of marginal costs, $4,000. Total revenues, $28,000, are also in excess of total costs, $24,000.[2]

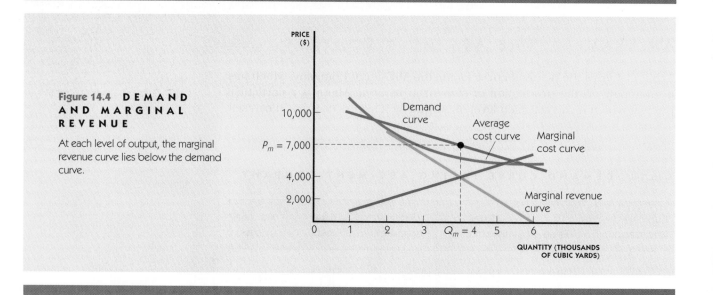

Figure 14.4 DEMAND AND MARGINAL REVENUE

At each level of output, the marginal revenue curve lies below the demand curve.

---

[2]In this example, the firm is indifferent between producing 3,000 or 4,000 cubic yards. If the marginal cost of producing the extra output exceeds $4,000 by a little, then it will produce 3,000 cubic yards; if the marginal cost is a little less than $4,000, then it will produce 4,000 cubic yards.

The relationship between monopoly and competitive prices can easily be calculated using the formula in the text:

$$MR = \text{marginal revenue} =$$
$$p\,(1 - 1/\text{elasticity of demand}).$$

A monopolist sets marginal revenue equal to marginal cost. Assume marginal cost is constant, at MC. Then

$$MC = p\,(1 - 1/\text{elasticity of demand})$$

or

$$p = \frac{MC}{1 - 1/\text{elasticity of demand}}$$

By contrast, we saw that in a competitive industry, price equals marginal cost,

$$p = MC.$$

Thus, in a monopoly, price is higher by the factor,

$$\frac{1}{1 - 1/\text{elasticity of demand}}$$

If the elasticity of demand everywhere along the demand curve is 2, we calculate,

$$\frac{1}{1 - 1/2} = 2.$$

The monopoly price is twice as high. If marginal cost is $1, the competitive price is a dollar and the monopoly price is $2.

What happens now if a tax is imposed on producers, raising the marginal cost of production from $1 to $1.50? In a competitive economy, the price increases by the full amount of the tax. Though the tax is imposed on the producers, the producers *shift* the burden of the tax on to consumers. In a monopoly, the price increases to $3.00. The price is more than fully shifted! A 50 cent tax results in consumers having to pay a dollar more for the product.

MONOPOLY PROFITS

Monopolists maximize their profits by setting marginal revenue equal to marginal cost. The total level of monopoly profits can be seen in two ways, as shown in Figure 14.5. Panel A shows total revenues and total costs (from Table 14.1) for each level of output of the ABC-ment Company. The difference between revenues and costs is profits—the distance between the two curves. This distance is maximized at the output $Q_m = 4{,}000$ cubic yards. We can see that at this level of output, profits are $4,000 ($28,000 − $24,000). Panel B calculates profits using the average cost diagram. Total profits are equal to the profit per unit multiplied by the number of units produced. The profit per unit is the difference between the unit price and the average cost, and total monopoly profits is the shaded area $ABCD$. Again, the sum is $4,000: ($7,000 − $6,000) × 4.

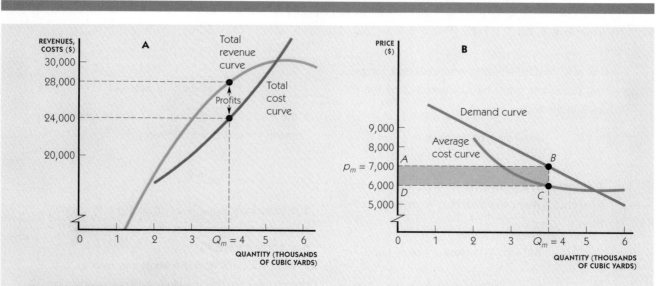

Figure 14.5 PRICE EXCEEDING AVERAGE COST MEANS PROFIT

Panel A shows profits to be the distance between the total revenue and total cost curves, maximized at the output $Q_m = 4,000$ cubic yards. Profits occur when the market price is above average cost, as in panel B, so that the company is (on average) making a profit on each unit it sells. Monopoly profits are the area *ABCD*, which is average profit per unit times the number of units sold.

A monopolist enjoys an extra return because it has been able to reduce its output and increase its price from the level that would have prevailed under competition. This return is called a **pure profit.** Because these payments are not required to elicit greater effort or production on the part of the monopolist (in fact, they derive from the monopolist's *reducing* the output from what it would be under competition), they are also called **monopoly rents.**

PRICE DISCRIMINATION

The basic objective of monopolists is to maximize profits, and they accomplish this by setting marginal revenue equal to marginal cost, so price exceeds marginal cost. Monopolists can also engage in a variety of other practices to increase their profits. Among the most important is **price discrimination,** which means charging different prices to different customers or in different markets.

Figure 14.6 shows a monopolist setting marginal revenue equal to marginal cost in the United States and in Japan. The demand curves the firm faces in the two countries are different. Therefore, though marginal costs are the same, the firm will charge different prices for the same good in the two countries. (By contrast, in competitive markets, price equals marginal cost, so that regardless of the shape of the demand curves, price will be the same in the

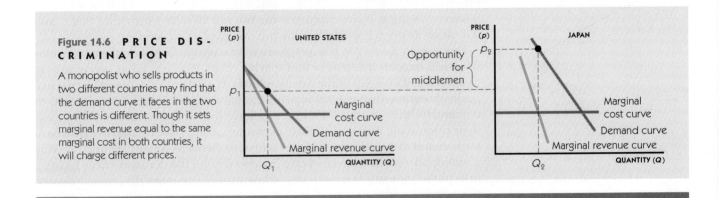

Figure 14.6 PRICE DIS-CRIMINATION

A monopolist who sells products in two different countries may find that the demand curve it faces in the two countries is different. Though it sets marginal revenue equal to the same marginal cost in both countries, it will charge different prices.

two markets, except for the different costs of delivering the good to each market.) With prices in the two countries differing, middlemen firms will enter the market, buying the product in the country with the low price and selling it in the other country. A company may attempt to thwart the middlemen—as many Japanese companies do—by, for instance, having distinct labels on the two products and refusing to provide service or honor any guarantees outside the country in which the good is originally delivered.

Within a country, a monopolist can also price discriminate *if* resale is difficult and *if* it can distinguish between buyers with high and low elasticities of demand. An electricity company can make its charge for each kilowatt hour depend on how much electricity the customer uses, because of restrictions on the retransmission of electricity. If the company worries that large customers faced with the same high prices that it charges small customers might install their own electric generators, or switch to some other energy source, it may charge them a lower price. An airline with a monopoly on a particular route might charge business customers a higher fare than vacationers. They do so knowing that business customers have no choice but to make the trip, while vacationers have many alternatives. They can travel elsewhere, on another day, or by car or train. Such business practices enable the monopolist to increase its profits relative to what they would be if it charged a single price in the market. Firms facing imperfect competition also engage in these practices as we will see. Airlines again provide a telling example. Though the Robinson-Patman Act, which Congress passed in 1936, was designed to restrict price discrimination, it is only partially successful.

IMPERFECT COMPETITION

In most markets, there is more than a single firm. In the perfectly competitive model of Part Two, firms compete against one another while believing they cannot affect the price—that if they raise their price, they will lose all their business. But outside agriculture, imperfect competition is more typical. Firms compete, often vigorously, against one another. But each believes that if it lowers its price, it can capture some but not all sales from other firms; and if it raises its price it will lose some but not all of its customers.

One way to assess the competitiveness of a particular market is to consider what will happen if a firm in that market raises its price. What percentage of its sales will it lose—in other words, what is its elasticity of demand? Firms in a perfectly competitive market face horizontal demand curves. The elasticity of demand for their output is infinite. Similarly, they are price takers. If they raise their price at all, they lose all their customers. They have no **market power,** a term meant to suggest the ability of a firm to throw its weight around, the way a monopoly can. As imperfect competition sets in, the demand curve facing a firm in the industry begins to slope downward. The more downward sloping the demand curve, the more market power the firm has.

Two factors affect the elasticity of the demand curve facing a firm, and, therefore, its market power. The first is the number of firms in the industry—more generally, how concentrated is production within a few firms. The second is how different are the goods produced by the various firms in the industry.

NUMBER OF FIRMS IN THE INDUSTRY

Competition is likely to be greater when there are many firms in an industry (textiles, shoes) than when a few companies dominate (home refrigerators and freezers, greeting cards, soft drinks). Table 14.2 gives the percentage of output that is produced by the top four firms in a variety of industries ranging from breakfast cereals to wood household furniture. The fraction of output produced by the top four firms in an industry is called the **four-firm concentration ratio,** one of several measures used to study industry concentration. When the four-firm percentage is high, as in the automobile or copper industry, companies have considerable market power. This is true even when they produce similar or identical products, as in the case of copper. When it is low, as in the case of furniture or women's clothes, market power is low; each firm faces a practically horizontal demand curve.[3]

PRODUCT DIFFERENTIATION

In addition to the number of firms in a market—and how concentrated production is—the amount of competition depends on how similar are the goods produced by different firms. In some industries, the goods produced are essentially identical—copper produced by Kennecott Copper is essentially identical to that produced by Anaconda Copper. More typically, the firms in an in-

Table 14.2 DEGREE OF COMPETITION IN VARIOUS INDUSTRIES

	Market share of top 4 firms (percent)
Breakfast cereals	81
Burial caskets	53
Motor vehicles and car bodies	92
Primary copper	92
Semiconductors and related devices	36
Women's suits and coats	14
Wood household furniture	15

Source: Census of Manufacturing (1982), vol. 7, Table 6.

---

[3]In both theory and practice, a critical issue in evaluating the extent of competition is defining the relevant market, an issue taken up in Chapter 16.

dustry with imperfect competition produce goods that are **imperfect substitutes**—goods sufficiently similar that they can be used for many of the same purposes, but different enough that one may be somewhat better than another, at least for some purposes or in some people's minds. Kellogg's Corn Flakes and the store brand may look alike. But more people purchase the Kellogg's version, even though it is more expensive.

The fact that similar products nonetheless differ from one another is referred to as **product differentiation.** Firms in imperfect markets spend considerable effort to produce goods that are slightly different from those of their competitors.

SOURCES OF PRODUCT DIFFERENTIATION

Many of the differences between products can be seen, heard, or tasted by consumers. But geography can also provide the basis for product differentiation. People are willing to pay more for service at a neighborhood garage, rather than drive fifty miles to a discount garage. They are willing to pay more for milk at the neighborhood grocery store than at the supermarket out on the main road.

In cases where consumers find it difficult to assess the quality of a product before they purchase it, they rely heavily on firm reputations. They may buy Bayer aspirin even though it is more expensive than the store brand, because they believe it is of a higher quality. (In fact, aspirin itself is just acetylsalicylic acid, nothing more or less. Still, the binding agents that hold the pill together may differ, so the effects may differ.) Consumers are often willing to pay more for goods with a trademark than for generic brands.

Ignorance and the costs of obtaining information often make the products of one firm an imperfect substitute for another. A consumer sees a dress for $45. She might know or suspect that some other store is selling the same dress for $35, but she does not know where, she is not sure it is in stock there, it will cost her money to drive around looking for it, and so she buys the dress at $45 anyway. If the store had raised its price to $55, she probably would have made the effort to search. If a store raises its prices, more customers decide to search out the bargains, and sales go down.

HOW PRODUCT DIFFERENTIATION IMPLIES IMPERFECT COMPETITION

When goods are perfect substitutes, individuals will choose whichever is cheapest. In an imaginary world where all brands of cornflakes really are perfect substitutes for all consumers, they would all sell at the same price. If one brand lowered its price slightly, all consumers (assuming they knew this) would switch to it. If it raised its price slightly, all consumers would switch to the rival brand. That is why the demand curve facing the manufacturer of a perfectly substitutable good is horizontal, as illustrated in Figure 14.7A.

By contrast, if most consumers view the different brands as imperfect substitutes, the demand curve facing each firm will be downward sloping as in panel B. This, we have already learned, implies a departure from perfect competition. Some individuals may prefer sogginess and be willing to pay more for cornflakes that rapidly become soggy. Others may prefer crispness and be

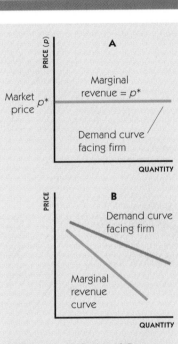

Figure 14.7 **DEMAND CURVES WITH PERFECT AND IMPERFECT COMPETITION**

Panel A shows the demand curve for a perfectly competitive firm: if it raises its price, all its customers will find substitutes. The marginal revenue curve for the firm is the same as its demand curve. Panel B shows the demand curve and marginal revenue curve facing a firm with only imperfect substitutes for its products.

willing to pay more for cereal that does not become soggy. Assume that Kellogg's Corn Flakes become soggy more slowly than the store brand. As the price for Kellogg's increases above that of the store brand, individuals who care less about crispness will switch to the store brand. They are not willing to pay the price differential. But some are willing to pay a lot more for crisp flakes. Hence, Kellogg's does not lose all its customers, even if it charges considerably more than the store brand. By the same token, when Kellogg's lowers its price below that of the store brand, it does not steal all the customers. Those who love sogginess will pay more for the store brand.

It matters little whether the differences between the brands are true or simply perceived differences. The store brand and Kellogg's Corn Flakes could be identical, but if Kellogg's advertisements have convinced some consumers that there is a difference, they will not switch even if the price of Kellogg's is higher. Numerous studies attest to the fact that consumers often see differences where none exist. One study put the same soap into two kinds of packages, one marked Brand A, the other marked Brand B. Homemakers were asked to judge which brand cleaned their clothes more effectively. Half saw no difference, but the other half claimed to see significant differences. Another study put the same beer into three kinds of bottles, one labeled premium, the second labeled standard, the third labeled discount. After drinking the differently bottled beers over an extended period of time, consumers were asked which they preferred. The "premium" beer was chosen consistently.

BASES OF PRODUCT DIFFERENTIATION

1. Differences in characteristics of products

2. Differences in location of different firms

3. Perceived differences, often induced by advertising

BARRIERS TO ENTRY: WHY IS COMPETITION LIMITED?

Normally, profits attract other firms to enter the market. For a monopoly to persist, some factors must prevent competition from springing up. Similarly, when there are profits with imperfect competition, some factors must prevent other firms' entering and eroding those profits. Such factors are called **barriers to entry.** They take a variety of forms, ranging from government rules that prohibit or limit competition (for reasons that may be good or bad), to technological reasons that naturally limit the number of firms in a market, to market strategies that keep potential competitors at bay.

When there are few barriers to entry, a monopoly can only be temporary—the profits of the monopolist will attract entry, and the firm's monopoly position will be lost. When there are many barriers, even if they only serve to delay entry, there *is* cause for concern, particularly when firms themselves take actions to create the barriers.

GOVERNMENT POLICIES

Many early monopolies were established by governments. In the seventeenth century, the British government gave the East India Company a monopoly on trade with India. The salt monopoly in eighteenth-century France had the exclusive right to sell salt. Even today, governments grant certain monopoly franchises; for example, government grants monopolies for electric and telephone service within a locality.

The most important monopolies granted by government today, however, are patents. As we learned in Chapter 1, a patent gives inventors the exclusive right to produce or to license others to produce their discoveries for a limited period of time, currently seventeen years. The argument for patents is that without them, copycat firms would spring up with every new invention, inventors would make little money from their discoveries, and there would be no economic incentive to invent. The framers of the U.S. Constitution thought invention so important that they included a provision enabling the newly created federal government to grant patents.

Occasionally governments set policies that restrict entry, allowing some, but only limited, competition. Licensing requirements in many of the professions (law, accounting, medicine), whose ostensible purpose is to protect consumers against incompetent practitioners, may at the same time limit the number of qualified practitioners, and thus limit competition.

SINGLE OWNERSHIP OF AN ESSENTIAL INPUT

Another barrier to entry and source of monopoly power is a firm's exclusive ownership of something that is not producible. For example, an aluminum company might attempt to become a monopolist in aluminum by buying all the sources of bauxite, the essential ingredient. A single South African company, De Beers, has come close to monopolizing the world's supply of diamonds. There are in fact relatively few instances of such monopolies.

INFORMATION

Information does not pass through the economy in the full and complete way envisioned in the basic competitive model of Part Two. In considering barriers to entry, we encounter two of many ways that information—and the lack

POLICY PERSPECTIVE: USING PATENTS TO MAINTAIN A MONOPOLY—THE CASE OF XEROX

Market strategies and patents can be—and have been—used in combination by companies to maintain a dominant position long after the initial patent has expired. While patents encourage innovation, abuses can lead not only to higher prices, but in some cases even a slower pace of innovation. But identifying abuses is not always easy.

You may have heard someone say, "I'm going to Xerox that document." What that person usually means is, "I'm going to photocopy that document on a machine that may or may not have been made by Xerox." Until the early 1970s, the Xerox company was almost synonymous with photocopying. The company had invented the photocopier; it held a group of more than 1,700 closely interrelated patents on the photocopying process; and it received about 95 percent of all copying machine sales in the United States.

In 1972, the Federal Trade Commission charged that Xerox was using its many patents as a way of monopolizing the photocopy market. Instead of using the patents to protect a new invention for a limited amount of time, the FTC argued, Xerox was making them part of a strategy to monopolize the market indefinitely.

After several years of investigation and argument, a "consent order" was announced. Essentially, Xerox did not admit it had done anything wrong, but it agreed to change anyway. In July 1975, Xerox agreed to allow other competitors to use its patents and even to give its competitors access to some future patents. In addition, Xerox was required to drop all outstanding lawsuits against other companies for infringing on its

patents. A spokesman for the FTC maintained that these steps (and some others) would "eliminate the principal sources of Xerox's dominance of the office copier industry."

No longer fearing a lawsuit for infringing on a Xerox patent, entrants started pouring into the photocopy market, led by the Japanese firm

thereof—affects market outcomes. First, firms engage in research to give them a technological advantage over competitors. Even if they do not get a patent, it will take time before what they learn disseminates to rivals. The fact that firms outside the industry do not know the trade secrets of the industry provides an important barrier to entry. Coca-Cola helps maintain its position in the soft drink market by guarding its formula with the greatest care.

Second, consumers have imperfect information concerning the products being sold by different firms. As a new firm, you must not only let potential buyers know about your product, you must convince them that the product is a better value than that of your rivals. When goods differ markedly in qualities that cannot easily be detected, it may not suffice simply to sell at a lower price. Customers may interpret the lower price as signaling lower quality. Thus, to get customers to try your product, you may have to advertise heavily and give away free samples. Entry costs like these constitute another significant barrier to entry.

ECONOMIES OF SCALE AND NATURAL MONOPOLIES

The technology needed to produce a good can sometimes result in a market with only one or very few firms. For example, it would be inefficient to have two firms construct power lines on each street in a city, with one company delivering electricity to one house and another company to the house next door. Likewise, in most locales, there is only one gravel pit or concrete plant. These situations are called **natural monopolies.**

A natural monopoly occurs whenever the average costs of production for a single firm are declining up to levels of output beyond those likely to emerge in the market. When the average costs of production fall as the scale of production increases, we say there are economies of scale, a concept first introduced in Chapter 11. In Figure 14.8, the demand curve facing a monopoly intersects the average cost curve at an output level at which average costs are still declining. At large enough outputs, average costs might start to increase, but that level of output is irrelevant to the actual market equilibrium. For instance, firms in the cement industry have U-shaped average cost curves, and

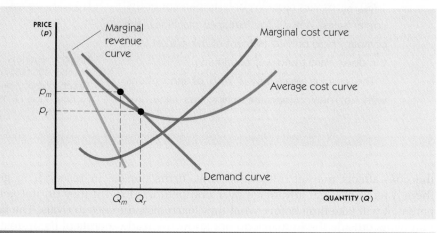

Figure 14.8 NATURAL MONOPOLY

In a natural monopoly, market demand intersects average cost in the downward-sloping portion of the average cost curve, at quantity Q_r and price p_r. Any firm that attempts to enter the market and produce less than Q_r will have higher average costs than the natural monopoly. Any firm that tries to enter the market and produce more than Q_r will find that it cannot sell all its output at a price that will cover its average costs.

the level of output at which costs are minimized is quite high. Accordingly, in smaller, isolated communities, there is a natural monopoly in cement.

A natural monopolist is protected by the knowledge that it can undercut its rivals should they enter. Since entrants typically are smaller and average costs decline with size, their average costs are higher. Therefore the monopolist feels relatively immune from the threat of entry. So long as it does not have to worry about entry, it acts like any other monopolist, setting marginal revenue equal to marginal cost, as in Figure 14.8, where it produces at the output Q_m and charges p_m.

Whether a particular industry is a natural monopoly depends on the size of the output at which average costs are minimized relative to the size of the market. With high enough demand, the monopolist will be operating along the rising part of the average cost curve. At this point, the monopolist can be undercut by an entrant, since a new firm that enters at the output at which average costs are minimized has costs that are lower. Thus, with high enough demand, the industry is no longer a natural monopoly. In medium-sized cities, there may be several producers of cement, so that instead of a monopoly, there is an oligopoly.

Among the most important determinants of market size are transportation costs. Among the most important determinants of the quantity of output at which average costs are minimized is the size of the fixed costs. The larger the expenditures of the firm just to begin production, the larger the scale of production at which average costs are minimized.

ECONOMIES OF SCALE AND IMPERFECT COMPETITION

Fixed costs also help explain why only a limited number of firms produce each variety of a good, and why the variety of goods is limited. Setting up dies to make a slight variant of an existing car, for example, may be very expensive. Similarly, automobile companies tend to produce cars in only a limited range of colors. Some individuals might prefer a car that is bright orange but most car manufacturers do not offer this option. Presumably this is because they realize that additional costs to paint some cars bright orange would exceed the marginal revenue they would receive from providing this option.

Because both technology and transportation costs may change over time, the number of firms in a market may change. Long-distance telephone service used to be a natural monopoly. Telephone messages were transmitted over wires, and it would have been inefficient to duplicate wires. As the demand for telephone services increased, and as alternative technologies like satellites developed, long-distance service ceased to be a natural monopoly. Today, a large number of firms compete to provide long-distance services.

MARKET STRATEGIES

Some monopolies and oligopolies cannot be explained by any of the factors discussed so far. They are not the result of government policies and are not natural monopolies; nor can information problems explain the lack of entry. Many firms, whose original monopoly position may have been based on some technological innovation or patent, manage to maintain their dominant positions even after their patents expire, at least for a time. IBM, Kodak, and Polaroid are three examples. These firms maintained their dominant positions by the pursuit of market strategies that deterred other firms from entering the market.

When a company thinks about entering an industry dominated by a single firm, it must assess not only the current level of profits being earned by that firm but also what profits will be like after it has entered. If a potential entrant believes that the incumbent firm is likely to respond to entry by lowering its price and fighting a fierce competitive battle, then the potential newcomer may come to believe that while prices and profits look high now, they are likely to drop precipitously if it actually does enter the market.

Established firms would thus like to pursue a strategy to convince potential entrants that even though they are currently making high levels of profit, these profits will disappear should the new firm enter the market. There are three major ways to create this belief, collectively called **entry-deterring practices:** predatory pricing, excess capacity, and limit pricing.

Predatory Pricing   If prices have fallen drastically in a certain market every time there has been entry in the past, then new firms may be reluctant to enter. An incumbent firm may deliberately lower its price below the new entrant's cost of production, in order to drive the new arrival out and discourage future entry. The incumbent also may lose money in the process, but it hopes to recoup the losses when the entrant leaves and it is free to raise prices to the monopoly level. This practice is called **predatory pricing** and is an illegal trade practice. However, shifting technologies and shifting demand often make it difficult to ascertain whether a firm has actually engaged in predatory pricing or simply lowered its price to meet the competition. Firms that lower their prices always claim that they were "forced" to do so by their competitors.

While allegations of predation are not uncommon, the courts have set high standards of proof. Thus, in one of the more recent cases, Liggett, a tobacco company that sells low-priced generic cigarettes that cut into name-brand sales, claimed that Brown & Williamson had engaged in predation. The charge was that B&W wanted Liggett to raise its prices and thus shift demand back to B&W's name brands. B&W lowered prices on its brands as a warning to Liggett to do B&W's bidding. In the lower court a jury found in favor of Liggett. The Supreme Court reversed the lower court's judgment, however, in a 1993 decision.

Excess Capacity   Another action firms can take to convince potential rivals that prices are likely to fall if they enter the market is to build up production facilities in excess of those currently needed. By building extra plants and equipment, even if they are rarely used, a firm poses an extra threat to potential entrants. A newcomer will look at this **excess capacity** and realize that the incumbent firm can increase production a great deal with minimal effort. The excess capacity serves as a signal that the incumbent is willing and able to engage in fierce price competition.

Limit Pricing   Other strategies for deterring entry involve clever patterns of pricing. A potential entrant may know what price is charged on the market and may have a good idea of its own costs of production. But it is not likely to know precisely the cost curve of the incumbent firm. The established firm can try to persuade potential entrants that its marginal costs are low, and that it could easily reduce its price if threatened with a new entrant to the market.

Suppose a potential entrant knows that a monopolist firm's marginal revenue is 70 percent of price. If the monopolist charges a price of $10, then the marginal revenue (the extra revenue from selling one more unit) is $7. Reasoning that the monopolist is setting marginal revenue equal to marginal cost, the potential entrant might use a $7 marginal cost figure in deciding whether it pays to enter.

The monopolist is aware that such a calculation is probably going on. Thus, it has an incentive to make its costs look lower than they are—and hence to make entry look less attractive than it really is. It can do this by lowering the price it charges. If it can persuade the potential entrant that marginal costs have to be below $6 (rather than $7) for entry to be profitable, it has protected its monopoly position that much better. This is an example of a broader practice known as **limit pricing,** in which firms charge less than the ordinary monopoly price and produce at a level beyond that at which marginal revenue equals marginal cost because they are afraid that at higher prices, entry will be encouraged. This may happen simply because a firm realizes that high profits attract attention. The more attention is focused on a market, the more likely it is that some entrepreneur will believe that entry is profitable.

Some entry-deterring devices, such as maintaining excess capacity, may be socially wasteful. Others, such as limit pricing, will benefit consumers, and partially temper deleterious effects of monopoly or limited competition.

BARRIERS TO ENTRY

Government policies: These include grants of monopoly (patents) and restrictions on entry (licensing).

Single ownership of an essential input: When a single firm owns the entire supply of a nonproducible input, entry is by definition precluded.

Information: Lack of technical information by potential competitors inhibits their entry; lack of information by consumers concerning the quality of a new entrant's product discourages consumers from switching to the new product, and thus inhibits entry.

Economies of scale: With a natural monopoly, economies of scale are so strong that it is efficient to have only one firm in an industry.

Market strategies: These include actions (such as predatory pricing, excess capacity, and limit pricing) aimed at convincing potential entrants that entry would be met with resistance, and thus would be unprofitable.

EQUILIBRIUM WITH MONOPOLISTIC COMPETITION

Barriers to entry are sufficiently weak in some markets that firms enter to the point where profits are driven to zero. But even then competition is imperfect, if products are differentiated. With each firm producing a slightly different product, each faces a downward-sloping demand curve. In this section, we analyze the case where fixed costs are sufficiently large to ensure that each firm faces a downward-sloping demand curve, but where there are *enough* firms so that each firm can ignore the consequences of its actions on others. This is the case of monopolistic competition, first analyzed by Edward Chamberlin of Harvard University in 1933.

Figure 14.9 illustrates a market in which there is monopolistic competition. Assume initially that all firms are charging the same price, say p_1. If one firm were to charge a slightly lower price, it would steal some customers away from other stores. If there were twenty firms in the market, this price-cutting firm would attract more than one-twentieth of the total market demand. And if it should raise its price above that of its rivals, it would lose customers to them. Each firm assumes that the prices charged by other firms will remain unchanged as it changes its price or the quantity it produces. The demand curve facing each firm is thus the one shown in the figure.

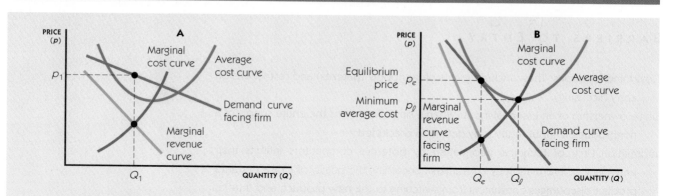

Figure 14.9 PROFIT-MAXIMIZING FOR A MONOPOLISTIC COMPETITOR

A monopolistic competitor chooses the quantity it will produce by setting marginal revenue equal to marginal cost (Q_1), and then selling that quantity for the price given on its demand curve (p_1). In panel A, the price charged is above average cost, and the monopolistic competitor is making a profit, enticing other firms to enter the market. As firms enter, the share of the market demand of each firm is reduced, and the demand curve facing each firm shifts to the left. Entry continues until the demand curve just touches the average cost curve (panel B). When the firm produces Q_e, it just breaks even; there is no incentive either for entry or exit.

In deciding how much to produce, the firm sets marginal revenue equal to marginal cost. The market equilibrium is (p_1, Q_1), with marginal revenue equaling marginal cost. In the equilibrium depicted in the figure, price exceeds average costs. One can think of this situation as a sort of minimonopoly, where each firm has a monopoly on its own brand name or its own store location.

But if existing firms are earning monopoly profits, there is an incentive for new competitors to enter the market until profits are driven to zero, as in the perfectly competitive model. *This is the vital distinction between monopolies and monopolistic competition.* In both cases, firms face downward-sloping demand curves. In both cases, they set marginal revenue equal to marginal cost. But in monopolistic competition, there are no barriers to entry. Entry continues so long as profits are positive. As firms enter, the share of the industry demand of each firm is reduced. The demand curve facing each firm thus shifts to the left, as depicted in panel B. This process continues until the demand curve just touches the average cost curve, at point (p_e, Q_e). At that point, profits are zero.

The figure also shows the firm's marginal revenue and marginal cost curves. As we have said, the firm sets its marginal revenue equal to its marginal cost. This occurs at exactly the level of output at which the demand curve is tangent to the average cost curve. This is because at any other point, average costs exceed price, so profits are negative. Only at this point are profits zero. Accordingly, this is the profit-maximizing output.

The monopolistic competition equilibrium has some interesting character-

CLOSE-UP: IBM—FROM THE EDGE OF MONOPOLY TO THE EDGE OF COMPETITION

IBM committed itself to computers in the 1950s, and rapidly asserted its dominance in the business of large "mainframe" computers. IBM machines were often the most technologically advanced, and in the few cases where they might not have been the best, they still had an extraordinary reputation for great service and support. Back in the days when computers were more than a little mysterious to most of their users, that reputation mattered a lot.

IBM was never a literal monopoly. Throughout the 1960s and 1970s, competition came from firms like Control Data, Honeywell, Sperry Univac, Burroughs, and NCR. But by 1980, IBM still had over 80 percent of the world market for mainframe computers. It was common for the company's sales to grow every year by double-digit percentages.

But by the early 1990s, its market share had slipped dramatically. In 1990, it had only 15 percent of the fastest-growing segment of the market, personal computers. Upstarts—Apple, Compaq, Dell, AST—as well as foreign producers—NEC and Toshiba—dominated the market. IBM was forced to make dramatic cutbacks. For the first time in its history, there were massive layoffs. It engaged in large-scale restructuring, trying to make itself "nimble" enough to compete in the fast-moving market. Less than two decades after the Justice Department had tried to break up IBM, charging that it was too close to a monopoly, it was scrambling for market share. It is a real world example of Joseph Schumpeter's vision of markets with dominant firms only able to maintain their position temporarily in the face of intense technological competition from new entrants (see page 358).

istics. Notice that in equilibrium, price and average costs exceed the minimum average costs at which the goods could be produced. *Less is produced at a higher price.* But there is a trade-off here. Whereas in the perfectly competitive market every product was a perfect substitute for every other one, in the world of monopolistic competition there is variety in the products available. People value variety, and are willing to pay a higher price to obtain it. Thus, the fact that goods are sold at a price above the minimum average cost does not necessarily mean that the economy is inefficient.

Whether the market results in too little or too much product variety remains a contested subject. Either can occur. The important point to realize here is that there is a trade-off. Greater variety can only be obtained at greater cost.

SCHUMPETERIAN COMPETITION

The famous Harvard economist Joseph Schumpeter envisaged a rather different form of monopolistic competition. He saw different markets dominated at different times by one or two firms, those that had technological superiority. The dominant firms were constantly subjected to competition for supremacy as new innovations supplanted old. Even when the lead firm is not supplanted by another, the threat of entry keeps it on its toes. While each company dominates the market, it acts like a monopolist: it sets marginal revenue equal to marginal cost, producing less than would be produced under perfect competition. But if it wishes to maintain its position, the firm must reinvest profits in further expenditures to make new products and to develop new, cheaper ways of producing. In Schumpeter's view, the disadvantage of the monopoly aspects of imperfect markets—the reduction in output—was more than offset by the advantages of the greater research the extra profits funded. Chapter 17 will take a closer look at these questions.

REVIEW AND PRACTICE

SUMMARY

1. Economists identify four broad categories of market structure: perfect competition, monopoly, oligopoly, and monopolistic competition (the last two are collectively referred to as imperfect competition).

2. A perfectly competitive firm faces a horizontal demand curve; it is a price taker. In markets in which there is imperfect or no competition, each firm faces a downward-sloping demand curve, and is a price maker.

3. Both monopolists and firms facing perfect competition maximize profit by producing at the quantity where marginal revenue is equal to marginal cost. However, marginal revenue for a perfect competitor is the same as the market price of an extra unit, while marginal revenue for a monopolist is less than the market price.

4. Since with a monopoly price exceeds marginal revenue, buyers pay more for the product than the marginal cost to produce it; there is less production in a monopoly than there would be if price were set equal to marginal cost.

5. Imperfect competition occurs when a relatively small number of firms dominate the market and/or when firms produce goods that are differentiated by their characteristics, by the location of the firms, or in the perception of consumers.

6. Monopolies and imperfect competition may be sustained by either natural or manmade barriers to entry.

7. With monopolistic competition, barriers to entry are sufficiently weak that entry occurs until profits are driven to zero; there are few enough firms that each faces a downward-sloping demand curve, but a sufficiently large number of firms that each ignores rivals' reactions to what it does.

KEY TERMS

monopoly
oligopoly
monopolistic
    competition
imperfect
    competition

pure profit or
    monopoly rents
price discrimination
product
    differentiation
barriers to entry

natural monopoly
predatory pricing
limit pricing

REVIEW QUESTIONS

1. What is the difference between perfect and imperfect competition? between oligopoly and monopolistic competition?

2. Why is price equal to marginal revenue for a perfectly competitive firm, but not for a monopolist?

3. How should a monopoly choose its quantity of production to maximize profits? Explain why producing either less or more than the level of output at which marginal revenue equals marginal cost will reduce profits. Since a monopolist need not fear competition, what prevents it from raising its price as high as it wishes to make higher profits?

4. What are the primary sources of product differentiation?

5. What are barriers to entry? Describe the principal ones.

6. What is a natural monopoly?

7. Describe market equilibrium under monopolistic competition. Why does the price charged by the typical firm exceed the minimum average cost, even though there is entry?

PROBLEMS

1. Explain how it is possible that at a high enough level of output, if a monopoly produced and sold more, its revenue would actually decline.

2. Assume there is a single firm producing cigarettes, and the marginal cost of producing cigarettes is a constant. Suppose the government imposes a

10-cent tax on each pack of cigarettes. If the demand curve for cigarettes is linear (that is, $Q = a - bp$, where Q = output, p = price, and a and b are constants), will the price rise by more or less than the tax?

3. With what strategies might a furniture firm differentiate its products?

4. Suppose a gas station at a busy intersection is surrounded by many competitors, all of whom sell identical gas. Draw the demand curve the gas station faces, and draw its marginal and average cost curves. Explain the rule for maximizing profit in this situation. Now imagine that the gas station offers a new gasoline additive called zoomine, and begins an advertising campaign that says: "Get zoomine in your gasoline." No other station offers zoomine. Draw the demand curve faced by the station after this advertising campaign. Explain the rule for maximizing profit in this situation, and illustrate it with an appropriate diagram.

5. Explain how consumers may benefit from predatory pricing in the short run, but not in the long run.

6. Why might it make sense for a monopolist to choose a point on the demand curve where the price is somewhat lower than the price at which marginal revenue equals marginal costs?

7. Assume the demand curve for some commodity is linear
$$Q = a - bp.$$
(a) Express how the price depends on the quantity produced.
(b) What is the relationship between revenue and the quantity produced?
(c) Assume that output increases slightly from Q to $(Q + \Delta Q)$. What happens to revenue? If ΔQ is a small number (much less than 1), then $(\Delta Q)^2$ is a *very* small number. Ignoring terms in $(\Delta Q)^2$, what is the relationship between marginal revenue and output?
(d) Show that the expression for marginal revenue can be reexpressed as
$$MR = 2p - a/b$$
(e) Assume that $b = 1$ and $a = 100$. Draw the demand and marginal revenue curves.
(f) If marginal cost is $1, what is the equilibrium competitive price and the monopoly price?
(g) If the producer is required to pay a tax of $.10 per unit of output produced, what happens to the price under monopoly? under perfect competition?

APPENDIX A: MONOPSONY

In any market, imperfections of competition can arise on either the buyer or seller side. In this chapter, we have focused on imperfect competition among the sellers of goods. When there is a single buyer in a market, the buyer is called a **monopsonist.** Though monopsonies are relatively rare, they do exist. The government is a monopsonist in the market for a variety of high-technology defense systems.

In some labor markets, a single firm may be close to a monopsonist. In many markets, an employer may face an upward-sloping supply curve for labor, or at least labor with particular skills. Firms in one-company towns—like Gary, Indiana, which was founded and is dominated by U.S. Steel—particularly when they are geographically isolated, are most likely to face such upward-sloping supply curves for labor.

The consequences of monopsony are similar to those for monopoly. The basic rule remains: produce at the point where marginal revenue equals marginal cost. The buyer firm is aware, however, that if it buys more units, it will have to pay a higher price. Then if the firm cannot price discriminate, the marginal cost of buying one more unit is not only what the company has to pay for the last unit, but also the higher price it must pay for all previously purchased units.

In the case of a labor market, Figure 14.10 illustrates the consequence. Chapter 12 showed that in competitive markets, firms hire labor up to the point where the value of the marginal product of labor (*MPL*) equals the wage, the marginal cost of hiring an additional worker. The figure shows the curve that represents the value of the marginal product of labor; it declines as the number of workers hired increases. The figure also shows the labor supply curve, which is upward sloping. From this, the firm can calculate the marginal cost of hiring an additional worker, the wage *plus* the increase in wage payments to all previously hired workers. Clearly, the marginal cost curve lies above the labor supply curve. The firm hires workers up to the point L^*, where the value of the marginal product of labor is equal to the marginal cost. Employment is lower than it would have been had the firm ignored the fact that as it hires more labor, the wage it pays increases.

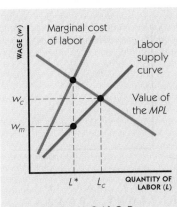

Figure 14.10 MONOP- SONY

As a monopsonist buys more of an input, it must pay not only a higher price for the marginal unit but a higher price for all the units it buys; thus, the marginal cost of buying an input exceeds the price. The monopsonist sets the marginal cost of the input equal to the value of its marginal product at employment level L^*, and sets the wage at w_m. In a competitive labor market, a firm hires labor up to L_c, at wage w_c. Thus, a monopsonist hires less labor at a lower wage than competitive firms would.

APPENDIX B: DEMAND FOR INPUTS UNDER MONOPOLY AND IMPERFECT COMPETITION

In Chapter 12, we saw that competitive firms hire labor up to the point where the value of the marginal product (the value of what an extra hour of labor would produce) is equal to the wage. Similarly, any other factor of production is demanded up to the point where the value of its marginal product is equal to its price. From this, we could derive the demand curve for labor (or any other input).

A quite similar analysis applies with imperfect competition. A monopolist hires labor up to the point where the extra revenue it produces—what economists call the marginal revenue product—is equal to the wage. In competitive markets, the value of the marginal product is just equal to the

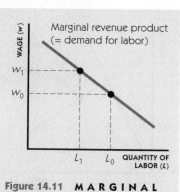

Figure 14.11 MARGINAL REVENUE PRODUCT CURVE

Firms hire labor up to the point where the marginal revenue product of an extra worker equals the marginal cost. In a competitive labor market, the marginal cost of labor is just the wage.

price of the output times the marginal physical product, the extra quantity that is produced. In a monopoly, the marginal revenue product *(MRP)* is equal to the marginal revenue yielded by producing one more unit *(MR)* times the marginal physical product *(MPP)*: $MRP = MR \times MPP$.

The quantity of labor that will be hired is illustrated in Figure 14.11, which shows the marginal revenue product curve. It is downward slop-ing, for two reasons: the more that is produced, the smaller the marginal physical product (this is just the law of diminishing returns), and the more that is produced, the smaller the marginal revenue. The firm hires labor up to the point where the marginal revenue product equals the wage, point L_0. If the wage increases from w_0 to w_1, the amount of labor hired will fall, from L_0 to L_1. Thus, the demand curve for labor is downward sloping with imperfect competition, just as it is with perfect competition.

15

Oligopolies

In industries characterized by monopolistic competition, there are enough firms that each assumes its actions have no effect on the actions of its competitors. But in many industries, called oligopolies, there are so few firms that each worries about how its rivals will react to anything it does. This is true of the airline, cigarette, aluminum, automobile, and a host of other industries. Airlines that offer frequent flier bonuses, for instance, can expect their competitors to respond with similar offers.

If an oligopolist lowers its price, it worries that rivals will do the same and it will gain no competitive advantage. Worse still, a competitor may react to a price cut by engaging in a price war and cutting the price still further. Different oligopolies behave in quite different ways. The oligopolist is always torn between its desire to outwit competitors and the knowledge that by cooperating with other oligopolists to reduce output, it will earn a portion of the higher industry profits.

This chapter examines the key question facing an oligopolistic firm—whether it will earn higher profits colluding with rivals to restrict output or competing with rivals by charging lower prices. The analysis of oligopoly behavior is divided into three sections. The first discusses collusion, or cooperation, and the problems firms confront in colluding. The second shows how firms may restrict competition, even when they do not formally collude. The third describes what happens if firms in an oligopoly compete.

KEY QUESTIONS

1. In what ways do oligopolies differ from the other market structures—monopoly, perfect competition, and monopolistic competition?

2. What are the incentives for the firms in an oligopoly to collude? Why is it hard to maintain the cooperative behavior required for cartels to be effective?

3. What practices do firms in an oligopoly engage in that facilitate collusion and, in the absence of collusion, that restrict the force of competition?

4. What are some of the different forms that competition among oligopolists takes?

COLLUSION

In some cases, oligopolists try to **collude** to maximize their profits. In effect, they act jointly as if they were a monopoly, and split up the resulting profits. The prevalence of collusion was long ago noted by Adam Smith, the founder of modern economics: "People of the same trade seldom meet together, even for merriment and diversion, but the conversation ends in a conspiracy against the public, or in some contrivance to raise prices."[1] A group of companies that formally operate in collusion is called a **cartel.** The Organization of Petroleum Exporting Countries (OPEC), for instance, acts collusively to restrict the output of oil, to raise oil prices and hence the profits of member countries.

In the late nineteenth century, two or more railroads ran between many major cities. When they competed vigorously, profits were low. So it did not take them long to discover that if they acted collusively, they could raise profits by raising prices.

In the steel industry at the turn of the century, Judge Elbert H. Gary, who headed the U.S. Steel Company, the largest of the steel firms, regularly presided over Sunday dinners for prominent members of his industry at which steel prices were set. But while cartels increase industry profits, it is hard to maintain the cooperative behavior required. We now look at three problems facing cartels.

THE PROBLEM OF SELF-ENFORCEMENT

Cartels seek to restrict output and thus to raise prices above marginal costs. The central difficulty facing cartels is that it pays any single member of the cartel to cheat. That is, if all other members of the cartel restrict output, so

[1] *Wealth of Nations* (1776), Book 1, Chapter 10, Part II.

that price exceeds marginal cost, it pays the last member of the cartel to increase its output and take advantage of the higher price. This firm is said to be free riding on the cartel—the other firms pay the price of collusion by restricting their output, while the free rider gets the higher price without giving up any sales. But if too many members of a cartel cheat by increasing their output beyond the agreed-upon levels, the cartel breaks down. This happened to the OPEC oil cartel during the 1980s. Producers (other than Saudi Arabia) systematically increased production beyond their allotted quotas.

The incentives for any member of a cartel to cheat are illustrated in Figure 15.1, in which all members of a cartel face the same constant marginal costs. The figure shows the market demand curve and the output, Q_c, and price, p_c, at which the cartel's joint profits are maximized—that is, where marginal revenue for the cartel as a whole equals marginal costs. But the marginal revenue for the cartel as a whole is not the marginal revenue for any one firm. Any firm thinks it can cheat on the cartel and get away with it. If it shaves its price just lower than p_c and increases its production, it makes a profit of approximately p_c minus the marginal cost on that additional unit. With a large gap between price and marginal costs, the incentives to cheat are strong.

A factor that further encourages some members of a cartel to cheat on the collusive agreement is that members frequently believe they are not getting their fair share. This problem has plagued the OPEC oil cartel. Each country within the cartel faces different economic circumstances. Oil-rich sheikdoms have per capita incomes among the highest in the world. But for poor countries like Indonesia, oil revenues are a potential resource for development. No simple principles exist to help these countries decide how much each should produce, or who should bear the burden of cutting back production in order to sustain a high market price. Those who feel they are being unfairly treated are most likely to try to cheat on the collusive agreement.

Thus, the first major problem facing cartels is how to enforce their collu-

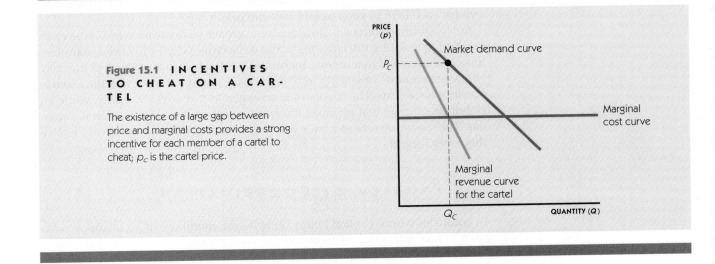

Figure 15.1 INCENTIVES TO CHEAT ON A CARTEL

The existence of a large gap between price and marginal costs provides a strong incentive for each member of a cartel to cheat; p_c is the cartel price.

Maintaining collusive behavior is difficult, particularly given the laws aimed at restricting it. Ironically, government is sometimes an accomplice in restricting competition. Such is commonly the case in alcoholic beverages, where state laws make it difficult for distributors in one state to sell in another. The dramatic effect of restrictions on selling across state lines was recently demonstrated by New York in the case of milk.

In the 1930s, the state passed a law prohibiting dairies outside New York from selling milk in the state. The law benefited New York milk producers at the expense of its consumers and milk producers in other states. In 1979, New Jersey–based Farmland Dairies challenged the New York law. After an eight-year legal battle, it won the right to sell milk in New York City. Before the decision, five milk producers controlled over 90 percent of the milk market in the city. After the decision, when

Farmland and others entered the market, milk prices in the city tumbled by as much as 70 cents a gallon. The new competition saves New York consumers as much as $100 million every year in lower milk prices.

sive arrangement on their members. This self-enforcement is a particular problem in the United States because both state and federal governments have passed **antitrust laws** prohibiting collusive behavior. This makes it impossible for firms to get together and sign legally binding contracts that would require each firm to keep output low and prices high.

But the profits from collusion can be so great that firms have taken the risks involved in violating the law. One of the most famous cases involved manufacturers of electrical machinery, including Westinghouse and General Electric, who were caught conspiring in their bids for major projects, like the electric turbines for a dam. The companies arranged to take turns winning, using an elaborate scheme that involved the phases of the moon and the lunar calendar. Their scheme was so clever that the conspiracy went on for years before they were caught.

THE PROBLEM OF COORDINATION

In countries where explicit collusion is illegal, members of an oligopoly who wish to take advantage of their market power must rely on **tacit collusion.** Tacit collusion is an implicit understanding that the oligopoly's interests are best served if its members do not compete too vigorously and particularly if they avoid price cutting. However, the interests of particular firms may not coincide exactly. And an implicit agreement by its very nature makes it difficult to specify what each firm should do in every situation. When cost or demand curves shift, perhaps because of changes in technology or changes in tastes, the members of a cartel need to get together to agree upon the appropriate changes in output and prices. A new technology or development may benefit one firm more than another, and that firm will wish to increase output more than the others. If the oligopolists could bargain together openly, they might be able to cut a deal. But since the law prohibits them from such a straightforward solution, inventive oligopolists have developed a number of ways to circumvent this coordination problem.

One approach is for a particular firm to become the **price leader.** That firm, often the second- or third-largest member of the industry, sets the price, and others follow. According to some economists, American Airlines used to be the price leader in its industry. As costs (say, of fuel) or demand conditions changed in the airline industry, American would announce new fare structures, and the other airlines would simply match them. It is hard to prove that collusion has occurred in this type of sequence—the firms simply claim that they are responding to similar market forces.

Sometimes communication among firms of an industry can be so subtle as to be almost undetectable. The Justice Department caught firms in the airline industry communicating through the airline reservation system. Farecodes are normally used to identify when a particular fare will be in effect, and other restrictions on availability. But the airlines devised a way (using farecodes for fares that were not actually being offered) in which they would communicate how they would respond to a proposed change in the fare in a particular market.[2]

Yet another approach is to develop **facilitating practices** that serve to make collusion easier. One example is the "meeting-the-competition clause," in which at least some members of the oligopoly commit themselves, often in advertisements, to charging no more than any competitor. Electronics shops often make such claims. To the consumer, this looks like a great deal. To see why this practice may actually lead to higher prices, think about it from the perspective of rival firms. Assume that the electronics store is selling for $100 an item that costs the store $90; its selling costs are $5, so it is making a $5 profit on the sale. Consider another store that would like to steal some customers away. It would be willing to sell the item for $95, undercutting the first store. But then it reasons that if it cuts its price, it will not gain any customers, since the first store has already guaranteed to match the lower price. Further, the second store knows that it will make less money on each sale to its current customers. Price cutting simply does not pay. It thus appears that a practice that seemingly is highly competitive in fact may facilitate collusion.

In many cases, oligopolists create a variety of cooperative arrangements that involve sharing inventories, research findings, or other information. In electronics and other high-technology industries, exchanging research

[2]Not surprisingly, the airlines denied the charge. But in 1993 they signed an agreement to no longer engage in the practice.

information is particularly important. In retail and wholesale markets, helping one another out in the case of inventory shortages is important. For example, one distributor of beer may provide beer to another when the latter's inventory is insufficient to meet his retailers' demand. Any firm that cheated on the collusive price arrangement would find itself cut out from these cooperative arrangements.

THE PROBLEM OF ENTRY

The third major problem cartels face is similar to the problem faced by a monopolist. High profits enjoyed by the members of the cartel attract entry from other firms or cause nonmembers of the cartel to expand production. This was one of the fates that befell OPEC. When its members raised the price of oil, noncartel countries like Britain, Canada, and Mexico increased their production of oil.

Some economists, such as William Baumol of New York and Princeton Universities, have argued that in some markets just the threat of entry is strong enough to keep prices low, even if a firm controls over 90 percent of the market. If prices were ever so slightly above costs of production, there would be rapid entry, forcing prices down. In these cases, **potential competition,** the possibility of entry, is sufficient to keep prices low. The costs of entry and exit have to be relatively small, however, for potential competition to be effective. Otherwise, firms will not enter, even when they see high prices, unless they have reason to believe that prices will remain high after entry.

Markets such as these, in which potential competition suffices to ensure competitive prices, are called **contestable.** At one time, advocates of the theory of contestable markets used airlines as the basic example of a contestable market. An airline could easily enter a market in which price exceeded costs (for example, the San Francisco–Los Angeles market), and thus potential competition would ensure low prices, even when there were only one or two airlines flying a particular route. But by the end of the 1980s, as airline prices skyrocketed on many routes on which competition was limited, potential competition did not seem strong enough to keep prices down. Potential entrants recognized that there were significant costs to entering a market—customers had to be informed, they had to be persuaded to switch from the usual carrier, airline offices had to be opened, and so forth—and experience had taught them that once they entered, prices would fall, making it impossible for them to recover these costs.

It is remarkable how many oligopolies persist with limited entry. There has been some entry into the film industry (Fuji), but it remains dominated by a few firms. Other oligopolies, such as the automobile, cigarette, and aluminum industries, have remained relatively intact over long periods of time. Even the number of attempts at entry has been limited; Tucker and Kaiser represent the two most famous cases of failure in automobiles. This suggests that if the barriers to entry discussed in Chapter 14 are strong enough, as appears to be the case in many situations, potential entry may not provide an adequate threat to prevent firms from charging prices in excess of marginal costs.

CLOSE-UP: PRICE FIXING IN ACTION

Price-fixing cases are often hard to prosecute, since the parties go to great lengths to hide their activities. Occasionally, however, a private conversation becomes public, as happened in a 1983 antitrust suit against American and Braniff Airlines. The following is part of a recorded telephone call between Robert Crandall, president of American Airlines, and Howard Putnam, president of Braniff Airlines, that was introduced at the trial. (The two companies had been acting as oligopolistic competitors and cutting prices as they competed in the Dallas market.)

> CRANDALL: I think it's dumb as hell . . . to sit here and pound the (deleted) out of each other and neither one of us making a (deleted) dime. . . . We can both live here and there ain't no room for Delta. But there's, ah, no reason that I can see, all right, to put both companies out of business.
>
> PUTNAM: Do you have a suggestion for me?
>
> CRANDALL: Yes, I have a suggestion for you. Raise your goddamn fares twenty percent. I'll raise mine the next morning. . . . You'll make more money, and I will too.

> PUTNAM: We can't talk about pricing.
>
> CRANDALL: Oh (deleted), Howard. We can talk about any goddamn thing we want to talk about.

The Justice Department released a transcript of the conversation as it charged American Airlines and Crandall with an attempt to monopolize airline routes and fix prices with Braniff. However, after some months of litigation, a federal judge dismissed the charge. The decision held that while the conversation was clearly an offer to raise prices, it was not an attempt to monopolize according to the meaning of the law. The judge also wrote that "Crandall's conduct was at best unprofessional and his choice of words distasteful," but concluded that since Putnam turned down the offer, no conspiracy to monopolize existed.

Crandall was lucky. If his phrasing had been a bit different, or if Putnam had taken him up on his offer, he could easily have been found guilty. But how many other, similar conversations are occurring among other executives today, without any government recording devices on the line?

Sources: Robert E. Taylor and Dean Rotbart, "American Air Accused of Bid to Fix Prices," *Wall Street Journal,* February 24, 1983, p. 2; Dean Rotbart, "American Air, Its President Gets Trust Suit Voided," *Wall Street Journal,* September 14, 1983, p. 2.

LIMITS TO COLLUSION

Self-enforcement; incentives for each firm to cheat
Coordination problems in responding to changed economic circumstances
Entry

GAME THEORY: THE PRISONER'S DILEMMA

In recent years, economists have used a branch of mathematics called game theory to study collusion among oligopolists. The participants in a game are allowed to make certain moves, defined by the rules of the game. The outcomes of the game—what each participant receives—are referred to as its payoffs, and depend on what each player does. Each participant in the game chooses a strategy; he decides what moves to make. In games in which each player has the chance to make more than one move (there is more than one round, or period), moves can depend on what has happened in previous periods. Game theory begins with the assumption that each player in the game is rational and knows that his rival is rational. Each is trying to maximize his own payoff. The theory then tries to predict what each player will do. The answer depends on the rules of the game and the payoffs.

One example of such a game is called the **Prisoner's Dilemma.** Two prisoners, A and B, alleged to be conspirators in a crime, are put into separate rooms. A police officer goes into each room and makes a little speech: "Now here's the situation. If your partner confesses and you remain silent, you'll get five years in prison. But if your partner confesses and you confess also, you'll only get three years. On the other hand, perhaps your partner remains silent. If you're quiet also, we can only send you to prison for one year. But if your partner remains silent and you confess, we'll let you out in three months. So if your partner confesses, you are better off confessing, and if your partner doesn't confess, you are better off confessing. Why not confess?" This deal is offered to both prisoners.

The diagram below shows the results of this deal. The upper left-hand box, for example, shows the result if both A and B confess. The upper right-hand box shows the result if prisoner A confesses but prisoner B remains silent. And so on.

		Prisoner B	
		Confesses	Remains silent
Prisoner A	Confesses	A gets 3 years B gets 3 years	A gets 3 months B gets 5 years
	Remains silent	A gets 5 years B gets 3 months	A gets 1 year B gets 1 year

From the combined standpoint of the two prisoners, the best option is clearly that they both remain silent and each serve their one year. But the self-interest of each individual prisoner says that confession is best, whether his partner confesses or not. However, if they both follow their self-interest and confess, they both end up worse off, each serving three years. The Prisoner's Dilemma is a simple game in which both parties are made worse off by independently following their own self-interest. Both would be better off if they could get together to agree on a story, and to threaten the other if he deviated from the story.

The Prisoner's Dilemma comes up in a variety of contexts. For example, during the years of the Cold War, the arms race between the United States and the former USSR was described in these terms. Each party reasoned that if the other side built weapons, it needed to match the buildup. And if the other side did not build, it could acquire an advantage by building. Even though both sides might have been better off by agreeing not to build, their incentives pushed them toward a situation where both continued to do so.

The game can also be directly applied to collusion between two oligopolists. (A market with two firms is called a duopoly.) Assume that both firms agree to cut back their production, so they obtain higher prices and higher profits. But each oligopolist reasons the following way. Whether my rival cheats or not, it pays for me to expand production. If my rival cheats, then he gets all the advantages of my restricting output but pays none of the price. And if he does not cheat and keeps production low, it pays for me to cheat. As both firms reason that way, production expands and prices fall to a level below that at which their joint profits are maximized.

In the examples of the Prisoner's Dilemma presented so far, each party makes only one decision. But if firms (or countries) interact over time, then they have additional ways to try to enforce their agreement. For example, suppose each oligopolist announces that it will refrain from cutting prices as long as its rival does. But if the rival cheats on the collusive agreement, then the first oligopolist will respond by increasing production and lowering prices. Won't this threat ensure that the two firms cooperate?

Consider what happens if the two firms expect to compete in the same market over the next ten years, after which time a new product is expected to come along and shift the entire configuration of the industry. It will pay each firm to cheat in the tenth year, when there is no possibility of retaliation, because the industry will be completely altered in the next year. Now consider what happens in the ninth year. Both firms can figure out that it will not pay either one of them to cooperate in the tenth year. But if they are not going to

USING ECONOMICS: GAME THEORY AND COLLUSION

Game theory helps explain why, in spite of the obvious advantages of collusion, cartels have a hard time maintaining themselves. The box below shows the problem of a duopoly, where each of the duopolists can either collude, restricting output, or compete. Numbers in the upper left triangle are the first duopolist's profits and in the bottom right triangle the second duopolist's profits.

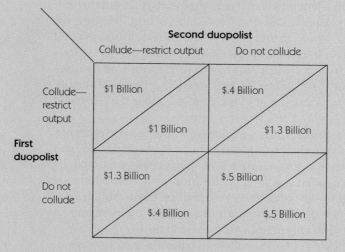

When they both collude, profits are high—in this example, each receives a profit of $1 billion. If the first duopolist restricts his output, and the second duopolist takes advantage of that, the first duopolists' profit falls to $400 million, while the second duopolists' profit increases to $1.3 billion. Industry profits are down ($1.7 billion versus $2 billion before); because only one firm is restricting its output, output is higher and price lower. The outcomes are symmetric, if the second duopolist restricts his output and the first does not. Finally, if both compete vigorously, price falls precipitously, and profits of each fall to $500 million. The gains from collusion in this example are enormous: profits are doubled. But in spite of that, in equilibrium, they will compete.

The first firm reasons: if my rival restricts his output, and I do too, my profits are $1 billion; but if I do not restrict my output, I can increase my profits to $1.3 billion. Clearly, in this case, I am better off not restricting my output. If my rival does not restrict his output, but I do, my profits are $400 million; but if I do not restrict my output, my profits increase to $500 million. In either case—no matter what my rival does—I am better off not restricting my output. The second firm reasons exactly the same way, and the outcome is clear: neither restricts his output, and each earns a profit of $500 million, half of what they would have earned had they colluded.

cooperate in the tenth year anyway, then the *threat* of not cooperating in the future is completely ineffective. Hence in the ninth year, each firm will reason that it pays to cheat on the collusive agreement by producing more than the agreed-upon amount. Collusion breaks down in the ninth year. Reasoning backward through time, this logic will lead collusion to break down almost immediately.

Economists have set up laboratory experiments, much like those used by other sciences, to test how individuals actually behave in these different games. The advantage of this sort of **experimental economics** is that the researcher can change one aspect of what is going on at a time, to try to determine what are the crucial determinants of behavior. One set of experiments has looked at how individuals cooperate with one another in situations like the Prisoner's Dilemma. These experiments have a tendency to show that participants often evolve simple strategies that, although they may appear irrational in the short run, can be effective in inducing cooperation (collusion) as the game is repeated a number of times. One common strategy is "tit for tat." If you increase your output, I will do the same, even if doing so does not maximize my profits. If the rival firm believes this threat, especially after it has been carried out a few times, the rival may decide that it is more profitable to cooperate and keep production low rather than to cheat. In the real world, such simple strategies may play an important role in ensuring that firms do not compete too vigorously in those markets where there are only three or four dominant firms.

RESTRICTIVE PRACTICES

If members of an oligopoly could easily get together and collude, they would. Their joint profits would thereby be increased. They would have a problem of how to divide the profits, but each of the members of the oligopoly could be better off than it would be if they competed. We have seen, however, that there are significant impediments to collusion. If the members of an industry cannot collude to stop competition and cannot prevent entry, at least they can act to reduce competition and deter entry.

Chapter 14 described some of the ways firms act to deter entry. Here, we look at practices firms engage in that may serve to *restrict* competition, called **restrictive practices.** Some of these practices were made illegal by the Federal Trade Commission Act of 1914. While these practices may not be quite as successful in increasing profits for the firms as the collusive arrangements discussed above, they do succeed in raising prices. In some cases, consumers may be even worse off than with outright collusion. Many restrictive practices are aimed at the wholesalers and retailers who sell a producer's goods. When one firm buys or sells another firm's products, the two companies are said to have a "vertical" relationship. Such restrictive practices are called **vertical restrictions,** as opposed to the price-fixing arrangements among producers or

Microsoft is the dominant producer of personal computer software in the world. Microsoft products account for almost two-thirds of installed PC operating systems and more than half of all spreadsheet applications. Its profits soared close to a billion dollars in 1993, and its market value is larger than that of GM. On July 16, 1994, Microsoft signed an out-of-court settlement of a case brought by the European Union and the U.S. Department of Justice alleging Microsoft engaged in practices designed to reduce competition. This marked the first time that two major law enforcement agencies from different parts of the world had collaborated in bringing and settling a suit.

Largeness in itself is not a crime. So why the suit? Competitors claimed, and the Department of Justice agreed, that Microsoft was engaging in unfair trade practices to establish and maintain its dominant market position. The contract it signed with PC manufacturers that installed programs like Microsoft Windows and DOS on their computers was cited as an example. Microsoft was basing its charges simply on the scale of the PC manufacturer's sales volume—such as the number of PCs delivered—not on the number on which Microsoft's programs were actually installed. Thus, if a competitor were to come up with a program that was in fact just as good, a manufacturer would have no incentive to install it, because it would have already paid for Microsoft's Windows and DOS programs. Microsoft denied any wrongdoing, but signing the consent decree involved an agreement to stop engaging in such practices.

Were the European Union and the U.S. Department of Justice right to accept the consent decree, or should they have gone farther? Critics say that the consent decree would not lessen Microsoft's hold on the market by much, because it was still allowed to use volume discounts, which kept the *marginal* charge for installing Windows and DOS very low. Since designing the operating system gave it a distinct advantage in developing applications programs for use with the system, some critics wanted Microsoft divided into two companies. One would develop operating systems and the other applications, and what is called a Chinese wall would separate them. This would put competitors on a level playing field in developing applications.

Microsoft supporters say the outcome represented an appropriate balance between concerns about innovation and competition. Their position is that the dominant position of Microsoft results from (1) its price competitiveness—it had been able to bring down the price of the operating systems to under $100—and (2) its innovativeness—new features were continually being added.

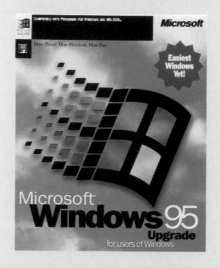

Source: *New York Times*, July 18, 1994, pp. D1–4.

among wholesalers selling in the same market, which are referred to as **horizontal restrictions.**

One example of a vertical restriction is that of **exclusive territories,** in which a producer gives a wholesaler or retailer the exclusive right to sell a good within a certain region. Beer and soft drink producers, for instance, typically give their distributors exclusive territories. Coca-Cola manufactures its own syrup, which it then sells to bottlers who add the soda water. Coca-Cola gives these bottlers exclusive territories, so the supermarkets in a particular area can buy Coke from only one place. A store in Michigan cannot buy the soft drink from Coca-Cola bottlers in New Jersey, even if the price in New Jersey is lower. Indiana passed a law prohibiting exclusive territories for beer within the state. As a result, beer prices there are substantially lower (adjusting for other differences) than in other states.

Another example of a restrictive practice is **exclusive dealing,** in which a producer insists that any firm selling its products not sell those of its rivals. When you go into an Exxon gas station, for instance, you can be sure you are buying gas refined by the Exxon Corporation, not Texaco or Mobil. Like most refiners, Exxon insists that stations that want to sell Exxon sell only its brand of gasoline.

A third example of a restrictive practice is **tie-ins,** in which a customer who buys one product must buy another. Mortgage companies, for example, used to insist that those who obtained mortgages from them purchase fire insurance as well. Nintendo designs its console so that it can only be used with Nintendo games. In effect, it forces a tie-in sale between the console and the computer games. In the early days of computers, IBM designed its computers so that they could only be used with IBM "peripherals," such as printers.

A final example of a restrictive practice is **resale price maintenance.** Under resale price maintenance, a producer insists that any retailer selling his product must sell it at the "list" price. Like exclusive territories, this practice is designed to reduce competitive pressures at the retail level.

CONSEQUENCES OF RESTRICTIVE PRACTICES

Firms engaging in restrictive practices *claim* they are doing so not because they wish to restrict competition, but because they want to enhance economic efficiency. Exclusive territories, they argue, provide companies with a better incentive to "cultivate" their territory. Exclusive dealing contracts, they say, provide incentives for firms to focus their attention on one producer's goods.

Regardless of these claims, restrictive practices often reduce economic efficiency. Exclusive territories for beer, for example, have limited the ability of very large firms, with stores in many different territories, to set up a central warehouse and distribute beer to their stores in a more efficient manner.

Regardless of whether they enhance or hurt efficiency, restrictive practices may lead to higher prices by limiting competitive pressures.

Some restrictive practices work by increasing the costs of, or otherwise impeding, one's rivals. In the 1980s, several major airlines developed computer reservation systems that they sold at very attractive prices to travel agents. If the primary goal of these systems had been to serve consumers, they would

FORMS OF RESTRICTIVE PRACTICES

Exclusive territories

Exclusive dealing

Tie-ins

Resale price maintenance

have been designed to display all the departures near the time the passenger desired. Instead, each airline's system provided a quick display for only its own flights—United's, for instance, focused on United flights—although with additional work, the travel agent could find out the flights of other airlines. Airlines benefited from these computer systems, not because they best met the needs of the consumer, but because they put competitors at a disadvantage and thereby reduced the effectiveness of competition.

An exclusive dealing contract between a producer and a distributor is another example of how one firm may benefit from hurting its rivals. The contract may force a rival producer to set up its own distribution system, at great cost. The already-existing distributor might have been able to undertake the distribution of the second product at relatively low incremental cost. The exclusive dealing contract increases total resources spent on distribution.

Courts have taken varying attitudes toward the legality of these and similar practices—in some circumstances ruling that they are illegal because they reduce competition, while in others allowing them, having been persuaded that they represent reasonable business practices.

THE MANY DIMENSIONS OF COMPETITION AMONG OLIGOPOLISTS

In the perfectly competitive markets of Part Two, competitive behavior is clear and simple. Firms work to lower their costs of production. They can sell as much as they want at the going market price. They don't have to worry about clever marketing strategies, new products, advertising: but these, and a host of other decisions, are the battlefields on which competition among oligopolists occurs. This competition is fierce with firms constantly trying to outwit rivals and anticipate their responses. It is like a game, but one in which not all the rules are clear, let alone written down. American Airlines might have thought it was getting a leg up on its rivals when it introduced its frequent flier program, and Delta Air Lines might have thought it was doing likewise when it offered triple mileage. But some of the rival airlines had more empty seats than either American or Delta. Since giving away free tickets may have been less costly for them, they could respond by offering even more attractive programs. Were American and Delta, then, really better off?

PRICE AND OUTPUT COMPETITION

Even in the limited domain on which we have focused so far, determining prices and output, the life of an oligopolist is complicated. At one level of analysis, the oligopolist firm is just like a firm facing monopolistic competition. The oligopolist faces a demand curve specifying how much output it believes it can sell at each price it charges, or what the firm believes it will receive if it tries to sell a particular quantity. The oligopolist chooses the point along that demand curve at which its profits are maximized. It sets, in other words, marginal revenue equal to marginal cost. But while true, this statement hides all the real difficulties in an analysis of oligopoly. What an oligopolist will sell at any particular price, or what the market price will be if it produces a particular level of output, depends on what its rivals do.

Economists have investigated the behavior of oligopolies under different assumptions concerning what each firm believes about what his rival will do.

COURNOT COMPETITION

An oligopolist firm may believe that its rivals are committed to producing a given quantity and selling it on the market, and that they will keep this quantity fixed no matter what level of output the firm chooses to produce. If the firm considers producing more, it expects that its rivals will cut their prices until they sell the production level to which they are committed. Competition where an oligopolist firm assumes its rivals' output levels are fixed is called **Cournot competition,** after Augustin Cournot, a French economist and engineer, who first studied it in 1838. Industries such as aluminum or steel, where the major part of the cost of production is the cost of machinery, and once capital goods are in place, variable costs are relatively unimportant, are often thought of as industries where Cournot competition prevails. Adding new machinery would be expensive, and not using machinery to its capacity would save the firm relatively little money. Output is then determined, at least in the short run, by the production capacity of the firm's capital goods.

BERTRAND COMPETITION

In Cournot competition, each firm maximizes profits by choosing what it will produce. In making its calculations, it assumes the level of output of its rivals is fixed. This assumption, we saw, is plausible for industries in which it takes time to change production capacity, and in which capital goods represent the bulk of all production costs. But in many industries it is easy to expand capacity. A taxicab company in a large city can easily buy a new car and hire new drivers. While increasing the total number of planes in service may take some time, an airline that wishes to increase the number of planes flying the Chicago–New York route can do so quickly. Firms in these industries can be thought of as choosing a price to charge, and adjusting their output to meet whatever demand arises at that price. They choose the price so as to maximize their profits, given their beliefs about the behavior of their rivals. One commonly made assumption is that rivals' prices are fixed. Oligopolies in which each firm chooses its price to maximize its profits on the assumption that rivals' prices are fixed are said to be characterized by **Bertrand competition,** after the French economist Joseph Bertrand, who first studied this form of competition in 1883.

If rivals keep their prices unchanged, then the oligopolist may steal many of its rivals' customers when it lowers its price. But as long as the goods produced by two rivals are imperfect substitutes (for any of the reasons discussed in Chapter 14), when one firm lowers its price below that of its rivals, it does not capture *all* the customers.

KINKED DEMAND CURVES

A third hypothesis about how oligopolistic rivals may respond says that rivals match price cuts but do not respond to price increases. In this situation, an oligopolist believes that it will not gain much in sales if it lowers its price, because rivals will match the price cut, but it will lose considerably if it raises its price, since it will be undersold by rivals who do not change their prices. The demand curve facing such an oligopolist appears kinked, as in Figure 15.2. The curve is very steep below the current price, p_1, reflecting the fact that few sales are gained as price is lowered. But it is relatively flat above p_1, indicating that the firm loses many customers to its rivals, who refuse to match the price increases.

The figure also presents the marginal revenue curve, which has a sharp drop at the output level corresponding to the kink. Why does the marginal revenue curve have this shape, and what are the consequences? Consider what happens if the firm wants to increase output by one unit. It must lower its price by a considerable amount since, as it does so, its rivals will match that price. Accordingly, the marginal revenue it garners is small. If the firm contemplates cutting back on production by one unit, it needs to raise its price only a little since rivals will not change their prices. Thus, the loss in revenue from cutting back output by a unit is much greater than the gain in revenue from increasing output by a unit. With a flat demand curve, price and marginal revenue are close together.

The drop in the marginal revenue curve means that at the output at which the drop occurs, Q_1, the extra revenue lost from cutting back production is much greater than the extra revenue gained from increasing production. This has one important implication. Small changes in marginal cost, from

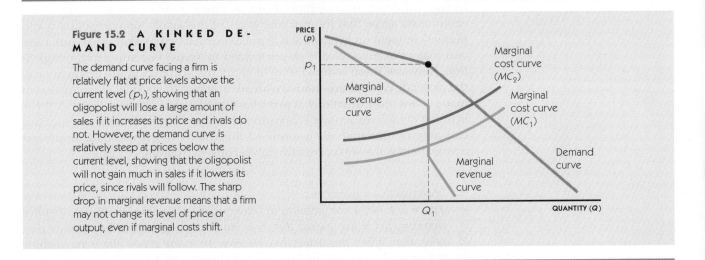

Figure 15.2 A KINKED DE-MAND CURVE

The demand curve facing a firm is relatively flat at price levels above the current level (p_1), showing that an oligopolist will lose a large amount of sales if it increases its price and rivals do not. However, the demand curve is relatively steep at prices below the current level, showing that the oligopolist will not gain much in sales if it lowers its price, since rivals will follow. The sharp drop in marginal revenue means that a firm may not change its level of price or output, even if marginal costs shift.

MC_1 to MC_2, have no effect on output or price. Thus, firms that believe they face a kinked demand curve have good reason to hesitate before changing their prices.

COMPETITION AMONG OLIGOPOLISTS

Cournot competition: Each firm believes its rivals will leave their output unchanged in response to changes in the firm's output.

Bertrand competition: Each firm sets its price believing its rivals will leave their own price unchanged in response to changes in the firm's price.

Kinked demand curves: Each firm believes its rivals will match price cuts but not price increases.

THE IMPORTANCE OF IMPERFECTIONS IN COMPETITION

Many of the features of the modern economy—from frequent-flyer mileage awards to offers to match prices of competitors, from brand names to the billions spent every year on advertising—not only cannot be explained by the basic competitive model, but are inconsistent with it. They reflect the imperfections of competition which affect so many parts of the economy. Most economists agree that the extreme cases of monopoly (no competition) and perfect competition (where each firm has *no* effect on market prices) are rare, and that most markets are characterized by some, but imperfect, competition. However, there is disagreement about the accuracy of the predictions of the perfectly competitive model, with advocates of that model claiming that in many, if not most situations, it provides a good approximation. Even so, there is broad consensus among economists that various phenomena and markets can only be understood in terms of limitations of competition. Imperfect competition is the subject of our eighth consensus point.

8   Imperfect Competition

There is limited competition in many markets. In imperfectly competitive markets, firms are aware that how much they sell, or other actions they take, may affect the price they receive. In many cases, firms must think strategically, considering how their rivals may react to their actions.

REVIEW AND PRACTICE

SUMMARY

1. Oligopolists must choose whether to seek higher profits by colluding with rival firms or by competing. They must decide what their rivals will do in response to any action they take.

2. A group of firms that have an explicit and open agreement to collude is known as a cartel. While the gains from collusion can be significant, there are important limits posed by the incentives to cheat and the necessity to rely on self-enforcement, by the coordination problems arising out of the necessity to respond to changing economic circumstances, and by new entry attracted by the cartel profits. Although cartels are illegal under U.S. law, firms have tried to find tacit ways of facilitating collusion—for example, by using price leaders and "meeting the competition" pricing policies.

3. If the threat of potential entry is sufficient to cause firms to set price and output at competitive levels, the industry is said to be contestable.

4. Even when they do not collude, firms attempt to restrict competition with practices like exclusive territories, exclusive dealing, tie-ins, and resale price maintenance. In some cases, a firm's profits may be increased by raising its rival's costs and making the rival a less effective competitor.

5. In Cournot competition, an oligopolist chooses its output under the assumption that its rivals' output levels are fixed.

6. In Bertrand competition, each firm chooses the price of its product on the assumption that its rivals' prices are fixed.

7. If the rivals to an oligopolist match all price cuts but do not match any price increases, then the oligopolist faces a kinked demand curve. A kinked demand curve will lead to a marginal revenue curve with a vertical segment, which implies that the firm will often not change its level of output or its price in response to small changes in costs.

KEY TERMS

cartel
antitrust laws
Prisoner's Dilemma
Cournot competition

Bertrand
   competition
kinked demand
   curve

contestable markets
potential
   competition

REVIEW QUESTIONS

1. Why is the analysis of oligopoly more complicated than that of monopoly, perfect competition, or monopolistic competition?

2. What are the gains from collusion? Why is there an incentive for each member of a cartel to cheat, to produce more than the agreed upon amount? What is the "Prisoner's Dilemma" and how is it related to the problem of cheating? What are the other problems facing cartels?

3. Name some ways that firms might use tacit collusion, if explicit collusion is ruled out by law.

4. What is a contestable market?

5. Name and define three restrictive practices.

6. What are the different forms of competition among oligopolies? How do they relate to *expectations* concerning how rivals will respond? Under what circumstances might each be more likely to be observed?

7. What expectations must an oligopolist have about the behavior of its rivals if it believes that it faces a kinked demand curve? Why might a firm that faces a kinked demand curve not change its price even when its costs change?

PROBLEMS

1. Explain why every member of a cartel has an incentive to cheat on its agreement. How does this fact strengthen the ability of antitrust laws that outlaw explicit collusion to do their job?

2. How might cooperative agreements between firms—to share research information, share the costs of cleaning up pollution, or help avoid shortfalls of supplies—end up helping firms to collude in reducing quantity and raising price?

3. Explain why each of the following might serve to deter entry of a competitor:
   (a) Maintaining excess production capacity.
   (b) Promising customers that you will undercut any rival.
   (c) Selling your output at a price below that at which marginal revenue equals marginal cost. (Hint: Assume entrants are unsure about what your marginal costs are. Why would they be deterred from entering if they believed you have low marginal costs? Why might a lower price lead them to think that you had low marginal costs?)
   (d) Offering a discount to customers who sign up for long-term contracts.

4. Explain why frequent-flyer programs (in which airlines give credits for each mile traveled, with the credits being convertible into travel awards) might reduce competition among airlines. Put yourself in the role of consultant to one of the airlines in the days before any airline had such programs. Would you have recommended that the airline adopt the program? What would you have *assumed* about the responses of other airlines? Would this have been important to your assessment?

5. At various times, Nintendo has been accused of trying to stifle its competitors. Among the alleged practices have been (a) not allowing those who produce games for Nintendo to produce games for others; and (b) discouraging stores that sell Nintendo from selling competing games, for instance, by not fulfilling their orders as quickly, especially in periods of shortages. Explain why these practices might increase Nintendo's profits.

6. Some industries are characterized by one large, highly efficient firm, and many smaller, less-efficient firms. Describe the equilibrium in this market. How does it depend on the level of demand? If the large firm becomes more efficient, what happens to price? profits?

7. Consider two oligopolists, with each choosing between a "high" and a "low" level of production. Given their choices of how much to produce, their profits will be:

		Firm A	
		High production	Low production
Firm B	High production	A gets $2 million profit / B gets $2 million profit	A gets $1 million profit / B gets $5 million profit
	Low production	A gets $5 million profit / B gets $1 million profit	A gets $4 million profit / B gets $4 million profit

Explain how firm B will reason that it makes sense to produce the high amount, regardless of what firm A chooses. Then explain how firm A will reason that it makes sense to produce the high amount, regardless of what firm B chooses. How might collusion assist the two firms in this case?

8. Use the Prisoner's dilemma analysis to describe what happens in the following two situations:

(a) Consider two rivals, say producers of cigarettes. If Benson and Hedges alone advertises, it diverts customers from Marlboro. If Marlboro alone advertises, it diverts customers from Benson and Hedges. If they both advertise, they retain their customer base.

Are they genuinely unhappy with government regulations prohibiting advertising? In practice, they have complained quite bitterly about such government restrictions, including those aimed at children. Why?

(b) Consider two rivals, say producers of camera film, Fuji and Kodak. Consumers want a film that accurately reproduces colors and is not grainy. Assume that initially, they had products that were comparable. If one does R & D and improves its product, it will steal customers from its rival. If they both do R & D, and develop comparable products, then they will continue to share the market as before. Thus, the hypothetical pay-off matrix (in millions of dollars) appears as below (the profits in the case of research take into account the expenditures on research):

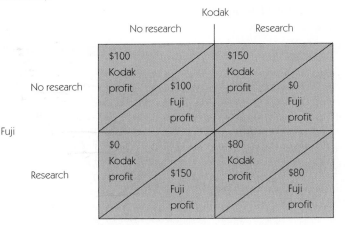

Explain why both will engage in research, even though their profits are lower. Could society be better off, even though profits are lower?

9. In 1990, Iraq invaded Kuwait, destroyed much of its oil fields, and, after losing a war, was essentially barred from selling oil. Assume Kuwait and Iraq were low-cost producers of oil. If OPEC, the oil cartel, operated to maximize joint profits, what would have been the effect of this on international oil prices? In 1996, there were plans to allow Iraq to sell a limited quantity of oil. What kind of response would one expect from OPEC?

10. Explain how exclusive territories, exclusive dealing, tie-ins, and resale price maintenance might help an oligopolist to make higher profits. How might a firm make the case that these practices add to efficiency?

APPENDIX: DESCRIBING THE MARKET EQUILIBRIUM FOR OLIGOPOLY

In this appendix, we take a closer look at how firms in an oligopoly behave and interact to determine the market equilibrium.

COURNOT COMPETITION

Under Cournot competition, each firm assumes its rival's output is constant. For simplicity, we focus on the case of a duopoly, a market in which there are only two firms, as illustrated in Figure 15.3.

The duopolist's demand curve in this case is simply the market demand curve shifted over to the left by the amount of output the rival is committed to producing.[3] Given this demand curve, we can draw the marginal revenue curve, and the firm produces at the point where marginal revenue equals marginal cost.

Figure 15.3 COURNOT COMPETITION IN A DUOPOLY

For a duopolist in a situation of Cournot competition, the firm's demand curve and the market demand curve are parallel, separated by the amount that the rival firm is committed to producing. Given the demand curve, the duopolist maximizes profit in the usual way, by setting its marginal revenue equal to marginal cost.

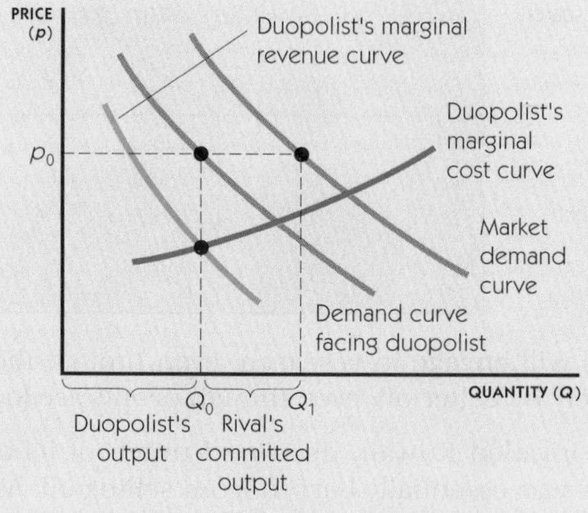

[3]This demand curve is sometimes referred to as the residual demand curve.

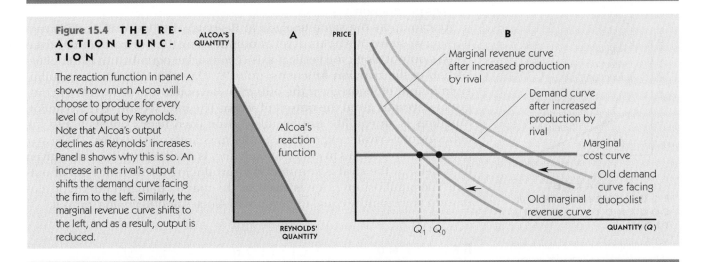

Figure 15.4 THE RE-ACTION FUNCTION

The reaction function in panel A shows how much Alcoa will choose to produce for every level of output by Reynolds. Note that Alcoa's output declines as Reynolds' increases. Panel B shows why this is so. An increase in the rival's output shifts the demand curve facing the firm to the left. Similarly, the marginal revenue curve shifts to the left, and as a result, output is reduced.

Normally, the equilibrium output with Cournot competition is less than with perfect competition but greater than with monopoly. Recall a firm sets marginal revenue equal to marginal cost. With perfect competition, marginal revenue is just price. With a monopoly, marginal revenue is lower than price. It is price minus what the firm loses on its earlier sales; that is, the reduction in price from producing one more unit. This is also the case with Cournot competition. Thus, output is lower than it is with perfect competition. But if there are two identical firms, each is producing only half the total output. Hence, what it loses in profits on earlier sales is smaller than under monopoly. Part of the lost revenue from lower prices is borne by the rival firm, which, under the Cournot assumption is expected to maintain its output. Marginal revenue is closer to price. So, because at any level of output the marginal revenue is higher with Cournot competition than with monopoly, equilibrium output is also higher.

To describe the market equilibrium, we need to see how the firms interact. The central tool in this analysis is the **reaction function,** which specifies the level of output of each firm given the level of output of the other firm. It shows, in other words, the reaction of one firm to the actions of the other. Consider the aluminum industry in the period after World War II; the two largest firms were Alcoa and Reynolds. The reaction function for Alcoa is plotted in Figure 15.4A. It is downward sloping.

To see why this is so, we need to recall how each Cournot oligopolist decides how much to produce. It sets marginal revenue equal to marginal cost, as in panel B. If Reynolds increases production, the demand facing Alcoa at any given price is reduced. Equivalently, if Alcoa wants to sell the same amount as before, it must lower its price. The figure shows the new demand and marginal revenue curves; they are to the left of the corresponding curves when Reynolds produced less. Accordingly, the optimal

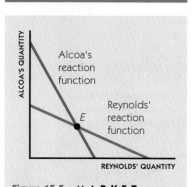

Figure 15.5 MARKET EQUILIBRIUM WITH COURNOT COMPETITION

Equilibrium will be at the intersection of the two reaction functions, where each firm is maximizing its profits given its belief that the output of the other firm is fixed. At that point, there is no pressure for either firm to change output.

level of output is lower: as Reynolds increases production, Alcoa decreases production.

We can apply the same analysis to Reynolds, in Figure 15.5. The reaction curve shows Reynolds' level of output along the horizontal axis, given Alcoa's output along the vertical axis. The market equilibrium is the intersection of the reaction functions, point E. This point depicts the equilibrium output of Alcoa given the output of Reynolds, and it depicts the output of Reynolds given the output of Alcoa. The intersection of the reaction functions is an equilibrium because, given each firm's beliefs about the behavior of its rival, neither firm wishes to change what it does. There are, in short, no pressures to change. Each firm is maximizing its profits, given its belief that the rival is committed to producing its current level of output. The equilibrium price is given by the market demand curve for aluminum at a quantity equal to the sum of Alcoa's and Reynolds' output.

BERTRAND COMPETITION

Figure 15.6 uses reaction functions to describe the market equilibrium of a Bertrand duopoly. A Bertrand duopolist assumes that its rival's price is fixed. This duopoly consists of two mattress companies, Supersleeper and Heavenlyrest, which produce imperfect substitutes. The reaction function in this case gives the price charged by one firm, given the price charged by its rival. As Supersleeper increases its price, Heavenlyrest finds it optimal to increase its own price. That is why the reaction function is positively sloped. The equilibrium is at E.

With price-setting (Bertrand) competition, firms believe that they face more elastic demand curves than they do with quantity-setting (Cournot) competition. This can easily be seen when we consider the extreme case where the two goods produced by two different firms are perfect substi-

Figure 15.6 MARKET EQUILIBRIUM WITH BERTRAND COMPETITION

Equilibrium will be at the intersection of the two reaction functions, where each firm is maximizing its profits given its belief that the price of the other firm is fixed. As one firm increases its price, the profit-maximizing price of its rival increases, so the reaction functions are positively sloped.

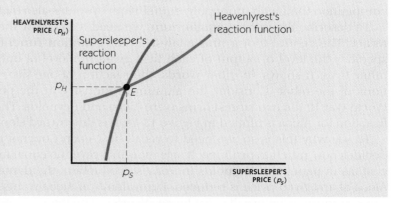

tutes. Then if one firm charges slightly less than its rival, it garners for itself the entire market; if it charges slightly more, it loses all of its sales. Each firm faces a horizontal demand curve. Thus, even when there are only two firms, if each believes the other has fixed its price and will not change the price in response to changes in prices it charges, and if the two firms produce *perfect* substitutes, the market outcome is competitive.

We can see this process of competition as follows. Assume both firms have constant marginal and average costs of production. Since each company believes its rival will not budge its price so long as price exceeds marginal costs, each one will find that it pays it to shave its price by a small amount. By doing so, it steals the whole market. But the rival firm, thinking the same way, then undercuts still further. The process continues until the price is bid down to the point where there are zero profits. It does not pay to cut prices any further.

In general, the products produced by two duopolists are not perfect substitutes but differ somewhat, so that each firm faces a downward-sloping demand curve. In equilibrium, price exceeds marginal costs. Output is less than it would be with perfect competition, but more than it would be with Cournot competition.

CHAPTER 16

GOVERNMENT POLICIES TOWARD COMPETITION

n the minds of most Americans, monopolies are not a good thing. They smell of income inequities and undemocratic concentrations of political power. To economists, however, the concern is economic efficiency. Motivated by both political and economic concerns, government has taken an active role in promoting competition and in limiting the abuses of market power. In this chapter, we review the economic effects of limited competition and look at government policies to reduce its negative effects.

KEY QUESTIONS

1. Why is government concerned with monopolies and imperfect competition? In what sense do markets with monopolies and imperfect competition result in inefficiency?

2. How have different governments attempted to address the problem posed by a natural monopoly?

3. How have governments used antitrust policies to break up monopolies, to impede the ability of any single firm to attain a dominant position in a market, and to outlaw practices designed to restrict competition?

THE DRAWBACKS OF MONOPOLIES AND LIMITED COMPETITION

Four major sources of economic inefficiency result from monopolies and other imperfectly competitive industries: restricted output, managerial slack, insufficient attention to research and development, and rent-seeking behavior. The problems can be seen most simply in the context of monopolies (the focus here), but they also arise in imperfectly competitive markets.

RESTRICTED OUTPUT

Monopolists, like competitive firms, are in business to make profits by producing the kinds of goods and services customers want. But monopolists can make profits in ways not available to competitive firms. One way is to drive up the price of a good by restricting output, as discussed in Chapter 14. They can, to use the popular term, gouge their customers. Consumers, by *choosing* to buy the monopolist's good, are revealing that they are better off than they would be without the product. But they are paying more than they would if the industry were competitive.

A monopolist who sets marginal revenue equal to marginal cost produces at a lower level of output than a corresponding competitive industry—an industry with the same demand curve and costs but in which there are many producers rather than one—where price equals marginal cost. Figure 16.1 shows that the monopoly output, Q_m, is much smaller than the competitive output, Q_c, where the price under competition, p_c, equals marginal cost. The price under monopoly, p_m, is much higher than p_c.

The price of a good, by definition, measures how much an individual is willing to pay for an extra unit of a good. It measures, in other words, the marginal benefit of the good to the purchaser. With perfect competition, price

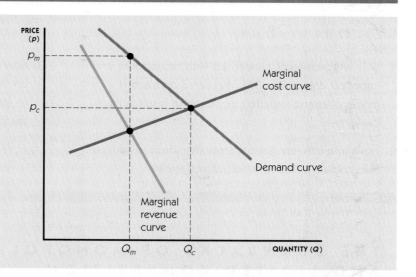

Figure 16.1 WHY MONOPOLY OUTPUT IS INEFFICIENT

With perfect competition price is set equal to marginal cost, with output at quantity Q_c and price p_c. A monopolist will set marginal revenue equal to marginal cost, and produce at quantity Q_m and price p_m, where the market price exceeds marginal cost.

equals marginal cost, so that in equilibrium the marginal benefit of an extra unit of a good to the individual (the price) is just equal to the marginal cost to the firm of producing it. At the monopolist's lower level of output, the marginal benefit of producing an extra unit—the price individuals are willing to pay for an extra unit—exceeds marginal cost.

By comparing the monopolist's production decision to the collective output decisions of firms in a competitive market, we can estimate the value of the loss to society when there is a monopoly. To simplify the analysis, in Figure 16.2 marginal cost is assumed to be constant, the horizontal line at the competitive price p_c. The monopolist produces an output of Q_m, at the point where marginal revenue equals marginal cost, and finds that it can charge p_m, the price on the demand curve corresponding to the output Q_m.

Two kinds of loss result, both related to the concept of consumer surplus introduced in Chapter 8. There we learned that the downward-sloping demand curve implies a bounty to most consumers. At points left of the intersection of the price line and demand curve, people are willing to pay more for the good than they have to. With competition, the consumer surplus in Figure 16.2 is the entire shaded area between the demand curve and the line at p_c.

The monopolist cuts into this surplus. First, it charges a higher price, p_m, than would be obtained in the competitive situation. This loss is measured by the rectangle *ABCD*, the extra price times the quantity actually produced and consumed. This loss to consumers is not a loss to society as a whole. It is a transfer of income as the higher price winds up as revenues for the monopoly. But second, it reduces the quantity produced. While production in a competitive market would be Q_c, with a monopoly it is the lower amount, Q_m. This second kind of loss is a complete loss to society, and is called the **dead-**

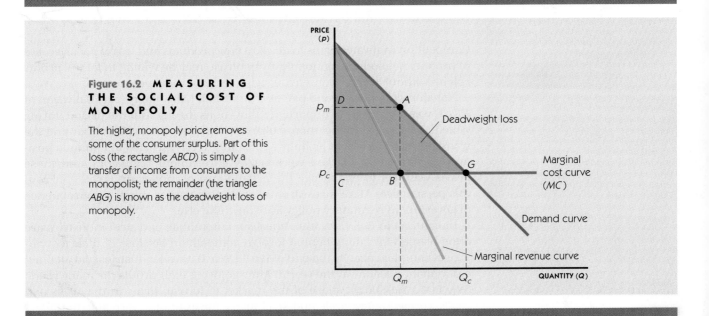

Figure 16.2 MEASURING THE SOCIAL COST OF MONOPOLY

The higher, monopoly price removes some of the consumer surplus. Part of this loss (the rectangle *ABCD*) is simply a transfer of income from consumers to the monopolist; the remainder (the triangle *ABG*) is known as the deadweight loss of monopoly.

weight loss of a monopoly. Consumers lose the surplus to the right of Q_m, denoted by *ABG,* with no resulting gain to the monopolist.

Some economists, such as Arnold Harberger of UCLA, have argued that these costs of monopoly are relatively small, amounting to perhaps 3 percent of the monopolist's output value. Others believe the losses from restricting output are higher. Whichever argument is right, output restriction is only one source of the inefficiencies monopolies introduce into the economy.

MANAGERIAL SLACK

Chapter 11 argued that any company wants to minimize the cost of producing whatever level of output it chooses to produce. But in practice, companies already making a lot of money without much competition often lack the incentive to hold costs as low as possible. The lack of efficiency when firms are insulated from the pressures of competition is referred to as **managerial slack.**

In the absence of competition, it can be difficult to tell whether managers are being efficient. How much, for instance, should it cost for AT&T to put a call through from New York to Chicago? In the days when AT&T had a monopoly on long-distance telephone service, it might have claimed that its costs were as low as possible. However, not even trained engineers could really tell whether this was true. When competition developed for intercity telephone calls, shareholders in AT&T could compare its costs with those of Sprint, MCI, and other competitors, and competition provided each company with an incentive to be as efficient as possible.

REDUCED RESEARCH AND DEVELOPMENT

Competition motivates firms to develop new products and less expensive ways of producing goods. A monopoly, by contrast, may be willing to let the profits roll in, without aggressively encouraging technological progress.

Not all monopolists stand pat, of course. Bell Labs, the research division of AT&T, was a fountain of important innovations throughout the period during which AT&T was a virtual monopolist in telephone service. The laser and the transistor are but two of its innovations. But AT&T was also in a unique position. The prices it charged were set by government regulators, and those prices were set to encourage the expenditure of money on research. From this perspective, AT&T's research contribution was as much a consequence of government regulatory policy as of anything else.

In contrast to Bell Labs, the American automobile and steel industries are often blamed for falling behind foreign competition because of their technological complacence. By the end of World War II, these industries had attained a dominant position in the world. After enjoying high profits for many years, they lost a significant share of the market to foreign firms in the 1970s and 1980s. Foreign automobile and steel firms, for example, were able to undersell their U.S. counterparts during the 1980s, not only because they paid lower wages but also because their technological advances had made production processes more efficient.

RENT SEEKING

The final source of economic inefficiency under monopoly is the temptation for monopolists to expend resources in economically unproductive ways. A major example is devoting resources to obtaining or maintaining their monopoly position by deterring entry. Since the profits a monopolist receives are called monopoly rents, the attempt to acquire or maintain already existing rents by acquiring or maintaining a monopoly position in some industry is referred to as **rent seeking.**

Sometimes a firm's monopoly position is at least partly the result of government protection. Many less-developed countries grant a company within their country a monopoly to produce a good, and they bar imports of that good from abroad. In these circumstances, firms will give money to lobbyists and politicians to maintain regulations that restrict competition so that they can keep their profits high. Such activities are socially wasteful. Real resources (including labor time) are used to win favorable rules, not to produce goods and services. There is thus legitimate concern that the willingness of governments to restrict competition will encourage firms to spend money on rent-seeking activities rather than on making a better product.

How much would a firm be willing to spend to gain and hold a monopoly position? The firm would be willing to spend up to the amount it would receive as monopoly profits. The waste from this rent-seeking activity can be much larger than the loss from the reduced output.

FURTHER DRAWBACKS OF LIMITED COMPETITION

We saw in Chapters 14 and 15 that markets in which a few firms dominated were more prevalent than monopolies. Relative to monopolies, some of the inefficiencies discussed above are smaller under limited competition. Output is lower than under perfect competition, but higher than under monopoly, for example. And competition to produce new products (research and development) is often intense, as we shall see in the next chapter. But other inefficiencies are worse in markets with limited competition than in monopoly markets. Firms under imperfect competition, for example, expend major resources on practices designed to deter entry, to reduce the force of competition, and to raise prices. Such expenditures may increase profits but they waste resources and make consumers worse off. Under imperfect competition firms may, for instance, maintain excess capacity to deter entry. A firm may gain a competitive advantage over its rival, not by lowering its own costs but by raising the rival's—for instance, by depriving it the use of existing distribution facilities. A firm may also spend money on uninformative (but persuasive) advertising.

POLICIES TOWARD NATURAL MONOPOLIES

If imperfect competition is as disadvantageous as the previous analysis has suggested, why not simply require that competition be perfect? To answer this question, we need to recall the reasons, discussed in Chapter 14, why competition is imperfect.

One reason is government-granted patents. Monopoly profits provide the return to inventors and innovators that is necessary to stimulate activities vital to a capitalist economy. We will discuss these issues more extensively in Chapter 17.

A second reason is that the cost of production may be lower if there is a single firm in the industry. This is the case with natural monopoly. In the case depicted in Figure 16.3, average costs are declining throughout the relevant levels of output, though marginal costs are constant. This is a case where there are very large fixed (overhead) costs. Natural monopolies present a difficult policy problem. Like any other firm, a natural monopolist will produce at the level where marginal revenue equals marginal cost, at Q_m in Figure 16.3. At this level, it will charge a price of p_m, which is higher than the marginal cost at that point. Thus, it will produce less and charge more than it would if price were equal to marginal cost, as would be the case with perfect competition (the output level Q_c and the price p_c in the figure).

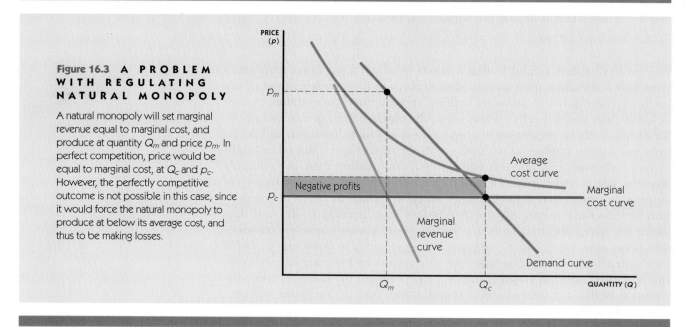

Figure 16.3 A PROBLEM WITH REGULATING NATURAL MONOPOLY

A natural monopoly will set marginal revenue equal to marginal cost, and produce at quantity Q_m and price p_m. In perfect competition, price would be equal to marginal cost, at Q_c and p_c. However, the perfectly competitive outcome is not possible in this case, since it would force the natural monopoly to produce at below its average cost, and thus to be making losses.

But in the case of natural monopoly, the very nature of the decreasing cost technology precludes perfect competition. Indeed, consider what would happen if price were set equal to marginal cost. With a natural monopoly, average costs are declining, and marginal costs are below average costs. Hence, if price were equal to marginal cost, it would be less than average costs, and the firm would be losing money. Profits would be negative, as shown by the shaded area in the figure. If the government wanted a natural monopoly to produce at the point where marginal cost equaled price, it would have to subsidize the company to offset these losses. Taxes would have to be raised to generate the money for the subsidies, which imposes other economic costs. Moreover, the government would likely have a difficult time ascertaining the magnitude of the subsidy actually required. Managers and workers in such a firm have a way of exaggerating their estimates of the high wages and other costs they "need" to produce the required output.

Following are three different solutions government has found to the problem of natural monopolies.

PUBLIC OWNERSHIP

In many foreign countries, government simply owns natural monopolies, such as electric power, gas, and water. There are problems with public ownership, however. Governments often are not particularly efficient as producers. Managers often lack adequate incentives to cut costs and modernize vigorously, particularly given the fact that government is frequently willing to subsidize the industry when it loses money. In addition, public ownership brings with it a number of political pressures. Political pressure may affect where public utilities, for example, locate their plants—politicians like to see jobs created in their home districts—and whether they prune their labor force to increase efficiency. Publicly run firms may also be under pressure to provide some services at prices below marginal cost, and make up the deficit from revenues from other services, a practice referred to as **cross subsidization.** Thus, business customers of utilities are sometimes charged more, relative to the costs of serving them, than are households. There is in effect a hidden tax and a hidden subsidy; businesses are taxed to subsidize households. The same phenomenon can be seen in our most important public monopoly, the U.S. postal service. It charges the same price for delivering mail to small rural communities as it does to major cities, in spite of the large differences in costs. Small communities have their mail services subsidized by larger ones.

How much less efficient the government is as a producer than the private sector is difficult to determine. Efficiency comparisons between government-run telephone companies in Europe and America's private firms provided much of the motivation for the **privatization** movement—the movement to convert government enterprises into private firms. Britain sold its telephone services and some other utilities, Japan its telephones and railroads, France its banks and many other enterprises. Not all publicly run enterprises are less efficient than their private counterparts, however. For example, Canada has two major rail lines, one operated by the government and one private, which differ little in the efficiency with which they are run. This may be because competition between the two forces the government railroad to be as efficient as the private. Many of the publicly owned enterprises in France seem to run as efficiently as private firms. This may be because of the high prestige afforded to those who work in the French civil service, which allows them to recruit from among the most talented people in their country. There may also be less difference between government enterprises and large corporations—particularly when both are subjected to some market pressure and competition—than popular conceptions of inefficient government would suggest.

REGULATION

Some countries leave the natural monopolies in the private sector but regulate them. This is generally the U.S. practice. Local utilities, for instance, remain private, but their rates are regulated by the states. Federal agencies regulate interstate telephone services and the prices that can be charged for interstate transport of natural gas.

The aim of regulation is to keep the price as low as possible, commensurate with the monopolist's need to obtain an adequate return on its investment. In other words, they try to keep price equal to average costs—where average costs include a "normal return" on what the firm's owners have invested in the firm. If the regulators are successful, the natural monopoly will earn no

Everyday 66 thousand planes fly across the country. With planes crisscrossing each other constantly in the sky, why are there not more collisions? The reason is the air traffic control system, currently run by the Federal Aviation Administration.

The system has not been kept up to date, however, because of budget pressure. Though it was one of the first government agencies to use computers on a large scale, many of its original outdated computers are still in use. The failure to make long-run investments, combined with government restrictions on procurement and personnel, have increased the cost of running the air traffic control system, and throw into question its capacity to meet the needs of the future.

In April 1994 the Clinton administration sent to Congress a proposal to **corporatize** the air traffic control system. Corporatization represents a halfway house towards privatization. Under the corporatization plan, the air traffic control system would be run much like a private corporation. Its revenues would come from "user fees" charged to the airlines and airplanes that use the system, and a ticket tax. Like regular corporations it could borrow funds. It would have a board of directors, composed, among others, of representatives from the airlines and government. Just as the government exercises safety supervision of private airlines, the government would continue to exercise safety supervision over the air traffic control system. The main difference between it and a private corporation would be that this "public" corporation could not sell shares. And its mandate would not be to maximize profits, but to provide the most efficient air traffic control services—for instance, minimizing unnecessary delay—at the lowest costs.

The privatized air traffic control system would, of course, be a monopolist, but since its major customers—the airlines—would serve on its board of directors, the scope for abusing its monopoly power would be limited. Still, there is concern that it could choose pricing or other policies that favor one group of users over another. Concern about such potential abuses provided the motivation for corporatization, as opposed to privatization, keeping the system within the public sector, with a strong public role in policy determination.

The major airlines were enthusiastic about the proposal. But supporters of general aviation—individually owned airplanes and corporate jets—were

against it. Cross subsidization is the reason. General aviation currently pays little for the services of the air traffic control system. Corporatization would stimulate potential pressure to eliminate this subsidy. Partly as a result of the resistance of this interest group, the proposal stalled in Congress.

monopoly profits. Such a regulated output and price are shown in Figure 16.4 as Q_r and p_r.

Two criticisms have been leveled against regulation as a solution to the natural monopoly problem. The first is that regulations often take an inefficient form. The sources of inefficiency are several. The intent is to set prices so that firms obtain a "fair" return on their capital. But to make the highest level of profit, firms respond by increasing their amount of capital as much as possible, which can lead to too much investment. In addition, the structure of prices may be set so that some groups, often businesses, may be charged extra-high prices to make it possible to subsidize other groups. This problem of cross subsidies is no less a problem for natural monopolies if they are privately owned and regulated than it is if they are owned and operated by the government. Further, firms' incentives to innovate are weakened if every time they lower costs, regulated prices are reduced commensurately. Recently regulators have recognized that unless they reward innovation, it will not happen. They have agreed to allow the utilities to retain much of the increased profits they obtain from improved efficiency, at least for a few years.

The second criticism is that the regulators lose track of the public interest. The theory of **regulatory capture** argues that regulators are pulled frequently

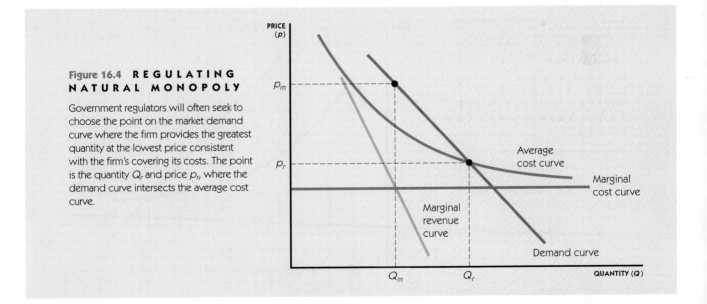

Figure 16.4 REGULATING NATURAL MONOPOLY

Government regulators will often seek to choose the point on the market demand curve where the firm provides the greatest quantity at the lowest price consistent with the firm's covering its costs. The point is the quantity Q_r and price p_r, where the demand curve intersects the average cost curve.

into the camps of those they regulate. This could happen through bribery and corruption, but the much likelier way is just that over time, employees of a regulated industry develop personal friendships with the regulators, who in turn come to rely on their expertise and judgment. Worse, regulatory agencies (of necessity) tend to hire from among those in the regulated industry. By the same token, regulators who demonstrate an "understanding" of the industry may be rewarded with good jobs in that industry after they leave government service.

ENCOURAGING COMPETITION

The final way government deals with the hard choices posed by natural monopolies is to encourage competition, even if imperfect. To understand this strategy, let us first review why competition may not be viable when average costs are declining over the relevant range of output.

If two firms divide the market between them, each faces higher average costs than if any one firm grabbed the whole market. As illustrated in Figure 16.5, Q_d denotes the output of each firm in the initial duopoly and AC_d its average costs. By undercutting its rival, a firm would be able to capture the entire market *and* have its average costs reduced. By the same token, a natural monopolist knows that it can charge a price above its average cost, AC_m, without worrying about entry. Rivals that might enter, trying to capture some of the profits, know that the natural monopolist has lower costs because of its larger scale of production, and so can always undercut them.

Even under these conditions, some economists have argued (as noted in

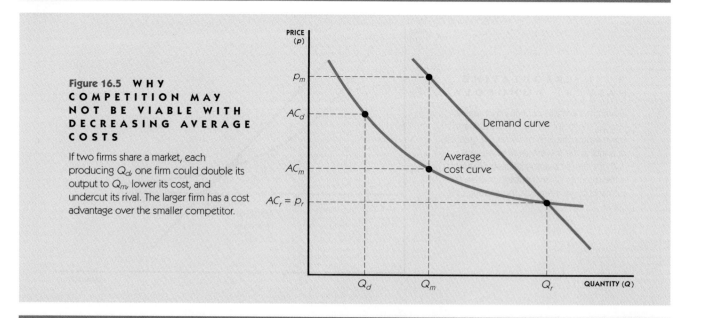

Figure 16.5 WHY COMPETITION MAY NOT BE VIABLE WITH DECREASING AVERAGE COSTS

If two firms share a market, each producing Q_d, one firm could double its output to Q_m, lower its cost, and undercut its rival. The larger firm has a cost advantage over the smaller competitor.

Chapter 15) that a monopolist would not in fact charge higher than average costs, because a rival could enter any time and grab the whole market. (The zero profit equilibrium is shown in the figure at output Q_r and price $AC_r = p_r$.) On this argument, all that is required to keep prices low is potential competition. Potential competition forces prices down to p_r, where the demand curve intersects the average cost curve.

Most economists are not so sanguine about the effectiveness of potential, as opposed to actual, competition. As we saw in Chapter 15, potential competition has not been able to keep airline prices down in those markets in which actual competition is limited to one or two carriers.

In the late 1970s and 1980s, as many governments became convinced that competition, however imperfect, might be better than regulation, and there began a process of deregulation. Deregulation focused on industries such as airlines, railroads, and trucking, where competition had a chance—there were, at most, limited increasing returns to scale. Government also sought to distinguish parts of an industry where competition might work from parts where competition was unlikely to be effective. In the telephone industry, for example, competition among several carriers was strong for long-distance telephone service, and there were few economies of scale in the production of telephone equipment. Accordingly, regulation of these parts of the industry was reduced or eliminated.

The virtues of competition have been borne out for the most part. Trucking—where the arguments for government regulation seemed most suspect—was perhaps the most unambiguous success story, with prices falling significantly. Railroads appear more financially sound than they did under regulation. But coal producers, who rely on railroads to ship their coal, complain that railroads have used their monopoly power to charge them much higher tariffs.

Airline deregulation has become more controversial in recent years. After its initial success—with new firms, lower fares, and more extensive routings—a rash of bankruptcies has reduced the number of airlines. Many airports, including those at St. Louis, Atlanta, and Denver, are dominated by one or two carriers, and these communities often face extremely high fares. A pattern of discriminatory pricing has developed, with businessmen who cannot make reservations weeks in advance paying four or more times the fare for the same seat as a vacationer.

APPROACHES TO NATURAL MONOPOLY

Public ownership

Regulation

Encouraging competition

CLOSE-UP: THE BREAKUP OF AT&T

When AT&T was broken up and the telephone industry partially deregulated in 1984, the general tone of discussion was resigned cynicism. The federal government had sought out one of the few things in life that worked—phone service—and decided to muck it up. AT&T had provided local and long-distance service to essentially everyone. After deregulation, a regional phone company (sometimes called a "Baby Bell") provided local phone service as a regulated monopoly, while the long-distance market was opened up to competition between AT&T, MCI, Sprint, and others. From the public reaction, you would have thought it was the end of modern communication. People complained about how confusing it was to receive two phone bills, one for local service and one for long-distance, and how phone service declined.

Well, fair is fair. The results are now coming in on how phone deregulation has worked, and they are reasonably positive. It is time to give the deregulation decision a little credit.

The technological story is clear. In the five years following deregulation, the cost of leasing a phone fell by half. New phone services like call waiting, phone mail, three-way calling, automatic redialing, and call forwarding have become popular. Of course, many of these technological changes would have happened over time, with or without phone deregulation. But the increased competitive pressure helped speed them up.

The price story, however, is a little more ambiguous. The price of long-distance service fell as much as 40 percent in these five years. However, local phone bills increased substantially; not enough to absorb all of that 40 percent, but enough to absorb much of it. Much of this change had been predicted by economists. Before deregulation, AT&T charged long-distance callers more heavily in order to subsidize local phone service. With deregulation, both local and long-distance service are now closer to paying their own way. Overall phone service (combining local and long-distance) was slowly getting cheaper before deregulation; it has continued to gradually fall in price.

Clearly, phone deregulation has had its benefits. Just as clearly, the main benefits have gone to those who make the most use of the new phone services and who use long-distance heavily. In 1996 Congress passed a new regulatory program for the telecommunications industry.

Deregulation has not yet extended to natural monopolies like water. But in the case of electricity a process for introducing some deregulation has begun. Some competition may be viable in electric power generation, which in general is not a natural monopoly, necessitating less government regulation. On the other hand, the transmission of electricity will continue to be a natural monopoly subject to regulation.

ANTITRUST POLICIES

Only some of the failures of competition arise from natural monopolies. Other imperfections, as we have seen, are the result of sharp business practices to develop market power by deterring entry or promoting collusion. When encouraging competition doesn't work, government sometimes resorts to enforcing competition through **antitrust policy.**

As we will see, these policies have often been controversial. Consumer groups and injured businesses tend to support them, arguing that, without them, firms would focus more on competition-reducing strategies than on efficiently producing products that customers like. Many businesses, however, claim that such policies interfere with economic efficiency. For instance, even if the most efficient way to distribute its products is through exclusive territories for distributors, the firm might worry that such a contract might be illegal under **antitrust law,** the body of law designed to restrict anticompetitive practices. Government antitrust efforts have followed the ebb and flow of concern about competition versus concern about the efficiency costs of antitrust restrictions.

The U.S. government has been officially concerned about the negative consequences of imperfect competition since the late nineteenth century. Table 16.1 lists the major landmarks of antitrust policy. These take the form of legislation and relevant judicial decisions. They fall into two categories: (1) limiting market domination, and (2) curbing restrictive practices.

LIMITING MARKET DOMINATION

In this section, we look at how government tries to limit economic power. In the decades following the Civil War, entrepreneurs in several industries attempted to form **trusts.** These were organizations that controlled a market. One individual has a controlling interest in a firm, which in turn had a controlling interest in all the other firms in the industry. By adding more layers—firms that controlled firms that controlled firms, and so on—a relatively small ownership stake could be leveraged into enormous economic power.

A controlling interest need not be a majority interest when the shares of a company are widely held. An individual or group of individuals owning only 10 or 20 percent of the shares can frequently exercise control, since the rest of the shareholders will either split their votes or be apathetic about the outcome. Among the most famous of the nineteenth-century trusts was the oil industry trust, with Rockefeller and his partners eventually controlling 90 percent of oil sold in America between 1870 and 1899. In the early 1900s, Andrew Carnegie and J. P. Morgan merged many smaller steel companies to form U.S. Steel, which in its heyday sold 65 percent of all American steel.

Concern about these robber barons led to passage of the Sherman Antitrust Act of 1890, which outlaws "every contract, combination in the form

Table 16.1 MAJOR ANTITRUST LEGISLATION AND LANDMARK CASES

Sherman Antitrust Act, 1890	Made acts in restraint of trade illegal.
Standard Oil and American Tobacco Cases, 1911	Broke up both firms (each of which accounted for more than 90% of their industry) into smaller companies.
Clayton Act, 1914	Outlawed unfair trade practices. Restricted mergers that would substantially reduce competition.
Establishment of the Federal Trade Commission, 1914	The Federal Trade Commission was established to investigate unfair practices and issue orders to "cease and desist."
Robinson-Patman Act, 1936	Strengthened provisions of the Clayton Act, outlawing price discrimination.
Alcoa Case, 1945	Alcoa, controlling 90% of the aluminum market, was found to be in violation of the Sherman Act.
Tobacco Case, 1946	The tobacco industry, a concentrated oligopoly, was found guilty of violation of the Sherman Act on the basis of tacit collusion.
Celler-Kefauver Act, 1950	Placed further restrictions on mergers that would reduce competition.
Du Pont Cellophane Case, 1956	Broadened the definition of market. Ruled that a 20% market share was insufficient to establish market power.

of a trust or otherwise, or conspiracy in restraint of trade or commerce." Further, "every person who shall monopolize, or attempt to monopolize, or combine or conspire with any other person or persons, to monopolize any part of the trade or commerce among the several States, or with foreign nations, shall be deemed guilty of a misdemeanor." (A 1974 amendment made violations felonies.) Two important decisions based on the Sherman Act were the breakups of Standard Oil and American Tobacco in 1911, each of which had dominated their respective industries.

The Sherman Act was supplemented by the Clayton Act in 1914, which forbade any firm to acquire shares of a competing firm when that purchase would substantially reduce competition. The act also outlawed interlocking directorates (in which the same individuals serve as directors of several firms) among firms that were supposedly in competition. These antimerger provisions were further strengthened in 1950 by the Celler-Kefauver Antimerger Act.

The government does not care about absolute size itself. In the 1960s, huge firms called conglomerates were formed, which brought together such disparate enterprises as a steel company, an oil company, and a company making films. For example, United Airlines bought Hertz rental cars and Westin

Hotels. But while large, these conglomerates generally did not have a dominant position in any one market, and thus the antitrust laws were not concerned with them. The early antitrust laws were particularly concerned with **horizontal mergers,** with competition within a market. These are distinguished from **vertical mergers,** in which a firm buys a supplier or a distributor, amalgamating the various stages in the production process within a firm. Thus, Ford made its own steel, and General Motors bought out Fisher Body (the maker of GM's car bodies), as well as many of the specialized firms that produced batteries, spark plugs, and other components.

Under current court interpretations, market power *per se* (by itself) is also not the primary concern. To be convicted of an antitrust violation, one must show that the firm acquired its market position by anticompetitive practices or that it used its market power to engage in anticompetitive practices.

DEFINING MARKETS

The question of whether a firm dominates a market is usually phrased, "What is its size relative to the market?" The debate thus centers on what is the relevant market. We have learned that the extent to which a firm's demand curve is downward sloping, so it can raise prices without losing all its customers—its market power—is related to both the number of firms in the industry and the extent of product differentiation. The problem of defining markets for the purposes of antitrust enforcement is related to both factors.

Market Bounds   During the last quarter century, international trade has become ever more important to the United States and the world economy. This change has affected all aspects of economic analysis, including the extent of competition in many markets. Today, imports exceed 9 percent of national output—three times the level in the 1950s and 1960s.

Thus while the degree of concentration among domestic producers of automobiles has increased—three firms are responsible for more than 90 percent of all U.S. auto production—the industry has become more competitive in the 1980s and 1990s, as foreign competition has increased and as foreign companies such as Toyota and Honda have established plants in the United States. It used to be that American firms could increase their price without worrying about their consumers switching to Japanese or European imports, but no longer. Today, the degree of competition in a market must be assessed from a global viewpoint, rather than looking simply at how many firms produce a good in the United States.

Product Differentiation   While all firms that produce the same good and sell in the same location are clearly in the same market, when the goods produced by different firms are imperfect substitutes, the definitional problem is more ambiguous.

What is the market for beer? Those in the industry might claim that premium beers and discount beers are really two different markets, with relatively few customers crossing over from one to the other. In the early 1950s,

Du Pont's cellophane had a virtual monopoly on the market for clear wrapping paper. In 1956, the company managed to fight off charges of monopoly by claiming that this market was part of a larger one for "wrapping materials." It claimed that brown paper was a good, though not perfect, substitute for cellophane, and in this broader market, Du Pont did not have a particularly large share (roughly 18 percent).

Legal Criteria   Today the courts look at two criteria for defining a market and market power. First, they consider the extent to which the change in prices for one product affects the demand for another. If an increase in the price of aluminum has a large positive effect on the demand for steel, then steel and aluminum may be considered to be in the same market—the market for metals. Second, if a firm can raise its price, say by 10 percent, and lose only a relatively small fraction of its sales, then it is "large"—that is, it has market power. (In a perfectly competitive market, a firm that raised its price by 10 percent would lose all its customers, so this is a workable approach to measuring the degree of competitiveness in the market.)

Before one large company can acquire a competitor or merge with another, it must convince the government that the acquisition would not seriously interfere with competition. Thus, although Dr. Pepper made up only a small part of the soft drink market, the government was concerned that the proposed acquisition of Dr. Pepper by Coca-Cola would have a significantly adverse affect on competition in a market that was already highly concentrated.

CURBING RESTRICTIVE PRACTICES

In addition to promoting competition by limiting the extent of concentration within an industry, the government works to limit restrictive practices. The history here begins with the 1914 Federal Trade Commission Act. The first ten words of the act read: "Unfair methods of competition in commerce are hereby declared unlawful." President Wilson defined the purpose of the new commission to "plead the voiceless consumer's case." Since then, a number of laws have been passed by Congress to make these general statements more specific.

Many of the restrictive practices targeted by the government involve the relations between a firm and its distributors and suppliers. Such practices include tying, exclusive dealing, and price discrimination. We have already encountered all three. Tying requires a buyer to purchase additional items when she buys a product. Exclusive dealing is when a producer says to a firm that wants to sell its product, "If you want to sell my product, you cannot sell that of my rival." Price discrimination entails charging different customers different prices, when those price differences are not related to the costs of serving those customers. The Robinson-Patman Act of 1936 strengthened the provisions outlawing price discrimination, making it easier to convict firms engaged in the practice. Other practices discussed in Chapters 14 and 15 designed to deter entry or promote collusion are illegal as well.

The precise definition of an illegal restrictive practice has changed over time with varying court interpretations of the antitrust laws. Some practices are illegal *per se*—firms conspiring together to fix prices, for example. In 1961, General Electric, Westinghouse, and other producers of electrical equipment were found guilty of this practice. They paid millions of dollars in fines, and some of their officials went to prison. Today, however, for most practices a "rule of reason" prevails. Under a rule of reason, the practice is acceptable if it can be shown to be reasonable business practice, designed to promote economic efficiency. The efficiency gains are balanced against the higher prices resulting from the reduced competition.

Thus, Budweiser beer delivers its product through distributors. In any area, there is only one distributor, and the distributors are not allowed to compete against one another. The New York attorney general has argued that this system, by restricting competition, raises prices. Anheuser-Busch has replied that the system of exclusive territories enhances the efficiency with which beer is delivered and is necessary to ensure that customers receive fresh beer. They have maintained that their distribution system satisfies the rule of reason, and thus far their view has been upheld by the courts.

ENFORCING THE ANTITRUST LAWS

Today antitrust laws are on the books at both state and federal levels, and are enforced by both criminal and civil courts. The government takes action not only to break up existing monopolies but also to prevent firms from obtaining excessive market power.

The Federal Trade Commission and the Antitrust Division of the Department of Justice are at the center of the government's efforts to promote competition. The FTC works like a law enforcement agency, investigating complaints it receives. It can provide advisory opinions on how an individual business should interpret the law, provide guidelines for entire industries, or even issue specific rules and regulations that businesses must follow. When necessary, the FTC enforces these decisions in court.

One interesting and controversial aspect of the antitrust laws is the use they make of *private* law enforcement. Any firm that believes it has been injured by the anticompetitive practices of another firm can sue, and if successful, can receive three times the dollar value of the damages and attorney fees incurred. The treble damage provision helps encourage private firms to call violations to the attention of the government. For example, MCI sued AT&T, claiming that the latter had used unfair trade practices to hurt MCI in its attempt to enter the long-distance telephone business. The jury estimated that MCI had, as a result of AT&T's activities, lost $600 million in profits, and ordered AT&T to pay triple that amount—$1.8 billion—in damages to MCI. The award was subsequently reduced on appeal to higher courts.

Two arguments favor private enforcement of antitrust laws. First, those who are injured by anticompetitive practices are in the best position to detect a violation of the law. Second, government may be lax in the enforcement of

USING ECONOMICS: COKE AND PEPSI PLAY MERGER MANIA

Coca-Cola Company and PepsiCo, Inc., dominate the market for carbonated soft drinks. Early in 1986, each proposed to grow larger through acquisition. In January, PepsiCo proposed buying 7-Up, the fourth largest soft drink manufacturer, for $380 million. In February, Coca-Cola proposed buying Dr. Pepper, the third largest, for $470 million.

The mergers would have made the big even bigger. Coca-Cola and PepsiCo already held 39 percent and 28 percent of the market, respectively, while Dr. Pepper had 7 percent and 7-Up had 6 percent. The next largest firm in the market after 7-Up was R. J. Reynolds (known for Canada Dry and Sunkist), which held 5 percent of the soft drink market.

The Federal Trade Commission announced that it would oppose the mergers. To assess the impact on competition, the government often uses in such cases what is called the Herfindahl-Hirschman Index (HHI). The HHI is calculated by summing the squares of the market shares. If the industry consists of a single firm, then the HHI is $(100)^2 = 10,000$. If the industry consists of 1,000 firms, each with .1 percent of the market, then the HHI is $(.1)^2 \times 1,000 = 10$. Thus, higher values of the HHI indicates less competitive industries.

Merger guidelines adopted by the federal government in 1982 divided markets into three categories, with different policy recommendations.

Before the mergers, a somewhat simplified HHI for the soft drink industry was (assuming that the 15 percent of the market not accounted for by the big four was divided equally among 15 small producers)

Level of HHI	Policy recommendation
Less than 1,000, unconcentrated	Mergers allowed without government challenge
Between 1,000 and 1,800, moderately concentrated	Mergers challenged if they raise the industry HHI by more than 100 points
Above 1,800, concentrated	Mergers challenged if they raise the industry HHI by more than 50 points

$$HHI = 39^2 + 28^2 + 7^2 + 6^2 + 5^2 + 15\,(1)^2$$

$$= 2,430.$$

If we plug in the 34 percent share that PepsiCo would have after acquiring 7-Up, the PepsiCo–7-Up merger would raise the HHI to 2,766. The two proposed mergers together would raise the HHI to 3,312.

With the announced FTC opposition to the merger, PepsiCo immediately gave up on purchasing 7-Up. Coca-Cola pushed ahead with its plan to buy Dr. Pepper until a federal judge ruled in August 1986 that it was a "stark, unvarnished" attempt to eliminate competition that "totally [lacked] any apparent redeeming feature."

The court case did bring a secret to the surface, however. The trial disclosed certain Coca-Cola company memos written after PepsiCo's offer for 7-Up had been made. In the memos, Coca-Cola executives expressed fear that the FTC might allow the PepsiCo merger, despite the merger guidelines. By announcing plans to buy Dr. Pepper, Coca-Cola hoped that the FTC would step in and these laws because of the potential political influence of cartels and dominant firms.

On the other side of the argument are concerns about the rising costs of antitrust litigation—the number of private suits doubled between the 1960s and the 1970s. And many worry that businesses use the threat of an antitrust suit as a way of raising a rival's costs. Thus, Chrysler charged General Motors with an antitrust violation when GM proposed a joint venture with a Japanese firm, only to drop the action when it found a Japanese partner for its own joint venture. Also, whenever a firm is successful in winning customers from a rival, the rival may accuse the firm of unfair practices and bring suit. Thus, firms may be reluctant to lower their prices when their efficiency has increased for fear they will be accused of predatory pricing.

CURRENT ANTITRUST CONTROVERSIES

Exactly how and when antitrust laws should be enforced remains one of the most controversial subjects of economic policy. In recent years, controversy has focused on two major issues.

First, how stringent should the standards be for allowing mergers of competing firms? In 1982, the government adopted new guidelines for such mergers, which many critics thought to be too lax. Those who favored the more lax rules argued that in today's international markets, competition is almost always sufficiently keen to ensure low prices and economic efficiency. Any firm that tried to exercise monopoly power by charging too high a price or that was slack in keeping costs down would be faced with an onslaught of competition. At most, the firm could enjoy a monopoly position for only a short time. For example, Ricoh, Canon, and a host of other firms unseated Xerox's monopoly position in copiers, and Fuji is now challenging Kodak's dominant position in film. Moreover, these advocates argue, attempts to restrict size penalize the more successful firms and inhibit their ability to take advantage of economies of scale and scope. Since foreign governments do not put similar restrictions on their own firms, American companies find themselves at a disadvantage. Size is particularly important for financing large-scale research endeavors, necessary if America is to keep its competitive edge.

Critics of this view contend that international competition cannot be relied upon—though admittedly, markets are more competitive with than without international competition. Furthermore, they question the importance of the economies of scale and scope. Many of America's leading exporters are relatively small companies, such as Compaq Computer. And the enhanced competition among firms in the United States not only makes consumers better off, through lower prices, but also sharpens the edge of businesses, making the more successful firms better able to compete not only at home but also abroad.

The second major controversial issue concerns what governmental policies should be toward restrictive practices—in particular, the contractual arrangements between firms and their suppliers and customers, such as exclusive dealing, tying, and exclusive territories—the so-called vertical restrictions discussed in Chapter 15. Those who, like Richard Posner (formerly of the University of Chicago, now a federal judge), believe that by and large competition is effective think there should be a presumption that such practices are legal. Others, like Steven Salop of Georgetown Law School, believe that frequently, while there is competition, it is limited. A review of the alleged "efficiency" gains of such practices suggests to these observers that the typical motive is to restrict competition further. If a change is needed from the current rule of reason, they argue, the presumption should be that these practices are restrictive. The burden would then be on any firm engaging in restrictive practices to show that the efficiency gains outweigh the losses from reduced competition.

ANTITRUST POLICIES

OBJECTIVE: ENSURE COMPETITIVE MARKETPLACE

Limit market domination

Curb restrictive practices

PROBLEMS

Defining markets

Practices may *both* reduce competition *and* enhance efficiency

Per se: practice is illegal (price fixing)

Rule of reason: balance anticompetitive and efficiency effects

ENFORCEMENT

Criminal

Civil–private law enforcement, treble damages

CURRENT CONTROVERSIES

Stringency of standards for allowing mergers

Policies toward vertical restraints

REVIEW AND PRACTICE

SUMMARY

1. Economists have identified four major problems resulting from monopolies and imperfect competition: restricted output; managerial slack; lack of incentives for technological progress; and wasteful rent-seeking expenditures.

2. Since for a natural monopoly average costs are declining over the range of market demand, a large firm can undercut its rivals. And since marginal cost for a natural monopoly lies below average cost, an attempt by regulators to require it to set price equal to marginal cost (as in the case of perfect competition) will force the firm to make losses.

3. Taking ownership of a natural monopoly allows the government to set price and quantity directly. But it also subjects an industry to political pressures and the potential inefficiencies of government operation.

4. In the United States, natural monopolies are regulated. Government regulators seek to keep prices as low and quantity as high as is consistent with the natural monopolist covering its costs. However, regulators are under political pressure to provide cross subsidies and are prone to being "captured" by the industry they are regulating.

5. In some cases, competition may be as effective as public ownership or government regulation at keeping prices low.

6. Antitrust policy is concerned with promoting competition, both by making it more difficult for any firm to dominate a market and by restricting practices that interfere with competition.

7. Under the "rule of reason," companies may seek to defend themselves from accusations of anticompetitive behavior by claiming that the behavior also leads to greater efficiency. In such cases, courts must often decide whether the potential efficiency benefits of restrictive practices outweighs their potential anticompetitive effects.

KEY TERMS

managerial slack	cross subsidization	vertical mergers
rent seeking	horizontal mergers	

REVIEW QUESTIONS

1. What does it mean when an economist says that monopoly output is "too little" or a monopoly price is "too high"? By what standard? Compared with what?

2. Why might a monopoly lack incentives to hold costs as low as possible?

3. Why might a monopoly lack incentives to pursue research and development opportunities aggressively?

4. What might an economist regard as a socially wasteful way of spending monopoly profits?

5. Explain why the marginal cost curve of a natural monopoly lies below its average cost curve. What are the consequences of this?

6. If government regulators of a natural monopoly set price equal to marginal cost, what problem will inevitably arise? How might government ownership or regulation address this problem? What are the problems of each?

7. What is the regulatory capture hypothesis?

8. Explain the difference between a horizontal and a vertical merger.

9. Explain how the government uses antitrust policies to encourage competition, by making it more difficult for a firm to dominate a market and by curbing restrictive practices. What are some of the problems in implementing antitrust policy and some of the current controversies surrounding it?

PROBLEMS

1. Before deregulation of the telephone industry in 1984, AT&T provided both local and long-distance telephone service. A number of firms argued that they could provide long-distance service between major cities more cheaply than AT&T, but AT&T argued against allowing firms to enter only the long-distance market. If those other firms (which had no technological advantage) could actually have offered long-distance service more cheaply, what does that imply about cross subsidies in AT&T's pricing of local and long-distance service? What would have happened if AT&T had been required to continue offering local service at the same price, but competition had been allowed in the long-distance market?

2. "The stories of $400 hammers and $1,000 toilet seats purchased by the Department of Defense prove that the private sector is more efficient than the public sector." Comment.

3. Explain the incentive problem involved if regulators assure that a natural monopoly will be able to cover its average costs.

4. Explain how some competition, even if not perfect, may be an improvement for consumers over an unregulated natural monopoly. Explain why such competition will not be as good for consumers as an extremely sophisticated regulator, and why it may be better than many real-world regulators.

5. Should greater efficiency be a defense against an accusation of an antitrust violation?

TECHNOLOGICAL CHANGE

F or much of the twentieth century, the United States has led in discovering and applying new technologies. Alexander Graham Bell and the telephone, the Wright brothers and the airplane, Thomas Edison and a host of electric devices—all are familiar early success stories. This tradition of innovation and invention continued as American inventors came up with products like the transistor and the laser. U.S. companies such as IBM, Eastman Kodak, and Xerox grew to become household names mostly because of the new products they brought to the market. More recently, Intel, Microsoft, and Genentech have experienced rapid growth and financial success based on their innovations.

The great strength of the market economy has been its ability to increase productivity, raise living standards, and innovate. Yet, the basic competitive model upon which we focused in Part Two simply *assumed* the state of technology as given.

If we are to understand what determines the pace of innovation, we must go beyond the standard competitive model.

KEY QUESTIONS

1. In what ways is the production of knowledge—including the knowledge of how to make new products and how to produce things more cheaply—different from the production of ordinary goods, like shoes and wheat?

2. Why is the patent system important in providing incentives to engage in research and development?

3. How may patents, as essential as they are for encouraging competition in research, at the same time reduce some aspects of competition?

4. How can government encourage technological progress?

First, industries in which technological change is important are almost necessarily imperfectly competitive. Second, the basic competitive model of Part Two assumes that individuals and firms receive all the benefits and pay all the costs of their actions. This assumption takes no account of the externalities produced by technological change. There is little doubt that we have all benefited from the multitude of inventions that have occurred in the last century. Just imagine what life would be like without the radio, television, cars, airplanes, washing machines, dishwashers—the list is endless. Alexander Graham Bell, Henry Ford, the Wright brothers were all rewarded for their inventions, some richly so. But the creation of these new products confers benefits beyond what consumers have to pay for them. Inventions possess certain characteristics of public goods and generate externalities.

This chapter shows why technological change is inevitably linked to imperfect competition. It then discusses the public good aspects of technological change and alternative ways to promote it.

LINKS BETWEEN TECHNOLOGICAL CHANGE AND IMPERFECT COMPETITION

In modern industrialized economies, much competition takes the form of trying to develop both new products and new ways of making existing products. Firms devote considerable resources to R & D—research (discovering new ideas, products, and processes) and development (perfecting, for instance, a new product to the point where it is brought to the market). In industries in which technological change and R & D is important, such as computers and drugs, firms strive to earn profits by introducing new and better (at least in the eyes of consumers) goods, or less costly methods of production. Only through such profits can the investment in R & D payoff.

Technological change and imperfect competition are inevitably linked for four major reasons. First, to make R & D expenditure pay, and therefore stimulate innovation, inventions are protected from competition by patents. Patents are specifically designed to limit competition. Second, industries where technological change is important typically have high fixed costs—costs that do not change as output increases. This implies decreasing average costs over a wide range of output, another characteristic that limits competition. Third, industries characterized by rapid technological change are also industries where the benefits of increasing experience in a new production technique can lead to rapidly decreasing costs. Finally, because banks are generally unwilling to lend funds to finance R & D, raising capital for new and small firms is difficult. All these make entry difficult, and reduce competition in the sense defined by the basic competitive model.

PATENTS

The U.S. Constitution, as noted in Part One, enables Congress to grant "for limited time to authors and inventors the exclusive right to their respective writing and discoveries." Economists refer to the output of this creative action as **intellectual property.** The "limited time" for inventors is currently seventeen years. During this period, other producers are precluded from producing the same good, or even making use of the invention in a product of their own, without the permission of the patent holder. A patent holder may allow others to use its patent or sell its product; in return the patent holder receives a payment called a royalty.

THE TRADE-OFF BETWEEN SHORT-RUN EFFICIENCY AND INNOVATION

The patent system grants the inventor a temporary monopoly, allowing her to appropriate some part of the returns on her inventive activity. In Chapter 16, we learned that, relative to a competitive market a monopoly produces a lower level of output that sells at a higher price. In spite of this, and in spite of the antitrust policies discussed there, why does government sanction these monopolies?

In Chapter 13, where we explained why competitive markets, with price equal to marginal cost, ensure economic efficiency, we assumed that the technology was given. We refer to the kind of economic efficiency that ignores concerns about innovation and invention as **static efficiency.**

But the overall efficiency of the economy requires balancing these short-run concerns with the long-run objectives of stimulating research and innovation. Innovation requires firms to reap a return on their investment, and that in turn requires some degree of monopoly power. An economy in which the balancing of short- and long-run concerns is appropriately done is said to be **dynamically efficient.**

A key provision of the patent law affecting the static efficiency versus the incentives for innovation necessary for dynamic efficiency is the **life of the patent.** If the life of a patent is short, then firms can appropriate the returns from their innovation for only a short time. There is less incentive to innovate than if the patent protection (and monopoly) lasted longer, but the economy has greater static efficiency. If the life of a patent is long, then there are large incentives to innovate, but the benefits of the innovation are limited. Consumers, in particular, must wait a long time before prices fall. The seventeen-year patent period is intended to strike a balance between the benefits to consumers and the return to investments in R & D.

AN EXAMPLE: THE SWEET MELON COMPANY

Figure 17.1 illustrates the effect of a patent owned by the Sweet Melon Company on a new, cheaper process for producing frozen watermelon juice. To make it simple, the marginal cost of production is constant in this example. Before the innovation, all producers face the same marginal cost of c_0. Sweet Melon's innovation reduces the marginal costs of production to c_1. Imagine that this industry is perfectly competitive before the innovation, so that price equals marginal cost, c_0. But now Sweet Melon is able to undercut its rivals. With patent protection, the firm sells the good for slightly less than p_0. Its rivals drop out of the market because at the new, lower price, they cannot break even. Sweet Melon now has the whole market. The company sells the quantity Q_1 at the price p_1, making a profit of AB on each sale. Total profits are shaded area $ABCD$ in the figure. The innovation pays off if the profits received exceed the cost of the research. (These profits may be thought of as "rents" associated with its superior technology.)

Figure 17.1 ECONOMIC EFFECT OF PATENTS

Here, an innovation has reduced the marginal cost of production from c_0 to c_1. Before the innovation, the equilibrium price is p_0, which equals c_0. However, an innovator with a patent will drop the price to p_1, just below p_0, and sell the quantity Q_1. Total profits are the shaded area $ABCD$. When the patent expires, competitors reenter the market, price falls to p_2, which equals c_1, and profits drop to zero.

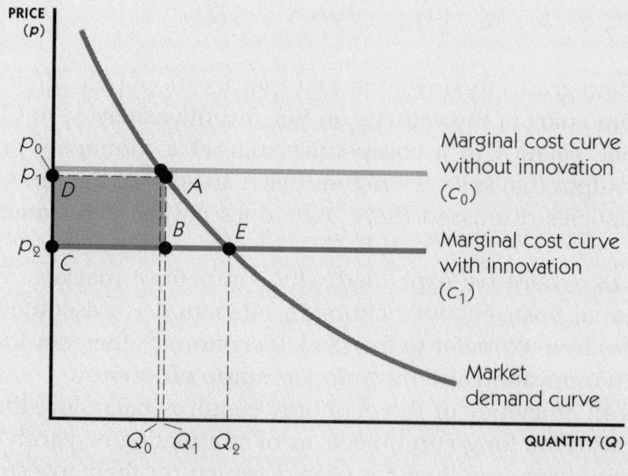

What happens when the patent expires? Other firms enter the industry, using the less expensive technology. Competition forces the price down to the now lower marginal costs, c_1, and output expands to Q_2. The new equilibrium is at E. Consumers are clearly better off. Static economic efficiency is enhanced, because price is now equal to marginal cost. But Sweet Melon reaps no further return from its expenditures on research and development.

If no patent were available, competitors would immediately copy the new juice-making process, and the price would drop to c_1 as soon as the innovation became available. Sweet Melon would receive absolutely no returns. (In practice, of course, imitation takes time, during which the company would be able to obtain *some* returns from the innovation.) If the patent were made permanent, consumers would benefit only a small amount from the innovation, since other companies could not compete. Output would remain at Q_1, slightly greater than the original output, and the price would remain high.

BREADTH OF PATENT PROTECTION

How broad a patent's coverage should be is as important as its duration. If an inventor comes up with a product quite similar to, but still slightly different from, one that has already been patented, can this inventor also get a patent for his variant? Or does the original patent cover "minor" variants? Chapter 1 discussed the patent claim of George Baldwin Selden, who argued that his patent covered all self-propelled, gasoline-powered vehicles. He tried to force Henry Ford and the other pioneers of the automobile industry to pay royalties to him, but Ford successfully challenged the patent claim. Recently controversies over patents have hit genetic engineering and superconductivity. Does a firm that decodes a fraction of a gene and establishes a use for that information, for example, get a patent? If so, does the patent cover the fraction in question or the whole gene?

The original innovators have every incentive to claim broad patent coverage, affecting their own product and those that are in any way related. Later entrants argue for narrow coverage, so that they will be allowed to produce variants and applications without paying royalties. As usual in economics, there is a trade-off. Broad coverage ensures that the first inventor reaps more of the returns of her innovation. But excessively broad coverage inhibits follow-on innovation, as others see their returns to further developing the idea squeezed by the royalties they must pay to the original inventor.

TRADE SECRETS

If patents protect the profits of innovation, why do many firms not bother to seek patent protection for their new products and processes? A major reason is that a firm cannot get a patent without disclosing the details of the new product or process—information that may be extremely helpful to its rivals in furthering their own R & D programs.

To prevent such disclosure, companies sometimes prefer to keep their own innovations a **trade secret.** A trade secret is simply an innovation or knowledge of a production process that a firm does not disclose to others. The formula for Coca-Cola, for example, is not protected by a patent. It is a trade secret. Trade secrets play an important role in metallurgy, where new alloys are usually not patented. Trade secrets have one major disadvantage over patents. If a rival firm *independently* discovers the same new process, say for making an alloy, it can use the process without paying royalties, even though it was second on the scene.

Some of the returns to an invention come simply from being first in the market. Typically, the firm that first introduces a new product has a decided advantage over rivals, as it builds up customer loyalty and a reputation. Latecomers often have a hard time breaking in, even if there is no patent or trade secret protection.

R & D AS A FIXED COST

Patents and trade secrets are not the only reason that industries in which technological change is important are generally not perfectly competitive. A second explanation is that R & D expenditures are fixed costs. That is, the cost of inventing something does not change according to how many times the idea is used in production.[1] The size of fixed costs helps determine how competitive an industry is. The larger the fixed costs relative to the size of the market the more likely that there will be few firms and limited competition.

Because expenditures on research and development are fixed costs, industries with large R & D expenditures face declining average cost curves up to relatively high levels of output. We saw in Chapter 11 that firms typically have U-shaped average cost curves. The presence of fixed costs means that average costs initially decline as firms produce more, but for all the reasons discussed in Chapter 11, beyond some level of output average costs increase. When there are large fixed costs, large firms will have lower average costs than small firms and enjoy a competitive advantage. (See Figure 17.2.) Industries with large fixed costs thus tend to have relatively few firms and limited competition. It is not surprising, therefore, that the chemical industry—where R & D is tremendously important—is highly concentrated.

Increased size also provides firms with greater incentives to undertake research. Suppose a small firm produces 1 million pens a year. If it discovers a better production technology that reduces its costs by $1 per pen, it saves $1 million a year. A large firm that makes the same discovery and produces 10 million pens a year will save $10 million a year. Thus, large firms have more incentive to engage in research and development, and as they do, they grow more than their smaller rivals do.

But while a large firm's research and development department may help the firm win a competitive advantage, it may also create managerial problems. Bright innovators can feel stifled in the bureaucratic environment of a large corporation, and they may also feel that they are inadequately compensated for their research efforts. In the computer industry, for example, many capable people have left the larger firms to start up new companies of their own.

---

[1]R & D expenditures can themselves be varied. Differences in the expenditure level will affect when new products will be brought to market and whether a firm will beat its rivals in the competition for new products.

Figure 17.2 COSTS OF RESEARCH AND DEVELOPMENT

R & D costs are fixed costs—they do not vary with the scale of production. In industries that are R & D intensive, average costs will be declining over a wide range of outputs. Firms with low levels of output (Q_1) have higher average costs than those with higher output (Q_2).

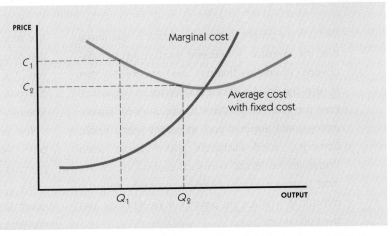

Thus, size has both its advantages and disadvantages when it comes to innovation. Important inventions and innovations, such as nylon, transistors, and the laser have been produced by major corporations; on the other hand, small enterprises and individual inventors have produced Apple computers, Polaroid cameras, and Kodak film, all of which became major corporations as a result of their success. One objective of antitrust policies is to maintain an economic environment in which small, innovative firms can compete effectively against established giants.

LEARNING BY DOING

Some increases in productivity occur not as a result of explicit expenditures on R & D, but as a by-product of actual production. As firms gain experience from production, their costs fall. This kind of technological change is called **learning by doing.** This systematic relationship between cumulative production experience and costs—often called the **learning curve**—was first discovered in the aircraft industry, where as more planes of a given type were produced, the costs of production fell dramatically.

This is the third reason why technological change and imperfect competition go together—because the marginal cost falls as the scale of production (and the experience accumulated) increases. The first firm to enter an industry has a particular advantage over other firms. Even if some of what the first company has learned spills over into other firms, not all of it does. Because of the knowledge the first firm has gained, its costs will be below those of potential rivals, and thus it can always undercut them. Since potential entrants know this, they are reluctant to enter industries where learning by doing has a significant impact on costs. By the same token, companies realize that if they can find a product that provides significant benefits from learning by doing,

CLOSE-UP: ELI WHITNEY AND THE COTTON GIN

Obtaining a patent does not necessarily guarantee that the inventor will receive a return on her discovery. Others may "infringe" on her patent— that is, use the idea without paying for it—in which case the inventor will have to sue. Suits for patent infringement are common. In recent years, Apple Computer sued Microsoft and Polaroid sued Kodak, to name but two such cases. One of the most famous examples of an inventor who found it difficult to enforce his patents is Eli Whitney and the cotton gin.

Late in the eighteenth century, the textile mills of England and the northern American states were up and humming, but there seemed to be a perpetual shortage of cotton. The kind of cotton grown in the southern United States could have filled the need, but someone had to find an inexpensive way to separate the seeds from the cotton. Eli Whitney invented the cotton gin to perform that task. Whitney did what an inventor is supposed to do. He applied for a patent and received one in 1794. He found a partner to put up the money, and then started a business to make machines that would clean the seeds out of cotton. The cotton gin turned out to be a wonder, bringing prosperity to the American South. But Whitney received little of the benefit.

The problem was that Whitney's machine was both very effective and very simple. Cotton planters found it easy to copy the cotton gin and make a few minor changes. When Whitney sued in court for patent infringement, courts in cotton-growing states tended to find that his patent had not actually been infringed. Eventually, the states of South Carolina, North Carolina, Tennessee, and Georgia agreed to pay a lump sum to Whitney to purchase the rights to his invention. The amount paid, though, was barely enough to allow Whitney and his partner to recoup their expenses.

Whitney continued his lifelong career as an inventor, but he never bothered to patent an invention again. As he once wrote: "An invention can be so valuable as to be worthless to the inventor." Whitney's experience was extreme. Today patent

Whitney's cotton gin

the profits they earn will be relatively secure. Hence, just as firms race to be the first to obtain a patent, so too they race to be the first to enter a product market in which there is a steep learning curve. This behavior is commonly displayed in the computer chip industry.

When learning by doing is important, firms will produce beyond the point where marginal revenue equals *current* marginal costs, because producing more today has an extra benefit. It reduces future costs of production. How much extra a firm produces depends on the steepness of the learning curve.

ACCESS TO CAPITAL MARKETS

Banks are generally unwilling to lend funds to finance R & D expenditures, because they are often very risky and these risks cannot be insured. When a bank makes a loan for a building, if the borrower defaults, the bank winds up with the building. If the bank lends for R & D and the research project fails, or a rival beats the firm to the patent office, the bank may wind up with nothing. Banks also often have a hard time judging the prospects of an R & D endeavor—inventors are always optimistic about their ideas. This difficulty is compounded because an inventor may be reluctant to disclose all the information about his idea, either to banks or potential investors, lest some among them steal his idea and beat him either to the market or the patent office.

For established firms in industries with limited competition and growing demand, financing their research expenditures presents no serious problem. They can pay for R & D out of their profits. That is why, for the economy as a whole, most research and development occurs in such firms. But raising capital is a problem for new and small firms, and also for firms in industries where intense competition limits the profits that any one company can earn. Thus, a firm's dominant position in an industry may be self-perpetuating. Its greater output means that it has more to gain from innovations that reduce the cost of production. And its greater profits give it more resources to expend on R & D.

Today much of the research and development in new and small companies is financed by venture capital firms. These firms raise capital, mainly from pension funds, insurance companies, and wealthy individuals, which they then invest in the most promising R & D ventures. Venture capital firms often demand, as compensation for their risk taking, a significant share of the new enterprise, and they usually keep close tabs on how their money is spent. They often specialize in particular areas, such as computer technology or biotechnology. In less glamorous industries, it is often difficult to find financing for research and development, because venture capital firms may be hesitant to invest in a higher-risk venture.

CLOSE-UP: JOSEPH SCHUMPETER AND SCHUMPETERIAN COMPETITION

The economist most known for emphasizing the role of innovation in market economies is Joseph Schumpeter. Schumpeter began his career in Austria (serving from spring to October 1919 as Minister of Finance to the Emperor of the Austro-Hungarian Empire), and ended his career as a distinguished professor of economics at Harvard. His vision of the economy was markedly different from that of the competitive equilibrium model. That model focuses on equilibrium, a state of the world in which there is no change. He questioned the very concept of equilibrium. To him the economy was always in flux and the economist's role was to understand the forces driving those changes.

Schumpeter argued that the economy was characterized by a process of creative destruction. An innovator could, through his new product or lower costs of production, establish a dominant position in a market. But eventually, that dominant position would be destroyed, as a new innovator took his place.*

He worried that the giant corporations he saw being formed during his life would stifle innovation and end this process of creative destruction. His fears, so far, have been unfounded; indeed, many of the largest firms, like IBM, have not been able to manage the innovative process in a way that keeps up with upstart rivals.

Modern day Schumpeterians often turn to biology to help them understand the process of change. They describe changes as *evolutionary*. They see a slow process of change, with many random elements, with firms that are the fittest—who, by luck or skill manage to discover new products or new ways of doing business that are better, in the particular environment, than their rivals—managing to survive and their practices spreading to other firms.

As respect for and understanding of the importance of innovation has grown, so too have the number of economists who think of themselves as Schumpeterians. And the Schumpeter Society of Austria provides an award every year to honor someone in the "Schumpeterian tradition." In 1994, the award went to an American, Ted Turner, founder of CNN.

*We discussed this kind of competition—a succession of monopolies—in Chapter 14, under the topic of **Schumpeterian competition**.

Joseph Schumpeter

COMPETITION AND TECHNOLOGICAL CHANGE

HOW COMPETITION AFFECTS TECHNOLOGICAL CHANGE

Competition spurs R & D:
> A new innovation enables firms to enjoy profits (profits are driven to zero in standard markets).
> Unless firms innovate, they will not survive.

Competition impedes R & D:
> Competitors may imitate, thus eroding returns from innovation.
> Competition erodes the profits required to finance R & D.

HOW TECHNOLOGICAL CHANGE AFFECTS COMPETITION

R & D spurs competition:
> R & D provides an alternative to prices as a way for firms to compete; it is one of the most important arenas for competition in modern economies.

R & D impedes competition:
> Patents give a single firm a protected position for a number of years.
> The fixed costs of R & D give large firms an advantage, and mean that industries in which R & D is important may have few firms.
> Learning by doing gives a decided advantage to the first entrant into a market.
> Limited access to capital markets for financing R & D is a disadvantage to new and small firms.

BASIC RESEARCH AS A PUBLIC GOOD

R & D expenditures on inventions or innovations almost always give rise to externalities. Externalities arise, as we learned in Chapter 7, whenever one individual's or firm's action produces costs or benefits to others. The total benefits produced by an R & D expenditure are referred to as its **social benefit.** Even with patents, inventors appropriate only a fraction of the social benefit of an invention. A firm that discovers a cheaper way of producing is likely to lower its price during the life of the patent to steal customers away from its rivals. This benefits consumers. After the patent expires, consumers benefit even more as rivals beat the price down further. And the benefits of an invention in one area spill over to other areas. The transistor, which revolutionized electronics, was invented at AT&T's Bell Laboratories. AT&T reaped the benefits from its direct application to telephone equipment. But the benefits in better radios, television sets, and other products accrued to others.

From society's viewpoint, a particularly valuable kind of R & D is **basic research.** Basic research is the kind of fundamental inquiry that produces a wide range of applications. Basic research in physics, for example, led to the ideas behind so many of the things we take for granted today—the laser, the transistor, atomic energy. The private returns to firms from any basic research they might undertake—which would dictate the amount of R & D spent on basic research in the absence of government intervention—are negligible in comparison to its social benefits. Indeed, the externalities flowing from basic research are so extreme that it can be considered a public good.

Public goods are defined by two properties. First, it is difficult to exclude anyone from the benefits of a public good. Basic research involves the discovery of underlying scientific principles or facts of nature. Such facts—like superconductivity, or even the fact that there exist certain materials that exhibit superconductivity at temperatures considerably above absolute zero—cannot be patented.

Second, the marginal cost of an additional individual enjoying a public good is zero. We say that consumption is nonrivalrous. An additional person being informed of a basic discovery does not detract from the knowledge that the original discoverer has, though it may, of course, reduce the profits the original discoverer can make out of the discovery. Indeed, sharing the fruits of basic research as soon as they are available can yield enormous benefits— as other researchers use this knowledge in their quest for innovations.

As with all public goods, private markets yield an undersupply of basic research. Accordingly, the government supports basic research through the National Science Foundation, the National Institutes of Health, and other organizations. Some of the expenditures of the Department of Defense on R & D also go into basic research. Still, there is increasing concern among economists that expenditures on basic research are inadequate.

Figure 17.3 shows that support by the federal government for R & D, outside of defense, has not increased, as a percentage of the nation's output, over

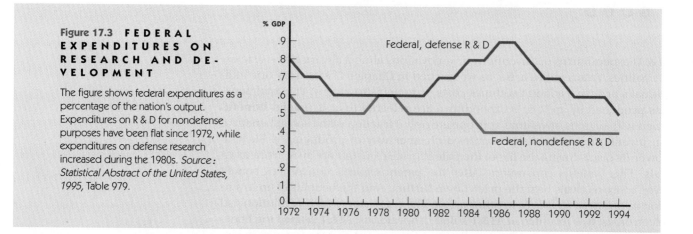

Figure 17.3 FEDERAL EXPENDITURES ON RESEARCH AND DEVELOPMENT

The figure shows federal expenditures as a percentage of the nation's output. Expenditures on R & D for nondefense purposes have been flat since 1972, while expenditures on defense research increased during the 1980s. *Source: Statistical Abstract of the United States, 1995,* Table 979.

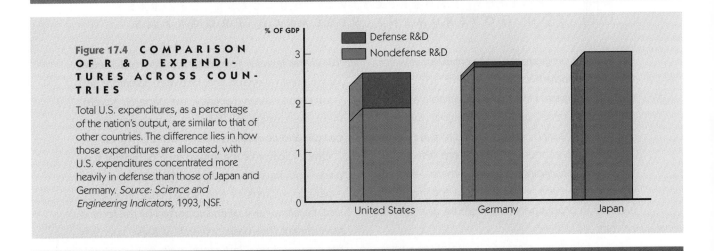

Figure 17.4 COMPARISON OF R & D EXPENDITURES ACROSS COUNTRIES

Total U.S. expenditures, as a percentage of the nation's output, are similar to that of other countries. The difference lies in how those expenditures are allocated, with U.S. expenditures concentrated more heavily in defense than those of Japan and Germany. *Source: Science and Engineering Indicators*, 1993, NSF.

the last two decades. With the end of the Cold War, there has been an attempt to shift more of the federal government's support of R & D away from defense towards civilian or **dual use** technologies (technologies which have both civilian and military use). Still, 55 percent of government R & D expenditures remain defense related. This explains why, while the United States devotes about the same proportion of its economy to R & D as do Japan and Germany, as shown in Figure 17.4, less of the total is spent in developing new products and processes to make American industry more competitive. And more is spent in developing better and more effective weapons. This may also partly explain why today foreigners are getting almost one out of every two patents granted by the U.S. Patent Office. (Inventors have the right to obtain a patent from a foreign country as well as their own.)

GOVERNMENT PROMOTION OF TECHNOLOGICAL PROGRESS

While there is widespread agreement that government should encourage innovative activity through the protection of intellectual property rights and through support of basic R & D, other ways by which the government promotes R & D have been more controversial.

SUBSIDIES

One way in which government has sought to encourage new technologies is through subsidies. This approach has been criticized with the argument that the government has a bad record in picking what to subsidize. As evidence, they note that the Concorde, the supersonic airplane developed with the support of the French and British governments, has never been able to pay for itself. Closer to home, the government spent billions of dollars in an unsuccessful attempt to develop synthetic fuels. Broad-based subsidies, such as R & D tax credits, do not depend on government selection of particular projects, but are controversial due to their relatively high cost to the government. Critics claim that little additional research is generated per dollar of tax revenue lost.

But there are still supporters of more active involvement of government in R & D, who claim there are large positive externalities associated with applied research, implying that the private sector underinvests in applied research. Policies aimed to support particular sectors of the economy are called **industrial policies,** even if those sectors are not industries as we conventionally think of them, such as agriculture.

Advocates of public support of applied R & D admit that government has not always picked winners. But they claim R & D is by its very nature risky, and a record of complete success cannot be expected. They also claim that, in fact, government's success record has been impressive. They point, for example, to the over 1,000 percent increase in the productivity of agriculture over the past century. This has resulted not only from research undertaken at the state agricultural colleges (which the federal government has helped for more than a century) but also from government-supported diffusion of knowledge, through the agricultural extension service.

Advocates of a more active government role in promoting technology argue that the objective is not so much to pick winners as to identify areas where, in the absence of government support, there would be significant underinvestment, for instance because there are large externalities or spillovers. There is not a sharp demarcation between basic and applied research, but rather a continuum, with many applied projects generating large knowledge spillovers. Substantial underinvestment is likely in sectors, such as agriculture, where there are a large number of small producers (in contrast to the chemical industry, for instance, where there are a few dominant firms.) Well-designed government research programs serve as a complement to private sector efforts, rather than as a substitute for them. On average, increases in government expenditures are associated with increases, not decreases, in private research expenditures.

Advocates of government technology programs argue, further, that government should work in partnership with industry to increase the effectiveness of its R & D investment. They advocate requiring industry to put up money of its own, and making the competition for funds very broad. New technology programs, established since the Clinton administration has taken office, take this approach. And hundreds of partnership agreements between private firms and government-run laboratories have been recently signed. It is too soon to assess the performance of these new efforts, but experience with earlier, similar programs has been encouraging. Sematech—a cooperative research venture of the electronics industry centered in Austin, Texas, and supported with $90 million annually in government subsidies—while it played an important role in the recovery of that industry in the 1980s, announced in October 1994 that it would no longer need government assistance as of fiscal 1997.

INTERNATIONAL COMPLICATIONS

Subsidies have, however, raised the specter of unfair competition in the international arena. Countries facing competition from foreign firms with government subsidies often impose countervailing duties, that is, taxes on imports that are intended to offset the benefits of these subsidies. The concern is if, for instance, Europe and the United States become engaged in a contest to support some industry, the industry will benefit, but at the expense of the taxpayers in both countries. Thus, international agreements have tried to reduce the extent of subsidization. Broad-based R & D subsidies (such as through the tax system) are still permitted, but more narrowly focused subsidies are either prohibited or put into the category of questionable practices.

PROTECTION

Firms in less developed countries often argue that they need to be insulated from competition from abroad in order to develop the knowledge base required to compete effectively in world markets. This is the **infant industry argument for protection.** Most economists are skeptical. They see this argument mainly as an attempt by rent-seeking firms who will use any excuse to insulate themselves from competition so they can raise prices and increase profits. The best way to learn to compete is to compete, not to be isolated from competition. If some help is needed to enable firms to catch up, it should be provided in the form of subsidies, the costs of which are explicit and obvious, unlike the hidden costs of higher prices that result from protection.

The billions of dollars it takes to develop a new aircraft have made the world's aircraft manufacturing industry into something akin to a world natural monopoly. Currently only two firms are actively designing large passenger jets—Boeing in the United States and Airbus inEurope.

Airbus has been subsidized by several European governments, which has stimulated complaints from the U.S. government about "unfair" competition. The U.S. government is in a weak position to complain, however, because it has been subsidizing the U.S. aircraft industry for decades, through the military. Private firms have only had to contribute a marginal investment in adapting military designs for civilian use.

The United States and Europe, recognizing the dangers of competition in subsidies, have signed an agreement to limit aircraft development subsidies on both sides. But there is now another potential threat to competition—the two firms involved are now discussing cooperation in the design of the next generation of jumbo jets. The firms argue that the development costs are so astronomical that cooperation is essential if innovation is to continue. Critics fear that Boeing and Airbus are really trying to "cartelize" the world market—thus creating what amounts to an unregulated monopoly—to enhance their own profits at the expense of consumers.

RELAXING ANTITRUST POLICIES

The antitrust policies explored in Chapter 16 were founded on the belief that government should push markets toward the model of perfect competition. But an increasing awareness of the importance of R & D in modern industrial economies has led some to argue for change.

A major argument for change is that cooperation aimed at sharing knowledge and coordinating research among firms in an industry has the effect of internalizing the externalities of R & D. But antitrust authorities long worried that cooperation in R & D could easily grow into cooperation in other areas, such as price setting, which would not serve the public interest. Public policy has tried to find an effective balance. In 1984, the National Cooperative Research Act was passed to allow some cooperative ventures. Ventures registered under the act are shielded from the risk of paying triple damages in a private antitrust suit, but not shielded from all antitrust risk. By the end of the 1980s, over a hundred such ventures had been registered. Among the best known are the Electric Power Research Institute, formed by electric power companies; Bell Communications Research, formed by local telephone companies; and Sematech.

TECHNOLOGICAL CHANGE AND THE BASIC COMPETITIVE MODEL

Basic competitive model	Industries in which technological change is important
Assumes fixed technology.	The central question is what determines the pace of technological change. Related issues include what determines expenditure on R & D and how learning by doing affects the level of production.
Assumes perfect competition, with many firms in industry.	Competition is not perfect; industries where technological change is important tend to have relatively few firms.
Perfect capital markets.	Firms find it difficult to borrow to finance R & D expenditures.
No externalities.	R & D confers benefits to those besides the inventor; even with patents, the inventor appropriates only a fraction of the social benefits of an invention.
No public goods.	Basic research is a public good: the marginal cost of an additional person making use of a new idea is zero (nonrivalrous consumption), and it is often difficult to exclude others from enjoying the benefits of basic research.

TECHNOLOGICAL CHANGE AND ECONOMIC GROWTH

Living standards in the United States are far higher today than they were 100 years ago. The reason is that productivity—output per hour—has increased enormously. Underlying these increases is technological change. While there are many stories of discoveries that occurred almost by accident (such as Fleming's discovery of penicillin), in the modern economy, most advances are a result of the deliberate allocation of resources to research and development. The importance—and consequences—of technological change constitutes our ninth point of consensus among economists.

9 Innovation

Modern economies are based on innovation. Imperfect competition is widespread in the sectors of the economy in which innovation is most important. Government plays a crucial role in innovation, not only protecting intellectual property (through patents and copyrights) but also in supporting basic research.

REVIEW AND PRACTICE

SUMMARY

1. Industries in which technological change is important are almost necessarily imperfectly competitive. Patents are one way the government makes it difficult and costly for firms to copy the technological innovations of others. A firm with a patent will have a government-enforced monopoly. The expenditures on R & D are fixed costs; when they are large, there are likely to be few firms in the industry, and price competition is more likely to be limited.

2. Long-lived and broad patents reduce competition (at least in the short run), but provide greater incentives to innovate. Excessively broad patent coverage may discourage follow-on innovation.

3. Learning by doing, in which companies (or countries) that begin making a product first enjoy an advantage over all later entrants, may be a source of technological advantage.

4. Research and development generally provides positive externalities to consumers and other firms. But since the innovating firm cannot capture all the social benefits from its invention, it will tend to invest less than a socially optimal amount.

5. Basic research has both the central properties of a public good: it is difficult to exclude others from the benefits of the research, and the marginal cost of an additional person making use of the new idea is zero.

6. A number of governmental policies encourage technological advance: patents; direct spending on research; tax incentives to encourage corporate R & D; temporary protection from technologically advanced foreign competitors; and relaxing antitrust laws to allow potential competitors to work together on research projects.

KEY TERMS

patent	learning curve	infant industry
trade secret	industrial policy	argument for
learning by doing		protection

REVIEW QUESTIONS

1. In what ways do industries in which technological change is important not satisfy the assumptions of the standard competitive model?

2. Why do governments grant patents, thereby conferring temporary mo-

nopoly rights? Explain the trade-off society faces in choosing whether to offer long-lived or short-lived patents, and whether to offer broad or narrow patents.

3. How does the existence of learning by doing provide an advantage to incumbent firms over prospective entrants?

4. Why might it be harder to raise capital for R & D than for other projects? How can established firms deal with this problem? What about start-up firms?

5. How do positive externalities arise from research and development? Why do externalities imply that there may be too little expenditure on research by private firms?

6. Explain how basic research can be thought of as a public good. Why is society likely to underinvest in basic research?

7. What are the arguments for and against industrial policies?

8. What possible trade-off does society face when it considers loosening its antitrust laws to encourage joint research and development ventures?

PROBLEMS

1. Imagine that Congress is considering a bill to reduce the current seventeen-year life of patents to eight years. What negative effects might this change have on the rate of innovation? What positive effect might it have for the economy?

2. Suppose that many years ago, one inventor received a patent for orange juice, and then another inventor came forward and requested a patent for lemonade. The first inventor maintained that the orange juice patent should be interpreted to cover all fruit juices, while the second inventor argued that the original patent included only one particular method of making one kind of juice. What trade-offs does society face in setting rules for deciding cases like these?

3. Although a patent assures a monopoly on that particular invention for some time, it also requires that the inventor disclose the details of the invention. Under what conditions might a company (like Coca-Cola) prefer to use trade secrets rather than patents to protect its formulas?

4. Why might a company invest in research and development even if it does not believe it will be able to patent its discovery?

5. Learning by doing seems to be important in the semiconductor industry, where the United States and Japan are the main producers. Explain why U.S. and Japanese firms may race to try to bring out new generations of semiconductors. If learning by doing is important in the semiconductor industry, why might other nations try to use an infant industry strategy to develop their own semiconductor industry?

18

IMPERFECT INFORMATION IN THE PRODUCT MARKET

t was never any secret to economists that the real world did not match the model of perfect competition. Theories of monopoly and imperfect competition such as those covered in Chapters 14–17 have been propounded from Adam Smith's time to the present.

Another limitation of the model of perfect competition has recently come to the fore: its assumption of **perfect information**—that market participants have full information about the goods being bought and sold. By incorporating **imperfect information** into their models, economists have come a long way in closing the gap between the real world and the world depicted by the perfect competition, perfect information model of Part Two.

This chapter provides a broad overview of the major information problems of the product market, the ways in which market economies deal with them, and how the basic model of Part Two has to be modified as a result. In the following chapters, we will see how information problems affect labor markets (Chapter 19), and capital markets and the management of firms (Chapter 20). In Parts Four and Five, we will see how many of the most important macroeconomic problems may be traced, at least in part, to information problems.

KEY QUESTIONS

1. Why is information different from other goods, such as hats and cameras? Why, in particular, do markets for information often not work well?

2. When does the market price affect the quality of what is being sold? How does the fact that consumers believe price affects quality influence how firms behave?

3. When customers have trouble differentiating good from shoddy merchandise, what are the incentives firms have to produce good merchandise? What role does reputation play?

4. Why is it that, in the same market, identical or very similar goods will sell at different prices? How does the fact that search is costly affect the nature of competition?

5. How does advertising affect firms' demand curves and profits? Why may the firms in an industry be better off if they collectively agree not to advertise?

6. What has government done to address some of the problems resulting from imperfect information? Why do these efforts have only limited success?

THE INFORMATION PROBLEM

The basic competitive model assumes that households and firms are well informed. This means that they know their opportunity set, or what is available and at what price. More striking, they know every characteristic of every good, including how long it will last. Were these assumptions true, shopping would be easy!

The model also assumes that consumers know their preferences, that is, they know what they like. They know not only how many oranges they can trade for an apple, but also how many oranges they are willing to trade. In the case of apples and oranges this may make sense. But how do students know how much they are going to enjoy, or even benefit from, a college education before they have experienced it? How does an individual know whether she would like to be a doctor or a lawyer? She gets some idea about what different professions are like by observing those who practice them, but her information is at best incomplete.

According to the basic model, firms too are perfectly well-informed. They all know the best available technology. They know the productivity of each applicant for a job. They know the prices at which inputs can be purchased from every possible supplier (and all of the inputs' characteristics). And they know the prices at which they can sell the goods, not only today, but in every possible circumstance in the future.

How Big a Problem?

That individuals and firms are not perfectly well informed is, by itself, not necessarily a telling criticism of the competitive model, just as the criticism that markets are not perfectly competitive does not cause us to discard the model. The relevant issue is, are there situations where the competitive model will mislead us? Are there important economic phenomena that can be explained only by taking into account imperfect information? Are there important predictions of the model that are incorrect as a result of the assumptions concerning well-informed consumers and firms?

Increasingly, over the past two decades, economists have come to believe that the answer to these questions is yes. For example, college graduates may receive a higher income than high school graduates not only because they have learned things in college that make them more productive, but because their college degree helps them through a sorting process. Employers cannot glean from an interview which applicants for a job will be productive workers. They therefore use a college degree to help them identify those who are better at learning. College graduates *are*, on average, more productive workers. But it is wrong to conclude from this that college has necessarily *increased* their productivity. It may simply have enabled firms to sort out more easily the more productive from the less productive.

How Prices Convey Information

The price system provides brilliant solutions for some information problems. We have seen how prices play an important role in coordinating production and communicating information about economic scarcity. Firms do not have to know what John or Julia likes, what their trade-offs are. The price tells the producer the marginal benefit of producing an extra unit of the good, and that is all he needs to know. Similarly, a firm does not need to know how much iron ore is left in Minnesota, the cost of refining iron ore, or a thousand other details. All it needs to know is the price of iron ore. This tells the company how scarce the resource is, how much effort it should expend in conserving. Prices and markets provide the basis of the economy's incentive system. But there are some information problems that markets do not handle, or do not handle well. And imperfect information sometimes inhibits the ability of markets to perform the tasks it performs so well when information is complete.

Markets for Information

Information has value; people are willing to pay for it. In this sense, we can consider information as a good similar to any other good. There is a market for information, with a price—just as there is a market for labor and a market for capital. Indeed, our economy is sometimes referred to as an information economy. Every year, investors spend millions of dollars on newsletters that give them information about stocks, bonds, and other investment opportunities. Magazines sell specialized information about hundreds of goods.

However, the markets for information are far from perfect, and for good reasons. The most conspicuous one is that information is *not* just like any other good. When you buy a chair, the furniture dealer is happy to let you look at it, feel it, sit on it, and decide whether you like it. When you buy information, you cannot do the same. The seller can either say, "Trust me. I'll tell you what you need to know," or show you the information and say, "Here's what I know. If this is what you wanted to know, please pay me." You would rightfully be skeptical in the first scenario, and might be unwilling to pay in the second. After you were given the information, what incentive would you have to pay?

In some cases, there is a basic credibility problem. You might think, if a stock tipster *really* knows that a stock is going to go up in price, why should he tell me, even if I pay him for the information? Why doesn't he go out and make his fortune with the information? Or is it that he really is not sure, and would just as soon have me risk my money rather than risk his?

Most important, even after the firm or consumer buys all the information he thinks is worth paying for, his information is still far from perfect. Some information is simply too costly to obtain relative to the benefit of having it. Let's look now at some of the consequences of imperfect information.

THE MARKET FOR LEMONS AND ADVERSE SELECTION

Have you ever wondered why a three-month-old used car sells for so much less—often 20 percent less—than a new car? Surely cars do not deteriorate that fast. The pleasure of owning a new car may be worth something, but in three months, even the car you buy new will be "used." But a couple of thousand dollars or more is a steep price to pay for this short-lived pleasure.

George Akerlof of the University of California at Berkeley has provided a simple explanation, based on imperfect information. Some cars are worse than others. They have hidden defects which become apparent to the owner only after she has owned the car for a while. Such defective cars are called lemons. One thing after another goes wrong with them. While warranties may reduce the financial cost of having a lemon, they do not eliminate the bother—the time it takes to bring the car into the shop, the anxiety of knowing there is a good chance of a breakdown. The owners, of course, know they have a lemon and would like to pass it along to someone else. Those with the worst lemons are going to be the most willing to sell their car. At a high used car price, they will be joined by owners of better quality cars who want to sell their cars, say, to buy the latest model. As the price drops, more of the good cars will be withdrawn from the market as the owners decide to keep them. And the average quality of the used cars for sale will *drop.* We say there is an

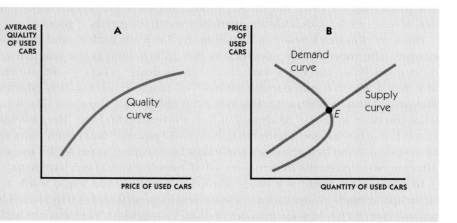

Figure 18.1 A MARKET WITH LEMONS

Panel A shows the average quality of a used car increasing as the price increases. Panel B shows a typical upward-sloping supply curve, but a backward-bending demand curve. Demand bends back because buyers know that quality is lower at lower prices, and they thus choose to buy less as the price falls. Panel B shows the market equilibrium is at point *E*.

adverse selection effect. The mix of those who elect to sell changes adversely as price falls. We encountered adverse selection in the insurance market in Chapter 6. We will encounter adverse selection again in our discussion of labor market (Chapter 19) and capital market (Chapter 20) imperfections.

Figure 18.1 shows the consequences of imperfect information for market equilibrium in the used car market. Panel A depicts, for each price (measured along the horizontal axis), the average quality of used cars being sold in the market. As price increases, average quality increases. Panel B shows the supply curve of used cars. As price increases, the number of cars being sold in the market increases, for all the usual reasons. The demand curve is also shown. This curve has a peculiar shape: upward as well as downward sloping. The reason is that as price increases, the average quality increases. But demand depends not just on price but on quality—on the "value" being offered on the market. If, as price falls, quality deteriorates rapidly, then quantity demanded will actually *fall* as price falls—consumers are getting less for their dollars. The equilibrium is depicted in panel B.

The situation just described is characterized by **asymmetric information** between sellers and buyers. That is, the seller of the used car has more information about the product than the buyer. Many markets are characterized by asymmetric information. One of the consequences of asymmetric information is that there may be relatively few buyers and sellers, far fewer than there would be with perfect information. Economists use the term **thin** to describe markets in which there are relatively few buyers and sellers. In some situations, a market may be so thin as to be essentially nonexistent. When there are important markets missing from an economy, it is said to have an **incomplete** set of markets. The used car market, for example, is a thin one. Buyers may know that there are some legitimate sellers, those who for one reason or another always want to drive a new car. But mixed in with these are people who are trying to dump their lemons. The buyers cannot tell the lemons apart from the good cars. Rather than risk it, they simply do not buy. (Of course, the fact that demand is low drives down the price, increasing the proportion of lemons. It is a vicious cycle.)

SIGNALING

If you have a good car and you want to sell it, you would like to persuade potential buyers that it is good. You could tell them that it is not a lemon, but why should they believe you? There is a simple principle: *actions speak louder than words*. What actions can you take that will convince buyers of the quality of your car?

The fact that Chrysler is willing to provide a five-year, fifty-thousand-mile warranty on its cars says something about the confidence Chrysler has in its product. The warranty is valuable, not only because it reduces the risks of having to spend a mint to repair the car, but also because the buyer believes that Chrysler would not have provided the warranty unless the chances of defects were low. Actions such as this are said to **signal** higher quality. A signal is effective if it differentiates goods—here between high-quality cars and low-quality cars. The cost to the producer of a five-year guarantee is much higher for a car that is likely to fall apart within five years than for a car that is unlikely to break down. Customers know this, and thus can infer that a firm willing to provide this warranty is selling high-quality cars.

When you go to a car dealer, you want to know that it will still be around if you have trouble. Some firms signal that they are not fly-by-nights by spending a great deal of money on their showroom. This indicates that it would be costly for them to just pack up and leave. (There are, of course, other reasons why they may spend money on a fancy showroom.)

Actions such as providing a better guarantee or a larger showroom are taken not just for the direct benefit that the consumer receives from them, but because those actions make consumers believe that the product is a better product or the firm is a better firm to deal with. In a sense, the desire to convey information "distorts" the decisions made relative to what they would have been in a perfect-information world. For example, if customers receive no direct benefit from the quality of the showroom, the cost of building and maintaining a luxurious showroom is a waste of resources.

JUDGING QUALITY BY PRICE

There is still another clue that buyers use to judge the quality of what they are about to purchase. This is price. Consumers make inferences about the quality of goods based on the price charged. For example, they know that on average, if the price of a used car is low , the chance of getting a lemon is higher. Many if not most sellers know that buyers know this.

In markets with imperfect information, firms *set* their prices. And in setting

CLOSE-UP: AUTOMOBILE BROKERS AND IMPERFECT INFORMATION

A broker is someone who arranges contracts between two parties. In older times, marriage brokers brought together prospective couples. Stockbrokers bring together buyers and sellers of stocks. Car brokers bring together buyers and sellers of cars.

In every case, though, a broker is someone whose job exists only because of imperfect information. After all, why can't a person just go out and choose a spouse or a stock or a car? The obvious problem is that many different varieties are available, and it costs time and energy and money to collect the information to make an informed decision. A good broker is out there in the market all the time, keeping track of what is going on. Having a relatively small number of people keeping track of buyers and sellers is certainly more efficient than having all buyers and sellers duplicating one another's efforts.

Consider how car brokers work, for example. You call up a broker (usually they are listed in the Yellow Pages of the phone book) and describe what sort of car you want—make, model, year, accessories. The broker then finds you the best deal.

Working as a broker may seem like a funny way to make a living. How can someone get paid for shopping for cars? The answer is that shopping for a car involves time and the energy of confronting dealers and haggling over price. Even if the buyer spends several days or weeks shopping, it is not clear she will find the best deal. Paying a knowledgeable broker will certainly save time and energy, and might result in a cheaper price too. A good broker will know the sales representative's typical commission or the "preparation fee" that dealers receive for getting a car ready to sell. By taking factors like this into account, the broker can often negotiate a better price.

Not everyone will need or want an automobile broker. But for those who feel their information about the car market is extremely imperfect, a broker may be a wise choice.

Source: "A Better Way to Buy a Car?" *Consumer Reports,* September 1989, pp. 593–95.

their prices, they take into account what customers will think about the quality of the good being sold. Concerns about consumers (correctly or incorrectly) making inferences about quality impede the effectiveness of price competition. In the used car example, we saw that, as price rose, the average quality of cars on the market increased. But if firms think customers believe that cars being sold at a lower price are lemons—that the quality deteriorates more than the price declines—they will not lower the price because to do so would scare away customers who perceive that such "bargains" must be lemons. Under such circumstances, even if firms cannot sell all they would like at the going price, they will still not cut prices.

A situation can be sustained in which there is a seeming excess supply of goods. Imperfect information means that equilibrium will be achieved away from the intersection of supply and demand curves. This is a profound result, one we will trace through many of the chapters that follow.

Information problems fascinate economists because they turn the basic competitive model upside down. Economists have long recognized that prices convey critical information about scarcity in a market economy. But only recently have the other informational roles of prices—and their consequences—become clear. Sellers will manipulate prices when they can to control the information conveyed. Buyers, for their part, see through these manipulations. And their concern that the seller is trying to pass off a lemon discourages trade. When information problems like these are severe, markets are thin or even nonexistent. Alternatively, price competition may be limited. Even when there is an excess supply of goods, firms may not cut their prices and the market may not clear.

SOLUTIONS TO ADVERSE SELECTION PROBLEMS IN MARKET ECONOMIES

Signaling

Judging quality by price

THE INCENTIVE PROBLEM

We have seen throughout this book that providing incentives that motivate individuals to make the best choices is one of the central economic problems. The central problem of incentives, in turn, is that individuals do not bear the full consequences of their actions. The multi-billion-dollar collapse of the savings and loan associations—though fraud may have played a part—is attributable largely to incorrect incentives. Because S & L deposits were guaranteed by the government, depositors had no incentives to check on what the S & Ls were doing. For the same reason, the owners of many S & Ls had an incentive to take high risks. If they were successful, they kept the gains. If they failed, the government picked up the loss.

When there is a misalignment of incentives such as occurred in the S & Ls, we say there is a problem of moral hazard, as noted in Chapter 6. The term originated in the insurance industry. Individuals who purchased insurance had an inadequate incentive to avoid the insured-against event—indeed, if they were insured for more than 100 percent of the loss, they would have an incentive to bring about the event. Doing so was considered immoral, hence the term. Today, economists think of these simply as incentive problems, with no moral overtones. Thus, an individual who has fire insurance has less of an incentive to avoid a fire. The benefit to him, for instance, of putting in a sprinkler system may not be worth the cost—though it would if he took into account the expected cost to the fire insurance company. That is why the fire insurance company is likely to require a sprinkler system, or to give a discount on the premium if an individual has one. It would thus pay to have a sprinkler system installed.

In the basic competitive model of Part Two, private property and prices provide incentives. Individuals are rewarded for performing particular tasks. The problem arises when an individual is not rewarded for what he does, or when he does not have to pay the full costs for what he does. In our economy, incentive problems are pervasive.

In product markets, firms must be given the incentive to produce quality products. Again, the incentive problem is an information problem. If customers could always tell the quality of the product they were getting, firms that produced higher-quality products would always be able to charge a higher price, and no company could get away with producing shoddy goods. Most of us have had the experience of going to a newly established restaurant, having a good meal, and then returning to find that the quality had deteriorated. Evidently something went wrong with incentives.

MARKET SOLUTIONS

In simple transactions, incentive problems can be solved by stipulating penalties and rewards. You would like a document typed. You sign a contract with someone to pay him $25 to deliver the typed document by tomorrow at 5:00 P.M. The contract stipulates that $.50 will be deducted for each typographical error, and $1.00 for every hour the paper is late. The contract has built-in incentives for the paper to be delivered on time and without errors.

But most transactions, even relatively simple ones, are more complicated than this one. The more complicated the transaction, the more difficult it is to solve the incentive problem. You want your grass mowed, and your neigh-

The soaring costs of Medicare (the government program providing health insurance for the aged) have prompted a number of proposals from policy makers, among these a proposal to establish *medical savings accounts* (MSAs). MSAs would encourage individuals to buy health insurance with large deductibles and co-payments. For instance, the insurance company would only pay 80 percent of the amount in excess of $1,000; in that case, there is a $1,000 deductible and a 20 percent co-payment. With such insurance, individuals have an incentive to economize on their use of health care, and the premium would, presumably, be considerably lower than the costs under the current system. Each individual would receive a check, representing the difference between what it costs the government under the old system and the premium under the new privately provided policies. Individuals could deposit this money in a tax-exempt medical savings account, and use it to pay for the uninsured costs, deductible, and co-payments.

Sounds like a good system: improved incentives reduce costs for both government and individuals. But the problems of adverse selection and incentives are often intertwined, and critics say that adverse selection effects will dominate the incentive effects. The rich and healthy will take the MSA option, transferring to the standard option when their health deteriorates. Thus, the *apparent* cost under the new option will be lower, but mostly because of the adverse selection effect, not improved incentives. Meanwhile, the same adverse selection effect will drive up the average costs of those remaining under the standard option. Thus, the net costs to the government could actually increase. This problem could be rectified if there were some way of adjusting payments to reflect the health condition of the individual. Such "risk adjusters" have been discussed for several years, but so far, no one has devised a satisfactory method of making the appropriate risk adjustments.

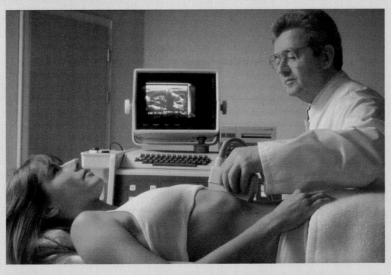

bor's twelve-year-old son wants to mow it. You want him to take care of your power mower. When he sees a rock in the mower's path, he should pick it up. But what incentive does he have to take care of the mower? If you plan to charge him for repairs if the mower does hit a rock, how can you tell whether the rock was hidden by the grass? If he owned his own mower, he would have the appropriate incentives. That is why private property combined with the price system provides such an effective solution to the incentive problem. But your neighbor's son probably does not have the money to buy his own power mower. Then an incentive problem is inevitable. Either you let him use your lawn mower and bear the risk of his mistreating it. Or you lend him money to buy his own, in which case you bear the risk of his not paying you back.

Many private companies must hire people to run machinery worth hundreds or thousands of times more than a lawn mower. Every company would like its workers to exert effort and care, to communicate clearly with one another and take responsibility. Beyond private property and prices, the market economy has other partial solutions to these incentive problems, loosely categorized as contract solutions and reputation solutions.

CONTRACT SOLUTIONS

When one party (firm) agrees to do something for another, it typically signs a contract, which specifies the conditions of the transaction. For example, a firm will agree to deliver a product of a particular quality at a certain time and place. There will normally be "escape" clauses. If there is a strike, if the weather is bad, and so on, the delivery can be postponed. These **contingency clauses** may also make the payment depend on the circumstances and manner in which the service is performed.

Contracts attempt to deal with incentive problems by specifying what each of the parties is to do in each situation. But no one can think of every contingency. And even if they could, it would take them a prohibitively long time to write down all the possibilities.

There are times when it would be extremely expensive for the supplier to comply with all the terms of the contract. He could make the promised delivery on time, but only at a very great cost; if the buyer would only accept a one-day delay, there would be great savings. To provide suppliers with the incentive to violate the terms only when it is really economically worthwhile, most contracts allow delivery delays, but with a penalty. The penalty gives the supplier the incentive to deliver in a timely, but not overly costly, way.

Sometimes the supplier may think it simply is not worth complying with the contract. If he violates the agreement, he is said to be in **breach** of the contract. When a contract has been breached, the parties usually wind up in court, and the legal system stipulates what damages the party breaking the contract must pay to the other side. Contracts, by stipulating what parties are supposed to do in a variety of circumstances, help resolve incentive problems. But no matter how complicated the contract, there will still be ambiguities and disputes. Contracts are incomplete and enforcement is costly, and thus they provide only a partial resolution of the incentive problem.

REPUTATION SOLUTIONS

Reputations play an extremely important role in providing incentives in market economies. A reputation is a form of guarantee. Even though you may know that you cannot collect from this guarantee yourself—it is not a "money-back" guarantee—you know that the reputation of the person or company will suffer if it does not perform well. The incentive to maintain a reputation is what provides firms with an incentive to produce high-quality goods. It provides the contractor with an incentive to complete a house on or near the promised date.

For reputation to be an effective incentive mechanism, firms must lose something if their reputation suffers. The "something" is, of course, profits. For reputations to provide incentives, there must be profits to lose.

Thus, we see another way that markets with imperfect information differ from markets with perfect information. In competitive markets with perfect information, competition drives price down to marginal cost. In markets in which quality is maintained as the result of a reputation mechanism, whether competitive or not, price must remain above marginal cost.

Why, in markets where reputation is important, doesn't competition lead to price cutting? If price is "too low," firms do not have an incentive to maintain their reputation. Consumers, knowing this, come to expect low-quality goods. This is another reason that cutting prices will not necessarily bring firms more customers. Most consumers, at one time or another, have encountered companies that tried to live off their reputation. For example, Head skis were the high-quality skis in the early 1970s. At high prices, of course, demand was limited. When the company lowered its price, sales increased. Consumers, knowing about the high quality, bought the skis thinking they were getting a bargain. But bargains are not so easy to come by. At the lower prices, profits were lower and Head had little incentive to maintain its reputation.

Reputation as a Barrier to Entry   Competition is frequently very imperfect in markets where reputation is important. The necessity of establishing a reputation acts as an important barrier to entry, and limits the degree of competition in these industries. Given a choice between purchasing the product of an

SOLUTIONS TO INCENTIVE PROBLEMS IN MARKET ECONOMIES

Private property and prices
Contracts
Reputations

One of the key issues in the 1992 U.S. presidential campaign was reform of the medical care industry. The United States spends a larger fraction of its national income on health care, but has a lower life expectancy and greater infant mortality rate than many other developed countries. Information problems and associated market failures are a large part of the reason. Moral hazard—the reduced incentive to economize on health care expenditures when a large fraction of the tab is picked up by insurance firms—is one source of market failure. Adverse selection—the attempt of each insurance firm to take the lowest-risk patients, leaving those with high medical costs to others—is another.

In the standard model, consumers are assumed to be well informed. But, consumers go to the doctor for information to find out what is wrong with them. Moreover, they typically must rely on the doctor's advice. Economists worry that under the fee-for-service system, where doctors are paid for each of the services they perform, there is an incentive to provide excessive care. Excessive means the marginal cost exceeds the marginal benefit to the patient.

Today, more and more doctors work in "managed care" organizations, where they are paid a flat fee up front. They then provide whatever care is needed and receive no extra income from doing extra procedures. On average, doctors working in managed care cost less and perform fewer surgeries, with no noticeable effect on patient health. Critics worry that with managed care, doctors have an incentive to underprovide, since they receive no compensation at all for providing care at the margin. But advocates argue that any managed care organization that did so would quickly lose its patients. Reputations provide effective discipline. When employers provide a level playing field between fee-for-service and managed care plans—contributing an equal amount for each, and making the employee pay for the extra cost if they choose the more expensive fee-for-service plans—more than half their employees, on average, choose the managed care plan. Evidently, the employees do not feel the benefits of the extra services provided under fee-for-service are worth the extra costs.

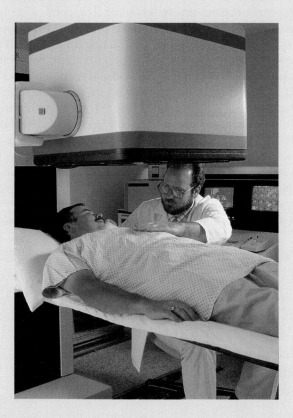

established firm with a good reputation and the product of a newcomer with no reputation at the same price, consumers will normally choose the established firm's good. In choosing a new TV you may choose a Sony over an equally priced new brand with no track record for quality and reliability. The newcomer must offer a sufficiently low price, often accompanied with strong guarantees. In some cases, newcomers have almost to give away their product in order to establish themselves. Entering a market thus becomes extremely expensive.

THE SEARCH PROBLEM

A basic information problem is that consumers must find out what goods are available on the market, at what price, and where. Households must learn about job opportunities as well as opportunities for investing their savings. Firms, by the same token, have to figure out the demand curve they face, and where and at what price they can obtain inputs. Both sides of the market need, in other words, to find out about their opportunity sets.

In the basic competitive model of Part Two, a particular good sells for the same price everywhere. If we see what look like identical shoes selling for two different prices at two neighboring stores—$25 at one and $35 at the other—it must mean (in that model) that the stores are really selling different products. If the shoes are in fact identical, then what the customer must be getting is a combination package, the shoes plus the service of having the shoes fitted. And the more expensive store is providing a higher quality of service.

In fact, however, essentially the same good may be sold at different stores for different prices. And you may not be able to account for the observed differences in prices by differences in other attributes, like the location of the store or the quality of the service provided. In these cases, we say there is **price dispersion.** If the act of finding out all prices were costless (or information perfect, as in the standard competitive model), consumers would search until they found the cheapest price. And no store charging more than the lowest price on the market would ever have any customers. But with costly information, a high-price store may still be able to keep some customers—and its higher profit per sale offsets its lower level of sales. Thus, price dispersion can persist.

Price dispersion, combined with variations in quality, means that households and firms must spend considerable energies in searching. Workers search for a good job. Firms look for good workers. Consumers search for the lowest prices and best values. The process by which this kind of information is gathered is called **search.**

Search is an important, and costly, economic activity. Because it is costly, a search stops before you have *all* the relevant information. You know there are bargains out there to be found, but it is just too expensive to find them. You might worry that you will be disappointed the day or week after buying a new computer, if you find it for sale at 10 percent less. But in truth, there should be no regrets. There was a chance that you would not find a better buy, or that

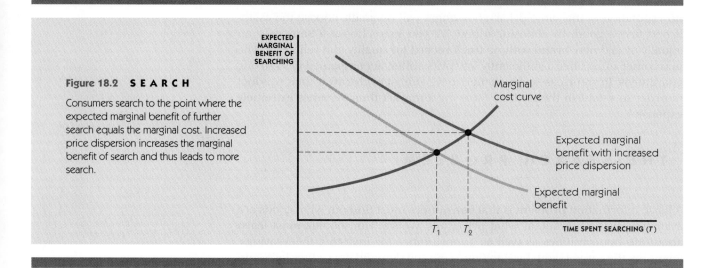

Figure 18.2 SEARCH

Consumers search to the point where the expected marginal benefit of further search equals the marginal cost. Increased price dispersion increases the marginal benefit of search and thus leads to more search.

next week you would not even be able to buy it at the price offered today. You looked at these risks, the costs of further search, the benefits of being able to get the computer today and use it now (compared with the benefits of waiting and the chance of finding it at a still lower price). After a careful balancing of the benefits and costs of further waiting, you decided to purchase now.

In Figure 18.2 the horizontal axis plots the time spent in searching, while the vertical axis measures the expected marginal benefit of searching. On the one hand, the expected marginal benefit of searching declines with the amount of search. In general, people search the best prospects first. As they search more and more, they look at less and less likely prospects. Say you are looking to buy a used car. You might first look in the newspaper, then go to local car dealers. Finally, you might drive the streets looking for cars with "for sale" signs. On the other hand, the marginal cost of additional search rises with increased search. This reflects the fact that the more time people spend in search, the less time they have to do other things. The opportunity cost of spending an extra hour searching thus increases. The amount of search chosen will be at the point where the expected marginal benefit just equals the marginal cost.

An increase in price (or quality) dispersion will normally increase the return to searching—there is a chance of picking up a really good bargain, and the difference between a good buy and a bad buy is larger. Thus, the expected marginal benefit curve shifts up, and the amount of search will increase from T_1 to T_2.

SEARCH AND IMPERFECT COMPETITION

Firms know search is costly, and take advantage of that fact. They know they will not lose all their customers if they raise their prices. And if a store lowers its price slightly, it will not immediately attract *all* the customers from the other stores. Customers have to learn about the competitive price advantage, and this takes time. Moreover, even when people do hear of the lower price, they may worry about the quality of the goods being sold, the nature of the service, whether the goods will be in stock, and so on.

The fact that search is costly means that the demand curve facing a firm will be downward sloping. Competition is necessarily imperfect.

Consider, for instance, the demand for a Walkman. When you walk into a store, you have some idea what it should sell for. The store asks $70 for it. You may know that somewhere you might be able to purchase it for $5 less. But is it worth the additional time, trouble, and gasoline to drive to the other stores that might have it, looking for a bargain? Some individuals are willing to pay the extra $5 simply to stop having to search. As the store raises its price to, say, $75, $80, or $85, some people who would have bought the Walkman at $70 decide that it is worth continuing to shop around. The store, as it raises its price, loses some but not all of its customers. Thus, it faces a downward-sloping demand curve. If search were costless, everyone would go to the store selling the Walkman at the lowest price, and any store charging more than that would have no sales. Markets in which search is costly are, accordingly, better described by the models of imperfect competition introduced in Chapters 14 and 15.

SEARCH AND INFORMATION INTERMEDIARIES

Some firms play an important role by gathering information and serving as intermediaries between producers and customers. These firms are part of the market for information discussed in the beginning of the chapter. One of the functions of good department stores, for example, is to economize on customers' search costs. The stores' buyers seek out literally hundreds of producers, looking for the best buys and the kinds of goods that their customers will like. Good department stores earn a reputation for the quality of their buyers. Customers still have a search problem—they may have to visit several department stores—but doing so is far less costly than if they had to search directly among producers. In addition magazines like *Consumer Reports* provide readers with detailed information on product quality and price, saving consumers considerable search cost.

ADVERTISING

Customers have an incentive to find out where the best buys are. Firms have a corresponding incentive to tell customers about the great deals they are providing. Companies may spend great sums on advertising to bring information about their products, prices, and locations to potential customers.

In the classic joke about advertising, an executive says, "We know half the money we spend on advertising is wasted, but we don't know which half."

That joke says a lot about the economics of advertising. In the United States, many firms spend 2 percent, 3 percent, or more of their total revenues on advertising. Today, total expenditures on advertising are over $130 billion, with slightly more than half spent on national advertising. To add some perspective, these expenditures are only slightly less than spending on all federal, state, and local public assistance.

Advertising can serve the important economic function of providing information about what choices are available. When a new airline enters a market, it must convey that information to potential customers. When a new product is developed, that fact has to be made known. When a business is having a sale, it must let people know. A firm cannot just lower its price, sit on its haunches, and wait, if it wants to be successful. Companies need to recruit new customers and convey information in an active way.

But not all advertising is designed to convey factual information about product prices or characteristics. Take the typical beer or car advertisement. It conveys almost no information about the product, but seeks to convey an image, one with which potential buyers will identify. That these advertisements succeed in persuading individuals either to try a product or to stick with that product and not try another—is a reminder that consumer behavior is much more complicated than the simple theories of competitive markets suggest. Few people decide to go out and buy a car or a new suit solely because they saw a TV ad. But decisions about what kinds of clothes to wear, what beer to drink, what car to drive, are affected by a variety of considerations, including, how peers view them or how they see themselves. These views, in turn, can be affected by advertising.

To emphasize the different roles played by advertising, economists distinguish between **informative advertising** and **persuasive advertising.** The intent of the former is to provide consumers with information about the price of a good, where it may be acquired, or what its characteristics are. The intent of persuasive advertising is to make consumers feel good about the product. This can even take the form of providing "disinformation"—to confuse consumers into thinking there is a difference among goods when there really is not.

ADVERTISING AND COMPETITION

Advertising is both a cause and a consequence of imperfect competition. In a perfectly competitive industry, where many producers make identical goods, it would not pay any single producer to advertise the merits of a good. You do not see advertisements for wheat or corn. If such advertising were successful, it would simply shift the demand curve for the product out. The total demand for wheat might increase, but this would have a negligible effect on the wheat grower who paid for the advertisement. If all wheat farmers could get together, it might pay them to advertise as a group. In recent years, associations representing producers of milk, oranges, almonds, raisins, and beef have done just that.

If, however, advertising can create in consumers' minds the perception that products are different, then firms will face downward-sloping demand curves. There will be imperfect competition. If imperfect competition exists, advertising can be used to increase the demand for a firm's products.

ADVERTISING AND PROFITS

The objective of advertising is not only to change the slope of the demand curve—by creating the perception of product differences—but also to shift the demand curve out, as in Figure 18.3. The increase in advertising by one firm may divert customers away from rivals, or it may divert customers away from other products. Advertising a particular brand of cigarettes may be successful in inducing some smokers to switch brands and in inducing some nonsmokers to smoke.

The increase in profits from shifting the demand curve consists of two parts. First, the firm can sell the same quantity it sold before but at a higher price—p_3, rather than p_1. Profits then increase by the original quantity (Q_1) times the change in price ($p_3 - p_1$), the rectangle $ABCD$ in the figure. Second, by adjusting the quantity it sells, it can increase profits still further. This is because the advertising has shifted the firm's marginal revenue curve up. As usual, the imperfectly competitive firm sets marginal revenue equal to marginal cost, so it

CLOSE-UP: ADVERTISING ORANGE JUICE

In the simple model of perfect competition, a new orange juice company would announce that its product was ready, match or beat the price prevailing in the market, and sell its product. When Procter and Gamble entered the orange juice business in 1983, it competed by setting the price for its Citrus Hill juice a little lower than the price for established competitors like Tropicana and Minute Maid, and by blanketing the country with Citrus Hill coupons. But Procter and Gamble evidently felt that something more was needed to get its product started. According to *Business Week,* it set an advertising and promotion budget of $75 to $100 million. (By comparison, only $2.5 billion worth of orange juice was being sold in a year by all existing companies.)

There are two lessons to be drawn from this and many similar episodes. First, by spending significant amounts of money on advertising, manufacturers demonstrate their belief that offering a lower price is not a sufficient way of competing. Second, manufacturers must believe that advertising helps to make people perceive their product as unique, even when, as in the case of orange juice, most consumers probably can barely distinguish the different brands. Companies are able to take advantage of such perceptions to earn higher profits.

Source: Business Week, October 31, 1983.

Figure 18.3 HOW ADVERTISING CAN SHIFT THE DEMAND CURVE

Successful advertising shifts the demand curve facing a firm. When the imperfect competitor equates its new marginal revenue with its old marginal cost, it will be able to raise both its price and its output.

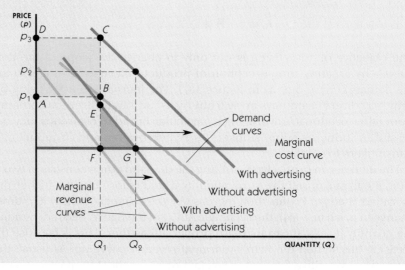

increases output from Q_1 to Q_2. The additional profits thus generated are measured by the area between the marginal revenue and marginal cost curves between Q_1 and Q_2. Marginal cost remains the same, so the second source of extra profits is the shaded area *EFG*. The net increase in profits is the area *ABCD* plus the area *EFG* minus the cost of advertising.

So far, in studying the effect of an increase in advertising on one firm's profits, we have assumed that other firms keep their level of advertising constant. The effect of advertising on both industry and firm profits is more problematical once the reactions of other firms in the industry are taken into account. To the extent that advertising diverts sales from one firm in an industry to another, advertising may, in equilibrium, have little effect on demand. For example, assume that Nike shoe ads divert customers from Reeboks to Nike and vice versa for Reebok ads. Figure 18.4 shows the demand curve facing Reebok (1) before advertising, (2) when only Reebok advertises, and (3) when both companies advertise. The final demand curve is the same as the initial demand curve. Price and output are the same; profits are lower by the amount spent on advertising. We have here another example of a Prisoner's Dilemma. If the firms could cooperate and agree not to advertise, they would both be better off. But without such cooperation, it pays each to advertise, regardless of what the rival does. The government-mandated ban on cigarette advertising on radio and TV may have partially solved this Prisoner's Dilemma for the tobacco industry—in the name of health policy.

In practice, when all cigarette firms advertise, the ads do more than just

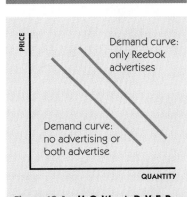

Figure 18.4 HOW ADVERTISING CAN CANCEL OTHER ADVERTISING

If only one company advertises, the demand curve for its product may shift out. But if both companies advertise, the resulting demand curve may be the same as it would if neither advertised.

CONSEQUENCES OF IMPERFECT INFORMATION

Adverse selection problems—quality may be affected by price

    Thin or nonexistent markets

    Signaling

    Markets may not clear

Incentive problems—weak or misdirected incentives

    Importance of contingency contracts, with contingency clauses

    Reputations, with price exceeding marginal cost

Search problems

    Price dispersion

    Imperfect competition

Advertising

    To change slope of demand curve—create perception of product differences

    To shift demand curve

cancel each other out. Some people who might not otherwise have smoked are persuaded to do so, and some smokers are induced to smoke more than they otherwise would have. But the shift in the demand curve facing a particular firm when all companies advertise is still much smaller than it is when only that firm advertises.

THE IMPORTANCE OF IMPERFECT INFORMATION

The modern economy has sometimes been called "the information economy." This is partly because the major advances in computer technology have greatly enhanced the capacity to process information, and partly because such a large fraction of economic activity revolves around collecting, processing, and disseminating information. Personnel officers focus on finding out about potential employees; lending officers attempt to assess the likelihood of default of potential borrowers; market researchers try to determine the potential market for some new product; large retail stores have buyers scouring the world for new suppliers of the clothes they sell. But no matter how much information we have, we seldom have as much as we would like.

Not only is information imperfect, but different people have different information. Information is asymmetric. The seller of a car knows more about his car's problems than the buyer. The worker may know more about his strengths and weaknesses than does the firm where he is interviewing for a job. The borrower may know more about some of the contingencies that may affect his ability to repay the loan than the lender. Because the parties to a transaction do not always have an incentive to be perfectly truthful, it may be difficult for the more informed party to convey convincingly what he knows to others.

In recent years, economists have come to agree that such imperfections of information fundamentally alter how individuals and markets behave. This agreement forms the basis of our tenth consensus point in economics.

10 Imperfect Information

The fact that individuals and firms typically make decisions based on imperfect information affects the behavior of markets in various ways. Firms and individuals compensate for the scarcity of information. In many markets where problems of adverse selection and moral hazard arise, firms adjust prices to convey information about quality. Individuals and firms may attempt to signal information about their characteristics and work to establish a reputation.

GOVERNMENT AND INFORMATION

The market inefficiencies resulting from information problems can take a number of forms. Governmental concern for the consequences of ill-informed consumers has motivated a number of pieces of **consumer protection legislation.** For example, the Wheeler-Lea Act of 1938 made "deceptive" trade practices illegal and gave the Federal Trade Commission power to stop false and deceptive advertising. Truth-in-lending legislation requires lenders to disclose the true interest rate being charged. Truth-in-packaging legislation makes it less likely that consumers will be misled by what is printed on the package. And the Securities and Exchange Commission, which regulates the sale of stocks and bonds, requires firms selling these securities to disclose a considerable amount of information.

Yet much of this legislation is of only limited effectiveness. One problem occurs when consumers try to absorb and process the information. A cereal manufacturer may disclose not only what is required, but a host of other information, which may or may not be of importance. How is the consumer to know what to pay attention to? He cannot absorb everything. Occasionally, as in the case of warnings about the dangers from smoking, government regulators, aware of these problems of information absorption, have required the disclosures to be of a specific form and size lettering to make them stand out. But that kind of intervention on a more massive scale would probably be, at the very least, extremely costly.

Another problem with outlawing deceptive advertising is the difficulty of drawing a clear line between persuasion and deception. Advertisers are good at walking along the edge of any line—a suggestive hint may do where an explicit claim might be called deceptive. Having congressmen or the courts draw a line between informative and noninformative advertising seems an impossible task.

REVIEW AND PRACTICE

SUMMARY

1. The basic competitive model assumes that participants in the market have perfect information about the goods being bought and sold and their prices. In the real world, information is often imperfect. Economists have modified the basic model to include a number of limitations on information.

2. A problem of adverse selection may arise when consumers cannot judge the true quality of a product. As the price of the good falls, the quality

mix changes adversely, and the quantity demanded at a lower price may actually be lower than at a higher price.

3. Producers of high-quality products may attempt to signal that their product is better than those of competitors, for instance by providing better warranties.

4. When consumers judge quality by price, there may be some price that offers the best value. Firms will have no incentive to cut price below this "best value" price, even when, at this price, the amount they would be willing to supply exceeds demand. As a result, the market can settle in an equilibrium with an excess supply of goods.

5. When there is perfect information, private property and prices provide correct incentives to all market participants. When information is imperfect, two methods of helping to provide correct incentives are contracts with contingency clauses, and reputations. For firms to have an incentive to maintain a reputation, there must be profits. The equilibrium price can exceed marginal cost. Reputation may serve as a barrier to entry.

6. With costly search, there may be price dispersion and imperfections of competition as each firm faces a downward-sloping demand curve.

7. Advertising attempts to change consumers' buying behavior, either by providing relevant information about prices or characteristics, by persuasion, or both.

KEY TERMS

imperfect information	thin or incomplete markets	contingency clauses
asymmetric information	adverse selection	price dispersion
	signal	consumer protection legislation

REVIEW QUESTIONS

1. Why are markets for information not likely to work as well as markets for goods like wheat?

2. Why would "lemons" not be a problem for consumers in a world of perfect information? Why do they lead to a backward-bending demand curve in a world of imperfect information?

3. Why is signaling unnecessary in a world of perfect information? What does it accomplish in a world of imperfect information?

4. Explain why, if consumers think that quality increases with price, there will be cases where firms will have no incentive to cut prices in an attempt to attract more business.

5. How do contingency clauses in contracts help provide appropriate incentives? What are some of the problems in writing contracts that provide for all the relevant contingencies?

6. What role does reputation have in maintaining incentives? What is required if firms are to have an incentive to maintain their reputations? How might the good reputation of existing firms serve as a barrier to the entry of new firms?

7. What are the benefits of searching for market information? What are the costs? How does the existence of price dispersion affect the benefits? Could price dispersion exist in a world of perfect information? How does the fact that search is costly affect the nature of competition in a market?

8. Describe how advertising might affect the demand curve facing a firm. How do these changes affect prices? profits?

9. "For most practical purposes, information problems can be solved by government requirements that information be disclosed to potential buyers and investors." Discuss.

PROBLEMS

1. The We Pick 'Em Company collects information about horse races, and sells a newsletter predicting the winners. Why might you possibly be predisposed to distrust the accuracy of the We Pick 'Em newsletter?

2. How might a house cleaning service try to signal that it will promptly and carefully clean your house every time?

3. Explain how the incentives of someone to look after a car she is renting may not suit the company that is renting the car. How might a contingent contract help to solve this problem? Is it likely to solve the problem completely?

4. L. L. Bean, a mail order company, has a long-standing policy that it will take back anything it has sold, at any time, for any reason. Why might it be worthwhile for a profit-maximizing firm to enact such a policy?

5. Would you expect to see greater price dispersion within a metropolitan area, or between several small towns that are fifty miles apart? Why?

6. How do costs of search help to explain the success of department stores?

IMPERFECTIONS IN THE LABOR MARKET

art Two emphasized the similarity between the labor market and markets for goods. Households demand goods and firms supply them, with the price system as intermediary. Likewise, firms demand labor and workers supply it, with the wage as intermediary. Firms hire labor up to the point where the value of the marginal product of labor is equal to the wage, just as they would buy coal up to the point where the value of the marginal product of coal is equal to the price of coal.

This chapter takes another look at the labor market. Just as we saw in the preceding five chapters some of the ways in which product markets differ from the way they are depicted in the basic competitive model, here we will see important ways in which labor markets differ from the way they are depicted in the basic competitive model. We will see that labor markets, like

KEY QUESTIONS

1. How do unions affect the wages of their workers? of workers in general? What limits the power of unions? Why have unions been declining in strength?

2. How do we explain the large differences in wages paid to different workers, even to workers that appear to have similar abilities? What role does discrimination play?

3. How do firms seek to motivate their workers, to ensure that they put out effort commensurate with their pay? In what sense can the problem of providing workers incentives be viewed as a consequence of imperfect or limited information?

product markets, are characterized by imperfect competition. Unions are the most obvious manifestation, and we will take a look at their history as well as their impact on wages and employment—the prices and quantities of the labor market.

Information problems have an even more significant impact on the labor market than on product markets. This is partly because workers are not like lumps of coal. They have to be motivated to work hard. And they are concerned with work conditions and how their pay compares with that of other firms. Firms are aware of the importance of these considerations in attracting and keeping employees and design employment and compensation policies that take them into account.

LABOR UNIONS

Labor unions are organizations of workers, formed to obtain better working conditions and higher wages for their members. The main weapon they have is the threat of a collective withdrawal of labor, known as a **strike.**

A BRIEF HISTORY

Labor unions are less important institutions in our economy than they used to be, and have always played a smaller role in the United States than they do in many European countries. Unionization in the United States began in the late nineteenth and early twentieth centuries. A variety of craft unions were established, consisting of skilled workers such as carpenters, plumbers, and printers. In 1886, the American Federation of Labor (AFL) was formed. Led by Samuel Gompers, the AFL gathered together a number of these craft unions to enhance their bargaining power.

The Rise of Unions In the 1930s, two events strengthened union power: the confederation of major industrial unions into the Congress of Industrial Organizations (CIO) and the passage of the Wagner Act, which provided legal status to unions. The CIO represented a major change in two respects. First, it embraced all workers, unskilled as well as skilled; and second, it represented all the workers in a company. These industrial unions, by uniting all workers together, enhanced workers' bargaining strength. The leaders of these unions, such as Walter Reuther of the United Automobile Workers (UAW), attained national prominence, and the unions were able to obtain for their workers substantial wage increases and improvements in working conditions. The 1935 Wagner Act set up the National Labor Relations Board, which established procedures for certification of labor unions and prevention of certain practices on the part of firms trying to prevent workers from unionizing.

The Decline of Unions Prompted by concern that the balance had swung too far in favor of unions, Congress passed the Taft-Hartley Act in 1947. This law addressed two issues. First, unions had claimed that when they negotiated a better contract or better working conditions, they were providing benefits to all workers at an establishment. Thus, they required all laborers at unionized companies to join the union, a requirement that established **union shops.** Critics of union shops thought that the right to work should not be limited to members of unions. The Taft-Hartley law left it to the individual states to decide whether to outlaw union shops, and many states subsequently passed **right-to-work laws.** The laws gave workers the right to hold a job without belonging to a union—or, to put it the way unions do, the right to receive union pay without paying union dues.

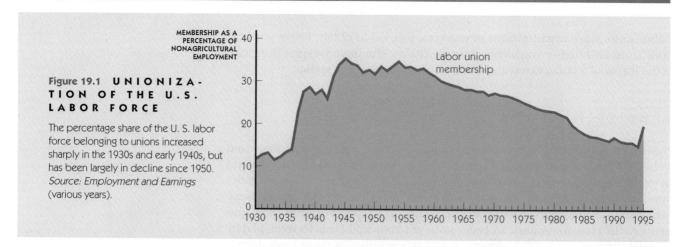

MEMBERSHIP AS A PERCENTAGE OF NONAGRICULTURAL EMPLOYMENT

Figure 19.1 UNIONIZA-TION OF THE U.S. LABOR FORCE

The percentage share of the U. S. labor force belonging to unions increased sharply in the 1930s and early 1940s, but has been largely in decline since 1950. *Source: Employment and Earnings* (various years).

Labor union membership

The second concern addressed by the Taft-Hartley Act was the devastating effect on the country of strikes by national unions. A shutdown of the railroads or the steel or coal industry could have ramifications far beyond the firms directly involved. The Taft-Hartley law gave the president the power to declare, when national welfare was at stake, an eighty-day cooling-off period, during which workers had to return to work.

Since the mid-1950s, union power has declined steadily in the United States. Figure 19.1 traces out the sharp increases of union membership in the 1930s, and again during World War II, when the government encouraged unionization in all military plants. But since then, unions have had only limited success in recruiting new members, so the union share of nonagricultural employment has been falling. It fell below 20 percent in 1984, where it remains today. In fact, not only has the union share been declining, the actual number of unionized workers has been falling. Today there are about seventeen million union members, 1 million less than there were in 1960.

These figures hide the even greater decline of unions in the private sector. In 1960 the percentage of union members working in the public sector was only 6 percent. Today it is more than 35 percent. Today only one out of ten nongovernment workers belongs to a union. Why the recent and continuing decline?

One explanation is that, whether as a result of union pressure or technological progress, working conditions for workers have improved enormously. Workers see less need for unions.

A second reason is related to the changing nature of the American economy. Unions have declined as the traditionally unionized sectors (like automobiles and steel) have weakened, and the service sector, in which unions have been and continue to be weak, has grown.

Third, unions may be less effective in competitive markets. When competition is limited, there are monopoly (or imperfect competition) profits or rents. Unions may be successful in obtaining for their workers a share in those rents. But when markets are competitive, firms cannot charge more than the market price for their goods, and if they are to survive, they simply cannot pay their workers more than the competitive wage.

In the late nineteenth and early twentieth centuries, for example, high wages in shoe and textile mills in New England drove plants to the nonunionized South. High wages also drive American firms to manufacture abroad. Unless unions manage to ensure that their workers are more productive than average, it is only when these sources of competition are restricted that unions can succeed in keeping their wages above average for long. In this view, the increased competition to which American industry was subjected in the 1970s and 1980s, both from abroad and from the deregulation of trucking, oil, airlines, banking, telephone service, and so on, led to a decline in the ability of unions in the private sector to garner higher wages for their workers.

A final explanation of the growth and decline of unions is the changing legal atmosphere. When laws support or encourage unions, unions prosper. When they do not, unions wither. Thus, the Wagner Act set the stage for the growth of unions in the 1930s. The Taft–Hartley Act paved the way for their decline in the post-World War II era.

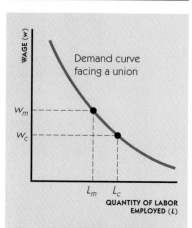

Figure 19.2 THE UNION AS A MONOPOLY SELLER OF LABOR

Unions can be viewed as sellers of labor, with market power. When they increase their wage demands, they reduce the demand for their members' labor services.

ECONOMIC EFFECTS

The source of union power is collective action. When workers join together in a union, they no longer negotiate as isolated individuals. The threat of a strike (or a work slowdown) poses many more difficulties for an employer than does the threat of any single employee quitting.

In the perfectly competitive model of labor markets, workers are price takers, facing a given market wage. But in situations where there is a downward-sloping demand curve for labor, as in Figure 19.2,[1] unions have some power to be price setters. As a result of this power, a worker at a given level of skill who works in a unionized establishment will be paid more than a comparable worker in a competitive industry. The firm would like to hire that lower-priced, nonunion worker, and the nonunionized worker could easily be induced to move, but the firm has a union contract that prevents it from doing so. But as the union raises the price of labor (the wage), firms will employ fewer workers. Higher wages are obtained at the expense of lower employment. In the figure, when wages rise from the competitive level w_c to w_m, employment is reduced from L_c to L_m.

SHORT-RUN GAINS AT THE EXPENSE OF LONG-RUN LOSSES

Sometimes unions can increase both employment and wages, at least for a time. They present the employer with, in effect, two alternatives: either pay a high wage *and* maintain an employment level above the labor demand curve for that wage, or go out of business. If the employer already has sunk costs in machines and buildings, he may concede to the union demands. In effect, the union takes away some of the employer's monopoly profits and/or return to capital. In competitive markets, where there are no monopoly profits, the higher wages can only come out of employers' return to capital. But these employers will lose interest in investing in more capital. As capital wears out, the employer has less and less to lose from the union threat. As he refuses to invest more, jobs decrease. Even if the union makes short-run gains, they come at the expense of a long-run loss in jobs.

EFFECTS ON NONUNION WORKERS

The gains of today's union members may not only cost future jobs, they may also be at the expense of those in other sectors of the economy, for two reasons. First, the higher wages may well be passed on to consumers in the form

---

[1] Chapter 12 showed how the demand curve for labor is derived in competitive markets. Firms hire labor up to the point where the wage equals the value of the marginal product of labor. The derivation of the demand curve for labor in monopolies and imperfectly competitive markets follows along similar lines. Firms hire labor up to the point where the marginal revenue, the extra revenue they obtain from selling the extra output they produce from hiring an extra unit of labor, is equal to the wage.

of higher prices, particularly if product markets are not perfectly competitive. Second, the increased wages (and reduced employment) in the union sector drives down wages in the nonunionized sector, as the supply of nonunion labor increases. Some argue the opposite—that high union wages "pull up" wages in nonunion firms. The nonunion firms may, for instance, pay higher wages to reduce the likelihood of unionization. In particular sectors this effect is important, but most economists believe that the overall effect on nonunion workers is negative.

JOB SECURITY AND INNOVATION

As explained in Chapter 17, the economy as a whole benefits from innovation, but particular groups are likely to suffer. In an innovative economy, those workers who are dislocated by new inventions are expected to learn new skills and seek out new jobs. Without labor shifting in response to changes in demand (resulting either from new technologies or changes in tastes), the economy will be inefficient.

Technological changes may threaten the job security unions seek for their members. As a result, unions have attempted to retard innovations that might decrease the demand for their members' labor services. Job transitions are necessary for economic efficiency, but they are costly and the costs are borne largely by the workers. Before the advent of unions and laws providing unemployment compensation, the human toll was considerable. Individuals could not buy insurance against these employment risks, but they could form unions, and union attempts to enhance job security were a response to this important problem. Today many countries are looking for ways of insulating workers against the risks of job transition without impeding the labor mobility that is so important for economic efficiency. For instance, the Swedish government has set up major programs to facilitate job transitions and job retraining.

UNIONS AND POLITICS

We have seen that the fortunes of unions depend, to a large extent, on the legal environment in which they operate. Unions have also learned that what they cannot get at the bargaining table they may be able to obtain through the political process. For example, they have actively campaigned for higher minimum wages.

At the same time, unions have shown in their political stances that they recognize the economic forces that determine both the strength of their bargaining positions and, more generally, the level of wages. Thus, they have been active supporters of policies of high employment. They have sought to restrict imports from abroad (believing that this will increase the demand for American products and therefore the demand for labor). And they have been proponents of restrictions on immigration (recognizing that increases in the supply of labor lead to reductions in wages).

Finally, unions have been strong advocates, through the political process, of safer working conditions. Today, the Occupational Safety and Health Administration (OSHA) attempts to ensure that workers are not exposed to unnecessary hazards. OSHA seeks to make the kinds of episodes such as occurred in the asbestos industry, where workers were exposed to life-threatening risks, much less likely today.

LIMITS ON UNION POWER

In the United States, no union has a monopoly on *all* workers. At most, a union has a monopoly on the workers currently working for a particular firm. Thus, the power of unions is partly attributable to the fact that a firm cannot easily replace its employees. When a union goes on strike, the firm may be able to hire some workers, but it is costly to bring in and train a whole new labor force. Indeed, most of the knowledge needed to train the new workers is in the hands of the union members. While one bushel of wheat may be very much like another, one worker is not very much like another. Workers outside the firm are not perfect substitutes for workers, particularly skilled ones, inside.

THE THREAT OF REPLACEMENT

In those industries in which skills are easily transferable across firms, or where a union has not been successful in enlisting the support of most of the skilled workers, a firm can replace striking workers, and union power will be limited. Caterpillar, a manufacturer of tractors and road-making equipment, weathered a prolonged strike by the United Auto Workers beginning June 21, 1993. Eventually management announced that if workers did not return to their jobs, they would be replaced. The union caved in shortly after the firm made good on its threat.

In many cases, however, workers' skills are firm-specific. Just as, from the employers' perspective, workers outside the firm are not perfect substitutes for workers within, from the workers' perspective, one job is not a perfect substitute for another. Thus, there is often value both to workers and firms in preserving ongoing employment relationships. The two parties are tied to each other in what is referred to as a bargaining relationship. The bargaining strengths of the two sides are affected by the fact that a firm, at a cost, can obtain other employees, and employees, at a cost, can get other jobs. The total amount by which the two sides together are better off continuing their relationship than ending it is referred to as the "bargaining surplus." A large part of the negotiations between unions and management are about how to split this surplus.

THE THREAT OF UNEMPLOYMENT

Unions have come to understand that in the long run, higher wages—other things being equal—mean lower levels of employment. When job opportunities in general are weak, concern about the employment consequences of union contracts increases. This was evident in the early 1980s, as a deep recession threatened a number of union jobs, especially in the automobile industry, which also faced the threat of Japanese imports.

CLOSE-UP: LESSONS FROM UNIONS IN OTHER COUNTRIES

Unions have been blamed for declining productivity growth in the United States, even though only one in six workers belongs to a union. This share is less than the share of the work force that in unionized in most developed countries. In Japan, for example, one in four workers belong to unions. The share in Germany is more than one third; Canada and the United Kingdom, 42 percent; and in Denmark and Sweden, it is over 70 percent.

Those who blame American unions for the decline of U.S. economic power must explain how nations like Japan and Germany have increased their rates of productivity with higher rates of unionization. And those who blame the decline in unionization on the growth of the service sector or greater global competition must explain why those factors have led to lower union membership in the United States but much higher levels in other countries.

Part of the explanation is the different nature of unions in different countries. In Finland and Portu-

gal, for example, unions negotiate with employers and the government on overall national policy. And in Germany, union negotiations tend to happen one industry at a time. By contrast, U.S. and Japanese unions tend to negotiate one *company* at a time.

In addition, a nation's legal environment can either encourage workers to form unions or make it easier for management to fight unions off. Margaret Thatcher, as prime minister of Britain in the 1970s, took as one of her main goals the redressing of what she saw as an imbalance of power in favor of unions.

This international perspective suggests that asking whether unions are generically "good" or "bad" is too simplistic. Instead, the question should be whether unions, in some form, have a potentially useful role to play in the U.S. economy. Richard Freeman, of Harvard University, thinks so. He argues: "Although Scandinavian levels of unionization seem to me to be infeasible and

undesirable in a large, diverse country like the United States . . . research supports the view that greater unionization is needed to give workers alternatives to the market or to governmental intervention in workplace arrangements." Freeman suggests that in the future, American unions will have to focus less attention on demanding higher wages and benefits and more on improving working conditions.

Just as American firms have been looking abroad to find alternative models for what makes success, unions in other countries may provide some alternative models for how American unions might help increase the country's productivity.

Sources: International Labour Office, *World Labour Report* (1992). Richard Freeman, "Is Declining Unionization of the U.S. Good, Bad, or Irrelevant?" in Lawrence Mishel and Paula Voos, eds., *Unions and Economic Competitiveness* (Armonk, N.Y.: Sharpe, 1992), pp. 143–72.

In the round of union negotiations that began in 1981, Ford Motor Company was the first auto company to settle with the United Automobile Workers. In the new thirty-month contract, the UAW agreed to give up annual wage increases for two years, to defer what had been automatic increases in wages in response to increases in the cost of living, and to eliminate a number of paid personal holidays. The contract also provided for new employees to be paid at only 85 percent of the normal rate, thus creating a two-tier wage system. For its part, Ford offered a moratorium on closing any plants, a guarantee that extra profits arising during the term of the contract would be shared with workers, increased worker participation in decision making, and greater job security for workers. General Motors made a similar deal a few months later, and Chrysler was able to negotiate a better deal because of its even

UNIONS AND IMPERFECT COMPETITION IN THE LABOR MARKET

Economic effects:

 Higher wages for union members, with fewer union jobs and lower wages for nonunion members

 Improved job security, sometimes at the expense of innovation and economic efficiency

 Minimum wages, restrictions on imports, improved working conditions, other gains achieved through the political process

Determinants of union power:

 Political and legal environment

 Economic environment: threat of replacement and unemployment worse financial condition. The dollar value of the total concessions from the union was estimated at about $3 billion for the contract period. Similar wage cuts occurred in the airline and steel industries, among others.

The deal between Ford and the UAW set the pattern for auto labor contracts in the 1980s. Unions made wage concessions in return for job security. For example, in 1984, in return for wage concessions, GM agreed not to lay off for the next six years any worker with at least one year's seniority who was displaced by new technology. Instead, such workers would stay on at their full salary while they were retrained and relocated.

WAGE DIFFERENTIALS

The basic competitive model suggests that if the goods being sold are the same, prices will also be the same. Wages are the price in the labor market; but even in the absence of unions, similar types of workers performing similar types of jobs are sometimes paid quite different wages. For example, some secretaries are paid twice as much as others. How can economists explain differences like these?

They begin by pointing to **compensating wage differentials.** Understanding compensating wage differentials begins with the observation that although different jobs may have the same title, they can be quite different. Some jobs are less pleasant, require more overtime, and are in a less convenient location. These are **nonpecuniary** attributes of a job. Other nonpecuniary attributes include the degree of autonomy provided the worker (that is, the closeness with which her actions are supervised) and the risk she must bear, whether in a physical sense or from the variability in income. Economists expect wages to adjust to reflect the attractiveness or unattractiveness of these nonpecuniary characteristics. Compensating wage differentials arise because firms have to compensate their workers for the negative aspects of a job.

Other differences are accounted for by differences in the productivity of workers. These are **productivity wage differentials.** Some workers are much more productive than others, even with the same experience and education.

Compensating and productivity wage differentials fall within the realm of the basic competitive model analysis. But other wage differentials are due to imperfect information. It takes time to search out different job opportunities. Just as one store may sell the same object for a higher price than another store, one firm may hire labor for a lower wage than another firm. The worker who accepts a lower-paying job simply because he did not know about the higher-paying one down the street faces an **information-based differential.**

Limited information has important implications for firms. First, in the standard competitive model, firms face a horizontal supply curve for labor. If they raise wages slightly above the "market" wage, they can obtain as much labor as they want. In practice, mobility is more limited. Even if workers at other firms knew about the higher wage offer, they might be reluctant to switch. They may worry that they are not well matched for the job, or that the employer is offering high wages because the work is unattractive.

Second, firms worry about the quality of their work force. If an employer offers a higher wage to someone working for another firm, and the worker accepts, the employer might worry about the signal his action sends about the quality of the worker. Did the worker's current employer—who presumably knows a lot about the worker's productivity—fail to match the job offer because the worker's productivity does not warrant the higher wage? Does the worker's willingness to leave demonstrate a "lack of loyalty," or an "unsettled nature"—in which case, he may not stick with the new firm long enough to make his training worthwhile? These concerns again impede labor mobility—as employers prefer to keep their existing labor force even when there are lower-paid workers with similar credentials whom they might recruit at a lower wage.

There are a variety of other impediments to labor mobility, including the costs of moving from one city to another.

Different groups of individuals may differ in their mobility. For instance, older workers may be much more reluctant to move than younger workers. Sometimes, firms take advantage of these differences, to pay lower wages. Knowing that older workers will not leave even if wages fail to keep pace with inflation, employers may hold back raises from them. This provides a rationale for employers to engage in age discrimination in wage setting.

DISCRIMINATION

Discrimination is said to occur if two workers of seemingly similar *work-related* characteristics are treated differently. Paying higher wages to more educated workers is not discrimination, as long as the higher level of education is related to higher productivity. If older workers are less productive, then paying them lower wages is not discrimination. But if older workers are just as productive as younger workers, then taking advantage of their lower mobility *is* discrimination.

Forty years ago, there was open and outright discrimination in the labor market. Some employers simply refused to hire African-Americans. Today much of the discrimination that occurs is more subtle. Firms seek to hire the best workers they can for each job at the lowest cost possible, operating with imperfect information. In making predictions about future performance, employers use whatever information they have available. On average, employers may have found that those receiving a degree from a well-established school are more productive than those receiving a degree from a less-established college. Of those African-Americans and Hispanics who have managed to get a college education, more may have gone to the less-established schools. Screening the applicant pool to pick those with degrees from well-established colleges effectively screens out many African-Americans and Hispanics. This more subtle form of discrimination is called **statistical discrimination.**

Some discrimination is neither old-fashioned prejudice nor statistical discrimination. Employers may just feel more comfortable dealing with people with whom they have dealt in the past. In a world in which there is so much uncertainty about who is a good worker, and in which a bad worker can do enormous damage, top management may rely on certain trusted employees for recommendations. And such judgments are inevitably affected by friendships and other ties. Many claim that if discrimination is to be eliminated, this form of discrimination, based on "old boy networks," has to be broken.

When firms pay lower wages to, say, women or minorities, it is called **wage discrimination.** Today, wage discrimination is perhaps less common than **job discrimination,** where disadvantaged groups have less access to better-paying jobs. Women are often said to face a "glass ceiling": they can climb up to middle management jobs, but can't get beyond that to top management.

Some market forces tend to limit the extent of discrimination. If a woman is paid less than a man of comparable productivity, it pays a firm to hire the woman. Not to hire her costs the firm profits. To put it another way, the firm pays a price for discriminating. If there are enough firms that put profits above prejudice, then the wages of women will be bid up toward the level of men of comparable productivity.

Beginning in the 1960s, the government has taken an increasingly active stance in combatting discrimination. In 1964, Congress passed the Civil Rights Act, which prohibited employment discrimination and set up the Equal Employment Opportunity Commission to prosecute cases of discrimination. The reach of these laws was extended in 1975 when the government banned age discrimination.

EXPLANATIONS OF WAGE DIFFERENTIALS

Unions: Unions may succeed in obtaining higher wages for their workers.

Compensating differentials: Wage differences may correspond to differences in the nature of the job.

Productivity differentials: Wage differences may correspond to differences in the productivity between workers.

Information-based differentials: Wage differences may reflect the fact that workers do not have perfect information about the opportunities available in the market, and employers do not view all workers as perfect substitutes.

Imperfect labor mobility: Differentials will not be eliminated by individuals moving between jobs.

Discrimination: Wage differentials and hiring and promotion decisions can sometimes be traced to nothing more than racial or gender differences.

Beyond this, the government has required its contractors to undertake **affirmative action.** They must actively seek out minorities and women for jobs, and actively seek to promote them to better-paying positions. In order to be effective, affirmative action has occasionally taken the form of quotas that specify that a certain number or fraction of positions be reserved for minorities or women. Critics claim that quotas are discriminatory—they imply that a minority individual would be chosen over a more qualified white male. One of the objectives of antidiscrimination laws was to discourage thinking in racial or gender terms. Courts have reaffirmed this, allowing quotas only in special circumstances such as redressing the effects of specific instances of past discrimination.

MOTIVATING WORKERS

The discussion to this point has treated workers as if they were machines. Workers have a price—the wage—analogous to the price of machines. But even to the most profit-hungry and coldhearted employer, people are different from machines. They bring adaptability and a multitude of skills and experiences to a job. Most machines can only do one task, and even robots can only do what they are programmed to do. However, machines have one advantage over humans. Except when they break down, they do what they are told. But workers have to be motivated if they are to work hard and to exercise good judgment.

This can be viewed as an information problem. In the basic competitive model of Part Two, workers were paid to perform particular tasks. The employer knew perfectly whether the worker performed the agreed-upon task in the agreed-upon manner. If the worker failed to do so, he did not get paid. The pay was the only form of motivation required. But in reality, workers frequently have considerable discretion. Employers have limited information about what a worker is doing at each moment. So they have to motivate their work force to exercise their abilities to the fullest.

To motivate workers, employers use both the carrot and the stick. They may reward workers for performing well by making pay and promotion depend on performance, and they may punish workers for shirking by firing them. Sometimes a worker is given considerable discretion and autonomy; sometimes he is monitored closely. The mix of carrots and sticks, autonomy and direct supervision, varies from job to job and industry to industry. It depends partly on how easy it is to supervise workers directly and how easy it is to compensate workers on the basis of performance.

PIECE RATES AND INCENTIVES

When workers can be paid for exactly what they produce, with their pay increasing for higher productivity and falling for lower productivity, they will have appropriate incentives to work hard. The system of payment in which a worker is paid for each item produced or each task performed is called a **piece-rate system.** But relatively few Americans are paid largely, let alone exclusively, on a piece-rate system. Typically, even workers within a piece-rate system get a base pay *plus* additional pay, which increases the more they produce.

Why don't more employers enact a piece-rate system, if it would improve incentives? One major reason is that piece rates leave workers bearing considerable risk. A worker may have a bad week because of bad luck. For example, salesmen, who are often paid commissions on the basis of sales—a form of piece rate—may simply find the demand for their products lacking.

A firm, by providing a certain amount of guaranteed pay, gives the worker a steady income and reduces the risk she must bear. But with lower piece-rate compensation, the worker has less incentive to work hard. There is thus a trade-off between risk and incentives. Compensation schemes must find some balance between offering security and offering incentives linked to worker performance. In many jobs, employers or managers achieve this balance by offering both a guaranteed minimum compensation (including fringe benefits) and bonuses that depend on performance.

A second reason more employers do not use piece-rate systems is a concern for quality. For workers on an assembly line, for example, the quantity produced may be easily measured, but quality cannot. If the workers' pay just depends on the number of items produced, the worker has an incentive to emphasize quantity over quality. The result may be less profitable for the firm than a lower level of higher-quality output.

In any case, most workers are engaged in a variety of tasks, only some of which can easily be defined and rewarded by means of a piece-rate system. For example, although employers would like experienced workers to train new workers, employees who are paid on a piece-rate system have little incentive to do this, or to help their co-workers in other ways. Similarly, when salesmen are paid on the basis of commissions, they have little incentive to provide information and service to potential customers whom they perceive as not likely to be immediate buyers. Even if providing information enhances the likelihood that a customer will return to the store to buy the good, there is a fair chance that some other salesperson will get the commission. To see this effect at work, visit a car dealer's showroom, make it clear that you are not going to buy a car that day, and see what service you get.

EFFICIENCY WAGES

When output is easily measured, then the carrot of basing pay at least partially on performance makes sense. And when effort is easily monitored, then using the stick of being fired for failure to exert adequate effort makes sense. But monitoring effort continuously is often expensive. An alternative is to monitor less frequently, and impose a big penalty if the worker is caught shirking. One way of imposing a big penalty is to pay above-market wages. Then, if a worker is fired, he suffers a big income loss. The higher the wage, the greater the penalty from being fired. Similarly, rewarding workers with higher pay who are observed to be working hard whenever they are monitored, provides incentives for workers to continue to work hard.

These are examples where higher wages help motivate workers and lead to increased productivity. There are additional reasons why it may pay a firm to pay high wages. High wages reduce labor turnover, lead to more loyalty and higher quality work by employees, and enable the firm to attract more productive workers. For all of these reasons it may pay firms to pay high wages—higher than are absolutely necessary to recruit the desired number of workers. The theory that higher wages increases workers' net productivity, either by reducing labor turnover, by providing better incentives, or by enabling the firm to recruit a higher quality labor force, is called the **efficiency wage theory.** While conventional theory emphasizes that increased productivity leads to higher wages, efficiency wage theory emphasizes that higher wages lead to increased productivity.

Efficiency wage theory provides an explanation for some wage differentials. In jobs where it is very costly to monitor workers on a day-to-day basis, or where the damage a worker can do is very great (where, for instance, by punching one wrong button the worker can destroy a machine), employers are more likely to rely on high wages to ensure workers perform well.

These "wages of trust" may explain why wages in more capital-intensive industries (that require massive investments) are higher for workers with otherwise comparable skills than wages in industries using less capital. They may also explain why workers entrusted with the care of much cash (which they could abscond with) are paid higher wages than are other workers of comparable skills. It is not so much that they receive high wages because they are trustworthy, but that they become more trustworthy because they receive high wages—and the threat of losing those high wages encourages honest behavior.

OTHER INCENTIVES

Other important incentives to increase job performance are enhanced promotion possibilities for those who perform well, with pay rising with promotions. But it is often hard to determine the difficulty of the task a worker is performing. One way to figure out who is performing well is to set up a contest among workers, with the winner receiving some valuable prize, like a cash bonus. Consider a firm trying to figure out how much to pay its sales force when it is promoting a new product. If a salesperson is successful, does that represent good salesmanship, or is the new product able to "sell itself"? All sales representatives are in roughly the same position. The representative who sells the most gets a bonus—and wins the contest.

At the top end of the corporate hierarchy, the top executives of America's largest firms are paid much higher average salaries than their counterparts in many other industrial economies, often running into the millions of dollars. Why is this? Economists continue to debate the issue. Some interpret these salaries as the payoffs of contests, others as reflecting the large contributions of these managers or wages of trust. But some suspect that top managers have

Legislating a minimum wage below which it is illegal to hire workers has been sharply criticized by economists as hurting exactly the people it is designed to help—those at the bottom of the wage scale.

Critics base their reasoning on the traditional demand and supply model of Part Two. There, an increase in wages above the market equilibrium results in lower employment. Those who manage to get jobs are better off; those who are forced into unemployment are worse off. If the objective is to reduce poverty, the minimum wage, in this perspective, seems counterproductive.

But as this chapter has pointed out, markets for labor are different from markets for many other commodities. Workers have to be motivated to work hard. High wages lead to increased productivity, less absenteeism, and lower labor turnover. Presumably, rational firms would take this into account in their wage setting. Even so, if the government forces firms to pay higher wages through minimum wage legislation, the increased productivity may largely offset the increased wages, so that the employment effect may be very small.

In labor markets in which there is imperfect competition, minimum wages could actually lead to increased employment. Because of imperfect mobility, firms face an upward-sloping supply schedule. Since all workers in a similar job have to be treated the same, the cost of hiring an additional worker may be high, above the wage it pays to its new employee. Not only must the firm raise the wage offered to the *new* worker, it must raise the wage paid to all existing workers. This discourages the firm from hiring additional employees. With a minimum wage, the cost of hiring an additional worker is just the minimum wage. Accord-

ingly, the marginal cost of hiring an additional worker when there is a minimum wage may actually be lower than when there is not, in which case firms will actually hire more workers.

These perspectives are consistent with several recent empirical studies which have shown there to be negligible, or even positive, employment effects from a minimum wage.

Some economists have also pointed to broader, positive consequences of minimum wages: they induce firms to invest more in their workers, to increase their workers' productivity. Gavin Wright, a distinguished economic historian at Stanford University, has argued that minimum wages played a vital role in the transformation of the South. It was

a region that had been vastly poorer than the North from the end of the Civil War to the Great Depression, with an economy largely based on very low wages. The minimum wage catalyzed changes which had dramatic effects on the South's economy, shifting them away from those low wage industries to dynamic industries paying higher wages.

A further alleged advantage of raising the minimum wage is that it increases the incentives to work, by increasing the difference between what someone on welfare receives and what a worker gets.

enough control over the firm to divert a considerable amount (though but a small fraction) of a firm's resources to their own betterment in the form of higher compensation.

In recent years, firms have explored the consequences of alternative ways of encouraging worker motivation and hence worker productivity. Some use teams. When pay depends on team performance, members of a team have an incentive to monitor and help one another. The Swedish automaker Volvo believes that such team arrangements have increased the productivity of its own work force. Some firms have encouraged worker participation in decision making. Such participation may help both sides see that there is more to be gained by cooperation than by conflict. For instance, new ways of producing goods can make both the firm and the workers better off; if the company sells more goods, all share in the benefits.

At least in the long run, wages and labor costs respond to reflect the attitudes of workers. If workers find that a certain firm provides an attractive workplace, the wages it must pay to recruit people may be lower than other firms' wages, and the people that it recruits will work harder and stay longer. If workers as a whole become concerned about having more autonomy, more say in decision making, or any other attribute of the workplace, it will pay firms to respond to their concerns.

WAYS OF MOTIVATING WORKERS

Piece rates, or pay based on measured output.

The threat of firing workers whose efforts or performance are deemed inadequate.

Efficiency wages introduce an extra cost to those dismissed for unsatisfactory performance.

Relative performance: promotions, contests.

Team rewards, pay based on team performance.

CLOSE-UP: FRINGE BENEFITS

The monetary pay a worker receives is often only a portion of his total compensation received. In 1993, for example, the average wage (or salary) received by a private industry worker in the United States was $11.90 per hour. However, the total compensation received was $16.70 per hour, a full 40 percent higher.

The difference is "fringe benefits." U.S. employers paid an average of $1.11 per hour to each employee for paid leave, including vacation time, paid holidays, and absence for illness, $.42 per hour for special bonuses and incentives, $1.19 per hour for insurance, mainly health insurance, and $.48 an hour for company pensions. Employers also paid $1.52 per hour per employee for government-required programs like Social Security and unemployment insurance. These payments clearly have value to workers, but they do not show up in take-home pay.

Fringe benefits complicate the straightforward model of the labor market presented earlier in this book. In that model, workers try to seek out the firm that will give them the highest pay, while employers try to seek out those who will work for the lowest pay. The existence of fringe benefits means that workers must look beyond take-home pay and take all forms of compensation into account.

Why do employers offer fringe benefits, rather than simply paying a straight salary to workers? One main reason involves the tax code; if employees are paid income and then purchase health insurance on their own, they must pay income tax on the money. But if the company buys the insurance for them, the fringe benefit is not counted as income. In addition, many employers use fringe benefits to offer an incentive for employees to stay with the company. For example, companies often require that the employee remain with the company for a period of several years before becoming eligible for the company pension plan. Such

"We have something with terrific fringe benefits. No salary—just fringe benefits."

benefits show that employers are not eager to lose their long-term employees, and would rather offer some added benefits than go through the cost and trouble of hiring and training new workers. But why—other than for tax reasons—they should rely so heavily on rewarding these workers through better fringe benefits rather than through cash bonuses remains unclear.

Source: Statistical Abstract of the United States (1994).

REVIEW AND PRACTICE

SUMMARY

1. The proportion of U.S. workers in unions has declined since the 1950s. Possible reasons include laws that have improved working conditions in general; the decline of manufacturing industries, where unions have traditionally been strong, relative to service industries; increased competition in the product market, providing firms with less latitude to pay above market wages; and a more anti-union atmosphere in the U.S. legal structure.

2. Union gains in wages are typically at the expense of lower employment, at least in the long run, and lower wages in the nonunion sector. Unions also have played an important role in enhancing job security, though sometimes at the expense of innovation. Some of the gains they have accomplished for workers have been through the political process, for instance, in pushing legislation that promotes occupational safety and health and the minimum wage.

3. Union power is limited by the ability of companies to bring in new, nonunion workers and by the threat of unemployment to union workers.

4. Explanations for wage differentials include compensating differentials (differences in the nature of jobs), productivity differentials (differences in productivity between workers), imperfect information (workers do not know all the job opportunities that are available), and discrimination.

5. Employers try to motivate workers and induce high levels of effort through a combination of direct supervision, incentives for doing well, and penalties for doing badly. They pay wages higher than workers could get elsewhere (efficiency wages), give promotions and bonuses, base pay on relative performance (contests), and grant team rewards.

KEY TERMS

union shops	compensating wage	piece-rate system
right-to-work laws	differentials	efficiency wage
		theory

REVIEW QUESTIONS

1. Has the power of unions in the U.S. economy been shrinking or growing in the last few decades? Why? In what sector has union growth been largest? Why might this be so?

2. What effect will successful unions have on the level of wages paid by unionized companies? on the capital investment for those companies? What effect will they have on wages paid by nonunionized companies?

3. How might greater job security for union workers possibly lead them to become less efficient?

4. Does it make sense for a union to resist the introduction of an innovation in the short run? in the long run?

5. What are alternative explanations for wage differentials?

6. How do piece rates provide incentives to work hard? Why is there not a greater reliance on piece-rate systems?

7. What is efficiency wage theory?

PROBLEMS

1. In what ways are labor markets similar to product markets? In what ways are they different?

2. Explain how both these points can be true simultaneously:
   (a) unions manage to raise the wage paid to their members;
   (b) unions do not affect the average level of wages paid in the economy.

3. How might each of the following factors affect the power of unions?
   (a) A state passes a right-to-work law.
   (b) Foreign imports increase.
   (c) The national unemployment rate falls.
   (d) Corporate profits increase.

4. Suppose a worker holding a job that pays $15 per hour applies for a job with another company that pays $18 per hour. Why might the second company be suspicious about whether the worker is really worth $18 per hour? How might the worker attempt to overcome those fears?

5. Imagine that a company knows that if it cuts wages 10 percent, then 10 percent of its employees will leave. How might adverse selection cause the amount of work done by the company to fall by more than 10 percent?

6. Advances in computer technology have allowed some firms to monitor their typists by a system that counts the number of keystrokes they make in a given workday. Telephone operators are sometimes monitored according to how many calls they take, and how long they spend on an aver-

age call. Would you expect these changes to increase productivity? Why or why not?

7. When someone is promoted from middle-management to top executive, his salary often doubles or more. Why does this seem puzzling, from the perspective of the theory of competitive markets? Why might a profit-maximizing firm do this?

CHAPTER 20

FINANCING, CONTROLLING, AND MANAGING THE FIRM

Who controls a company? The simple answer is the executives do. Presidents, vice presidents, chief executive officers—these are the people who make decisions, and they deserve a major share of the responsibility for a company's actions. But executives of most corporations are not entirely autonomous. There is an old saying: "He who pays the piper calls the tune." In the context of corporate behavior, investors who provide money to a firm certainly have some control over the executives who manage it.

In Chapter 9 we looked at equity and debt from the perspective of the household investing its funds. Here we use the perspective of the corporation that issues securities and receives the money. The branch of economics concerned with how firms raise capital—and the consequences of alternative methods—is called **corporate finance.** The importance of this topic to modern economics was recognized by the Nobel Foundation in 1990, when it awarded the Nobel Memorial Prize in economics to William Sharpe of Stanford University, Merton Miller of the University of Chicago, and Harry Markowitz of the City College of New York for their pioneering work in the field.

1. What difference does it make whether a firm raises capital through debt or through equity? How do concerns about taxes, bankruptcy, and managerial incentives affect firms' choices of financial structure?

2. Why is credit frequently rationed? And why, in spite of the advantages in risk sharing, is so little new capital raised in the form of equity?

3. What is the relationship between financial structure and control of the firm?

4. What role do takeovers play in enhancing the efficiency of the economy? Why is there such criticism of takeovers?

5. What are the central problems facing organizations in which the manager is not the sole owner?

6. What difference does it make whether decision making is centralized or decentralized? What are the pros and cons to each?

7. What determines what a firm produces itself as opposed to what it purchases from other companies? What determines, in other words, the boundaries of the firm?

Curiously enough, none of the issues we will be concerned with here arises in the basic competitive model of Part Two. There, firms all have a single objective, to maximize their profits or market value. That is also what all investors want. And because there is unanimity about what firms should do, the issue of "control" never arises. Indeed, even the issue of how the firm should raise its capital—through debt or equity financing—turns out to make no difference in the basic competitive model. In the real world, issues of finance and control not only grab headlines but also absorb the attention of Wall Street and firm managers. And for a good reason, as we will see.

THE FIRM'S LEGAL FORM

Business firms in the United States take one of three legal forms: proprietorship, partnership, or corporation. A **proprietorship** is the simplest form. The firm has a single owner. If you went into business selling class notes to other students, your business would be listed as a proprietorship by the IRS. Because of the advantages of incorporation (which we will see below), only the smallest firms remain proprietorships.

When two or more individuals decide to go into business together, they typically form a **partnership.** As with proprietorships, most partnerships are small—Sally and Sue's Delicatessen, or Bob and Andy's Laundromat. However, some partnerships are much larger. Many of the major national accounting firms are organized as partnerships, with hundreds of partners. Likewise, many law firms with one hundred or more lawyers are organized as partnerships.

The final form of organization is the **corporation.** Corporations divide ownership into shares, also known as the stock of a company. The purchase of a corporation's stock entitles the purchaser to a corresponding share of ownership in the firm with proportional voting rights and entitlements to the firm's profits. The key feature of the corporation, and the one that has made possible the huge firms we know today—like IBM, General Motors, and Exxon—is **limited liability.**

With proprietorships and partnerships, there is no limit to the liability of the owner(s). Consider Joe Smith, who decides to open up a restaurant and has not yet hired a lawyer to advise him of the advantages of the corporate form of business. He invests $50,000 of his savings and borrows $200,000 to buy furniture for the restaurant, to decorate it, and to pay for a five-year lease. Unfortunately, he has limited talents both as a chef and as a businessman, and fails to attract customers. After trying it for a year, he closes his business. But he is still responsible for the debts of the firm. Not only has he lost the $50,000 he took out of his savings, but he may be forced to sell his home to repay the $200,000 in loans because he is fully liable for them.

In partnerships, each partner is fully liable for all the debts of the firm. Now, when Joe Smith and his partner, Alfred Jones, go into business together, they each put up $25,000 and together borrow $200,000. If Alfred has no house or other form of wealth and thus cannot help to pay off the debt when the restaurant goes bankrupt, Joe will again find himself fully liable for the $200,000 debt.

By choosing the corporate form, owners avoid full liability. If Joe Smith sets his restaurant up as a corporation (and he can invite Alfred Jones and any others to purchase shares and join him as owners of the company), he can put his $50,000 into the corporation and have the corporation borrow the $200,000. The corporation is liable for all the debts it incurs, and in the case of bankruptcy, its assets will be sold. The money recouped in this way will go first to those who have lent the firm money (banks, bondholders), and then, if any is left over, to Joe and his fellow shareholders. In the event of bankruptcy, the shareholders are likely to lose all the money they invested in the corporation, but *they will not lose any more*. When Eastern Airlines declared bankruptcy in March 1989, the airline's shareholders did not have to worry about selling their houses to help pay off the billions of dollars of Eastern's debts.

Limited liability provides larger corporations with another important advantage over other forms of organization: it facilitates public trading of the company's shares. Buying such a share always involves the risk that the investor will lose all the money invested, as we have seen. Yet this risk may be tiny compared with the risk faced by the investor in a partnership. In the latter, each partner is liable for all the partnership's bills, if his fellow partners cannot pay their share. Therefore, an investor purchasing a partnership share needs to know something about the wealth of each of the other partners in order to know how much risk he faces. Such information is unnecessary to the investor in a corporation, which means the potential pool of investors in corporations is much, much larger. The limited liability feature of corporations is attractive enough that today most businesses, small and large, are set up as corporations. Even the single proprietor, if he has a good lawyer, is likely to set his business up as a corporation to protect his family's assets.

There is another important distinction among the three legal forms. When there is a single proprietor, there is no question about who makes the final decisions. When there are many owners, whether they are partners or shareholders, there are potential disagreements. There must be a set of rules concerning how these disagreements are to be resolved. For instance, shareholders elect directors, who choose managers. If a majority of shareholders do not like what their board of directors is doing, they can elect new directors—though this seldom happens.

CORPORATE FINANCE

Corporations can finance their investments in many ways. We focus on three alternatives. A corporation can borrow funds, either from a bank or directly from investors by issuing bonds. It can issue new shares of stock, the buyers of which become entitled to a share of whatever profits the firm distributes to its owners in dividends. Or, if its profits are high enough, the corporation can finance its investment with its own earnings, rather than paying them out in dividends.

Figure 20.1 provides a schematic representation of a corporation's cash flow. The corporation receives cash in three forms: income from the sale of

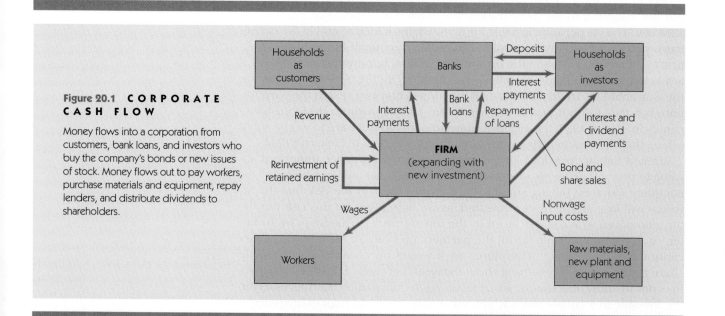

Figure 20.1 CORPORATE CASH FLOW

Money flows into a corporation from customers, bank loans, and investors who buy the company's bonds or new issues of stock. Money flows out to pay workers, purchase materials and equipment, repay lenders, and distribute dividends to shareholders.

its products, borrowed funds from banks and bond sales, and funds from sales of new shares. The corporation uses its cash to pay its expenses—wages, raw materials, and other costs of production. It also pays back outstanding loans. Any cash left over after expenses and debt payments may be distributed to the shareholders as dividends. Or some cash—called **retained earnings**— may be kept by the firm for the corporation to use for further investments or as a cash reserve.

In Chapters 6 and 9, we learned the attributes of investments: average return, risk, tax treatment, and liquidity. There we took the perspective of the investor. Bonds yielded a lower average return and had lower risks than stocks. Stocks yielded returns in the form of both dividends and capital gains. And capital gains had major tax advantages.

Here, we take the corporation's perspective. A corporation's management wants to raise capital in a way that best serves the interests of its shareholders. In particular, managers want to maximize the value of the firm's shares. Traditional theory reasons that in deciding between debt and equity financing, a firm's treasurer focuses on two issues. First is the cost of capital, what the firm must pay to *new* investors in return for using their funds—the "average return" to investors. The average return paid to those who supply debt capital is lower than the average return paid to those who supply equity capital. Thus, debt is less attractive from the viewpoint of new investors but more attractive from the viewpoint of the firm.

The second issue is risk, particularly the risk of bankruptcy. While firms do not have to pay their shareholders on any fixed schedule, they do have fixed obligations to pay certain amounts at certain times to bondholders and other lenders. Debt therefore imposes greater risks on the firm. If it does not have the cash to meet those obligations, and cannot get the cash by borrowing from someone else, then the company goes into bankruptcy. The more the firm borrows, the greater these fixed obligations, and the greater the chance that it will not be able to meet them. Thus, while to the investor debt appears safer, to the firm debt is riskier. On this account equity is preferable to the firm.

The traditional analysis of corporate finance sees the firm as facing a risk-return trade-off. In general, the greater the debt, the lower the costs (lower payments, on average, to those who provided the capital), but the higher the risk, in terms of the likelihood of bankruptcy. The problem of the corporate treasurer in this scenario is to choose the appropriate balance between risk and return.

The nature of the trade-off between risk and return is complicated. Assume the firm only cares about its *average* cost of capital. Since what it pays to bondholders is less than what it pays to equity holders, it might be tempted to issue more and more debt. But as it borrows more—that is, as it becomes more **highly leveraged**—the equity becomes riskier. The return on equity is simply what is left over after paying debtholders. The more it borrows, the more likely it is that there will be nothing left over for equity holders. As a result, the return it has to pay in order to raise equity must be increased.

In 1958, Franco Modigliani of MIT and Merton Miller of the University of Chicago proved a remarkable theorem. They showed that under what seemed like quite general conditions, how firms raised funds still made no difference, because the increasing cost of equity, as more debt is issued, just offsets the savings from the reduced cost of capital raised from debt.

We can liken the firm in the Modigliani-Miller perspective to a pie. Bondholders and shareholders get different pieces of the pie. But the size of the pie—the real value of the firm—is not affected at all by how it is sliced. The corporation's financial structure affects *who* gets the dollars earned by the corporation—how the profits pie is divided and who bears the risk of the firm—but that is all.

WHY CORPORATIONS CARE ABOUT FINANCIAL STRUCTURE

The Modigliani-Miller theorem is like the simple model of profit-maximizing firms in perfectly competitive markets. It provides a useful starting point and organizing framework for thinking about the central issues. Describing when the corporate finance decision does not matter helps focus attention on what is truly important about corporate financial structure. The sections that follow examine the confounding factors of bankruptcy, taxation, management incentives, the market perception of a firm's value, and corporate control. Each provides an explanation of why, in particular cases, a firm may care a great deal about its financial structure, its blend of debt and equity.

CONSEQUENCES FOR BANKRUPTCY

As we have already seen, increased debt imposes a greater risk of bankruptcy on a corporation. Modigliani and Miller's analysis ignored any direct costs associated with bankruptcy. And there are hundreds of thousands of bankruptcies a year. Bankruptcy has high *direct* costs—to shareholders, creditors, and managers. While 700,000 new businesses were incorporated in 1993, there were 86,000 filings of bankruptcy in that year. These statistics are typical. And they include major firms like International Harvester, once one of the world's largest manufacturers of agricultural machinery, Western Union, Railroad Express, Pennsylvania Central Railroad, and Eastern Airlines. Were it not for the fact that lenders limit the amounts they are willing to lend and monitor closely the firms to which they have lent money, bankruptcy rates might be substantially higher.

Concerns about bankruptcy thus provide an important limit on the use of debt. Banks are likely to limit the amount they are willing to lend. And even if they were willing to lend more, at high enough interest rates to compensate them for the risk of default, borrowers would limit the amount they borrow, recognizing that borrowing more exposes them to an excessively high risk of bankruptcy.

TAX CONSEQUENCES

Taxes affect a firm's choice of financial structure because, while interest payments are tax deductible, payments to shareholders (dividends) are not. Thus, the firm would rather pay interest than dividends, if these are its options. Of course, the firm also should take into account the taxes that its investors have to pay on their individual incomes. The tax law treats differently capital gains, dividends, and interest. Under the current tax law, capital gains receive slightly favored treatment. Since much of the return to stocks takes the form of capital gains, this aspect of the tax code gives shares a slight advantage over debt to individuals. Still, the net effect of the tax code appears to be in favor of corporate borrowing.

MANAGERIAL INCENTIVES

Another reason a firm cares about how it is financed is that debt and equity provide managers with different incentives. A backs-to-the-wall theory of corporate finance holds that firms should be encouraged to borrow, so that managers are forced to work hard to avoid bankruptcy. If a firm is financed by equity and is making at least some money, according to this theory, managers have little incentive to push for greater efficiency.

In the 1970s, for example, the sharp increase in the price of oil yielded enormous profits to oil companies. Flush with profits, the firms invested unwisely, resulting in a rash of takeovers, financed largely with debt. There is evidence that under the pressure of the increased debt, the management of these firms did become more effective.

But the higher chance of bankruptcy that accompanies high debt loads can also cause a problem. All the managers' efforts may be directed at keeping the firm alive, not at making the sound investments necessary for long-run prosperity. Firms near the threshold of bankruptcy may also undertake excessive risks. Management may gamble—knowing that if they fail they won't lose much since they probably would have gone broke anyway, but if the gamble pays off they may be able to get the firm back on its feet. Thus, finding the right financial structure represents a real challenge. Too little debt, and the firm's resources may be inefficiently used; too much debt, and the bankruptcy threat will distort the incentives to invest wisely for the longer term.

CONSEQUENCES FOR MARKET PERCEPTION OF VALUE

A firm's financial structure may also affect the market's beliefs about the firm's prospects. Most investors believe that a firm's managers are in a better position to judge the company's prospects than outsiders are. If the managers believe there is little risk, they will be willing to issue more debt, because they can do so without incurring a risk of bankruptcy. Their willingness to issue debt thus conveys in a forceful and concrete way management's confidence in the firm—a far more convincing display of confidence than a glossy and glowing report on the firm's future. Because debt both leads managers to work hard and convinces prospective shareholders about the value of the firm's prospects, issuing debt reduces the overall cost of capital to the firm and increases the company's market value.

We have seen that three of the factors discussed so far—tax considerations, managerial incentives, and market perceptions of value—tend to steer firms in the direction of debt financing, when they can obtain it. In practice, established firms finance most of their investments, in excess of retained earnings, by borrowing from banks or issuing bonds.

FINANCE AND CONTROL

There is a final, important respect in which debt and equity financing differ, and it relates to who controls the firm.

Previous chapters treated the "firm" as a monolithic entity. The firm decided what to produce, how to produce it, and how much to produce in order to maximize profits or the market value of the firm. In practice, however, individuals within the firm make these decisions. The interests and beliefs of different individuals differ. The interests of individuals within the firm may not be perfectly aligned with the objectives of profit maximization. And even if they are aligned, it may not be obvious what actions the firm should take to accomplish those goals. In the world of perfect information of Part Two, it was easy to answer the basic questions of what to produce, how to produce it, and how much to produce. But in practice, even the simplest question is fraught with uncertainties. Should GM invest more in robotics? (In this particular case, GM took a gamble of heavy investment in robotics in the 1980s, which, at least so far, does not appear to have paid off.) Can machines really replace men? Should we wait until the technology improves? Or should we invest now to get ahead of our competitors?

Because different individuals might answer the basic questions of what the firm should do differently, it matters who makes these decisions. Who controls the firm and how it is controlled are key issues to understanding how firms behave.

How firms raise capital has implications for control. An entrepreneur needing additional cash often is reluctant to issue equity, since shareholders have the right to elect the board of directors—which nominally controls the firm by appointing the officers who run it. Every entrepreneur is familiar with the story of Steven Jobs, who co-founded Apple Computer, but was pushed out of the company a few years later when Apple faced financial problems. By contrast, bondholders and banks have no formal role in the management of the corporation, except when there is a bankruptcy.

In reality, however, shareholders may have less control over a firm's decisions than banks and other lenders. This is because information and incentive problems weaken shareholders' control. They have to rely on managers for information, who will, to the extent possible, tell them what they want them to hear. And they have little incentive to invest the effort and resources required to become really well informed about management quality, because they typically own such a small proportion of the shares. In most large American firms, no shareholder has more than a few percent of the outstanding shares. This is a classic public goods problem. All shareholders would benefit from better management, but none has the full incentive to get the information necessary to make informed judgments about management.

WHY FINANCIAL POLICY MATTERS

The amount of debt affects the likelihood of bankruptcy.

Debt and equity receive different tax treatment.

The amount of debt affects managerial incentives.

The firm's choice of financial structure may affect the market's perception of the firm's value and risk.

Bonds, bank finance, and new equities have different implications for who controls the firm.

Banks and other lenders are in a more powerful position, because most firms are critically dependent on them for funds—at least from time to time—and lenders at any time can withdraw the credit they have extended. Corporation managers, accordingly, pay close attention to their bankers' views. Because banks often lend considerable amounts to a large firm, they have both the incentive and capacity to keep abreast of the firm's financial state and the quality of management decisions.

The safest course for an entrepreneur who worries about the loss of control is to finance her investments with retained earnings. But if her retained earnings are small, as is typically the case with new firms, and if she believes that the return to additional investment is high enough, she will be tempted to turn to outside sources for funds. In this case, she believes the expected return is worth risking loss of control.

Limited Financial Options

We have seen that the advantages and disadvantages of raising funds by alternative means help explain the choices that individual firms make in financing new investments. But in many circumstances, firms may not be able to borrow or issue new equities, except at very disadvantageous terms. A company may then be forced to limit its investment to retained earnings.

CREDIT RATIONING

When individuals or firms are willing to pay the current interest rate but simply cannot obtain funds at that rate, they are said to be **credit rationed.** To understand credit rationing, picture a medium-sized corporation, Checkout Systems, that produces software. This software, when used with retailers' checkout registers, handles inventory and all other accounting functions as well. The software has been popular, but Checkout Systems realizes that it would be much more successful if it also sold the hardware—computer systems, terminals, and cash register drawers—that stores must have in order to use the software. Checkout can get the hardware from a computer manufacturer, but it needs $2 million for warehouse and inventory. The company is fully confident that the $2 million expansion will produce a steady return of at least 30 percent. However, it has no retained earnings with which to pay for the expansion.

This is only the beginning of Checkout's problems. Let the going interest rate for loans to small firms be 14 percent. The company has a line of credit at the going rate of $400,000. But its banker refuses to make a loan to finance expansion. Checkout executives offer to pay a higher price—16 percent interest for the $2 million. The bank turns the company down. Is there any interest rate at which the bank would be willing to lend, the Checkout executives ask? The bank replies no.

The bank knows that some borrowers are more likely to default than others, but it has no way of knowing which ones are most likely to do so. Thus, it faces an adverse selection problem. As it raises interest rates to accommodate firms like Checkout, its average returns may actually decrease. The reason for this is that at higher interest rates, the "best" borrowers—those with the lowest likelihood of default—decide not to borrow.

Figure 20.2 shows the return to a lender being maximized at the interest rate r_0. The bank will not raise its interest rates beyond this level, even though at this rate the demand for funds may exceed the supply.

Let's look now at the market for funds for a particular category of loans, say small mortgages (under \$100,000) for owner-occupied houses. The supply curve for funds for loans differs from the supply curve depicted in the basic model. Figure 20.3, which is based on the information in Figure 20.2, shows the supply curve for funds as backward bending. This shape reflects the reasonable assumption that as the average return to loans (which should not be confused with the interest rate charged for these loans) increases, the supply of funds increases. The supply curve thus bends backward beyond r_0. As the interest rate charged rises to this point, average returns increase and so does the supply of funds; but at interest rates beyond this point, average returns decline and so does the supply of funds.

Credit rationing takes three forms. Some borrowers get funds, but less than they would like. Some loan applicants are denied credit, even though similar applicants receive credit. And some whole categories of applicants are simply denied credit. A bank may, for instance, refuse to give loans for vacations or to finance a college education or to buy a house in a particular part of the town. In each of these cases, those who have their credit denied or limited will not be any more successful in obtaining credit if they offer to pay a higher interest rate.

If lenders had perfect information, there would be no rationing. They would charge higher interest rates to reflect differences in the likelihood of default, but all applicants willing to pay the appropriate rate would get loans. Thus, underlying credit rationing is lack of information. No matter how many

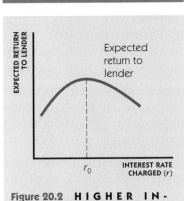

Figure 20.2 HIGHER INTEREST RATES, LOWER RETURN

As the interest rate increases, safe borrowers tend to drop out of the market, and only risky borrowers remain. Beyond some point, rises in the interest rate increase defaults on loans by enough to reduce the expected return to a lender. At higher interest rates, borrowers may also undertake greater risks, again lowering lenders' expected returns.

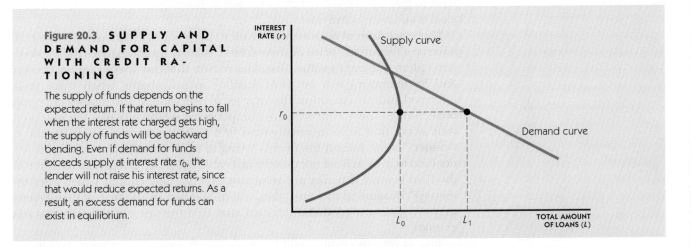

Figure 20.3 SUPPLY AND DEMAND FOR CAPITAL WITH CREDIT RATIONING

The supply of funds depends on the expected return. If that return begins to fall when the interest rate charged gets high, the supply of funds will be backward bending. Even if demand for funds exceeds supply at interest rate r_0, the lender will not raise his interest rate, since that would reduce expected returns. As a result, an excess demand for funds can exist in equilibrium.

forms are filled out, references requested, or interviews held, lenders know there is a residual amount of missing information. They therefore develop rules of thumb for loans. Yes to well-run, small businesses. No to vacation loans for college students or to new high-tech computer software firms, both of whom typically have high rates of default.

The lower the interest rate charged, of course, the greater the demand for funds. As the demand curve is drawn in Figure 20.3, average returns are maximized at interest rate r_0, but the supply of funds is less than the demand at this point. There is credit rationing; L_0 loans are actually made, while total demand is L_1. Many qualified borrowers would like to take out loans at the going interest rate but cannot. The magnitude of the credit rationing is measured by the gap between the demand, L_1, and the supply, L_0.

In addition to imperfect information, there is a second reason for credit rationing. Let's return to the example of Checkout Systems. The bank knows that Checkout's executives can engage in excessively risky behavior, some of which the bank will find impossible to monitor. It may worry that the higher the interest rate charged, the more likely that such risk-taking behavior occurs. The greater the risk taking, the higher the probability of bankruptcy, the lower the possibility that the lender will be able to recoup his funds, and thus the lower the expected return to the loan. As in Figure 20.2, expected returns to the bank may actually decrease as the interest rate charged increases, because of this adverse incentive effect.

EQUITY RATIONING

We might suppose that firms that are unable to borrow would raise money by issuing more stock. However, established firms seldom raise capital in this way. In recent years, less than a tenth of new financing has occurred through the sale of equity. The reason is not hard to see—when firms issue new equity, the price of existing shares tends to decline, often by a significant amount. For example, say that a firm worth $1 million issues $100,000 worth of new shares, and the price of the stock falls by 5 percent. The firm's existing shareholders have to give up $50,000 to raise $100,000 in funds from new investors. This is clearly an unattractive deal.

There are several reasons why issuing more equity frequently has such an adverse effect on the price of shares. First, issuing equity reduces the market's perception of a firm's value. Investors reason that the firm's original owners and its managers will be most anxious to sell shares when these well-informed individuals think the market is overvaluing the shares currently outstanding. These concerns are compounded by the fact that the market is well aware that firms normally turn first to banks to raise funds. Investors wonder, "Is the reason the firm is trying to issue new shares that banks will not lend to it, or at least not on very favorable terms, or at least not as much as the firm wants? If banks are reluctant to lend, why should I turn over my money?" Reasoning this way, they will only invest in the firm if they believe they are getting a good enough deal, that is, if the price of the shares is low enough.

Also, as we saw earlier, debt has a positive incentive effect on managers. By the same token, giving the firm more money to play with, without any fixed commitment to repay—which is exactly what new issues of equity do—may have an adverse effect on incentives.

For these and other reasons, the issue of new shares on average depresses the share value. Accordingly, only infrequently do established firms raise new capital by issuing shares.

OVERVIEW: THE LIFE CYCLE OF A FIRM

We have now identified various considerations affecting the relative attractiveness of different ways of raising capital. In the life cycle of a firm these considerations play out in different ways. In its early days, a firm typically finds it impossible to issue shares and has difficulty borrowing. Owners must rely on their own savings and investments of friends and relatives. In some high technology areas, they may turn to providers of venture capital (see Chapter 6). Such businesses provide not only capital but also managerial help, in return for a substantial share in the firm. As the young firm gets more established, it will find access to borrowing easier, and eventually, it may issue an IPO (initial public offering) on the stock market. Throughout the remainder of its life, it will finance much of its investment through retained earnings. In its later years, it may even turn to buying back its shares.

TAKEOVERS, CONTROL OF FIRMS, AND THE MARKET FOR MANAGERS

If you are a small shareholder, and you think management is not using the company's assets in ways that maximize profits, there is little you can do other than sell your shares. But if you are rich—or if you have access to others' capital—you can attempt to buy enough of the shares to gain control of the firm. This need not be a majority of the shares. You may be able to persuade other shareholders to vote their shares in support of you. You may even be able to persuade the existing management to leave quietly (by providing them with generous pensions) and to support the change in control. When one management team (one firm) takes over the control of another, it is called a **takeover.** When the second firm resists, it is called a **hostile takeover.** Sometimes takeovers occur through mergers. That is, the two firms combine, with shareholders in the new firm getting shares in the new combined firm in exchange for their shares in the original firm. Sometimes takeovers occur through acquisitions, when one firm buys another outright.

Takeovers increased sharply in the 1980s, as seen in Figures 20.4 and 20.5. So did the size of the companies taken over. It used to be thought that a company the size of TWA, Marathon Oil, or Nabisco would be immune from a takeover attempt. Who, after all, had the capital required to buy the shares? But size has not turned out to be a barrier—in 1988, RJR Nabisco was bought for over $20 billion.

Figure 20.4 NUMBER OF ACQUISITIONS IN RE- CENT YEARS

The number of acquisitions rose sharply in the mid-1980s, nearly tripling between 1981 and 1988. Acquisitions then tapered off before resurging in the mid-1990s. *Source: Mergerstat Review 1995* (1996), p. 35.

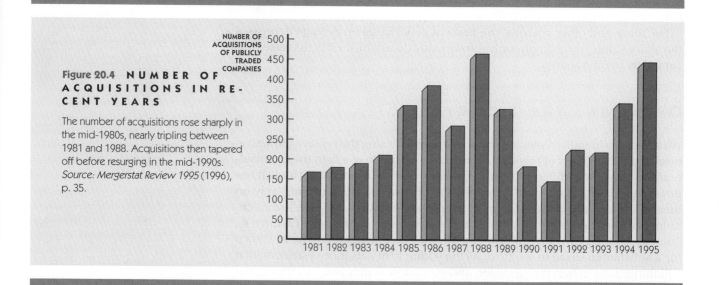

Figure 20.5 VALUE OF ACQUISITIONS IN RECENT YEARS

The value of publicly traded companies acquired also rose sharply in the mid-1980s, nearly tripling from 1981 to 1988. The dollar value of acquisitions dropped after 1988, but returned to a high level in 1995. (The dollar values given are adjusted for inflation, reflecting 1995 dollars.) *Source: Mergerstat Review 1995* (1996), p. 35.

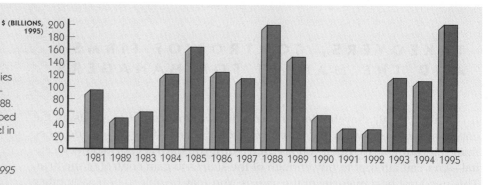

Mergers and acquisitions began to decline after 1988, for a variety of reasons. Many of the mergers and acquisitions had been financed by **junk bonds** carrying interest rates of 15 percent or higher. Even these seemingly high interest rates underestimated the true risk of default. Company after company found itself unable to meet its debt obligations, particularly as the economy began to go into recession in 1990. After the recession, takeovers returned to high levels in 1994 and 1995. Changes in economic structure and industrial regulations may explain the resurgence. For instance, rapid changes in the telecommunications industry, including anticipated changes in government regulations, spawned a series of mergers and acquisitions by telecommunications firms.

The takeover movement of the mid-1980s got a bad reputation because of the unsavory practices of some of its leading practitioners. Several, such as Michael Milken, wound up in jail. The government—in order to ensure that the markets are viewed as a "level playing field"—does not allow managers of firms who have access to inside information about their firms to trade on their information (as noted in Chapter 9). Thus, if you are president of an oil company, and you know that your firm has just made a major oil discovery, you cannot go out and buy more shares of the firm's stock. Nor can you tell your wife and family to do the same. The courts have extended this basic "insider" principle to those involved in buying and selling companies. If you know that your firm is about to make an offer to acquire another firm, which will send that firm's share prices soaring, you cannot use that information for private gain. In one year alone, Milken made more than a billion dollars, at least some of which was attributed to exactly this kind of insider trading.

Another unsavory practice was **greenmail,** so called because of its similarity to blackmail. Takeover artists would buy shares in a firm and then threaten a takeover. Their intent was not to actually buy the company but to get a "bribe" to go away—to get the company to buy back their shares at a premium to ward off a takeover.

Opposition to takeovers came not only from the management that was displaced, but also from workers in the affected firms. Often, following a takeover, faced with heavy debt, firms tightened their belts, laying off workers and even shutting down whole plants. Of course, some of these changes were exactly the reason for the takeover: previous management had not been effective in minimizing costs.

TAKEOVERS: PROS AND CONS

The debate about takeovers is often a debate about how well markets work—in this case the markets for managers and for financial assets.

The central argument in favor of takeovers is that they represent a successful way to replace ineffective managers. Under existing management, a firm may be worth $1 million, with 100,000 shares that trade at $10. An alternative management team may be able to use the firm's resources better, raising its value to $2 million ($20 per share). Even if the acquiring firm (the firm making the takeover) pays a 10 percent premium for the shares—that is, pays $1.1 million for the firm—it makes a profit of $900,000 on the deal. From this perspective, takeover battles are like auctions. The firm is sold to the bidder willing to pay the highest price, the one that thinks it can most effectively utilize the firm's resources.

Having won the auction, the highest bidder must get the company to earn enough money to justify its bid. If the post-takeover managers can indeed do a better job, the takeover firm realizes a profit. From this perspective, then, takeovers reflect the competition to be managers. They are evidence that the market for managers works. Much of the takeover activity of the 1980s in the oil industry was an attempt by various investors to redirect America's oil companies toward more profitable activities.

Thus, takeovers provide an important discipline device even for managers not threatened with one. Managers know that if they do not work hard, they may be threatened with a hostile takeover. They also know that a well-managed firm is unlikely to be taken over, because outsiders will recognize the quality of the management and know they are unlikely to raise the firm's profits. Even if the typical small shareholder does not look over the shoulder of the existing management team, an army of corporate raiders is always on the lookout for a mismanaged firm that could be turned around under new management.

Takeovers are particularly important, because the other methods of controlling managers of large corporations are relatively ineffective. We saw earlier, for instance, that most shareholders have neither the information, the incentives, nor the tools to exercise much control over management. The one way they have of exercising control is voting to elect members of the board of directors. Most investors, if they become dissatisfied with how the firm is being run, just sell their shares. In addition, supporters of takeovers (and of free markets) tend to believe that since shareholders are the real owners of a company, they should have a chance to sell what they own to the highest bidder when they desire to do so.

PUBLIC POLICY TOWARD TAKEOVERS

During their heyday in the late 1980s, takeovers became a source of public policy concern. As the memory of the collapse of the junk bond market and the unsavory practices fades, the takeover movement may well recover, and with it the public policy debate.

Many economists believe that the virtues of takeovers have been overstated. They argue that takeovers do not necessarily replace one management with a more efficient management, but rather often represent the unbridled quest of one firm's management to aggrandize more power for itself. There is some evidence for this view. On average, the shares of the firms taking over do not increase as a result of the takeover activity. This is particularly true in companies where management owns a relatively small share of the stock—in which case management may have little incentive to pay close attention to how their activities affect the market price. Professor Andrei Shleifer of Harvard University has shown that managers with large egos—who, for instance, place their picture prominently within the company's annual report—are more likely to engage in takeovers.

Critics claim that even the threat of a takeover has bad consequences, because it forces companies to make themselves look like unattractive candidates for a takeover. To accomplish this, a corporation may do several things. On the positive side, it can try to make itself more efficient. But it may choose efficiency-reducing alternatives instead. It may be tempted, for example, to sacrifice long-term projects for short-term profits, in the hope that short-term profits will trick investors into thinking the company is better managed than it actually is. Additionally, since corporations with a lot of free cash are particularly attractive takeover targets, the corporation might be induced to

In early 1990, Pennsylvania passed a law aimed at allowing companies to block takeovers. The new law had three main provisions. One made it very difficult for anyone who bought a large block of stock within twelve months of a takeover bid to vote either for or against the takeover. A second provision allowed corporate directors to put the interests of a firm's employees and customers above the interests of the company's shareholders. A third provision required that if a raider made any profits while attempting a takeover that turned out to be unsuccessful, those profits would have to be given to the target of the takeover.

One might think that companies would welcome this sort of protection. However, the law also allowed companies to choose to be exempt from any or all of the antitakeover provisions if they wished. About two dozen of Pennsylvania's largest companies (including Westinghouse, H. J. Heinz, Mellon Bank, Allegheny Ludlum, and Quaker Chemical) chose not to be protected against takeovers in at least one of these ways.

Why would any company choose to remain vulnerable? Many shareholders, especially big institutional investors like state pension funds, shy away from owning the stock of companies that are sheltered against takeovers, since eliminating the threat of a takeover may mean less pressure for efficiency. When a number of large buyers no longer demand a company's stock, the share price falls. Indeed, the stocks of Pennsylvania-based companies did 7 percent worse than the average performance of stocks from the time the antitakeover law was first proposed until it was passed.

With passage of the antitakeover law, Pennsylvania companies faced a trade-off. They could be protected against takeovers but know that some investors would be reluctant to invest in their company and their stock price would suffer. Or they could remain vulnerable to a takeover but manage their business in such a way that their stock price stayed high, making them an unattractive target.

Source: Leslie Wayne, "Many Companies in Pennsylvania Reject State's Takeover Protection," *New York Times,* July 20, 1990, p. A1.

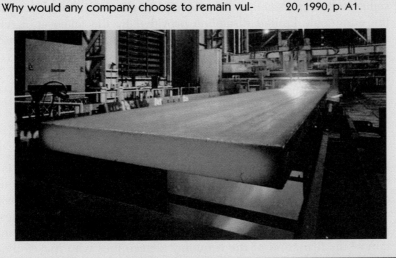

Slab casting at U.S. Steel

spend its free cash so quickly that it makes bad investment decisions. Or it may take on huge debts so that the return on the stock becomes riskier. Such actions rarely accord with the long-run interests of the corporation.

Finally, critics point out that a company that spends its scarce management time thwarting takeovers is less able to spend its time increasing efficiency and making better products.

Curiously, both those who believe strongly in the competitive model and those who have great reservations about that model often side together in opposing legislation curbing takeovers. Economists who believe strongly in the market system argue that hostile takeovers, like any change, produce gainers and losers, and that overall, the discipline that the market imposes makes the economy more efficient and most individuals better off.

Economists with less faith in the perfectly competitive markets envisioned in Part Two, including Andrei Shleifer of Harvard University and Rob Vishny of the University of Chicago Business School, argue that without the threat—and reality—of hostile takeovers, management would be even more entrenched, more pursuant of its own interests, than it is today. While they recognize potential abuses of a system that permits takeovers, such as greenmail, they argue, in the imperfect world we live in, the gains from the discipline provided by takeovers exceed the costs of any of the abuses.

Despite these concerns, legislation has been enacted that would alter market outcomes. Some states have allowed corporations to create "poison pills," devices that provide for the partial destruction of the firm in the event of a successful takeover, making the takeover less attractive. And Congress—motivated partly by interest-group politics and partly by concern that the large debts accumulated to finance the takeovers might increase the chance of a wave of bankruptcies—has debated whether to remove some of the tax advantages of debt when used as part of a hostile takeover. But the fact is that laws restricting takeovers work to the detriment of shareholders for several reasons. Shareholders do not benefit from the competition for shares that results from takeover battles. The likelihood of incompetent management being replaced through takeover is reduced. And current management, freed from the admittedly limited discipline provided by the takeover mechanism, is more likely to take actions that benefit the managers at the expense of shareholders.

MAKING DECISIONS

In Chapter 1, we listed four basic questions: What and how much is to be produced, how it is to be produced, for whom it is produced, and *who makes these decisions*. Most of this book focuses on the first three questions. The question of who controls the firm goes to the heart of the final question: Who makes these decisions? The rest of this chapter addresses how the organization of the firm, and of the economy, determines who makes the decisions and how they make them.

DELEGATION AND THE PRINCIPAL-AGENT PROBLEM

Even if the firm were owned by a single individual, there would be a problem of control, because the owner cannot make all the decisions himself. He must *delegate* some to subordinates, who, in turn, must engage in further delegation. The central problem is how to ensure that these managers act in the same way that the owner would have acted. This is an example of a broad class of incentive problems.

Chapter 6 noted that incentive problems arise whenever an individual does not bear, or receive, the full consequences of her action. If the manager makes a good decision, the firm prospers and the shareholders benefit. If she makes a bad decision, they suffer. Thus, shareholders would like to motivate the manager to act in a way that maximizes the value of their shares. In this form, the incentive problem is referred to as the **principal-agent problem.** The principal (here, the owner) would like to motivate the agent (here, the manager) to act in the principal's interests. But both parties know the owner cannot judge whether the manager has taken the appropriate action simply by the observable results.

The interests of managers and owners frequently differ. The manager going on a business trip may choose to buy a ticket on a more expensive airline because he is trying to accumulate frequent flier points for himself on that airline, rather than a cheaper alternative. The sales representative for a computer firm may give some account especially close attention, not because of the prospects of increased sales but because he is trying to land a new job.

There are two important aspects of the principal-agent problem: how hard the agent works, and what risks the agent takes. If a manager works especially hard, for example, the owners of the firm (often the shareholders) will receive some of the reward. But because the manager does not receive all the reward, she may have insufficient incentives for exerting maximum effort.

The manager's taste for risk will rarely match the owner's interests. On the one hand, managers may act in a more risk-averse (cautious) manner than the owners of the firm might like. After all, the managers know that should projects under their supervision fail, they may be denied promotions or even lose their jobs. On the other hand, managers may be willing to take risks when the owners would not be willing to do so. They are gambling with someone else's money. If the project is a flop, the firm loses money; if it is successful, the manager will be called a "genius." The consensus among economists is that under most circumstances, managers act in a way that is *more* risk averse than the owners would like.

Ownership as a Solution   The most obvious solution to the principal-agent problem would be for the owner of the firm to sell each manager the portion of the firm under his responsibility. As the owner, the manager would have all the right incentives. If he worked harder, he would reap the rewards. If he took more risks, he would receive the gains and bear the losses. In general,

CLOSE-UP: THE BEST EXECUTIVES FOR THE MONEY?

As the table here shows, some top executives earn mind-bending sums of money, sometimes millions of dollars a year. Defenders of these high salaries point out that top executives make life-or-death decisions for their companies and that they deserve to be compensated for making those decisions wisely. Much of top executive pay comes in the form of stock options. Their high pay is therefore due in part to the fact that the company's stock did well, which offers an incentive for top management to look out for the interests of shareholders.

However, in the past few years, critics of high executive salaries have become considerably more vocal. Here are some of their main arguments:

1. Pay for top executives has grown disproportionately. In 1974, for example, the typical chief executive officer (CEO) received pay that was 35 times that of the average manufacturing worker. In the early 1990s, the typical CEO earned about 120 times the pay of an average manufacturing worker.

2. Pay for U.S. top executives is out of line with what foreign companies pay. In Japan, the average CEO earns 20 times the pay of the average worker;

in the United Kingdom, he earns 35 times the pay of the average worker. These large differences from U.S. practice are not reflected in productivity differences.

3. Pay for top executives does not offer a true incentive, because it often rises even when the company does badly. During the recession in 1990, for example, average corporate profits fell by 7 percent, but compensation for top executives rose by 7 percent.

Critics of high executive pay point out that compensation levels are often set by a board of directors chosen by the top executive, with the help of an outside consultant who is also chosen by the top executive. They argue that, although a well-designed plan of linking the top executives' pay to the long-term price of the company's stock can provide useful incentives, too many stock plans have become a way to funnel money to the top executive, without limit or control.

Sources: "How High can CEO Pay Go?," *Business Week,* April 22, 1996; Graef Crystal, *In Search of Excess* (New York: Norton, 1991).

THE 10 HIGHEST-PAID CHIEF EXECUTIVES FOR 1995

Name	Company	Total pay in 1995
1. Lawrence Coss	Green Tree Financial	$65.6 million
2. Sanford Weill	Travelers Group	$49.8 million
3. John Welch Jr.	General Electric	$22.1 million
4. Gordon Binder	Amgen	$21.5 million
5. James Donald	DSC Communications	$19.2 million
6. Casey Cowell	U. S. Robotics	$18.6 million
7. Floyd English	Andrew Corp.	$17.7 million
8. Howard Solomon	Forest Laboratories	$17.0 million
9. Stanley Gualt	Goodyear Tire and Rubber	$16.6 million
10. Edward Brennan	Sears, Roebuck	$16.4 million

however, the manager does not have the requisite capital to buy the firm, and even if he did, he might not be willing to buy it. An owner's income is a lot more variable than a paycheck, depending not only on his own efforts but also on the vagaries of the market. A manager may not be willing to take that risk.

In any case, most modern corporations cannot be split into the right parts to make each manager an owner and still operate efficiently. We can sometimes divide a large corporation into several parts, each run separately. But within each of these parts, there remain large principal-agent problems.

Incentive Pay as a Solution A second-best solution to the principal-agent problem is to include in the agent's compensation package incentives that reflect the principal's interest. Thus, sales representatives earn commissions, and many workers can qualify for performance bonuses if they or their department exceeds production quotas. One form of incentive program for top managers is the **stock option** bonus, the value of which depends on how well their firms perform. Suppose stock in a particular company is currently selling for $30. The stock option allows the manager to purchase a specified number of shares at $30 for a specified period of time. For instance, the manager may be given the option to buy 100,000 shares at $30 any time during the next three years. If the firm's shares rise in value to $40, the manager can purchase the shares for $3 million and then immediately resell them for $4 million, receiving a bonus—presumably as a reward for her contribution in increasing the value of the firm—of $1 million. It is common for firms to provide their top managers with stock option bonuses valued in the millions of dollars.

Monitoring as a Solution Appropriately designed compensation schemes help align the interests of the agent with that of the principal. But they do not fully resolve the problem. Principals further reduce the scope for agents to take actions which are not in their interests by monitoring and obtaining information not only about what the agent *is* doing, but also about what she *should* be doing.

It is not easy for owners or top management to know what is going on in a large corporation. They can, of course, easily tell whether the factories are producing, but are they really doing what it takes to maximize profits? An

DELEGATION

The principal-agent problem
    Work effort of agent
    Risk taking of agent

Solutions
    Ownership
    Incentive pay
    Monitoring

Close-up: What is Good Management?

Despite conflicts of interests between managers and shareholders, American managers do see themselves as trying quite hard to do the best job that they can for their firm. The bestseller list for books almost invariably includes one or two that promise a better way to manage a firm. The popularity of these books is testimony to the widespread concern about how to be a good manager; the fact that one book is followed by another with contradictory advice is testimony to the everlasting hope of American managers that the promised success formulas are just around the corner.

Back in the 1950s and 1960s, books often taught management skills as if following a few basic steps would always lead to a correct decision. Managers were urged to clarify their objectives, outline how best to attain those objectives, and constantly monitor the extent to which their objectives were being attained; good advice, but of only limited help. The simple prescriptions of forty years ago offered no assistance in dealing with the uncertainty and limited information that pervade decision making within firms; neither did they offer solutions for the difficulties of motivating individuals—the principal-agent problem.

More recent examples of this genre of books do not have a much better record of success. In 1983, Tom Peters and Robert Waterman wrote a bestseller, *In Search of Excellence.* The book's main theme was that managers of businesses should learn from the example of the excellent companies identified in the book. The distinguishing feature of these companies was their commitment to excellence and the concern they showed for their employees.

However, the next couple of years were not kind to many of the "excellent" companies identified by Peters and Waterman. For example, an airline called People Express, which had been growing like a weed for several years by offering no-frill flights, was cited as an excellent company with innovative personnel policies. It went bankrupt and was bought by Continental Airlines two years after the book came out. In fact, the firms selected as role models for excellence fared not much better over the five years following the book's publication than any randomly chosen group of firms.

But only five years later, both authors were back with new books that contained new guesses for success. In 1988, Tom Peters's, *Thriving on Chaos* argued that "there are no excellent companies."

essential aid in gathering requisite information are the accounting systems that all modern corporations employ. They are intended to provide top management with essential information concerning, for instance, the relative profitability of each of its parts.

Still, monitoring is imperfect. Long-term relationships between most principals and agents improve the effectiveness of even imperfect monitoring because both sides see the gains from continuing the relationship. An employee will not take advantage of every opportunity to gain at the expense of the firm. She knows that even if the firm does not detect self-serving behavior every time, it is likely to observe it some of the time, and that even if the firm does not fire her, her behavior might affect prospects for promotion.

CENTRALIZATION AND DECENTRALIZATION

The most basic issue in a firm's decision-making structure is the extent to which decision making is **centralized** or **decentralized.** A firm in which the president or chief executive officer (CEO) makes all decisions is highly centralized, just as an economy where all decisions are made by a central Ministry of Economics is highly centralized. However, all large organizations involve some degree of decentralization. The president of a corporation simply does not have the time, much less the information, with which to make all the day-to-day decisions.

The consequence of decentralization is that the firm's subunits have considerable autonomy—freedom to make their own decisions. Should the Chevrolet division of General Motors be allowed to make its own decisions concerning what kind of new car to develop, or should the corporation's CEO be consulted? Which decisions are of sufficient importance that the CEO needs to be involved? Which decisions should the CEO actually make? These fundamental decisions are faced by every economic organization.

There are trade-offs to differing degrees of centralization and decentralization. Centralized decision making usually involves a hierarchical structure. A project must pass through a set of well-defined approval layers, like a fine sieve. This reduces the likelihood that bad projects are approved. But the process of sifting also leads to good projects being rejected. Decentralized decision making provides fewer checks on any project. Some bad projects are more likely to get adopted. By the same token, fewer good projects are rejected.

ADVANTAGES OF CENTRALIZATION

Hierarchical decision making may allow for better coordination across the divisions of a large corporation; this may be important in instances where there are externalities—where, for instance, the fruits of research in one part of the firm may be of benefit to another. Thus, in developing a new motor—an expensive endeavor—it might pay the different divisions of General Motors to coordinate their research and development efforts. Even if, in the end, the different units decide to produce different motors, they will still find it profitable to coordinate their research programs and develop, for instance, new, lighter materials from which to make a motor.

Another argument in favor of centralized decision making is that it avoids the duplication that results from operating autonomous corporate divisions, where personnel from several units are often engaged in quite similar activities. Thus, advocates of centralization claim that it is inefficient for each division of a firm to have its own legal staff or its own marketing department.

ADVANTAGES OF DECENTRALIZATION

Some of the arguments used by advocates of greater centralization can be turned on their head and used as arguments for decentralization. For example, supporters of decentralization point out that having different units within an organization doing similar things may have decided advantages: the resulting competition not only provides a strong motivation for members of the different production units, but also provides a basis for judging whether one unit is doing better than another, and hence for making decisions about who is performing well and who should receive more funds.

Decentralized decision making also enables a production unit to adapt decisions to its own particular circumstances, so that they reflect the diversity of attitudes and skills among workers. As hard as they may try, centralized authorities have difficulty in obtaining the requisite information from those who are actually engaged in the production process. Decentralization also allows a range of experimentation greater than that found under more centralized regimes, and enables projects to be approved more quickly.

Its advantages are sufficiently great that many firms have considerable decentralization. Large corporations, like General Motors, are separated into divisions, each of which may have considerable autonomy, at least over some functions (such as marketing). While there may be centralization in certain issues—like the design of a new motor or body frame—there is great decentralization in others. Pontiac and Buick see their markets as slightly different, and even if they have the same basic engineering, each division believes it can adapt the car—with its own interior design, for example—and adopt a marketing strategy aimed at its part of the market far better than central headquarters could do. The computer company Hewlett-Packard divides itself into a large number of units, each of which has the authority to undertake research projects.

CENTRALIZATION AND DECENTRALIZATION WITHIN THE ECONOMY AS A WHOLE

The advantages and disadvantages of centralization within firms parallel those of the economy as a whole. The U.S. economy is characterized by a high degree of decentralization. Each firm in the economy decides for itself which projects to undertake. Projects and ideas that are rejected by one firm are taken up by others. There is a widespread consensus that decentralization is desirable. The gains in increasing the likelihood that good projects get developed outweigh the disadvantages of having the same idea reexamined in what appears to be a duplicative manner. There are many stories of inventors and entrepreneurs who needed the chances provided by a decentralized system in order to find one backer for their brilliant idea.

Despite the decentralization of the U.S. economy as a whole, many of its autonomous firms have only limited decentralization and retain a fairly strong hierarchy. Even multibillion-dollar companies like Exxon maintain a fairly high degree of centralization. Thus, our economy can be viewed as involving a mixture of decentralization and centralization. The question is one of balance. And the balance between centralization and decentralization is one that will continually be debated, both within firms and, more broadly, within society as a whole.

CENTRALIZED VERSUS DECENTRALIZED DECISION MAKING

CENTRALIZED	DECENTRALIZED
Fewer bad projects are accepted.	More good projects are accepted.
There is greater coordination; externalities are taken into account.	Comparison between competing units provides (a) incentives and (b) bases of selection.
Duplication is avoided.	There is greater diversity and experimentation

THE BOUNDARIES OF THE FIRM

Many firms sell personal computers. Most of them are "assemblers." They buy circuit boards, cases, monitors, and keyboards in bulk, assemble the parts into personal computers, and sell them. Why don't they expand, and make their own circuit boards, cases, monitors, and keyboards? To turn the question around, why don't those who make these parts assemble them? After all, firms always want more profits, and these expansions seem to be prime areas for growth.

Economists are interested in the conditions that cause a firm to limit itself in size or in the number of products it manufactures. What determines the boundaries of firms? Or to put the same question in a different way, when does a company find it easier to deal with another company through the market, rather than produce what it needs itself? What are the advantages and disadvantages of markets? In modern economies, the degree of centralization and decentralization is closely related to the issue of what is produced within the firm, and what each firm purchases from other firms.

In the case of the personal computer market, there is a great deal of decentralization. Companies make extensive use of the market. The circuit board manufacturers have a much larger market than just personal computers, so they can achieve economies of scale they would not enjoy if they restricted their output to supplying circuit boards for personal computers. They also fear the risk entailed in putting all their eggs in the personal computer market "basket." The same is true for those who make the other parts. This pattern of specialization, however, leaves a profit opportunity for the assemblers, who can buy the parts from outside and still wind up with a computer they can sell at a good profit.

But the degree of decentralization within the personal computer market is unusual. Much economic activity occurs within firms, rather than between firms. That is, companies produce intermediate products that are used as inputs for the goods the company eventually sells, and firms may even produce the inputs that are used in these intermediate products. Such activity is known as **vertical integration.** (By contrast, **horizontal integration** involves bringing together firms producing the same goods.) At one time, U.S. Steel owned its own iron ore mines and its own fleet of vessels to transport the iron ore. It not only produced the pig iron, it also used the pig iron to make more finished steel products, such as the beams used in construction. Ford Motor Company at one time owned its own steel mill, for producing the steel used in making its cars.

Table 20.1 shows that the output of several large, vertically integrated firms is as large as the entire output of several medium-sized countries.[1] Within these firms, relationships are controlled by commands—direct decisions by the managers—though those commands themselves may be affected by accounting profits and prices (which can differ significantly from market prices and profits).

There are a number of factors that go into the decisions about whether to vertically integrate—that is, whether to produce the inputs used to produce the goods—or whether to use the market. One important factor is **transactions costs**—the extra costs (beyond the price of the purchase) of conducting

Table 20.1 COMPARING LARGE CORPORATIONS AND SMALL COUNTRIES

1993 sales of large U.S. corporations	
General Motors	$134 billion
Ford	$109 billion
Exxon	$ 98 billion
IBM	$ 63 billion
1992 national output of medium-sized economies	
Norway	$113 billion
Thailand	$110 billion
Greece	$ 67 billion
Egypt	$ 34 billion

Source: Fortune, April 18, 1994; *World Development Report* (1994).

[1]The comparison is not perfect. The appropriate comparison would be between the value added of U.S. corporations—the difference between their sales and the goods and services they purchase from other firms. Even in these terms, General Motors and Ford are larger than Egypt and Greece.

a transaction, whether those costs are money, time, or inconvenience. Ronald Coase of the University of California at Los Angeles was awarded the Nobel Prize in 1991 partly for his work in identifying the role of transactions costs in determining the "boundaries" of the firm—what activities occur within a firm and what activities occur between firms.

Consider, for instance, the problem of a large manufacturing company that offers health insurance to its employees. The company could continue to pay premiums to an outside insurance company that would then be liable for any claims. Because of its large work force, however, the option of paying its employees' medical bills directly has become economically viable. The company could set up a division to run its health insurance, but then it will face all the managerial problems discussed in this chapter. Although this company is good at manufacturing, it has no comparative advantage at running a health insurance company, and its managerial talent is scarce. Accordingly, the firm may find it cheaper, once these transactions costs are taken into account, to continue with the outside health insurance company. It is more efficient to make use of the market in obtaining health insurance services.

In other cases, transactions costs may be lower if the firm vertically integrates. Consider a chemical firm eager for new products to sell. It could hire an outside laboratory to try to develop a new drug, and use outside sales representatives to sell existing ones. But how can the company make sure that the outside laboratory really tries to make a breakthrough discovery? How can the company make sure that the outside sales firm makes a sincere effort to sell its products?

Transactions costs are every bit as real as the costs of production. Indeed, as innovations in manufacturing (such as the invention of the assembly line) have reduced production costs, transactions costs have taken on increasing importance. Many of the innovations of the past two decades, in turn, have reduced transactions costs. Computers, for example, have enhanced our ability to keep track of records and process other information required for engaging in transactions.

Finding a balance between centralization and decentralization and between what the firm produces and what it purchases from other firms are thus two of the central problems facing managers of all large enterprises.

REVIEW AND PRACTICE

SUMMARY

1. The three main forms of business ownership are proprietorships, partnerships, and corporations. Only corporate ownership has the advantage of limited liability, which means that investors are not liable for debts incurred by the company.

2. The Modigliani-Miller theorem argues that under a simplified set of conditions, the manner in which a firm finances itself is a matter of

indifference. However, issues of bankruptcy, taxation, management incentives, and corporate control mean that firms care about their financial structure.

3. Shareholders have nominal control of corporations, but when share ownership is widely distributed, shareholders may not exercise effective control. While lenders (like banks) have nominal control over a corporation only if it declares bankruptcy, their ability to control the immediate flow of capital to the firm may give them a fair amount of say in what the firm does.

4. Credit rationing occurs when a borrower cannot find a source of funds even when he is willing to pay a higher-than-market interest rate. Lenders fear their average return may *decrease* (the chance of default is greater) as the nominal interest rate increases.

5. Firms will not be willing to issue new equity if doing so results in large decreases in the market value of outstanding shares.

6. The argument for takeovers is that they provide a means by which less efficient management teams can be replaced by more efficient teams. The argument against is that takeovers often are more matters of power or ego rather than efficiency, and that the threat of takeovers diverts companies from focusing on their actual business.

7. The problem owners of firms have in motivating the managers to work hard and make decisions about risk in the general interests of the firm, rather than in their own personal interest, is known as the principal-agent problem.

8. A major problem facing all economic organizations (firms or whole economies) is the extent of centralization or decentralization. In principle, greater centralization can improve coordination, provide a more effective way of dealing with externalities, reduce duplication, and reduce the chances of "bad" projects being adopted. Decentralization provides a basis for experimentation and comparison, allows for greater adaptability and faster decision making, and increases the chances that "good" projects will be adopted.

9. Every firm must decide whether to make a product or provide a service inside the firm or buy it in the marketplace. The choice depends, in part at least, on transactions costs.

KEY TERMS

proprietorship	Modigliani-Miller theorem	centralization
partnership	credit rationing	decentralization
corporation	principal-agent problem	transactions costs

REVIEW QUESTIONS

1. Explain the difference between a proprietorship, a partnership, and a corporation.

2. Explain how the risk of bankruptcy and the tax treatment of dividends and interest payments affect the attractiveness of equity to a business. How does debt provide incentives for management to work harder?

3. Why might the market interpret the issue of new equity as a negative signal concerning the value of a company?

4. Do banks or small shareholders have greater effective control over a corporation? Is your answer the same for large shareholders?

5. What is credit rationing? Why does it occur?

6. What are the arguments for and against takeovers?

7. What is a principal-agent problem? How might ownership and incentive pay address this problem?

8. What are the advantages and disadvantages of centralized and decentralized decision making within a firm?

9. When will a firm try to do a job itself, and when will it try to hire someone to do it in the market?

PROBLEMS

1. Consider a firm that needs $350,000 in capital to get started. First, think about this firm organized as a proprietorship, where you put up $50,000 and borrow the rest from a bank. Second, think about this firm organized as a partnership, where you and nine friends each put up $5,000 and borrow the rest from a bank. Third, think about the firm organized as a corporation, where you and nine friends each buy $5,000 worth of stock and then borrow the rest from a bank. If the firm goes broke without earning any money, how large are your potential losses in each case?

2. The bankruptcy laws of the United States were changed in the mid-1980s to make it easier and less costly for a firm to declare bankruptcy. Would you expect these laws to lead to more partnerships or to more corporations? Why?

3. Speak Software, a small firm attempting to design new computer software, applies for a bank loan to purchase some new computer hardware. The bank turns the company down for the loan. When Speak Software offers to pay a higher interest rate, the bank still turns it down. Explain why the bank might practice this form of credit rationing, using a diagram that compares the interest rate charged with the bank's expected return.

4. The Kitbits Company, which makes cat treats, has a stock price of $40 per share. A raider is trying to take over the company and is offering $50 per share. Shareholders must decide whether to sell their stock to the raider and take a $10 per share gain, or to hold on to the stock. Consider the effect of future management of the company. When might it make sense to hold on to the stock?

5. How might a firm harm itself in attempting to avoid a takeover? How might it strengthen itself in attempting to avoid a takeover?

6. Think up an incentive scheme that would encourage managers to take more risks.

7. A company is considering setting up two new divisions. One division would own a corporate fleet of cars, as an alternative to renting cars from existing firms. The other division would be an R & D laboratory, as an alternative to contracting out projects to labs. Consider issues of transactions costs and comparative advantage, and analyze why these functions might be set up inside the company or bought from outside.

8. In several European countries, there have been strong movements for worker participation in management, entailing, for instance, unions sending representatives to sit on the board of directors. Discuss the problem of getting worker representatives to act in the interests of the workers in terms of the principal-agent problem.

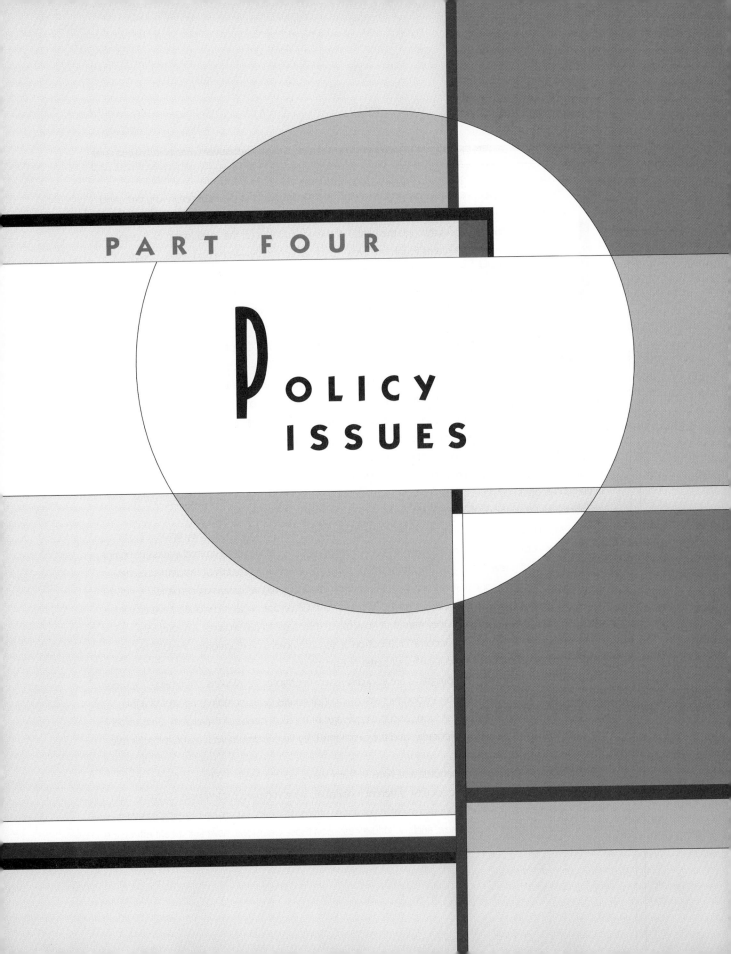

PART FOUR

Policy Issues

The basic competitive model presented in Part Two focused on the private sector—on firms and households. Yet government plays a central role in our modern economy. About a third of the economy's output passes through the hands of the government (at the local, state, or federal level). Government programs touch our lives—and our economy—in myriad ways. Chapter 7 presented a brief overview of the economic role of government, and in Part Three we saw how government sought to encourage competition and promote technological change. But we have yet to discuss some of the most important activities of the government—both what the government does, and why.

In Chapter 21 we return to the subject of externalities—introduced in Chapter 7—considering the impact of negative externalities upon the environment. In the last twenty-five years, government efforts to limit environmental degradation have enjoyed great success. We will explore the market failures which give rise to pollution, and review the alternative ways in which governments have attempted to remedy those failures. We will also examine the depletion of natural resources, a growing concern in recent years. Do markets provide adequate incentives to conserve natural resources such as oil and mineral resources? Chapter 21 answers this question. Finally, Chapter 21 discusses an important category of circumstances in which the consumption of certain products is mandated (as in compulsory education) or prohibited (as in illegal narcotics) by government. Here, government intervention is not only based on economic efficiency, but stands on other grounds.

Even when markets are efficient, how they allocate resources among individuals may appear to be socially unacceptable. Such concerns are raised by poverty, homelessness, and limited access to health care, to name but a few examples. The distribution of income is a major concern of modern societies and their governments, one that has grown in the United States due to the increasing disparity of income and wealth between the most well off and the least well off. Of course, what individuals have to spend depends not only on how much they earn, but how much they have to pay in taxes. Chapter 22 discusses recent changes in U.S. income distribution. It also provides a description of the U.S. tax system, and evaluates that system in terms of certain basic criteria.

Government social insurance programs are also discussed in Chapter 22. Markets often fail to provide insurance against some of the most important risks which individuals face, including the loss of a job, being disabled so that one cannot work, and the coverage of medical needs of the elderly. Chapter 22 looks at these social insurance programs, and the problems they face today, as well as the broader role of government in redistribution.

Government differs from households and firms in many ways, not the least of which is the form of decision making. In a democratic society, different individuals have different preferences. Some would like the government to spend more money on education, others on parks, others on building bombers. How *collective* decisions are made, and the influences upon those decisions, have significant effects on the allocation of resources. Chapter 23 discusses these issues and some of the problems facing collective decision making. While we have seen that markets often fail to provide efficient resource allocations, or socially acceptable resource allocations, government interventions are also subject to failure. Chapter 23 analyzes some of the systematic reasons for these public failures.

In Part Four we will complete our discussion of the many ways in which the real world is different from the basic model—except for one. The basic model assumes that all markets clear, including the labor market. But at times involuntary unemployment becomes a fact of life. At times, such as during the Great Depression when one out of four workers was without a job, there is massive unemployment. Later parts of the book will address the causes of this unemployment, and what government can do about it.

21

EXTERNALITIES AND THE ENVIRONMENT

I n this and the next two chapters, we probe the economic role of government, a topic first treated in broad terms in Chapter 7. Beyond providing a legal framework within which economic relations take place, government may have an economic role to play when markets fail to produce efficient outcomes. This justification is known as the **market failures approach** to the role of government.

We already know several ways in which markets can fail to produce efficient outcomes. For example, competition may be less than envisaged by the basic model, and less-than-perfect competition produces inefficient economic outcomes. Competitive markets may, for all the reasons set forth in Chapter 17, fail to produce the technological innovation needed by a thriving economy. Government has responded with patent laws and other legislative efforts to spur innovation.

Markets may also fail in the face of information problems described in Chapters 18 and 19. For instance, producers tend to know more about their products than they reveal to customers. Government has responded with truth-in-advertising laws.

One market failure has not yet been adequately discussed. This failure arises when there are externalities—costs and benefits of a transaction that are not fully reflected in the market price. When we first encountered externalities in Chapter 7, our focus was on positive externalities, such as those associated with goods that are publicly provided. Here we shift the focus to negative externalities and the issues of environmental protection.

KEY QUESTIONS

1. Why do externalities such as pollution result in a market failure? What alternatives can government employ to remedy this market failure?

2. What are the market forces that lead to an efficient use of society's natural resources? What may impede markets from using scarce natural resources efficiently?

NEGATIVE EXTERNALITIES AND OVERSUPPLY

The basic competitive model assumes that the costs of producing a good and the benefits of selling it all accrue to the seller, and that the benefits of receiving the good and the costs of buying it all accrue to the buyer. This is often not the case. As was explained in Chapter 7, the extra costs and benefits not captured by the market transaction are called externalities.

Externalities can be either positive or negative, depending on whether individuals enjoy extra benefits they did not pay for or suffer extra costs they did not incur themselves. Goods for which there are positive externalities—such as research and development—will be undersupplied in the market. In deciding how much of the good to purchase, each individual or firm thinks only about the benefits it receives, not the benefits conferred upon others. By the same token, goods for which there are negative externalities, such as air and water pollution, will be oversupplied in the market. The fact that the market might not fully capture the costs and benefits of a trade provides a classic example of a market failure and a possible role for the public sector.

Figure 21.1A shows the demand and supply curves for a good, say steel. Market equilibrium is the intersection of the curves, the point labeled E, with output Q_p and price p_p. Chapter 13 explained why, in the absence of externalities, the equilibrium E is efficient. The price reflects the marginal benefit individuals receive from an extra unit of steel (it measures their marginal willingness to pay for an extra unit). The price also reflects the marginal cost to the firm of producing an extra unit. At E, marginal benefits equal marginal costs.

Consider what happens if, in the production of steel, there is an externality—producers are polluting the air and water without penalty. The **social marginal cost**—the marginal cost borne by all individuals in the economy—will now exceed the **private marginal cost**—the marginal cost borne by the producer alone. Note that in a competitive industry, the supply curve corresponds to the horizontal sum of all producers' *private* marginal cost curves. Panel B contrasts the two situations. It shows the social marginal cost curve for producing steel lying above the private marginal cost curve. Thus, with so-

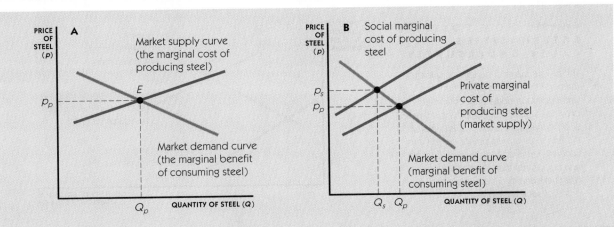

Figure 21.1 HOW NEGATIVE EXTERNALITIES CAUSE OVERSUPPLY

In a perfectly competitive market, the market supply curve is the (horizontal) sum of the marginal cost curves of all firms, while market demand reflects how much the marginal consumer is willing to pay or how much the marginal unit is worth to any consumer. In panel A, the intersection or equilibrium, at quantity Q_p and price p_p, will be where private marginal cost is equal to the marginal benefit.

The private marginal cost includes just the costs actually paid by the producing firm. If there are broader costs to society as a whole, like pollution, then the social marginal costs will exceed the private costs. If the supplier is not required to take these additional costs into account (as in panel B), production will be at Q_p, greater than Q_s, where price equals social marginal cost, and the quantity produced will exceed the amount where marginal cost is equal to marginal benefit for society as a whole.

cial marginal costs equated to social marginal benefits, the economically efficient level of production of steel will be lower, *at Q_s*, than it would be, at Q_p, if private costs were the only ones.

Thus, the level of production of steel, which generates negative externalities, will be too high in a free market. We can also ask, what about the level of expenditure on pollution abatement? Such expenditures confer a positive externality on others—the benefits of the equipment, the cleaner air, accrue mainly to others. Figure 21.2 shows a firm's demand curve for pollution-abatement equipment in the absence of government regulation. It is quite low, reflecting the fact that the firm itself derives little benefit. That is, the firm's marginal private benefit from expenditures on pollution-abatement equipment are small. The firm sets its marginal private benefit equal to the marginal cost of pollution abatement, which results in a level of expenditure on pollution abatement at *E*. The figure also depicts the marginal social benefit of pollution abatement, which is far greater than the marginal private benefit. Efficiency requires that the marginal social benefit equal the marginal cost, point *E'*. Thus, economic efficiency requires greater expenditures on pollution abatement than there would be in the free market.

One of government's major economic roles is to correct the inefficiencies resulting from externalities. Among the many types of negative externalities, perhaps the most conspicuous are those that harm the environment.

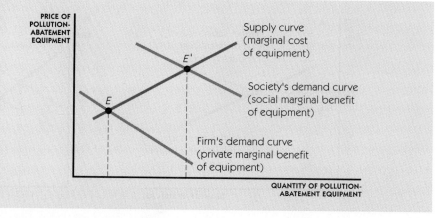

Figure 21.2 HOW POSITIVE EXTERNALITIES CAUSE UNDERSUPPLY

The private marginal benefit includes just the benefits received by the firm, but since pollution-abatement equipment provides a positive externality, it will have a social marginal benefit that is higher. If the firm takes only its private benefit into account, it will operate at point E, using less equipment than at the point where marginal benefits are equal to marginal costs for society as a whole (E').

ENVIRONMENTAL PROTECTION AND CONSERVATION: EXAMPLES

Freon gas, used as the propellant in aerosol cans and as a coolant in air conditioners, appears to have destroyed some of the ozone layer of the atmosphere—risking major climatic changes and possibly exposing individuals to radiation that may cause cancer. This is a worldwide externality. A major treaty among the nations of the world was signed in early 1990 that would eventually ban the use of this and related gases. The nature of the externality in this case was clear: the use of the gas anywhere could have disastrous effects on everyone.

Another major international treaty was signed in Rio de Janeiro in 1992. Since the beginning of the industrial revolution, enormous quantities of fossil fuels—coal, oil, and gas—have been burned. When they burn, they produce carbon dioxide (CO_2). Carbon dioxide is absorbed into the oceans and used by plants in photosynthesis. But the rate of emissions in recent decades has been far greater than the rate of absorption—so much so that the concentration of CO_2 in the atmosphere is 25 percent higher than it was at the beginning of the industrial revolution. Worse, in the next few decades, it is projected to double, or more, unless strong actions are taken. The United Nations convened an international panel of scientists to assess both the extent of these dramatic changes in the earth's atmosphere and their consequences. Their findings were alarming. These and other gases create a "greenhouse gas" effect, trapping radiation arriving at the earth, and leading to global warming. While the magnitude of the warming effect is likely to be small—only a few degrees—the potential harm is great: a partial melting of the earth's ice caps, a rise in sea levels, a flooding of low-lying countries such as Bangladesh, an increase in the spread of deserts.

At Rio, the developed countries agreed to restrain their level of emissions, returning them to their 1990 level by the year 2000. Since emissions increase with energy use, and energy use normally increases with economic growth, achieving this goal will require both substantial increases in energy efficiency and switching from energy sources (such as coal) that produce high levels of emissions to those that produce little or none (such as hydroelectric power).

These are examples of global externalities. Most externalities are more local. Many of the world's cities are choking with smog, for example, caused largely by automobile exhausts. Many rivers, streams, and lakes are so polluted that they are unsafe to drink from or to swim in.

POLICY RESPONSES TO PROBLEMS IN THE ENVIRONMENT

As the negative externalities associated with pollution and other environmental issues are increasingly recognized, the alternative ways government can curtail their bad effects have received considerable attention from economists and others. This section evaluates several of the major options.

PROPERTY RIGHTS RESPONSES

Large-scale environmental degradation is a conspicuous form of negative externalities. Having identified them as market failures, what can the government do to improve matters? Some economists, led by Nobel laureate Ronald Coase of the University of Chicago Law School, argue that government should simply rearrange property rights. **Coase's theorem** says that, with appropriately designed property rights, markets could take care of externalities without direct government intervention. Consider, for example, the case of a small lake in which anyone can fish without charge. Each fisherman ignores the fact that the more fish he takes out of the lake, the fewer fish there are for others to take out. If the government were to rearrange property rights and grant to a single individual the right to fish, then he would have every incentive to fish efficiently. There would be no externalities. He would take into account the long-run interests as well as the short-run. He would realize that if he fished too much this year, he would have fewer fish next year. If it were a large lake, he might let others do the fishing and charge them for each fish caught or regulate the amount of fish they could catch. But the prices he charged and the regulations he imposed would be designed to ensure that the lake was not overfished.

The point of this example is that the problem of overfishing is solved with only limited government intervention. All the government has to do is assign the property rights correctly.

This kind of problem arises repeatedly. The U.S. government leases public land to cattle ranchers. Since the ranchers only lease the land, they often impose a negative externality on future potential users by overgrazing the land, which leads to environmental damage like soil erosion. If the property rights were altered so that the land was sold to the ranchers, they would have reason to look after the land. In deciding on how many cattle to graze this year, they would take into account the effect on the pasture, and thus on the number of cattle they could graze next year.

Coase envisioned that once property rights were assigned, market solutions or bargaining among potential users would ensure efficient outcomes. Consider the conflict between smokers and nonsmokers over whether to allow smoking in a room. Smokers confer a negative externality on nonsmokers. Coase suggests a simple solution. Give the rights to the air to one individual, say a smoker. He has the right to decide whether to allow smoking or not. For simplicity, assume that there are only two individuals in the room, one a smoker and the other a nonsmoker. If the value of fresh air to the nonsmoker exceeds the value of smoking to the smoker, the nonsmoker would offer the smoker enough money to compensate him not to smoke. Conversely, if the property rights were given to the nonsmoker, and if the value of smoking to the smoker exceeded the value of fresh air to the nonsmoker, then the smoker could compensate the nonsmoker.

Coase argued not only that assigning property rights ensures an efficient outcome, but that how the property rights are assigned affects only the distribution of income, not economic efficiency. Whether smoking would be allowed would depend simply on whether the value of smoking to smokers exceeded or was less than the value of fresh air to nonsmokers.

The appeal of Coase's theorem is that it assigns a minimal role to government. Government simply makes the property rights clear, and leaves the efficient outcome to private markets. Opportunities to apply the theorem are limited, however, because the costs of reaching an agreement may be high, particularly when large numbers of individuals are involved. Imagine the difficulties of assigning property rights to the atmosphere, and having all the individuals adversely affected by air pollution negotiating with all those contributing to it!

Today there is general agreement that while assigning property rights clearly may take care of some externality problems, most externalities, particularly those concerning the environment, require more active government intervention. Some forms this intervention might take include regulatory measures, financial penalties, subsidization of corrective measures, and creating a market for the externality.

REGULATION

Government's first response to the need for intervention to address environmental externalities was to regulate. Electric utilities that burned high-sulfur coal would not be allowed to emit sulfur dioxide into the atmosphere. They would be required to install scrubbers, devices that removed the sulfur from

CLOSE-UP: THE MARKET FOR WHALES

The average American eats sixty-three pounds of beef, fifty pounds of pork, and forty-six pounds of chicken in a year, and one never hears concerns that this consumption will drive cows or pigs or chickens into extinction. Relatively few Americans eat whale meat, yet in certain countries like Japan, whale meat is considered a delicacy. In 1986, fearing that whales were being hunted into extinction, an international convention passed a moratorium on all commercial whaling. Why does the market system work to assure plenty of cows and pigs and chickens, but threaten to exterminate certain breeds of whales?

Economists approach this question by analyzing the property rights in each case. The farmers who raise cows and pigs and chickens own them, and thus have an incentive to build up the supply of animals. But no country or individual owns the ocean or the whales in it. Thus, although there is an economic incentive to hunt whales and sell their meat, there is no individual or company with a direct economic incentive to help nurture and increase the overall number of whales.

This pattern has been called "the tragedy of the commons." When an area is owned in common, like the ocean, everyone has an economic incentive to exploit it, but no one has an economic incentive to care for it. The result can be the disappearance of the whales in the ocean.

Of course, the problem of the commons is not limited to whales. The decimation of the bison on the commonly owned American prairie is another example, as is the pollution in the commonly owned air and water.

Soon after the moratorium on whaling for commercial purposes was passed in 1986, several countries felt a sudden need to hunt whales for scientific purposes. Japan, for example, announced in 1987 an urgent need to kill for research purposes nearly half the number of whales they had been catching for commercial purposes. Iceland announced that it would be shipping much of the whale meat from its "research whales" to Japan, where the meat would sell at premium prices. More recently, international agreements have placed tight limits on the number of whales that can be caught. As a result, the number of Minke whales quickly made a recovery, to the point where limited commercial whaling has begun once again.

Sources: Figures on meat consumption from *Statistical Abstract of the United States* (1994) information about whaling in 1986 and 1987 comes from Timothy Appel, "Japan Finds Loophole in Whaling Ban," *Christian Science Monitor,* April 15, 1987, p. 1.

the fumes. And cars would be required to have catalytic converters. This approach is sometimes called the **command and control approach.**

It quickly ran into problems. The same environmental benefits often could be achieved at much lower costs than the specificity of the regulations demanded. This was partly because the regulations did not (and could not) allow for the myriad of variations in circumstances facing different firms, and partly because the regulatory process is always slow (at best) in incorporating newly developing technologies. Worse still, the command and control approach failed to provide incentives for the development of new technologies to reduce environmental damage, since it often would not allow the technologies, even if they did a better job.[1]

Moreover, politics inevitably intrudes into the setting of regulations, resulting in higher than necessary costs. High-sulfur coal producers worried that the cost of scrubbers would put them at a competitive disadvantage relative to low-sulfur coal producers. (This is the correct market outcome from the viewpoint of economic efficiency, of course, because the social cost of high-sulfur coal—including the negative environmental impacts—was greater than that of the low-sulfur coal.) So they succeeded in getting Congress to mandate that low-sulfur coal also had to have unnecessary scrubbers. In another example, ethanol producers (dominated by a single firm, ADM) succeeded in getting regulators to require a corn-based gasoline additive to reduce pollution rather than an oil-based one—even though the latter was cheaper, and may be better environmentally.[2]

TAXES AND SUBSIDIES

Most economists believe that taxes and subsidies provide a better way than regulation to encourage the behavior society wants. Taxes are the stick, while subsidies are the carrot. Both share the aim of adjusting private costs to account for social costs.

Taxes on pollution are similar to fines for violating regulations in one respect—they both increase the cost of and thereby discourage pollution. But taxes differ from regulation in a fundamental way. Regulations are a clumsy weapon. They penalize firms for polluting over a specified level, but polluters who stay just below that level get off scot-free. Pollution taxes can be set so that they reduce aggregate pollution by the same amount as a regulator would under a command and control system. But the economic effects are very different. Taxes add the cost of pollution to the costs a company has to cover to remain in business. As a result, companies have the incentive to reduce their pollution as far as possible and to find new, low-cost ways of reducing pollution, rather than keeping it just below the legal standard. This is "efficient pollution abatement," with the producers who pollute less having their reward in lower costs.

---

[1] On the other side, advocates argue that in some cases the tight regulations have "forced" development of new technologies to meet environmental standards that could not be met with existing technologies.

[2] As this book goes to press, the courts have issued a stay on this regulation.

Subsidies such as tax credits for pollution-abatement devices are an alternative way of providing incentives to reduce pollution. Subsidies are economically inefficient. Take the case of a steel firm. With subsidies, firms are not paying the full costs. Part of the costs are being picked up by the government. This allows producers to sell (and users to buy) steel at lower than its full cost of production, and it keeps steel and pollution production above the socially efficient level. Clearly, firms prefer subsidies to taxes.

THE MARKETABLE PERMIT RESPONSE

Still another approach to curbing pollution is **marketable permits.** Companies purchase (or are granted) a permit from the government that allows them to emit a certain amount of pollution. Again, the government can issue the amount of permits so that the company produces the same level of pollution that there would be under the command and control approach. However, companies are allowed to sell their permits. Thus, if a company cuts its pollution in half, it could sell some of its permits to another company that wants to expand production (and hence its emission of pollutants).

The incentive effects of marketable permits are very much like those of taxes. A market for pollution permits encourages development of the best possible antipollution devices, rather than keeping the pollution just under some government-set limit. If the government wishes to reduce pollution over time, the permits can be designed to reduce the amount of pollution they allow by a set amount each year. In the United States, this sort of shrinking marketable permit was used to reduce the amount of lead in gasoline during the early 1980s. Variants of this idea have recently been adopted to help control other forms of air pollution, such as sulfur dioxide.

WEIGHING THE ALTERNATIVE APPROACHES

Incentive programs, such as taxes or marketable permits, have an important advantage over direct controls, like regulations. The issue of pollution is not whether it should be allowed—after all, it is virtually impossible to eliminate all pollution in an industrial economy. Nor would it be efficient; the costs of doing so would far exceed the benefits. The real issue is how sharply pollution should be limited. The *marginal* benefits have to be weighed against the marginal costs. This is not done under regulation. If government ascertains the marginal social cost of pollution and sets charges or marketable permits accordingly, private firms will engage in pollution control up to the point at which the marginal cost of pollution control equals the marginal social return of pollution abatement (which is, of course, just the marginal cost of pollution). Each firm will have the correct marginal incentives.

Governments often prefer direct regulations because they believe that they can control the outcomes better. But such control can be illusory. If an unreachable standard is set, it is likely to be repealed. For example, as automobile companies have found the costs of various regulations to be prohibitive, they have repeatedly appealed for a delay in the enforcement of the regulations, often with considerable success.

It must also be kept in mind that choosing the socially efficient method of pollution abatement is the easy part of the policy problem. Figuring out the

SOLVING THE PROBLEM OF EXTERNALITIES

Externalities, which occur when the extra costs and benefits of a transaction are not fully reflected in the market price, give rise to market failure. Four main solutions have been proposed and used:

1. The reassignment of property rights
2. Regulations that outlaw the negative externality
3. Tax and subsidy measures to encourage the behavior society wants
4. Marketable permits

POLICY PERSPECTIVE: UNFUNDED MANDATES, TAKINGS, AND COST-BENEFIT ANALYSIS

In the new, Republican-controlled Congress that convened in January 1995, three issues dominated the environmental debate: unfunded mandates (federal requirements laid on states and localities without accompanying funding); takings (a legal term meaning reduction in property value because of government regulations); and cost-benefit analysis (verifying the costs and benefits in assessing whether—and how—to regulate).

Unfunded Mandates The federal government imposes certain environmental regulations on states and localities that entail costs for which the federal government does not provide funds. Critics of environmental regulation said that if the government imposed mandates, it should provide the money. Environmentalists worried that, since federal funding is hard to come by, such a requirement would end environmental regulation. Economists tried to point out that, when well designed, environmental regulations align social and private costs. This is true whether the action is one undertaken by a private firm or a municipal sewage authority. If the sewage authority is imposing externalities on others, through its effect of discharges on water quality, it should bear some extra costs, such as those required to stop the externality. (To be sure, not all of the federally imposed mandates were correcting an externality.)

Takings The takings, for the private sector, are what the unfunded mandate is for the public sector. Take the case of a farmer being ordered not to drain a wetlands area and plant on it. Critics said

that if the government took actions that had adverse effects on property values, the government should provide compensation. Environmentalists again worried that, without funds, such a requirement would end environmental regulation. They agreed that the Constitution prohibited the taking of private property without compensation, but said that the courts should adjudicate whether and when a taking occurred. Courts in fact have taken a fairly narrow view: only in extreme cases would they declare that a taking had occurred. The problem is that virtually every government action affects property values. A change in the interest rates engineered by the Federal Reserve Board can have huge effects on market values. These are not actionable as takings. Where do you draw the line?

Cost-Benefit Analysis The rising costs of environmental regulation, now estimated to exceed $100 billion a year, have made the demand for better analysis when designing regulation almost irresistible. Such analysis should look at the cost and benefit of regulations, encouraging government to only undertake regulations where benefits exceed costs, and to focus on areas where environmental risks are greatest. These principles, supported by most economists, would seem to be unexceptional, and are in fact reflected in Executive Orders issued by both President Bush and President Clinton to guide the implementation of regulations. But some environmentalists take a "purist" stand. They argue that a child's health is not an issue for the cold calculus of costs and benefits. And they worry about "paralysis by analysis"—that the process of doing the cost-benefit analysis studies will effectively bring environmental regulation to a halt.

"right" level of pollution to aim for is much harder. Uncertainty about the consequences of pollution abounds and how to value certain options is an issue of hot debate. To what extent can environmental degradation be reversed? How much value should be placed on the extinction of a species like the spotted owl, or the preservation of the Arctic wilderness? No matter what approach is chosen to externalities and the environment, such questions will remain controversial.

NATURAL RESOURCES

A recurrent theme among environmentalists is that our society is squandering its natural resources too rapidly. We are using up oil and energy resources at an alarming rate, hardwood timber forests that took hundreds of years to grow are being cut down, and supplies of vital resources like phosphorus are dwindling. There are repeated calls for government intervention to enhance the conservation of our scarce natural resources. Those who believe in the infallibility of markets reply, nonsense! Prices give the same guidance to the use of natural resources that they give to any other resource, these people say. Prices measure scarcity, and send consumers and firms the right signals about how much effort to expend to conserve resources, so long as consumers and firms are well informed, and so long as there is not some other source of market failure.

There is, in fact, some truth in both positions. Prices, in general, do provide signals concerning the scarcity of resources, and *in the absence of market failures,* those signals lead to economic efficiency. We have seen some cases where a private market economy without government intervention will not be efficient—when there are negative externalities (pollution) or when a resource (like fish in the ocean) is not priced.

But what about a privately owned resource, like bauxite (from which aluminum is made) or copper? The owner of a bauxite mine has a clearly defined property right. Let's assume that he pays a tax appropriate to any pollution his mining operation causes. Thus, the price he charges will reflect both social and private costs. The question of resource depletion now boils down to the question of whether his bauxite is worth more to him in the market today or left in the ground for future extraction. The answer depends on what bauxite will be worth in the future, say thirty years from now. If it is worth enough more thirty years from now (to compensate for waiting), he will keep the bauxite in the ground even though he may not be alive. That way he maximizes the value of his property, and he can enjoy his wise decision by selling the mine when he retires. The price at which he sells it should reflect the present discounted value of the bauxite.

If this miner and all other bauxite producers choose to bring the bauxite to market today, depleting the world's supply of bauxite, there are two possible reasons. Either, this is the socially efficient outcome—society values bauxite more highly today than it will tomorrow. Or, the miners have miscalculated the value of bauxite thirty years from now and underestimated future prices, though they have every incentive to get as accurate a forecast as they can. If they have indeed miscalculated, we might view the result as a market failure; but there would be no reason to expect a government bureaucracy to do any better than the firms at guessing future prices.

However, from society's viewpoint there are two plausible reasons why private owners may undervalue future benefits of a natural resource. First, in countries where property rights are not secure, owners of a resource may feel that if they do not sell it soon, there is a reasonable chance that the resources will be taken away from them. There may be a revolution, for example, in which the government will take over the resource with no or only partial compensation to the owners. Even in countries like the United States, where owners are not worried about government confiscating their property, increased regulations might make it more expensive to extract the resource in the future, or higher taxes might make it less attractive to sell the resource in the future. Second, individuals and firms often face limited borrowing opportunities and very high interest rates. In these circumstances, capital markets discount future returns at a high rate, far higher than society or the government would discount them.

Higher interest rates induce a more rapid depletion of resources. Suppose an oil company is deciding whether to extract some oil today or to wait until next year. For simplicity, assume there are no extraction costs, so the net return to selling the oil is just its price. If the price of a barrel of oil is the same today as a year from now, the firm's decision is simple. The firm will sell the oil today. But what if the price of oil is expected to go up 10 percent? Now the firm must compare the present discounted value of the oil sold a year from now with what it could receive today. To calculate the present discounted value, we simply divide next year's price by 1 plus the interest rate. If the interest rate is 10 percent, then a dollar a year from now is worth 10 percent less than a dollar today. So if the interest rate is less than 10 percent, it pays the firm to wait; if the interest rate is more than 10 percent, it pays the firm to extract the oil today. At higher interest rates, firms have a greater incentive to extract oil earlier.

Sometimes government has aggravated the waste of natural resources. In the United States, for example, much of the timber lies on government lands. The government, in making the land available, has paid less attention to concerns about economic efficiency than it has to the pleading of timber interest groups. Government policies aimed at restricting the import of foreign oil have also encouraged the use of domestic resources, a seemingly perverse policy of "drain America first." Government policies in keeping the price of water for farmers low has led to many negative outcomes: excessive use of water, draining water from underground basins built up over centuries, lowering the water table, and in some cases, leaching out the soil. In each of these cases, private property rights and market outcomes would have supplied solutions that almost everyone in society would regard as better than what happened.

MERIT GOODS AND BADS

In this chapter, we have explained why market failures—such as externalities—provide a rationale for government intervention. To some people, how we treat the environment and the earth's natural resources is not just a matter of economic efficiency; it is a moral issue. They argue that the issue of allowing whaling should not be approached narrowly from the perspective of economic costs and benefits. This is but one of many examples in which government becomes involved not just because markets have failed to produce efficient outcomes, but because government believes there are values that supersede those reflected in individual preferences, and it has the right and duty to impose those values on its citizens. It rejects the basic premise of *consumer sovereignty*, which holds that individuals are the best judges of their own welfare, and argues that in certain selected areas, there is a role for *paternalism*—government can make better choices in some matters than individuals. Goods that the government mandates to be consumed—like compulsory education—are called **merit goods,** and goods that it prohibits on these grounds—such as drugs, pornography, and, from 1919 to 1933, alcohol—are called **merit bads.** These goods are proscribed not just because of their adverse effects on others (externalities).

REVIEW AND PRACTICE

SUMMARY

1. Government may have a role in the economy when markets fail to produce an efficient outcome. When positive or negative externalities exist, markets will not provide an efficient outcome.

2. One way to deal with externalities is to assign clear-cut property rights.

3. Governments may deal with environmental externalities by imposing regulatory measures (the command and control approach), levying taxes and granting subsidies, or issuing marketable permits.

4. In a perfect market, natural resources are used up at an efficient rate. However, privately owned resources may be sold too soon, for two reasons. First, owners may fear that if they do not sell the resources soon, new government rules may prevent them from selling at all or, in any case, lower the return from selling it in the future. Second, interest rates facing owners may be high, so they may value future income less than society in general. High interest rates lead to a faster exploitation of natural resources.

KEY TERMS

market failure approach	private marginal cost	command and control approach
social marginal cost	Coase's theorem	

REVIEW QUESTIONS

1. Name several market failures. Why do economists see the existence of these market failures as a justification for government action?

2. Why will a free market produce too much of goods that have negative externalities, like pollution? Why will a free market produce too little of goods that have positive externalities, like pollution control?

3. What are the advantages and limitations of dealing with externalities by assigning property rights?

4. What are the advantages of marketable permits over command and control regulation? What are the advantages of using taxes for polluting rather than subsidies for pollution-abatement equipment?

5. How do markets work to allocate natural resources efficiently? In what cases will markets fail to give the correct signals for how quickly a resource like oil should be depleted?

PROBLEMS

1. Marple and Wolfe are two neighboring dormitories. Wolfe is considering giving a party with a very loud band, which will have a negative externality, a sort of sound pollution, for Marple. Imagine that the school

administration decides that any dormitory has the right to prevent another dorm from hiring a band. If the band provides a negative externality,
how might the residents of Wolfe apply the lessons of Coase's theorem to
hire the band they want?

Now imagine that the school administration decides that no dormitory
can prevent another dorm from hiring a band, no matter how loud. If the
band provides a negative externality, how might the residents of Marple
apply the lessons of Coase's theorem to reduce the amount of time they
have to listen to the band? How would your answer change if the band
provided a positive externality?

2. The manufacture of trucks produces pollution of various kinds; for the
purposes of this example, let's call it all "glop." Producing a truck creates
one unit of glop, and glop has a cost to society of $3,000. Imagine that the
supply of trucks is competitive, and market supply and demand are given
by the following data:

Price (thousand $)	19	20	21	22	23	24	25
Quantity supplied	480	540	600	660	720	780	840
Quantity demanded	660	630	600	570	540	510	480

Graph the supply curve for the industry and the demand curve. What are
equilibrium price and output? Now graph the social marginal cost curve.
If the social cost of glop were taken into account, what would be the new
equilibrium price and output?

If the government is concerned about the pollution emitted by truck
plants, explain how it might deal with the externality through fines or
taxes and through subsidies. Illustrate the effects of taxes and subsidies by
drawing the appropriate supply and demand graphs. (Don't bother worrying about the exact units.) Why are economists likely to prefer fines to
subsidies?

3. Consider a small lake with a certain number of fish. The more fish that
one fisherman takes out, the fewer fish are available for others to take out.
Use graphs depicting private and social costs and benefits to fishing to describe the equilibrium and the socially efficient level of fishing. Explain
how a tax on fishing could achieve the efficient outcome. Explain how giving a single individual the property right to the fish in the lake might also
be used to obtain an efficient outcome.

The more fish taken out this year, the less fish will be available next
year. Explain why if there is a single owner for the lake, the fish will be efficiently extracted from it. Assume that anyone who wants to fish can do
so. Would you expect that too many fish would be taken out this year?

4. Consider a crowded room with an equal number of smokers and nonsmokers. Each smoker would be willing to pay $1.00 to have the right to
smoke. Each nonsmoker would be willing to pay $.50 to have the room
free from smoke. Assume there is a rule that says than no smoking is allowed. Could everyone be made better off if smoking is allowed? How? If
property rights to clean air are assigned to the nonsmokers, how might

the efficient outcome be obtained? What difference does it make to the outcome whether there is initially a rule that smoking is allowed or smoking is not allowed? What problems might you envision occurring if no smoking is allowed unless all the nonsmokers agree to allow smoking?

TAXES, TRANSFERS, AND REDISTRIBUTION

D uring this century, governments have become increasingly involved in reducing inequality in the distribution of income provided by the market. Without help, some families have too little income to do more than barely survive. Children who have the bad fortune to be born into impoverished families face bleak life prospects. Most developed countries have therefore sought to provide a safety net for the poor. Some have taken the more active stance of promoting equality of opportunity. Many have also developed benefit programs that help people, regardless of income, in times of need (such as illness, unemployment, or old age).

Income redistribution is inextricably linked to taxation. After a look at the case for income redistribution, this chapter takes up the two major ways government alters the distribution of income: taxes and public benefit programs (transfers).

KEY QUESTIONS

1. What are the characteristics of a good tax system, and how does America's current tax system fare under these criteria? What are the various ways government raises revenues?

2. What do economists mean when they talk about a fair or equitable tax system? What arguments are used to decide how the burden of taxation should be shared among various groups in the population?

3. What are the basic programs designed to provide assistance for the poor? What are the trade-offs between equity and efficiency in the design of these programs?

4. What is the rationale for social insurance programs? What are some of the current public policy controversies surrounding them?

THE CASE FOR INCOME REDISTRIBUTION

Income redistribution policies are justified in ways different from other governmental economic policies. The roles of government developed in earlier chapters are based on the premise that public sector intervention may be appropriate to ensure efficient outcomes when there are market failures— whether from lack of competition, imperfect information, or the presence of externalities. In such situations, markets fail to provide completely satisfactory answers to some of the basic economic questions: "What goods are produced, and in what quantities?" and "How are the goods produced?"

When it comes to the question "For whom are the goods produced?," to which this chapter is devoted, the rationale for public sector intervention is different. Individuals' incomes determine who consumes the goods produced in a market economy. People with higher skills or more capital, for instance, earn higher incomes and therefore get to consume more of the goods produced. Labor and capital markets may be efficient, in the sense that wages and returns to capital get the incentive structure right for the economy. But the market-determined distribution of income may result in some individuals having billions of dollars and others being homeless, with inadequate food and medical care. Thus, the case for income redistribution is not based on the pursuit of economic efficiency. It is based on overriding social values. There is a general consensus that when the market results in incomes so low that people cannot sustain a minimally decent standard of living, government should help out. *How* it helps out is crucial, however, because redistribution programs often interfere with economic efficiency.

THE CHANGING U.S. INCOME DISTRIBUTION

Concern about income distribution has risen as the wage differential between skilled and unskilled workers has become more pronounced over the past two decades. Real wages of unskilled workers have fallen dramatically over this time span. At the same time, real wages of skilled workers have held steady or fallen modestly, increasing the wage differential between skilled and unskilled workers. (See Figure 22.1.) Though lower-income families have made up for some of the difference by working longer hours (often with both parents working), the poorest families have still seen a decline in their real incomes. Moreover, changing family structures have increased the proportion of single-parent households. These patterns, in turn, have increased the number of poor children to the point where almost one in four children in this country now lives below the poverty threshold.

What to do about the increased inequality depends on the time frame. The long-run strategy focuses on improved education and training. In the short run, attention focuses on tax and benefit programs.

TAXES

The U.S. government raises tax revenues from a variety of sources. There are taxes on the earnings of individuals and corporations, known as **individual income taxes** and **corporation income taxes.** Real estate—buildings and

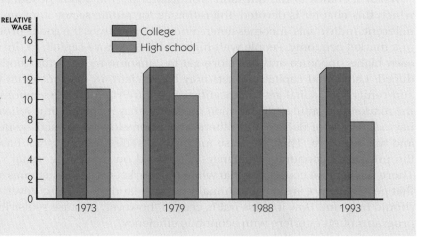

Figure 22.1 INCREASING INCOME INEQUALITY

During the past two decades the wage differential between skilled and unskilled workers has become more pronounced. This trend is evident in a comparison of the average real wages of high school and college graduates who recently entered the labor force. The real wages of high school graduates have decreased consistently since 1973, falling a total of 30 percent between 1973 and 1993. During the same period, the average real wages of college graduates changed little. *Source:* John Bound and George Johnson, "What Are the Causes of Rising Wage Inequality in the United States?", *FRBNY Economic Policy Review* (January 1995), p. 11.

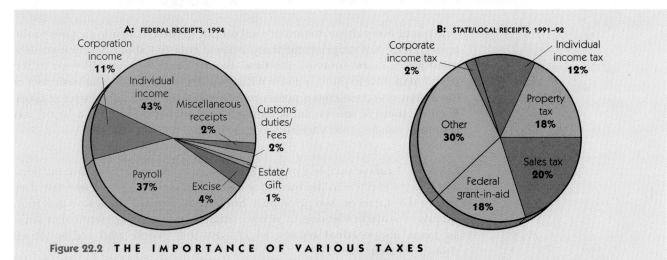

Figure 22.2 THE IMPORTANCE OF VARIOUS TAXES

At the federal level, the largest share of taxes come from the individual income tax, followed by the payroll tax and the corporate income tax, as shown in panel A. Sources of revenue at the state and local level are more fragmented, as seen in panel B, but include sales and property taxes, as well as revenue received from other levels of government. *Source: Economic Report of the President* (1996), Tables B-78, B-82.

land—is subject to taxation by most states; these taxes are known as **property taxes.** Large bequests and gifts are taxed, through **gift** and **estate taxes.** There are special provisions relating to the taxation of capital gains (the increase in value of an asset between the time an individual purchases it and the time she sells it). Furthermore, wage income is subject not only to the income tax, but also to the **payroll tax** (the tax levied on a company's payroll, half of which is deducted from employees' paychecks). Revenues from the payroll tax are intended to finance the Social Security (retirement income) and Medicare (medical care for the aged) programs.

There are also taxes on the purchase of specific goods and services, known as **excise taxes.** The two heaviest excise taxes are on alcohol and tobacco, also known as **sin taxes.** The excise taxes on air travel and gasoline are sometimes called **benefit taxes** because the proceeds go for benefits, like airports and roads, to those who purchase the good. Excise taxes on perfume, large cars, yachts, and expensive fur coats, targeted to the rich, are referred to as **luxury taxes.** Other excise taxes, such as the one on telephone services, have no particular justification other than raising revenue. Most states impose a general tax on purchases of goods and services, known as a **sales tax,** though typically a wide variety of items (such as food) are exempted.

As this list indicates, few transactions in our economy escape taxation. Figure 22.2 shows the relative importance of various taxes at the federal and the state/local levels. At the federal level (panel A), the single most important source of revenue is the tax on individuals' income (contributing almost half of total revenue), followed by the payroll tax. At the state/local levels (panel B), the sales tax is the most important revenue source.

CHARACTERISTICS OF A GOOD TAX SYSTEM

One out of every three dollars of total output of the U.S. economy goes to the government. Not surprisingly, there is great concern about how the government raises its revenue. At one time, the art of taxation was likened to the problem of how to pluck a goose without making it squawk. The basic fact of life is that everyone enjoys government services but few enjoy paying taxes. Even so, there is substantial agreement about what constitutes a "good" tax system. It has five characteristics.

Fairness   In most people's minds, the first criterion is fairness. But fairness, like beauty, is often in the eyes of the beholder. In trying to define fairness, economists focus on two principles: **horizontal equity,** which says that individuals who are in identical or similar situations should pay identical or similar taxes, and **vertical equity,** which says that people who are better off should pay more taxes.

Tax systems in which the rich pay a larger fraction of their income than the poor are said to be **progressive,** while those in which the poor pay a larger fraction of their income than the rich are called **regressive.** If rich people pay more taxes than the poor but not proportionately more, the tax system is still considered regressive.

The U.S. income tax is progressive, since the rates that apply to higher incomes are larger than for lower incomes. Taxes on tobacco and alcohol are examples of regressive taxes, since poor individuals spend a larger fraction of their income on these goods. States sales taxes, on the whole, are regressive, since in general not all goods—such as vacations in Europe—are taxed, and the fraction of income of the rich that thus escapes taxation is larger than that of the poor.

Efficiency   The second criterion for a good tax system is efficiency. The tax system should interfere as little as possible with the way the economy allocates resources, and it should raise revenue with the least cost to taxpayers. Very high taxes may discourage work and savings, and therefore interfere with the efficiency of the economy. Taxes that select out particular goods to be taxed—such as excise taxes on perfume, boats, and airline tickets—discourage individuals from purchasing those goods, and therefore also interfere with efficiency.

The U.S. income tax system has many provisions that have the effect of encouraging some types of economic activity and discouraging others. For instance, the U.S. income tax allows certain child care payments to be taken as a credit against tax payments owed. The government thus subsidizes child care. Similarly, when firms spend money on R & D, their expenditures may reduce the amount they have to pay in taxes. Such arrangements are called **tax subsidies.** These subsidies cost the government money just as if the government paid out money directly for child care or research. Accordingly, the revenue lost from a tax subsidy is called a **tax expenditure.**

Today, capital gains received favorable treatment in a number of ways. The maximum tax rate is 28 percent, rather than the 39.6 percent tax rate on other income. In addition, taxes are paid only when assets are sold, not when the gain is accrued. This postponement of payment is equivalent to a reduction in the tax rate of a quarter or more (7 percentage points). In addition, when an individual dies, the assets are passed on to his or her heirs and the accrued capital gain completely escapes taxation—at an estimated cost to the Treasury of $30 billion a year. And there are major tax breaks if you hold investments in new companies for at least five years.

But prior to 1986, capital gains received even more favorable treatment—they were taxed at 40 percent of the rate of ordinary income. Many investors would like a return to the good old days. Reinforcing that perspective is a bit of budget gimmickry. When capital gains taxes are lowered (particularly if the reduction is viewed to be temporary), some households are induced to sell their assets earlier than they otherwise would. This yields a temporary *increase* in tax revenues. Of course, though households pay their taxes earlier, the total taxes they pay is reduced. Thus, in the long run, government revenues are lowered (and the deficit increased). There is another possibility: some individuals who would have held assets until death—and thus managed to escape taxation—might be enticed by the lower capital gains tax rates to sell their assets early. Even so, the statistical evidence that tax revenues would increase is, at best, weak.

Advocates for cutting the capital gains tax believe that lower taxes will provide a greater stimulus to the economy, and the higher rate of growth will itself generate more revenues. This is the same argument as was used in 1981 when taxes were lowered. At the time, the economy was operating far below full employment, so there was room for expansion; even under these conditions, the tax cut did not generate increased tax revenues.

Critics of a capital gains tax cut argue that with the economy at full employment, there is little room for extra expansion. And in any case, capital gains taxation distorts the pattern of investment. If greater investment is desired, the best way to elicit efficient investment is through lowering interest rates. The focus should be on policies, such as deficit reduction, which allow lower interest rates. The benefits of capital gains tax reductions go disproportionately to the rich, since wealth is even more concentrated than income; and, extending the preferential tax treatment to investments already made has no incentive effect.

In spite of these criticisms, as this book goes to press, the prospects of a capital gains tax cut remain good. In an era of budget stringency, the official accounting of the cost of capital gains tax reductions focuses only on the impact over seven years, and employs high estimates of induced realizations of capital gains. This accounting method makes the capital gains tax cut appear to be one of the most affordable forms of tax reduction. In some versions, cutting the tax actually provides more revenue within the seven-year period.

Administrative Simplicity   The third criterion is administrative simplicity. It is costly—to the government and to those who must pay taxes—to collect taxes and administer a tax system. In addition to the costs of running the IRS, billions of hours are spent each year in filling out tax forms, hours that might be spent producing goods and services. Billions of dollars are spent on accountants and lawyers by taxpayers and by the IRS in the annual ritual of preparing and processing tax forms. Finally, with a good tax system, it should be difficult to evade the taxes imposed.

Flexibility   The fourth criterion is flexibility. As economic circumstances change, it may be desirable to change tax rates. With a good tax system, it should be relatively easy to do this.

Transparency   The fifth criterion is transparency. A good tax system is one in which it can be ascertained what each person is paying in taxes. The principle of transparency is analogous to the principle of "truth in advertising." Taxpayers are consumers of public services. They should know what they (and others) are paying for the services they are getting.

GRADING THE U.S. TAX SYSTEM

How well does the U.S. tax system fare, based on these five criteria? Equally important, have the major changes in the tax laws over the past decade improved the tax system?

Fairness   As noted, the U.S. federal income tax system is, over all, progressive. Low-income individuals are exempted from paying any income tax whatsoever. Beyond a certain level of income (depending on the size of the family—for a family of four, the critical level in 1995 was $16,550), the tax rate is 15 percent. This means that for each extra $100 an individual earns, he must pay an extra $15 of taxes; this is his **marginal tax rate.** At a still higher level of income, the marginal tax rate increases to 28 percent, then to 39.6 percent.

The **average tax rate** gives the ratio of taxes to taxable income. While there are big jumps in the marginal tax rate, the average tax rate increases smoothly. Figure 22.3 shows the 1995 marginal and average income tax rates for a typical family of four that did not itemize its deductions.

The income tax is only one of several income-related taxes that U.S. citizens pay. The payroll (Social Security) tax is another one that increases with income up to some level. An **earned-income tax credit** is designed to supplement the income of low-income workers with families; as a person's income increases beyond some level, the payments he *receives* under this program decrease. Figure 22.4 collects together all income-related federal taxes: the income tax, the earned-income credit, and the payroll tax. The figure is remarkable because of its irregular shape—a consequence of the interaction of the various parts of the tax system—but also because for so much of the income distribution, there is so little variability in the marginal tax rate.

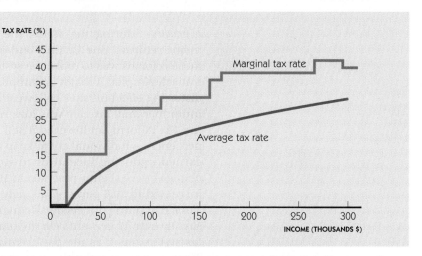

Figure 22.3 MARGINAL AND AVERAGE TAX RATES

Marginal tax rates change by jumps, as shown in the table, but average tax rates increase gradually. *Source:* Internal Revenue Service, Form 1040 (1995).

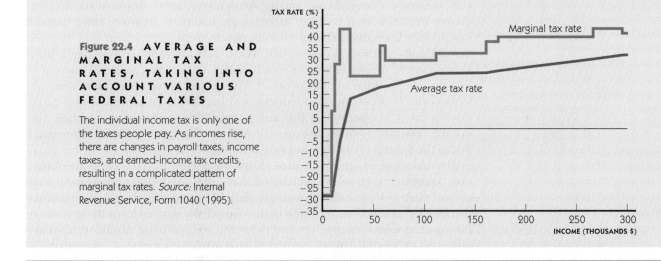

Figure 22.4 AVERAGE AND MARGINAL TAX RATES, TAKING INTO ACCOUNT VARIOUS FEDERAL TAXES

The individual income tax is only one of the taxes people pay. As incomes rise, there are changes in payroll taxes, income taxes, and earned-income tax credits, resulting in a complicated pattern of marginal tax rates. *Source:* Internal Revenue Service, Form 1040 (1995).

To assess the overall progressiveness of the U.S. tax system, we have to look not only at the federal income tax but at all taxes—including the corporation income tax and state and local taxes.

Many state and local taxes are regressive. This is because lower- and middle-income individuals spend a larger fraction of their income on items that are subject to state sales taxes than do the rich. Our current *total* tax system— combining the slightly progressive federal tax system with the slightly regressive state and local tax system—is, in the judgment of most economists, only slightly progressive.

Efficiency During the 1980s, the U.S. income tax system underwent two major reforms, one in 1981 and another in 1986. The announced intent of these reforms was to make the system more efficient, more fair, and administratively simpler. A major accomplishment of these reforms was to reduce the distorting effect of taxes by lowering the marginal tax rate. In 1981, the maximum marginal tax rate was lowered from 70 percent to 50 percent. In 1986, the Tax Reform Act lowered it still further to 33 percent. With a tax rate of 70 percent, the individual got to keep less than one out of every three dollars she earned, reducing incentives to work harder and increase earnings. These changes were slightly reversed in 1993, when the top marginal tax bracket was increased to 39.6 percent (actually, when the medicare insurance and provisions that phase out certain deductions are included, the top marginal rate is slightly over 42 percent). On the other hand, several distorting elements of the tax system, such as the preferential treatment of gas and oil, were retained. Thus, in the area of efficiency, the U.S. tax system today, while considerably better than it was fifteen years ago, still has much room for improvement.

Administrative Simplicity Americans live in a complex society, and their tax laws reflect and contribute to this complexity. As they have sought to make sure that the tax laws are fair and apply uniformly to all people in similar situations, the laws have become increasingly complex. High tax rates make it worthwhile for individuals and businesses to think hard about how to avoid taxes (legally, without going to jail). With high tax rates, it may pay a businessperson to devote almost as much energy to how he can avoid taxes as to how he can produce a better product. The tax law has evolved out of this constant battle between the government and taxpayers; as each new way of reducing taxes is discovered, the law is modified to close the loophole. Inevitably another hole is discovered, and another repair job is attempted. Today the federal tax law amounts to a multitude of volumes.

The objective of administrative simplicity seems to have been an elusive one. Many economists are convinced that the United States could have a tax system that is truly administratively simple, but to do so, other objectives would have to be given up. Some of the complexity derives from the attempt to have a progressive income tax and to tax the income from capital. But preferential treatment of capital income is also a major source of complexity, as rules have to be made to stop the conversion of other income into forms receiving preferential treatment.

Flexibility One of the weakest aspects of the U.S. tax system is its lack of flexibility. Any time a tax change is proposed, all of the issues discussed here are raised. There are debates about how different groups would be affected and about how efficiency is affected. Basic issues of values—how progressive should the tax system be?—are aired once again. Special-interest groups try to take the opportunity of any change in the tax law to get favorable treatment. It has turned out to be extremely difficult—and time-consuming—to change the tax law.

Transparency   Of all the parts of the tax system, the ultimate burden of corporation income tax is perhaps the least transparent. Although corporations write the check to the IRS, most economists agree that much of the burden is shifted to individuals and households, through reduced wages and/or higher product prices. The 1986 Tax Reform Act increased the relative importance of the corporation income tax, and thus on average made the tax system less transparent. The sales tax ranks second lowest on the transparency scale. Politicians love the sales tax, because they know that many, perhaps most, individuals never figure out the total amount they are actually spending on government services.

TRANSFERS

In addition to tax policy, government affects the income distributions through **transfer programs.** Transfers are payments that households receive without having to engage in any current productive activity in return. Transfer payments can be private, such as company pensions or scholarships from private universities. Government engages in a wide range of transfer programs. Two major groups of government transfer programs concern us here: **income-tested transfers,** the direct purpose of which is to redistribute income from upper-income to lower-income Americans, and **social insurance,** which protects individuals, irrespective of income, in times of need.

NEED-BASED TRANSFER PROGRAMS

Politicians frequently appeal to voters by expressing their concern for the poor. Compassion for others not as fortunate is a fundamental human value. Government programs to aid the poor reflect the belief that all citizens have a collective responsibility to take care of those among them who are in need. Though the extent to which responsibility should be borne by government or by voluntary charities is a matter of debate, governments in all the developed countries have assumed a major role in providing at least a safety net to protect the most disadvantaged.

There are currently five major public benefit programs for low-income Americans. AFDC (Aid to Families with Dependent Children), what most people refer to as "welfare," provides cash assistance to poor families (mostly households with only one parent present). Medicaid provides health care for those on AFDC and to other poor children as well. The food stamp program provides vouchers for the purchase of food. SSI (supplemental security income) provides cash assistance to the low-income elderly and disabled, to supplement their social security benefits. Housing assistance programs include public housing and rental vouchers. In addition to these five program areas, states and localities provide general assistance to those who fall between the cracks. Food stamps and SSI are federal programs (states can supplement SSI benefits). The other programs vary from state to state, with the federal government typically providing only broad program guidelines, but footing much of the bill.

Our discussion here focuses on the two most controversial program areas: welfare and housing.

WELFARE

AFDC is the most controversial of the programs providing benefits that depend on income. In his 1992 campaign, President Clinton promised to "end welfare as we know it," a sentiment shared by many Republicans. In 1996 Congress passed, and the president signed, major welfare reform legislation, which ended the federal entitlement to welfare, left most of the details of welfare programs up to the states, and provided the states with a fixed amount of money (bloc grants) with which to run the programs. Underlying the reforms were three principles:

1. Encouraging work. There is now a strong consensus that welfare should be, for all who are capable, a transition to work. Recipients need incentives to work—carrots and sticks. The earned income tax credit (EITC) provides a big carrot by subsidizing the wages of low-income workers. The stick embodied in the new welfare legislation is the threat to cut off welfare payment after two years of receipt ("time-limited welfare").
2. Increasing opportunity. To obtain work, individuals must have the skills required by the marketplace. Hence, most welfare reform proposals include provision for training and job search.
3. Fostering responsibility. Most proposals also include measures designed to make parents provide financial support for their children, and to encourage a sense of responsibility—in particular, the responsibility that comes with parenthood.

A goal of the 1996 reform was the reduction of welfare costs, but the success of the initiative may require new expenditures, such as spending on child care and training.

HOUSING

Public housing projects have been described as "warehouses of the poor," and the description has merit. By failing to integrate the poor more thoroughly into the communities in which they live, public housing projects help perpetuate the cycle of poverty. Moreover, many housing programs are inequitable. They provide generous benefits to those lucky enough to receive them, but many with the same income and family size get nothing. Worse still, providing a subsidy that is tied to a particular dwelling impedes labor mobility. Finally, the costs of public housing are high, and its quality is often much lower than housing of similar cost in the private sector.

All these drawbacks to public housing have led the government to reduce its role in directly supplying low-income housing and to turn increasingly to more market-based solutions. This is done by subsidizing the cost of housing for the poor through rental vouchers. As recipients use the vouchers, increasing demand for low-income housing, more builders are induced to provide

The official poverty line determines how many people the government counts as "poor." But what determines the poverty line itself?

In the late 1960s, an official at the Social Security Administration, Molly Orshansky, developed a method of measuring poverty from a survey of household expenditures. She found that a typical family spent one-third of its income on food. She then gathered information on minimum food budgets for families of various sizes, and multiplied that number by three to get an estimate of the poverty line for the different family sizes. With minor changes, Orshansky's poverty line was officially adopted in 1969 and has been increased by the overall rate of inflation since then.

There are a number of questions one can ask about how poverty is measured: here are three.

First, the survey Orshansky relied on to find that households spent one-third of their income on food was taken in 1955. Since then, household expenditures have shifted. Households now spend a much lower percentage of income on food, perhaps one-fourth or one-fifth. If the minimum food budget were accordingly multiplied by four or five, the poverty line would be much higher.

Second, the poverty line does not take in-kind benefits into account. In-kind benefits include any benefits that are not received in cash form, like Medicaid, food stamps, and subsidized school lunches. If those benefits are measured as additional income, the number of people below the poverty line falls by about 20 percent.

Finally, some critics have proposed that poverty should be thought of as a relative rather than an absolute concept. They argue that those at the bottom of society, say the bottom 5 or 10 or 20 percent, are poor relative to everyone else. Poverty is more appropriately viewed as an extreme case of inequality.

For many, this last criticism goes too far. They fear that a relative concept of poverty might reduce the moral urgency of fighting poverty. There is broad social support for efforts to assure that people have basic levels of food, housing, clothing, and medical care, even if defining those amounts is controversial.

In 1995, a National Academy of Sciences study proposed major revisions in how we measure poverty. While there was agreement about including noncash income, the difficult problems of how best to include health care expenditures were not

fully resolved. Should a sick, poor person who receives $150,000 for a kidney transplant have that added to his income, in which case he now appears to be in an upper income bracket? The study proposed an adjustment in the poverty level that went beyond just taking into account inflation, but it did not propose increasing the poverty level in proportion to increases in average income, which would have made poverty a purely relative phenomenon. But even this compromise generated a strong dissent from one of the members of the Academy's panel.

Sources: Joyce E. Allen and Margaret C. Simms, "Is a New Yardstick Needed to Measure Poverty?" *Focus,* February 1990, pp. 6–8; *Measuring Poverty: A New Approach,* National Academy of Sciences, 1996.

housing for them. Vouchers have several other advantages. They allow for individuals to shop for their housing over broader areas, not just the inner cities, and they can be made "portable," so that individuals can relocate due to job opportunities without losing their housing subsidy.

SOCIAL INSURANCE

Most Americans are neither rich nor poor. They belong to the "middle class." They have seen the poor get free medical care. They have heard about the rich hiring accountants to duck taxes by taking advantage of loopholes. They feel squeezed and unfairly treated. Some of this is a matter of perception. The middle class actually receives the benefits of many "hidden" loopholes that reduce their taxes. For instance, fringe benefits (health insurance, retirement funds), often representing between a quarter to a third of a person's salary, generally escape taxation. In addition, the United States has a variety of what are referred to as **middle-class entitlement programs,** so named because individuals do not have to demonstrate poverty to receive benefits. The most important of these are the social insurance programs. Social insurance programs are like private insurance, in that people nominally pay for their own protection through a tax on wage income, the payroll tax. But in other, important ways, they are *not* like private insurance, as we will see in the paragraphs that follow.

THE BURDEN OF SOCIAL INSURANCE PROGRAMS

The first myth about social insurance concerns who pays for it. Social Security is supported by a tax on wages, 50 percent paid by the employer, 50 percent by the employee. This division of the tax is entirely superficial; the consequences of the tax are essentially the same as they would be if the worker paid the entire tax.

Figure 22.5 uses demand and supply curves for labor to show this. Consider a payroll tax imposed on the employer based on what she pays her workers. The vertical axis measures the wage *received* by the employee. Since the cost of a worker is the wage received by the employee *plus* the tax, the tax shifts the demand curve down. In the new equilibrium, workers' wages have fallen.

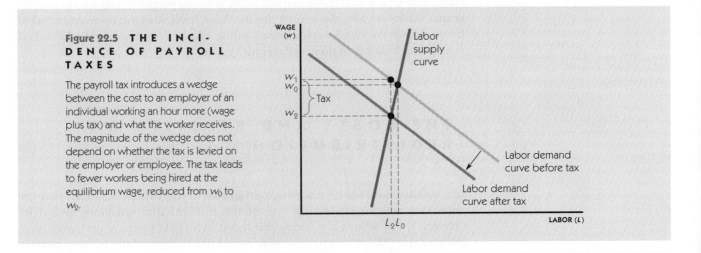

Figure 22.5 THE INCIDENCE OF PAYROLL TAXES

The payroll tax introduces a wedge between the cost to an employer of an individual working an hour more (wage plus tax) and what the worker receives. The magnitude of the wedge does not depend on whether the tax is levied on the employer or employee. The tax leads to fewer workers being hired at the equilibrium wage, reduced from w_0 to w_2.

The wage received by a worker is precisely the same as it would have been had the same tax been imposed on the worker directly. While normally the wage falls by less than the amount of the tax, the extent to which it falls depends on the elasticity of the demand and supply curves. The figure shows the "normal" case where the supply of labor is relatively inelastic, in which case wages fall almost by the full amount of the tax.

HOW SOCIAL INSURANCE IS MORE THAN AN INSURANCE PROGRAM

The second myth about social insurance programs is that they have no redistribution effect. In any insurance program, some individuals receive back more than they contribute, some less. That, in a sense, is the whole purpose of insurance. No one knows whether she will be sick enough next year to need hospitalization. So people buy hospital insurance. Those who are lucky enough not to need hospitalization in effect help pay for the hospitalization of those who need it. But with private insurance, on average, the premiums (what you pay for the insurance) cover the costs of what you receive (including the costs of administration, which are often substantial). With the social insurance programs, however, there is often no close connection between the amount contributed and the amount received back. For instance, on average, single high-wage earners receive less back per dollar contributed than do low-wage families with a single earner. Thus, Social Security performs a redistributive as well as an insurance function.

To the extent that social insurance provides insurance that individuals want and the market has failed to provide, it performs an important economic function. To the extent that social insurance is popular because everyone believes someone else is picking up the tab, its role and function need to be reexamined. Social insurance is popular partly because it seems to benefit the majority of the population, the middle class. The problem facing the middle class, however, is that there are not enough "rich" people to pay for these programs, so the middle class must pay for them itself. And the taxes required to finance them may have serious disincentive effects. These have to be balanced against the benefits of their redistributive role.

THE COSTS AND BENEFITS OF REDISTRIBUTION

Tax, welfare, and social insurance programs in the United States all play an important role in answering one of the fundamental questions posed in Chapter 1: For whom are goods produced (who gets to enjoy the goods that are available)? Each group in society would like to pay as little in taxes as possible and receive as many benefits as possible, and complaints about fairness abound. But issues of what is fair may never be resolved. And economists worry that at least some attempts to make sure everyone has a fair slice may so reduce the size of the economic pie to be divided that almost everyone is worse off.

EQUITY-EFFICIENCY TRADE-OFFS

Economists enter the discussion of redistribution to clarify the costs and consequences of various programs, including different tax systems. Systems that tax the rich more heavily or provide support for poor people even if they could work (but only if they remain unemployed) are likely to have adverse effects on incentives. Economists try to calculate precisely how important these effects are.

All economists agree that as government redistributes more income to the poor, it has to raise taxes on the rich and middle-income individuals, which weakens their incentives to work. But economists disagree about the magnitudes of the trade-offs. Most economists agree that at high enough tax rates, incentives are greatly reduced. The high marginal tax rates of 60 percent or more that used to prevail in Europe probably had large negative effects on efficiency. But whether at current marginal tax rates in the United States, an increase in taxation would have a *large* effect on incentives is much more debatable.

Economists focus on the trade-offs—between equity (how the pie is divided) and efficiency (the size of the pie); and between reductions in the risks of life (through the provision of social insurance) and economic incentives. Beyond these trade-offs lie basic issues of social values, of what kind of society we want to have *recognizing the economic constraints on the choices that we can make.* These values touch not only on issues of efficiency, equality, and risk protection (economic security), but also on individual rights and social responsibilities.

HOW WELL DOES THE UNITED STATES DO?

Taking all of the government programs into account—the tax system, welfare, social insurance—does the government succeed in changing the answer to the question "Who gets the goods produced in the economy?" To answer this question, we need some way of measuring the distribution of income.

Economists often represent the degree of inequality in an economy by a diagram called the **Lorenz curve.** The Lorenz curve shows the cumulative fraction of the country's total income going to the poorest 5 percent, the poorest 10 percent, the poorest 15 percent, and so on. Figure 22.6A shows Lorenz curves for the United States, both before and after government tax and transfer programs have had their effect. If there were complete equality, then 20 percent of the income would accrue to the lowest 20 percent of the population, 40 percent to the lowest 40 percent, and so on. The Lorenz curve would be a straight 45-degree line. If incomes were very concentrated, then the lowest 80 percent might receive almost nothing, and the top 5 percent might receive 80 percent of total income; in this case, the Lorenz curve would be very bowed. Twice the

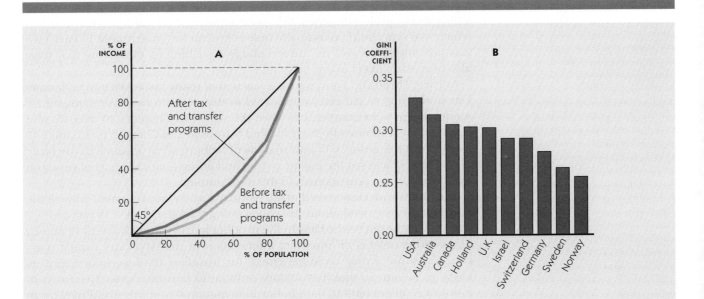

Figure 22.6 INEQUALITY MEASURES

Taxes and subsidies affect the distribution of income. Panel A shows two Lorenz curves for the United States in 1989, one for income before taxes have been levied and government transfers have been received, and the other after. Clearly, some redistribution does take place through these mechanisms, as they move the Lorenz curve toward greater equality. Panel B shows how other developed countries rank relative to the United States on one standard measure of inequality, the Gini coefficient. The United States ranks number one: it has the most unequal distribution of income among the ten. *Sources: Current Population Reports (1990), p. 5, Table B; Luxembourg Income Study Database (1989).*

area between the 45-degree line and the Lorenz curve is a commonly employed measure of inequality, called the **Gini coefficient.**

As can be seen, the after-tax curve for the United States is decidedly inside the pre-tax, indicating that the combined effect of government redistribution programs is to make incomes more equal than the market would have made them. Thus, while the efficiency costs are a matter of debate, the redistributive gains are undeniable.

Still, income inequality in the United States remains much larger than in other developed economies. Panel B of Figure 22.6 gives the measure of inequality for ten developed countries. The United States ranks number one: it has the most *unequal* distribution of income among the ten.

THE ROLES OF GOVERNMENT: A REVIEW

Part Two, which set forth the basic competitive model, closed with a chapter that explained how the market system envisioned by that model will produce efficient economic outcomes. Beyond establishing a legal framework within which markets could operate, the only role seen for government in Part Two was possibly to correct the unacceptable distributions of income that have also been the subject of this chapter.

In Parts Three and Four, we have learned of many instances in which markets in the real world can be expected to depart from the basic competitive model. Failures of competition were discussed in Chapters 14 and 15, and government responses to them formed the subject of Chapter 16. Chapter 17 pointed out the absence of any analysis of technological advance in the basic model, and discussed the patent system and government support of research and development as responses to this shortcoming.

The basic model assumes that parties to transactions are armed with all the information they need about the goods being traded. Chapter 18 pointed out why this might not be the case in the product market, and Chapters 19 and 20 discussed problems of imperfect information in the labor and capital markets. Consumers may be ill-informed, for instance, because information is costly to obtain, so that it is seldom optimal to become perfectly informed; moreover, sellers tend to have better information than buyers and may try to take advantage of this. Government has responded with truth-in-advertising laws designed to protect consumers from this information imbalance. Similarly, the regulations surrounding securities trading were promulgated largely out of concern that buyers needed more information than they were given. In certain insurance and loan markets, where systematic information problems create a thin market—or no market at all—government has stepped in to supply the insurance or loans itself.

Chapter 21 discussed another market failure, externalities, which have so adversely affected our environment in recent decades, and the steps government has taken to remedy the situation.

When the market is efficient—or when government interventions success-fully correct market failures—no one can be made better off without some-one being made worse off. But even under these circumstances, there may be dissatisfaction with the market which leads to government action. For in-stance, sometimes there is a profound distrust of consumer sovereignty—as in the case of merit goods. But the most important reasons for government action is its role in income distribution and social insurance. Even when mar-kets produce economically efficient outcomes, there is no guarantee that the income shares they produce will be socially acceptable. As we have seen in this chapter, both taxes and expenditures—including the important social in-surance programs—are sensitive to concerns about income distribution. Progressive taxes are designed to ensure that upper income individuals pay a larger fraction of their income and taxes, and the social insurance and wel-fare programs are designed to provide a safety net for poorer households, and especially for poor children and the elderly.

GOVERNMENT RESPONSES TO MARKET FAILURES

Market failures	Government responses
Failure to ensure efficiency	
Market not competitive 　　Product markets (Chapters 14–17) 　　Labor markets (Chapter 19)	Antitrust policies
Public goods and externalities 　　(Chapters 7, 21)	Regulation of pollution; provision of 　　national defense
Basic research as a public good; 　　externalities associated with 　　R & D (Chapter 17)	Public support of basic research; 　　patents
Imperfect information and thin or 　　nonexistent markets (Chapters 　　18, 20)	Consumer protection legislation 　　(including securities 　　regulations); government loan 　　and insurance programs
Imperfect annuity markets 　　　　(Chapter 22)	Social Security
Absence of unemployment and 　　　　disability insurance (Chapter 22)	Unemployment and disability 　　insurance programs
Problems in health insurance market 　　　　for the aged (Chapter 22)	Medicare
Failure to produce socially desirable outcomes	
Merit goods and bads; distrust of 　　consumer sovereignty (Chapter 21)	Compulsory education; prohibition 　　against drugs
Socially unacceptable income 　　distribution (high levels of 　　poverty) (Chapter 22)	Welfare and other safety net programs; 　　social insurance programs; tax 　　structure reflecting redistributive 　　objectives

Finally, we should note one more category of market failures. Even though resources are scarce, periodically, the economy fails to utilize them fully. The result is unemployment—occasionally massive unemployment. The reason for this market failure, and what governments can do about it, are among the central questions of macroeconomics, and lie beyond our concerns here.

REVIEW AND PRACTICE

SUMMARY

1. Even if markets are efficient, there may be dissatisfaction with the resulting distribution of income.

2. Inequality—both in terms of wages and income—in the United States has been increasing.

3. At the federal level, the largest share of taxes comes from the individual income tax. At the state level, the main source of revenue is the sales tax.

4. A tax system can be judged by five criteria: horizontal and vertical equity, efficiency, administrative simplicity, flexibility, and transparency.

5. All public assistance programs force society to balance the concerns of equity, which involve helping those in need, with the concerns of efficiency, which involve making sure that both poor people and taxpayers have good incentives to work and invest.

6. Social insurance programs, like Social Security and Medicare, are entitlement programs for everyone, regardless of income. But although everyone is entitled to benefits, some redistribution takes place, with some people getting back more than they contribute.

KEY TERMS

individual income tax	payroll tax	regressive tax
corporate income tax	excise tax	transfer programs
property tax	horizontal equity	Lorenz curve
	vertical equity	Gini coefficient
	progressive tax	

REVIEW QUESTIONS

1. Will an efficient market necessarily produce a fairly equal distribution of income? Discuss.

2. What is the main source of federal revenue? of state revenue?

3. What are the five characteristics of a good tax system? How well does the U.S. tax system fare in terms of these criteria? What is the difference between horizontal equity and vertical equity? What is the difference between a progressive and a regressive tax?

4. How can redistribution take place through an entitlement program like Social Security, where all workers contribute and all retirees receive benefits?

5. How do tax and redistribution programs affect incentives? How do social insurance programs affect incentives? Describe some of the trade-offs involved?

6. What is a Lorenz curve? What does it reveal?

PROBLEMS

1. Explain how a tax subsidy for a good with positive externalities (like research and development) can help economic efficiency. Then explain how a tax subsidy for other goods without such externalities could injure efficiency.

2. Assume that a country has a simple tax structure, in which all income over $10,000 was taxed at 20 percent. Evaluate a proposal to increase the progressivity of the tax structure by requiring all those with incomes over $100,000 to pay a tax of 80 percent on income in excess of $100,000. Draw a high-wage earner's budget constraint. How does the surtax affect his budget constraint? What happens to his incentives to work? Is it possible that imposing the tax actually will reduce the tax revenues the government receives from the rich?

3. Imagine that Congress decided to fund an increase in Social Security benefits by increasing the payroll tax on employers. Would this prevent employees from being affected by the higher tax? Draw a diagram to illustrate your answer.

4. Draw Lorenz curves for the following countries. Which country has the greatest and least inequality?

| | Percentage of total income received by | | | | |
	Lowest fifth	Second fifth	Third fifth	Fourth fifth	Top fifth
United States	4.7	11.0	17.4	25.0	41.9
Japan	8.7	13.2	17.5	23.1	37.5
Germany	6.8	12.7	17.8	24.1	38.7

5. Consider an individual contemplating whether to quit her job and go on welfare. How might the fact that welfare is time limited affect her decision? Is it possible that time-limited welfare may not only lead people to leave welfare, but reduce the number who go on welfare?

23

PUBLIC DECISION MAKING

E
xcept in a dictatorship, government actions do not reflect the preference of any single individual. Rather, they are the result of public choices. The importance of public choice theory was recognized when James Buchanan of George Mason University was awarded the Nobel Prize for his pioneering work on this topic.

In this chapter we look at how public choices are made. We look at some of the problems, at both the theoretical and practical levels, facing public decision making in a democracy. What are the problems associated with majority voting? What role do interest groups play and why? In recent years, there has been considerable dissatisfaction with government. The analysis of this chapter may provide insights into why government often fails to live up to our expectations. Also, in recent years, there has been a strong movement to give government "back to the people," by giving more responsibility to the state and local governments, and taking responsibility away from the federal government. In this chapter, we see what economic analysis has to say about the appropriate assignment of responsibilities for different functions of government.

1. How does majority voting provide answers to questions about the public allocation of resources? Why may voting fail to give clear answers?

2. What is the role of bureaucrats and interest groups in decision making in a democracy?

3. Why does government frequently fail to achieve its stated objectives? What are the sources of government failure?

4. What should be the relationship between federal and state governments? What activities should be undertaken at each level?

DECISION MAKING IN A DEMOCRACY

In a democracy, the wishes of the majority are supposedly reflected in the actions government takes. But the United States is not a direct democracy, where citizens vote for or against each law. Rather Americans vote for the president and members of Congress, along with state and local elected officials, who, in turn, make our laws. Federal laws have to be introduced and passed by both houses, and signed by the president. The president can veto the legislation, and that veto can be overridden by a two-thirds vote in each house. Political scientists focus on the whole range of issues and actors that define the political process, including coalition formation, interest groups, and the media. Economists have a narrower focus, analyzing how rational individuals express their preferences through the political process of voting, and how, in models of the political process, their votes are reflected in the public choices that mark collective decision making.

COLLECTIVE DECISION MAKING

Chapter 8 provided a simple description of how an individual allocates his income: he chooses the most preferred point along his budget constraint. Communities, states, and the federal government also face budget constraints in allocating public resources. For example, they can buy more bombers and spend less on schools, or provide better Social Security benefits and spend less on medical care for the aged. The big difference between individual and collective decision making is that individuals may have different views about public decisions. The aged may want more spending on Social Security; the family with children may want more on education; and the businessperson may see more profits from increased defense spending. Somehow, from these disparate views, a decision must be formed.

There are many theories describing how public decision making occurs—including those that focus on the role of interest groups—but the simplest theory focuses directly on the voting process. In a democracy, the majority is supposed to rule. What does this imply for resource allocation?

MAJORITY VOTING AND THE MEDIAN VOTER

Consider a simple issue like how much to spend on public schools. Some individuals want more to be spent, some less. Whose preferences dominate? The **median voter theory** provides a remarkably simple prediction of the outcome in the case of majority voting. It is the median voter—half of the population want more to be spent than this voter, and half want less—whose preferences dominate. For instance, assume the median voter wants $5,000 to be spent per pupil and there are 40,001 voters. In any vote between $5,000 per pupil and a lesser amount, say $3,000, $5,000 will win. Likewise, in any vote between $5,000 and a greater amount, $5,000 will win again. The median voter will always join those wanting the amount closest to $5,000, ensuring that $5,000 wins. This is the choice the median voter would have made if the decision had been left to her.

Voters, of course, do not decide most issues directly, but elect politicians who vote on issues. Politicians, however, want to get elected. To increase the likelihood that they get elected, they take positions that will increase the amount of votes they receive. If politicians of both parties take positions to maximize their votes, both will take positions reflecting the views of the median voter.

To understand this point, imagine that the amounts different individuals would like the government to spend are arranged from the smallest to the largest. Suppose there are two parties, and one party takes the position reflecting the individual at the 40th percentile. That is, 40 percent would like the government to spend less, 60 percent would like it to spend more. The other party will win simply by taking a position close to that of the voter representing the 41st percentile. That party would get 59 percent of the vote—a landslide. Of course, the first party knows this and tries to find a position such that the opposition cannot undercut it and win a majority. There are thus strong incentives for both parties to take positions closely reflecting the views of the median voter.

This theory explains why voters often feel that they do not have a choice: the two parties are both trying to find the middle position, so that they will not be defeated. It also gives us a way of forecasting government behavior: government will approximate the interests of the median voter.[1]

---

[1] The principle that both parties will gravitate toward the center (reflecting the views of the median voter) was first analyzed by the economist-statistician Harold Hotelling, who taught at Columbia University and North Carolina State.

THE VOTING PARADOX

Governments are not always consistent in their actions. This may not be surprising, given that government choices do not reflect the preferences of a single individual. More fundamentally, majority voting may not yield a determinate outcome even when only three people choose among only three alternatives, as was noted more than two hundred years ago by the Frenchman Marquis de Condorcet. This is referred to as the **voting paradox.** Consider the simple example of three people who want to go to a movie together. They have narrowed their choices down to three movies, which they rank in this way.

	Jessica's preferences	Ralph's preferences	Brutus's preferences
First choice:	*Young and Romantic*	*Third and Goal to Go*	*Automatic Avengers*
Second choice:	*Third and Goal to Go*	*Automatic Avengers*	*Young and Romantic*
Third choice:	*Automatic Avengers*	*Young and Romantic*	*Third and Goal to Go*

When they compare each of the movies, they find that *Young and Romantic* is preferred over *Third and Goal to Go* by a 2–1 margin and *Third and Goal to Go* is preferred to *Automatic Avengers*, also by a 2–1 margin. Taking this information alone, they might reason that—since *Young and Romantic* is preferred over *Third and Goal to Go* and *Third and Goal to Go* is preferred over *Automatic Avengers*—*Young and Romantic* is also preferred to *Automatic Avengers*. But when they put it to a vote, they find that *Automatic Avengers* is preferred to *Young and Romantic* by a 2–1 margin. There is no majority winner. Majority voting can compare any two of these choices, but is incapable of ranking all three of them.

Nobel laureate Kenneth Arrow proved an even more remarkable result. All voting systems (two-thirds majority, weighted majority, or any other), under some circumstances, yield the same kind of indecision. Inconsistencies are simply inherent in the decision-making process of any democratic government. The only way around this problem, to ensure that consistent choices are made, is to entrust a single individual with all decisions. Such a system yields consistent choices, but is hardly democratic!

Inconsistencies in democratic decision making, such as illustrated by the above example, are fortunately not inevitable. For instance, with majority voting, if there is a single variable being voted upon—say, the level of expenditure on education—and different individuals have a "most preferred" level and vote for outcomes closer to that level, then the median voter will always determine the outcome. But some preferences are more complicated—for instance, some individuals prefer a high level of expenditures on public education, in which case they send their children to public schools. But if expenditures are viewed to be inadequate, they send their children to private schools, and so would vote for a very low level of expenditures over a "moderate" level. When alternatives cannot be simply ranked in terms of "more" or "less" (as in the three-movie example given earlier) the voting paradox will arise and there is no clear theoretical prediction of the outcome of the electoral process.

INTEREST GROUPS AND RENT SEEKING

The median voter theory provides a clear answer to how decisions are made in a democracy, but frequently government action does not even remotely reflect the interests of the median voter. Rather, it more nearly represents interests of particular groups.

One economic explanation for this has to do with the increasing needs of candidates for funds to run successfully for election, and the willingness of special-interest groups to provide those funds as long as their interests are served. In American politics, these groups argue that it is in the general interest for their special interests to be served. Thus, the gas and oil industries argue for huge subsidies through the tax system, stressing the importance of energy for the American economy.

Economists refer to these activities as rent seeking. Rents, as we learned in Chapter 12, are returns enjoyed by a factor of production that go beyond those required to elicit its supply. As we saw in Chapter 16, the term rent seeking is used when individuals or firms devote their energies to the procurement of rents or other special favors from the government. Government, through its power to tax, set tariffs, provide subsidies, and intervene in other ways in private markets, can affect the profitability of various enterprises enormously. For example, the attempt by U.S. car producers in the 1980s to restrict foreign competition is a case of rent seeking. As a result of protection from foreign competition, they can get higher prices for their products and make bigger profits.

In the budget debates of 1995 and 1996, attention was drawn to special interest provisions under the title of "corporate welfare." In a period in which sacrifices were being asked from a wide range of groups—such as welfare, Medicaid, and Medicare recipients—it was argued that it was only fair for corporations to pay their fair share. While much of the cost of tariffs and other restrictions is borne directly by consumers in the form of higher prices, the Treasury loses billions of dollars each year from preferential tax provisions and other subsidies, often hidden (such as the sale of timber at below market price). The Clinton administration, as part of its plan to reduce the deficit, proposed eliminating more than $40 billion of such subsidies over a seven-year period.

As long as the government has the discretion to grant rents and other special favors, firms and individuals will find it pays to engage in rent-seeking behavior—that is, to persuade government to grant them tariffs or other benefits—and the decisions of government accordingly get distorted. It makes little difference whether this behavior comes in the form of direct bribes, as is frequently the case in less developed countries, or campaign contributions that serve to influence how congressional representatives vote. Either way,

The most important determinant of political outcomes often comes down to the simple question of who turns out to vote. In some sense, it is not *rational* for an individual to vote. It is costly to become informed. It is costly, in terms of time, to vote. And the likelihood that any individual will have an effect on the outcome is negligible. Ensuring that government is well run is a public good—all benefit when governments function well—and like any public good, there is a tendency for undersupply.

The fact that individuals have so little incentive to vote—and that who votes makes a big difference to outcomes—has not gone unnoticed by politicians. Although all parties pay lip service to the principle that everyone should be encouraged to vote, the party that expects to gain from participation of the nonvoter is more likely to go after those votes. Thus, soon after he took office in 1993, President Clinton proposed a law that would make it easier for individuals to register to vote. The bill, called the Motor Voter bill—because it would enable people to register at the same time they got their driver's license—was opposed by some Republicans. The reason given was that more noncitizens, not eligible to vote, might slip through onto the electoral rolls. The Republican governor of California, Pete Wilson, also claimed the law was a case of an unfunded mandate: a requirement placed on states without funds to carry it out. But Democratic skeptics suspected that the real concern was its effect on the electoral process.

the consequences are likely to be similar: governments respond to the rent-seeking behavior of special-interest groups.

BUREAUCRACIES

The final aspect of government behavior that we will take up is the theory of bureaucracy, which involves a principal-agent problem. The government consists not only of elected officials, but also of those appointed by elected officials and the civil service, whose job it is to administer government programs. Just as in the private sector managers' interests may not perfectly coincide with those of shareholders, in the government sector public managers may not do what the electorate, or their elected representatives would ideally like—or what is, in some broader sense, in the public interest.

Even if they are partly concerned with doing a good job, bureaucrats are also concerned with their own careers. For instance, concern about making mistakes may lead them to act in a risk-averse manner. Because it is so difficult to assess the "output" of administrators, performance may be judged more on the extent to which an individual has conformed to certain "bureaucratic" procedures, which partially accounts for the proliferation of red tape. Bureaucrats may have an interest in expanding their spheres of influence, just as any businessperson has an interest in the growth of her business. But while a businessperson expands her business by providing a good at a cheaper price, bureaucrats expand their influence by persuading the legislature either that they need more funds or personnel to do what has to be done, or that there should be more of whatever it is they do. This leads to a form of competition among bureaucrats that may have deleterious effects.

AGRICULTURE: A CASE STUDY IN MIXED MOTIVES

Government agricultural programs provide an opportunity for studying the mixed motives of government as well as the public and market failures that so frequently characterize government activities. The United States has a major program of subsidies for agriculture—amounting, at their peak in 1986, to more than $25 billion per year. The total cost to the American consumer, however, is far higher, because a major objective of the program is to raise the prices farmers receive—and therefore the prices consumers pay.

Government gives two justifications for its agriculture programs. One is the enormous variability of prices and output in agriculture, risks against which a farmer cannot obtain adequate insurance. Thus, the programs are sometimes rationalized on the basis of "stabilizing" prices. But prices are not just stabilized around an average market price, as they would be if the objective were truly risk reduction. Rather, prices are stabilized around a higher level, necessitating huge government purchases of some goods in order to sustain the prices and restrictions on production. Moreover, the risk that farmers really

Close-up: Economics, Liability, and Legal Reform

When the Republican members and prospective members of Congress signed their "Contract with America," prior to the November 1994 election, among their pledges was reform in the U.S. liability laws that compensate someone for damages as a result of another's actions.

Through the nineteenth century, one could only be held liable in a court case for behavior that deviated greatly from the norm—for example, if you kept explosives in your back garden and they blew up the neighbor's house. By definition, actions that are very different from normal do not happen all that often, so liability law was quite restricted. By the early twentieth century, this sort of liability law was felt to be inadequate. After all, many people are injured in the normal course of events—in the workplace, while driving, while using various products, and so on. If liability only applied to the ab-

normal, most people injured through no fault of their own would receive no compensation.

In the 1930s and 1940s economists pointed out that if employers, drivers, or manufacturers could impose negative externalities on others without having to pay a price, they would have insufficient incentives to avoid negligence. Moreover, the liability system could be viewed as a sort of insurance system. To "insure" against liabilities for injuries caused by products, for example, manufacturers would charge a little more to everyone (like an insurance premium) and use the money to pay off the lawsuits of those who were injured.

By the 1960s, the legal rule had evolved into "strict" liability, under which all parties were held responsible for *all* harm they did, whether they had behaved abnormally or not. This was viewed as a useful way to encourage safer behavior and

assure that victims of accidents received compensation. But strict liability ran into problems. While it reduced the occurrence of negative externalities, it led to an explosion of lawsuits, some of them frivolous, with a corresponding increase in liability insurance premiums. Moreover, since manufacturers were held liable for any harm resulting from a product, no matter how carefully they had tested it beforehand, they became more hesitant to innovate.

These were among the motivations for inclusion of liability reform in the list of ten major initiatives in the Contract with America. Courts have even allowed "punitive damages"—damages in excess of the losses incurred—as a way of providing further incentives for firms to ensure that the products they produce are safe. But critics worry that juries have gone too far. The Contract with America attempts to restore balance, by restricting punitive damages. Whether the proposal will restore a balance, or tilt the balance the other way, is the central question at issue.

care about is the risk to their income. Price stabilization programs do not eliminate *income* risk. Income depends on the price of outputs, the level of output, and costs. Price stabilization programs only affect one of the three variables. If risk reduction were really the objective, it would be possible to design a better program to meet that objective. Indeed, today there are markets where farmers can effectively ensure that they get a certain price when they harvest their crop, making the role of government even more questionable.

The second justification given is to help the rural poor (small farms). This justification has little merit because, by their very nature, programs that provide support by raising the prices result in large farmers receiving more than small farmers. This is because the more farmers sell, the greater their subsidy. In assessing whether poverty alleviation is really the objective, one needs to ask two questions. Is there any reason why the United States should be more concerned about the poor in the rural sector than poor elsewhere in the economy? And even if a reason could be found for a program directed at poor farmers, couldn't a program be designed that got at this problem more directly, rather than also providing large subsidies to large farmers? In fact, average farm income today is higher than average nonfarm income, and, while in recent years, total farm payments have declined, the average *payment* per farm household now exceeds $30,000, close to the U.S. average family *income*.

Worse still, the farm programs have in many instances contributed to environmental degradation. Because of peculiar provisions in the farm law, farmers' benefits are often reduced when they engage in crop rotation, even though crop rotation increases soil fertility. The high payment rates also often encourage excessive use of fertilizer and pesticides. The new farm legislation passed in 1996 went some way in reducing these distortions.

The explanation for the farm programs is simple: special-interest groups try to increase the income of their members, at the expense of taxpayers and consumers at large. Consider the rice and tobacco programs. Many of the rice farms are in California, on irrigated land. Even with large government subsidies, rice farming is profitable largely because the price of water is heavily subsidized. Why, in a state that is facing major water shortages, is the government subsidizing rice production? And why did the government spend large amounts of money on the message that smoking is bad for your health at the same time it spent money subsidizing tobacco farmers?

More generally, how can we explain the seeming disproportionate influence of certain small interest groups, like farmers, who constitute less than 2 percent of Americans and have succeeded in getting huge subsidies from the federal government? The answer suggested by Nobel laureate Gary Becker is that the free-rider problem is smaller the smaller the group. "Bribing" representatives to support one's special interest is a public good. All wheat farmers benefit from a wheat subsidy. All steel or car producers benefit from trade barriers that keep out less expensive foreign steel or cars. But these are small groups, making it easier to persuade all to contribute to the cost of lobbying. Each of these programs also has losers. And the losers are not only far more numerous, but together, they lose more than the special-interest groups gain. But each of the losers loses a little, while each of the gainers gains a lot. Opposing the special-interest groups is also a public good, and each opponent has an incentive to be a free rider. As a result, it is harder for groups representing broad groups, such as consumers, to be organized than it is for special-interest groups representing industries or other concentrated beneficiaries.

PUBLIC FAILURES

That markets are, by and large, the most efficient way of providing goods and services is well accepted today, as is the idea that there are particular circumstances—such as the externalities associated with environmental pollution—in which markets fail. The role of government in correcting such market failures is more hotly debated, with many Americans believing that—no matter how bad the market failure—government is likely to make matters worse, not better.

The evidence is more mixed than much of the antigovernment rhetoric suggests. Government has long played an important role in the economy, and the list of commonly accepted successes is correspondingly long. The amazing increase in agricultural productivity over the past seventy-five years is generally attributed to the government's support of research, and its dissemination of knowledge of new technologies to farmers. Major scientific breakthroughs, from atomic energy to the discovery of the AIDS virus, occurred in government laboratories. Key advances in computer technology and jet engines were the result of government support. The development of the important telecommunications sector has been based on government support—from Samuel Morse's first telegraph line between Baltimore and Washington in 1842 to the development of the Internet in the 1970s and 1980s. America was brought together as a nation in part through the intercontinental railroads, made possible through huge land grants. We are better able to breathe the air in our cities and to drink and swim in the water from our lakes and rivers, largely because of actions undertaken by government.

Even the evidence on the comparative inefficiency of government is mixed. The government-run Canadian National Railroad appears to be as efficient as the privately run Canadian Pacific Railroad. And even the much maligned post office has managed to score productivity improvements in the past fifteen years that exceed the average for the U.S. economy.

Still, failures of government are impressive, from public housing projects that rival the worst provided by any slumlord, to cost overruns on defense projects. And some of the government successes have had questionable side effects: the interstate highway system, while greatly reducing transportation time, contributed to the urban sprawl that plagues many of our cities. Many of the worst problems have been the result of complex interactions between the private and public sectors. The failure of savings and loan associations, costing U.S. taxpayers upwards of $200 billion, was the result of excessively speculative investments made by *private* S & Ls. But government-provided deposit insurance allowed depositors to give their money to S & Ls without worrying how the money would be used. Thus, S & Ls undertook increasingly speculative investments without considering their depositors. And government regulators failed to take strong actions in the face of worsening balance sheets, increasing the final costs of the debacle to the taxpayers.

What should be the role of government? And how can it perform better? To answer these questions, we have to understand the *systemic* reasons for government failure. Three major factors underlie systemic government failure: incentive problems, budgeting problems, and unintended consequences of government action.

INCENTIVES AND CONSTRAINTS

Unlike private organizations, government has the power of coercion. It can force people to pay taxes. It can prohibit people from paying less than the minimum wage if they engage in interstate commerce. And so on. But since this power carries with it enormous potential for abuse, certain procedures have been developed to protect the public against arbitrary use of government power. These procedures are called **due process.**

A good example to illustrate the potential incentive problems of due process procedures is the set of rules governing civil service employment. These rules are designed to ensure that there is no discrimination or other arbitrary treatment of government workers. But the rules are often inflexible and make it difficult to pay comparable salaries to public officials who do their jobs as well as similarly qualified and dedicated persons in the private sector—or to offer them the same opportunities for rapid promotion. It is even more difficult for government to demote or fire incompetent and lazy workers. Thus, the public sector's ability to recruit and manage staff for maximum efficiency is typically limited.

In addition to the constraints of due process, the government has trouble making long-term commitments that are perceived to be binding. The

Republicans who signed the 1994 Contract with America—with its guarantees about taxes, the deficit, and the like—may or may not live up to their contract. But if they do not, the American voters will have no *legal* recourse. Any Congress can reverse decisions made by previous Congresses, though it may try to design both legislation and legislative rules in ways that make it more difficult to do so. Such limitations on the government's ability to make binding commitments can have major economic consequences. Take, for example, a government promise that it will pursue a policy of interest rate stability. The current government may convince investors of its commitment to keeping interest rates low. But it has no control at all over what happens in the next election. Investors know that and make their own assessments of interest rate risk, which may interfere with the effectiveness of what the government is trying to do today. The government today can make it more costly for future governments to increase the rate of inflation; for instance, it can issue short-term bonds, so that the interest cost to the government would rise quickly if inflation started to pick up.

Another factor that can undermine government efficiency, and lead to perverse decisions against the broad interests of society, is the political pressures inherent in the democratic process. A prime example here is legislators' concerns about the next election. These can lead to so-called "pork barrel" projects that create jobs in a pivotal legislator's home district but make no economic sense from a national perspective. In addition to the incentives to invest in projects that will aid the reelection chances of politicians, the enormous cost of running for office provides incentives for elected officials to pay particular attention to the views and needs of those who contribute to their campaign funds. Through this route, lobbyists, for example, can wield influence way out of proportion to the importance of the interests they represent.

BUDGETING AND SPENDING PROCEDURES

The budgeting and spending constraints facing government decision makers differ from those of the private sector in three major ways. The first is the severity of the budget constraint facing public decision makers. Unlike a private firm, which faces the prospect of bankruptcy if enough of its ventures yield losses, a public enterprise can more easily turn to the government for budgetary help. This is the problem of **soft budget constraints.** Amtrak, for example, continues to make losses in its overall railroad operations, in spite of government promises to the contrary. A major reason for the continuing loss is a set of labor rules *imposed by the government*—which require that workers be compensated if they are laid off or forced to relocate even a short distance. Soft budget constraints such as these weaken the incentives for public management to be efficient. There is nothing quite like the threat of bankruptcy to focus managerial attention.

The second budgetary difference between the private and public sectors—a factor that works in the opposite way from the soft budget constraints—is the annual appropriations process. This can force short-term spending constraints on the public sector that are not cost-effective in the long run. Limited investment flexibility is a particularly unfortunate fallout from the annual appropriations system. One of the major reasons the Clinton administration proposed corporatizing the air traffic control system, for example, was to remove this rigidity. Although the air traffic control system had done a truly impressive job in preventing accidents, many saw a disaster waiting to happen. The computers used by the system were so outmoded that many still used vacuum tubes—indeed they were probably the largest purchaser of these outmoded products, which are no longer manufactured in the United States, and must be imported from Poland. The government simply did not have the estimated $30 billion on hand in a given year to update the system.

The third budgetary constraint on government is the antiefficiency effects of some of the procedures implemented to ensure strict cost control. No one likes to see public money wasted, least of all taxpayers or the congressional representatives who risk the taxpayers' wrath. Government has instituted detailed accounting, competitive bidding, and other procurement procedures to avoid waste and corruption. Yet these procedures can cost more than they save and not only because of the extra bureaucracy involved. Competitive bidding is an example highlighted by Vice President Gore's National Performance Review. When purchasing T-shirts, for example, the government in its efforts to ensure that the specifications were accurate and precise—so that bidders were competing to supply *exactly* the same product—created 30 pages of fine print documentation which prospective bidders have to follow carefully. These types of bureaucratic red tape reduce the supply of bidders willing to sell to the government and increase the cost to the government of goods and services. Gore's project recommended, among many other things, that the government purchase such ordinary items "off the shelf." Procurement reforms such as this were enacted into law in the 1994 Federal Acquisitions Streamlining Act, and are expected to save billions of dollars a year.

UNINTENDED CONSEQUENCES

Information problems plague government just as they plague the private sector. But one aspect of uncertainty is much more problematic for government—the problem of unforeseen consequences, particularly the unanticipated effects of government actions on incentives, both public and private. For example, subsidizing medical care for the elderly through Medicare greatly increased the elderly's demand for medical services, leading to increases in costs far beyond those originally projected. (Since the Medicare program was passed in the 1960s, the ability to project behavioral consequences and their cost implications has vastly improved. But the problem of unanticipated consequences has by no means been solved.)

Two frequently cited examples are the interstate highway program and the urban renewal programs. The interstate highway program was designed to provide a suitable highway system for the rapid expansion of automobiles after World War II. But the expansion of the highways made it easier for people

Recognizing a problem is only the first step in addressing it. There has been wide recognition that government often fails to deliver on its promise, and the government is often inefficient. But addressing the problem is a greater challenge—one which Vice President Gore set out to meet in his National Performance Review (NPR) in 1993, often referred to as his initiative to "reinvent government."

The basic thrust of his recommendations was that government should organize itself more like successful firms. Government should think of those they serve as their "customers" or "clientele." They should be customer oriented, taking into account the costs they impose on those with whom they deal (such as waiting time) and the kinds of services that their customers want. As a result of the emphasis on customer orientation, one survey noted that the Social Security Administration's telephone service rivaled that of the best private companies.

The NPR also emphasized that, where possible, performance criteria should be developed, and agencies and managers should be evaluated in terms of how well they do on these performance criteria.

The NPR also recommended that, where possible, government activities should be corporatized or privatized. In corporatization, a government agency functions like a corporation, though ownership remains with the government. Government corporations include the TVA (the Tennessee Valley Authority), the postal service, and the Uranium Enrichment Corporation (the USEC, which produces nuclear fuel for electric power plants). NPR recommended that the air traffic control system be corporatized. Privatization entails going one step further—turning over ownership to the private sector. The most recent privatization has been the sale of the U.S. government's helium production. Some have recommended that USEC be privatized, though others have worried that doing so might have adverse security consequences; and others have recommended that the air traffic control system be privatized, though this proposal also has its strong critics.

to commute from the suburbs and thereby facilitated the widespread movement of people from cities to suburbs. This suburban flight—with the associated decay of the inner city—was thus an unintended consequence of a program designed to improve our highway system.

Urban renewal programs were designed to stop urban decay, by tearing down old buildings and putting in their place new housing and facilities for new businesses. But the housing that was destroyed was low-income housing, and the housing with which it was replaced was largely housing for middle and upper-income households. Thus, the urban renewal programs unintentionally contributed to the plight of the poor—the shortage of housing which they could afford—and, over time, to homelessness.

SOURCES OF PUBLIC FAILURES

Incentives and constraints
> Due process
> Constrained ability to make long-term commitments
> Political pressures
>> Pork barrel projects
>> Power of lobbyists who make campaign contributions

Budgeting and spending constraints
> Soft budget constraints
> Annual appropriations process
> Rigid procurement rules

Unintended consequences
> Unforeseen changes in behavior resulting from government action

DECENTRALIZATION AND THE FEDERAL ROLE

Ever since the United States was first formed, debate has raged not only about government's role generally, but also about the role of the federal government in contrast to the role of states and localities. The U.S. Constitution provided that those activities not explicitly delegated to the federal government were reserved to the states and the people. This provision has been interpreted in different ways over the years, changing the role of government as economic circumstances have changed. The "interstate commerce clause," which gives the federal government the right to regulate interstate commerce, has been used very flexibly to cover a host of activities.

The fundamental debate is over the virtues of centralization versus decentralization in government decision making and action. **Decentralization** in this context refers to provision of government goods and services at the state or local levels. Since markets are a decentralized way of producing private goods and services, market failure analysis provides insight into why decentralization will *not* work.

First, when there are externalities, leaving matters to the states or localities will *not* result in efficient outcomes. Pollution in Chicago leads to acid rain in New York. Children who receive an inadequate education in one state may become a welfare burden in another state when they grow up and move. This is a negative externality. There are also positive externalities. Again, education is an example. Some states, such as Wisconsin, provide strong support to their state university systems. These systems yield benefits that extend far beyond the state residents whose taxes make them possible.

Second, although some public goods benefit only residents of a particular area—called **local public goods** (such as local libraries and local roads)—others benefit the whole nation. Protection against foreign aggression, for example, is a national public good. Efficiency requires that national public goods be provided at the federal level.

Third, just as we cannot count on markets to yield a socially acceptable distribution of income, we cannot rely on particular states and localities to ensure an acceptable distribution of income. By lowering benefits to the poor, for example, each state or locality can reduce its poor population as they move elsewhere to survive. This has been called "a race to the bottom."

The instances just listed—of circumstances when decentralization does not yield the outcomes society wants—are matched by circumstances in which decentralization has marked advantages. The first important point here is that federal responses may be clumsy solutions to problems that require adaptation to different community preferences and different state or local needs. States and localities have good incentives to be aware of and respond to needs that are specific to their communities' political, social, and economic conditions. The second major point is that decentralization allows different states to try out different solutions to common problems. In this sense, the states are like a set of laboratories, with the successful experiments providing examples for imitation elsewhere. To take one example, the Medicaid program is partly funded and regulated by the states. This has allowed individual states to experiment with cost controls. Minnesota, for example, is one of the states pushing Health Maintenance Organizations (HMOs) as part of Medicaid. These HMOs reduce the incentive to overtreat by charging a fixed fee per enrollee, regardless of medical condition or services received. Oregon has reduced the range of services provided in exchange for expanding the number of individuals covered.

Many public programs entail shared responsibilities among different levels of government. A typical form of sharing is for the federal government to pick up much of the tab and set broad guidelines, but for the states/localities to implement the programs within these guidelines. This type of sharing does not always work well. If the federal government pays most of the bill, the incentives for state and local bureaucrats to spend the money cost-effectively are correspondingly weakened. The federal government currently picks up as much as 90 percent of highway maintenance costs. This gives the states a strong incentive to use their allotment fully, even when they know the money is not being used cost-effectively (the states would not spend the money in this manner if they had the alternative of using it elsewhere).

Twice in recent times, debate over the federal role has taken center stage. Early in his presidency, Ronald Reagan proposed a New Federalism—a redefinition that proposed transferring responsibility for a number of then-federal social programs to the states. Overshadowing the debate over principles at that time were the potential fiscal consequences for states. The governors did not mind taking over the responsibilities for running programs but they were very concerned that the federal government was also transferring to the states the responsibility for paying a greater share of the costs.

The election of November 1994, which ended with Republican majorities in both the House and Senate, brought principles of decentralization to the forefront of policy debate: (1) states should be given more flexibility to use funds as they want; (2) many of what are now separate programs should be consolidated into grants to the states; and (3) performance measures should be used to measure program performance, both to provide efficiency incentives for states and localities and to evaluate their success in meeting federal objectives. There are large elements of a consensus on these principles, but many disputed issues remain. For instance, Congress passed, and the president signed, a measure limiting legislation which imposes costs on states and localities without providing funds (the so-called unfunded mandates). Information about the magnitude of the costs must be made available before the legislation may be passed. Critics said this did not go far enough; others argued that in some cases, unfunded mandates were just like federal requirements on private producers not to pollute—that the federal government should have the right to impose restrictions against one state dumping garbage in the water of a neighboring state.

Perhaps the most contentious issues in the 1995 to 1996 debate concerned Medicaid: should there be a *national* entitlement, for instance, for children to receive a minimal level of health care, or should the federal government simply provide funds for states to spend on health care however they wished? Providing funds without restrictions is called **bloc granting.** Clearly, there is a wide range between the extremes—no restrictions or no state discretion. Much of the real debate concerns where in that range to place various programs in which there is a shared federal and state responsibility.

DECENTRALIZATION

Limitations
- Externalities
- National public goods
- Income redistribution
    - Race to the bottom

Advantages
- Local public goods
- Adaptation to local preferences and needs
- Experimentation
    - Different solutions to common problems

The debate over the appropriate federal–state division of responsibilities—in particular the activities for which lower levels of government should take fiscal responsibility—has been going on since the colonies split from the British crown. It is unlikely to stop any time soon.

REVIEW AND PRACTICE

SUMMARY

1. Different voters have different views about what the government should do. In some cases majority voting may not yield a determinate outcome. In other cases the choices made in majority voting reflect the preferences of the median voter.

2. Government actions sometimes reflect the interests of particular groups, who seek special favors. The activities they engage in to get these special favors are called rent-seeking activities.

3. Sources of systemic public failure include weak or distorted incentives, budgeting and spending rigidities, and inability to foresee fully the consequences of government programs, particularly changes in behavior.

4. Centralized (federal) provision of public goods and services is preferred in the case of externalities extending beyond a state's jurisdiction and national public goods or when income distribution issues are involved. Decentralized (state and local) provision is preferred for local public goods, may be more responsive to community preferences and needs, and facilitates experimentation in different ways to solve common problems.

KEY TERMS

voting paradox	public choice theory	due process
median voter theory	public failure	soft budget
rent seeking		constraints

REVIEW QUESTIONS

1. What is the voting paradox?

2. What is the median voter? Why does the median voter matter so much in a system of majority rule?

3. What role do special-interest groups and bureaucrats play in determining what government does?

4. In what ways do government enterprises face different constraints from those facing firms in the private sector? What effects do the differences have on incentives?

5. Describe the advantages and disadvantages of providing public goods and services at the local or state level versus the national level?

PROBLEMS

1. The president is trying to decide which of three goals he should put at the top of his agenda—deficit reduction (*d*), a middle-class tax cut (*m*), and preserving the safety net for the poor (*p*). He puts the matter before his advisers in three separate meetings. Assume he has three advisers, and he takes a vote in each meeting. His political adviser's ranking is {*m–d–p*}, his economic adviser's ranking is {*d–p–m*}, and his health care adviser's ranking is {*p–m–d*}. What is the outcome?

2. Suppose you are considering building a food stand along a mile-long strip of beach, but you know that one other vendor is planning to build a stand too. If visitors are evenly distributed along the beach, and people will buy from whichever food stand is closest to them, where should you decide to build your stand? If the goal is to have the shortest possible average distance for people to get to food, where should the two stands be located? (Hint: Think about the situation of two political parties competing for the median voter.)

3. While the median voter theory predicts that the two political parties will converge toward the center, in practice the two parties often seem far apart. Use median voter theory to predict the outcome of a two-stage election. In the first stage, voters within each party choose their candidate. If, in the first stage, voters do not vote strategically—that is they vote for their preferred candidate, not for the candidate that they think will win—describe the outcome of the political process. How might the fact that voters at the extremes of the political spectrum are more likely to vote affect the outcome?

4. In some programs, the federal government pays half of all expenditures but leaves it to the states to decide how much will be spent. How might this cost-sharing arrangement affect the level of expenditure? How might the wealth of a state affect the extent to which it takes advantage of such programs?

5. Evaluate the advantages and disadvantages of transferring responsibility to states and localities for the following programs: (a) interstate highways; (b) local streets; (c) welfare programs; (d) cash assistance to the poor; (e) assistance to the poor for medical expenses; (f) job training programs.

6. In 1996, the welfare system was reformed. Each state was given a bloc grant (a fixed sum of money), where previously it had been given a match-

ing grant, with the fraction paid by the federal government somewhat higher for poor states than for rich states. Focusing on incentives and marginal costs, explain why a state that received exactly as much as before might *choose* to spend less on welfare. Some critics worried that matters would be worse: there would be a race to the bottom, with each state lowering welfare payments to encourage welfare recipients to move to a neighboring state. Explain why this is consistent with median voter theory.

7. In virtually every election, there are complaints about the undue influence of special interest groups, resulting from their large campaign contributions. Prohibiting an individual from spending money on his own behalf is viewed as interfering with First Amendment rights of free speech; prohibiting campaign contributions is viewed as putting those who are not rich at an unfair disadvantage in the political arena, relative to those who can pay for their campaigns. Discuss the consequences and desirability of (a) public financing of campaigns; or (b) prohibiting campaign contributors from lobbying the person to whom they have contributed for a period of, say, one year after the contribution.

8. Special interest groups often are thought of as representing particular industries, like steel or automobiles. More recently, however, attention has turned to the American Association of Retired Individuals (AARP), which tries to represent the interests of the retired. There has been increasing concern among economists about the long-term fiscal situation of the United States. As the baby boomers reach retirement age, enormous demands will be placed on Social Security, Medicare, and Medicaid. Why might median voter theory give a different prediction about how the political system responds to this problem than do theories focusing on special interests?

GLOSSARY

absolute advantage: a country has an absolute advantage over another country in the production of a good if it can produce that good more efficiently (with fewer inputs)

acquired endowments: resources a country builds for itself, like a network of roads or an educated population

adaptive: expectations are adaptive when events of the recent past are extrapolated into the future

adverse selection: the phenomenon that as an insurance company raises its price, the best risks (those least likely to make a claim) drop out, so the mix of applicants changes adversely; now used more generally to refer to effects on the mix of workers, borrowers, products being sold, and so forth resulting from a change in wages (interest rates, prices) or other variables

affirmative action: actions by employers to seek out actively minorities and women for jobs, and to provide them with training and other opportunities for job promotion

aggregate savings: the sum of the savings of all individuals in society

aggregate savings rate: the fraction of national income that is saved; it is calculated by dividing aggregate savings by national income

antitrust laws: laws that discourage monopoly and restrictive practices and encourage greater competition

antitrust policy: policies designed to promote competition and to restrict anti-competitive practices

arbitrage: the process by which assets with comparable risk, liquidity, and tax treatment are priced to yield comparable expected returns

asset: any item that is long-lived, purchased for the service it renders over its life and for what one will receive when one sells it

assistance in kind: public assistance that provides particular goods and services, like food or medical care, rather than cash

asymmetric information: a situation in which the parties to a transaction have different information, as when the seller of a used car has more information about its quality than the buyer

average costs: the total costs divided by the total output

average productivity: the total quantity of output divided by the total quantity of input

average tax rate: the ratio of taxes to taxable income

average variable costs: the total variable costs divided by the total output

barriers to entry: factors that prevent firms from entering a market, such as government rules or patents

basic competitive model: the model of the economy that pulls together the assumptions of self-interested consumers, profit-maximizing firms, and perfectly competitive markets

basic research: fundamental research; it often produces a wide range of applications, but the output of basic research itself usually is not of direct commercial value; the output is knowledge, rather than a product; the output of basic research typically cannot be patented

benefit tax: a tax that is levied on a particular product, the revenues of which go for benefits to those who purchase the product

bequest savings motive: people save so that they can leave an inheritance to their children

Bertrand competition: an oligopoly in which each firm believes that its rivals are committed to keeping their prices fixed and that customers can be lured away by offering lower prices

bilateral trade: trade between two parties

black market: an illegal market in which proscribed trades occur. For instance, in war time, when coupons are required to buy certain basic commodities, it may be illegal to buy and sell coupons; black markets typically develop in which these coupons are in fact traded

bloc granting: providing grants to states and localities without restrictions

breach: an individual is said to be in breach of a contract if he violates the agreement

budget constraint: the limitations on consumption of different goods imposed by the fact that households have only a limited amount of money to spend (their budget). The budget constraint *defines* the opportunity set of individuals, when the only constraint that they face is money

capital: funds used for investment; the term is also used for the value of an individual's investment or a firm's capital stock

capital gain: the increase in the value of an asset between the time it is purchased and the time it is sold

capital goods: machines and buildings used to produce goods

capital goods investment: investments in machines and buildings (to be distinguished from investments in inventory, in research and development, or in training (human capital)

capital goods markets: the markets in which capital goods are traded

capital inflow: the inflow of capital (money) from abroad, to buy investments, to be deposited in U.S. banks, to buy U.S. government bonds, or to be lent in America for any reason

capital loss: a capital loss occurs when an asset is sold at a price below the price at which it was purchased; the difference is the magnitude of the capital loss

capital market: the various institutions concerned with raising funds and sharing and insuring risks; it includes banks, insurance markets, bond markets, and the stock market

capital outflows: the outflow of capital (money) to abroad

cartel: a group of producers with an agreement to collude in setting prices and output

categorical assistance: public assistance aimed at a particular category of people, like the elderly or the disabled

causation: the relationship that results when a change in one variable is not only correlated with but actually causes a change in another variable; the change in the second variable is a consequence of the change in the first variable, rather than both changes being a consequence of a change in a third variable

centralization: organizational structure in which decision making is concentrated at the top

centrally planned economy: an economy in which most decisions about resource allocation are made by the central government

certificate of deposit (CD): an account in which money is deposited for a preset length of time, that yields a slightly higher return to compensate for the reduced liquidity

circular flow: the way in which funds move through the capital, labor, and product markets between households, firms, the government, and the foreign sector

Coase's theorem: the assertion that if property rights are properly defined, then people will be forced to pay for any negative externalities they impose on others, and market transactions will produce efficient outcomes

collude: when firms act jointly (more nearly as they

would if there were a monopolist) to increase overall profits

command-and-control approach: the approach to controlling environmental externalities in which the government provides detailed regulations about what firms can and cannot do, including what technologies they can employ

comparative advantage: a country has a comparative advantage over another country in one good as opposed to another good if its *relative* efficiency in the production of the first good is higher than the other country's

compensating wage differentials: differences in wages that can be traced to nonpecuniary attributes of a job, such as the degree of autonomy and risk

competitive equilibrium price: the price at which the quantity supplied and the quantity demanded are equal to each other

competitive model: the basic model of the economy, in which profit-maximizing firms interact with rational, self-interested consumers in competitive markets, in which all participants are price takers (that is, assume that prices are unaffected by their actions)

complement: two goods are complements if the demand for one (at a given price) decreases as the price of the other increases

compound interest: interest paid on interest; a savings account pays compound interest when, say, interest is credited to the account every day, so that on subsequent days, interest is earned not only on the original principal, but also on the credited interest

constant returns: a production function has constant returns when increases in an input (keeping all other inputs fixed) increase output proportionately

constant returns to scale: a production function has constant returns to scale when equiproportionate increases in all inputs increase output proportionately

consumer protection legislation: laws aimed at protecting consumers, for instance by assuring that consumers have more complete information about items they are considering buying

consumer surplus: the difference between what a person would be willing to pay and what he actually has to pay to buy a certain amount of a good

contestable markets: markets in which there is strong potential (or actual) competition; the theory of con-

testable markets predicts that even in a market with only one firm, that firm will make zero profits, so long as there is strong potential competition (which will be the case if sunk costs are low)

contingency clauses: statements within a contract that make the level of payment or the work to be performed conditional upon various factors

corporate finance: the branch of economics concerned with how firms raise capital and the consequences of alternative methods of raising capital

corporate income tax: a tax based on the income, or profit, received by a corporation

corporation: a firm with limited liability, owned by shareholders, who elect a board of directors that chooses the top executives

correlation: the relationship that results when a change in one variable is consistently associated with a change in another variable

coupon rationing: a system of rationing (often used in wartime) in which, in order to buy some commodity, such as a pound of sugar, a coupon is required in addition to the dollar price. Each individual or household is issued so many coupons for certain essential commodities each month

Cournot competition: an oligopoly in which each firm believes that its rivals are committed to a certain level of production and that rivals will reduce their prices as needed to sell that amount

credentials competition: the trend in which prospective workers acquire higher educational credentials, not so much because of anything they actually learn in the process but to convince potential employers to hire them by signaling that they will be more productive employees than those with weaker credentials

credit rationing: credit is rationed when no lender is willing to make a loan to a borrower or the amount lenders are willing to lend to borrowers is limited, even if the borrower is willing to pay more than other borrowers of comparable risk who are getting loans

cross subsidization: the practice of charging higher prices to one group of consumers in order to subsidize lower prices for another group

dead-weight loss: the difference between what producers gain and (the monetary value of) what consumers lose, when output is restricted under imperfect competition; also, the difference between what the government gains and what consumers lose, when taxes are imposed

debt: capital, such as bonds and bank loans, supplied to a firm by lenders; the firm promises to repay the amount borrowed plus interest

decentralization: organizational structure in which many individuals or subunits can make decisions

decision tree: a device for structured decision making that spells out the choices and possible consequences of alternative actions

demand curve: the relationship between the quantity demanded of a good and the price, whether for an individual or for the market (all individuals) as a whole

demographic effects: effects that arise from changes in characteristics of the population such as age, birthrates, and location

deregulation: the lifting of government regulations to allow the market to function more freely

diminishing marginal rate of substitution: the principle that as the individual gets more and more of one good, less and less of the other good is required to compensate her for a one unit decrease in consumption of the first good; since the marginal rate of substitution is the slope of the indifference curve, the principle of diminishing marginal rate of substitution is equivalent to the slope of the indifference curve becoming flatter as the quantity on the horizontal axis increases

diminishing marginal rate of technical substitution: the principle that as the firm uses more and more of one input, less and less of the other input is required to compensate it for a one unit decrease in the first input; since the marginal rate of technical substitution is the slope of the indifference curve, the principle of diminishing marginal rate of technical substitution is equivalent to the slope of the isoquant curve becoming flatter as the quantity of input on the horizontal axis increases

diminishing marginal utility: the principle that says that as an individual consumes more and more of a good, each successive unit increases her utility, or enjoyment, less and less

diminishing returns: the principle that says that as one input increases, with other inputs fixed, the resulting increase in output tends to be smaller and smaller

discount: assets which sell at a price below that which might be expected, given their expected returns, are

said to sell at a discount; the term is also used to refer more specifically to assets which sell at a price below that which might be expected, given their observable attributes. Because the price of such assets is low, the return per dollar invested is high; the higher return is said to reflect a *risk premium*

disposable income: income after paying taxes

dissaving: negative savings; an individual is dissaving when consumption exceeds income

diversification: spreading one's wealth among a large number of different assets

dividends: that portion of corporate profits paid out to shareholders

division of labor: dividing a production process into a series of jobs, with each worker focusing on a limited set of tasks; the advantage of division of labor is that each worker can practice and perfect a particular set of skills

dual-use technologies: technologies that have both a civilian and a military use

due process: procedures designed to protect the public against arbitrary use of government power

duopoly: an industry with only two firms

dynamically efficient: an economy that appropriately balances short-run concerns (static efficiency) with long-run concerns (focusing on encouraging R & D)

earned income tax credit: a reduction in taxes provided to low income workers based on the amount of income they earn and the size of their family

econometrics: the branch of statistics developed to analyze the particular kinds of problems that arise in economics

economic rents: payments made to a factor of production that are in excess of what is required to elicit the supply of that factor

economics: the social science that studies how individuals, firms, governments, and other organizations make choices, and how those choices determine the way the resources of society are used

economies of scope: the situation that exists when it is less expensive to produce two products together than it would be to produce each one separately

efficiency wage theory: the theory that paying higher wages (up to a point) lowers total production costs, for instance by leading to a more productive labor force

efficient market theory: the theory that all available information is reflected in the current price of an asset

elastic: see relatively elastic

elasticity of labor supply: the percentage change in labor supplied resulting from a 1 percent change in wages

elasticity of supply: see **price elasticity of supply**

eminent domain: the right of government to seize private property for public use, provided it compensates the owner fairly

entrepreneurs: people who create new businesses, bring new products to market, and develop new processes of production

entry-deterring practices: practices of incumbent firms designed to deter the entry of rivals into the market

equilibrium: a condition in which there are no forces (reasons) for change

equilibrium price: the price at which demand equals supply

equilibrium quantity: the quantity demanded (which equals the quantity supplied) at the equilibrium price, where demand equals supply

equity, shares, stock: terms that indicate part ownership of a firm; the firm sells these in order to raise money, or capital

equity capital: capital, such as shares (or stock), supplied to a firm by shareholders; the returns received by the shareholders are not guaranteed but depend on how well the firm does

estate tax: a tax on the estate (wealth) that an individual leaves to his heirs

excess capacity: capacity in excess of that currently needed, sometimes used by an incumbent firm to discourage new entrants

excess demand: the situation in which the quantity demanded at a given price exceeds the quantity supplied

excess supply: the situation in which the quantity supplied at a given price exceeds the quantity demanded

exchange efficiency: the condition in which whatever the economy produces is distributed among people in such a way that there are no gains to further trade

excise tax: a tax on a particular good or service

exclusive dealing: a restrictive practice in which a producer insists that any firm selling its products not sell those of its rivals

exclusive territories: a vertical restriction in which a producer gives a wholesaler or retailer the exclusive right to sell a good within a certain region

exit the market: a consumer exits the market when he decides that at that price, he would prefer to consume none of it

expected return: the average return—a single number that combines the various possible returns per dollar invested with the chances that each of these returns will actually be paid

experimental economics: the branch of economics which analyzes certain aspects of economic behavior in a controlled, laboratory setting

exports: goods produced domestically but sold abroad

externality: a phenomenon that arises when an individual or firm takes an action but does not bear all the costs (negative externality) or receive all the benefits (positive externality)

facilitating practices: practices used by members of an oligopoly to make collusion easier

factor demand: the amount of an input demanded by a firm, given the price of the input and the quantity of output being produced; in a competitive market, an input will be demanded up to the point where the value of the marginal product of that input equals the price of the input

factors of production: the inputs that are used in the production process

federal governmental structure: a system in which government activity takes place at several levels—national, state, county, city, and others

fixed costs: the costs resulting from fixed inputs, sometimes called **overhead costs**

fixed or **overhead inputs:** (a) inputs that do not change depending on the quantity of output, (b) fixed inputs also sometimes refer to inputs that are fixed in the short run—that is, they do not depend on *current* output—but may depend on output in the long run

four-firm concentration ratio: the fraction of output produced by the top four firms in an industry

free-market economists: economists who believe that

free markets are the best way by which the economy can achieve economic efficiency; typically, they believe that the basic competitive model provides a good description of most markets most of the time

free-rider: someone who enjoys the benefit of a (public) good without paying for it; because it is difficult to preclude anyone from using a pure public good, those who benefit from the goods have an incentive to avoid paying for them, that is, to be a free rider

gains from trade: the benefits that each side enjoys from a trade

general equilibrium: the full equilibrium of the economy, when all markets clear simultaneously

general equilibrium analysis: a simultaneous analysis of all capital, product, and labor markets throughout the economy; it shows, for instance, the impact on all prices and quantities of immigration or a change in taxes

gift and estate tax: a tax imposed on the transfers of wealth from one generation to another

Gini coefficient: a measure of inequality (equal to twice the area between the 45-degree line and the Lorenz curve)

greenmail: a practice in which takeover artists buy shares in a firm and threaten a takeover unless they are compensated by the firm repurchasing their shares at an inflated price

highly leveraged: a firm is highly leveraged if it has a high ratio of debt to equity; it has, through borrowing, "highly leveraged" its equity

horizontal equity: the principle that says that those who are in identical or similar circumstances should pay identical or similar amounts in taxes

horizontal integration: the integration of a firm with other firms producing the same product (at the same level of production)

horizontal merger: a merger between two firms that produce the same goods

horizontal restrictions: restrictions (such as an agreement not to compete in price or to enter each others' markets) by competing firms (at the same level of production, for instance, among producers, or among wholesalers, or among retailers)

hostile takeover: when one management team (one firm) takes over the control of another, against the will of the second firm

human capital: the stock of accumulated skills and experience that make workers more productive

imperfect competition: any market structure in which there is some competition but firms face downward-sloping demand curves

imperfect information: a situation in which market participants lack information (such as information about prices or characteristics of goods and services) important for their decision making

imperfect market economists: economists who see significant discrepancies between the basic competitive model and the conditions observed in market economies

imperfect markets: markets that do not satisfy the assumptions of the basic competitive model, such as when competition is less than perfect, information is less than complete, or when there are externalities or markets are missing

imperfect substitutes: goods that can substitute for each other, but imperfectly so

imports: goods produced abroad but bought domestically

incentive-equality trade-off: in general, the greater the incentives, the greater the resulting inequality

income effect: the reduced consumption of a good whose price has increased that is due to the reduction in a person's buying power, or "real" income; when a person's real income is lower, normally she will consume less of all goods, including the higher-priced good

income elasticity of demand: the percentage change in quantity demanded of a good as the result of a 1 percent change in income (the percentage change in quantity demanded divided by the percentage change in income)

income-tested transfer: transfers to particular groups of individuals (such as the aged) based on their income

incomplete markets: situations in which no market may exist for some good or for some risk, or in which some individuals cannot borrow for some purposes

increasing returns: a production function has increasing returns when increases in an input (keeping all other inputs fixed) increase output more than proportionately

increasing, constant, or diminishing returns to scale: when all inputs are increased by a certain proportion, output increases by a greater, equal, or smaller proportion, respectively; increasing returns to scale are also called **economies of scale**

indexed funds: mutual funds that simply buy a fixed portfolio of stocks, usually linked to a market index, such as Standard & Poor's 500 Index. An S & P 500 indexed fund buys shares in the S & P index (in the proportion that they are within the index), or attempts to emulate the behavior of the S & P 500 closely

indifference curves: indifference curves give the combinations of goods among which an individual feels for equally (that is, which yield the same level of utility)

individual income tax: a tax based on the income received by an individual or household

industrial policies: government policies designed to promote particular sectors of the economy

industry: the collection of firms making the same product is called an industry

inelastic: see relatively inelastic

infant industry argument for protection: the argument that industries must be protected from foreign competition while they are young, until they have a chance to acquire the skills to enable them to compete on equal terms

inferior good: a good the consumption of which falls as income rises

infinite elasticity of demand: the situation that exists when any amount will be demanded at a particular price, but nothing will be demanded if the price increases even a small amount

infinite elasticity of supply: the situation that exists when any amount will be supplied at a particular price, but nothing will be supplied if the price declines even a small amount

information-based differential: a wage differential that results from imperfect information, for instance, the fact that a worker does not know the wage being offered by other employers, and that it would be costly for him to search to find out

informative advertising: advertising designed to provide consumers with information about the price of a good, where it may be acquired, or what its characteristics are

inputs: the various material, labor, and other factors used in production

inside traders: individuals who buy and sell shares of companies for which they work, making use of the inside information that they are thereby able to glean

intellectual property: proprietary knowledge, such as that protected by patents and copyright

interest: the return a saver receives in addition to the original amount she deposited (loaned), and the amount a borrower must pay in addition to the original amount he borrowed

intertemporal trades: trades that occur *between* two periods of time

investment: the purchase of an asset that will provide a return over a long period of time

investors: those who supply capital to the capital market (including individuals who buy shares of stock in a firm or lend money to a business)

isocost: different combinations of inputs that cost the same

isoquants: different combinations of inputs that produce the same quantity of output

job discrimination: discrimination in which disadvantaged groups have less access to better paying jobs

joint products: products that are naturally produced together, such as wool and mutton

junk bonds: bonds which are especially risky, that is, have a high probability of default

kinked demand curve: the demand curve perceived by an oligopolist who believes that rivals will match any price cuts but will not match price increases

labor force participation decision: the decision by an individual to actively seek work, that is, to participate in the labor market

labor market: the market in which labor services are bought and sold

law of supply and demand: the law in economics that holds that *in equilibrium* prices are determined so that demand equals supply. Changes in prices thus reflect shifts in the demand or supply curves

learning by doing: the increase in productivity that occurs as a firm gains experience from producing, and that results in a decrease in the firm's production costs

learning curve: the curve describing how costs of production decline as cumulative output increases over time

life-cycle savings motive: people save during their working lives so that they can consume more during retirement

limited liability: corporations have limited liability; with limited liability, the amount an investor in a corporation can lose is limited to the amount that he has invested in the firm

limit pricing: the practice of charging a lower price than the level at which marginal revenue equals marginal cost, as a way of deterring entry by persuading potential competitors that their profits from entering are likely to be limited

linear demand curve: a demand curve that is a straight line, that is, in which demand is a linear function of price

liquidity: the ease with which an asset can be sold

local public goods: public goods that benefit only residents of a particular local area

long-term bonds: bonds with a maturity of more than ten years

Lorenz curve: a curve that shows the cumulative proportion of income that goes to each cumulative proportion of the population, starting with the lowest income group

lottery: a process, such as picking a name from a hat, through which goods are allocated randomly

luxury tax: an excise tax imposed on luxuries, goods typically consumed disproportionately by the wealthy

macroeconomics: the top-down view of the economy, focusing on aggregate characteristics

managerial slack: the lack of managerial efficiency (for instance, in cutting costs) that occurs when firms are insulated from competition

marginal cost: the additional cost corresponding to an additional unit of output produced

marginal costs and benefits: the extra costs and benefits that result from choosing a little bit more of one thing

marginal product: the amount output increases with the addition of one unit of an input

marginal rate of substitution: the slope of an indifference curve; the marginal rate of substitution tells how much of one good an individual is willing to give up in return for one more unit of another

marginal rate of technical substitution: the slope of an isoquant; the marginal rate of technical substitution tells how much of one input a firm can give up in return for one more unit of another, and still leave output unchanged

marginal rate of transformation: the slope of the production possibilities schedule; the extra output of one commodity resulting from a decrease in output of another commodity in an economy in which all resources are fully and efficiently used

marginal revenue: the extra revenue received by a firm for selling one additional unit of a good

marginal tax rate: the rate of tax at the margin; the extra tax that will have to be paid as a result of an additional dollar of income

marginal utility: the extra utility, or enjoyment, a person receives from the consumption of one additional unit of a good

marketable permits: a permit issued by the government which can be bought and sold that allows a firm to emit a certain amount of pollution

market clearing: the situation that exists when supply equals demand, so there is neither excess supply nor excess demand

market demand: the total amount of a particular good or service demanded in the economy

market demand curve: the total amount of a particular good or service demanded in the economy at each price; it is calculated by "adding horizontally" the individual demand curves, that is, at any given price, it is the sum of the individual demands

market economy: an economy that allocates resources primarily through the interaction of individuals (households) and private firms

market failure: the situation in which a market economy fails to attain economic efficiency

market failures approach: the argument that government may have an economic role to play when markets fail to produce efficient outcomes

market for risk: the market (the institutions and

arrangements) in which risks are transferred (exchanged), transformed, and shared

market labor supply curve: the relationship between the wage paid and the amount of labor willingly supplied, found by adding up the labor supply curves of all the individuals in the economy

marketplace: the place where, in traditional societies, goods were bought and sold. In today's economy, only in the case of a few goods and services is there a well-defined marketplace

market power: a firm is said to have market power if it can significantly affect price through its actions (such as sales)

markets: the place where goods or services (including labor) are bought, sold, and traded. The term is used today metaphorically; there is no single marketplace where any particular good is bought and sold; the collection of all the places where exchanges take place is thought of as "the market." See also **capital market**

market structure: term used to describe the organization of the market, such as whether there is a high degree of competition, a monopoly, an oligopoly, or monopolistic competition

market supply: the total amount of a particular good or service that all the firms in the economy supply

market supply curve: the total amount of a particular good or service that all the firms in the economy together would like to supply at each price; it is calculated by "adding horizontally" the individual firm's supply curves, that is, it is the sum of the amounts each firm is willing to supply at any given price

market surplus: there is a market surplus (or surplus) if at the going price, the amount firms are willing to produce exceeds the amount households demand

maturity: the length of time before a loan or bond is due to be paid in full; a bond with a maturity of ten years will be paid off in full in ten years

median voter: the voter such that half the population have preferences on one side of this voter (for instance, they want higher government expenditures and taxes), while the other half of the population have preferences on the other side of this voter (they want lower taxes and expenditures)

merit goods and bads: goods that are determined by government to be good or bad for people, regardless of whether people desire them for themselves or not

microeconomics: the bottom-up view of the economy, focusing on individual households and firms

middle-class entitlement program: programs that provide benefits automatically to individuals meeting certain criteria (such as age), irrespective of their income, most of the benefits of which accrue to middle-class individuals

missing market: when there is a good or service which individuals would like to purchase (at a price at which that good could be profitably produced) but which is not available in the market, the market for that good or service is said to be missing. More generally, when there is no market in which a good or service can be bought or sold, the market is said to be missing

mixed economy: an economy that allocates resources through a mixture of public (governmental) and private decision making

model: a set of assumptions and data used by economists to study an aspect of the economy and make predictions about the future or about the consequences of various policy changes

Modigliani-Miller theorem: the theorem that says that under a simplified set of conditions, the manner in which a firm finances itself does not matter

monetarists: economists who emphasize the importance of money in the economy; they tend to believe that an appropriate monetary policy is all the economy needs from government, and market forces will otherwise solve any macroeconomic problems

monopolist: the single firm in a monopoly, that is, in an industry in which there is a single firm

monopolistic competition: the form of imperfect competition in which the market has sufficiently few firms that each one faces a downward-sloping demand curve, but enough that each can ignore the reactions of rivals to what it does

monopoly: a market consisting of only one firm

monopoly rents: the profits that accrue to a monopolist (as a result of its reducing its output from the competitive level to the monopoly level)

monopsonist: the single buyer of a good or service

moral hazard: the principle that says that those who purchase insurance have a reduced incentive to avoid what they are insured against

multilateral trade: trade between more than two parties

mutual fund: a fund that gathers money from different

investors and purchases a range of assets; each investor then owns a portion of the entire fund

myopic expectations: expectations are myopic when they are "short sighted," for instance, simply assuming that today's prices will continue into the future

nationalization: the process whereby a private industry is taken over by the government, whether by buying it or simply seizing it

natural endowments: a country's natural resources, such as good climate, fertile land, or minerals

natural monopoly: a monopoly that exists because average costs of production are declining beyond the level of output demanded in the market, thus making entry unprofitable and making it efficient for there to be a single firm

negative sloped curve: a curve in which as the variable measured along the horizontal axis is increased, the variable measured along the vertical axis decreases

net capital inflows: total capital inflows minus total capital outflows

net exports: total exports minus total imports

nominal interest rate: the percentage return on a deposit, loan, or bond; the nominal interest rate does not take into account the effects of inflation

nonexcludability: it costs a great deal to exclude any individual from enjoying the benefits of a pure public good; in the extreme, it may be impossible to exclude

nonpecuniary: aspects of a job other than the wage it pays

nonrivalrous: the property possessed by pure public goods that the consumption or enjoyment of the good by one individual does not subtract from that of other individuals

normal good: a good the consumption of which rises as income rises

normative economics: economics in which judgments about the desirability of various policies are made; the conclusions rest on value judgments as well as facts and theories

Okun's law: the observation that as the economy pulls out of a recession, output increases more than proportionately to increases in employment

oligopoly: the form of imperfect competition in which

the market has several firms, sufficiently few that each one must take into account the reactions of rivals to what it does

opportunity cost: the cost of a resource, measured by the value of the next-best, alternative use of that resource

opportunity sets: a summary of the choices available to individuals, as defined by budget constraints and time constraints

outputs: the outcomes of a production process

overhead costs: the costs a firm must pay just to remain in operation. They do not depend on the scale of production

Pareto efficient: a resource allocation is said to be Pareto efficient if there is no rearrangement that can make anyone better off without making someone else worse off

partial equilibrium analysis: an analysis that focuses on only one or a few markets at a time

partnership: a business owned by two or more individuals, who share the profits and are jointly liable for any losses

patent: a government decree giving an inventor the exclusive right to produce, use, or sell an invention for a period of time

paternalism: the making of judgments by government about what is good for people to have, rather than letting people choose on their own

payroll tax: a tax based on payroll (wages) that is used to finance the Social Security and Medicare programs

perfect competition: a situation in which each firm is a price taker—it cannot influence the market price; at the market price, the firm can sell as much as it wishes, but if it raises its price, it loses all sales

perfect information: a state in which market participants have full information about the goods being bought and sold (including the prices at which they are available at every location and all of the relevant characteristics)

perfectly elastic: infinite elasticity; a demand or supply curve is perfectly elastic if it is horizontal

perfectly inelastic: zero elasticity; a demand or supply curve is perfectly inelastic if it is vertical, so the demand or supply is completely insensitive to price

permanent-income savings motive: people save in good years to tide them over in bad years; they choose their pattern of saving and spending year by year to average, or smooth, their consumption over good years and bad

persuasive advertising: advertising designed to make consumers feel good about the products that are being sold and more inclined to purchase them; it does not inform them about price or any characteristic of the product

physical capital: investments in plant and equipment; the term is used to distinguish these investments from investments in people, called human capital

piece-rate system: a compensation system in which workers are paid specifically for each item produced

portfolio: an investor's entire collection of assets and liabilities

positive economics: economics that describes how the economy behaves and predicts how it might change—for instance, in response to some policy change

positively sloped curve: a curve in which as the variable measured along the horizontal axis is increased, the variable measured along the vertical axis increases

potential competition: competitive pressures that arise from the potential of firms to enter a market

precautionary savings motive: people save so that they will be able to meet the costs of an unexpected illness, accident, or other emergency

predatory pricing: the practice of cutting prices below the marginal cost of production to drive out a new firm (or to deter future entry), at which point prices can be raised again

premium: assets that sell at a price above that which might be expected, given their expected returns, are said to sell at a premium; the term is also used to refer more specifically to the higher price that an asset might sell at, above that which might be expected, given its observable attributes

present discounted value: how much an amount of money to be received in the future is worth right now

price: the price of a good or service is what must be given in exchange for the good

price ceiling: a maximum price above which market prices are not legally allowed to rise

price discrimination: the practice of a firm charging different prices to different customers or in different markets

price dispersion: a situation that occurs when the same item is sold for different prices by different firms

price elasticity of demand: the percentage change in quantity demanded of a good as the result of a 1 percent change in price (the percentage change in quantity demanded divided by the percentage change in price)

price elasticity of supply: the percentage change in quantity supplied of a good as the result of a 1 percent change in price (the percentage change in quantity supplied divided by the percentage change in price)

price floor: a minimum price below which market prices are not legally allowed to fall

price leader: in some oligopolies, a particular firm, called the price leader, sets the price, with other firms quickly following suit

price makers: firms that affect, or make, the price as a result of their actions, especially as a consequence of their level of production

price system: the economic system in which prices are used to allocate scarce resources

price takers: firms that take the price for the good or service they sell as given; the price is unaffected by their level of production

principal: the original amount a saver deposits in a bank (lends) or a borrower borrows

principal-agent problem: any situation in which one party (the principal) needs to delegate actions to another party (the agent), and thus wishes to provide the agent with incentives to work hard and make decisions about risk that reflect the interests of the principal

principle of consumer sovereignty: the principle that holds that each individual is the best judge of what makes him better off

principle of substitution: the principle that holds that in general there are large possibilities for substitution, both by consumers and by firms, so that an increase in the price of say an input will lead the firm to substitute other inputs in its place

Prisoner's Dilemma: a situation in which the noncooperative pursuit of self-interest by two parties makes them both worse off

private marginal cost: the marginal cost of production borne by the producer of a good; when there is a negative externality, such as air pollution, private marginal cost is less than social marginal cost

private property: ownership of property (or other assets) by individuals or corporations; under a system of private property, owners have certain property rights, but there may also be legal restrictions on the use of property

privatization: the process whereby functions that were formerly undertaken by government are delegated instead to the private sector

product differentiation: the fact that similar products (like breakfast cereals or soft drinks) are perceived to differ from one another and thus are imperfect substitutes

production efficiency: the condition in which firms cannot produce more of some goods without producing less of other goods; the economy is on its production possibilities curve

production function: the relationship between the inputs used in production and the level of output

production possibilities: the combination of outputs of different goods that an economy can produce with given resources

productivity wage differential: wage differentials among individuals arising from differences in productivity

product market: the market in which goods and services are bought and sold

product-mix efficiency: the condition in which the mix of goods produced by the economy reflects the preferences of consumers

profits: total revenues minus total costs

progressive tax: a tax in which the rich pay a larger fraction of their income than the poor

property rights: the rights of an owner of private property; these typically include the right to use the property as she sees fit (subject to certain restrictions, such as zoning) and the right to sell it when and to whom she sees fit

property tax: a tax based on the value of property

proprietorship: a business owned by a single person, usually a small business

protectionism: the policy of protecting domestic industries from the competition of foreign-made goods

public good: a good, such as national defense, that costs little or nothing for an extra individual to enjoy, and the costs of preventing any individual from the enjoyment of which are high; public goods have the properties of nonrivalrous consumption and nonexcludability

pure profit or **monopoly rents:** the profit earned by a monopolist that results from its reducing output and increasing the price from the level at which price equals marginal cost

pure public good: a good which possesses the property of nonexcludability (in which it is *impossible* to exclude any individual from enjoying the benefits of the good) and nonrivalrousness (the consumption or enjoyment of the good by one individual does not subtract at all from that of other individuals)

random walk: a term used to describe the way the prices of stocks move; the next movement cannot be predicted on the basis of previous movements

rational choice: a choice process in which individuals weigh the costs and benefits of each possibility, and in which the choices made are those within the opportunity set that maximize net benefits

rational expectations: expectations are rational when people make full use of all relevant available past data in their formation of expectations

rationed goods: when individuals get less of a good than they would like at the terms being offered, the good is said to be rationed

rationing system: any system of allocating scarce resources, applied particularly to systems other than the price system. Rationing systems include rationing by coupons and rationing by queues

reaction function: in the analysis of oligopolies, the reaction function gives the level of output of one firm, given the level of output of other firms (in Cournot competition) or the level of price of one firm, given the prices of other firms (in Bertrand competition)

real income: income measured by what it can actually buy, rather than by the amount of money

real interest rate: the real return to saving, equal to the nominal interest rate minus the rate of inflation

real product wage: the wage divided by the price of the good being produced

regressive tax: a tax in which the poor pay a larger fraction of their income than the rich

regulatory capture: a term used to describe a situation in which regulators serve the interests of the regulated rather than the interests of consumers

relatively elastic: a good is said to be relatively elastic when the price elasticity of its demand is greater than unity

relatively inelastic: a good is said to be relatively inelastic when the price elasticity of its demand is less than unity

relative performance compensation: pay based on performance on the job relative to others who have similar responsibilities and authority

relative price: the ratio of any two prices; the relative price of apples and oranges is just the ratio of their prices

rent: see **economic rent**

rent control: limitations on the level or rate of increase of rents which landlords can charge

rent seeking: the name given to behavior that seeks to obtain benefits from favorable government decisions, such as protection from foreign competition

reputation: the "good will" of a firm resulting from its past performance; maintaining one's reputation provides an incentive to maintain quality

resale price maintenance: a restrictive practice in which a producer insists that any retailer selling his product sell it at the "list price"

reservation wage: the wage below which an individual chooses not to participate in the labor market

restrictive practices: practices of oligopolists designed to restrict competition, including vertical restrictions like exclusive territories

retained earnings: that part of the net earnings of the firm that are not paid out to shareholders, but retained by the firm

revenue curve: the relationship between a firm's total output and its revenues

revenues: the amount a firm receives for selling its products, equal to the price received multiplied by the quantity sold

right-to-work laws: laws that prevent union membership from being a condition of employment

rigid prices: prices that do not adjust when demand differs from supply

risk averse, risk loving, risk neutral: given equal expected returns and different risks, risk-averse people will choose assets with lower risk, risk-loving people will choose assets with higher risk, and risk-neutral individuals will not care about differences in risk

risk premium: the additional interest required by lenders as compensation for the risk that a borrower may default; more generally, the extra return required to compensate an investor for bearing risk

sales tax: a tax imposed on the purchase of goods and services

scarcity: term used to describe the limited availability of resources, so that if no price were charged for a good or service, the demand for it would exceed its supply

screening: the process of differentiating among job candidates, when there is incomplete information, to determine who will be the most productive

search: the process by which consumers gather information about what is available in the market, including prices, or by which workers gather information about the jobs that are available, including wages

shortage: a situation in which demand exceeds supply at the current price

short-run production function: the relationship between output and employment in the short run, that is, with a given set of machines and buildings

short-term bonds: bonds that mature within a few years

signaling: conveying information, for example a prospective worker's earning a college degree to persuade an employer that he has desirable characteristics that will enhance his productivity

simple interest: a savings account pays simple (rather than compound) interest when interest is paid only against the original principal (deposit)

sin tax: an excise tax on alcohol and tobacco

slope: the amount by which the value along the vertical axis increases as the result of a change in one unit along the horizontal axis; the slope is calculated by dividing the change in the vertical axis (the "rise") by the change in horizontal axis (the "run")

Smith's "invisible hand": the idea that if people act in their own self-interest, they will often also be acting in a broader social interest, as if they had been directed by an "invisible hand"

smoothing consumption: consuming similar amounts in the present and future, rather than letting year-to-year income dictate consumption

social benefit: the benefits which accrue to society as a whole; the social benefit of an innovation includes not only the profits of the innovator, but the benefits that accrue to others, either as a result of the knowledge produced in the innovative process or because the new product is available at a price below that which the individual would be willing to pay

social insurance: insurance provided by the government to individuals, for instance, against disabilities, unemployment, or health problems (for the aged)

social marginal cost: the marginal cost of production, including the cost of any negative externality, such as air pollution, borne by individuals in the economy other than the producer

social science: a branch of science which studies human social behavior; the social sciences include economics, political science, anthropology, sociology, and psychology

soft budget constraints: budget constraints facing public enterprises, which can always turn to government for assistance in the event of a loss

static efficiency: the efficiency of the economy with given technology; taxes used to finance basic research and monopoly power resulting from patents result in a loss in static efficiency

statistical discrimination: differential treatment of individuals of different gender or race that is based on the use of observed correlations (statistics) between performance and some observable characteristics; it may even *result* from the use of variables like education in which there is a *causal* link to performance

sticky prices: prices that do not adjust or adjust only slowly toward a new equilibrium

stock option: an option to buy a share of a stock at a particular price (usually within a particular period of time); if the value of the share increases (above that price), the value of the option increases; stock options are often used to reward corporate executives

strike: the collective withdrawal of labor (usually organized by a union)

substitute: two goods are substitutes if the demand for one increases when the price of the other increases

substitution effect: the reduced consumption of a good whose price has increased that is due to the changed trade-off, the fact that one has to give up more of other goods to get one more unit of the high-priced good; the substitution effect is associated with a change in the slope of the budget constraint

sunk cost: a cost that has been incurred and cannot be recovered

supply curve: the relationship between the quantity supplied of a good and the price, whether for a single firm or the market (all firms) as a whole

surplus: the magnitude of the gain from trade, the difference between what an individual would have been willing to pay for a good and what she has to pay. See also **market surplus**

tacit collusion: collusive behavior among the firms of an oligopoly based on an implicit understanding that it is in each firm's best interest not to compete too vigourously; they tacitly understand that it is undesirable to undercut each others' prices, but there is no open discussion about price fixing

takeover: when one management team (one firm) takes over the control of another

target savings motive: people save for a particular target, for example to make a down payment on a house or to pay college tuition

tax expenditures: the revenue lost from a tax subsidy

tax-favored assets: the return on these assets receives favorable tax treatment, such as tax-exempt municipal bonds

tax subsidies: subsidies provided through the tax system to particular industries or to particular expenditures, in the form of favorable tax treatment

theorem: a logical proposition that follows from basic definitions and assumptions

theory: a set of assumptions and the conclusions derived from those assumptions put forward as an explanation for some phenomena

thin markets: markets with relatively few buyers and sellers

tie-ins: a restrictive practice in which a customer who buys one product must buy another

time constraints: the limitations on consumption of different goods imposed by the fact that households have only a limited amount of time to spend (twenty-four hours a day). The time constraint defines the opportunity set of individuals if the only constraint that they face is time

time value of money: the fact that a dollar today is worth more than a dollar in the future is called the time value of money

total costs: the sum of all fixed costs and variable costs

trade deficit: the excess of imports over exports

trade-offs: the amount of one good (or one desirable objective) that must be given up to get more of another good (or to attain more of another desirable objective)

trade secret: an innovation or knowledge of a production process that a firm does not disclose to others

transactions costs: the extra costs (beyond the price of the purchase) of conducting a transaction, whether those costs are money, time, or inconvenience

transfer programs: programs directly concerned with redistribution, such as AFDC and Medicaid, that move money from one group in society to another

transplants: plants constructed in one country by firms based in another. U.S. factories producing Mazdas and Toyotas are Japanese transplants

Treasury bills (T-bills): bills the government sells in return for a promise to pay a certain amount in a short period, usually less than 180 days

trusts: organizations that attempted to control certain markets in the late nineteenth century; they were designed to allow an individual or group owning a small fraction of the total industry to exercise control

unemployment rate: the fraction of the labor force (those unemployed *plus* those seeking jobs) who are seeking jobs but are unable to find them

union shops: unionized firms in which all workers are required to join the union as a condition of employment

unitary price elasticity: a demand curve has unitary price elasticity if the demand for the commodity decreases by one percent when the price increases by one percent. If demand has unitary elasticity, then expenditures on the good do not depend at all on price. A sup-

ply curve has unitary price elasticity if the supply of the commodity increases by one percent when the price increases by one percent

utility: the level of enjoyment an individual attains from choosing a certain combination of goods

utility possibilities curve: a curve showing the maximum level of utility that one individual can attain, given the level of utility attained by others

value of the marginal product of labor: the value of the extra output produced by an extra unit of labor; it is calculated by multiplying the marginal product of labor times the price of the good which is being produced

variable: anything that can be measured and that changes; examples of variables are prices, wages, interest rates, quantities bought and sold

variable costs: the costs resulting from variable inputs

variable inputs: inputs that rise and fall with the quantity of output

vertical equity: the principle that says that people who are better off should pay more taxes

vertical integration: the integration of a firm with its supplier or customer

vertical merger: a merger between two firms, one of which is a supplier or distributor for the other

vertical restrictions: restrictions imposed by a producer on wholesalers and retailers who distribute its products; more generally, restrictions imposed by a firm on those to whom it sells its products

voting paradox: the fact that under some circumstances there may be no determinate outcome with majority voting: choice A wins a majority over B, B wins over C, and C wins over A

wage discrimination: paying lower wages to women or minorities

zero elasticity: a demand (or supply) curve has zero elasticity if the quantity demanded (or supplied) does not change at all if price changes; the demand (supply) curve is vertical

CREDITS

CREDITS

I NDEX